Microeconomics

Canadian Edition

R. Glenn Hubbard
Columbia University

Anthony Patrick O'Brien
Lehigh University

Apostolos Serletis
University of Calgary

Jason Childs
University of Regina

PEARSON

Toronto

Vice-President, Editorial Director: Gary Bennett
Managing Editor: Claudine O'Donnell
Senior Marketing Manager: Leigh-Anne Graham
Program Manager: Karen Townsend
Project Manager: Rachel Thompson
Developmental Editor: Mary Watt
Media Editor: Imee Salumbides
Media Producer: Olga Avdyeyeva
Production Services: Cenveo Publisher Services
Permissions Project Manager: Joanne Tang
Photo Permissions Research: Cordes Hoffman
Text Permissions Research: Jill Dougan
Art Director: Zeneth Denchik
Cover and Interior Designer: Anthony Leung
Cover Image: (c) Izabela Habur/Getty Images

10 9 8 7 6 5 4 3 2 1 [CKV]

Library and Archives Canada Cataloguing in Publication

Hubbard, R. Glenn, author
      Microeconomics / R. Glenn Hubbard, Columbia University, Anthony
Patrick O'Brien, Lehigh University, Apostolos Serletis, University of Calgary,
Jason Childs, University of Regina. -- Canadian edition.
      Includes indexes.
      ISBN 978-0-13-702209-0 (pbk.)

      1. Microeconomics--Textbooks. I. O'Brien, Anthony Patrick, author
II. Serletis, Apostolos, 1954-, author III. Childs, Jason, 1974-, author IV. Title.
      HB172.H78 2014   338.5   C2013-907061-3

ISBN 978-0-13-702209-0

For Aglaia, Adia, and Alia.
—Apostolos Serletis

For Marla, Nora, Ed, and Leslie.
—Jason Childs

Glenn Hubbard, policymaker, professor, and researcher. R. Glenn Hubbard is the dean and Russell L. Carson Professor of Finance and Economics in the Graduate School of Business at Columbia University and professor of economics in Columbia's Faculty of Arts and Sciences. He is also a research associate of the National Bureau of Economic Research and a director of Automatic Data Processing, Black Rock Closed-End Funds, KKR Financial Corporation, and MetLife. He received his Ph.D. in economics from Harvard University in 1983. From 2001 to 2003, he served as chairman of the White House Council of Economic Advisers and chairman of the OECD Economy Policy Committee, and from 1991 to 1993, he was deputy assistant secretary of the U.S. Treasury Department. He currently serves as co-chair of the nonpartisan Committee on Capital Markets Regulation. Hubbard's fields of specialization are public economics, financial markets and institutions, corporate finance, macroeconomics, industrial organization, and public policy. He is the author of more than 100 articles in leading journals, including *American Economic Review, Brookings Papers on Economic Activity, Journal of Finance, Journal of Financial Economics, Journal of Money, Credit, and Banking, Journal of Political Economy, Journal of Public Economics, Quarterly Journal of Economics, RAND Journal of Economics,* and *Review of Economics and Statistics.* His research has been supported by grants from the National Science Foundation, the National Bureau of Economic Research, and numerous private foundations.

Tony O'Brien, award-winning professor and researcher. Anthony Patrick O'Brien is a professor of economics at Lehigh University. He received his Ph.D. from the University of California, Berkeley, in 1987. He has taught principles of economics for more than 15 years, in both large sections and small honors classes. He received the Lehigh University Award for Distinguished Teaching. He was formerly the director of the Diamond Center for Economic Education and was named a Dana Foundation Faculty Fellow and Lehigh Class of 1961 Professor of Economics. He has been a visiting professor at the University of California, Santa Barbara, and the Graduate School of Industrial Administration at Carnegie Mellon University. O'Brien's research has dealt with such issues as the evolution of the U.S. automobile industry, sources of U.S. economic competitiveness, the development of U.S. trade policy, the causes of the Great Depression, and the causes of black-white income differences. His research has been published in leading journals, including *American Economic Review, Quarterly Journal of Economics, Journal of Money, Credit, and Banking, Industrial Relations, Journal of Economic History,* and *Explorations in Economic History.* His research has been supported by grants from government agencies and private foundations. In addition to teaching and writing, O'Brien also serves on the editorial board of the *Journal of Socio-Economics.*

Apostolos Serletis is a professor of economics at the University of Calgary. Since receiving his Ph.D. from McMaster University in 1984, he has held visiting appointments at the University of Texas at Austin, the Athens University of Economics and Business, and the Research Department of the Federal Reserve Bank of St. Louis.

Professor Serletis' teaching and research interest focus on monetary and financial economics, macroeconometrics, and nonlinear and complex dynamics. He is the author of 12 books, including *The Economics of Money, Banking, and Financial Markets: Fifth Canadian Edition,* with Frederic S. Mishkin (Pearson, 2014); *Macroeconomics: A Modern Approach: First Canadian Edition,* with Robert J. Barro (Nelson, 2010); *The Demand for Money: Theoretical and Empirical Approaches* (Springer, 2007); *Financial Markets and Institutions: Canadian Edition,* with Frederic S. Mishkin and Stanley G. Eakins (Addison-Wesley, 2004); and *The Theory of Monetary Aggregation,* co-edited with William A. Barnett (Elsevier, 2000).

In addition, he has published more than 200 articles in such journals as the *Journal of Economic Literature, Journal of Monetary Economics, Journal of Money, Credit, and Banking, Journal of Econometrics, Journal of Applied Econometrics, Journal of Business and Economic Statistics, Macroeconomic Dynamics, Journal of Banking and Finance, Journal of Economic Dynamics and Control, Economic Inquiry, Canadian Journal of Economics, Econometric Reviews,* and *Studies in Nonlinear Dynamics and Econometrics.*

Professor Serletis is currently an Associate Editor of two academic journals, *Macroeconomic Dynamics* and *Energy Economics,* and a member of the Editorial Board at the *Journal of Economic Asymmetries* and the *Journal of Economic Studies.* He has also served as Guest Editor of the *Journal of Econometrics, Econometric Reviews,* and *Macroeconomic Dynamics.*

Jason Childs is an Associate Professor of Economics at the University of Regina. He received his PhD from McMaster University in 2003. He has taught introductory economics (both microeconomics and macroeconomics) his entire career. He began his teaching career with the McCain Postdoctoral Fellowship at Mount Allison University. After this fellowship he spent six years at the University of New Brunswick, where he received one teaching award and was nominated for two others. Since joining the University of Regina, he has continued to teach introductory-level economics courses and was instrumental in designing a graduate-level program applying economics to problems of public policy. While in Saskatchewan, he has also consulted for the Ministry of Education on the social science curriculum. Professor Childs' research has dealt with a wide variety of issues ranging from the voluntary provision of public services, uncovered interest rate parity, rent controls, to lying. His work has been published in leading journals, including the *Journal of Public Economics, Review of International Economics, Computational Economics,* and *Economics Letters.*

BRIEF CONTENTS

CONTENTS

*These end-of-chapter resource materials repeat in all chapters.

PART 3: Firms in the Domestic and International Economies

PART 6: Labour Markets, Public Choice and the Distribution of Income

There have been dramatic advances in microeconomics over the past 40 years and the field is changing rapidly. The roles of uncertainty and information, the analysis of pricing by firms with market power, and game theory and competitive strategy play a central role in microeconomic theory today. Yet, in the aftermath of the global financial crisis, a number of economists, the media, and policymakers have argued that modern microeconomics cannot capture the complexity of the real world.

We believe that with increasing uncertainty and interdependence of real economies, there is a need for increasingly relevant and applicable microeconomics. However, most first-year books do not help students understand many of the issues and economic events and the managerial and public policy responses to them. We realized that the Fourth U.S. Edition of Hubbard and O'Brien's *Principles of Microeconomics* is the kind of textbook that makes modern microeconomics valuable and applicable. It is the textbook that we always wanted to use in our classes and for this reason we decided to work on the Canadian edition of the book.

The Canadian edition of *Principles of Microeconomics* is completely widget free. It delivers complete economics coverage using many fresh, lively, real world examples from newspapers, magazines, websites, and professional journals from around the world. By building from the specific example to the general case, this text fosters student engagement. In testing early drafts of the text in the classroom, we found the degree of student engagement was substantially improved by placing real-world examples and applications at the forefront rather than treating them as add-ons or afterthoughts. The approach is attractive to both instructors and students because it captures the richness and interactions of the real-world while demonstrating the value and applicability of modern microeconomics.

Highlights of this Edition

The severe global financial crisis that began in 2007 with the bursting of the housing bubble in the United States and the Great Recession and European debt crisis that followed are still affecting the world economy today. In many countries, unemployment has risen to levels not seen in decades. The crisis in the financial system has been the worst since the Great Depression of the 1930s. Managerial and public policy debates have intensified as governments around the world introduced the largest packages of spending increases and tax cuts in history. Central banks, including the Bank of Canada, have sailed into uncharted waters as they develop new policy tools to deal with the unprecedented financial turmoil. Other long-running managerial and public policy debates continue as well, as huge long-run budget deficits, environmental problems, income inequality, and changes to the tax system all receive attention from economists, policymakers, and the public.

Principles of Microeconomics, The Canadian edition, helps students understand recent economic events and the managerial and public policy responses to them. It places applications at the forefront of the discussion. We believe that students find the study of microeconomics more interesting and easier to master when they see microeconomic analysis applied to real-world issues that concern them.

The Foundation: Contextual Learning and Modern Organization

We believe a course is a success if students can apply what they have learned in both personal and business settings and if they have developed the analytical skills to understand what they read in the media. That's why we explain economic concepts by using many real-world business examples and applications in the chapter openers, graphs, *Making the Connection* features, *An Inside Look* features, and end-of-chapter problems. This approach helps both business majors and liberal arts majors become educated consumers, voters, and citizens. In addition to our widget-free approach, we also have a modern organization and discuss interesting policy topics early in the book to pique student interest.

We are convinced that students learn to apply economic principles best if they are taught in a familiar context. Whether they open an art studio, do social work, trade on Bay Street, work for the government, or tend bar, students benefit from understanding the economic forces behind their work. And though business students will have many opportunities to see economic principles in action in various courses, liberal arts students may not. We therefore use many diverse real-world business and policy examples to illustrate economic concepts and to develop educated consumers, voters, and citizens.

Notable features of this book are:

- **A strong set of introductory chapters.** The introductory chapters provide students with a solid foundation in the basics. We emphasize the key ideas of marginal analysis and economic efficiency. In Chapter 4, "Economic Efficiency, Government Price Setting, and Taxes," we use the concepts of consumer surplus and producer surplus to measure the economic effects of price ceilings and price floors as they relate to the familiar examples of rental properties and the minimum wage. (We revisit consumer surplus and producer surplus in Chapter 7, "Comparative Advantage and the Gains from International Trade," where we discuss outsourcing and analyze government policies that affect trade, and in Chapter 13, "Monopoly and Antitrust Policy," where we examine the effect of market power on economic efficiency. In the online Chapter 16, "Pricing Strategy," we examine the effect of firm pricing policy on economic efficiency.) In the online Chapter 17, "Firms, the Stock Market, and Corporate Governance," we provide students with a basic understanding of how firms are organized, how they raise funds, and how they provide information to investors. We also illustrate how in a market system entrepreneurs meet consumer wants and efficiently organize production.

- **Early coverage of policy issues.** To expose students to policy issues early in the course, we discuss immigration in Chapter 1, "Economics: Foundations and Models"; rent control and the minimum wage in Chapter 4, "Economic Efficiency, Government Price Setting, and Taxes"; air pollution, global warming, and whether the government should run the health care system in Chapter 5, "Externalities, Environmental Policy, and Public Goods"; and government policy toward illegal drugs in Chapter 6, "Elasticity: The Responsiveness of Demand and Supply."

- **Complete coverage of monopolistic competition.** We devote a full chapter—Chapter 11, "Monopolistic Competition: The Competitive Model in a More Realistic Setting"—to monopolistic competition prior to covering oligopoly and monopoly in Chapter 12, "Oligopoly: Firms in Less Competitive Markets," and Chapter 13, "Monopoly and Antitrust Policy." Although many instructors cover monopolistic competition very briefly or dispense with it entirely, we think it is an overlooked tool for reinforcing the basic message of how markets work in a context that is much more familiar to students than are the agricultural examples that dominate other discussions of perfect competition. We use the monopolistic competition model to introduce the downward-sloping demand curve material usually introduced in a monopoly chapter. This helps students grasp the important point that nearly all firms—not just monopolies—face downward-sloping demand curves. Covering monopolistic competition directly after perfect competition also allows for the early discussion of topics such as brand management and sources of competitive success. Nevertheless, we wrote the chapter so that instructors who prefer to cover monopoly (Chapter 13, "Monopoly and Antitrust Policy") directly after perfect competition (Chapter 10, "Firms in Perfectly Competitive Markets") can do so without loss of continuity.

- **Extensive, realistic game theory coverage.** In Chapter 12, "Oligopoly: Firms in Less Competitive Markets," we use game theory to analyze competition among oligopolists. Game theory helps students understand how companies with market power make strategic decisions in many competitive situations. We use familiar companies such as Apple, Hewlett-Packard, Coca-Cola, PepsiCo, and Dell in our game theory applications.

- **Unique coverage of pricing strategy.** In the online Chapter 16, "Pricing Strategy," we explore how firms use pricing strategies to increase profits. Students encounter pricing strategies everywhere—when they buy a movie ticket, book a flight for spring break, or research book prices online. We use these relevant, familiar examples to illustrate how companies use strategies such as price discrimination, cost-plus pricing, and two-part tariffs.

Special Features: A Real-World, Hands-on Approach to Learning Economics

Business Cases and *An Inside Look* News Articles

Each chapter-opening case provides a real-world context for learning, sparks students' interest in economics, and helps to unify the chapter. The case describes an actual company facing a real situation. The company is integrated in the narrative, graphs, and pedagogical features of the chapter. Many of the chapter openers focus on the role of entrepreneurs in developing new products and bringing them to the market. For example, Chapter 3 covers Bill Gates of Microsoft and Steve Jobs of Apple, the online Chapter 17 covers the founding of the Hudson's Bay Company and the Facebook initial public offering, and Chapter 11 covers Howard Schultz of Starbucks. Here are a few examples of companies we explore in the chapter openers in this new edition:

- Apple (Chapter 3, "Where Prices Come From: The Interaction of Demand and Supply")
- Hudson's Bay Company and Facebook (online Chapter 17, "Firms, the Stock Market, and Corporate Governance")
- Starbucks (Chapter 11, "Monopolistic Competition")

An Inside Look is a two-page feature that shows students how to apply the concepts from the chapter to the analysis of a news article. Select articles deal with policy issues and are titled *An Inside Look*. Articles are from sources such as the *Hamilton Spectator*, *The Economist*, *National Post*, *Toronto Star*, and the *Montreal Gazette*. *An Inside Look* feature presents an excerpt from an article, analysis of the article, a graph(s), and critical thinking questions.

Here are some examples of the articles featured in *An Inside Look:*

- Peaking Gas Prices Set New Records—"Breaking Down the Price of Gasoline" (Chapter 6, "Elasticity: The Responsiveness of Demand and Supply")
- Adding Value Through Association with Star Power?—"Celebrity Endorsements: Do They Make Products More Appealing to You?" (Chapter 8, "Consumer Choice and Behavioural Economics")
- Competing in the Wireless Spectrum—"Telus CEO Entwistle Warns of 'Bloodbath' if Verizon Has Advantage in Wireless Spectrum Auction (Chapter 9, "Technology, Production, and Costs")
- Competing: Intel's "Ultrabook" Against Apple's MacBook Air—"Intel Taps into New Computing at Taiwan Show" (Chapter 12, "Oligopoly: Firms in Less Competitive Markets")

Economics in Your Life

After the chapter-opening real-world business case, we have added a personal dimension to the chapter opener with a feature titled *Economics in Your Life*, which asks students to consider how economics affects their own lives. The feature piques the interest of students and emphasizes the connection between the material they are learning and their own experiences.

Economics in Your Life

Red Bull or Beaver Buzz Energy: What's Your Beverage?

Suppose you are about to buy an energy drink and you are choosing between a Red Bull and a Beaver Buzz Energy. As the more established, well-known brand, Red Bull has many advantages over a recent entrant like Beaver Buzz Energy. One strategy DD Beverage Company can use to overcome Red Bull's advantages is to have Beaver Buzz Energy compete based on price and value. Would you choose to buy a can of Beaver Buzz Energy if it had a lower price than a can of Red Bull? Would you be less likely to drink Beaver Buzz Energy if your income dropped? As you read this chapter, see if you can answer these questions. You can check your answers against those we provide on page 82 at the end of this chapter.

At the end of the chapter, we use the chapter concepts to answer the questions asked at the beginning of the chapter.

Economics in Your Life

Red Bull or Beaver Buzz Energy: What's Your Beverage?

At the beginning of the chapter, we asked you to consider two questions: Would you choose to buy a can of Beaver Buzz Energy if it had a lower price than a can of Red Bull? Would you be less likely to drink Beaver Buzz Energy if your income dropped? To determine the answer to the first question, you have to recognize that Beaver Buzz Energy and Red Bull are substitutes. If you consider the two drinks to be very close substitutes, then you are likely to buy the one with the lower price. In the market, if consumers generally believe that Beaver Buzz Energy and Red Bull are close substitutes, a fall in the price of Beaver Buzz Energy will increase the quantity of Beaver Buzz Energy demanded and decrease the demand for Red Bull. Suppose that you are currently leaning toward buying Red Bull because you believe that it is better tasting than Beaver Buzz Energy. If a decrease in your income made you more likely to buy Beaver Buzz Energy, then you consider Beaver Buzz Energy as an inferior good.

The following are examples of the topics we cover in the *Economics in Your Life* feature:

- How Much Do Gas Prices Matter to You? (Chapter 6, "Elasticity: The Responsiveness of Demand and Supply")
- Have You Ever Been Urged to "Buy Canadian"? (Chapter 7, "Comparative Advantage and the Gains From International Trade")
- Why Does Toronto Have Only One NHL Team? (Chapter 13, "Monopoly and Antitrust Policy")

Solved Problems

Many students have great difficulty handling applied economics problems. We help students overcome this hurdle by including two or three worked-out problems tied to select chapter-opening learning objectives. Our goals are to keep students focused on the main ideas of each chapter and to give students a model of how to solve an economic problem by breaking it down step by step. Additional exercises in the end-of-chapter Problems and Applications section are tied to every *Solved Problem*. Additional *Solved Problems* appear in the Instructor's Manual and the print Study Guide. In addition, the Test Item Files include problems tied to the *Solved Problems* in the main book.

Table 3.3

How Shifts in Demand and Supply Affect Equilibrium Price (P) and Quantity (Q)

	Supply Curve Unchanged	Supply Curve Shifts Right	Supply Curve Shifts to the Left
Demand curve unchanged	Q unchanged	Q increases	Q decreases
	P unchanged	P decreases	P increases
Demand curve shifts right	Q increases	Q increases	Q increases or decreases
	P increases	P increases or decreases	P increases
Demand curve shifts left	Q decreases	Q increases or decreases	Q decreases
	P decreases	P decreases	P increases or decreases

Solved Problem 3.2

High Demand and Low Prices in the Lobster Market

For many communities in the Maritimes, the lobster fishery is an essential part of the local economy. Lobster is fished only in season, and different communities are allowed to fish at different times of the year. For example, the fishing season for the area of Yarmouth, Nova Scotia, is from late November to the end of May. It isn't uncommon for the price of lobster to fluctuate during the season. In some cases, it can change from below $5 per pound to $8 or $9 per pound. A patch of really bad weather can drive up the price quickly, but so does Christmas (lobster tends to be a popular part of winter festivities in Canada, Europe, and other parts of the world).

What would happen if the weather just before Christmas was particularly good, allowing fishers to spend more time on the water and catch more lobster?

Solving the Problem

Step 1: Review the chapter material. This problem is about how shifts in demand and supply curves affect the equilibrium price, so you may want to review the section "The Effect of Shifts in Demand and Supply over Time."

Step 2: Draw the demand and supply graph. Draw a demand and supply graph,

Step 3: Add a demand and supply curve. Add a demand curve to account for the increase in the demand for lobster from Europe. Add a supply curve to account for the nicer-than-usual weather.

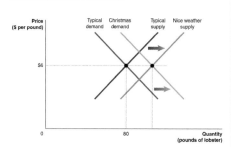

Step 4: Explain the graph. After studying the graph, you should see how the two events of increased demand from Europe and the nicer-than-usual weather combine to move the equilibrium price. The increase in supply due to the nicer-than-usual weather is offset by some of the increase in demand from Europeans. We can't say for sure which way the price will go. The price of lobster will rise if the shift in demand is greater than the shift in supply. If the shift in supply is greater than the shift in demand, prices will actually fall. All that we can say for certain is that the quantity of lobster sold (and eaten) will go up.

Source: Province of Nova Scotia, "Lobster Fishing Seasons in Atlantic Canada," *Nova Scotia Fisheries and Aquaculture*, May 17, 2012, http://www.gov.ns.ca/fish/marine/map/lobarea.shtml.

Your Turn: For more practice, do related problems 4.3 and 4.4 on page 88 at the end of this chapter.

Don't Let This Happen to You

We know from many years of teaching which concepts students find most difficult. Each chapter contains a feature called *Don't Let This Happen to You* that alerts students to the most common pitfalls in that chapter's material. We follow up with a related question in the end-of-chapter Problems and Applications section.

Don't Let This Happen to You

Remember: A Change in a Good's Price Does *Not* Cause the Demand or Supply Curve to Shift

Suppose a student is asked to draw a demand and supply graph to illustrate how an increase in the price of oranges would affect the market for apples, other variables being constant. He draws the graph on the left below and explains it as follows: "Because apples and oranges are substitutes, an increase in the price of oranges will cause an initial shift to the right in the demand curve for apples, from D_1 to D_2. However, because this initial shift in the demand curve for

apples results in a higher price for apples, P_2, consumers will find apples less desirable, and the demand curve will shift to the left, from D_2 to D_3, resulting in a final equilibrium price of P_3." Do you agree or disagree with the student's analysis?

You should disagree. The student has correctly understood that an increase in the price of oranges will cause the demand curve for apples to shift to the right. But the second demand curve shift the student describes, from D_2 to D_3, will not take place. Changes in the price of a product do not result in shifts in the product's demand curve. Changes in the price of a product result only in movements along a demand curve.

Making the Connection

Each chapter includes two to four *Making the Connection* features that provide real-world reinforcement of key concepts and help students learn how to interpret what they read on the web and in newspapers. Most *Making the Connection* features use relevant, stimulating, and provocative news stories focused on businesses and policy issues. Each *Making the Connection* has at least one supporting end-of-chapter problem to allow students to test their understanding of the topic discussed. Here are some of the *Making the Connection* features:

- Chapter 1: Should the Government of Ontario Increase the Minimum Wage?
- Chapter 6: Price Elasticity, Cross-Price Elasticity, and Income Elasticity in the Market for Alcoholic Beverages
- Chapter 8: Why Do Firms Pay Sidney Crosby to Endorse Their Products?
- Chapter 10: The Rise and Fall of Canada's Technology Darling
- Chapter 11: The Tim Hortons Coffee War in Canadian Cities

Graphs and Summary Tables

Graphs are an indispensable part of a principles of economics course but are a major stumbling block for many students. Each chapter except Chapter 1 includes end-of-chapter problems that require students to draw, read, and interpret graphs. Interactive

Making the Connection

Is Beer an Inferior Good?

For most Canadians, a beverage on a hot summer afternoon is part of the culture. In 2012, Canadians drank 8.1 litres of alcohol in various forms per person, including 80.3 litres of beer. This is a profitable industry with the LCBO (Liquor Control Board of Ontario) paying a dividend to the Government of Ontario of $1.63 billion.

How does income affect the choices Canadians make at the liquor store? As Canadians have gotten wealthier, they have changed their drinking habits. There is an underlying trend: Instead of buying beer at the lowest possible price, more and more Canadians are opting for local micro-brewery beer or local wine. In 2009, New Brunswick's alcohol retailer (Alcool NB Liquor) launched its own brand of beer, which provided New Brunswickers with a low-cost alternative, but in July 2011, that brand was discontinued due to lack of sales. During the 2011 fiscal year, the LCBO noticed that the sales of its premium products recovered from the slump that started around the same time as the financial crisis; in Ontario, the volume of sales of alcoholic beverages changed little.

Alcool NB Liquor discontinued its low cost brand of beer as the economy recovered from recession.

What we're seeing from beer sales in particular is that Canadians have begun to treat mainstream beer as an inferior good. As the average income of Canadians rises, they switch from low-cost beverages to more expensive ones. Recall that when economists describe a product as inferior, they aren't necessarily saying it is of poor quality, they're just saying that consumers buy less of it when their incomes rise.

Sources: Statistics Canada – CANSIM Table 183-0019 Series v28463248; David Pett and Jared Lindzon, Financial Post Jun. 3, 2011; Cigdem Iltan on Thursday, July 7, 2011, MacLean's Magazine.

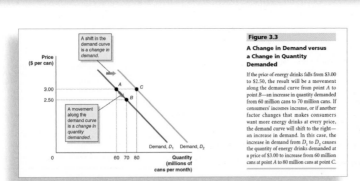

Figure 3.3

A Change in Demand versus a Change in Quantity Demanded

If the price of energy drinks falls from $3.00 to $2.50, the result will be a movement along the demand curve from point A to point B—an increase in quantity demanded from 60 million cans to 70 million cans. If consumers' incomes increase, or if another factor changes that makes consumers want more energy drinks at every price, the demand curve will shift to the right—an increase in demand. In this case, the increase in demand from D_1 to D_2 causes the quantity of energy drinks demanded at a price of $3.00 to increase from 60 million cans at point A to 80 million cans at point C.

graphing exercises appear on the book's supporting website. We use four devices to help students read and interpret graphs:

1. Detailed captions

2. Boxed notes

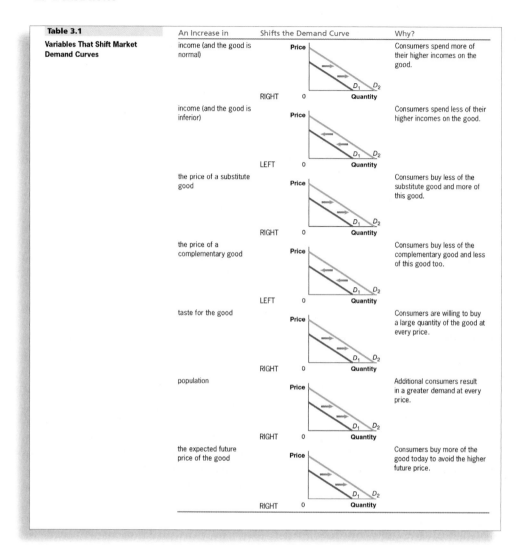

Table 3.1	An Increase in	Shifts the Demand Curve	Why?
Variables That Shift Market Demand Curves	income (and the good is normal)	RIGHT	Consumers spend more of their higher incomes on the good.
	income (and the good is inferior)	LEFT	Consumers spend less of their higher incomes on the good.
	the price of a substitute good	RIGHT	Consumers buy less of the substitute good and more of this good.
	the price of a complementary good	LEFT	Consumers buy less of the complementary good and less of this good too.
	taste for the good	RIGHT	Consumers are willing to buy a large quantity of the good at every price.
	population	RIGHT	Additional consumers result in a greater demand at every price.
	the expected future price of the good	RIGHT	Consumers buy more of the good today to avoid the higher future price.

3. Colour-coded curves

4. Summary tables with graphs (see pages 68, 72, and 163 for examples)

Review Questions and Problems and Applications

Every exercise in a chapter's Problems and Applications section is available in MyEconLab. Using MyEconLab, students can complete these and many other exercises online, get tutorial help, and receive instant feedback and assistance on exercises they answer incorrectly. Also, student learning will be enhanced by having the summary material and problems grouped together by learning objective, which will allow students to focus on the parts of the chapter they found most challenging. Each major section of the chapter, paired with a learning objective, has at least two review questions and three problems.

   We include end-of-chapter problems that test students' understanding of the content presented in the *Solved Problem*, *Making the Connection*, and *Don't Let This Happen to You* special features in the chapter. Instructors can cover a feature in class and assign the corresponding problem for homework. The Test Item Files also include test questions that pertain to these special features.

Integrated Supplements

The authors and Pearson Canada have worked together to integrate the text, supplements, and media resources to make teaching and learning easier.

MyEconLab

MyLab and Mastering, our leading online learning products, deliver customizable content and highly personalized study paths, responsive learning tools, and real-time evaluation and diagnostics. MyLab and Mastering products give educators the ability to move each student toward the moment that matters most—the moment of true understanding and learning. MyEconLab for Hubbard, Canadian Edition, can be used as a powerful out-of-the-box resource for students who need extra help, or instructors can take full advantage of its advanced customization options. Students can also benefit from MyEconLab's Study Play, now powered by a sophisticated adaptive learning engine that tailors learning material to meet their unique learning needs.

Pearson eText gives students access to the text whenever and wherever they have access to the Internet. eText pages look exactly like the printed text, offering powerful new functionality for students and instructors. Users can create notes, highlight text in different colours, create bookmarks, zoom, click hyperlinked words and phrases to view definitions, and view in single-page or two-page view. Pearson eText allows for quick navigation to key parts of the eText using a table of contents and provides full-text search. The eText may also offer links to associated media files, enabling users to access videos, animations, or other activities as they read the text.

Other Resources for the Instructor

Instructor's Manual

The Instructor's Manual includes chapter-by-chapter summaries grouped by learning objectives, teaching outlines incorporating key terms and definitions, teaching tips, topics for class discussion, new *Solved Problems*, new *Making the Connection* features, new *Economics in Your Life* scenarios, and solutions to all review questions and problems in the book. The Instructor's Manual is available for download from the Instructor's Resource Center (www.pearsoned.ca/highered). The text authors—Jason Childs and Apostolos Serletis—prepared the solutions to the end-of-chapter review questions and problems.

Two Test Item Files

This edition is accompanied by two Test Item Files. Each Test Item File includes 2,000 class-tested multiple-choice, true/false, short-answer, and graphing questions. The first Test Item File will be available upon publication of the text; the second Test Item File of 2,000 questions will be added a year following publication in order to incorporate market feedback and to provide a fresh and updated store of questions. There are questions to support each key feature in the book. The Test Item Files are available in print and for download from the Instructor's Resource Center (www.pearsonhighered.com/hubbard). Test questions are annotated with the following information:

- **Difficulty:** 1 for straight recall, 2 for some analysis, 3 for complex analysis
- **Type:** multiple-choice, true/false, short-answer, essay
- **Topic:** the term or concept the question supports
- **Learning outcome**
- **AACSB** (see description that follows)
- **Page number**
- **Special feature in the main book:** chapter-opening business example, *Economics in Your Life, Solved Problem, Making the Connection, Don't Let This Happen to You,* and *An Inside Look*

The Association to Advance Collegiate Schools of Business (AACSB)

The Test Item File author has connected select questions to the general knowledge and skill guidelines found in the AACSB Assurance of Learning Standards.

TestGen

The computerized TestGen package allows instructors to customize, save, and generate classroom tests. The test program permits instructors to edit, add, or delete questions from the Test Item Files; analyze test results; and organize a database of tests and student results. This software allows for extensive flexibility and ease of use. It provides many options for organizing and displaying tests, along with search and sort features. The software and the Test Item Files can be downloaded from the Instructor's Resource Center (www .pearsonhighered.com/hubbard).

PowerPoint Lecture Presentation

Two sets of PowerPoint slides are available:

1. A comprehensive set of animated PowerPoint slides can be used by instructors for class presentations or by students for lecture preview or review. These animated slides include all the graphs, tables, and equations in the textbook.

2. A second set of PowerPoint slides without animations is available for those who prefer a more streamlined presentation for class use.

CourseSmart for Instructors

CourseSmart goes beyond traditional expectations—providing instant, online access to the textbooks and course materials you need at a lower cost for students. And even as students save money, you can save time and hassle with a digital eTextbook that allows you to search for the most relevant content at the very moment you need it. Whether it's evaluating textbooks or creating lecture notes to help students with difficult concepts, CourseSmart can make life a little easier. See how when you visit www.coursesmart.com /instructors.

Learning Solution Consultants

Pearson's Technology Specialists work with faculty and campus course designers to ensure that Pearson technology products, assessment tools, and online course materials are tailored to meet your specific needs. This highly qualified team is dedicated to helping students take full advantage of a wide range of educational resources by assisting in the integration of a variety of instructional materials and media formats. Your local Pearson Canada sales representative can provide you with more details about this service program.

Pearson Custom Library

For enrollments of at least 25 students, you can create your own textbook by choosing the chapters that best suit your own course needs. To begin building your custom text, visit www.pearsoncustomlibrary.com. You may also work with a dedicated Pearson Custom editor to create your ideal text—publishing your own original content or mixing and matching Pearson content. Contact your local Pearson Representative to get started.

ACKNOWLEDGEMENTS

The guidance and recommendations of the following instructors helped us develop our plans for the first Canadian edition and the supplements package. While we could not incorporate every suggestion from every reviewer, we do thank each and every one of you and acknowledge that your feedback was indispensable in developing this text. We greatly appreciate your assistance in making this the best text it could be; you have helped teach a whole new generation of students about the exciting world of economics. We also wish to acknowledge Michael Leonard and his fine contributions to the Canadian research and examples in this volume.

Fred Aswani, McMaster University
Iris Au, University of Toronto – Scarborough
Vasyl Golovetsky, Simon Fraser University
Frank Trimnell, Ryerson University
Chris Wilmore, University of Victoria
Constantin Colonescu, Grant MacEwan University
Sigrid Ewender, Kwantlen Polytechnic University
Hannah Holmes, McMaster University
Bernnan Thompson, Ryerson University
Michael G. Lanyi, University of Lethbridge
Sandra Wellman, Seneca College
Vladimir Dvoracek, University of the Fraser Valley
David Gray, University of Ottawa
Neil Roberts, Kwantlen Polytechnic University
Robert Jefferson, Wilfrid Laurier University
Narine Grigoryan, Camosun College
Hussein Alzyoud, Athabasca University
Duanne Rockerbie, University of Lethbridge
Andrew Wong, Grant MacEwan University
Carol Derksen, Red River College
Karl Pinno, University of Calgary
Nargess Kayhani, Mount Saint Vincent University
Fiona T. Rahman, University of Waterloo

A WORD OF THANKS

We greatly appreciate the efforts of the Pearson team. Managing Editor Claudine O'Donnell's energy and direction made this first Canadian edition possible. Developmental Editor Mary Wat and Project Manager Rachel Thompson worked tirelessly to ensure that this text was as good as it could be. We are grateful for the energy and creativity of marketing manager Leigh-Anne Graham. Karen Townsend and Imee Salumbides ably managed the extensive MyLab and supplement package that accompanies the book. Anthony Leung and Jerilyn Bockorick turned our manuscript pages into a beautiful published book. We received excellent research assistance from Mike Sherar and Michael Leonard. We thank copy editor Laurel Sparrow and proofreader Cat Haggert for their careful copy editing and proofreading.

Economics: Foundations and Models

© oah1611/Fotolia

Chapter Outline and Learning Objectives

You versus Caffeine

As you study economics, you will start to see the complexity and interconnectedness of the world around you. Something as simple as your morning cup of coffee is actually the result of hundreds of individual choices made by people you have never met.

If you are like 65 percent of Canadians, you had a cup of coffee this morning—you might even be drinking one now. In Colombia, over 3500 kilometres away, someone decided to plant coffee, somebody else picked it, and another group of people brought it to a port. A different group of people loaded it onto a ship, and other people sailed the ship to North America. The coffee beans were then unloaded, transported to a roaster, roasted and ground, and packaged, all by more different people. Finally, the coffee arrived at your local coffee shop, where

yet another group of people brew the coffee for you. This amazing sequence of events happens without any one person or group of people planning it. Yet you get the benefit of all this work by all these different people for less than $5. It's amazing to consider all that's involved in something so simple.

This interconnectedness of people's choices can have major implications for you. In 2011, heavy rains in Colombia reduced the amount of coffee grown there. This change in the weather, so far from Canada, changed what all Canadians had to pay for their morning cup.

AN INSIDE LOOK on **page 16** discusses some of the factors that can change the price of coffee and which types of companies are most likely to change their prices.

Economics in Your Life

How Much Will You Pay for a Cup of Coffee?

The price of coffee is likely to go up in the next year or two. There was a time not long ago when a cup of coffee cost less than a dollar. Suppose you are waiting in line to buy the cup of coffee you count on to keep you awake during class. Is the price likely to be higher than it was last week? We all complain when the price of something we buy regularly goes up, but what determines that price? Consider what might change if the price of coffee doubled over the next six months. As you read this chapter, see if you can answer this question. You can check your answer against the one we provide on page 15 at the end of this chapter.

In this book, we use economics to answer a wide variety of questions. Just a few examples:

- How are the prices of things you buy every day determined?
- How does government spending and taxation affect the economy?
- Why do governments control the prices of some goods?
- Why are some countries wealthier than others?

Economists don't always agree on the answers to these questions and a lot of others. In fact, there are a number of lively debates on a lot of different issues. In addition, new problems and issues are constantly arising. So, economists are always at work developing new methods to analyze economic questions.

Scarcity A situation in which unlimited wants exceed the limited resources available to fulfill those wants.

All the issues we discuss in this text illustrate a basic fact of life: People have to make choices. We all have to make choices because of **scarcity**. Scarcity means that we don't have enough resources to do everything we want to. Our needs and wants are infinite, but our planet and time are finite. You likely had to choose between spending money on tuition or taking a trip to Europe. Even the richest people in the world have to deal with scarcity of time. Bill Gates, one of the wealthiest people in the world, has to choose between working with his charitable foundation or spending time with his children. Every hour he spends on charity work is an hour he can't spend with his family. **Economics** is the study of the choices consumers, business managers, and government officials (in short, *people*) make in their efforts to make the best use of scarce resources in achieving their goals.

Economics The study of the choices people make to attain their goals, given their scarce resources.

We begin this chapter by discussing three important economic ideas that will come up throughout this book. *People are rational, people respond to incentives*, and *optimal decisions are made at the margin*. We then introduce you to the three basic economic decisions that all societies have had to find answers to since society began: *What* goods and services will be produced? *How* will the goods and services be produced? and *Who* will receive the goods and services produced? Next, we introduce you to the idea of economic models and their role in analyzing economic issues. **Economic models** are simplifications of reality used to analyze real-world issues. We will explain why economists use models and how they construct them. Finally, we will discuss the difference between microeconomics and macroeconomics and introduce you to some of the other important terms that are part of economists' language.

Economic model A simplified version of reality used to analyze real-world economic situations.

Three Key Economic Ideas

1.1 LEARNING OBJECTIVE

Explain these three key economic ideas: People are rational, people respond to incentives, and optimal decisions are made at the margin.

As you go through your day-to-day life, you interact with many people directly and thousands more indirectly. Whether you are looking for a part-time job, downloading the latest app, or getting a quick cup of coffee, you are interacting with other people through markets. A **market** is a group of buyers and sellers and the institutions (rules) or arrangements by which they come together to trade. Most of economics involves analyzing what happens in markets. Throughout this book, as we study how people make choices and interact in markets, we will return to three important ideas:

Market A group of buyers and sellers of a good or service and the institutions or arrangements by which they come together to trade.

1. People are rational.
2. People respond to incentives.
3. Optimal decisions are made at the margin.

People are Rational

Economists generally assume that people are rational. This does not mean that economists think that people are computers with no emotions. It means that people make decisions and take the actions that they *believe* will make them happy. Economists tend to think people consider the costs and benefits of something and only do the things with more benefit than cost. When you buy a cup of coffee, an economist assumes that you thought the benefit was worth at least as much as the time, effort, and money you had to spend getting it. You might be wrong, it could be the worst cup of coffee you have ever had, but when you paid $2, you believed it was worth it. Put simply, economists don't think people deliberately do things to make themselves worse off.

People Respond to Incentives

Many factors go into determining the benefit of something. You might see benefits in terms of religious fulfillment, jealousy, compassion, or even greed. Economists emphasize that consumers and firms consistently respond to *economic* incentives. This fact may seem obvious, but it is often overlooked. For a great example of this, take a look at your local bank and then think of banks shown in American movies. Banks in American movies often have bullet resistant shields and security guards to deter bank robbers. Bullet-resistant plastic shields and armed security guards are unheard of at Canadian bank branches. Why? The shields are expensive, costing up to $20 000. The average loss during a robbery is around just $1200. The economic incentives for banks are clear: It is less costly to put up with robberies and tell staff not to resist robbers than to take additional security measures. Some people are surprised by the lack of security in Canadian banks, but economists aren't.

In each chapter, the *Making the Connection* feature discusses a news story or another application related to the chapter material. Read the following *Making the Connection* for a discussion of whether people respond to incentives even when deciding to have children.

Making the Connection	**Will Women in Quebec Have More Babies if the Government Pays Them to?**

The population of Canada is aging as birthrates decline and people live longer. An aging population makes social and pension programs harder to afford as there are fewer young workers paying into the programs and more people drawing benefits. The result will require either reducing payments to seniors or increasing taxes on young workers.

For the population of a country to be relatively stable (without immigration), women must have, on average, 2.1 children each. Canadian women have about 1.6 children on average. This figure is well below what is needed to keep the population stable. To deal with this shortage of people, governments can encourage people from other countries to move to Canada or they can try to encourage Canadian women to have more children.

While some provinces have focused on immigration, Quebec has opted to encourage women to have more children. The provincial government pays parents $500 for their first child, $1000 for their second, and $6000 for their third. While $6000 may not seem like a lot of money for having a child, women in Quebec have more children than the Canadian average (1.72 compared with 1.58). It could be that some women who had just barely decided not to have a third child were convinced by the extra incentive offered by the government.

Sources: Based on Daniel Parent and Ling Wang, "Tax Incentives and Fertility in Canada: Quantum vs Tempo Effects," *Canadian Journal of Economics* 40, no. 2(2007): 371–400; and Statistics Canada, "Crude Birth Rate, Age-Specific and Total Fertility Rates (Live Births), Canada, Provinces and Territories," CANSIM Table 102-4505, http://www5.statcan.gc.ca/cansim/a05?lang=eng&id=1024505.

Your Turn: Test your understanding by doing related problems 1.3 and 1.4 on page 19 at the end of this chapter.

MyEconLab

Optimal Decisions are Made at the Margin

Economics is sometimes referred to as the *marginal science* because of how economists tend to think about decisions. Some decisions are "all or nothing." When you finish your undergraduate degree, you can choose to either get a job or go to graduate school. However, most decisions are not the all-or-nothing type and involve doing a little more or a little less. For example, when you have a job, your choices are not whether to spend everything you earn or to save it all, but how much to save.

Economists use the term *marginal* to mean "extra" or "additional." Should you spend your next hour playing an online game or spend it studying? The *marginal benefit (MB)* of playing another hour is the enjoyment you receive. The *marginal cost (MC)* is the lower grade you receive because you studied less. You aren't the only one who has to make decisions at the margin. McCain Foods has to decide how many kilograms of frozen french-fries to produce per year. Should the company make another million kilos? The marginal benefit of this would be the extra revenue it gets from selling the extra french-fries, and the marginal cost would be the extra wages, materials, and equipment needed to make them. If your goal is to make the *net benefit* (benefit minus cost) as big as possible, then you have a really simple decision rule—*do more of any activity with a marginal benefit greater than the marginal cost*. As long as MB > MC, do more. If you've gotten as much net benefit as possible, you'll find that MB is pretty close to MC. In fact, MB = MC is an easy way of deciding when to do no more of something. When it comes to a firm's profit (revenue – cost), if producing the next unit increases revenue (MB) more than costs (marginal cost), making that unit will increase your profits. If producing the next unit increases costs more than revenue, making that unit will actually reduce profits. If producing the next unit increases revenue by the same amount as it increases costs, stop! You've now maximized profits and net benefits.

People often apply this rule without really thinking about it. Usually you will know whether the extra enjoyment of another hour of gaming is worth the additional cost of spending one hour less studying for your economics midterm without a mathematical formula. However, business people often have to make careful calculations using spreadsheets and such to determine whether the extra revenue of increased production is greater than or less than the additional costs. Economists refer to this sort of analysis as **marginal analysis**.

Marginal analysis Analysis that involves comparing marginal benefits and marginal costs.

In each chapter of this book, you will see the special feature *Solved Problem*. This feature will enhance your understanding of the material by leading you through the steps of solving an applied economic problem. After reading the problem, you can test your understanding by working out the related problems at the end of the chapter and in the study guide. You can also find more *Solved Problems* and tutorials at MyEconLab.

Solved Problem **1.1**

McCain Foods Makes a Decision at the Margin

Suppose McCain Foods is currently selling 10 million kilograms of frozen french-fries per year. Managers at McCain Foods are thinking about increasing production to 11 million kilograms per year. One manager argues, "Increasing production from 10 million to 11 million is good because we will make a total profit of $500 million if we make 11 million kilograms." Do you agree with her reasoning? What, if any, additional information do you need to have to decide whether McCain Foods should produce the extra 1 million kilograms of french-fries? When would making the extra french-fries be a good idea? When would it be a bad idea?

Solving the Problem

Step 1: Review the chapter material. This problem is about making decisions, so you may want to review the section "Optimal Decisions Are Made at the Margin," which begins on this page. Remember to "think marginal" whenever you see the words *additional* or *extra* in economics.

Step 2: Explain whether you agree with the manager. We have seen that any activity should be continued up to the point where marginal benefit is equal to marginal cost. In this case, that means making french-fries up to the point where the additional revenue McCain Foods gets from selling more french-fries is equal to the extra cost of making them. The McCain Foods' manager has not done a marginal analysis, so you should not agree with the manager's reasoning, *yet*. Her statement about total profit doesn't help you decide whether to make the extra french-fries. The manager could be right that making the extra french-fries is a good idea, but she hasn't provided proof—you need more information to know for sure.

Step 3: Explain what additional information you need. You need more information to make the correct decision. You need to know the additional revenue that would be generated by selling the extra french-fries. You also need to know how much the extra potatoes, oil, labour, etc. will cost. In short, you need to know the marginal cost (extra costs) and the marginal benefit (extra revenue).

Step 4: Compare marginal cost and marginal benefit. Once you know the marginal cost and marginal benefit of making the extra million kilograms of french-fries, compare the two. If the marginal cost is greater than the marginal benefit, then making the extra fries is a bad idea. If the marginal cost is less than the marginal benefit, then making the extra french-fries is a good idea.

Your Turn: For more practice, do related problem 1.5 on page 19 at the end of this chapter.

MyEconLab

The Economic Problems all Societies must Solve

Living in a world of scarcity means that we face **trade-offs**: Doing more of one thing means that we have to do less of something else. The best way to measure the cost of something is the value of what we give up to get it. The value of what we give up to engage in an activity is called the **opportunity cost**. To be accurate, the opportunity cost of something (such as a good or service) is the value of the next best alternative. What is the opportunity cost of spending an extra hour studying? It depends on what you would have chosen to do if you weren't studying. If you would have spent the hour watching TV, then that is the opportunity cost, never mind that you could have spent the same time studying. The easiest way to demonstrate what opportunity cost is all about is with an example. Let's say that a federal government employee, who is currently earning $80 000 a year, is thinking about leaving his or her job to start a consulting company. The opportunity cost of starting the consulting company is the $80 000 salary that is no longer received from the government, even if the person doesn't pay him or herself a salary in the new business.

Since all societies face trade-offs, they must make choices when answering the following three fundamental economic questions:

1. *What* goods and services will be produced?
2. *How* will the goods and services be produced?
3. *Who* will receive the goods and services produced?

Throughout this book, we'll return to these questions. For now, we briefly introduce each one.

What Goods and Services will be Produced?

How will a society decide whether to make more economics textbooks or more video games? More daycare spaces or more sports arenas? Of course, "society" doesn't make decisions, individual people do. The answer to the question of what to produce is determined by the choices that consumers, firms, and governments make. Due to the

1.2 LEARNING OBJECTIVE

Discuss how a society answers these three key economic questions: What goods and services will be produced? How will the goods and services be produced? Who will receive the goods and services produced?

Trade-off The idea that because of scarcity, producing more of one good or service means producing less of another good or service.

Opportunity cost The highest-valued alternative that must be given up to engage in an activity.

structure of the Canadian economy, every day you help decide what goods and services firms in Canada and around the world make. When you choose to spend your money at the movies instead of at the bookstore, you encourage firms to make more movies and fewer books. Similarly, Bombardier must decide whether it will devote resources to producing new planes or trains. The federal government must also make decisions about what to produce. Will it devote resources to the military or increase payments to parents with children? In each case, consumers, firms, and governments deal with scarcity by trading off one good or service for another. Each choice made comes with an opportunity cost, measured by the value of the best alternative given up.

How will the Goods and Services be Produced?

After figuring out what to make, societies must figure out how to make it. In the Canadian context, we generally think of firms or government making this decision. Producers of goods and services face a trade-off between using more workers and using more machines. For example, movie studios have to choose whether to produce animated films using highly skilled animators to draw each frame by hand or to use fewer animators and powerful computers and software. Firms also have to decide whether to produce in Canada using few workers and many machines or produce in developing countries using many workers with few machines.

Who will Receive the Goods and Services Produced?

In Canada, who receives what is produced depends largely on how income is distributed. Individuals with the highest incomes have the ability to buy the most goods and services. Governments levy taxes and use part of the money to provide income to some people. Governments also use the money collected in taxes to supply goods and services that are not being provided in other ways. The debate over how much taxation and government spending is appropriate will continue as long as societies must address the three fundamental questions.

Centrally Planned Economies versus Market Economies

Societies answer the three questions— what, how, and for whom?—in different ways. We'll talk briefly about the two extremes, but remember that all countries use a combination of both.

Centrally planned economy An economy in which the government decides how economic resources will be allocated.

One extreme is the **centrally planned economy**, in which an individual or group of people (generally the government) directly answers all three questions. From 1917 to 1991, the most important centrally planned economy was the Soviet Union's. In the Soviet Union, government agencies decided what to produce, what production techniques to use, and who would get the goods once they were made. People managing factories and stores reported to the government. These managers had to follow the instructions of government even when what they were producing wasn't what consumers (people) wanted. Centrally planned economies like the Soviet Union's have not been successful in producing low-cost (plentiful), high-quality goods and services. As a result, the material standard of living of the average person in a centrally planned economy tends to be low. All centrally planned economies have also been dictatorships. Dissatisfaction with low living standards and political repression finally led to the collapse of the Soviet Union in 1991. Today only a few small countries, such as Cuba and North Korea, still have largely centrally planned economies. Recently Cuba, under Raúl Castro, has begun to move away from central planning.

Market economy An economy in which the decisions of households and firms interacting in markets allocate economic resources.

At the other end of the spectrum is the **market economy**. Market economies rely on privately owned firms to produce goods and services and to decide how to produce them. A *market* is all potential buyers and sellers of a good or service as well as the rules that determine how buyers and sellers interact. Markets, rather than a government employee, determine who receives the goods and services produced. In this type of economy, firms must produce goods and services that people want to buy or they go out of business. In that sense, it is ultimately consumers who decide what will be produced and how. In a market economy, all trades must be agreed to by all the people involved.

In a market economy, people's income is mostly determined by what they have to sell. For example, if you're a civil engineer and firms are willing to pay you $85 000 a year, that's what you will have to spend on goods and services. If you own a house that you rent out to your friends or own shares in a company, your income will be even higher. Market economies have two distinguishing features: (1) markets directly reward people's hard work, and (2) decision making is shared by everyone in the market. Overall, in a market economy the answers to the three basic questions are provided by everyone.

Market economies do have drawbacks. Luck, both good and bad, plays a role in determining a person's income, and sometimes markets don't work the way we would like them to. In particular, markets are not good at providing important goods and services such as roads, national defence, or health care.

The Modern Mixed Economy

We've seen that there are flaws in how both centrally planned economies and market economies answer the three basic questions. As a result, all modern economies are "**mixed economies**" that use elements of both centrally planned and market economies. In Canada, most of the things you buy in stores—electronics, coffee, food, etc.—are produced by privately owned firms in response to the demands of consumers: The availability of these goods results from a market system answering the three basic questions. At the same time, other goods and services are provided by the government, such as roads, national defence, health care, etc. Even the United States and China are mixed economies that rely on a combination of both the market and central planning to provide people with a variety of goods and services.

Mixed economy An economy in which most economic decisions result from the interaction of buyers and sellers in markets, but in which the government plays a significant role in the allocation of resources.

Most debates about central planning and markets are about the extent each plays in answering the three questions. Very few people actually still advocate for a total market economy or a completely centrally planned economy. Keep this in mind when listening to the debates of leaders of political parties.

Efficiency and Equity

Market economies tend to be more efficient than centrally planned economies. Before we can understand why this is, we must explore two types of efficiency: *productive efficiency* and *allocative efficiency*. **Productive efficiency** occurs when a good or service is produced at the lowest possible cost. **Allocative efficiency** occurs when a country's resources are used to produce the mix of goods and services that consumers want. Markets tend to be efficient because they rely on **voluntary exchange**. When an exchange is voluntary, both the buyer and the seller are made better off by the transaction, or they wouldn't have agreed to it. The voluntary nature of exchange promotes competition that encourages producers to find cheaper methods of producing the goods and services they want to sell, as consumers always wish to pay less. This leads to productive efficiency, as firms that can't match others' low costs go out of business. Competition also promotes allocative efficiency. A firm that uses scarce resources to produce goods and services that consumers don't want to buy goes out of business.

Productive efficiency A situation in which a good or service is produced at the lowest possible cost.

Allocative efficiency A state of the economy in which production is in accordance with consumer preferences; in particular, every good or service is produced up to the point where the last unit provides a marginal benefit to society equal to the marginal cost of producing it.

Markets and competition promote efficiency, but they don't guarantee it. Inefficiency can arise from a variety of sources. It often takes time to achieve an efficient outcome. When Blu-ray players were first introduced, firms didn't instantly achieve productive efficiency, as they had to experiment to find the lowest cost method of producing them. Some production processes cause environmental damage. In this case, government intervention can actually increase efficiency; without government action, firms will ignore the cost of damaging the environment, leading to the production of more goods than is in society's best interest.

Voluntary exchange A situation that occurs in markets when both the buyer and seller of a product are made better off by the transaction.

An economically efficient outcome is not necessarily a desirable one. Many people prefer economic outcomes that they consider fair or equitable, even if those outcomes are less efficient. **Equity** is harder to define than *efficiency*, but it usually involves a fair distribution of economic benefits. For some people, equity involves a more equal distribution of economic benefits than would result from an emphasis on efficiency alone.

Equity The fair distribution of economic benefits.

For example, some people support raising taxes on people with higher incomes to provide funds for programs that aid the poor. Although governments may increase equity by reducing the incomes of high-income people and increasing the incomes of the poor, efficiency may be reduced. People have less incentive to open new businesses, to supply labour, and to save if the government takes a significant amount of the income they earn from working or saving. The result is that fewer goods and services are produced, and less saving takes place. As this example illustrates, *there is often a trade-off between efficiency and equity.* Government policymakers often confront this trade-off.

1.3 LEARNING OBJECTIVE

Understand what economic models are and aren't, and why they're a good idea.

Economic Models

Economists rely on economic theories, or models (we use the words *model* and *theory* interchangeably in this text), to analyze real-world issues from coffee prices to immigration. As mentioned earlier, economic models are simplifications of reality. Economists are not the only ones using models: An engineer may use a computer model of a bridge to test its resistance to earthquakes; a biologist may make a physical model of a nucleic acid to better understand its properties. The main point of a model is to allow people to focus on the interactions between two or more things. Thus a model makes ideas sufficiently explicit and concrete so that individuals, firms, or the government can use them to make decisions. For example, we will see in Chapter 3 that the model of demand and supply is a simplified version of how the prices of products are determined by interactions among buyers and sellers in markets.

Economists use models to answer questions. For example, consider the question from the chapter opener: "How much will you be paying for a cup of coffee?" While this seems like a fairly simple question, it is actually quite complicated. To answer such complex questions like this one, economists use several models to look at different aspects of the issue. For example, they may use a model of how wages are determined to analyze the flexibility different firms have in their cost structures. They may use another model to consider how often people will change their purchasing patterns. Yet another model might be used to explore how growers will react to a change in the price of raw coffee. Sometimes economists can use existing models to analyze an issue, but in other cases, they must develop a new model. To develop a new model, economists generally follow these steps:

1. Decide on the assumptions to use in developing the model.
2. Formulate a testable hypothesis.
3. Use economic data to test the hypothesis.
4. Revise the model if it fails to explain the economic data well.
5. Retain the revised model to help answer similar economic questions in the future.

The Role of Assumptions in Economic Models

Any model, in any discipline, is based on assumptions because models have to be simple to be useful. We cannot analyze an economic issue unless we reduce its complexity at least a little. For example, economic models make *behavioural assumptions* about the motives of consumers and firms. Economists assume that consumers will buy the goods and services that will maximize their well-being or their satisfaction. Similarly, economists assume that firms act to maximize their profits. These assumptions are simplifications because we know they don't describe the motives of every firm or every consumer exactly. How can we know if the assumptions in a model are too simple or too limiting? We discover this when we form hypotheses based on these assumptions and test the hypotheses using real-world information.

Forming and Testing Hypotheses in Economic Models

Economic variable Something measurable that can have different values, such as the price of coffee.

An **economic variable** is something measurable, such as the wages paid to Tim Hortons employees. A *hypothesis* in an economic model is a statement about an economic variable that may be either correct or incorrect. Most hypotheses take the form of predictions. An example of a hypothesis in an economic model is the statement that extreme weather in Colombia will increase the price of coffee in Canada. An economic hypothesis is usually about a *causal relationship*; in this case, the hypothesis states that weather patterns in Colombia *cause* higher prices for coffee in Canada.

All hypotheses need to be tested before they are accepted. To test a hypothesis, we analyze statistics on the relevant economic variables. In our coffee example, we would gather data on coffee prices and other variables that we think might have an impact on the people buying or selling coffee. Testing a hypothesis can be tricky. For example, showing that coffee prices rose following a spate of bad weather in Colombia is not enough to demonstrate that Colombian weather *caused* the price increase. Just because two things are *correlated*—that is, they happen together—does not mean that one caused the other. In this example, perhaps the price increase was caused by an increase in the wages paid to coffee shop employees. Many different economic variables change over any given period of time, which makes testing hypotheses a challenge.

Note that hypotheses must be statements that could, in fact, turn out to be incorrect. Statements such as "high coffee prices are bad" or "high wages for baristas are good" are value judgments rather than hypotheses because there is no way to disprove them.

Economists accept and use an economic model if it leads to hypotheses that are confirmed by statistical analysis. In many cases, the acceptance is tentative pending the gathering and analysis of new data. In fact, economists often refer to a hypothesis having been "not rejected," rather than "accepted." But what if statistical analysis rejects a hypothesis? For example, what if a model generates the hypothesis that bad weather in Colombia leads to higher coffee prices in Canada, but analysis of the data rejects the hypothesis? In this case, the model must be reconsidered. It may be that an assumption used in the model was too simplistic or limiting. What if the model used to determine the effect of weather on Canadian coffee prices didn't take into account Canadian weather patterns—people drink more hot beverages when it's cold outside. If the bad weather in Colombia occurred during the Canadian summer, we might not see an impact on coffee prices.

The process of developing models, testing hypotheses, and revising models occurs not just in economics but in disciplines like physics, chemistry, and biology. This process is often referred to as the *scientific method*. Economics is called a *social science* because it applies the scientific method to the study of interactions among people.

Normative and Positive Analysis

Throughout this book, as we build economic models and use them to answer questions, we need to keep the distinction between *positive analysis* and *normative analysis* in mind. **Positive analysis** concerns facts or logic. Positive statements are concerned with what is and can potentially be disproven. **Normative analysis** is about value judgments, or what *ought* to be. Economics is about positive analysis, which measures the costs and benefits of different courses of action.

Positive analysis Analysis concerned with what is.

Normative analysis Analysis concerned with what ought to be.

We can use a provincial government's minimum wage laws to compare positive and normative analysis. In 2013 Nova Scotia had the highest minimum wage of any province in Canada (Nunavut had an even higher minimum wage). In Nova Scotia, it is illegal to pay a worker less than $10.30 an hour. Without the minimum wage law, some firms and some workers would voluntarily agree to a lower wage. Because of the minimum wage law, some workers have a hard time finding work, and some firms end up paying more for workers. A positive analysis of the minimum wage law uses an economic model to estimate how many workers lose their jobs (or are unable to find one) when the minimum wage increases, the impact of an increase on firms' costs and profits, and the gains to those workers who find jobs at a higher rate of pay. After economists complete this positive analysis, the decision as to whether an increase in the minimum wage was a good idea or a bad idea is a normative one and depends on how people view the trade-offs involved. Supporters of minimum wage laws feel that the losses to employers and to newly unemployed workers are more than offset by the gains to workers who see their pay increase. Opponents of minimum wage laws think the losses are greater than the gains. The assessment depends, in part, on a person's values and political views. The positive analysis an economist provides would play a role in the decision but can't by itself decide the issue one way or another.

In each chapter, you will see a *Don't Let This Happen to You* box like the one below. This box alerts you to common pitfalls in thinking about economic ideas. After reading this box, test your understanding by working out the related problem at the end of the chapter.

Don't Let This Happen to You

Don't Confuse Positive Analysis with Normative Analysis

"Economic analysis has shown that an increase in the minimum wage is a bad idea because it causes unemployment." Is this statement accurate? In 2012, legislation in British Columbia prevented anyone from paying a worker less than $10.25 per hour. This wage is higher than some employers are willing to pay some workers. If the minimum wage were lower, some people who currently can't find a job would be able to find work at a lower wage. Therefore, positive economic analysis indicates that an increase in the minimum wage causes unemployment (although there is a lot of disagreement on how much). *But,* those people who find jobs benefit from the increased minimum wage because they get paid more. In other words, increasing the minimum wage creates both losers (those who end up unemployed because of the minimum wage legislation and the firms that have to pay workers more) and winners (people who get paid more than they would have before the minimum wage increase).

Should we value the gains to the winners more than the losses to the losers? The answer to this question involves normative analysis. Positive economic analysis can only show you what the consequences of a policy are, not whether a policy is "good" or "bad." The statement at the beginning of this box is incorrect.

MyEconLab

Your Turn: Test your understanding by doing related problem 3.5 on page 20 at the end of this chapter.

Economics as a Social Science

Since economics studies the actions of people, it is a social science. Economics is similar to other social science disciplines like psychology, political science, and sociology. As a social science, economics is all about human behaviour—particularly decision making—in every context, not just the context of business. Economists study issues such as how families decide how many children to have, why some people have a hard time losing weight, and why people often ignore important information when making decisions. Economics also has much to contribute to questions of government policy. As we'll see throughout this book, economists have played an important role in formulating government policies in areas such as the environment, health care, and poverty.

Making
the
Connection | ## Should the Government of Ontario Increase its Minimum Wage?

The current minimum wage in Ontario is $10.25 per hour, despite the fact that Toronto is one of the most expensive places to live in Canada. Should Ontario increase the minimum wage? Like most questions about economic policy, the answer is, it depends. There are costs and benefits to increasing the minimum wage.

An increase in the minimum wage tends to reduce the number of entry-level jobs. When firms have to pay workers more, they hire fewer people. Entry-level jobs, which tend to be filled by young people, can be the first step in developing a successful career. Youth unemployment is a growing problem in a number of countries, such as Spain and France, that have restrictive labour laws. Moreover, a person's early employment history has a huge impact on lifelong earnings.

Higher labour costs are also difficult for some firms to deal with. Having to pay more for labour means that firms that are able to substitute machinery for workers will have an advantage over those that can't. Increasing the minimum wage tends to give larger firms an advantage over smaller ones, because they can afford the complex machinery to replace people. (Do you think a small retail store could afford the self-scan checkout you see at major retailers?)

Increasing the minimum wage also offers important benefits. Those who can find or keep their jobs get bigger pay cheques. An increase in income can go a long way toward improving the lives of people who depend on minimum wage work for their livelihoods. People with lower incomes may spend more of what they earn than those with higher incomes, so increasing the minimum wage may create more economic opportunities for other people as well.

Whether Ontario should increase its minimum wage rate is a normative question. The answer to that question will be based on how the people of Ontario feel the costs and benefits compare.

Your Turn: Test your understanding by doing related problem 3.3 on page 20 at the end of this chapter.

Should Ontario raise its minimum wage?

MyEconLab

Microeconomics and Macroeconomics

1.4 LEARNING OBJECTIVE

Distinguish between microeconomics and macroeconomics.

Economic models can be used to analyze decision making in many areas. We group some of these areas together as *microeconomics* and others as *macroeconomics*. **Microeconomics** is the study of how individual economic agents make choices, how these choices come together to determine what happens in a single market, and the impact of government interventions on market outcomes. When you're talking about microeconomics, you're generally talking about *one* person, *one* firm, or *one* market. Microeconomic issues include explaining how consumers react to changes in prices and how firms decide what prices they should charge. Microeconomics is also used to analyze other issues, such as how individual women decide whether to have children, who is most likely to take illegal drugs, and how to reduce pollution in the most efficient way.

Microeconomics The study of how households and firms make choices, how they interact in markets, and how the government attempts to influence their choices.

Macroeconomics is the study of the economy as a whole. When you're talking about macroeconomics, you're generally talking about a country, province, or region. Macroeconomics focuses on topics such as inflation, unemployment, and economic growth. Some of the big questions in macroeconomics are why economies experience a cycle of booms and busts, why some economies grow much faster than others, and why prices rise faster in some places than in others. Macroeconomics also involves a lot of different policy issues, such as whether and how the government can intervene to prevent recessions.

Macroeconomics The study of the economy as a whole, including topics such as inflation, unemployment, and economic growth.

The division between microeconomics and macroeconomics is not always clear-cut. Many situations have *both* a microeconomic and a macroeconomic aspect. For example, the level of total investment by firms in new machinery and equipment helps determine how quickly an economy grows, which is a macroeconomic issue, but understanding the decisions made by each firm about what to invest in and when to do it is a microeconomic issue.

The Language of Economics

1.5 LEARNING OBJECTIVE

Define important economic terms. (It's not *all* Greek.)

In the following chapters, you'll encounter a number of important economic terms again and again. Becoming familiar with these terms is a necessary step in learning economics—you have to learn to speak the language. Here we provide a brief introduction to a few of these terms. We will discuss them all in greater detail later in the book.

- **Production.** *Production* is the process of making goods and services, often undertaken by entrepreneurs.

- **Entrepreneur.** An *entrepreneur* is someone who operates a business. In a market system, entrepreneurs decide what goods and services to produce and how to produce them. An entrepreneur starting a new business often puts his or her own money at risk. If an entrepreneur is wrong about what consumers want or about the best way to produce goods or services, the money he or she puts up to start the business can be lost. This is not an unusual occurrence: About half of all new businesses close within a few years. Without entrepreneurs willing to take on the risk of starting and running businesses, economic progress would be impossible.

- **Innovation.** There is a difference between *invention* and *innovation*. An invention is the development of a new good or a new process for making a good. An innovation is the practical application of an invention. (Innovation may also be used to refer to any significant improvement in a good or way of making a good.) A lot of time can pass between the appearance of a new idea and its development for widespread use. The first digital electronic computer, the ENIAC—which was the size of a small house (167 m^2)—was developed in 1945. ENIAC can be thought of as an invention. However, the first personal computer (an innovation) wasn't introduced until 1981, and it has only been since the 1990s that computers (which experience continual innovations) have become common in workplaces and homes.

- **Technology.** A firm's *technology* is the processes it uses to turn inputs into outputs (i.e., goods and services). In an economic sense, a firm's technology depends on many factors, such as the skill of its managers, the education of its workers, and the quality of its equipment.

- **Firm, company, or business.** A *firm* is an organization that produces a good or service. Most firms produce goods or services in order to earn profit, but there are also non-profit firms, such as universities. Economists tend to use the terms *firm, company,* and *business* interchangeably.

- **Goods.** *Goods* are tangible items that people want, such as books, computers, clothing, etc.

- **Services.** *Services* are activities done for others, such as cutting hair, cleaning houses, or conducting banking transactions.

- **Revenue.** A firm's *revenue* is all the money it receives when it sells goods or services. It is calculated by multiplying the price per unit by the number of units sold.

- **Profit.** A firm's *profit* is the difference between its revenue and its costs. Economists distinguish between *accounting profit* and *economic profit*. In calculating accounting profit, the costs of some economic resources the firm doesn't explicitly pay for are left out—accounting profit only worries about *explicit costs*. Economic profit includes all the costs associated with operating a firm, including *implicit costs* (particularly opportunity costs). When we use the term *profit* in this book, we're referring to *economic profit*. It is very important that you don't confuse profit with revenue.

- **Household.** A *household* consists of all the people occupying a home that make decisions together. Households are the suppliers of all the factors of production (particularly labour) used by firms to make goods and services. Households are also the consumers of all the goods and services produced in an economy.

- **Factors of production or economic resources.** Firms use *factors of production* to produce goods and services. The main factors of production are labour, capital, natural resources—including land—and entrepreneurial ability. Households earn income by supplying firms with these factors of production.

- **Capital.** The word *capital* can refer to *financial capital* or to *physical capital*. Financial capital includes stocks and bonds issued by firms, bank accounts, and holdings of money. However, in economics, *capital* refers to physical capital, which is any manufactured good that is used to make other goods. Examples of physical capital are computers, factory buildings, tools, and trucks. The total amount of physical capital available in a country is referred to as the country's *capital stock*.

- **Human capital.** *Human capital* is the accumulated training, skills, and knowledge that a person has. For example, university-educated workers generally have more skills and are more productive than workers with only high school education. Therefore, people with a university degree are said to have more human capital than people with only a high school diploma.

Economics in Your Life

How Much Will You Pay for a Cup of Coffee?

At the start of the chapter, we asked you "How much will you be paying for a cup of coffee?" Some information that will help you think about the answer to this question appears in *Making the Connection* on page 12. The price of a good is determined by how much someone, like you, is willing to pay for it and how much someone else is willing to sell it for. The costs of producing a cup of coffee, including the opportunity costs, play a very important role in how much you have to lay out for that all important first cup of the day. As the minimum wage increases, coffee-growing lands become increasingly scarce, and more people want to have a cup, the price of coffee will increase. As the price goes up, people will also change their behaviour, and some people might stop drinking coffee all together.

Conclusion

The best way to think of economics is as a group of useful ideas about how individuals make choices. Economists have put these ideas into practice by developing economic models. Consumers, business managers, and government policymakers use these models every day to help make choices. In this book, we explore many key economic models and give examples of how to apply them in the real world. Most students taking an introductory economics course do not major in economics or become professional economists. Whatever your major or career path, the economic principles you'll learn in this book will improve your ability to make choices in many aspects of your life. These principles will also improve your understanding of how decisions are made in business and government.

Reading newspapers and websites is an important part of understanding the current political, economic, and business climates and learning how to apply economic concepts to a variety of real-world issues. At the end of each chapter, you will see a two-page feature titled *An Inside Look*. This feature consists of an excerpt that relates to the company or economic issue introduced at the start of the chapter and also the concepts discussed throughout the chapter. A summary and an analysis, as well as other material, highlight the key economic point of the article. Read *An Inside Look* on the next page to explore some of the key factors that determine the price of a cup of coffee. Test your understanding by answering the *Thinking Critically* questions.

Coffee Prices Set to Soar

HAMILTON SPECTATOR

Canadians will be paying more for store bought coffee in the New Year, as a shrinking global supply and increasing demand continues to push up the price.

A recent spate of extreme weather in Colombia paired with a growing taste for higher quality beans and a diminished global stockpile could result in a 30 to 50 per cent spike in prices, according to one U.S. analyst.

On Wednesday Kraft Canada confirmed that the company's Maxwell House and Nabob Roast & Ground coffees will go up in price on January 30, 2011, the price of roast and ground coffees will go up 7 to 10 per cent. Distributors were informed of the boost a few weeks ago, the company said.

Kraft Canada said the increase "stems from the significant increase in world prices for green coffee." The company boosted prices twice on popular coffee brand products in 2010, the last increasing roast and ground coffee by as much as 12 percent and instant coffee by 16 percent.

South of the border Kraft Foods Inc. cited the same cause was behind Wednesday's boost for Maxwell House and Yuban coffees, with roast and ground coffee prices up 12 per cent and instant coffee prices up about 4 per cent.

Shawn Hackett, president of Hackett Financial Advisors, Inc., a brokerage firm specializing in agricultural commodities in Boynton Florida, predicts "actual coffee prices" or the cost of beans and cups of coffee could rise anywhere from 30 to 50 per cent by 2012.

Coffee closed on the U.S. futures market for (U.S.) $2.175 a pound [Note: like most global markets, the market for coffee uses U.S. Dollars and U.S. units.], about double the cost reported the same time last year. That price is well below historic highs of (U.S.) $3.35 per pound reported in 1977.

Hackett said based on current price increases a conservative estimate would be (U.S.) $4 per pound by the end of 2011.

Caffeine addicts should try to relax. Tim Hortons has no immediate plans to charge more.

"Typically, Tim Hortons books its coffee contracts for at least six months at a time, which protects its restaurant owners and customers from jumps in worldwide future markets," said a spokesperson in an email.

Starbucks said no one was available to comment.

The shortage is being caused by several factors, but poor weather in Colombia is key, he said.

Torrential rainstorms have resulted in loss of life and heavy damage to the current crop. Last year production was down 35 per cent and it was hoped they would recoup those losses in 2010, said Hackett.

Colombia is the largest producer of high-quality, mild washed Arabica. "That is your Starbucks kind of coffee," said Hackett. "The shortest supply is in that kind of coffee which is in the highest demand."

In previous years stockpiles of coffee in Brazil were released to relieve pressure when the market became too tight, but those supplies were depleted this year, said Hackett.

He said because of the massive profits large companies like Starbucks make selling coffee most can afford to eat cost increases until prices stabilize.

Ken Hardy, a professor emeritus of marketing for the Richard Ivey School of Business, said the smaller increase like the one from Kraft are unlikely to impact consumer habits.

Hardy, a board member for Williams Coffee Pub, noted that coffee is a central part of our social habits and a slight price hike won't deter us from buying.

He said if the price for over the counter coffee was going to rise in Canada, the cycle would start with Tim Hortons.

"I think they are the dominant buyer and dominant retail chain . . . they would be the price setter for most coffees."

If prices do rise above $4 and a hefty price hike is passed down to consumers people may start rethinking how much they drink and from where, he said.

Some companies, like Starbucks, don't have a great deal of room to manoeuvre, he said.

"They are already near the ceiling of price tolerance."

Key Points in the Article

This article discusses the impact that weather and tastes in different parts of the world have on the prices Canadians have to pay for a cup of coffee. Bad weather in Colombia means less coffee is available for the entire world. As the global population grows and becomes wealthier, more and more people want to start their day with a cup of coffee. These factors combine to increase the price of coffee.

Analyzing the News

a Coffee beans are bought and sold in a global market; companies from all over the world come together to buy and sell coffee beans. It is this global market that determines the price of the basic ingredient of your morning brew. Price changes in this market change the price of coffee not only for Canadians but also for people all over the world.

If suddenly coffee became very unpopular in a country like the United States, Canadians would likely have to pay less for a cup as there would be less competition for the coffee that was grown.

b The weather in another part of the world can have a large impact on your life. Bad weather in Colombia can make your morning cup of coffee more expensive, an earthquake in Japan can make electronics harder to get, and brush fires in Russia can make bread cost more here.

c Some companies are so important to their markets that other companies follow their lead. In the Canadian coffee shop market, Tim Hortons is the leader. Many smaller firms like Starbucks or Second Cup are hesitant to increase their prices if Tim Hortons does not. This competition among sellers can limit the impact of raw material price changes on consumers, at least for a while.

When the price of something goes up, people often respond by changing their behaviour. For example, if the price of coffee were to double and stay high, you might switch to drinking tea, hot chocolate, or another less-expensive beverage before class starts to save some money. Some people might start bringing their own coffee to work or school in travel mugs. Other people might give up something else, such as going to the movies, so that they can still have their morning coffee at the local coffee shop. People can change their behaviour in response to a change in prices in a number of ways.

Thinking Critically

1. According to the article, heavier-than-normal rains in Colombia reduced the amount of coffee grown there, which led to an increase in the world price of coffee. What do you think would happen if the weather in Colombia was particularly good for growing coffee this year? What do you think will happen to the price of coffee if weather patterns all over the world become more extreme?

2. How do you think you would react if the price of a cup of coffee doubled? How do you think most people would react? What do you think that would mean for the owner of your local coffee shop?

Chapter Summary and Problems

Key Terms

Allocative efficiency, p. 9

Centrally planned economy, p. 8

Economic model, p. 4

Economic variable, p. 10

Economics, p. 4

Equity, p. 9

Macroeconomics, p. 13

Marginal analysis, p. 6

Market, p. 4

Market economy, p. 8

Microeconomics, p. 13

Mixed economy, p. 9

Normative analysis, p. 11

Opportunity cost, p. 7

Positive analysis, p. 11

Productive efficiency, p. 9

Scarcity, p. 4

Trade-off, p. 7

Voluntary exchange, p. 9

Summary

*LO **1.1 Economics** is the study of the choices consumers, business managers, and government officials make to attain their goals, given their scarce resources. We must make choices because of **scarcity**, which means that although our wants are unlimited, the resources available to fulfill those wants are limited. Economists assume that people are rational in the sense that consumers and firms use all available information as they take actions intended to achieve their goals. Rational individuals weigh the benefits and costs of each action and choose an action only if the benefits outweigh the costs. Although people act from a variety of motives, ample evidence indicates that they respond to economic incentives. Economists use the word **marginal** to mean extra or additional. The optimal decision is to continue any activity up to the point where the marginal benefit equals the marginal cost.

LO **1.2** Society faces **trade-offs**: Producing more of one good or service means producing less of another good or service. The **opportunity cost** of any activity—such as producing a good or service—is the highest-valued alternative that must be given up to engage in that activity. The choices of consumers, firms, and governments determine what goods and services will be produced. Firms choose how to produce the goods and services they sell. In Canada, who receives the goods and services produced depends largely on how income is distributed in the marketplace. In a **centrally planned economy**, most economic decisions are made by the government. In a **market economy**, most economic decisions are made by consumers and firms. Most economies, including Canada's, are **mixed economies** in which most economic decisions are made by consumers and firms but in which the government also plays a significant role. There are two types of efficiency: productive efficiency and allocative efficiency. **Productive efficiency** occurs when a good or service is produced at the lowest possible cost. **Allocative efficiency** occurs when production is in accordance with consumer preferences. **Voluntary exchange** is a situation that occurs in markets when both the buyer and seller of a product are made better off by the transaction. **Equity** is more difficult to define than efficiency, but it usually involves a fair distribution of economic benefits. Government policymakers often face a trade-off between equity and efficiency.

LO **1.3** An **economic variable** is something measurable that can have different values, such as the wages of software programmers. Economists rely on economic models when they apply economic ideas to real-world problems. **Economic models** are simplified versions of reality used to analyze real-world economic situations. Economists accept and use an economic model if it leads to hypotheses that are confirmed by statistical analysis. In many cases, the acceptance is tentative, however, pending the gathering of new data or further statistical analysis. Economics is a social science because it applies the scientific method to the study of the interactions among individuals. Economics is concerned with positive analysis rather than normative analysis. **Positive analysis** is concerned with what is. **Normative analysis** is concerned with what ought to be. Because economics is based on studying the actions of individuals, it is a social science. As a social science, economics considers human behaviour in every context of decision making, not just in business.

LO **1.4 Microeconomics** is the study of how households and firms make choices, how they interact in markets, and how the government attempts to influence their choices. **Macroeconomics** is the study of the economy as a whole, including topics such as inflation, unemployment, and economic growth.

LO **1.5** Becoming familiar with important terms is a necessary step in learning economics. These important economic terms include *capital, entrepreneur, factors of production, firm, goods, household, human capital, innovation, production, profit, revenue, services,* and *technology.*

MyEconLab   Log in to MyEconLab to complete these exercises and get instant feedback.

---

*'Learning Objective' is abbreviated to 'LO' in the end of chapter material.

Review Questions

LO 1.1

1.1 Briefly discuss each of the following economic ideas: People are rational, people respond to incentives, and optimal decisions are made at the margin.

1.2 What is scarcity? Why is scarcity central to the study of economics?

LO 1.2

2.1 Why does scarcity imply that every society and every individual face trade-offs?

2.2 What are the three economic questions that every society must answer? Briefly discuss the differences in how cen-

trally planned, market, and mixed economies answer these questions.

LO 1.3

3.1 Why do economists use models? How are economic data used to test models?

3.2 Describe the five steps by which economists arrive at a useful economic model.

3.3 What is the difference between normative analysis and positive analysis? Is economics concerned mainly with normative analysis or with positive analysis? Briefly explain.

LO 1.4

4.1 Briefly discuss the difference between microeconomics and macroeconomics.

Problems and Applications

LO 1.1

1.1 Bank robberies are on the rise in New Jersey, and according to the FBI, this increase has little to do with the economic downturn. The FBI claims that banks have allowed themselves to become easy targets by refusing to install clear acrylic partitions, called "bandit barriers," which separate bank tellers from the public. Of the 193 banks robbed in New Jersey in 2008, only 23 had these barriers, and of the 40 banks robbed in the first 10 weeks of 2009, only 1 had a bandit barrier. According to a special agent with the FBI, "Bandit barriers are a great deterrent. We've talked to guys who rob banks, and as soon as they see a bandit barrier, they go find another bank." Despite this finding, many banks have been reluctant to install these barriers. Wouldn't banks have a strong incentive to install bandit barriers to deter robberies? Why, then, do so many banks not do so?

Richard Cowen, "FBI: Banks Are to Blame for Rise in Robberies," NorthJersey.com, March 10, 2009.

1.2 The grading system is a powerful resource for teachers. In their book *Effective Grading: A Tool for Learning and Assessment,* Barbara Walvoord and Virginia Anderson state that "teachers must manage the power and complexity of the grading system" and that "teachers must consider grading in their first deliberations about a course."

a. How could the grading system a teacher uses affect the incentives of students to learn the course material?

b. If teachers put too little weight in the grading scale on a certain part of the course, such as readings outside the textbook, how might students respond?

c. Teachers often wish that students came to class prepared, having read the upcoming material. How could a teacher design the grading system to motivate students to come to class prepared?

Barbara E. Walvoord and Virginia Johnson Anderson, Effective Grading: A Tool for Learning and Assessment, Jossey-Bass: San Francisco, 1998, pp. xvii–xviii.

1.3 [**Related to** Making the Connection **on page 5**] Most provincial governments and the federal government in Canada

offer programs and payments to encourage Canadians to have more children. The federal government currently pays all parents with children under six years old $100 per month (this is the Universal Child Care Benefit). Why would the Government of Canada make a cash payment to people with small children? How do you think most people respond to this program?

1.4 [**Related to** Making the Connection **on page 5**] Daniel Parent and Ling Wang have found that changes in government subsidies to people who have children don't have an impact on the number of children people have, only on when people have children. They found that more generous subsidies lead people to have children earlier in life than they would have without the subsidies, but that the total number of children people have doesn't change.

a. Why might a government program affect when people have children?

b. Why might a government subsidy not change the number of children people have?

Based on Parent, D. and Wang, L. (2007), Tax incentives and fertility in Canada: quantum vs tempo effects. Canadian Journal of Economics/Revue canadienne d'économique, 40: 371–400. doi: 10.1111/j.1365-2966.2007.00413.x

1.5 [**Related to** Solved Problem 1.1 **on page 6**] Two students are discussing *Solved Problem 1.1:*

Joe: "I think the key additional information you need to know in deciding whether McCain Foods should make 11 million rather than 10 million kilograms of french-fries is the amount of profit they currently make while selling 10 million kilograms. Then we can compare the profit earned from making 11 million to the profit earned from making 10 million. This information is more important than the additional revenue and additional cost of making 1 million more kilograms."

Jill: "Actually, Joe, knowing how much profit changes when McCain Foods makes 1 million more kilograms is exactly the same as knowing the additional revenue and the additional cost."

Briefly evaluate their arguments.

Based on Lauren A. E. Schuker, "Can 3-D Save Hollywood?" Wall Street Journal, March 20, 2009; and "3D Films Struggle," The Economist, July 23–29, 2011.

1.6 [**Related to** Solved Problem 1.1 **on page 6**] Late in the semester, a friend tells you, "I was going to drop my psychology course so I could concentrate on my other courses, but I had already put so much time into the course that I decided not to drop it." What do you think of your friend's reasoning? Would it make a difference to your answer if your friend has to pass the psychology course at some point to graduate? Briefly explain.

Based on Lauren A. E. Schuker, "Can 3-D Save Hollywood?" Wall Street Journal, March 20, 2009; and "3D Films Struggle," The Economist, July 23–29, 2011.

LO 1.2

2.1 Why does Bill Gates, one of the richest people in the world, face scarcity? Does everyone face scarcity? Are there any exceptions?

2.2 Centrally planned economies have been less efficient than market economies.
   a. Has this difference in efficiency happened by chance, or is there some underlying reason?
   b. If market economies are more economically efficient than centrally planned economies, would there ever be a reason to prefer having a centrally planned economy rather than a market economy?

2.3 In a recent paper, economists Patricia M. Flynn and Michael A. Quinn state the following:

> We find evidence that Economics is a good choice of major for those aspiring to become a CEO [chief executive officer]. When adjusting for size of the pool of graduates, those with undergraduate degrees in Economics are shown to have had a greater likelihood of becoming an S&P 500 CEO than any other major.

A list of famous economics majors published by McMaster University includes business leaders Steve Ballmer (CEO of Microsoft), Warren Buffet, Sam Walton (Founder of Walmart), and Scott McNealy (CEO of SUN Microsystems). The list also includes politicians Ronald Reagan (former US president), Stephen Harper (Prime Minister of Canada), Manmohan Singh (Prime Minister of India), and Kofi Annan (former Secretary-General of the United Nations). Why might studying economics be particularly good preparation for being the top manager of a corporation or a leader in government?

Based on Patricia M. Flynn and Michael A. Quinn, " Economics: A Good choice of Major for Future CEOs," Social Science Research Network, November 28, 2006; and Famous Economics Majors, McMaster University; http://www.economics.mcmaster.ca/documents/Famous_Econ.pdf, accessed Feb. 12, 2012.

2.4 Suppose that a local radio station has decided to give away 100 tickets to an Arcade Fire performance it's promoting. It announces that tickets will be given away at 7:00 a.m. on Monday at the radio station's studio.
   a. What groups of people will be most likely to try to get the tickets? Think of specific examples and then generalize.
   b. What is the opportunity cost of distributing tickets in this way?

   c. Productive efficiency occurs when a good or service, such as the distribution of tickets, is produced at the lowest possible cost. Is this an efficient way to distribute the tickets? If possible, think of a more efficient method of distributing the tickets.
   d. Is this an equitable way to distribute the tickets? Explain.

LO 1.3

3.1 Do you agree with the following assertion: "The problem with economics is that it assumes that consumers and firms always make the correct decision. But we know everyone's human, and we all make mistakes."

3.2 Dr. Strangelove's theory is that the price of mushrooms is determined by the activity of subatomic particles that exist in another universe parallel to ours. When the subatomic particles are emitted in profusion, the price of mushrooms is high. When subatomic particle emissions are low, the price of mushrooms is also low. How would you go about testing Dr. Strangelove's theory? Discuss whether this theory is useful.

3.3 [**Related to** Making the Connection **on page 12**] *Making the Connection* explains that there are both positive and normative elements to the debate over raising the minimum wage. What economic statistics would be most useful in evaluating the positive elements of the debate? Assuming that these statistics are available or could be gathered, are they likely to resolve the normative issues in this debate?

3.4 [**Related to the Chapter Opener on page 3**] Recently, Tim Hortons decided to change the sizes of coffee it sold. It essentially increased the size of each cup, so that what was a large is now a medium.
   a. Many other food items, like crackers, are now being sold in smaller quantities than was traditionally the case. Why is takeout coffee different from other goods?
   b. How have the economic incentives for selling coffee changed over the last few years?

3.5 [**Related to** Don't Let This Happen to You **on page 12**] Explain which of the following statements represent positive analysis and which represent normative analysis:
   a. A 50-cent-per-pack tax on cigarettes will lead to a 12 percent reduction in smoking by teenagers.
   b. The federal government should spend more on AIDS research.
   c. Rising paper prices will increase textbook prices.
   d. The price of coffee at Starbucks is too high.

LO 1.4

4.1 Briefly explain whether each of the following is primarily a microeconomic issue or a macroeconomic issue:
   a. The effect of higher cigarette taxes on the quantity of cigarettes sold
   b. The effect of higher income taxes on the total amount of consumer spending
   c. The reasons for the economies of East Asian countries growing faster than the economies of sub-Saharan African countries
   d. The reasons for low rates of profit in the airline industry

4.2 Briefly explain whether you agree with the following assertion: "Microeconomics is concerned with things that happen in one particular place, such as the unemployment rate in one city. In contrast, macroeconomics is concerned with things that affect the country as a whole, such as how the rate of teenage smoking in the United States would be affected by an increase in the tax on cigarettes."

Appendix A

LO

Review the use of graphs and formulas.

Using Graphs and Formulas

Graphs are used to illustrate key economic ideas. Graphs appear not just in economics textbooks but also on websites and in newspaper and magazine articles that discuss events in business and economics. Why the heavy use of graphs? Because they serve two useful purposes: (1) They simplify economic ideas, and (2) they make the ideas more concrete so they can be applied to real-world problems. Economic and business issues can be complicated, but a graph can help cut through complications and highlight the key relationships needed to understand the issue. In that sense, a graph can be like a street map.

For example, suppose you take a bus to Toronto to see the CN Tower. After arriving at the downtown bus station, you will probably use a map similar to the one shown below to find your way to the CN Tower.

Maps are very familiar to just about everyone, so we don't usually think of them as being simplified versions of reality, but they are. This map does not show much more than the streets in this part of Toronto and some of the most important places. The names, addresses, and telephone numbers of the people who live and work in the area aren't given. Almost none of the stores and buildings those people work and live in are shown either. The map doesn't indicate which streets allow curbside parking and which don't. In fact, the map shows almost nothing about the messy reality of life in this section of Toronto, except how the streets are laid out, which is the essential information you need to get from the bus station to the CN Tower.

Think about someone who says, "I know how to get around in the city, but I just can't figure out how to read a map." It certainly is possible to find your destination in a

© Valentino Visentini / Alamy

city without a map, but it's a lot easier with one. The same is true of using graphs in economics. It is possible to arrive at a solution to a real-world problem in economics and business without using graphs, but it is usually a lot easier if you do use them.

Often, the difficulty students have with graphs and formulas is a lack of familiarity. With practice, all the graphs and formulas in this text will become familiar to you. Once you are familiar with them, you will be able to use them to analyze problems that would otherwise seem very difficult. What follows is a brief review of how graphs and formulas are used.

Graphs of One Variable

Figure 1A.1 displays values for market shares in the Canadian automobile market, using two common types of graphs. Market shares show the percentage of industry sales accounted for by different firms. In this case, the information is for groups of firms: the "Big Three"—Ford, General Motors, and Chrysler—as well as Japanese firms, European firms, and Korean firms.

Information on economic variables is also often displayed in time-series graphs. Time-series graphs are displayed on a coordinate grid. In a coordinate grid, we can measure the value of one variable along the vertical axis (or *y*-axis) and the value of another variable along the horizontal axis (or *x*-axis). The point where the vertical axis intersects the horizontal axis is called the *origin*. At the origin, the value of both variables is zero. The points on a coordinate grid represent values of the two variables. In Figure 1A.2, we measure the number of automobiles and trucks sold worldwide by Ford Motor Company on the vertical axis, and we measure time on the horizontal axis. In time-series graphs, the height of the line at each date shows the value of the variable measured on the vertical axis. Both panels of Figure 1A.2 show Ford's worldwide sales during each year from 2001 to 2010. The difference between panel (a) and panel (b) illustrates the importance of the scale used in a time-series graph. In panel (a), the scale on the vertical axis is truncated, which means it does not start with zero. The slashes (//) near

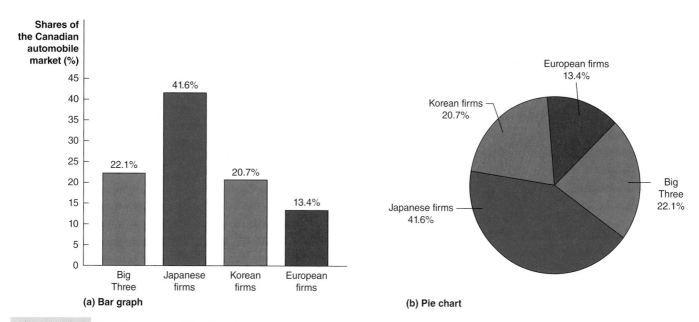

Figure 1A.1 **Bar Graphs and Pie Charts**

Values for an economic variable are often displayed as a bar graph or as a pie chart. In this case, panel (a) shows market share data for the Canadian automobile industry as a *bar graph*, where the market share of each group of firms is represented by the height of its bar. Panel (b) displays the same information as a *pie chart*, with the market share of each group of firms represented by the size of its slice of the pie.

Source: Data from Global Economic Research, Global Auto Report, Oct. 4, 2012. http://www.gbm.scotiabank.com/English/bns_econ/bns_auto.pdf

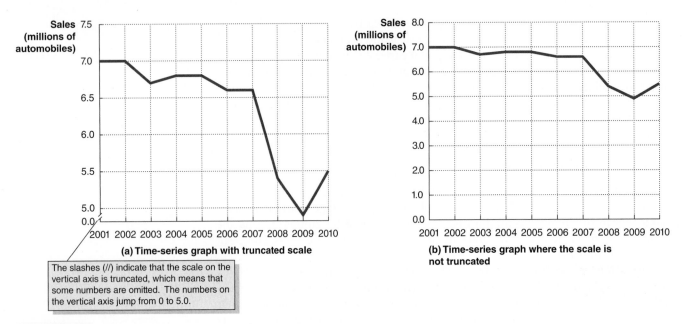

Figure 1A.2 **Time-Series Graphs**

Both panels present time-series graphs of Ford Motor Company's worldwide sales during each year from 2001 to 2010. Panel (a) has a truncated scale on the vertical axis, and panel (b) does not. As a result, the fluctuations in Ford's sales appear smaller in panel (b) than in panel (a).

Source: Data from Ford Motor Company, Annual Report, various years.

the bottom of the axis indicate that the scale is truncated. In panel (b), the scale is not truncated. In panel (b), the decline in Ford's sales during 2008 and 2009 appears smaller than in panel (a). (Technically, the horizontal axis is also truncated because we start with the year 2001, not the year 0.)

Graphs of Two Variables

We often use graphs to show the relationship between two variables. For example, suppose you are interested in the relationship between the price of a pepperoni pizza and the quantity of pizzas sold per week in the small town of Sackville, New Brunswick. A graph showing the relationship between the price of a good and the quantity of the good demanded at each price is called a *demand curve*. (As we will discuss later, in drawing a demand curve for a good, we have to hold constant any variables other than price that might affect the willingness of consumers to buy the good.) Figure 1A.3 shows the data collected on price and quantity. The figure shows a two-dimensional grid on which we measure the price of pizza along the y-axis and the quantity of pizza sold per week along the x-axis. Each point on the grid represents one of the price and quantity combinations listed in the table. We can connect the points to form the demand curve for pizza in Sackville, NB. Notice that the scales on both axes in the graph are truncated. In this case, truncating the axes allows the graph to illustrate more clearly the relationship between price and quantity by excluding low prices and quantities.

Slopes of Lines

Once you have plotted the data in Figure 1A.3, you may be interested in how much the quantity of pizza sold increases as the price decreases. The slope of a line tells us how much the variable we are measuring on the y-axis changes as the variable we are measuring on the x-axis changes. We can use the Greek letter delta (Δ) to stand for the change in a variable. The slope is sometimes referred to as the *rise* over the *run*. So, we have several ways of expressing slope:

Price (dollars per pizza)	Quantity (pizzas per week)	Points
$15	50	A
14	55	B
13	60	C
12	65	D
11	70	E

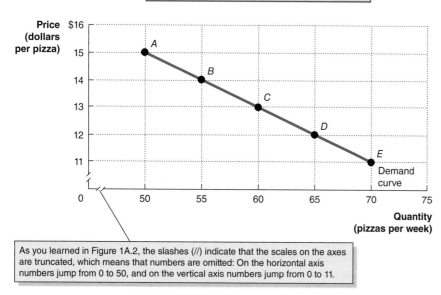

As you learned in Figure 1A.2, the slashes (//) indicate that the scales on the axes are truncated, which means that numbers are omitted: On the horizontal axis numbers jump from 0 to 50, and on the vertical axis numbers jump from 0 to 11.

Figure 1A.3

Plotting Price and Quantity Points in a Graph

The figure shows a two-dimensional grid on which we measure the price of pizza along the vertical axis (or *y*-axis) and the quantity of pizza sold per week along the horizontal axis (or *x*-axis). Each point on the grid represents one of the price and quantity combinations listed in the table. By connecting the points with a line, we can better illustrate the relationship between the two variables.

$$\text{Slope} = \frac{\text{Change in value on the vertical axis}}{\text{Change in value on the horizontal axis}} = \frac{\Delta y}{\Delta x} = \frac{\text{Rise}}{\text{Run}}.$$

Figure 1A.4 reproduces the graph from Figure 1A.3. Because the slope of a straight line is the same at any point, we can use any two points in the figure to calculate the slope of the line. For example, when the price of pizza decreases from $14 to $12, the quantity of pizza sold increases from 55 per week to 65 per week. Therefore, the slope is:

$$\text{Slope} = \frac{\Delta \text{Price of pizza}}{\Delta \text{Quantity of pizza}} = \frac{(\$12 - \$14)}{(65 - 55)} = \frac{-2}{10} = -0.2.$$

The slope of this line gives us some insight into how responsive consumers in Sackville are to changes in the price of pizza. The larger the value of the slope (ignoring the negative sign), the steeper the line will be, which indicates that not many additional pizzas are sold when the price falls. The smaller the value of the slope, the flatter the line will be, which indicates a greater increase in pizzas sold when the price falls.

Taking into Account More Than Two Variables on a Graph

The demand curve graph in Figure 1A.4 shows the relationship between the price of pizza and the quantity of pizza demanded, but we know that the quantity of any good demanded depends on more than just the price of the good. For example, the quantity of pizza demanded in a given week in Sackville can be affected by other variables, such as the price of hamburgers, whether an advertising campaign by local pizza parlours has begun that week, and so on. Allowing the values of any other variables to change will cause the position of the demand curve in the graph to change.

Suppose, for example, that the demand curve in Figure 1A.4 were drawn holding the price of hamburgers constant, at $1.50. If the price of hamburgers rises to $2.00, some consumers will switch from buying hamburgers to buying pizza, and more pizzas will be demanded at every price. The result on the graph will be to shift the line

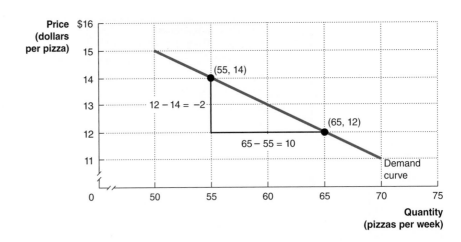

Figure 1A.4

Calculating the Slope of a Line

We can calculate the slope of a line as the change in the value of the variable on the *y*-axis divided by the change in the value of the variable on the *x*-axis. Because the slope of a straight line is constant, we can use any two points in the figure to calculate the slope of the line. For example, when the price of pizza decreases from $14 to $12, the quantity of pizza demanded increases from 55 per week to 65 per week. So, the slope of this line equals –2 divided by 10, or –0.2.

representing the demand curve to the right. Similarly, if the price of hamburgers falls from $1.50 to $1.00, some consumers will switch from buying pizza to buying hamburgers, and fewer pizzas will be demanded at every price. The result on the graph will be to shift the line representing the demand curve to the left.

The table in Figure 1A.5 shows the effect of a change in the price of hamburgers on the quantity of pizza demanded. For example, suppose that at first we are on the line labelled *Demand curve₁*. If the price of pizza is $14 (point *A*), an increase in the price of hamburgers from $1.50 to $2.00 increases the quantity of pizzas demanded from 55 to 60 per week (point *B*) and shifts us to *Demand curve₂*. Or, if we start on *Demand curve₁* and the price of pizza is $12 (point *C*), a decrease in the price of hamburgers from $1.50 to $1.00 decreases the quantity of pizzas demanded from 65 to 60 per week (point *D*) and shifts us to *Demand curve₃*. By shifting the demand curve, we have taken into account the effect of changes in the value of a third variable—the price of hamburgers. We will use this technique of shifting curves to allow for the effects of additional variables many times in this book.

Positive and Negative Relationships

We can use graphs to show the relationships between any two variables. Sometimes the relationship between the variables is negative, meaning that as one variable increases in value, the other variable decreases in value. This was the case with the price of pizza and the quantity of pizzas demanded. The relationship between two variables can also be positive, meaning that the values of both variables increase or decrease together. For example, when the level of total income—or personal disposable income—received by households in Canada increases, the level of total consumption spending, which is spending by households on goods and services, also increases. The table in Figure 1A.6 shows the values (in millions of dollars) for income and consumption spending for the years 2008–2011. The graph plots the data from the table, with personal disposable income measured along the horizontal axis and consumption spending measured along the vertical axis. Notice that the four points do not all fall exactly on the line. This is often the case with real-world data. To examine the relationship between two variables, economists often use the straight line that best fits the data.

Determining Cause and Effect

When we graph the relationship between two variables, we often want to draw conclusions about whether changes in one variable are causing changes in the other variable. Doing so, however, can lead to incorrect conclusions. For example, suppose you graph the number of homes in a neighbourhood that have a fire burning in the fireplace and the number of leaves on trees in the neighbourhood. You would get a relationship like that shown in panel (a) of Figure 1A.7: The more fires burning in the neighbourhood, the fewer leaves the trees have. Can we draw the conclusion from this graph that using a fireplace causes trees to lose their leaves? We know, of course, that such a conclusion

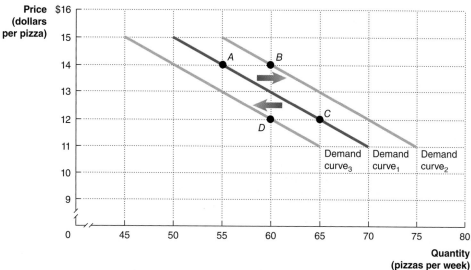

Quantity (pizzas per week)			
Price (dollars per pizza)	When the Price of Hamburgers = $1.00	When the Price of Hamburgers = $1.50	When the Price of Hamburgers = $2.00
$15	45	50	55
14	50	55	60
13	55	60	65
12	60	65	70
11	65	70	75

Figure 1A.5

Showing Three Variables on a Graph

The demand curve for pizza shows the relationship between the price of pizzas and the quantity of pizzas demanded, holding constant other factors that might affect the willingness of consumers to buy pizza. If the price of pizza is $14 (point *A*), an increase in the price of hamburgers from $1.50 to $2.00 increases the quantity of pizzas demanded from 55 to 60 per week (point *B*) and shifts us to *Demand curve*$_2$. Or, if we start on *Demand curve*$_1$ and the price of pizza is $12 (point *C*), a decrease in the price of hamburgers from $1.50 to $1.00 decreases the quantity of pizza demanded from 65 to 60 per week (point *D*) and shifts us to *Demand curve*$_3$.

would be incorrect. In spring and summer, there are relatively few fireplaces being used, and the trees are full of leaves. In the fall, as trees begin to lose their leaves, fireplaces are used more frequently. And in winter, many fireplaces are being used and many trees have lost all their leaves. The reason that the graph in Figure 1A.7 is misleading about cause and effect is that there is obviously an omitted variable in the analysis—the season

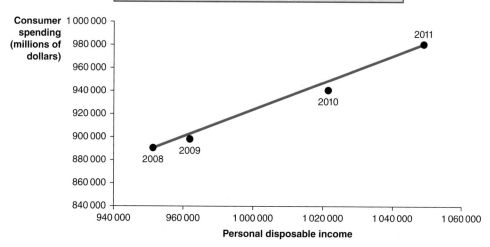

Year	Personal Disposable Income (millions of dollars)	Consumption Spending (millions of dollars)
2008	$953 568	$890 601
2009	966 269	898 215
2010	1 013 778	940 620
2011	1 046 827	980 629

Figure 1A.6

Graphing the Positive Relationship between Income and Consumption

In a positive relationship between two economic variables, as one variable increases, the other variable also increases. This figure shows the positive relationship between personal disposable income and consumption spending. As personal disposable income in Canada has increased, so has consumption spending.

Source: Data from Statistics Canada.

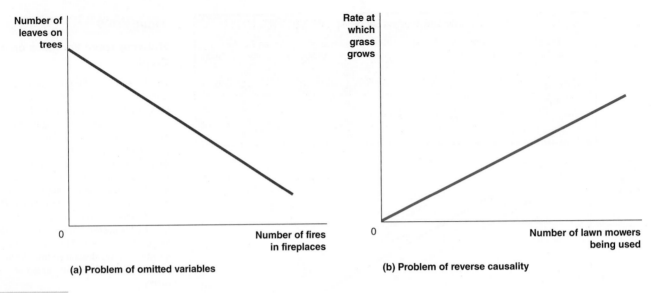

(a) Problem of omitted variables

(b) Problem of reverse causality

Figure 1A.7 **Determining Cause and Effect**

Using graphs to draw conclusions about cause and effect can be hazardous. In panel (a), we see that there are fewer leaves on the trees in a neighbourhood when many homes have fires burning in their fireplaces. We cannot draw the conclusion that the fires cause the leaves to fall because we have an *omitted variable*—the season

of the year. In panel (b), we see that more lawn mowers are used in a neighbourhood during times when the grass grows rapidly and fewer lawn mowers are used when the grass grows slowly. Concluding that using lawn mowers causes the grass to grow faster would be making the error of *reverse causality*.

of the year. An omitted variable is one that affects other variables, and its omission can lead to false conclusions about cause and effect.

Although in our example the omitted variable is obvious, there are many debates about cause and effect where the existence of an omitted variable has not been clear. For instance, it has been known for many years that people who smoke cigarettes suffer from higher rates of lung cancer than do nonsmokers. For some time, tobacco companies and some scientists argued that there was an omitted variable—perhaps a failure to exercise or a poor diet—that made some people more likely to smoke and more likely to develop lung cancer. If this omitted variable existed, then the finding that smokers were more likely to develop lung cancer would not have been evidence that smoking caused lung cancer. In this case, however, nearly all scientists eventually concluded that the omitted variable did not exist and that, in fact, smoking does cause lung cancer.

A related problem in determining cause and effect is known as *reverse causality*. The error of reverse causality occurs when we conclude that changes in variable X cause changes in variable Y when, in fact, it is actually changes in variable Y that cause changes in variable X. For example, panel (b) of Figure 1A.7 plots the number of lawn mowers being used in a neighbourhood against the rate at which grass on lawns in the neighbourhood is growing. We could conclude from this graph that using lawn mowers causes the grass to grow faster. We know, however, that in reality, the causality is in the other direction: Rapidly growing grass during the spring and summer causes the increased use of lawn mowers. Slowly growing grass in the fall or winter or during periods of low rainfall causes decreased use of lawn mowers.

Once again, in our example, the potential error of reverse causality is obvious. In many economic debates, however, cause and effect can be more difficult to determine. For example, changes in the money supply, or the total amount of money in the economy, tend to occur at the same time as changes in the total amount of income people in the economy earn. A famous debate in economics was about whether the changes in the money supply caused the changes in total income or whether the changes in total income caused the changes in the money supply. Each side in the debate accused the other side of committing the error of reverse causality.

Are Graphs of Economic Relationships Always Straight Lines?

The graphs of relationships between two economic variables that we have drawn so far have been straight lines. The relationship between two variables is linear when it can be represented by a straight line. Few economic relationships are actually linear. For example, if we carefully plot data on the price of a product and the quantity demanded at each price, holding constant other variables that affect the quantity demanded, we will usually find a curved—or nonlinear—relationship rather than a linear relationship. In practice, however, it is often useful to approximate a nonlinear relationship with a linear relationship. If the relationship is reasonably close to being linear, the analysis is not significantly affected. In addition, it is easier to calculate the slope of a straight line, and it also is easier to calculate the area under a straight line. So, in this book, we often assume that the relationship between two economic variables is linear, even when we know that this assumption is not precisely correct.

Slopes of Nonlinear Curves

In some situations, we need to take into account the nonlinear nature of an economic relationship. For example, panel (a) of Figure 1A.8 shows the hypothetical relationship between Apple's total cost of producing iPhones and the quantity of iPhones produced.

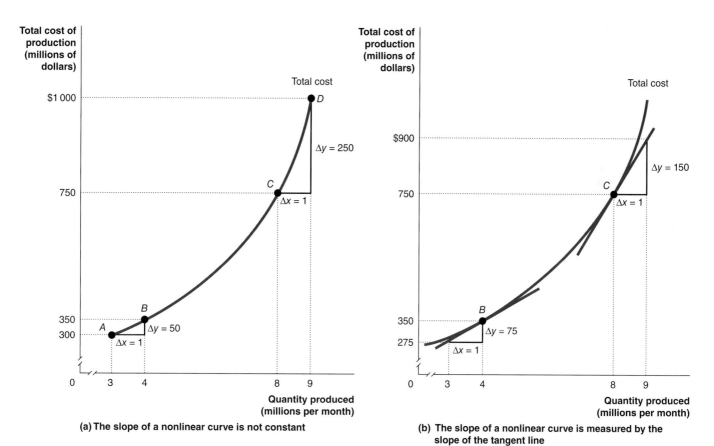

(a) The slope of a nonlinear curve is not constant

(b) The slope of a nonlinear curve is measured by the slope of the tangent line

Figure 1A.8   The Slope of a Nonlinear Curve

The relationship between the quantity of iPhones produced and the total cost of production is curved rather than linear. In panel (a), in moving from point A to point B, the quantity produced increases by 1 million iPhones, while the total cost of production increases by $50 million. Farther up the curve, as we move from point C to point D, the change in quantity is the same—1 million iPhones—but the change in the total cost of production is now much larger: $250 million.

Because the change in the y variable has increased, while the change in the x variable has remained the same, we know that the slope has increased. In panel (b), we measure the slope of the curve at a particular point by the slope of the tangent line. The slope of the tangent line at point B is 75, and the slope of the tangent line at point C is 150.

The relationship is curved rather than linear. In this case, the cost of production is increasing at an increasing rate, which often happens in manufacturing. Put a different way, as we move up the curve, its slope becomes larger. (Remember that with a straight line, the slope is always constant.) To see this effect, first remember that we calculate the slope of a curve by dividing the change in the variable on the y-axis by the change in the variable on the x-axis. As we move from point A to point B, the quantity produced increases by 1 million iPhones, while the total cost of production increases by $50 million. Farther up the curve, as we move from point C to point D, the change in quantity is the same—1 million iPhones—but the change in the total cost of production is now much larger: $250 million. Because the change in the y variable has increased, while the change in the x variable has remained the same, we know that the slope has increased.

To measure the slope of a nonlinear curve at a particular point, we must measure the slope of the *tangent line* to the curve at that point. A tangent line will touch the curve only at that point. We can measure the slope of the tangent line just as we would the slope of any other straight line. In panel (b), the tangent line at point B has a slope equal to:

$$\frac{\Delta \text{Cost}}{\Delta \text{Quantity}} = \frac{75}{1} = 75.$$

The tangent line at point C has a slope equal to:

$$\frac{\Delta \text{Cost}}{\Delta \text{Quantity}} = \frac{150}{1} = 150.$$

Once again, we see that the slope of the curve is larger at point C than at point B.

Formulas

We have just seen that graphs are an important economic tool. In this section, we will review several useful formulas and show how to use them to summarize data and to calculate important relationships.

Formula for a Percentage Change

One important formula is the percentage change. The percentage change is the change in some economic variable, usually from one period to the next, expressed as a percentage. An important macroeconomic measure is the real gross domestic product (GDP). GDP is the value of all the final goods and services produced in a country during a year. "Real" GDP is corrected for the effects of inflation. When economists say that the Canadian economy grew 3.0 percent during 2011, they mean that real GDP was 3.0 percent higher in 2011 than it was in 2010. The formula for making this calculation is:

$$\frac{\text{GDP}_{2011} - \text{GDP}_{2010}}{\text{GDP}_{2010}} \times 100$$

or, more generally, for any two periods:

$$\text{Percentage change} = \frac{\text{Value in the second period} - \text{Value in the first period}}{\text{Value in the first period}} \times 100.$$

In this case, real GDP was $1 279 586 million in 2010 and $1 316 622 million in 2011. So, the growth rate of the Canadian economy during 2011 was:

$$\left(\frac{\$1\ 316\ 622 - \$1\ 279\ 586}{\$1\ 279\ 586} \right) \times 100 = 2.89\%.$$

Notice that it doesn't matter that in using the formula, we ignored the fact that GDP is measured in millions of dollars. In fact, when calculating percentage changes, *the*

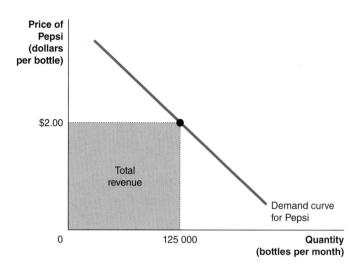

Figure 1A.9

Showing a Firm's Total Revenue on a Graph

The area of a rectangle is equal to its base multiplied by its height. Total revenue is equal to quantity multiplied by price. Here, total revenue is equal to the quantity of 125 000 bottles times the price of $2.00 per bottle, or $250 000. The area of the green-shaded rectangle shows the firm's total revenue.

units don't matter. The percentage increase from $1 279 586 million to $1 316 622 million is exactly the same as the percentage increase from $1 279 586 to $1 316 622.

Formulas for the Areas of a Rectangle and a Triangle

Areas that form rectangles and triangles on graphs can have important economic meaning. For example, Figure 1A.9 shows the demand curve for Pepsi. Suppose that the price is currently $2.00 and that 125 000 bottles of Pepsi are sold at that price. A firm's total revenue is equal to the amount it receives from selling its product, or the quantity sold multiplied by the price. In this case, total revenue will equal 125 000 bottles times $2.00 per bottle, or $250 000.

The formula for the area of a rectangle is:

$$\text{Area of a rectangle} = \text{Base} \times \text{Height}.$$

In Figure 1A.9, the green-shaded rectangle also represents the firm's total revenue because its area is given by the base of 125 000 bottles multiplied by the price of $2.00 per bottle.

We will see in later chapters that areas that are triangles can also have economic significance. The formula for the area of a triangle is:

$$\text{Area of a triangle} = \frac{1}{2} \times \text{Base} \times \text{Height}.$$

The blue-shaded area in Figure 1A.10 is a triangle. The base equals 150 000 – 125 000, or 25 000. Its height equals $2.00 – $1.50, or $0.50. Therefore, its area equals 1/2 × 25 000 × $0.50, or $6250. Notice that the blue area is a triangle only if the demand curve is a straight line, or linear. Not all demand curves are linear. However, the formula for the area of a triangle will usually still give a good approximation, even if the demand curve is not linear.

Summary of Using Formulas

You will encounter several other formulas in this book. Whenever you must use a formula, you should follow these steps:

1. Make sure you understand the economic concept the formula represents.

2. Make sure you are using the correct formula for the problem you are solving.

3. Make sure the number you calculate using the formula is economically reasonable. For example, if you are using a formula to calculate a firm's revenue and your answer is a negative number, you know you made a mistake somewhere.

Figure 1A.10

The Area of a Triangle

The area of a triangle is equal to 1/2 multiplied by its base multiplied by its height. The area of the blue-shaded triangle has a base equal to 150 000 – 125 000, or 25 000, and a height equal to $2.00 – $1.50, or $0.50. Therefore, its area equals 1/2 × 25 000 × $0.50, or $6 250.

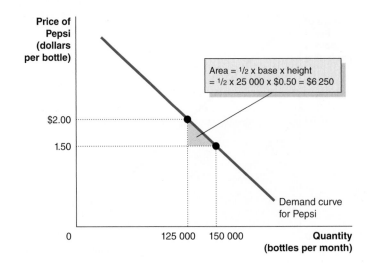

MyEconLab   Log in to MyEconLab to complete these exercises and get instant feedback.

Problems and Applications

LO Review the use of graphs and formulas.

1A.1 The following table shows the relationship between the price of custard pies and the number of pies Jacob buys per week:

Price	Quantity of Pies	Week
$3.00	6	July 2
2.00	7	July 9
5.00	4	July 16
6.00	3	July 23
1.00	8	July 30
4.00	5	August 6

    a. Is the relationship between the price of pies and the number of pies Jacob buys a positive relationship or a negative relationship?

    b. Plot the data from the table on a graph similar to Figure 1A.3 on page 25. Draw a straight line that best fits the points.

    c. Calculate the slope of the line.

1A.2 The following table gives information on the quantity of glasses of lemonade demanded on sunny and overcast days:

Price (dollars per glass)	Quantity (glasses of lemonade per day)	Weather
$0.80	30	Sunny
0.80	10	Overcast
0.70	40	Sunny
0.70	20	Overcast
0.60	50	Sunny
0.60	30	Overcast
0.50	60	Sunny
0.50	40	Overcast

Plot the data from the table on a graph similar to Figure 1A.5 on page 27. Draw two straight lines representing the two demand curves—one for sunny days and one for overcast days.

1A.3 Using the information in Figure 1A.2 on page 24, calculate the percentage change in auto sales from one year to the next. Between which years did sales fall at the fastest rate?

1A.4 Real GDP in 2008 was $13 162 billion. Real GDP in 2009 was $12 703 billion. What was the percentage change in real GDP from 2008 to 2009? What do economists call the percentage change in real GDP from one year to the next?

1A.5 Assume that the demand curve for Pepsi passes through the following two points:

Price per Bottle of Pepsi	Number of Bottles Demanded
$2.50	100 000
1.25	200 000

a. Draw a graph with a linear demand curve that passes through these two points.

b. Show on the graph the areas representing total revenue at each price. Give the value for total revenue at each price.

1A.6 What is the area of the blue triangle shown in the following figure?

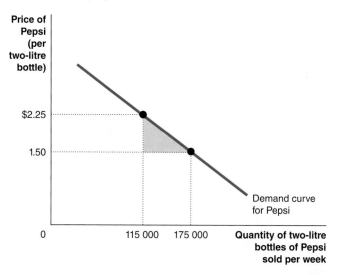

1A.7 Calculate the slope of the total cost curve at point *A* and at point *B* in the following figure.

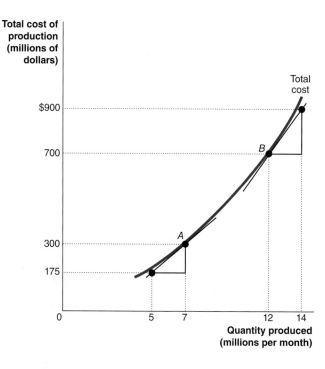

CHAPTER 2

Trade-offs, Comparative Advantage, and the Market System

Chapter Outline and Learning Objectives

OMEO GACAD/AFP/Getty Images

Managers Make Choices at Toyota

When you think of major automakers, Toyota is likely one of the first companies on your list. Founded in Japan in 1937, Toyota is the largest automaker in the world, selling 9.2 million vehicles in 2012. To compete in the automotive market, the managers of Toyota must make many decisions, such as whether to introduce new car models. Toyota doesn't just sell gasoline-powered cars, it also sells diesel-powered cars, hybrids, and is developing all-electric vehicles.

Toyota's managers must also decide whether to concentrate production in Japanese facilities or build new ones in overseas markets. Keeping production in Japan makes it easier for Toyota's managers to supervise production and to employ Japanese workers, who generally have high skill levels and few labour disputes. By building plants in the countries in which it sells its vehicles, Toyota can benefit from paying lower wages, lower transportation costs, and the reduced political friction that

results from investing in local economies. Toyota has assembly plants in Cambridge and Woodstock, Ontario, in which it builds the Toyota Corolla, Matrix, and RAV4, and the Lexus RX 350.

Managers also face smaller-scale business decisions. For instance, they must decide how many Toyota Corolla sedans and Lexus RX 350 SUVs to build in the company's Cambridge plant each month. Like other decisions people make, this one involves a trade-off: Producing more Corolla sedans means making fewer RX 350 SUVs.

AN INSIDE LOOK on **page 54** discusses how managers decide between producing hybrid cars and diesel cars, and improving existing gasoline-powered models.

Sources: "GM Loses Global Sales Crown to Toyota," *Globe and Mail*, January 14, 2013, http://www.theglobeandmail.com/globe-investor/gm-loses-global-sales-crown-to-toyota/article7319056/; and Toyota.ca.

Economics in Your Life

The Trade-offs When You Buy a Car

When you buy a car, you probably consider features such as safety, fuel efficiency, and, of course, cost. Most newer cars are more fuel-efficient than older cars. Fuel-efficiency standards have been improving almost continuously over the last 40 years. Of course, newer cars are more expensive than older ones. Very old, inefficient cars can sometimes be bought for very little. Under what circumstances would you be better off buying an older, less fuel-efficient car than a new highly efficient one? Who do you think is most likely to want a car with high fuel efficiency? As you read this chapter, see if you can answer these questions. You can check your answers against those we provide on page 52 at the end of this chapter.

Scarcity A situation in which unlimited wants exceed the limited resources available to fulfill those wants.

Factors of production The inputs used to make goods and services.

All economics starts with the recognition of **scarcity**. Scarcity exists because we have unlimited wants but only limited resources available to fulfill those wants. *Scarcity requires trade-offs.* When resources are scarce, having more of one thing means having less of something else. The economic resources, or **factors of production**—the inputs used to make goods and services, such as workers, capital, natural resources, and entrepreneurial ability—are scarce. This means goods and services are scarce. Your time is scarce, which means that you face trade-offs: If you spend an hour studying for an economics exam, you have one less hour to spend playing video games. If your university decides to use some of its scarce budget to buy new computers for the computer labs, those funds will not be available to expand parking lots. In a market system, managers at all firms must make decisions like those made by Toyota's managers. If Toyota decides to devote some of the scarce workers and machinery in its Cambridge plant to producing more RX 350 SUVs, those resources will not be available to produce more Corolla sedans.

Canadian households and firms make many of their decision in markets. Trade is a key activity that takes place in markets. Trade involves the decisions of millions of households and firms spread all over the world. By engaging in trade, people can raise their standard of living. In this chapter, we provide an overview of how the market system coordinates the independent decisions of millions of people. We begin our analysis of the economic consequences of scarcity, the benefits of trade, and the workings of the market system by introducing an important economic model: the *production possibilities frontier*.

Use a production possibilities frontier to analyze opportunity costs and trade-offs.

Production Possibilities Frontiers and Opportunity Costs

As we saw in the chapter opener, Toyota operates plants in Cambridge and Woodstock, Ontario, where it assembles Toyota sedans and Lexus RX 350 SUVs. Because the firm's resources—workers, machinery, materials, and entrepreneurial skills—are limited, Toyota faces a trade-off: For example, resources devoted to building sedans can't be used to build RX 350 SUVs, and vice versa. Chapter 1 explained that economic models can be useful to analyze a number of questions. We can use a simple model called the *production possibilities frontier* to analyze the trade-offs Toyota faces in its Cambridge plant. A **production possibilities frontier (PPF)** is a curve showing the maximum attainable combinations of two products that may be produced with available resources and technology. For our purposes, let's assume that Toyota produces only Corolla sedans and RX 350 SUVs at its Cambridge plant, using workers, robots, materials, and other machinery.

Production possibilities frontier (PPF) A curve showing the maximum attainable combinations of two products that may be produced with available resources and current technology.

Graphing the Production Possibilities Frontier

Figure 2.1 uses a production possibilities frontier to illustrate the trade-offs that Toyota faces. The numbers on the table are plotted on the graph. The line in the graph is Toyota's production possibilities frontier. If Toyota uses all its resources to produce Corolla sedans, it can make 800 per day—point *A* at one end of the production possibilities frontier. If Toyota uses all its resources to produce RX 350 SUVs, it can produce 800 per day—point *E* at the other end of the production possibilities frontier. If Toyota devotes resources to producing both types of vehicles, it could be at a point like *B* where it produces 600 Corolla sedans and 200 RX 350 SUVs.

All the combinations on the frontier (such as *A*, *B*, *C*, *D*, and *E*) or inside it (such as point *F*) are *attainable* with the resources and technology Toyota currently has. Combinations on the frontier are (productively) *efficient* because all available resources are being fully used, and the fewest possible resources are being used to produce a given amount of output. Toyota is getting the most it can. Combinations inside the frontier, such as point *F*, are inefficient because maximum output is not being obtained from the available resources. We can tell *F* is inefficient because Toyota could make 500 SUVs at this factory and still

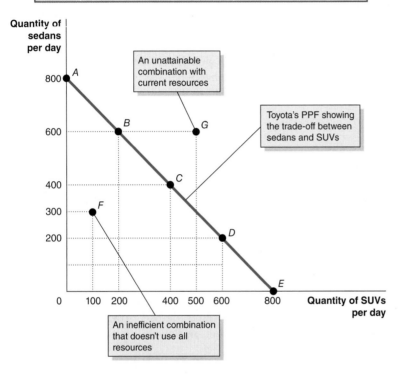

Toyota's Production Possibilities at Its Cambridge Plant		
Choice	Quantity of Corolla Sedans Produced	Quantity of RX 350 SUVs Produced
A	800	0
B	600	200
C	400	400
D	200	600
E	0	800
F	300	100
G	600	500

Figure 2.1

Toyota's Production Possibilities Frontier

Toyota faces a trade-off: To build one more sedan, it must build one less SUV. The production possibilities frontier illustrates the trade-off Toyota faces. Combinations on the production possibilities frontier—such as points A, B, C, D, and E—are *technically efficient* because the maximum output is being obtained from the available resources. Combinations inside the frontier—such as point F—are *inefficient* because some resources are not being used. Combinations outside the frontier—such as point G—are *unattainable* with current resources.

make 300 sedans, instead of only making 100 SUVs and 300 sedans. This would happen if the managers decided to hire a number of workers, but didn't give them anything to do.

Toyota, like most firms, would like to be beyond the frontier—at a point like G, where it would be producing 600 sedans and 500 SUVs—but points outside the production possibilities frontier are unattainable with the workers, equipment, materials, and technology currently in use. To be able to produce 600 sedans and 500 SUVs, Toyota would have to hire more workers and buy more equipment.

Notice that if Toyota is producing efficiently and is on the production possibilities frontier, the only way to produce more of one type of vehicle is to produce fewer of another type. Recall from Chapter 1 that the **opportunity cost** of any activity is the highest-valued alternative that must be given up to engage in that activity. For Toyota, the opportunity cost of producing one more SUV is the number of sedans it will not be able to produce because it has shifted those resources to making SUVs. For example, in moving from point B to point C, the opportunity cost of producing 200 more SUVs per day is the 200 fewer sedans that can be made.

Being on the production possibilities frontier is a good idea, but what point on the production possibilities frontier is best? Choosing the best point on the production possibilities frontier is called **allocative efficiency**. Allocative efficiency occurs when a society is making the combination of goods and services that are most valued by consumers. For example, if consumers want SUVs more than they do sedans (as they did in the 1990s and 2000s), then the allocatively efficient point is likely a point like E. If consumers want sedans more than they do SUVs (as they tend to when the price of gas is high) the allocatively efficient point is more likely a point like point A.

Opportunity cost The highest-valued alternative that must be given up to engage in an activity.

Allocative efficiency A state of the economy in which production is in accordance with consumer preferences; in particular, every good or service is produced up to the point where the last unit provides a marginal benefit to society equal to the marginal cost of producing it.

Solved Problem **2.1**

Drawing a Production Possibilities Frontier for Pat's Pizza Pit

Pat's Pizza Pit makes both root beer and pizza. Pat has 5 hours a day to spend on making either pizzas or root beer. In 1 hour, Pat can make 2 pizzas or 1 litre of root beer.

a. Use the information given to complete the table below.

	Hours Spent Making		Quantity Made	
Choice	Root Beer	Pizza	Root Beer (litres)	Pizza
A	5	0		
B	4	1		
C	3	2		
D	2	3		
E	1	4		
F	0	5		

b. Use the data from the table you just completed to draw a production possibilities frontier graph illustrating Pat's trade-offs between making pizza and making root beer. Label the vertical axis "Quantity of pizzas made" and the horizontal axis "Quantity of root beer made." Make sure to label the values where Pat's PPF intersects the vertical and horizontal axes.

c. Label the points representing choice *B* and choice *C*. If Pat is at choice *B*, what is her opportunity cost of making more root beer?

Solving the Problem

Step 1: Review the chapter material. This problem is about using production possibilities frontiers to analyze trade-offs, so you may want to review the section "Graphing the Production Possibilities Frontier," which begins on page 36.

Step 2: Answer part (a) by filling in the table. If Pat can produce 1 litre of root beer in one hour, then with choice *A*, she will make 5 litres of root beer and no pizza. Because she can produce 2 pizzas in 1 hour, with choice *B*, she will make 4 litres of root beer and 2 pizzas. Using similar reasoning, you can fill in the remaining cells of the table as follows:

	Hours Spent Making		Quantity Made	
Choice	Root Beer	Pizza	Root Beer (litres)	Pizza
A	5	0	5	0
B	4	1	4	2
C	3	2	3	4
D	2	3	2	6
E	1	4	1	8
F	0	5	0	10

Step 3: Answer part (b) by drawing the production possibilities frontier graph. Using the data in the table shown in Step 2, you should have a graph that looks something like this:

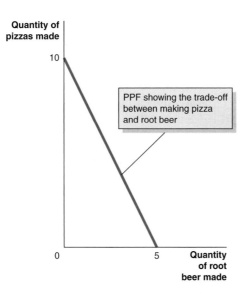

If Pat devotes all 5 hours to making pizza, she will have 10 pizzas. Therefore, her production possibilities frontier will intersect the vertical axis at 10. If she spends all her time making root beer, she will have 5 litres. Therefore, her production possibilities frontier will intersect the horizontal axis at 5.

Step 4: **Answer part (c) by showing choices *B* and *C* on your graph.** The points for choices *B* and *C* can be plotted using the information in the table, which gives you the following:

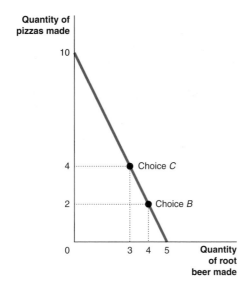

Moving from choice *B* to choice *C* increases Pat's production of pizza from 2 to 4, but lowers her production of root beer by 1 litre (from 4 to 3).

Your Turn: For more practice, do related problem 1.4 on page 57 at the end of this chapter.   MyEconLab

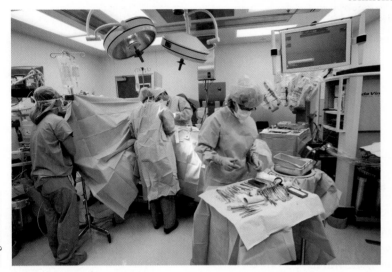

ImageBroker/Glow

Spending more on health care means spending less on other goods and services.

Making the Connection

Facing the Trade-offs of Health Care Spending

Governments have to deal with scarcity. If your provincial government spends more on health care, say by paying doctors or nurses more, it has less to spend on other areas such as education. Health care expenditures are the single biggest item in the budgets of all provincial governments, accounting for about 40 percent of spending. The federal government also supports health care spending through the Canada Health Transfer, which is the single biggest transfer of funds from the federal government to provincial governments. In 2011–2012, the federal government transferred about $27 billion dollars to provincial governments to pay for health care.

Canada's population is aging; the number of people who are over 65 is greater than ever before and that number is growing. As the population ages, two things will happen. First, older people need more health care than younger adults, which means governments will be asked to provide more money for health care spending. Second, there will be fewer people of working age to pay the taxes that support health care spending. Moreover, the money to pay for all government spending will become even scarcer than it is now.

Spending more on health care would mean that less funding is available for all the other government programs, such as education, housing, infrastructure, and so on. If governments increase taxes to fund higher health care costs (instead of cutting spending in other areas), people will have less money for the purchases they want to make. Very soon governments will have to make real and meaningful choices about the areas that will receive funding. If doctors and nurses are paid more or more doctors and nurses are hired, who are we going to pay less or what services will receive less funding? Will there be fewer teachers? Fewer police officers? More roads in disrepair? Will we have less money to spend on ourselves? Scarcity of resources means that these sorts of trade-offs have to be made.

Sources: "Canada's demographic time bomb," Financial Post via CBCnews website, April 2, 2011: http://www.cbc.ca/fp/story/2011/04/02/4544389.html#ixzz1RzxLnJHa; Geddes, John, "The health care time bomb," McLean's Magazine, April 12, 2010.

MyEconLab

Your Turn: Test your understanding by doing related problems 1.5 and 1.6 on page 57 at the end of this chapter.

Increasing Marginal Opportunity Costs

We can use the production possibilities frontier to explore issues concerning the economy as a whole. For example, suppose we divide all the goods and services produced in the economy into just two types: government-provided goods and privately provided goods. In Figure 2.2, we let operations represent government-provided goods and cars represent privately provided goods. If all the country's resources are devoted to producing government-provided goods, 400 operations could be performed in one year. If all the country's resources are devoted to producing privately provided goods, 500 cars could be produced in one year. Devoting resources to producing both types of goods results in the economy being at other points along the production possibilities frontier.

Notice that this production possibilities frontier looks different from the one in Figure 2.1. This PPF is bowed outward rather than a straight line. The fact that the PPF

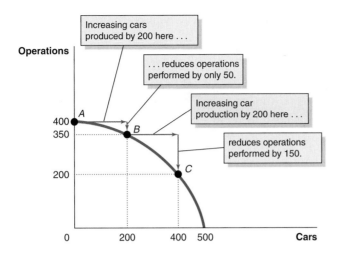

Figure 2.2

Increasing Marginal Opportunity Costs

As the economy moves down the production possibilities frontier, it experiences *increasing marginal opportunity costs* because increasing car production by a given quantity requires larger and larger decreases in the number of operations performed. For example, to increase car production from 0 to 200—moving from point *A* to point *B*—the economy has to give up only 50 operations. But to increase production of cars by another 200 vehicles—moving from point *B* to point *C*—the economy has to give up 150 operations.

is bowed outward tells us that the opportunity cost of producing more cars depends on where the economy currently is on the production possibilities frontier. For example, to increase the production of cars from 0 to 200—moving from point *A* to point *B*—the economy has to give up only 50 operations. To increase the number of cars by another 200 (for a total of 400)—moving from point *B* to point *C*—the economy has to give up another 150 operations.

As the economy moves down the production possibilities frontier, it experiences *increasing marginal opportunity costs*. Marginal opportunity costs increase because some workers, machines, and other resources are better suited to some uses than others. At point *A*, some resources that are best suited to making cars are used to perform operations. To move from point *A* to point *B*, the resources best suited to producing cars (and worst suited to performing operations) are shifted to car production. The result is a large gain in cars made while giving up few operations. As more cars are produced, resources that are better suited to performing operations are switched into car production. As a result, an increasing number of operations must be given up to get the same increase in the production of cars. Economists generally think that production possibilities frontiers are bowed outward (as in this example) rather than linear (as in the Toyota example earlier in the chapter).

The idea of increasing marginal opportunity costs illustrates an important economic concept: *The more resources already devoted to an activity, the smaller the payoff to devoting additional resources to that activity.* For example, the more hours you have already spent studying economics, the smaller the increase in your test grade from each additional hour you spend studying—and the greater the opportunity cost of using the hour in that way. The more funds a firm devotes to research and development during a given year, the smaller the amount of useful knowledge it receives from each additional dollar—and the greater the opportunity cost of using funds in that way. The more money the federal government spends cleaning up the environment during a given year, the smaller the reduction in pollution from each additional dollar—and, once again, the greater the opportunity cost of using the money in that way.

Economic Growth

At any given time, the total resources available to an economy are fixed. Therefore, if Canada produces more cars, it must produce less of something else, operations in our example. Over time the resources available to an economy may increase. For example, both the labour force and the capital stock—the amount of physical capital available to a country—may increase. The increase in the available labour force and the capital stock shifts the production possibilities frontier outward for the Canadian economy and makes it possible to produce more of *both* operations and cars. Panel (a) of Figure 2.3 shows that when an economy gets more resources, it can move from point *A* to point *B*, producing more cars *and* performing more operations.

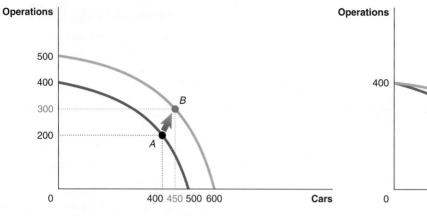

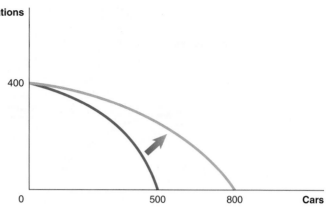

(a) Shifting out the production possibilities frontier

(b) Technological change in the automotive industry

Figure 2.3 **Economic Growth**

Panel (a) shows that as more economic resources become available and technological change occurs, the economy can move from point *A* to point *B*, performing more operations and producing more cars. Panel (b) shows the results of technological change in the automobile industry that increases the quantity of

cars workers can produce per year while leaving unchanged the maximum quantity of operations that can be performed. Shifts in the production possibilities frontier represent *economic growth*.

Similarly, technological change makes it possible to produce more goods with the same number of workers and the same amount of machinery, which also shifts the production possibilities frontier outward. Technological progress doesn't necessarily affect all sectors of the economy. Panel (b) of Figure 2.3 shows the results of technological progress in the automotive industry—for example, the invention of a better welding robot—that increases the number of cars produced per year but leaves the number of operations performed per year unchanged.

Shifts in the production possibilities frontier represent **economic growth** because they allow the economy to increase the production of goods and services, which ultimately raises the standard of living. In Canada, and other higher income countries, the market system has aided the process of economic growth, which over the past 200 years has greatly increased the well-being of the average person.

Economic growth The ability of an economy to produce increasing quantities of goods and services.

2.2 LEARNING OBJECTIVE

Understand comparative advantage and explain how it is the basis for trade.

Trade The act of buying and selling.

Comparative Advantage and Trade

In Chapter 1 we talked about all the steps and people involved in getting you a cup of coffee. All of these steps and people rely on *trade*. We can use the ideas of production possibilities frontiers and opportunity costs to understand the basic economic activity of **trade**, which is the act of buying and selling. Markets are fundamentally about trade. Sometimes we trade directly, as when children trade one hockey card for another, or you help your friend with her economics homework in exchange for help with your chemistry homework. We often trade indirectly: We sell our labour services as, say, an economist, salesperson, or nurse for money, and then we use the money to buy goods and services. Although in these cases, trade takes place indirectly, ultimately the economist, salesperson, and nurse are trading their services for food, clothing, or video games. One of the great benefits of trade is that it makes it possible for people to become better off by increasing both their production and consumption.

Specialization and Gains from Trade

Consider the following situation: You and your neighbour both have fruit trees on your property. Initially, suppose you have only apple trees and your neighbour only has cherry trees. In this situation, if you both like apples and cherries, there is an obvious opportunity for you both to gain from trade: You give your neighbour some apples and she gives you some cherries, making you both better off.

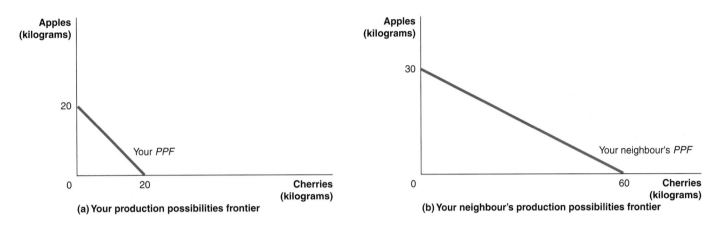

	You		Your Neighbour	
	Apples (kg)	Cherries (kg)	Apples (kg)	Cherries (kg)
Pick nothing but apples	20	0	30	0
Pick nothing but cherries	0	20	0	60

(a) Your production possibilities frontier

(b) Your neighbour's production possibilities frontier

Figure 2.4   Production Possibilities for You and Your Neighbour, without Trade

The table in this figure shows how many kilograms of apples and how many kilograms of cherries you and your neighbour can each pick in one week. The graphs in the figure use the data from the table to construct production possibilities frontiers (PPFs) for you and your neighbour. Panel (a) shows your PPF. If you devote all your time to picking apples and none of your time to picking cherries, you can pick 20 kilograms. If you devote all your time to picking cherries, you can pick 20 kilograms. Panel (b) shows that if your neighbour devotes all her time to picking apples, she can pick 30 kilograms. If she devotes all her time to picking cherries, she can pick 60 kilograms.

What if you both had apple and cherry trees in your yards? In that case, there could still be gains from trade. For example, if your neighbour was really good at picking cherries and you were really good at picking apples, it would make sense for each of you to focus on picking just one kind of fruit and trading after you were done. Things get a little more complicated if your neighbour is better at picking both apples and cherries than you are, but as we will see there are still gains from trade.

We can use production possibilities frontiers to show how you and your neighbour can benefit from trading with you *even if she is better at picking both apples and cherries.* (For simplicity, and because it doesn't change the conclusions, we assume that the PPFs are straight lines.) The table in Figure 2.4 shows how many apples and how many cherries you and your neighbour can pick in one week. The graph in the figure uses the same data to draw PPFs. Panel (a) shows your PPF and Panel (b) shows your neighbour's PPF. If you spend all week picking apples you'll end up with 20 kilograms of apples and no cherries. If you spend all week picking cherries you'll get 20 kilograms of cherries and no apples. If your neighbour spends all week picking apples she will have 30 kilograms of apples and no cherries, while if she spends the week picking nothing but cherries she will have 60 kilograms of cherries and no apples.

The PPFs in Figure 2.4 show how many apples and cherries you and your neighbour can *consume*, if you do not trade. Suppose that when you don't trade with your neighbour you decide to pick and eat 8 kilograms of apples and 12 kilograms of cherries a week (point *A* in panel (a) of Figure 2.5). This combination of apples and cherries is represented by point *A* in panel (a) of Figure 2.5. When your neighbour doesn't trade with you, she picks and consumes 9 kilograms of apples and 42 kilograms of cherries. This combination of apples and cherries is point *C* in panel (b) of Figure 2.5.

After years of ignoring each other—picking and eating apples and cherries independently—suppose your neighbour comes to you with the following proposal: She offers to trade you 15 kilograms of her cherries for 10 kilograms of your apples next week. Should

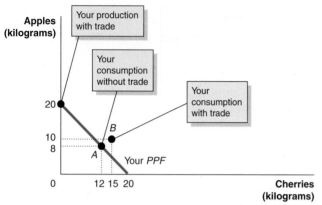

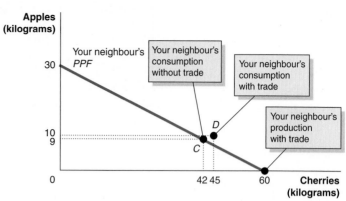

(a) Your production and consumption after trade

(b) Your neighbour's production and consumption with trade

Figure 2.5 **Gains from Trade**

When you don't trade with your neighbour, you pick and consume 8 kilograms of apples and 12 kilograms of cherries per week—point *A* in panel (a). When you neighbour doesn't trade with you, she picks and consumes 9 kilograms of apples and 42 kilograms of cherries per week—point *C* in panel (b). If you specialize in picking apples, you can pick 20 kilograms. If your neighbour specializes in picking

cherries, she can pick 60 kilograms. If you trade 10 kilograms of apples for 15 kilograms of your neighbour's cherries, you will be able to consume 10 kilograms of apples and 15 kilograms of cherries—point *B* in panel (a). You neighbour can now consume 10 kilograms of apples and 45 kilograms of cherries—point *D* in panel (b). You and your neighbour are both better off as a result of the trade.

you accept this offer? Yes! You should accept because you will end up with more apples and more cherries to consume. To take advantage of her proposal, you should specialize in picking only apples rather than splitting your time between picking apples and cherries. This would allow you to pick 20 kilograms of apples. You can then trade 10 kilograms of your apples for 15 kilograms of cherries. As a result of this trading, you end up with 10 kilograms of apples and 15 kilograms of cherries (point *B* in panel (a) of Figure 2.5), 2 kilograms of apples, and 3 kilograms of cherries more than you had last week. You now get to consume a combination of apples and cherries that was unattainable (outside your PPF) to you before!

It might seem like you've got the better of your neighbour, but she is better off too. By specializing in picking cherries, she can pick 60 kilograms. She trades 15 kilograms of cherries to you for 10 kilograms of apples. She ends up with 10 kilograms of apples and 45 kilograms of cherries (point *D* in panel (b) of Figure 2.5), which is 1 kilogram more apples and 3 kilograms more cherries than she had before trading with you. She too can now consume a combination of apples and cherries that was unattainable last week. Table 2.1 summarizes the changes in production and consumption that results from trading with your neighbour. (In this example, we chose one specific rate of trading cherries for apples—15 kilograms of cherries for 10 kilograms of apples. There are, however, many other rates of trading cherries for apples that would also make you and your neighbour both better off.)

Absolute Advantage versus Comparative Advantage

One of the most remarkable aspects of the previous example is that both you and your neighbour benefit from trading, even though your neighbour is better than you at

Table 2.1

A Summary of the Gains from Trade

	You		Your Neighbour	
	Apples (kg)	Cherries (kg)	Apples (kg)	Cherries (kg)
Production and consumption *without* trade	8	12	9	42
Production *with* trade	20	0	0	60
Consumption *with* trade	10	15	10	45
Increased consumption (gains from trade)	2	3	1	3

picking both apples and cherries. **Absolute advantage** is the ability of an individual, a firm, or a country to produce more of a good or service than potential trading partners, using the same amount of resources. Your neighbour has an absolute advantage over you in producing both apples and cherries because she can pick more of each fruit than you can with the same amount of time. Although it seems like you have nothing to offer and she should pick her own apples and cherries, we have already seen that she is (and you are too) better off specializing in cherry picking and leaving the apple picking to you.

We can consider why both you and your neighbour benefit from specializing in picking only one fruit in more detail. First, think about the opportunity cost to each of you of picking each type fruit. We saw from the PPF in Figure 2.4 that if you devoted all your time to picking apples, you would be able to pick 20 kilograms of apples per week. As you move down your PPF and shift time away from picking apples to picking cherries, you have to give up 1 kilogram of apples for each kilogram of cherries you pick (the slope of your PPF is −1). (For a refresher on calculating slopes, see Appendix A, which follows Chapter 1.) Therefore, your opportunity cost of picking 1 kilogram of cherries is 1 kilogram of apples. Put slightly differently, for every kilogram of cherries you pick, you have to give up 1 kilogram of apples. If you were to start off picking nothing but cherries and were thinking about picking some apples, every kilogram of apples you picked would cost you 1 kilogram of cherries. Your opportunity cost of picking apples is 1 kilogram of cherries per kilogram of apples.

Your neighbour's PPF has a different slope, so she faces a different trade-off: As she shifts time from picking apples to picking cherries, she has to give up 0.5 kilogram of apples for every kilogram of cherries she picks (the slope of your neighbour's PPF is −0.5). Her opportunity cost of picking cherries is 0.5 kilogram of apples per kilogram of cherries. If she were going the other way, shifting time from picking cherries to picking apples, she would have to give up 2 kilograms of cherries in order to pick 1 kilogram of apples. Your neighbour's opportunity cost of picking apples is 2 kilograms of cherries per kilogram of apples.

Table 2.2 summarizes the opportunity costs for you and your neighbour of picking apples and cherries. Note that even though your neighbour can pick more of both apples and cherries than you can, the *opportunity cost* of picking apples is higher for her than it is for you, meaning that it costs you less to pick apples than it costs her. Even though she has an absolute advantage in picking both apples and cherries, you have a *comparative advantage* in picking apples. **Comparative advantage** is the ability of an individual, a firm, or a country to produce a good or service at a lower opportunity cost than potential trading partners. In our example, your neighbour has an absolute advantage in picking apples, while you have the comparative advantage in apple picking. At the same time, your neighbour has both the absolute and comparative advantage in picking cherries. As we demonstrated, you are better off specializing in picking apples, and your neighbour is better off specializing in picking cherries. Determining whether a specific trade will lead to gains requires that we know the *exchange ratio*—in this case, the number of kilograms of cherries you would get for each kilogram of apples (or, more often, a price in terms of dollars).

Comparative Advantage and the Gains from Trade

We have just derived an important economic principle: *The basis for trade is comparative advantage, not absolute advantage.* The fastest apple pickers do not necessarily do much apple picking. If the fastest apple pickers have a comparative advantage in something

Absolute advantage The ability of an individual, a firm, or a country to produce more of a good or service than potential trading partners, using the same amount of resources.

Comparative advantage The ability of an individual, a firm, or a country to produce a good or service at a lower opportunity cost than potential trading partners.

	Opportunity Cost of Apples	Opportunity Cost of Cherries
You	1 kg of cherries	1 kg of apples
Your neighbour	2 kg of cherries	0.5 kg of apples

Table 2.2

Opportunity Costs of Picking Apples and Cherries

Don't Let This Happen to You

Don't Confuse Absolute Advantage and Comparative Advantage

First, make sure you know the definitions:

- **Absolute advantage.** The ability of an individual, a firm, or a country to produce more of a good or service than potential trading partners using the same amount of resources. In our example, your neighbour has an absolute advantage over you in both picking apples and picking cherries.
- **Comparative advantage.** The ability of an individual, a firm, or a country to produce a good or service at a lower opportunity cost than potential trading partners. In our example, your neighbour has a comparative advantage in picking cherries, while you have the comparative advantage in picking apples.

Keep these two key points in mind:

1. It is possible to have an absolute advantage in producing something without having a comparative advantage. This is the case with your neighbour and picking apples.
2. It is possible to have a comparative advantage without having an absolute advantage. In our example, you have the comparative advantage in picking apples, even though your neighbour can pick more than you.

MyEconLab

Your Turn: Test your understanding by doing related problem 2.2 on page 57 at the end of this chapter.

else—for example, picking cherries, playing hockey, or being economists—they are better off specializing in that other activity *and so is everyone else.* Individuals, firms, and countries are better off if they specialize in producing goods and services in which they have a comparative advantage and trade to get the other goods and services they aren't producing.

Solved Problem **2.2**

Comparative Advantage and the Gains from Trade

Suppose that Canada and the United States both produce video games and nacho chips. These are the combination of the two goods that each country can produce in one day:

Canada		United States	
Video Games (titles)	Nacho Chips (tonnes)	Video Games (titles)	Nacho Chips (tonnes)
0	60	0	200
10	45	10	160
20	30	20	120
30	15	30	80
40	0	40	40
		50	0

a. Who has the comparative advantage in producing nacho chips? Who has the comparative advantage in producing video games?
b. Suppose that Canada is currently producing (and consuming) 30 video games and 15 tonnes of nacho chips, while the United States is currently producing (and consuming) 10 video games and 160 tonnes of nachos. Demonstrate that Canada and the United States can both be better off if they specialize in producing only one good and engage in trade.
c. Illustrate your answer to question (b) by drawing a PPF for Canada and a PPF for the United States. Show on your PPFs the combinations of video games and nachos produced and consumed in each country before and after trade.

Solving the Problem

Step 1: Review the chapter material. This problem is about comparative advantage, so you may want to review the section "Absolute Advantage versus Comparative Advantage," which begins on page 44.

Step 2: **Answer part (a) by calculating the opportunity costs of each activity for each country and comparing your results to see who has the comparative advantage.** Remember that a country has a comparative advantage when they can produce something at a lower opportunity cost. When Canada produces 1 more video game title, it produces 1.5 tonnes fewer nacho chips. When the United States produces 1 more video game title, it produces 4 tonnes fewer nacho chips. Therefore, Canada's opportunity cost of producing video game titles—1.5 tonnes of nacho chips per video game title—is lower than that of the United States—4 tonnes of nacho chips per video game title. When Canada produces 1 more tonne of nacho chips, it produces 0.67 fewer video game titles. When the United States produces 1 more tonne of nacho chips, it produces 0.25 fewer video game titles. Therefore, the United States' opportunity cost of producing nacho chips—0.25 video game titles per tonne of nacho chips—is lower than Canada's—0.67 video game titles per tonne of nacho chips. We can conclude that Canada has the comparative advantage in producing video game titles and the United States has the comparative advantage in producing nacho chips.

Step 3: **Answer part (b) by showing that specialization makes both Canada and the United States better off.** We know that Canada should specialize where it has a comparative advantage, and so should the United States. This means that Canada should produce video games and the United States should produce nacho chips. If both countries specialize completely, Canada will produce 40 video game titles and 0 tonnes of nacho chips, while the United States will produce 0 video game titles and 200 tonnes of nacho chips. After both countries specialize, Canada could then trade 10 video game titles to the United States in exchange for 20 tonnes of nacho chips. (You should be aware that a lot of other mutually beneficial trades are possible as well.) We can summarize the results in a table:

	Before Trade		After Trade	
	Video Games (titles)	Nacho Chips (tonnes)	Video Games (titles)	Nacho Chips (tonnes)
Canada	30	15	30	20
United States	10	160	10	180

Canadians are better off after trade because they can consume the same number of video games and 5 *more* tonnes of nachos than they could before trade. Americans are better off after trade because they can consume the same amount of nacho chips and 10 *more* video games than before trade.

Step 4: **Answer part (c) by drawing the PPFs.**

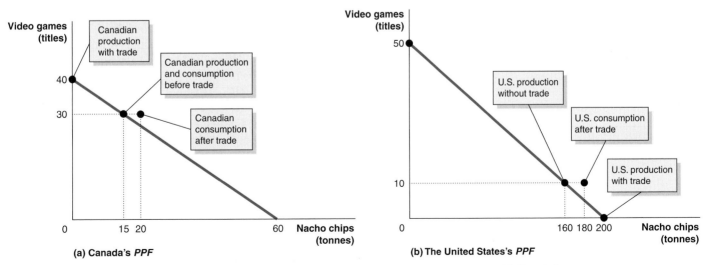

(a) Canada's *PPF*   (b) The United States's *PPF*

Your Turn: For more practice, do related problem 2.3 on page 57 at the end of this chapter.   MyEconLab

The Market System

We have seen that households, firms, and the government face trade-offs and incur opportunity costs because resources are scarce. We have also seen that trade allows people to specialize according to their comparative advantage. By engaging in trade, people can raise their material standard of living—the amount of goods, and services that they get to consume. Of course, trade in the modern world is a lot more complicated than it was in the examples we have considered so far. Trade today involves the decisions of billions of people around the world. But how does an economy make trade possible, and how are the decisions of these billions of people coordinated? In Canada and most other countries, trade is carried out in markets. It is also through markets that these billions of people determine the answers to the three fundamental questions discussed in Chapter 1: What goods and services will be produced? How will the goods and services be produced? Who will receive the goods and services produced?

Market A group of buyers and sellers of a good or service and the institutions or arrangements by which they come together to trade.

Recall that the definition of **market** is a group of buyers and sellers of a good or service and the institutions or arrangements by which they come together to trade. Markets take many forms: They can be physical places, such as a farmers' market, a grocery store, or even the Toronto Stock Exchange, or virtual places such as eBay. In a market, the buyers are the people that demand goods or services (demanders), and the sellers are the people willing to supply them (suppliers). Households and firms interact in two types of markets: *product markets* and *factor markets*. **Product markets** are markets for goods—such as computers—or services—such as haircuts. In product markets, households demand the goods and services supplied by firms. **Factor markets** are markets for the *factors of production*. As mentioned earlier, *factors of production* are the inputs used to make goods and services; they are divided into four broad categories:

Product market A market for goods—such as computers—or services—such as haircuts.

Factor market A market for the factors of production, such as labour, capital, natural resources, and entrepreneurial ability.

- *Labour* includes all types of work, from the part-time labour of teens working at McDonald's to the work of CEOs of large corporations.

- *Capital* refers to physical capital, such as computers, machines, and buildings that are used to make other goods.

- *Natural resources* include land, water, oil, iron ore, and other raw materials (or "gifts of nature") that are used in producing goods.

Entrepreneur Someone who operates a business, bringing together factors of production—labour, capital, and natural resources—to produce goods and services.

- An **entrepreneur** is someone who operates a business. *Entrepreneurial ability* is the ability to bring the other factors of production together to successfully produce and sell goods and services.

The Circular Flow of Income

Two key groups of people participate in markets:

- A *household* consists of all the individuals in a home. Households are the owners and suppliers of factors of production—particularly labour—employed by firms to make goods and services. Households use the income they receive from selling their factors of production to purchase the goods and services produced by firms. We are familiar with households as suppliers of labour because the majority of people earn most of their money by going to work, which means they are selling their labour services to firms in the labour market. Households also own all the other factors of production, either directly or indirectly, by owning the firms that have these resources. All firms are owned by households. Small firms, like a local coffee shop, might be owned by one person. Large firms, like Toyota, are owned by millions of households that own shares of stock in them. When firms pay profits to the people who own them, the firms are paying for using the capital and natural resources that are supplied to them by those owners. So, we can generalize by saying in factor markets, households are suppliers and firms are demanders.

- *Firms* are suppliers of goods and services. Firms use the funds they receive from selling goods and services to buy the factors of production needed to make the goods and services they sell.

We can use a simple economic model called the **circular-flow diagram** to see how participants in markets are linked. Figure 2.6 shows that in factor markets, households supply labour and other factors of production in exchange for wages and other payments from firms. In product markets, households use the payments they earn in factor markets to purchase the goods and services supplied by firms. Firms produce these goods and services using the factors of production supplied by households. In the figure, the blue arrows show the flow of factors of production from households through factor markets to firms. The red arrows show the flow of goods and services from firms through product markets to households. The green arrows show the flow of funds from firms through factor markets to households and the flow of spending from households through product markets to firms.

Like all models, the circular-flow diagram is a simplified version of reality. For example, Figure 2.6 leaves out the important role of government in buying goods from firms and in making payments, such as employment insurance, to households. The figure also leaves out the roles played by banks, the stock and bond markets, and other parts of the financial system in aiding the flow of funds from lenders to borrowers. Finally, the figure does not show that some goods and services purchased by Canadian households are produced in other countries and some goods and services produced by Canadian firms are sold to households in foreign countries. (The government, financial systems, and international sector are explored in later chapters.) Despite these simplifications, the circular-flow diagram in Figure 2.6 is useful for seeing how product markets, factor markets, and their participants are linked together. One of the great wonders of the market system is that it manages to successfully coordinate the independent activities of so many households and firms.

Circular-flow diagram A model that illustrates how participants in markets are linked.

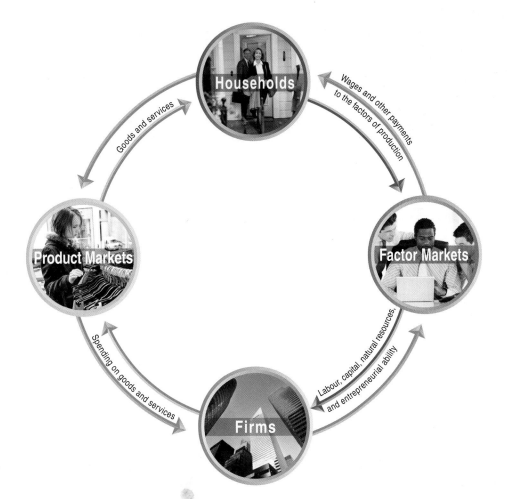

Figure 2.6

A Simple Circular-Flow Diagram

Households and firms are linked together in a circular flow of production, income, and spending. The blue arrows show the flow of the factors of production. In factor markets, households supply labour, entrepreneurial ability, and other factors of production to firms. Firms use these factors of production to make goods and services that they supply to households in product markets. The red arrows show the flow of goods and services from firms to households. The green arrows show the flow of funds. In factor markets, households receive wages and other payments from firms in exchange for supplying the factors of production. Households use these wages and other payments to purchase goods and services from firms in product markets. Firms sell goods and services to households in product markets, and they use the funds to purchase the factors of production from households in factor markets.

Photo credits: (Clockwise) JupiterImages; Alamy; Mikael Damkier/Alamy; Elena Elisseeva/Shutterstock

The Gains from Free Markets

Free market A market with few government restrictions on how goods or services can be produced or sold, on who can buy or sell goods or services, or on how factors of production can be employed.

A **free market** exists when the government places few restrictions on how goods or services can be produced or sold, on who can buy or sell goods or services, or on how factors of production can be employed. Governments in all modern economies intervene in markets, so no market in the world is completely free. In that sense, we can think of the free market as being a theoretical benchmark against which we can judge actual markets. There are relatively few government restrictions on economic activity in Canada, the United States, Western Europe, Japan, and many other countries. So these countries come fairly close to the free market benchmark. In countries such as Cuba and North Korea, the free market system has been rejected in favour of centrally planned economies with extensive government control of product and factor markets. Countries that come closest to the free market benchmark have much higher standards of living than those with centrally planned economies.

Scottish philosopher Adam Smith is considered the father of modern economics because his book *An Inquiry into the Nature and Causes of the Wealth of Nations*, published in 1776, was an early and very influential argument for the free market system. Smith was writing at a time when extensive government restrictions on markets were

Making
the
Connection

A Story of the Market System in Action: How Do you Make a PlayBook?

Chris Ratcliffe/Bloomberg via Getty Images

The market coordinates the activities of the many people spread around the world who contribute to the making of such products as a BlackBerry PlayBook.

BlackBerry makes smartphones and used to make the PlayBook. Given that BlackBerry's headquarters are in Waterloo, Ontario, you might think that PlayBooks were made in Ontario. In fact, BlackBerry didn't produce any of the physical parts of the PlayBook, nor did it assemble them to make the finished product. Far from being produced entirely by one company in one place, the PlayBook required the coordinated activities of thousands of workers and many firms from all over the world.

The PlayBook used a CPU made by Texas Instruments, based in Dallas, Texas. But Texas Instruments didn't make the memory components for the PlayBook. Those were produced by SanDisk, which has its headquarters in Milpitas, California, but has manufacturing facilities throughout Asia. These and other PlayBook components—such as screens, speakers, accelerometers, and batteries—were brought together by Quanta Computer in Taiwan for assembly. Once assembled, the PlayBook was shipped all over the world by yet other companies.

All told, a PlayBook contained hundreds of different parts that were designed and manufactured by firms all over the world. Many of these firms were not even aware of which other firms were also producing parts for the PlayBook. Few of the managers of these firms were likely to have met managers of the other firms or have shared knowledge or production schedules with them. In fact, no one person—including Thorsten Heins, the CEO of BlackBerry, and any of the developers of the PlayBook's operating system—knew how to manufacture all the components that went into a PlayBook. Instead, the invisible hand of the market has led the firms involved in producing the PlayBook to contribute their knowledge and resources to the process that ultimately resulted in a PlayBook being available for purchase to people all over the world.

Source: Based on UBM TechInsights, "RIM BlackBerry Playbook Teardown Analysis," http://www.ubmtechinsights.com/teardowns/blackberry-playbook-teardown/.

MyEconLab **Your Turn:** Test your understanding by doing related problem 3.2 on page 58 at the end of this chapter.

very common. In many parts of Europe, the *guild system* still prevailed. Under this system, governments would give guilds (organizations of producers) the authority to control the production of a good. For example, the shoemakers' guild controlled who was allowed to produce shoes, how many shoes they could produce, and what price they could charge. In France, the cloth makers' guild even dictated the number of threads in cloth.

Smith argued that such restrictions reduced the income, or wealth, of a country and its people by restricting the quantity of goods produced. Some people at the time supported the restrictions of the guild system because it was in their financial interest to do so. If you were a member of a guild, the restrictions served to reduce the competition you faced. But other people sincerely believed that the alternative to the guild system was economic chaos. Smith argued that these people were wrong and that a country could enjoy a smoothly functioning economic system if firms were freed from guild restrictions.

The Legal Basis of a Successful Market System

As noted earlier, in a free market, government imposes few restrictions. However, the market system cannot work without government, as you can see if you look at some of the failed states around the world. Government must take active steps to provide a *legal environment* that will allow the market system to succeed.

Protection of Private Property For the market system to work well, individuals must be willing to take risks. Someone with $250 000 can be cautious and keep it safely in a bank—or even as cash. But the market system won't work unless a lot of people are willing to risk their savings by investing them in businesses. Investing in businesses is risky in any country. Many businesses fail every year in Canada and other high-income countries. But in high-income countries, someone who starts a new business or invests in an existing business doesn't have to worry that the government, the military, or a criminal gang might decide to seize the business or demand payments for not destroying the business. Unfortunately, in many poor countries, owners of businesses are not well protected from having their businesses seized by government or from having their profits taken by criminals. Where these problems exist, opening a business can be extremely risky. Cash can be concealed easily, but a business is a lot harder to hide and difficult to move.

Property rights are the rights individuals or firms have to the exclusive use of their property, including the right to buy or sell it. Property can be tangible, physical property such as a house, store, or factory. Property can also be intangible, such as the rights to an idea, image, or process.

Property rights The rights individuals or firms have to the exclusive use of their property, including the right to buy or sell it.

Property rights in Canada are based on the system of common law that was in effect when Canada was a British colony (with the exception of Quebec, where matters of provincial jurisdiction are based on the civil code system). Both the federal and provincial governments play a role in property rights. The federal government is responsible for intellectual property rights, while provincial governments are responsible for personal and real property. Provincial property rights legislation that concerns goods and services other than land generally has the same name in each province—the Sale of Goods Act. Specifically, this set of acts outlines the obligations of people entering into contracts to buy and sell goods and services. The sale and purchase of land is governed by each province's real estate law, as well as common law (or the civil code, in the case of Quebec). Although seldom used, the federal government has the power to require people to sell their land, which is called *expropriation*. Expropriation law requires that the government "fairly" compensate those from whom it takes land. Unfortunately, many developing countries do not provide the same protection of land property rights.

Enforcement of Contracts and Property Rights Business activity often involves someone agreeing to carry out some action in the future. For example, you borrow

$20 000 to buy a car and promise the bank—by signing a loan contract—that you will pay back the money (with interest) over the next five years. BlackBerry might also sign a contract with Texas Instruments agreeing to buy 10 000 CPUs for smartphones at a specific price. Usually these agreements take the form of legal contracts. For the market system to work, businesses and individuals have to rely on these contracts being honoured. If one party to a legal contract does not fulfill its obligations—perhaps Texas Instruments doesn't deliver the CPUs on time—the other party to the contract can take Texas Instruments to court to have the deal enforced. Similarly, if one company believes that another has violated a patent or copyright, a lawsuit is likely to follow.

Going to court to enforce a contract or private property rights will be successful only if the court system is independent and judges are able to make impartial decisions on the basis of the law. In Canada and other high-income countries, the court systems have enough independence from other parts of the government and enough protection from threats from outside forces—such as criminals—that they are able to make the decision based on the law. In many developing countries, the court systems lack this independence and will not provide a remedy if the government violates private property rights or if a person with powerful political allies decides to violate a business contract.

If property rights are not well enforced, fewer goods and services will be produced. This reduces economic efficiency, leaving the economy inside its production possibilities frontier and people worse off.

Economics in Your Life

The Trade-offs When You Buy a Car

At the beginning of the chapter, we asked you to think about two questions: Under what circumstances would you be better off buying an older, less fuel-efficient car than a new highly efficient one? Who do you think is most likely to want a car with high fuel efficiency? To answer the first question, you have to think about the trade-off between fuel efficiency and current price. If you buy an older car, you will have to pay less now, but you will have to pay more (in gas) when you drive somewhere. The trade-off is between paying now or paying later. This trade-off would look a lot like the relationship in Figure 2.1 on page 37. What you decide will likely depend on how far or often you plan to drive. If you don't think you will drive much, a cheaper car is probably better for you. That is, you might find you are willing to give up fuel efficiency (future savings) for a lower price (savings now). To have a cheaper and more fuel-efficient car, automakers would have to discover new technologies for making cars. This would shift the PPF out, as in panel (a) of Figure 2.3 on page 42.

To answer the second question, think about the trade-off between purchase price and fuel efficiency. The people most likely to want a fuel-efficient car are people who drive a lot. For them, the savings in gasoline expenses would be more important than the initial purchase price.

Conclusion

We have seen that by trading in markets, people are able to specialize and pursue their comparative advantage. Trading on the basis of comparative advantage makes all participants in trade better off. The key role of markets is to facilitate trade. In fact, the market system is a very effective way of coordinating the decisions of billions of consumers, workers, and firms. At the centre of the market system is the consumer. To be successful, firms must respond to the desires of consumers. These desires are communicated to firms through prices. To explore how markets work, we must study the behaviour of consumers and firms. We continue this exploration of markets in Chapter 3, where we develop the model of demand and supply. Before moving on to Chapter 3, read *An Inside Look* on the next page to learn how managers decide between producing hybrid cars or improving the fuel efficiency of other types of engines.

NATIONAL POST

Diesels vs. Hybrids: Who Wins?

Go to any new vehicle launch and invariably one wag will ask whether the car du jour will ever be available with a diesel engine. Ask that question at a Toyota launch and you might need to book off the rest of the morning for the answer.

Toyota, which does supply diesel offerings in markets outside North America, is very adamant about why it thinks diesel is the last thing North America needs.

"We believe in investing in technology that you can use elsewhere rather than in antiquated technology that barely meets the regulatory requirements," says engineer John-Paul Farag, with Toyota Canada's advanced powertrain department.

Antiquated technology? That's fightin' words in some camps. But Farag points to the hiatus diesel vehicles had to take in 2008 when emissions standards changed and the then-current range of diesel vehicles no longer quali-

fied. It took new technology, such as selective catalytic conversion and a system to spray urea in catalytic converters, to bring them back to being legal. But the standards are likely to become more restrictive soon, he claims, "and they're right on the edge."

Farag says the technology to clean up diesel fuel emissions runs counter to fuel efficiency, particularly the need to run the engine with a rich fuel mixture at times to generate enough heat to activate the catalytic conversion process.

"I wouldn't be surprised if diesel's on the outside looking in in the near future."

Farag says Toyota is investing heavily in hybrid vehicles because it believes it has greater applications, is more adaptable to future technology and can work with whatever fuel supply is in play. If gasoline gives way to biofuel or hydrogen, the basic concept of hybrid technology applies. Hybrid technology also provides a solid foundation to work toward vehicles that are all-electric, he says.

Porsche has been driving some of its technology toward hybrids, in particular a Panamera hybrid and a Cayenne hybrid, but it hasn't ruled out diesels.

Laurance Yap, public relations manager for Porsche Cars Canada, says the company's interest in hybrids is driven by customer demand, particularly for high-revving, high-performance engines. But it also sells a diesel Cayenne elsewhere in the world and "we're probably going to bring that to Canada as well," he says.

"Diesel will always be complicated to keep within regulations," Yap says, agreeing that diesel is an easier case to make in Europe where the fuel is cleaner than the diesel sold here. "In Europe, cars are taxed on the amount of CO_2 they release, and diesels do release less CO_2 than gasoline models, but they're higher in the stuff that's not taxed—the nitrous oxides and other emissions."

Key Points in the Article

This article discusses the trade-offs managers at Toyota, Porsche, and other automakers face in attempting to increase fuel efficiency and meet pollution standards. In Canada, emissions standards have become more stringent, requiring that automakers design cars that produce lower emissions. To meet these standards, automakers have had to make a variety of choices. Given that resources are limited, they have faced a trade-off between investing in research and development on hybrids and research and development on cars that burn diesel fuel. In recent years, automakers have focused on research and development on hybrids that use electric batteries or batteries combined with gasoline engines, and have given up on improving diesel engines.

Analyzing the News

ⓐ While Toyota produces diesel-powered cars for other markets, it doesn't offer them to North American consumers. Toyota doesn't offer these cars because emission standards are expensive to meet. In 2008, when the emission standards changed, many manufacturers had to take diesel engines off the market because they generated too much pollution. Toyota's engineer expects that emissions standards will become even tougher in the future, making diesel-powered cars even more expensive.

ⓑ To have diesel-powered cars meet emissions standards, automakers would have to redesign these cars in a way that would increase the amount of fuel they currently use. The increase in fuel use creates an important trade-off for automakers and car buyers. If there is another technology, such as the hybrid engine, that allows cars to be fuel efficient and pollute less, it makes sense for automakers to invest in that technology.

ⓒ Companies face trade-offs in the type of research and development they pursue. Toyota has chosen to invest in hybrid rather than diesel technology. This choice will change the PPF over time, causing it to pivot, as in panel (b) of Figure 2.3 on page 42. When companies successfully invest in research and development, they are able to produce more of their goods or services with the same amount of labour and capital. If Toyota had chosen to invest in both diesel and hybrid engines, its PPF would be represented like the PPF in panel (a) of Figure 2.3.

Thinking Critically

1. Continuing to produce diesel-powered cars will mean that Toyota can produce fewer hybrids than it could if it were to switch all its production to hybrids. Given the generally agreed upon bright future for hybrids, why would Toyota continue to produce diesel-powered cars?

2. Assume that the graph below accurately represents Toyota's production possibilities frontiers at its Canadian plants for 2013 and 2015. Also assume that in 2015 it has customer orders for 500 hybrids per week and 400 diesel-powered cars per week. Explain whether Toyota can fill all of these orders from its Canadian plants.

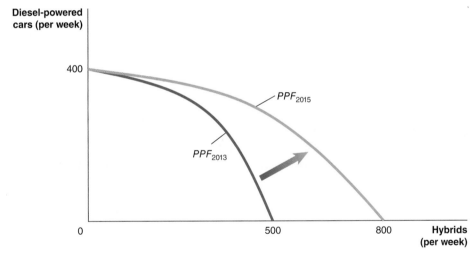

Chapter Summary and Problems

Key Terms

Absolute advantage, p. 45

Allocative efficiency, p. 37

Circular-flow diagram, p. 49

Comparative advantage, p. 45

Economic growth, p. 42

Entrepreneur, p. 48

Factor market, p. 48

Factors of production, p. 36

Free market, p. 50

Market, p. 48

Opportunity cost, p. 37

Product market, p. 48

Production possibilities
frontier (PPF), p. 36

Property rights, p. 51

Scarcity, p. 36

Trade, p. 42

Summary

*LO 2.1 The *production possibilities frontier (PPF)* is a curve that shows the maximum attainable combinations of two products that may be produced with available resources. The PPF is used to illustrate the trade-offs that arise from scarcity. Points on the frontier are technically efficient. Points inside the frontier are inefficient, and points outside the frontier are unattainable. The *opportunity cost* of any activity is the highest-valued alternative that must be given up to engage in that activity. Because of increasing marginal opportunity costs, production possibilities frontiers are usually bowed out rather than straight lines. This illustrates the important economic concept that the more resources that are already devoted to any activity, the smaller the payoff from devoting additional resources to that activity is likely to be. *Economic growth* is illustrated by shifting a production possibilities frontier outward.

LO 2.2 Fundamentally, markets are about *trade*, which is the act of buying or selling. People trade on the basis of *comparative advantage*. An individual, a firm, or a country has a comparative advantage in producing a good or service if it can produce the good or service at the lowest opportunity cost. People are usually better off specializing in the activity for which they have a comparative advantage and trading for the other goods and services they need. It is important not to confuse comparative advantage with absolute advantage. An individual, a firm, or a country has an *absolute advantage* in producing a good or service if it can produce more of

that good or service using the same amount of resources. It is possible to have an absolute advantage in producing a good or service without having a comparative advantage.

LO 2.3 A *market* is a group of buyers and sellers of a good or service and the institutions or arrangements by which they come together to trade. *Product markets* are markets for goods and services, such as computers and haircuts. *Factor markets* are markets for the *factors of production*, such as labour, capital, natural resources, and entrepreneurial ability. A *circular-flow diagram* shows how participants in product markets and factor markets are linked. Adam Smith argued in his 1776 book *The Wealth of Nations* that in a *free market*, where the government does not control the production of goods and services, changes in prices lead firms to produce the goods and services most desired by consumers. If consumers demand more of a good, its price will rise. Firms respond to rising prices by increasing production. If consumers demand less of a good, its price will fall. Firms respond to falling prices by producing less of a good. An *entrepreneur* is someone who operates a business. In the market system, entrepreneurs are responsible for organizing the production of goods and services. The market system will work well only if there is protection for *property rights*, which are the rights of individuals and firms to use their property.

MyEconLab   Log in to MyEconLab to complete these exercises and get instant feedback.

Review Questions

LO 2.1

1.1 What is a production possibilities frontier? How can we show economic efficiency on a production possibilities frontier? How can we show inefficiency? What causes a production possibilities frontier to shift outward?

1.2 What does *increasing marginal opportunity costs* mean? What are the implications of this idea for the shape of the production possibilities frontier?

LO 2.2

2.1 What is absolute advantage? What is comparative advantage? Is it possible for a country to have a comparative advantage in producing a good without also having an absolute advantage? Briefly explain.

2.2 What is the basis for trade: absolute advantage or comparative advantage? How can an individual or a country gain from specialization and trade?

LO 2.3

3.1 What is a circular-flow diagram, and what does it demonstrate?

*'Learning Objective' is abbreviated to 'LO' in the end of chapter material.

3.2 What is a free market? In what ways does a free market economy differ from a centrally planned economy?

3.3 What are private property rights? What role do they play in the working of a market system? Why are independent courts important for a well-functioning economy?

Problems and Applications

LO 2.1

1.1 Draw a production possibilities frontier that shows the trade-off between the production of cotton and the production of soybeans.

    a. Show the effect that a prolonged drought would have on the initial production possibilities frontier.

    b. Suppose genetic modification makes soybeans resistant to insects, allowing yields to double. Show the effect of this technological change on the initial production possibilities frontier.

1.2 [**Related to the** Chapter Opener **on page 35**] One of the trade-offs Toyota faces is between safety and gas mileage. For example, adding steel to a car makes it safer but also heavier, which results in lower gas mileage. Draw a hypothetical production possibilities frontier that Toyota engineers face that shows this trade-off.

1.3 Suppose you win free tickets to a movie plus all you can eat at the snack bar for free. Would there be a cost to you to attend this movie? Explain.

1.4 [**Related to** Solved Problem 2.1 **on page 38**] You have exams in economics and chemistry coming up, and you have five hours available for studying. The following table shows the trade-offs you face in allocating the time you will spend in studying each subject:

	Hours Spent Studying		Midterm Score	
Choice	Economics	Chemistry	Economics	Chemistry
A	5	0	95	70
B	4	1	93	78
C	3	2	90	84
D	2	3	86	88
E	1	4	81	90
F	0	5	75	91

    a. Use the data in the table to draw a production possibilities frontier graph. Label the vertical axis "Score on economics exam," and label the horizontal axis "Score on chemistry exam." Make sure to label the values where your production possibilities frontier intersects the vertical and horizontal axes.

    b. Label the points representing choice *C* and choice *D*. If you are at choice *C*, what is your opportunity cost of increasing your chemistry score?

    c. Under what circumstances would choice *A* be a sensible choice?

1.5 [**Related to** Making the Connection **on page 40**] Suppose the minister responsible for Health Canada is trying to decide whether the federal government should spend more on research to find a cure for heart disease. She asks you,

one of her economic advisers, to prepare a report discussing the relevant factors she should consider. Use the concepts of opportunity cost and trade-offs to discuss some of the main issues you would deal with in your report.

1.6 [**Related to** Making the Connection **on page 40**] Suppose your provincial government is deciding which of two sports programs it will pay for (assuming that only one program will be funded). The choices are Sport A, which will allow 24 students to play for 8 months and costs $37 500 per year, and Sport B, which will allow 20 students to play for 8 months and costs $15 000 per year. What factors should the provincial government take into account in making this decision?

LO 2.2

2.1 Look again at the information in Figure 2.4 on page 43. Choose a rate of trading cherries for apples different from the rate used in the text (15 kilograms of cherries for 10 kilograms of apples) that will allow you and your neighbor to benefit from trading apples and cherries. Prepare a table like Table 2.1 on page 44 to illustrate your answer.

2.2 [**Related to** Don't Let This Happen to You **on page 46**] In the 1950s, economist Bela Balassa compared 28 manufacturing industries in the United States and Britain. In every one of the 28 industries, Balassa found that the United States had an absolute advantage. In these circumstances, would there have been any gain to the United States from importing any of these products from Britain? Explain.

2.3 [**Related to** Solved Problem 2.2 **on page 46**] Suppose that France and Germany both produce schnitzel and wine. The following table shows combinations of the goods that each country can produce in a day:

France		Germany	
Wine (bottles)	Schnitzel (kilograms)	Wine (bottles)	Schnitzel (kilograms)
0	8	0	15
1	6	1	12
2	4	2	9
3	2	3	6
4	0	4	3
		5	0

    a. Who has a comparative advantage in producing wine? Who has a comparative advantage in producing schnitzel?

    b. Suppose that France is currently producing 1 bottle of wine and 6 kilograms of schnitzel, and Germany is currently producing 3 bottles of wine and 6 kilograms of schnitzel. Demonstrate that France and Germany can both be better off if they specialize in producing only one good and then engage in trade.

2.4 Can an individual or a country produce beyond its production possibilities frontier? Can an individual or a country consume beyond its production possibilities frontier? Explain.

2.5 Is specialization and trade between individuals and countries more about having a job or about obtaining a higher standard of living? Individually, if you go from a situation of not trading with others (you produce everything yourself) to a situation of trading with others, do you still have a job? Does your standard of living increase? Likewise, if a country goes from not trading with other countries to trading with other countries, does it still have jobs? Does its standard of living increase?

2.6 Some people argue that Canada should import only products that could not be produced here. Do you believe that this would be a good policy? Explain.

LO 2.3

3.1 Identify whether each of the following transactions will take place in the factor market or in the product market and whether households or firms are supplying the good or service or demanding the good or service:
  a. George buys a Toyota Camry hybrid.
  b. Toyota increases employment at its Cambridge plant.
  c. George works 20 hours per week at McDonald's.
  d. George sells land he owns to McDonald's so it can build a new restaurant.

3.2 [**Related to** Making the Connection **on page 50**] In *The Wealth of Nations*, Adam Smith wrote the following (Book I, Chapter II): "It is not from the benevolence of the butcher, the brewer, or the baker, that we expect our dinner, but from their regard to their own interest." Briefly discuss what he meant by this.

3.3 Evaluate the following argument: "Adam Smith's analysis is based on a fundamental flaw: He assumes that people are motivated by self-interest. But this isn't true. I'm not selfish, and most people I know aren't selfish."

3.4 Some economists have been puzzled that although entrepreneurs take on the risk of losing time and money by starting new businesses, on average their incomes are lower than those of people with similar characteristics who go to work at large firms. Economist William Baumol believes part of the explanation for this puzzle may be that entrepreneurs are like people who buy lottery tickets. On average, people who don't buy lottery tickets are left with more money than people who buy tickets because lotteries take in more money than they give out. Baumol argues that "the masses of purchasers who grab up the [lottery] tickets are not irrational if they receive an adequate payment in another currency: psychic rewards."

William J. Baumol, The Microtheory of Innovative Entrepreneurship, (Princeton, NJ: Princeton University Press, 2010).

a. What are "psychic rewards"?

b. What psychic rewards might an entrepreneur receive?

c. Do you agree with Baumol that an entrepreneur is like someone buying a lottery ticket? Briefly explain.

William J. Baumol, The Microtheory of Innovative Entrepreneurship, (Princeton, NJ: Princeton University Press, 2010).

3.5 The 2009 International Property Rights Index study states:

> Data shows that countries that protect the physical and intellectual property of their people enjoy nearly nine times higher [income per person] . . . than countries ranking lowest in property rights protections. The study . . . compared the protections of physical and intellectual property to economic stability in 115 countries. . . .

How would the creation of property rights be likely to affect the economic opportunities available to citizens of those countries ranking lowest in property rights protections?

Kelsey Zahourek, "Report: Property Rights Linked to Economic Security," International Property Rights Index 2009 Report.

MyEconLab MyEconLab is an online tool designed to help you master the concepts covered in your course. It will create an adaptive, highly personalized study plan to stimulate and measure your learning. Log in to take advantage of this powerful study aid, and to access quizzes and other valuable course-related material.

Where Prices Come From: The Interaction of Supply and Demand

Chapter Outline and Learning Objectives

PhotoXpress/ZUMAPRESS/Newscom

Red Bull and the Market for Energy Drinks

Markets for some products suddenly explode. This was the case in the market for energy drinks. Red Bull was developed in Austria by Dietrich Mateschitz, who based it on a drink he discovered being sold in pharmacies in Thailand. Before Red Bull entered the market, few soft drinks included caffeine. Red Bull didn't enter the Canadian market until 2004, likely due to soft drink regulations. In Canada, caffeine may not be added to a traditional soft drink other than a cola. For example, Mountain Dew sold in the United States has a relatively high amount of caffeine, but the version sold in Canada contains none. Red Bull and other energy drinks are sold in Canada as natural health products, and are therefore subject to different regulations. Despite not being available in Canada before 2004, the Canadian sports and energy drink sector saw $876 million in retail sales in 2012. The market for energy drinks has found a particularly valuable niche with students wanting an extra boost of energy for sports, gaming, or studying. Some people have speculated that energy drinks might replace coffee as the morning drink for the current generation.

The success of Red Bull, Monster Energy, and Rockstar Energy Drink has attracted the attention of huge multinational beverage corporations as well as entrepreneurs looking to introduce new products into a hot market. Coca-Cola signed an agreement to distribute Monster Energy in Canada, 20 US states, and 6 Western European countries, and Pepsi struck a similar deal with Rockstar Energy Drink. A Canadian company that has recently entered the market, DD Beverage Company, produces Beaver Buzz Energy and other energy and sports beverages. Well over 200 energy drinks are now available in the North American marketplace.

The intense competition among firms selling energy drinks is a striking example of how the market responds to changes in consumer tastes. Although intense competition is not always good news for firms trying to sell products, it is great news to consumers. Competition among firms increases the variety of products available and reduces the price consumers pay for those products.

AN INSIDE LOOK on **page 84** discusses Kickstart, PepsiCo's latest high-energy breakfast drink, which the company hopes will attract young consumers who enjoy energy drinks but are looking for an alternative with the promise of health benefits.

Sources: http://www4.agr.gc.ca/AAFC-AAC/display-afficher.do?id=1288818173139&lang=eng, The Calgary Herald, February 3, 2005; "The Buzz Surrounding Energy Drinks", National Geographic, "Why We Love Caffeine", January, 2005.

Economics in Your Life

Red Bull or Beaver Buzz Energy: What's Your Beverage?

Suppose you are about to buy an energy drink and you are choosing between a Red Bull and a Beaver Buzz Energy. As the more established, well-known brand, Red Bull has many advantages over a recent entrant like Beaver Buzz Energy. One strategy DD Beverage Company can use to overcome Red Bull's advantages is to have Beaver Buzz Energy compete based on price and value. Would you choose to buy a can of Beaver Buzz Energy if it had a lower price than a can of Red Bull? Would you be less likely to drink Beaver Buzz Energy if your income dropped? As you read this chapter, see if you can answer these questions. You can check your answers against those we provide on page 82 at the end of this chapter.

I n Chapter 1, we explored how economists use models to predict human behaviour. In Chapter 2, we used the production possibilities frontier model to analyze scarcity and trade-offs. In this chapter, we explore the model of demand and supply, which is the most powerful tool in economics, and use it to explain how prices are determined.

Recall from Chapter 1 that because economic models rely on assumptions, they are simplifications of reality. In some cases, the assumptions of the model may not seem to match the economic situation being analyzed. For example, the model of demand and supply assumes that we are analyzing a *perfectly competitive market*. In a **perfectly competitive market**, there are many buyers and sellers, all the products sold are identical to consumers, and there are no barriers to new firms entering the market. These assumptions are very restrictive and only really describe a very small number of real world markets, such as the global market for wheat or a few other agricultural products. Experience has shown, however, that the model of demand and supply can be very useful in analyzing markets where competition among sellers is intense, even if there are relatively few sellers and the products being sold are not identical. In fact, in recent studies, the model of demand and supply has been successful analyzing markets with as few as four buyers and four sellers. In the end, the usefulness of a model depends on how well it can predict outcomes in a market. As we will see in this chapter, the model of demand and supply is often very useful in predicting changes in quantities and prices in many markets.

We begin exploring the model of demand and supply by discussing consumers and the demand side of the market, before turning to firms and the supply side. As you will see, we will apply this model throughout this book to understand business, the economy, and economic policy.

Perfectly competitive market A market that meets the conditions of (1) many buyers and sellers, (2) all firms selling identical products, and (3) no barriers to new firms entering the market.

3.1 LEARNING OBJECTIVE

Discuss the variables that influence demand.

The Demand Side of the Market

Chapter 2 explained that in a market system, consumers ultimately determine which goods and services will be produced. The most successful businesses are those that respond best to consumer demand. But what determines consumer demand for a product? Many, many things influence the willingness of consumers to buy a particular product. For example, consumers who are considering buying an energy drink, such as Red Bull or Beaver Buzz Energy, will make their decisions based on, among other factors, the amount of money they can spend (income) and the effectiveness of advertising campaigns. The main factor in consumer decisions, however, will be the price. So, it makes sense to begin with price when analyzing the decision of consumers to buy a product. It is important to note that when we discuss demand, we are considering not what a consumer *wants* to buy but what the consumer is both willing and *able* to buy.

Demand Schedules and Demand Curves

Tables that show the relationship between the price of a product and the quantity of the product demanded are called **demand schedules**. The table in Figure 3.1 shows the number of cans of energy drinks consumers would be willing to buy over the course of a month at five different prices. The amount of a good or service that a consumer is willing and able to purchase at a given price is the **quantity demanded**. The graph in Figure 3.1 plots the numbers from the table as a **demand curve**, a curve that shows the relationship between the price of a product and the quantity of the product demanded. (Note that for convenience, we made the demand curve in Figure 3.1 a straight line, or linear. There is no reason to believe that all demand curves are straight lines.) The demand curve in Figure 3.1 shows the **market demand**, or the demand by all the consumers of a given good or service. The market for a product, such as restaurant meals, that is purchased locally would include all the consumers in a city or a relatively small area. The market for a product that is sold internationally, such as energy drinks, would include all the consumers in the world.

Demand schedule A table that shows the relationship between the price of a product and the quantity of the product demanded.

Quantity demanded The amount of a good or service that a consumer is willing and able to purchase at a given price.

Demand curve A curve that shows the relationship between the price of a product and the quantity of the product demanded.

Market demand The demand by all the consumers of a given good or service.

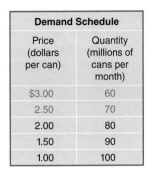

Demand Schedule	
Price (dollars per can)	Quantity (millions of cans per month)
$3.00	60
2.50	70
2.00	80
1.50	90
1.00	100

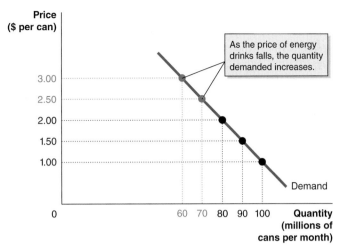

As the price of energy drinks falls, the quantity demanded increases.

Figure 3.1

A Demand Schedule and Demand Curve

As the price changes, consumers change the quantity of energy drinks they are willing to buy. We can show this as a *demand schedule* in a table or as a *demand curve* on a graph. The table and graph both show that as the price of energy drinks falls, the quantity demanded increases. When the price of an energy drink is $3.00, consumers buy 60 million cans per month. When the price drops to $2.50, consumers buy 70 million cans per month. Therefore, the demand curve for energy drinks is downward sloping.

The demand curve in Figure 3.1 slopes downward because consumers will buy more cans over the same time period when the price falls. When the price is $3.00 per can, consumers buy 60 million cans per month. If the price is $2.50 per can, consumers buy 70 million cans per month. Buyers demand a larger quantity of a product as the price falls because the product becomes less expensive relative to other products and because they can afford to buy more at a lower price.

The Law of Demand

The inverse relationship between the price of a product and the quantity of the product demanded is known as the **law of demand**: Holding *everything else* constant, when the price of a product falls, the quantity demanded of the product will increase, and when the price of a product rises, the quantity demanded of the product will decrease. The law of demand holds for any market demand curve. Economists have found only a very few exceptions (after more than 100 years of research).

Law of demand The rule that, holding everything else constant, when the price of a product falls, the quantity demanded of the product will increase, and when the price of a product rises, the quantity demanded of the product will decrease.

What Explains the Law of Demand?

It makes sense that consumers will buy more of a good when the price falls and less of a good when the price rises, but let's take a closer look at why this is true. When the price of energy drinks falls, consumers buy a larger quantity because of two effects, the *substitution effect* and the *income effect*.

The Substitution Effect The **substitution effect** refers to the change in the quantity demanded of a good that results from a change in the relative price of that good. The *relative price* of a good is how much it costs compared with a good that could be purchased instead, a *substitute* good. When the price of energy drinks falls and becomes less expensive relative to coffee (a substitute good), consumers will buy *more* energy drinks and *less* coffee.

Substitution effect The change in the quantity demanded of a good that results from a change in price making the good more or less expensive relative to other goods, holding constant the effect of the price change on consumer purchasing power.

The Income Effect The **income effect** of a price change refers to the change in the quantity demanded of a good that results from the effect of a change in the good's price on consumers' purchasing power. *Purchasing power* is the quantity of goods (and services) a consumer can buy with a fixed amount of income. When the price of a good falls, a consumer can buy more of everything with the same amount of money, including the product whose price fell in the first place. For example, if the price of energy drinks falls, the increased purchasing power of consumers' incomes means that they can buy more energy drinks and other goods with the same amount of money. When the price of a good rises, the decreased purchasing power of consumers' incomes will usually lead them to purchase fewer goods, including the good whose price became higher.

Income effect The change in the quantity demanded of a good that results from the effect of a change in the good's price on consumers' purchasing power.

Note that although we can analyze them separately, the substitution effect and the income effect happen simultaneously whenever a price changes. Thus, a fall in the price of energy drinks leads consumers to buy more energy drinks, both because the cans are now less expensive relative to substitute products (such as coffee) and because the purchasing power of their incomes has increased.

That Magic Latin Phrase *Ceteris Paribus*

Ceteris paribus ("all else equal") condition The requirement that when analyzing the relationship between two variables—such as price and quantity demanded—other variables must be held constant.

You likely noticed that the definition of the law of demand contains the phrase *holding everything else constant*. In constructing the market demand curve for energy drinks, we focused only on the effect that changes in the price of energy drinks would have on how many cans consumers would be willing and able to buy. We were holding constant all other variables that might affect the willingness of consumers to buy energy drinks. Economists refer to the necessity of holding all other variables constant in constructing a demand curve (or any other model) as the **ceteris paribus condition**: *ceteris paribus* is Latin for "all else equal."

What would happen if we allowed a change in a variable—other than price—that might affect the willingness of consumers to buy energy drinks? Consumers would then change the quantity they demanded at each price. We can illustrate this effect by shifting the market demand curve. A shift of a demand curve is *an increase or a decrease in demand*. A movement along a demand curve is *an increase or a decrease in the quantity demanded*. As Figure 3.2 shows, we shift the demand curve to the right if consumers decide to buy more of the good even when the price doesn't change, and we shift the demand curve to the left when consumers decide to buy less of a good even if the price doesn't change.

Variables That Shift Market Demand

Many variables other than price can influence how much of a product consumers are willing and able to buy. These five are the most important:

*   Income
*   Prices of related goods
*   Tastes
*   Population and demographics
*   Expectations

Figure 3.2

Shifting the Demand Curve

When consumers increase the quantity of a product they want to buy at a given price, the market demand curve shifts to the right, from D_1 to D_2. When consumers decrease the quantity of a production they want to buy at a given price, the demand curve shifts to the left from D_1 to D_3.

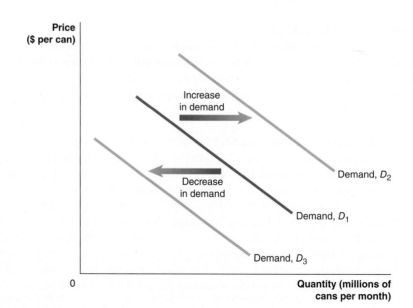

We next discuss how changes in each of these variables affect the market demand curve.

Income   The income that consumers have available to spend affects their willingness and ability to buy a good. Suppose the market demand curve in Figure 3.1 on page 63 represents the willingness of consumers to buy energy drinks when average household income is $60 000. If household income rises to $65 000, the demand for energy drinks will increase, which we show by shifting the demand curve to the right. A good is a **normal good** when demand increases following a rise in income and decreases following a fall in income. Most goods are normal goods, but the demand for some goods falls when income rises and rises when income falls. For instance, when your income rises, you might buy fewer hot dogs and more steak. A good is an **inferior good** when demand decreases following a rise in income and increases following a fall in income. So, for you, hot dogs would be an example of an inferior good. Remember, when economists say a good is inferior, they aren't saying anything about the quality of the good, just that the amount people buy falls when income rises.

Normal good A good for which the demand increases as income rises and decreases as income falls.

Inferior good A good for which the demand increases as income falls and decreases as income rises.

Prices of Related Goods   The price of other goods can also affect consumers' demand for a product. Goods and services that can be used for the same purpose—such as energy drinks and coffee—are **substitutes**. Two goods are substitutes if, when you

Substitutes Goods and services that can be used for the same purpose.

Making the Connection	**Is Beer an Inferior Good?**

For most Canadians, a beverage on a hot summer afternoon is part of the culture. In 2012, Canadians drank 8.1 litres of alcohol in various forms per person, including 80.3 litres of beer. This is a profitable industry with the LCBO (Liquor Control Board of Ontario) paying a dividend to the Government of Ontario of $1.63 billion.

How does income affect the choices Canadians make at the liquor store? As Canadians have gotten wealthier, they have changed their drinking habits. There is an underlying trend: Instead of buying beer at the lowest possible price, more and more Canadians are opting for local micro-brewery beer or local wine. In 2009, New Brunswick's alcohol retailer (Alcool NB Liquor) launched its own brand of beer, which provided New Brunswickers with a low-cost alternative, but in July 2011, that brand was discontinued due to lack of sales. During the 2011 fiscal year, the LCBO noticed that the sales of its premium products recovered from the slump that started around the same time as the financial crisis; in Ontario, the volume of sales of alcoholic beverages changed little.

Alcool NB Liquor discontinued its low cost brand of beer as the economy recovered from recession.

Brent Lewin/Bloomberg via Getty Images

What we're seeing from beer sales in particular is that Canadians have begun to treat mainstream beer as an inferior good. As the average income of Canadians rises, they switch from low-cost beverages to more expensive ones. Recall that when economists describe a product as inferior, they aren't necessarily saying it is of poor quality, they're just saying that consumers buy less of it when their incomes rise.

Sources: Statistics Canada – CANSIM Table 183-0019 Series v28463248; David Pett and Jared Lindzon, Financial Post· Jun. 3, 2011; Cigdem Iltan on Thursday, July 7, 2011, MacLean's Magazine.

Your Turn: Test your understanding by doing related problem 1.4 on page 87 at the end of this chapter.

MyEconLab

buy more of one, you buy less of the other. A decrease in the price of a substitute causes the demand curve for a good to shift to the left. An increase in the price of a substitute causes the demand curve for a good to shift to the right.

Suppose that the market demand curve in Figure 3.1 represents the willingness and ability of consumers to buy energy drinks during a week when the average price of coffee is $2.00. If the average price of coffee falls to $1.50, how will the market for energy drinks change? Consumers will demand fewer cans of energy drinks at every price. We show this impact by shifting the demand curve for energy drinks to the left.

Complements Goods and services that are used together.

Goods and services that are used together—like hamburgers and buns—are **complements**. When two goods are complements, the more consumers buy of one, the more they will buy of the other. A decrease in the price of a complement causes the demand curve for a good to shift to the right. An increase in the price of a complement causes the demand curve to shift to the left.

Many people drink Red Bull, Monster Energy, or Beaver Buzz Energy when working out. So, for these people, energy drinks and gym memberships are complements. Suppose that the market demand curve in Figure 3.1 represents the willingness of consumers to buy energy drinks when the average price of a gym membership is $40 per month. If the price of gym memberships drops to $30 per month, consumers will buy more gym memberships *and* more energy drinks, making the demand curve for energy drinks shift to the right.

Tastes Consumers can be influenced by an advertising campaign for a product. If the firms making Red Bull, Monster Energy, Beaver Buzz Energy, or other energy drinks begin to advertise heavily online, consumers are more likely to buy cans at every price, and the demand curve will shift to the right. An economist would say that the advertising campaign has affected consumers' *taste* for energy drinks. Taste is a catchall category that refers to the many subjective elements that can enter into a consumer's decision to buy a product. A consumer's taste for a product can change for many reasons. Sometimes trends play a substantial role. For example, the popularity of low-carbohydrate diets caused a decline in demand for some goods, such as bread and donuts, and an increase in the demand for meat. In general, when consumers' taste for a product increases, the demand curve will shift to the right, and when consumers' taste for a product decreases, the demand curve for the product will shift to the left.

Demographics The characteristics of a population with respect to age, race, and gender.

Population and Demographics Population and demographic factors can affect the demand for a product. As the population of Canada increases, so will the number of consumers, and the demand for most products will increase. The **demographics** of a population refers to its characteristics, with respect to age, race, and gender. As the demographics of a country or region change, the demand for particular goods will increase or decrease because different people have different tastes or preferences for those goods. For example, the population of Indo-Canadians (people whose ancestors originate from India) has increased over the last 20 years. Currently there are around 1 million Indo-Canadians, and this number is expected to rise. The increase in the Indo-Canadian population will expand the demand for Indian-made "Bollywood"

Making the Connection | **The Aging Baby Boomers**

The average age of Canadians is increasing. After World War II ended in 1945, Canada experienced a "baby boom" as birthrates rose and remained high through the early 1960s. Falling birthrates after 1965 mean that the baby boom generation is larger than the generation before it or those after it. The figure below uses data from Statistics Canada to show how people over the age of 65 have become a significant portion of the population.

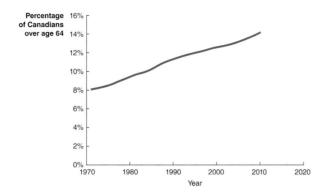

Source: Statistics Canada. Table 051-0001 - Estimates of population, by age group and sex for July 1, Canada, provinces and territories, annual (persons unless otherwise noted) (table), CANSIM (database), Using E-STAT (distributor). Reproduced and distributed on an "as is" basis with the permission of Statistics Canada.

What effects will the aging of the baby boom generation have on the economy? Older people need more medical care than younger adults, which means that there will be greater demand for doctors, nurses, and hospital facilities in the future. In Canada, a growing number of foreign-trained nurses and doctors are being recruited to help meet the growing demand for health care services.

Aging baby boomers will also have an impact on the housing market. Older folks often "downsize" their housing by moving from large, single-family homes with high maintenance costs to smaller homes, condominiums, or apartments. Hence, in coming years, demand for smaller homes may increase, while demand for large homes falls.

Source: Kaleigh Rogers, "Foreign physician Recruits Helping Meet City's Growing Need for Doctors," *CBC.ca*, March 21, 2013, http://www.cbc.ca/hamilton/news/story/2013/03/20/hamilton-foreign-doctors.html.

Your Turn: Test your understanding by doing related problem 1.5 on page 87 at the end of this chapter.

MyEconLab

films and Indo-Canadian cable television channels, as well as other cultural goods and services.

Expectations Consumers choose not only which products to buy but also when to buy them. For instance, if enough consumers become convinced that houses will be selling for lower prices in three months, the demand for houses will decrease now, as some consumers delay their purchases to wait for prices to fall. Alternatively, if enough consumers become convinced that house prices will rise over the next three months, the demand for houses will rise now as some people try to avoid the expected increase in prices.

Expected future prices aren't the only important expectations that affect consumer demand. Consumers also change their purchasing habits when their expected income changes. Most of you are probably consuming more now than your income would suggest. This is because you expect that your income will be higher in the future, meaning that you believe you can afford to consume more now. When the economy slows down and people expect their incomes to be lower in the future, they often put off major purchases or buy different things. How an expected income change affects the demand for a product depends on whether the product is a normal or an inferior good. When incomes are generally falling (e.g., when the economy is doing poorly), people tend to buy more inferior goods, even if their incomes haven't actually changed.

Table 3.1 summarizes the most important variables that cause market demand curves to shift. Note that the table shows the shift in the demand curve that results from an *increase* in each of the variables. A *decrease* in these variables would cause the demand curve to shift in the opposite direction.

Table 3.1

Variables That Shift Market Demand Curves

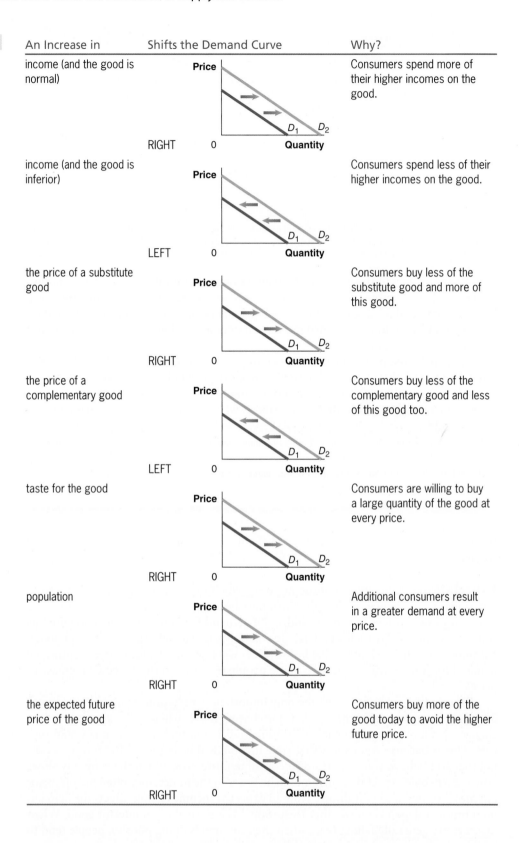

An Increase in	Shifts the Demand Curve	Why?
income (and the good is normal)	RIGHT	Consumers spend more of their higher incomes on the good.
income (and the good is inferior)	LEFT	Consumers spend less of their higher incomes on the good.
the price of a substitute good	RIGHT	Consumers buy less of the substitute good and more of this good.
the price of a complematary good	LEFT	Consumers buy less of the complematary good and less of this good too.
taste for the good	RIGHT	Consumers are willing to buy a large quantity of the good at every price.
population	RIGHT	Additional consumers result in a greater demand at every price.
the expected future price of the good	RIGHT	Consumers buy more of the good today to avoid the higher future price.

A Change in Demand versus a Change in Quantity Demanded

It is important to understand the difference between a *change in demand* and a *change in quantity demanded*. A change in demand refers to a shift of the demand curve. A shift occurs if there is a change in one of the variables, *other than the price of the product,* that

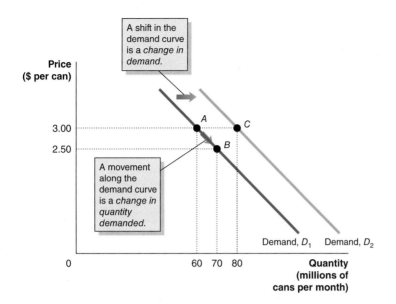

Figure 3.3

A Change in Demand versus a Change in Quantity Demanded

If the price of energy drinks falls from $3.00 to $2.50, the result will be a movement along the demand curve from point *A* to point *B*—an increase in quantity demanded from 60 million cans to 70 million cans. If consumers' incomes increase, or if another factor changes that makes consumers want more energy drinks at every price, the demand curve will shift to the right— an increase in demand. In this case, the increase in demand from D_1 to D_2 causes the quantity of energy drinks demanded at a price of $3.00 to increase from 60 million cans at point *A* to 80 million cans at point *C*.

affects the willingness of consumers to buy the product. A change in quantity demanded refers to a movement along the demand curve as a result of a change in the product's price. Figure 3.3 illustrates this important distinction. If the price of energy drinks falls from $3.00 to $2.50 per can, the result will be a movement along the demand curve from point *A* to point *B*—an increase in quantity demanded from 60 million to 70 million. If consumers' incomes increase, or if another factor changes that makes consumers want more energy drinks *even if the price doesn't change*, the demand curve will shift to the right—an increase in demand. In this case, the increase in demand from curve D_1 to D_2 causes the quantity of energy drinks demanded at a price of $3.00 to increase from 60 million at point *A* to 80 million at point *C*.

The Supply Side of the Market

Just as many variables influence the willingness and ability of consumers to buy a good or service, many variables also influence the willingness and ability of firms to sell a good or service. The most important of these variables is price. The amount of a good or service that a firm is willing and able to supply at a given price is the **quantity supplied**. Holding all other variables constant (recall the Latin phrase *ceteris paribus*), when the price of a good rises, producing (and selling) that good is more profitable, and the quantity supplied will increase. When the price of a good falls, the good is less profitable to produce, and the quantity supplied will decrease. In addition, as we saw in Chapter 2, devoting more and more resources to the production of a specific good results in increasing marginal costs. If, for example, Red Bull, Monster Energy, and DD Beverage Company increase production of their energy drinks during a given time period, they are likely to find that the cost of producing additional cans increases as they run existing factories for longer hours and pay higher prices for ingredients and higher wages for workers. As the marginal costs of making a product rises as output increases, a firm will supply more of that product only if the price is higher.

Supply Schedules and Supply Curves

A **supply schedule** is a table that shows the relationship between the price of a product and the quantity of the product supplied. The table in Figure 3.4 is a supply schedule showing the quantity of energy drinks that firms would be willing to supply per month at different prices. The graph in Figure 3.4 plots the numbers from the supply schedule as a *supply curve*. A **supply curve** shows the relationship between the price of a product

3.2 LEARNING OBJECTIVE

Discuss the variables that influence supply.

Quantity supplied The amount of a good or service that a firm is willing and able to supply at a given price.

Supply schedule A table that shows the relationship between the price of a product and the quantity of the product supplied.

Supply curve A curve that shows the relationship between the price of a product and the quantity of the product supplied.

Figure 3.4

A Supply Schedule and Supply Curve

As the price changes, Red Bull, Monster Energy, DD Beverage Company, and other firms producing energy drinks change the quantity they are willing to supply. We can show this as a *supply schedule* in a table or a *supply curve* on a graph. The supply schedule and supply curve both show that as the price of energy drinks rises, firms will increase the quantity they supply. At a price of $2.50 per can, firms will supply 90 million cans. At a price of $3.00 per can, firms will supply 100 million cans.

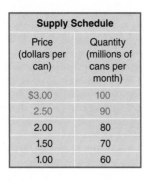

Supply Schedule	
Price (dollars per can)	Quantity (millions of cans per month)
$3.00	100
2.50	90
2.00	80
1.50	70
1.00	60

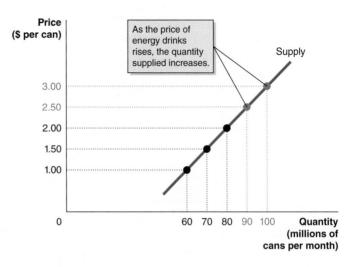

and the quantity of the product supplied. The supply schedule and the supply curve both show that as the price of energy drinks rises, firms will increase the quantity they supply. At a price of $2.50 per can, firms will supply 90 million cans per month. At the higher price of $3.00, firms will supply 100 million. (Once again, we are assuming that the relationship is linear—even though most supply curves are not actually straight lines.)

The Law of Supply

Law of supply The rule that, holding everything else constant, increases in price cause increases in the quantity supplied, and decreases in price cause decreases in the quantity supplied.

The *market supply curve* in Figure 3.4 is upward sloping. We expect most supply curves to be upward sloping based on the **law of supply**, which states that, holding everything else constant, increases in price cause increases in the quantity supplied, and decreases in price result in decreases in the quantity supplied. Notice that the definition of the law of supply—just like the definition of the law of demand—contains the phrase *holding everything else constant*. If only the price of the product changes, there is a movement along the supply curve, which is *an increase or a decrease in the quantity supplied*. As Figure 3.5 shows, if any other variable that affects the willingness of firms to supply a good changes, the supply curve will shift, which is *an increase or a decrease in the quantity supplied*. When firms increase the quantity of a product they would like to sell at a given price, the supply curve shifts to the right. The shift from S_1 to S_3 represents *an*

Figure 3.5

Shifting the Supply Curve

When firms increase the quantity of a product they want to sell at a given price, the supply curve shifts to the right. The shift from S_1 to S_3 represents *an increase in supply*. When firms decrease the quantity of a product they want to sell at a given price, the supply curve shifts to the left. The shift from S_1 to S_2 represents *a decrease in supply*.

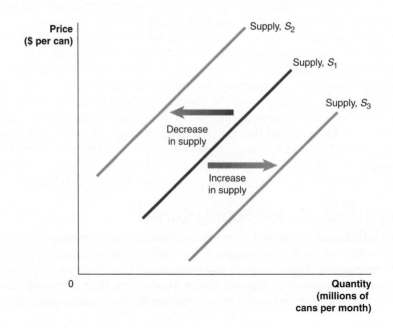

increase in supply. When firms decrease the quantity of a product they would like to sell at a given price, the supply curve shifts to the left. The shift from S_1 to S_2 represents *a decrease in supply*.

Variables That Shift Market Supply

The following are the most important variables that shift the market supply curve:

- Price of inputs
- Technological change
- Prices of substitutes in production
- Number of firms in the market
- Expected future prices

We next discuss how each of these variables affects the market supply curve.

Prices of Inputs The factor most likely to cause the supply curve for a product to shift is a change in the price of an *input*. An input is anything used in the making of a good or service. For instance, if the price of guarana (a stimulant in many energy drinks) rises, the cost of producing energy drinks will increase, and energy drinks will be less profitable at every price. The supply of energy drinks will decline, and the market supply curve for energy drinks will shift to the left. Similarly, if the price of an input falls, the supply of energy drinks will increase, and the market supply curve for energy drinks will shift to the right. Any time something like wages or interest rates (the price of labour and capital) change, the market supply curve will shift.

Technological Change A second factor that causes a change in supply is *technological change*. **Technological change** is a positive or negative change in the ability of a firm to produce a given level of output from a given quantity of inputs. Positive technological change occurs when a firm is able to produce *more* output with the same amount of inputs. This change will happen when the *productivity* of workers or machines increases. If a firm can produce more output with the same amount of inputs, its costs will be lower, and the good will be more profitable to produce at any given price. As a result, when positive technological change occurs, a firm will want to sell more of its product at every given price, making the market supply curve shift to the right. Normally, we expect technological change to have a positive impact on a firm's willingness to supply a product.

Negative technological change is rare, although it might be caused by a natural disaster or a war that reduces a firm's ability to supply as much output with a given amount of inputs. Negative technological change will raise a firm's costs, and the good will be less profitable to produce. Therefore, negative technological change causes the market supply curve to shift to the left.

Technological change A change in the quantity of output a firm can produce using a given quantity of inputs.

Prices of Substitutes in Production Firms often have to choose which goods they will produce at a particular time. Alternative products that a firm could produce with the same inputs are called *substitutes in production*. A number of companies produce both energy drinks and traditional soft drinks. For instance, the Coca-Cola Company produces Full Throttle in addition to the many varieties of Coke it sells. PepsiCo produces Amp in addition to Pepsi, Mountain Dew, and other drinks. If the price of colas falls, producing Pepsi and Coke will be less profitable, and Coca-Cola, PepsiCo, and other soft drink manufacturers will shift some of their productive capacity out of cola production and into making energy drinks. As a result, each company will offer more energy drinks for sale, even if the price doesn't change, so the market supply curve for energy drinks will shift to the right.

Number of Firms in the Market A change in the number of firms in the market will change supply. When new firms *enter* a market, the supply curve shifts to the right,

Table 3.2

Variables That Shift Market Supply Curves

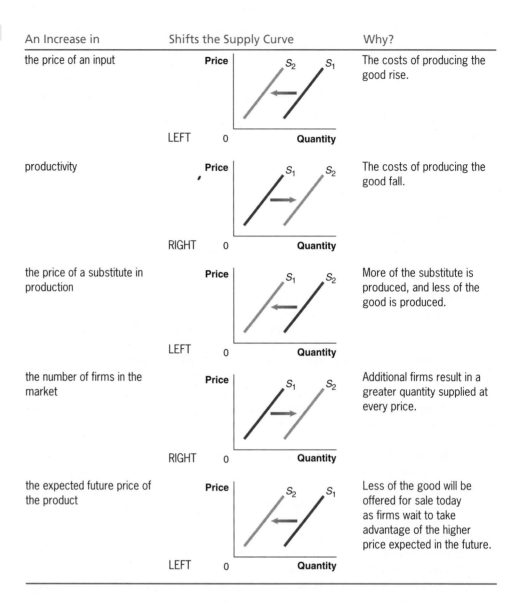

An Increase in	Shifts the Supply Curve	Why?
the price of an input	LEFT	The costs of producing the good rise.
productivity	RIGHT	The costs of producing the good fall.
the price of a substitute in production	LEFT	More of the substitute is produced, and less of the good is produced.
the number of firms in the market	RIGHT	Additional firms result in a greater quantity supplied at every price.
the expected future price of the product	LEFT	Less of the good will be offered for sale today as firms wait to take advantage of the higher price expected in the future.

and when existing firms leave, or *exit*, a market, the supply curve shifts to the left. For example, when Beaver Buzz Energy was introduced, the market supply curve for energy drinks shifted to the right.

Expected Future Prices If a firm expects that the price of its product will be higher in the future than it is today, it has an incentive to decrease supply now and increase supply in the future. For example, if Red Bull believes that prices for energy drinks are temporarily low—perhaps due to low incomes of consumers—it may store some of its production today to sell later on, when it expects prices to be higher.

Table 3.2 summarizes the most important variables that cause market supply curves to shift. Note that the table shows the shift in the supply curve that results from an *increase* in each of the variables. A *decrease* in these variables would cause the supply curve to shift in the opposite direction.

A Change in Supply versus a Change in Quantity Supplied

We noted earlier the important difference between a change in demand and a change in quantity demanded. There is a similar difference between a *change in supply* and a *change in quantity supplied*. A change in supply refers to a shift in the supply curve. The supply curve will shift when there is a change in one of the variables, *other than the price*

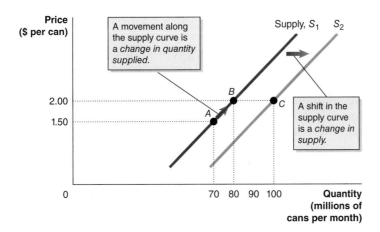

Figure 3.6

A Change in Supply versus a Change in Quantity Supplied

If the price of energy drinks rises from $1.50 to $2.00 per can, the result will be a movement up the supply curve from point A to point B—an increase in quantity supplied of Red Bull, Monster Energy, Beaver Buzz Energy, and other energy drinks from 70 million to 80 million cans. If the price of an input decreases or another factor changes that causes sellers to supply more of the product at every price, the supply curve will shift to the right—an increase in supply. In this case, the increase in supply from S_1 to S_2 causes the quantity of energy drinks supplied at a price of $2.00 to increase from 80 million cans to 100 million cans.

of the product, that affects the willingness of firms to sell the product. A change in quantity supplied refers to a movement along the supply curve as a result of a change in the product's price. Figure 3.6 illustrates this important distinction. If the price of energy drinks rises from $1.50 to $2.00 per can, the result will be a movement up the supply curve from point A to point B—an increase in quantity supplied from 70 million cans per month to 80 million cans per month. If the price of an input decreases (or another factor makes sellers supply more of the product at every price), the supply curve will shift to the right—an increase in supply. In this case, the increase in supply from S_1 to S_2 causes the quantity of energy drinks supply to increase from 80 million to 100 million per month even if the price remains at $2.00 per can (note the move from point B to point C in the figure).

Market Equilibrium: Putting Buyers and Sellers Together

3.3 LEARNING OBJECTIVE

Use a graph to illustrate market equilibrium.

The purpose of markets is to bring buyers and sellers together. As we saw in Chapter 2, instead of being chaotic and disorderly, the interaction of buyers and sellers in markets ultimately results in firms being led to produce the goods and services that consumers want. To understand how this happens, we first need to see how markets work to reconcile the plans of buyers and sellers.

In Figure 3.7, we bring the market demand curve and the market supply curve together. Notice that the demand curve crosses the supply curve at only one point.

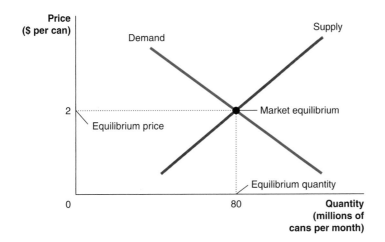

Figure 3.7

Market Equilibrium

Where the demand curve crosses the supply curve determines market equilibrium. In this case, the demand curve for energy drinks crosses the supply curve at a price of $2.00 and a quantity of 80 million cans. Only at this point is the quantity of energy drinks consumers want to buy equal to the quantity of energy drink suppliers are willing to sell: The quantity demanded is equal to the quantity supplied.

Market equilibrium A situation in which quantity demanded equals quantity supplied.

Competitive market equilibrium A market equilibrium with many buyers and many sellers.

This point represents the price of $2.00 and a quantity of 80 million cans. Only at this point is the quantity of energy drinks consumers are willing to buy equal to the quantity of energy drinks firms are willing to sell. This is the point of **market equilibrium**. Only at market equilibrium will the quantity demanded equal the quantity supplied. In this case, the *equilibrium price* is $2.00 and the *equilibrium quantity* is 80 million. As we noted at the beginning of the chapter, markets that have many buyers and many sellers are competitive markets, and equilibrium in these markets is a **competitive market equilibrium**. In the market for energy drinks, there are many buyers but only about 80 firms. Whether 80 firms are enough for our model of demand and supply to apply to this market is a matter of judgment. In this chapter, we are assuming that the market for energy drinks has enough sellers to be treated as competitive.

How Markets Eliminate Surpluses and Shortages: Getting to Equilibrium

A market that is not in equilibrium moves toward equilibrium. Once a market is in equilibrium, it remains in equilibrium. To see why, consider what happens if the market is not in equilibrium. For instance, suppose that the price in the market for energy drinks is $3.00, rather than the equilibrium price of $2.00. As Figure 3.8 shows, at a price of $3.00 the quantity of energy drinks demanded would be 60 million cans per month, while the quantity supplied would be 100 million cans per month. The quantity supplied is 40 million more than the quantity demanded (100 million − 60 million). When the quantity supplied is greater than the quantity demanded, there is a **surplus** in the market. A surplus means that firms will be unable to sell all the goods they would like and the goods they're producing start piling up. Fortunately, firms have a handy method of getting rid of unwanted inventory, they put it on sale. Remember a sale is just a reduction in price. Cutting the price will simultaneously increase the quantity demanded and decrease the quantity supplied. This adjustment will reduce the surplus, but as long as the price remains above the equilibrium of $2.00, there will be unsold energy drinks and downward pressure on the price. Only when the price has fallen to $2.00 will firms have a reason to stop reducing the price.

Surplus A situation in which the quantity supplied is greater than the quantity demanded.

What if the price was below market equilibrium, say $0.50? If this were the case the quantity demanded would be 110 million and the quantity supplied would be only 50 million, as shown in Figure 3.8. When the quantity demanded is greater than the quantity supplied, there is a **shortage** in the market. In this case, the shortage is 60 million cans (110 million − 50 million). When a shortage occurs, some consumers will be unable to buy energy drinks at the current price. When this happens, firms will realize they can raise the price without losing sales. A higher price means a decrease in the quantity demanded and an increase in the quantity supplied. The increase in price will reduce the size of the shortage, but as long as the price remains below the equilibrium price of $2.00 there will be a shortage and firms will have an incentive to increase the prices they charge. Only when the price has risen to $2.00 will the market be in equilibrium.

Shortage A situation in which the quantity demanded is greater than the quantity supplied.

At a competitive equilibrium, all consumers willing to pay the market price will be able to buy as much of the product as they want, and all firms willing to accept the market price will be able to sell as much as they want. As a result, neither consumers nor suppliers will have a reason to do anything differently. This means that the price of energy drinks will stay at $2.00, unless the demand curve, the supply curve, or both shift.

Demand and Supply Both Count

Keep in mind that the interaction of demand and supply determines the equilibrium price. Neither consumers nor firms can dictate what the equilibrium price will be. No firm can sell anything, at any price, unless it can find a willing buyer, and no consumer can buy anything, at any price, without finding a willing seller.

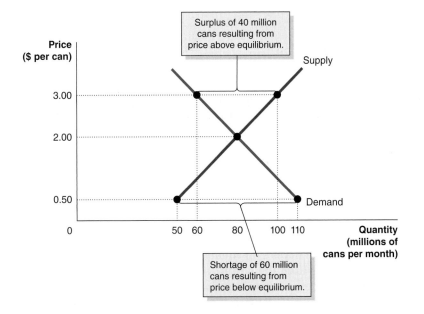

Figure 3.8

The Effect of Surpluses and Shortages on the Market

When the market price is above equilibrium, there will be a *surplus*. In the figure, a price of $3.00 per energy drink results in 100 million cans being supplied but only 60 million cans being demanded, or a surplus of 40 million cans. As the firms that produce Red Bull, Monster Energy, Beaver Buzz Energy, and other drinks cut the price to dispose of the surplus, the price will fall to the equilibrium of $2.00. When the market price is below equilibrium, there will be a *shortage*. A price of $0.50 results in 110 million cans being demanded, but only 50 million cans being supplied, or a shortage of 60 million cans. As firms find that consumers who are unable to find energy drinks for sale are willing to pay more for them, the price will rise to the equilibrium of $2.00.

Solved Problem **3.1**

Demand and Supply Both Count: A Tale of Two Cards

Which hockey card do you think is worth more: Sidney Crosby's rookie card or one of Jacques Plante's distributed free in a box of Quaker Oats? Sidney Crosby is one of the most popular hockey players in recent memory; his jersey sells exceptionally well even though he has missed many games due to concussions and other injuries. Jacques Plante was a goaltender from 1946 to 1975 and played for a number of NHL teams, including the Montreal Canadiens and the Edmonton Oilers. The demand for Sidney Crosby's rookie card is much higher than the demand for Jacques

Plante's cereal-box card. However, at auction, a Sidney Crosby rookie card can be expected to sell for about $5000, while a Jacques Plante cereal-box card can be expected to fetch about $12 000. Use a demand and supply graph to explain how it is that a card of a player from 50 years ago that was distributed free in a box of cereal has a higher price than a card of one of the most popular modern players that was sold in a sealed foil pack, even though the demand for Sidney Crosby's card is certain to be greater than the demand for Jacques Plante's card.

Solving the Problem

Step 1: **Review the chapter material.** This problem is about prices being determined at market equilibrium, so you may want to review the section "Market Equilibrium: Putting Buyers and Sellers Together."

Step 2: **Draw demand curves that illustrate the greater demand for Sidney Crosby's card.** Begin by drawing two demand curves. Label one "Demand for Crosby's card" and the other "Demand for Plante's card." Make sure that the Crosby demand curve is much farther to the right than the Plante demand curve. Make sure you label your axes.

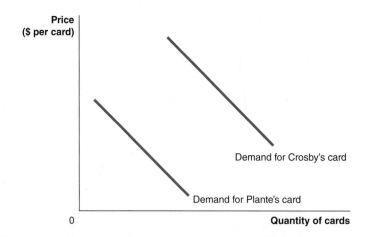

Step 3: **Draw supply curves that illustrate the equilibrium price of Plante's card being higher than the equilibrium price of Crosby's card.** Based on the demand curves you have just drawn, think about how it might be possible for the market price of Crosby's card to be lower than the market price of Plante's card. The only way this can be true is if the supply of Crosby's card is much greater than the supply of Plante's card. (Plante's card was distributed in a cereal box and were therefore easily damaged). In your graph, draw a supply curve for Crosby's card and a supply curve for Plante's card that will result in an equilibrium price of Plante's card of $12 000 and an equilibrium price of Crosby's card of $5000. You have now solved the problem.

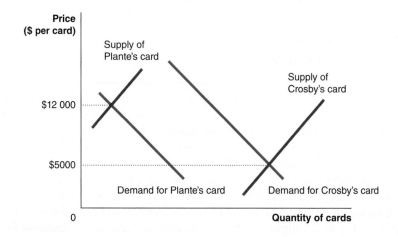

Extra credit: The explanation for this puzzle is that both demand and supply count when determining market price. The demand for Crosby's card is much greater than the demand for Plante's card, but the supply of Crosby's card is also much greater. (Note that the supply curves for the cards of Plante and Crosby are upward sloping, even though only a fixed number of each of these types of cards is available and no more can be produced. The supply curves slope upwards because a higher price will induce more cards to be offered for sale by their current owners.) Try and come up with your own examples of goods with very low demand but very high prices and goods with high demand and very low prices.

Source: http://bleacherreport.com/articles/812055-nhl-the-15-most-valuable-hockey-cards-of-all-time/page/8 and http://bleacherreport.com/articles/812055-nhl-the-15-most-valuable-hockey-cards-of-all-time/page/5

MyEconLab   **Your Turn:** For more practice, do related problem 3.2 on page 88 at the end of this chapter.

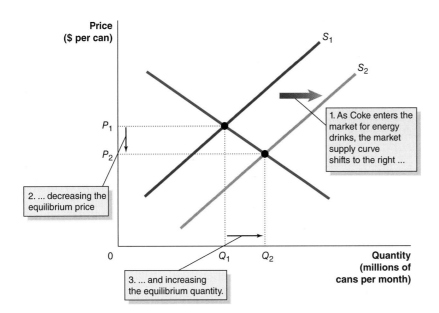

Figure 3.9

The Effect of an Increase in Supply on Equilibrium

If a firm enters a market, as Coca-Cola Company did when it introduced Full Throttle, the equilibrium price will fall, and the equilibrium quantity will rise:

1. As Coke enters the market for energy drinks, a larger quantity of energy drinks will be supplied at every price, so the market supply curve shifts to the right, from S_1 to S_2, which causes a surplus of energy drinks at the original price, P_1.

2. The equilibrium price falls from P_1 to P_2.

3. The equilibrium quantity rises from Q_1 to Q_2.

The Effect of Demand and Supply Shifts on Equilibrium

We have seen that the interaction of demand and supply in markets determines the quantity of a good that is produced and the price at which it sells. We have also seen that several variables cause demand curves to shift, and other variables cause supply curves to shift. As a result, demand and supply curves in most markets are constantly moving around, and the prices and quantities that represent equilibrium are constantly changing. In this section, we look at how shifts in demand and supply curves affect equilibrium price and quantity.

The Effect of Shifts in Supply on Equilibrium

When Coke started selling the energy drink Full Throttle, the market supply curve for energy drinks shifted to the right. Figure 3.9 shows the supply curve shifting from S_1 to S_2. When the supply curve shifts to the right, there will be a surplus at the original equilibrium price, P_1. The surplus is eliminated as the equilibrium price falls to P_2, and the equilibrium quantity rises from Q_1 to Q_2. If existing firms exit the market, the supply curve will shift to the left, causing the equilibrium price to rise and the equilibrium quantity to fall.

3.4 LEARNING OBJECTIVE

Use demand and supply graphs to predict changes in prices and quantities.

Making the Connection | **The Falling Price of LCD TVs**

Research on flat-screen televisions using liquid crystal displays (LCDs) began way back in the 1960s. However, it was surprisingly difficult to produce a television with a price low enough for many consumers to purchase. One researcher noted, "In the 1960s, we used to say 'In 10 years, we're going to have the TV on the wall.' … We said the same thing in the "70s and then in the "80s." A key technical problem in manufacturing LCD TVs was making glass large, thin, and clean enough to be used as LCD screens. Finally in 1999, Corning Inc., developed a manufacturing process that produced glass that was less than 1 millimetre thick and very clean because it didn't come into contact with machinery.

Corning's breakthrough led to what the *Wall Street Journal* described as a "race to build new, better factories." For years, the leading firms were Korea's Samsung Electronics and LG Phillips LCD, Taiwan's AU Optronics, and Japan's Sharp Corporation. But in recent years, new firms, such as Vizio, and existing firms, such as Matsushita (the makers of Panasonic), have entered the market or expanded their offerings. Matsushita's Japanese factory can produce as many as 15 million LCD screens a year. The figure below shows how the entry of new firms and the expansion of existing firms has driven down the price of LCD TVs.

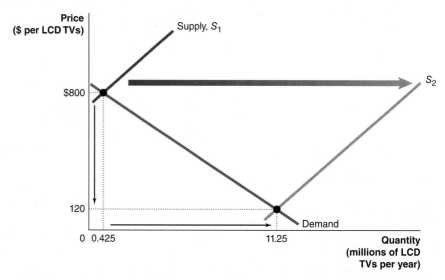

Sources: Daisuke Wakabayashi and Christopher Lawton, "TV Makers Confront a Stakeout," *Wall Street Journal*, January 20, 2009; David Richards, "Sony and Panasonic Flat Screen Kings," Smarthouse.com, February 13, 2007; and Evan Ramstad, "Big Display: Once a Footnote, Flat Screens Grow into Huge Industry," Wall Street Journal, August 30, 2004.

MyEconLab **Your Turn:** Test your understanding by doing related problem 4.7 on page 89 at the end of this chapter.

The Effect of Shifts in Demand on Equilibrium

Because energy drinks are generally a normal good, when incomes increase, the market demand for energy drinks shifts to the right. Figure 3.10 shows the effect of a demand curve shifting to the right, from D_1 to D_2. This shift causes a shortage at the original

Figure 3.10

The Effect of an Increase in Demand on Equilibrium

Increases in income will cause equilibrium price and quantity to rise:

1. Because energy drinks are a normal good, as income grows, the quantity demanded increases at every price, and the market demand curve shifts to the right, from D_1 to D_2, which causes a shortage of energy drinks at the original price, P_1.

2. The equilibrium price rises from P_1 to P_2.

3. The equilibrium quantity rises from Q_1 to Q_2.

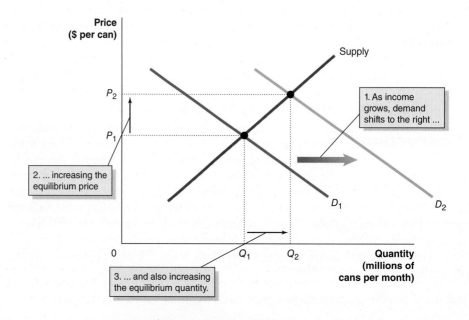

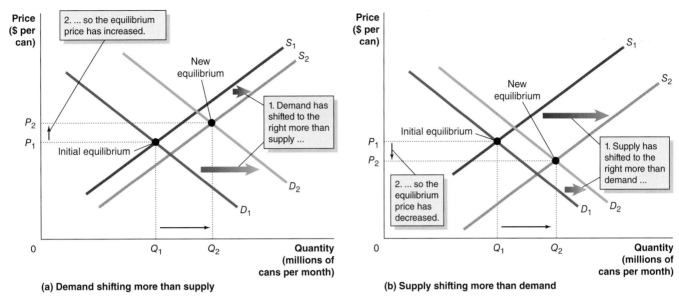

Figure 3.11 Shifts in Demand and Supply

Whether the price of a product rises or falls over time depends on whether demand shifts to the right more than supply. In panel (a), demand shifts to the right more than supply, and the equilibrium price rises:

1. Demand shifts to the right more than supply.
2. The equilibrium price rises from P_1 to P_2.

In panel (b), supply shifts to the right more than demand, and the equilibrium price falls:

1. Supply shifts to the right more than demand.
2. The equilibrium price falls from P_1 to P_2.

equilibrium price, P_1. To eliminate this new shortage, equilibrium price rises to P_2, and the equilibrium quantity rises from Q_1 to Q_2. In contrast, if the price of a substitute good, such as coffee, were to fall, the demand for energy drinks would decrease, shifting the demand curve for energy drinks to the left. When the demand curve shifts to the left, the equilibrium price and quantity both decrease.

The Effect of Shifts in Demand and Supply over Time

Whenever only demand or only supply shifts, we can easily predict the effect on equilibrium price and quantity. Things are more complicated when *both* supply and demand shift at the same time. For instance, in many markets, the demand curve shifts to the right over time as populations and incomes grow. The supply often shifts to the right over time too, as new firms enter the market or technology improves. Whether the equilibrium price rises or falls over time depends on which shift is bigger. If the shift in the demand curve is bigger than the shift in the supply curve, the price will rise. If the shift in the supply curve is bigger than the shift in the demand curve, the price will fall. Panel (a) of Figure 3.11 shows that when demand shifts to the right more than supply, the equilibrium price rises. But as panel (b) shows, when supply shifts to the right more than demand, the equilibrium price falls.

Table 3.3 summarizes all possible combinations of shifts in demand and supply over time and the effects of the shifts on equilibrium price (P) and quantity (Q). For example, the entry in red in the table shows that if the demand curve shifts to the right and the supply curve also shifts to the right, the equilibrium quantity will increase, while the equilibrium price may increase, decrease, or remain unchanged. To be sure you understand each entry in the table, draw demand and supply graphs to check whether you can reproduce the predicted changes in equilibrium price and quantity. If the entry in the table says the predicted change in equilibrium price or quantity can be either an increase or a decrease, draw two graphs similar to panels (a) and (b) of Figure 3.11—one showing the equilibrium price or quantity increasing and the other showing it decreasing. Note also that in the ambiguous cases where either price or quantity might increase or decrease, it is also possible that price or quantity might remain unchanged. Be sure you understand why.

Table 3.3

How Shifts in Demand and Supply Affect Equilibrium Price (*P*) and Quantity (*Q*)

	Supply Curve Unchanged	Supply Curve Shifts Right	Supply Curve Shifts to the Left
Demand curve unchanged	Q unchanged P unchanged	Q increases P decreases	Q decreases P increases
Demand curve shifts right	Q increases P increases	Q increases P increases or decreases	Q increases or decreases P increases
Demand curve shifts left	Q decreases P decreases	Q increases or decreases P decreases	Q decreases P increases or decreases

Solved Problem 3.2

High Demand and Low Prices in the Lobster Market

For many communities in the Maritimes, the lobster fishery is an essential part of the local economy. Lobster is fished only in season, and different communities are allowed to fish at different times of the year. For example, the fishing season for the area of Yarmouth, Nova Scotia, is from late November to the end of May. It isn't uncommon for the price of lobster to fluctuate during the season. In some cases, it can change from below $5 per pound to $8 or $9 per pound. A patch of really bad weather can drive up the price quickly, but so does Christmas (lobster tends to be a popular part of winter festivities in Canada, Europe, and other parts of the world).

What would happen if the weather just before Christmas was particularly good, allowing fishers to spend more time on the water and catch more lobster?

Solving the Problem

Step 1: **Review the chapter material.** This problem is about how shifts in demand and supply curves affect the equilibrium price, so you may want to review the section "The Effect of Shifts in Demand and Supply over Time."

Step 2: **Draw the demand and supply graph.** Draw a demand and supply graph, showing the market equilibrium before the Christmas rush and with normal weather. Label the equilibrium price $6.00. Label both the demand and supply curves "Typical."

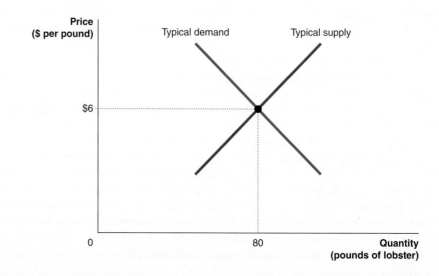

Step 3: **Add a demand and supply curve.** Add a demand curve to account for the increase in the demand for lobster from Europe. Add a supply curve to account for the nicer-than-usual weather.

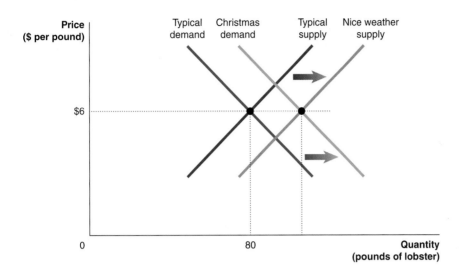

Step 4: **Explain the graph.** After studying the graph, you should see how the two events of increased demand from Europe and the nicer-than-usual weather combine to move the equilibrium price. The increase in supply due to the nicer-than-usual weather is offset by some of the increase in demand from Europeans. We can't say for sure which way the price will go. The price of lobster will rise if the shift in demand is greater than the shift in supply. If the shift in supply is greater than the shift in demand, prices will actually fall. All that we can say for certain is that the quantity of lobster sold (and eaten) will go up.

Source: Province of Nova Scotia, "Lobster Fishing Seasons in Atlantic Canada," *Nova Scotia Fisheries and Aquaculture*, May 17, 2012, http://www.gov.ns.ca/fish/marine/map/lobarea.shtml.

Your Turn: For more practice, do related problems 4.3 and 4.4 on page 88 at the end of this chapter.   MyEconLab

---

Don't Let This Happen to You

Remember: A Change in a Good's Price Does *Not* Cause the Demand or Supply Curve to Shift

Suppose a student is asked to draw a demand and supply graph to illustrate how an increase in the price of oranges would affect the market for apples, other variables being constant. He draws the graph on the left below and explains it as follows: "Because apples and oranges are substitutes, an increase in the price of oranges will cause an initial shift to the right in the demand curve for apples, from D_1 to D_2. However, because this initial shift in the demand curve for

apples results in a higher price for apples, P_2, consumers will find apples less desirable, and the demand curve will shift to the left, from D_2 to D_3, resulting in a final equilibrium price of P_3." Do you agree or disagree with the student's analysis?

You should disagree. The student has correctly understood that an increase in the price of oranges will cause the demand curve for apples to shift to the right. But the second demand curve shift the student describes, from D_2 to D_3, will not take place. Changes in the price of a product do not result in shifts in the product's demand curve. Changes in the price of a product result only in movements along a demand curve.

The graph on the right below shows the correct analysis. The increase in the price of oranges causes the demand curve for apples to increase from D_1 to D_2. At the original price, P_1, the increase in demand initially results in a shortage of apples equal to $Q_3 - Q_1$. But, as we have seen, a shortage causes the price to increase until the shortage is eliminated. In this case, the price will rise to P_2, where the quantity demanded and the quantity supplied are

both equal to Q_2. Notice that the increase in price causes a decrease in the *quantity demanded*, from Q_3 to Q_2, but does not cause a decrease in demand.

MyEconLab

Your Turn: Test your understanding by doing related problems 4.6 and 4.7 on page 89 at the end of this chapter.

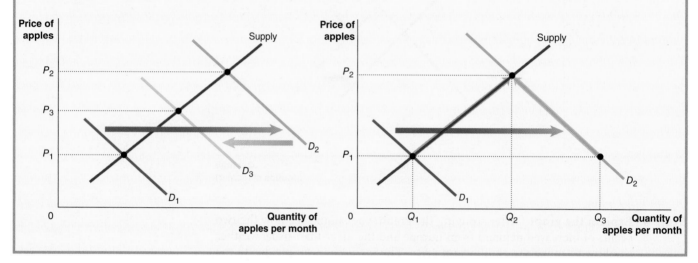

Shifts in a Curve versus Movements along a Curve

When analyzing markets using demand and supply curves, it is important to remember that *when a shift in a demand or supply curve causes a change in equilibrium price, the change in price does not cause a further shift in demand or supply.* For instance, suppose an increase in supply causes the price of a good to fall, while everything else that affects the willingness of consumers to buy the good is constant. The result will be an increase in the quantity demanded, but not an increase in demand. For demand to increase, the whole curve must shift. The point is the same for supply: If the price of the good falls but everything else that affects the willingness of sellers to supply the good is constant, the quantity supplied decreases, but the supply does not. For supply to decrease, the whole curve must shift.

Economics in Your Life

Red Bull or Beaver Buzz Energy: What's Your Beverage?

At the beginning of the chapter, we asked you to consider two questions: Would you choose to buy a can of Beaver Buzz Energy if it had a lower price than a can of Red Bull? Would you be less likely to drink Beaver Buzz Energy if your income dropped? To determine the answer to the first question, you have to recognize that Beaver Buzz Energy and Red Bull are substitutes. If you consider the two drinks to be very close substitutes, then you are likely to buy the one with the lower price. In the market, if consumers generally believe that Beaver Buzz Energy and Red Bull are close substitutes, a fall in the price of Beaver Buzz Energy will increase the quantity of Beaver Buzz Energy demanded and decrease the demand for Red Bull. Suppose that you are currently leaning toward buying Red Bull because you believe that it is better tasting than Beaver Buzz Energy. If a decrease in your income made you more likely to buy Beaver Buzz Energy, then you consider Beaver Buzz Energy as an inferior good.

Conclusion

The interaction of demand and supply determines market equilibrium. The model of demand and supply is a powerful tool for predicting how changes in the actions of consumers and firms will cause changes in equilibrium prices and quantities. As we have seen in this chapter, we can use the model to analyze markets that do not meet all of the requirements for being perfectly competitive. As long as there is intense competition among sellers, the model of demand and supply can often successfully predict changes in prices and quantities.

Before moving on to Chapter 4, read *An Inside Look* on the next page for a discussion of PepsiCo's Kickstart, a high-energy breakfast drink that the company hopes will help it capture part of the market for energy drinks.

PepsiCo Tries to Create a New Category of Drinks That Promises Energy and Health Benefits

MAIL ONLINE

Mountain Dew for Breakfast? Soda Giant's New Morning Beverage Is Packed with Caffeine and Vitamins (Just Don't Call It an Energy Drink)

If you don't like coffee or tea, Mountain Dew has a new breakfast drink that might perk you up.

PepsiCo Inc. is rolling out a new drink called Kickstart this month that has Mountain Dew flavour but is made with 5% juice and Vitamins B and C, along with an extra jolt of caffeine.

The company, based in Purchase, N.Y., is hoping to boost sales by reaching Mountain Dew fans at a new time of day: morning.

PepsiCo said it doesn't consider Kickstart to be an energy drink, noting that it still has far less caffeine than drinks such as Monster and Red Bull and none of the mysterious ingredients that have raised concerns among lawmakers and consumer advocates.

But Kickstart, which comes in flavours such as "energizing orange citrus" and "energizing fruit punch," could nevertheless give the company a side-door into the fast-growing energy drink market without getting tangled in any of its controversies.

It also comes in the same 16-ounce cans as popular energy drinks made by Monster Beverage Corp., which also offers options with juice content.

Simon Lowden, chief marketing officer for PepsiCo's Americas beverages, says the idea for Kickstart came about after the company learned through consumer research that Mountain Dew fans were looking for an alternative to traditional morning drinks such as coffee, tea and juice.

Kickstart was developed independently from a Taco Bell breakfast drink last year.

"They didn't really see anything that fit their needs," he said.

Lowden said Kickstart was developed independently from a Taco Bell breakfast drink introduced last year that combines Mountain Dew and orange juice.

With the growth of energy drinks such as Monster and Red Bull expected to slow, Kickstart could also signal the emergence of a new category that plays off the promise of energy and other health benefits, said John Sicher, publisher of the trade journal *Beverage Digest*.

In a nod to the growing concerns about sugary drinks, for example, Kickstart also uses artificial sweeteners to reduce its caloric content to about half that of regular soda; a can has 80 calories.

"It's a very interesting experiment capturing a number of attributes," Sicher said, likening it to Starbucks' Refreshers drinks, which promise "natural energy" from green coffee extract.

PepsiCo and the Coca-Cola Co. have largely watched the growth of energy drinks from the sidelines.

The promise of "energy" has been a big seller in the beverage industry in recent years, with the energy drink market increasing 17% in 2011 even as broader soft drink consumption has continued to decline, according to *Beverage Digest*. PepsiCo and the Coca-Cola Co. have largely watched that growth from the sidelines, however, with players such as Monster Beverage and Red Bull dominating the market.

But the surging popularity of energy drinks has also led to sharper scrutiny. This summer, New York's attorney general launched an investigation into the marketing prices of energy drink makers including Monster and PepsiCo, which also makes Amp. Lawmakers and consumer advocacy groups have also called on the Food and Drug Administration to investigate the safety of the high levels of caffeine in energy drinks for younger people.

Although Kickstart may look like an energy drink, it has far less caffeine, at 92 milligrams for a 16-ounce can. A comparable amount of regular Mountain Dew would have 72 milligrams of caffeine while a can of PepsiCo's Amp energy drink has 142 milligrams, according to the Center for Science in the Public Interest.

By comparison, a 16-ounce cup of Starbucks coffee has 330 milligrams of caffeine.

Source: Associated Press, "Mountain Dew for Breakfast? Soda Giant's New Morning Beverage Is Packed with Caffeine and Vitamins (Just Don't Call It an Energy Drink)," *Mail Online*, February 11, 2013, http://www.dailymail.co.uk/femail/article-2277065/Mountain-Dew-breakfast-Soda-giants-new-morning-beverage-packed-caffeine-vitamins-just-dont-energy-drink.html.

Key Points in the Article

PepsiCo has introduced a new product intended to fill the space between traditional coffee/tea and the more caffeinated energy drinks. Soft drink giants Coca Cola and PepsiCo hadn't entered the caffeinated drink market with the same intensity they have other drinks markets, but PepsiCo is now focusing on increasing its sales in this market. Kickstart is based on a mix of orange juice and Mountain Dew, which was developed by Taco Bell (that's owned by Yum! Brands Inc., which was part of PepsiCo).

Analyzing the News

(a) In addition to the growth in the demand for energy drinks, demand for healthier drinks has expanded as well. PepsiCo is hoping to capture parts of both markets by offering a product that fits into both categories. The new product also addresses some of the concerns about the large amount of caffeine in energy drinks by offering much less in Kickstart.

(b) The energy drink market has been dominated by Red Bull and Monster Energy, two firms that are not part of either major soft drink maker (Coca Cola and PepsiCo). Kickstart also offers less sugar than many other soft drinks by using artificial sweeteners, thereby reducing the calories in the new product. By trying to meet the concerns of different consumers, PepsiCo is entering not only the energy drink market, but also the market for vitamin-fortified drinks at the same time.

(c) As energy drinks have become more popular, many people have become concerned about the impact of large doses of caffeine on health, particularly in younger consumers. Kickstart has much less caffeine than an energy drink or even a medium-sized coffee at some of the most popular coffee shops in Canada.

Thinking Critically

1. How would you show the impact of the launch of Kickstart on the market for energy drinks in a graph?
2. If health researchers find strong evidence that high-caffeine beverages damage the health of younger consumers, what would be the impact on the market for energy drinks?

Chapter Summary and Problems

Key Terms

Ceteris paribus ("all else equal") condition, p. 64

Competitive market equilibrium, p. 74

Complements, p. 66

Demand curve, p. 62

Demand schedule, p. 62

Demographics, p. 66

Income effect, p. 63

Inferior good, p. 65

Law of demand, p. 63

Law of supply, p. 70

Market demand, p. 62

Market equilibrium, p. 74

Normal good, p. 65

Perfectly competitive market, p. 62

Quantity demanded, p. 62

Quantity supplied, p. 69

Shortage, p. 74

Substitutes, p. 65

Substitution effect, p. 63

Supply curve, p. 69

Supply schedule, p. 69

Surplus, p. 74

Technological change, p. 71

Summary

*LO 3.1 The model of demand and supply is the most powerful tool in economics. The model applies exactly only to *perfectly competitive markets*, where there are many buyers and sellers, all the products sold are identical, and there are no barriers to new sellers entering the market. But the model can also be useful in analyzing markets that don't meet all these requirements. The *quantity demanded* is the amount of a good or service that a consumer is willing and able to purchase at a given price. A *demand schedule* is a table that shows the relationship between the price of a product and the quantity of the product demanded. A *demand curve* is a graph that shows the relationship between the price of a good and the quantity of the good demanded. *Market demand* is the demand by all consumers of a given good or service. The *law of demand* states that *ceteris paribus*—holding everything else constant—the quantity of a product demanded increases when the price falls and decreases when the price rises. Demand curves slope downward because of the *substitution effect*, which is the change in quantity demanded that results from a price change that makes one good more or less expensive relative to another good, and the income effect, which is the change in quantity demanded of a good that results from the effect of a change in the good's price on consumer purchasing power. Changes in income, the prices of related goods, tastes, population and demographics, and expectations all cause the demand curve to shift. *Substitutes* are goods that can be used for the same purpose. *Complements* are goods that are used together. A *normal good* is a good for which demand increases as income increases. An *inferior good* is a good for which demand decreases as income increases. *Demographics* refers to the characteristics of a population with respect to age, race, and gender. A change in demand refers to a shift of the demand curve. A change in quantity demanded refers to a movement along the demand curve as a result of a change in the product's price.

LO 3.2 The *quantity supplied* is the amount of a good that a firm is willing and able to supply at a given price. A *supply*
schedule is a table that shows the relationship between the price of a product and the quantity of the product supplied. A *supply curve* shows on a graph the relationship between the price of a product and the quantity of the product supplied. When the price of a product rises, producing the product is more profitable, and a greater amount will be supplied. The *law of supply* states that, holding everything else constant, the quantity of a product supplied increases when the price rises and decreases when the price falls. Changes in the prices of inputs, technology, the prices of substitutes in production, expected future prices, and the number of firms in a market all cause the supply curve to shift. *Technological change* is a positive or negative change in the ability of a firm to produce a given level of output with a given quantity of inputs. A change in supply refers to a shift of the supply curve. A change in quantity supplied refers to a movement along the supply curve as a result of a change in the product's price.

LO 3.3 *Market equilibrium* occurs where the demand curve intersects the supply curve. A *competitive market equilibrium* has a market equilibrium with many buyers and many sellers. Only at this point is the quantity demanded equal to the quantity supplied. Prices above equilibrium result in *surpluses*, with the quantity supplied being greater than the quantity demanded. Surpluses cause the market price to fall. Prices below equilibrium result in *shortages*, with the quantity demanded being greater than the quantity supplied. Shortages cause the market price to rise.

LO 3.4 In most markets, demand and supply curves shift frequently, causing changes in equilibrium prices and quantities. Over time, if demand increases more than supply, equilibrium price will rise. If supply increases more than demand, equilibrium price will fall.

MyEconLab   Log in to MyEconLab to complete these exercises and get instant feedback.

---

*'Learning Objective' is abbreviated to 'LO' in the end of chapter material.

Review Questions

LO 3.1

1.1 What is a demand schedule? What is a demand curve?

1.2 What is the difference between a change in demand and a change in the quantity demanded?

1.3 What are the main variables that will cause the demand curve to shift? Give an example of each.

LO 3.2

2.1 What is a supply schedule? What is a supply curve?

2.2 What is the difference between a change in supply and a change in the quantity supplied?

2.3 What is the law of supply? What are the main variables that will cause a supply curve to shift? Give an example of each.

LO 3.3

3.1 What do economists mean by *market equilibrium*?

3.2 What do economists mean by a *shortage*? By a *surplus*?

3.3 What happens in a market if the current price is above the equilibrium price? What happens if the current price is below the equilibrium price?

LO 3.4

4.1 Draw a demand and supply graph to show the effect on the equilibrium price in a market in the following two situations:
  a. The demand curve shifts to the right.
  b. The supply curve shifts to the left.

4.2 If, over time, the demand curve for a product shifts to the right more than the supply curve does, what will happen to the equilibrium price? What will happen to the equilibrium price if the supply curve shifts to the right more than the demand curve? For each case, draw a demand and supply graph to illustrate your answer.

Problems and Applications

LO 3.1

1.1 For each of the following pairs of products, state which are complements, which are substitutes, and which are unrelated.
  a. Gasoline and electric car batteries
  b. Houses and household appliances
  c. UGG boots and Kindle e-readers
  d. iPads and Kindle e-readers

1.2 [**Related to the** Chapter Opener **on page 61**] Many people are concerned about the health effects of consuming large quantities of energy drinks. In fact, Health Canada began a review of its regulation of the energy drink industry in 2012. One proposal, not made by Health Canada but by others, is that energy drinks only be sold in pharmacies or liquor stores. What impact do you think this proposal would have on the market for energy drinks? What do you think will happen to the price of these products?

1.3 Imagine that the table below shows the quantity demanded of UGG boots at five different prices in 2012 and in 2013:

	Quantity Demanded	
Price	2012	2013
$160	5000	4000
170	4500	3500
180	4000	3000
190	3500	2500
200	3000	2000

Name two different variables that could cause the quantity demanded of UGG boots to change as indicated from 2012 to 2013.

1.4 [**Related to** Making the Connection **on page 65**] A student makes the following argument:

The chapter says that Canadian consumers, as a group, have begun to treat mainstream beer as an inferior good and wine as a normal good. But I like the taste of mainstream beer better than I like the taste of wine, so for me wine is an inferior good and beer is a normal good.

Do you agree with the student's reasoning? Briefly explain.

1.5 [**Related to the** Making the Connection **on page 67**] Name three products whose demand is likely to increase rapidly if the following demographic groups increase at a faster rate than the population as a whole:
  a. Teenagers
  b. Children under age five
  c. Recent immigrants

1.6 Suppose the following table shows the price of a base model Toyota Prius hybrid and the quantity of Priuses sold for three years. Do these data indicate that the demand curve for Priuses is upward sloping? Explain.

Year	Price	Quantity
2010	$24 880	35 265
2011	24 550	33 250
2012	25 250	36 466

1.7 Richard Posner is a US federal court judge who also writes on economic topics. A newspaper reporter summarized Posner's view on the effect of online bookstores and e-books on the demand for books:

Posner's [argument] is that the disappearance of bookstores is to be celebrated and not mourned, partly because e-books and online stores will reduce the cost of books and thus drive up demand for them.

Do you agree with Posner's statements as given by the reporter? Briefly explain.

Christopher Shea, "Judge Posner Hails the Demise of Bookstores," *Wall Street Journal*, January 13, 2011.

LO 3.2

2.1 Briefly explain whether each of the following statements describes a change in supply or a change in the quantity supplied:

  a. To take advantage of high prices for snow shovels during a snowy winter, Alexander Shovels, Inc., decides to increase output.

  b. The success of the Apple iPad leads more firms to begin producing tablet computers.

  c. In the six months following the Japanese earthquake and tsunami in 2011, production of automobiles in Japan declined by 20 percent.

2.2 Suppose that the following table shows the quantity supplied of UGG boots at five different prices in 2012 and in 2013:

	Quantity Supplied	
Price	2012	2013
$160	300 000	200 000
170	350 000	250 000
180	400 000	300 000
190	450 000	350 000
200	500 000	400 000

Name two different variables that would cause the quantity supplied of UGG boots to change as indicated in the table from 2012 to 2013.

2.3 Will each firm in the tablet computer industry always supply the same quantity as every other firm at each price? What factors might cause the quantity of tablet computers supplied by different firms to be different at a particular price?

2.4 If the price of a good increases, is the increase in the quantity of the good supplied likely to be smaller or larger, the longer the time period being considered? Briefly explain.

LO 3.3

3.1 Briefly explain whether you agree with the following statement: "When there is a shortage of a good, consumers eventually give up trying to buy it, so the demand for the good declines, and the price falls until the market is finally in equilibrium."

3.2 [**Related to** Solved Problem 3.1 **on page 75**] In *The Wealth of Nations*, Adam Smith discussed what has come to be known as the "diamond and water paradox":

  Nothing is more useful than water: but it will purchase scarce anything; scarce anything can be had in exchange for it. A diamond, on the contrary, has scarce any value in use; but a very great quantity of other goods may frequently be had in exchange for it.

  Graph the market for diamonds and the market for water. Show how it is possible for the price of water to be much lower than the price of diamonds, even though the demand for water is much greater than the demand for diamonds.

  Adam Smith, An Inquiry into the Nature and Causes of the Wealth of Nations, Vol. I, (Oxford, UK: Oxford University Press, 1976 original edition, 1776).

3.3 If a market is in equilibrium, is it necessarily true that all buyers and all sellers are satisfied with the market price? Briefly explain.

LO 3.4

4.1 As oil prices rose during 2006, the demand for alternative fuels increased. Ethanol, one alternative fuel, is made from corn. According to an article in the *Wall Street Journal*, the price of tortillas, which are made from corn, also rose during 2006: "The price spike [in tortillas] is part of a ripple effect from the ethanol boom."

  a. Draw a demand and supply graph for the corn market and use it to show the effect on this market of an increase in the demand for ethanol. Be sure to indicate the equilibrium price and quantity before and after the increase in the demand for ethanol.

  b. Draw a demand and supply graph for the tortilla market and use it to show the effect on this market of an increase in the price of corn. Once again, be sure to indicate the equilibrium price and quantity before and after the increase in the demand for ethanol.

  c. During 2009, the demand for gasoline had fallen, lowering its price. The demand for ethanol had declined as well. In response, ethanol producers asked regulators to raise the allowable amount of ethanol in gasoline blends from 10 percent to 15 percent. If regulators were to agree to this proposal, what would be the likely effect on tortilla prices?

  Based on Stephen Power, "Industry Seeks to Raise Ethanol Levels in Fuel," Wall Street Journal, March 7, 2009; and Mark Gongloff, "Tortilla Soup," Wall Street Journal, January 25, 2007.

4.2 [**Related to** Making the Connection **on page 77**] During 2013, the demand for LCD TVs appeared to be falling. At the same time, some industry observers expected that several smaller TV manufacturers might exit the market. Use a demand and supply graph to analyze the effects of these factors on the equilibrium price and quantity of LCD TVs. Clearly show on your graph the old equilibrium price and quantity and the new equilibrium price and quantity. Can you tell for certain whether the new equilibrium price will be higher or lower than the old equilibrium price? Briefly explain.

4.3 [**Related to** Solved Problem 3.2 **on page 80**] The demand for watermelons is highest during summer and lowest during winter. Yet watermelon prices are normally lower in summer than in winter. Use a demand and supply graph to demonstrate how this is possible. Be sure to carefully label the curves in your graph and to clearly indicate the equilibrium summer price and the equilibrium winter price.

4.4 [**Related to** Solved Problem 3.2 **on page 80**] Tourism is an important part of the economies of the Maritime provinces. The tourist season is generally the summer months; with June, July, and August being the most popular months. Shediac, New Brunswick, and Prince Edward Island as a whole are particularly popular with tourists. The lobster fishing season in Shediac doesn't begin until mid-August and ends in mid-October. Use a demand and supply graph to explain whether lobster prices would be higher or lower if the lobster fishing season were to begin in June and end in August.

4.5 An article in the *Wall Street Journal* noted that the demand for Internet advertising was declining at the same time that the number of websites accepting advertising was increasing. After reading the article, a student argues: "From this information, we know that the price of Internet ads should fall, but we don't know whether the total quantity of Internet ads will increase or decrease." Is the student's analysis correct? Illustrate your answer with a demand and supply graph.

Based on Martin Peers, "Future Shock for Internet Ads?" *Wall Street Journal*, February 17, 2009.

4.6 **[Related to** Don't Let This Happen to You **on page 81]** A student writes the following: "Increased production leads to a lower price, which in turn increases demand." Do you agree with the student's reasoning? Briefly explain.

4.7 **[Related to** Don't Let This Happen to You **on page 81]** A student was asked to draw a demand and supply graph to illustrate the effect on the tablet computers market of a fall in the price of displays used in tablet computers, holding everything else constant. She drew the graph below and explained it as follows:

> Displays are an input to tablet computers, so a fall in the price of displays will cause the supply curve for tablets to shift to the right (from S_1 to S_2). Because this shift in the supply curve results in a lower price (P_2), consumers will want to buy more tablets, and the demand curve will shift to the right (from D_1 to D_2). We know that more tablets will be sold, but we can't be sure whether the price of tablets will rise or fall. That depends on whether the supply curve or the demand curve has shifted farther to the right. I assume that the effect on supply is greater than the effect on demand, so I show the final equilibrium price (P_3) as being lower than the initial equilibrium price (P_1).

Explain whether you agree or disagree with the student's analysis. Be careful to explain exactly what—if anything—you find wrong with her analysis.

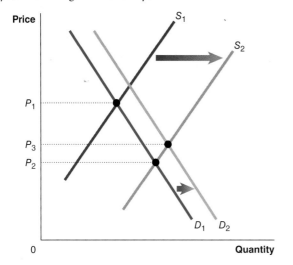

4.8 Proposals have been made to increase government regulation of firms providing child-care services by, for instance, setting education requirements for child-care workers. Suppose that these regulations increase the quality of child-care and cause the demand for child-care services to increase. At the same time, assume that complying with the new government regulations increases the costs of firms providing child-care services. Draw a demand and supply graph to illustrate the effects of these changes in the market for child-care services. Briefly explain whether the total quantity of child-care services purchased will increase or decrease as a result of regulation.

4.9 The following graphs show the supply and demand curves for two markets. One of the markets is for BMW automobiles, and the other is for a cancer-fighting drug, without which lung cancer patients will die. Briefly explain which graph most likely represents which market.

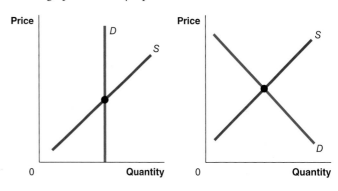

Appendix B

LO
Use quantitative demand and supply analysis.

Quantitative Demand and Supply Analysis

Graphs help us understand economic change *quantitatively*. For instance, a demand and supply graph can tell us that if household incomes rise, the demand curve for a normal good will shift to the right, and its price will rise. Often, though, economists, business managers, and policymakers want to know more than the qualitative direction of change; they want a *quantitative estimate* of the size of the change.

In this chapter, we carried out qualitative analysis of market equilibriums. We saw that an increase in demand would increase the market price and an increase in supply would decrease the market price. To better understand how different shifts in the market impact price and quantity, we need to know how large the effects are. A quantitative analysis of market equilibrium will tell us how much prices and quantities change after a demand or supply curve shifts.

Demand and Supply Equations

The first step in a quantitative analysis is to supplement our use of demand and supply curve with demand and supply *equations*. We noted briefly in this chapter that economists often statistically estimate equations for demand curves. Supply curves can also be statistically estimated. For example, suppose that economists have estimated that the demand for apartments in Toronto is:

$$Q^D = 3\,000\,000 - 1000P$$

and the supply of apartments is:

$$Q^S = -450\,000 + 1300P.$$

We have used Q^D for the quantity of apartments demanded per month, Q^S for the quantity of apartments supplied per month, and P for the apartment rent, in dollars per month. In reality, both the quantity of apartments demanded and quantity of apartments supplied will depend on more than just the rental price of apartments in Toronto. For instance, the demand for apartments in Toronto will also depend on the average incomes of families in the Toronto area and on the rents of apartments in surrounding cities. For simplicity, we will ignore these other factors.

The competitive market equilibrium occurs when the quantity demanded equals the quantity supplied, or:

$$Q^D = Q^S.$$

We can use this equation, which is called an *equilibrium condition*, to solve for the equilibrium monthly apartment rent by setting the quantity demanded from the demand equation equal to the quantity demanded from the supply equation:

$$3\,000\,000 - 1000P = -450\,000 + 1300P$$

$$3\,450\,000 = 2300P$$

$$P = \frac{3\,450\,000}{2300} = \$1500.$$

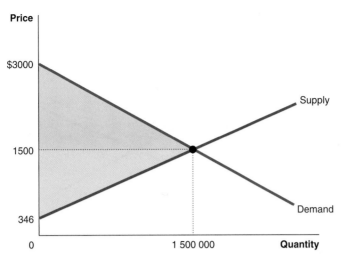

(a) Determining the equilibrium apartment price (monthly rent) in Toronto

Figure 3B.1a

Graphing Supply and Demand Equations

After statistically estimating supply and demand equations, we can use the equations to draw supply and demand curves. In this case, as panel (a) shows, the equilibrium rent for apartments is $1500 per month, and the equilibrium quantity of apartments rented is 1 500 000. The supply equation tells us that at a rent of $346, the quantity of apartments supplied will be zero. The demand equation tells us that at a rent of $3000, the quantity of apartments demanded will be zero. Panel (b), below, shows the shift in the equilibrium price from $1500 to $1283 when the demand for apartments decreases.

We can then substitute this price back into either the demand equation or the supply equation to find the equilibrium quantity of apartments rented:

$$Q^D = 3\,000\,000 - 1000P = 3\,000\,000 - 1000(1500) = 1\,500\,000$$

$$Q^S = -450\,000 + 1300P = -450\,000 + 1300(1500) = 1\,500\,000.$$

Panel (a) of Figure 3B.1 shows in a graph *the same information as we just found using algebra.*

If the economy of Toronto is not performing as well as it has in the past, fewer people are likely to want to live in Toronto, all else being equal. We can represent this idea by reducing the number of apartments that would be rented at every price. This makes the new demand equation:

$$Q^D = 2\,500\,000 - 1000P$$

and the supply equation remains unchanged:

$$Q^S = -450\,000 + 1300P.$$

The new equilibrium price is:

$$2\,500\,000 - 1000P = -450\,000 + 1300P$$

$$2\,950\,000 = 2300P$$

$$P = \frac{2\,950\,000}{2300} = \$1283.$$

The new quantity of apartments rented can be found by substituting this price into either the demand equation or the supply equation:

$$Q^D = 2\,500\,000 - 1000P = 2\,500\,000 - 1000(1283) = 1\,217\,000$$

$$Q^S = -450\,000 + 1300P = -450\,000 + 1300(1283) = 1\,217\,000.$$

When the demand for apartments decreases, the equilibrium price falls from $1500 to $1283, and the equilibrium number of apartments rented falls from 1 500 000 to 1 217 000. Panel (b) of Figure 3B.1 illustrates the result of this shift. Notice that the qualitative results (a decrease in price and quantity) match the quantitative results we just found.

Figure 3B.1b

Graphing Supply and Demand Equations

The process of finding the new equilibrium remains the same no matter whether the demand curve, the supply curve, or both shifts. You set the quantity demanded equal to the quantity supplied and solve for price. Then you substitute the price you found into either the demand equation or the supply equation.

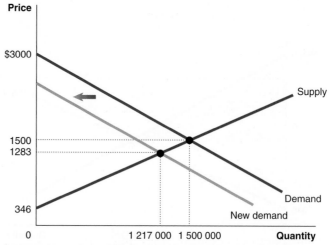

(b) Determining the equilibrium apartment price (monthly rent) in Toronto: when demand decreases

MyEconLab   Log in to MyEconLab to complete these exercises and get instant feedback.

LO Use quantitative demand and supply analysis.

Review Questions

3B.1 In a linear demand equation, what economic information is conveyed by the intercept on the price axis? Similarly, what information is conveyed by the intercept on the price axis in a linear supply equation.

Problems and Applications

3B.1 Suppose that you have been hired to analyze wages in a simple market. The demand for labour and supply of labour can be represented by the following equations:

$$\text{Demand:} \quad L^D = 100 - 4W$$

$$\text{Supply:} \quad L^S = 6W$$

a. Calculate the equilibrium wage (price) and quantity of labour employed in this market.
b. A new employer enters the market causing labour demand to become:

$$\text{New Demand: } L^D = 120 - 4W$$

Calculate the new equilibrium wage (price) and quantity of workers employed in this market.

3B.2 Suppose the demand and supply of leather shoes can be represented by the following equations:

$$Q^D = 200 - 2P$$

$$Q^S = 2P$$

a. Calculate the equilibrium price and quantity in this market.
b. Assume that an increase in the cost of leather causes the supply of shoes to change to:

$$Q^S = -50 + 2P$$

Calculate the new equilibrium price and quantity in this market.
c. Assume that in addition to the increase in the price of leather, the demand for leather shoes falls due to a change in fashion and is now as follows:

$$150 - 2P$$

Calculate the equilibrium price and quantity in this market. Remember to use the same supply curve as in part (b).

Economic Efficiency, Government Price Setting, and Taxes

Chapter Outline and Learning Objectives

SnapshotPhotos/Shutterstock

Should the Government Control Apartment Rents?

One of the single biggest expenses for students—after tuition, of course—is rent. If you live in British Columbia, Manitoba, Ontario, or Quebec, the provincial government has a direct influence over the amount you pay for rent. In each of these provinces, the government restricts what landlords can charge for an apartment. This sort of restriction is generally known as rent control when talking about apartments, and as a price ceiling more generally.

In most cases, rent control applies to some apartments and not others. Tenants in rent-controlled apartments generally pay a lot less in rent than those in otherwise identical apartments that aren't rent controlled.

Despite being intended to improve the affordability of housing for poor people, rent controls can also benefit wealthier people. In Ontario and British Columbia, for example, the provincial government limits the rate of rent increases for occupied apartments, but not rent increases for new tenants. The result is often wildly different prices being paid for exactly the same good. This system makes it possible for a university professor living in Toronto to pay much less in rent than the student living next door.

AN INSIDE LOOK on **page 116** shows both sides of the rent control debate during the 2011 provincial election in Saskatchewan. Fast economic and population growth in Saskatchewan's two largest cities caused rents to increase sharply in a short period of time. The result was a political debate that highlights the costs and benefits of rent controls.

Economics in Your Life

Does Rent Control Make It Easier for You to Find an Affordable Apartment?

Suppose you have job offers in two cities. One factor in deciding which job to accept is whether you can find an affordable apartment. If one city has rent control, are you more likely to find an affordable apartment in that city, or would you be better off looking for an apartment in a city without rent control? As you read the chapter, see if you can answer this question. You can check your answer against the one we provide on page 115 at the end of this chapter.

Price ceiling A legally determined maximum price that sellers may charge.

Price floor A legally determined minimum price that sellers may receive.

We saw in Chapter 3 that in a competitive market the price adjusts to ensure that the quantity demanded equals the quantity supplied. Stated another way, in equilibrium, every consumer willing to pay the market price is able to buy as much of the product as the consumer wants, and every firm willing to accept the market price can sell as much as it wants. Even so, consumers would naturally prefer to pay a lower price, and sellers would prefer to receive a higher price. Normally, consumers and firms have no choice but to accept the equilibrium price if they wish to participate in the market. Occasionally, however, consumers succeed in having the government impose a **price ceiling**, which is a legally determined maximum price that sellers may charge. Rent control is an example of a price ceiling. Firms also sometimes succeed in having the government impose a **price floor**, which is a legally determined minimum price that sellers may receive. In markets for farm products such as eggs, chickens, turkeys, and milk, the federal and provincial governments have been setting price floors that are above the equilibrium market price since the 1960s. Recent trade negotiations between Canada and the European Union, as well as Asia, have made the future of these supply management systems uncertain.

Another way the government intervenes in markets is by imposing taxes. The government relies on the revenue raised from taxes to finance its operations. Unfortunately, whenever the government imposes a price ceiling, a price floor, or a tax, there are predictable negative economic consequences. It is important for government policymakers and voters to understand the negative consequences when evaluating these policies. Economists have developed the concepts of *consumer surplus*, *producer surplus*, and *economic surplus* to analyze the economic effects of price ceilings, price floors, and taxes.

4.1 LEARNING OBJECTIVE

Distinguish between the concepts of consumer surplus and producer surplus.

Consumer Surplus and Producer Surplus

Consumer surplus measures the dollar benefit consumers receive from buying goods or services in a particular market. Producer surplus measures the dollar benefit firms receive from selling goods or services in a particular market. Economic surplus in a market is the sum of consumer surplus plus producer surplus. As we will see, *when the government imposes a price ceiling or a price floor, the amount of economic surplus in a market is reduced*—in other words, price ceilings and price floors reduce the total benefit to consumers and firms from buying and selling in a market. To understand why this is true, we need to understand how consumer surplus and producer surplus are determined.

Consumer Surplus

Consumer surplus The difference between the highest price a consumer is willing to pay for a good or service and the price the consumer actually pays.

Consumer surplus is the difference between the highest price a consumer is willing to pay for a good or service and the price the consumer actually pays. For example, suppose you are in Walmart, and you see a coffee maker on the shelf. No price is indicated on the package, so you take it over to the register to check the price. As you walk to the register, you think to yourself that $18 is the highest price you would be willing to pay. At the register, you find out that the price is actually $12, so you buy the coffee maker. Your consumer surplus in this example is $6: the difference between the $18 you were willing to pay and the $12 you actually paid.

Marginal benefit The additional benefit to a consumer from consuming one more unit of a good or service.

We can use the demand curve to measure the total consumer surplus in a market. Demand curves show the willingness of consumers to purchase a product at different prices. Consumers are willing to purchase a product up to the point where the marginal benefit of consuming a product is equal to its price. The **marginal benefit** is the additional benefit to a consumer from consuming one more unit of a good or service. As a simple example, suppose there are only four consumers in the market for chai tea: Theresa, Tom, Terri, and Tim. Because these four consumers have different tastes for tea and different incomes, the marginal benefit each of them receives from consuming a cup of tea will be different. Therefore, the highest price each is willing to pay for a cup

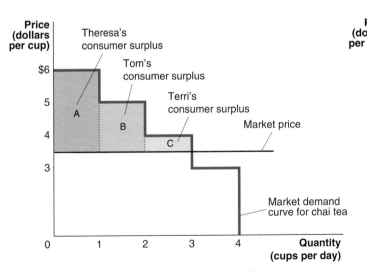

Figure 4.1

**Deriving the Demand Curve
for Chai Tea**

With four consumers in the market for chai
tea, the demand curve is determined by
the highest price each consumer is willing
to pay. For prices above $6, no tea is sold
because $6 is the highest price any con-
sumer is willing to pay. For prices of $3 and
below, every one of the four consumers is
willing to buy a cup of tea.

of tea is also different. In Figure 4.1, the information from the table is used to construct
a demand curve for chai tea. For prices above $6 per cup, no tea is sold because $6 is the
highest price any of the consumers is willing to pay. At a price of $4.50, both Theresa
and Tom are willing to buy tea, so two cups are sold. At prices below $3, all four con-
sumers are willing to buy tea, and four cups are sold.

Suppose the market price of tea is $3.50 per cup. As Figure 4.2 shows, the demand
curve allows us to calculate the total consumer surplus in this market. In panel (a), we

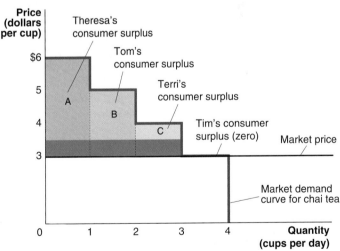

(a) Consumer surplus with a market price of $3.50

(b) Consumer surplus with a market price of $3.00

Figure 4.2   Measuring Consumer Surplus

Panel (a) shows the consumer surplus for Theresa, Tom, and Terri when the price
of tea is $3.50 per cup. Theresa's consumer surplus is equal to the area of rectan-
gle *A* and is the difference between the highest price she would pay—$6—and
the market price of $3.50. Tom's consumer surplus is equal to the area of rect-
angle *B*, and Terri's consumer surplus is equal to the area of rectangle *C*. Total

consumer surplus in this market is equal to the sum of the areas of rectangles
A, *B*, and *C*, or the total area below the demand curve and above the market
price. In panel (b), consumer surplus increases by the shaded area as the
market price declines from $3.50 to $3.00.

Figure 4.3

Total Consumer Surplus in the Market for Chai Tea

The demand curve tells us that most buyers of chai tea would have been willing to pay more than the market price of $2.00. For each buyer, consumer surplus is equal to the difference between the highest price he or she is willing to pay and the market price actually paid. Therefore, the total amount of consumer surplus in the market for chai tea is equal to the area below the demand curve and above the market price. Consumer surplus represents the benefit to consumers in excess of the price they paid to purchase the product.

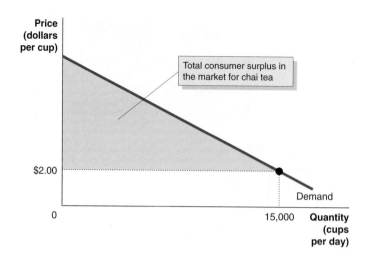

can see that the highest price Theresa is willing to pay is $6, but because she pays only $3.50, her consumer surplus is $2.50 (shown by the area of rectangle *A*). Similarly, Tom's consumer surplus is $1.50 (rectangle *B*), and Terri's consumer surplus is $0.50 (rectangle *C*). Tim is unwilling to buy a cup of tea at a price of $3.50, so he doesn't participate in this market and receives no consumer surplus. In this simple example, the total consumer surplus is equal to $2.50 + $1.50 + $0.50 = $4.50 (or the sum of the areas of rectangles *A*, *B*, and *C*). Panel (b) shows that a lower price will increase consumer surplus. If the price of tea drops from $3.50 per cup to $3.00, Theresa, Tom, and Terri each receive $0.50 more in consumer surplus (shown by the shaded areas), so total consumer surplus in the market rises to $6.00. Tim now buys a cup of tea but doesn't receive any consumer surplus because the price is equal to the highest price he is willing to pay. In fact, Tim is indifferent between buying the cup or not—his well-being is the same either way.

The market demand curves shown in Figures 4.1 and 4.2 do not look like the smooth curves we saw in Chapter 3. This is because this example uses a small number of consumers, each consuming a single cup of tea. With many consumers, the market demand curve for chai tea will have the normal smooth shape shown in Figure 4.3. In this figure, the quantity demanded at a price of $2.00 is 15,000 cups per day. We can calculate total consumer surplus in Figure 4.3 the same way we did in Figures 4.1 and 4.2: by adding up the consumer surplus received on each unit purchased. Once again, we can draw an important conclusion: *The total amount of consumer surplus in a market is equal to the area below the demand curve and above the market price.* Consumer surplus is shown as the blue area in Figure 4.3 and represents the benefit to consumers in excess of the price they paid to purchase the product—in this case, chai tea.

The consumer surplus generated by Gros Morne National Park is much more than the price of admission.

Making the Connection

The Consumer Surplus from Visits to National Parks

Consumer surplus allows us to measure the benefit consumers receive in excess of the price they paid to purchase something. This includes things like visits to national parks. National parks in Canada charge relatively little for access to vast and unique areas of the country. For example, Gros Morne National Park in Newfoundland and Labrador is a UNESCO heritage site visited by approximately 120,000 people each year. The park charges just over $44 for an adult entry fee that represents only the minimum value of the experience for visitors; these people's consumer surplus will be much higher. Economists Roberto Martinez-Espineira and Joe Amoako-Tuffour estimated the demand for visits to the park as well as the consumer surplus the park generated.

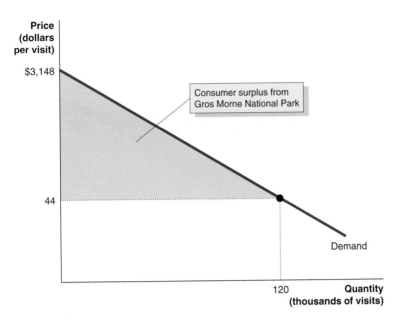

The demand curve shows the marginal benefit consumers receive from visiting the park rather than staying home. The area below the demand curve and above the $44 price line represents the difference between the price consumers would have paid and the $44 they did pay. The shaded area of the graph represents the total consumer surplus generated by Gros Morne National Park. Martinez-Espineira and Amoako-Tuffour estimate that the value of this area is $1,596 per person on average, so the total area with 120,000 visitors would be $191,520,000 or approximately $192 million.

Based on Roberto Martinez-Espineira and Joe Amoako-Tuffour, "Recreation Demand Analysis Under Truncation, Overdispersion, and Endogenous Stratification: An Application to Gros Morne National Park," *Journal of Environmental Management, 88(4)*, September 2008, 1320–1332.

Your Turn: Test your understanding by doing related problem 1.6 on page 119 at the end of this chapter.

MyEconLab

Producer Surplus

Just as demand curves show the willingness of consumers to buy a product at different prices, supply curves show the willingness of firms to supply a product at different prices. The willingness to supply a product depends on the cost of producing it. Firms will supply an additional unit of a product only if they receive a price equal to the additional cost of producing that unit. **Marginal cost** is the additional cost to a firm of producing one more unit of a good or service. Consider the marginal cost to the firm Heavenly Tea of producing one more cup: In this case, the marginal cost includes the ingredients to make the tea and the wages paid to the worker preparing the tea. Often, the marginal cost of producing a good increases as more of the good is produced during a given period of time. This is the key reason—as we saw in Chapter 3—that supply curves are upward sloping.

Panel (a) of Figure 4.4 shows Heavenly Tea's producer surplus. For simplicity, we show Heavenly producing only a small quantity of tea. The figure shows that Heavenly's marginal cost of producing the first cup of tea is $1.25. Its marginal cost of producing the second cup is $1.50, and so on. The marginal cost of each cup of tea is the lowest price Heavenly is willing to accept to supply that cup. The supply curve, then, is also a marginal cost curve. Suppose the market price of tea is $2.00 per cup. On the first cup of tea, the price is $0.75 higher than the lowest price Heavenly is willing to accept. **Producer surplus** is the difference between the lowest price a firm would be willing to accept for a good or service and the price it actually receives. Therefore, Heavenly's

Marginal cost The additional cost to a firm of producing one more unit of a good or service.

Producer surplus The difference between the lowest price a firm would be willing to accept for a good or service and the price it actually receives.

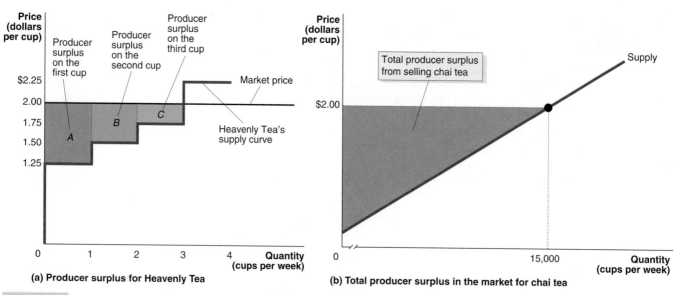

Figure 4.4   Measuring Producer Surplus

Panel (a) shows Heavenly Tea's producer surplus. Producer surplus is the difference between the lowest price a firm would be willing to accept and the price it actually receives. The lowest price Heavenly Tea is willing to accept to supply a cup of tea is equal to its marginal cost of producing that cup. When the market price of tea is $2.00, Heavenly receives producer surplus of $0.75 on the first cup (the area of rectangle A), $0.50 on the second cup (rectangle B), and $0.25 on the third cup (rectangle C). In panel (b), the total amount of producer surplus tea sellers receive from selling chai tea can be calculated by adding up for the entire market the producer surplus received on each cup sold. In the figure, total producer surplus is equal to the area above the supply curve and below the market price, shown in red.

producer surplus on the first cup is $0.75 (shown by the area of rectangle A). Its producer surplus on the second cup is $0.50 (rectangle B). Its producer surplus on the third cup is $0.25 (rectangle C). Heavenly will not be willing to supply the fourth cup because the marginal cost of producing it is greater than the market price. Heavenly Tea's total producer surplus is equal to $0.75 + $0.50 + $0.25 = $1.50 (or the sum of rectangles A, B, and C). A higher price will increase producer surplus. For example, if the market price of chai tea rises from $2.00 to $2.25, Heavenly Tea's producer surplus will increase from $1.50 to $2.25. (Make sure you understand how the new level of producer surplus was calculated, assuming they make four cups.)

The supply curve shown in panel (a) of Figure 4.4 does not look like the smooth curves we saw in Chapter 3 because this example uses a single firm producing only a small quantity of tea. With many firms, the market supply curve for chai tea will have the normal smooth shape shown in panel (b) of Figure 4.4. In panel (b), the quantity supplied at a price of $2.00 is 15,000 cups per day. We can calculate total producer surplus in panel (b) the same way we did in panel (a): by adding up the producer surplus received on each cup sold. Therefore, *the total amount of producer surplus in a market is equal to the area above the market supply curve and below the market price.* The total producer surplus tea sellers receive from selling chai tea is shown as the red area in panel (b) of Figure 4.4.

What Consumer Surplus and Producer Surplus Measure

We have seen that consumer surplus measures the benefit to consumers from participating in a market, and producer surplus measures the benefit to producers from participating in a market. It is important, however, to be clear about what this means. In a sense, consumer surplus measures the *net* benefit to consumers from participating in a market rather than the *total* benefit. That is, if the price of a product were zero, the consumer surplus in a market would be all of the area under the demand curve. When the price is not zero, consumer surplus is the area below the demand curve and above the market price. So, consumer surplus in a market is equal to the total benefit received by consumers minus the total amount they must pay to buy the good or service.

Similarly, producer surplus measures the *net* benefit received by producers from participating in a market. If producers could supply a good or service at zero cost, the producer surplus in a market would be all of the area below the market price. When cost is not zero, producer surplus is the area below the market price and above the supply curve. So, producer surplus in a market is equal to the total amount firms receive from consumers minus the cost of producing the good or service.

The Efficiency of Competitive Markets

4.2 LEARNING OBJECTIVE

Understand the concept of economic efficiency.

In Chapter 3, we defined a *competitive market* as a market with many buyers and many sellers. An important advantage of the market system is that it results in efficient economic outcomes. But what do we mean by *economic efficiency*? The concepts we have developed so far in this chapter give us two ways to think about the economic efficiency of competitive markets. We can think in terms of marginal benefit and marginal cost. We can also think in terms of consumer surplus and producer surplus. As we will see, these two approaches lead to the same outcome, but using both can increase our understanding of economic efficiency.

Marginal Benefit Equals Marginal Cost in Competitive Equilibrium

Figure 4.5 again shows the market for chai tea. Recall from our discussion that the demand curve shows the marginal benefit received by consumers, and the supply curve shows the marginal cost of production. To achieve economic efficiency in this market, the marginal benefit from the last unit sold should equal the marginal cost of production. The figure shows that this equality occurs at competitive equilibrium where 15,000 cups per day are produced and marginal benefit and marginal cost are both equal to $2.00. Why is this outcome economically efficient? Because every cup of chai tea has been produced where the marginal benefit to buyers is greater than or equal to the marginal cost to producers.

Another way to see why the level of output at competitive equilibrium is efficient is to consider what the situation would be if output were at a different level. For instance, suppose that output of chai tea were 14,000 cups per day. Figure 4.5 shows that at this level of output, the marginal benefit from the last cup sold is $2.20, whereas the marginal cost is only $1.80. This level of output is not efficient because 1,000 more cups could be produced for which the additional benefit to consumers would be greater than the additional cost of production. Consumers would willingly purchase those cups, and

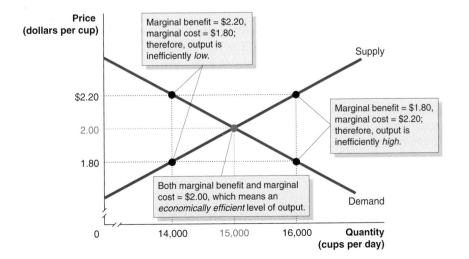

Figure 4.5

Marginal Benefit Equals Marginal Cost Only at Competitive Equilibrium

In a competitive market, equilibrium occurs at a quantity of 15,000 cups and a price of $2.00 per cup, where marginal benefit equals marginal cost. This is the economically efficient level of output because every cup has been produced where the marginal benefit to buyers is greater than or equal to the marginal cost to producers.

Figure 4.6

Economic Surplus Equals the Sum of Consumer Surplus and Producer Surplus

The economic surplus in a market is the sum of the blue area, representing consumer surplus, and the red area, representing producer surplus.

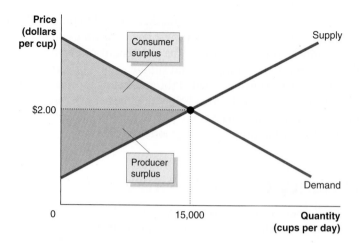

tea sellers would willingly supply them, making both consumers and sellers better off. Similarly, if the output of chai tea were 16,000 cups per day, the marginal cost of the 16,000th cup is $2.20, whereas the marginal benefit is only $1.80. Tea sellers would only be willing to supply this cup at a price of $2.20, which is $0.40 higher than consumers would be willing to pay. In fact, consumers would not be willing to pay the price tea sellers would need to receive for any cup beyond the 15,000th.

To summarize, we can say this: *Equilibrium in a competitive market results in the economically efficient level of output, where marginal benefit equals marginal cost.*

Economic Surplus

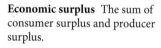

Economic surplus The sum of consumer surplus and producer surplus.

Economic surplus in a market is the sum of consumer surplus and producer surplus. In a competitive market, with many buyers and sellers and no government restrictions, economic surplus is at a maximum when the market is in equilibrium. To see this, let's look one more time at the market for chai tea shown in Figure 4.6. The consumer surplus in this market is the blue area below the demand curve and above the line indicating the equilibrium price of $2.00. The producer surplus is the red area above the supply curve and below the price line.

Deadweight Loss

To show that economic surplus is maximized at equilibrium, consider a situation in which the price of chai tea is *above* the equilibrium price, as shown in Figure 4.7. At a price of $2.20 per cup, the number of cups consumers are willing to buy per day drops from 15,000 to 14,000. At competitive equilibrium, consumer surplus is equal to the sum of areas *A*, *B*, and *C*. At a price of $2.20, fewer cups are sold at a higher price, so consumer surplus declines to just the area of *A*. At competitive equilibrium, producer surplus is equal to the sum of areas *D* and *E*. At the higher price of $2.20, producer surplus changes to be equal to the sum of areas *B* and *D*. The sum of consumer and producer surplus—economic surplus—has been reduced to the sum of areas *A*, *B*, and *D*. Notice that this is less than the original economic surplus by an amount equal to areas *C* and *E*. Economic surplus has declined because at a price of $2.20, all the cups between the 14,000th and the 15,000th, which would have been produced in competitive equilibrium, are not being produced. These "missing" cups are not providing any consumer or producer surplus, so economic surplus has declined. The reduction in economic surplus resulting from a market not being in competitive equilibrium is called the **deadweight loss**. In the figure, it is equal to the sum of yellow triangles *C* and *E*.

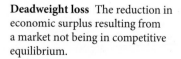

Deadweight loss The reduction in economic surplus resulting from a market not being in competitive equilibrium.

Economic Surplus and Economic Efficiency

Consumer surplus measures the benefit to consumers from buying a particular product, such as chai tea. Producer surplus measures the benefit to firms from selling a particular

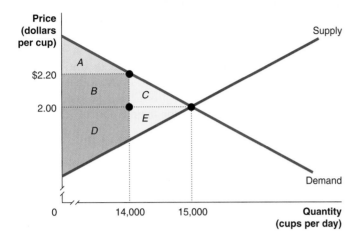

	At Competitive Equilibrium	At a Price of $2.20
Consumer Surplus	A + B + C	A
Producer Surplus	D + E	B + D
Deadweight Loss	None	C + E

Figure 4.7

When a Market Is Not in Equilibrium, There Is a Deadweight Loss

Economic surplus is maximized when a market is in competitive equilibrium. When a market is not in equilibrium, there is a deadweight loss. When the price of chai tea is $2.20 instead of $2.00, consumer surplus declines from an amount equal to the sum of areas A, B, and C to just area A. Producer surplus increases from the sum of areas D and E to the sum of areas B and D. At competitive equilibrium, there is no deadweight loss. At a price of $2.20, there is a deadweight loss equal to the sum of areas C and E.

product. Therefore, economic surplus—which is the sum of the benefit to firms plus the benefit to consumers—is the best measure we have of the benefit to society from the production of a particular good or service. This gives us a second way of characterizing the economic efficiency of a competitive market: *Equilibrium in a competitive market results in the greatest amount of economic surplus, or total net benefit to society, from the production of a good or service.* Anything that causes the market for a good or service not to be in competitive equilibrium reduces the total benefit to society from the production of that good or service.

Now we can give a more general definition of *economic efficiency* in terms of our two approaches: **Economic efficiency** is a market outcome in which the marginal benefit to consumers of the last unit produced is equal to its marginal cost of production and in which the sum of consumer surplus and producer surplus is at a maximum.

Economic efficiency A market outcome in which the marginal benefit to consumers of the last unit produced is equal to its marginal cost of production and in which the sum of consumer surplus and producer surplus is at a maximum.

Government Intervention in the Market: Price Floors and Price Ceilings

Notice that we have *not* concluded that every *individual* is better off if a market is at competitive equilibrium. We have only concluded that economic surplus, or the *total* net benefit to society, is greatest at competitive equilibrium. Any individual producer would rather receive a higher price, and any individual consumer would rather pay a lower price, but usually producers can sell and consumers can buy only at the competitive equilibrium price.

Producers or consumers who are dissatisfied with the competitive equilibrium price can lobby the government to legally require that a different price be charged. In Canada, the government occasionally overrides the market outcome by setting prices. When the government does intervene, it can either attempt to aid sellers by requiring that a price be above equilibrium—a price floor—or aid buyers by requiring that a price be below equilibrium—a price ceiling. To affect the market outcome, the government must set a price floor that is above the equilibrium price or set a price ceiling that is below the equilibrium price. Otherwise, the price ceiling or price floor will not be *binding* on buyers and sellers. The preceding section demonstrates that moving away from competitive equilibrium will reduce economic efficiency. We can use the concepts of consumer

4.3 LEARNING OBJECTIVE

Explain the economic effect of government-imposed price floors and price ceilings.

surplus, producer surplus, and deadweight loss to see more clearly the economic inefficiency of price floors and price ceilings.

Price Floors: Government Policy in Agricultural Markets

If you live near the Canada–U.S. border you've likely noticed that milk costs a lot less in the U.S. than it does in Canada. It's not that American cows produce more milk, but rather that the Canadian federal and provincial governments have intervened in the market for milk and certain other agricultural products for years. The Canadian Wheat Board controlled the purchase of wheat from farmers in Alberta, Saskatchewan, Manitoba, and parts of British Columbia from the 1930s until 2012. Production of eggs, chickens, turkeys, broiler hatching eggs, and milk has been controlled since the 1960s. The marketing boards controlling the production and sale of these products are to ensure that farmers receive a "fair" price for their products, which effectively means setting a price floor.

To see how a price floor in an agricultural market works, suppose that the equilibrium price in the market for milk is $1 per litre, but the government decides to set a price floor of $1.50 per litre. As Figure 4.8 shows, the price of milk rises from $1 to $1.50, and the quantity of milk sold falls from 85 billion litres per year to 78 billion litres per year. Initially, suppose that production of milk also falls to 78 billion litres.

Just as we saw in the earlier examples of the market for chai tea (shown in Figure 4.7), the producer surplus received by dairy farmers increases by an amount equal to the area of the red rectangle *A* and falls by an amount equal to the area of the yellow triangle *C*. The area of the red rectangle represents a transfer from consumer surplus to producer surplus. The fall in consumer surplus is equal to the area of the red rectangle *A* plus the area of the yellow triangle *B*. Dairy farmers benefit from this program, but consumers lose. There is also a deadweight loss equal to the areas of the yellow triangles *B* and *C*, which represents the decline in economic efficiency due to the price floor. There is a deadweight loss because the price floor has reduced the amount of economic surplus in the market for milk. Or, looked at another way, the price floor has caused the marginal benefit of the last litre of milk sold to be greater than the marginal cost of producing it. We can conclude that a price floor reduces economic efficiency.

We assumed initially that farmers reduce their production of milk to the amount consumers are willing to buy. In fact, as Figure 4.8 shows, a price floor will cause the quantity dairy farmers want to supply to increase from 85 billion litres to 92 billion litres. Because the higher price also reduces the amount of milk consumers want to buy, the result is a surplus of 14 billion litres of milk (the 92 billion litres supplied minus the 78 billion litres demanded).

Figure 4.8

The Economic Effect of a Price Floor in the Milk Market

If dairy farmers convince the government to impose a price floor of $1.50 per litre, the amount of milk sold will fall from 85 billion litres a year to 78 billion litres a year. If we assume that farmers produce 78 billion litres, producer surplus then increases by the red rectangle *A*—which is transferred from consumer surplus—and falls by the yellow triangle *C*. Consumer surplus declines by the red rectangle *A* plus the yellow triangle *B*. There is a deadweight loss equal to the yellow triangles *B* and *C*, representing the decline in economic efficiency due to the price floor. In reality, without further government intervention, a price floor of $1.50 would cause farmers to expand their production from 85 billion litres to 92 billion litres, resulting in a surplus of milk.

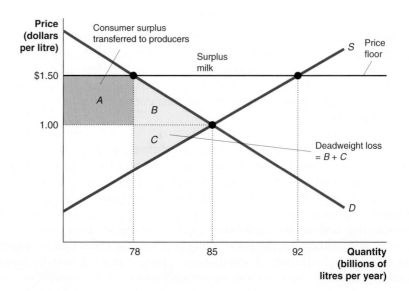

In order to ensure that we don't end up with a huge surplus of milk that just ends up going sour, the government restricts the supply of milk by issuing licences to produce milk. In order to legally produce and sell milk commercially, every dairy farmer must have a milk market quota. The legal limit on milk production is set so that supply is equal to demand at the price set by the government; in our example, this quantity is 78 billion litres.

<table>
<tr><td>

Making
the
Connection
</td><td>

Price Floors in Labour Markets: The Debate Over Minimum Wage Policy

The minimum wage may be the most controversial "price floor." Supporters see the minimum wage as a way of raising
</td></tr>
</table>

the incomes of low-skilled workers. Opponents argue that it results in fewer jobs and imposes large costs on small businesses.

Each province and territory in Canada sets its own hourly minimum wage, ranging from $11.00 in Nunavut to $9.40 in Alberta. It is illegal for an employer to pay less than this wage. For most workers, the minimum wage is irrelevant because it is well below the wage employers are voluntarily willing to pay them. But for low-skilled workers—such as workers in fast-food restaurants—the minimum wage is above the wage they would otherwise receive. The following figure shows the effect of the minimum wage on employment in the market for low-skilled labour.

Without a minimum wage, the equilibrium wage would be W_1 and the number of workers hired would be L_1. With a minimum wage set above the equilibrium wage, the number of workers demanded by employers declines from L_1 to L_2, and the quantity of labour supplied increases to L_3, leading to a surplus of workers unable to find jobs equal to $L_3 - L_2$. The quantity of labour supplied increases because the higher wage attracts more people to work. For instance, some teenagers may decide that working after school is worthwhile at the minimum wage but would not be worthwhile at a lower wage.

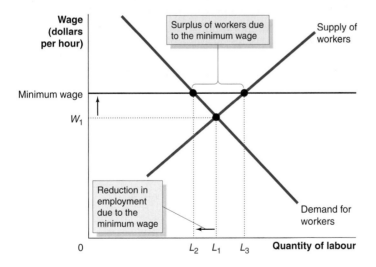

This analysis is very similar to our analysis of the milk market in Figure 4.8. Just as a price floor in the milk market leads to less milk being consumed, a price floor in the labour market should lead to fewer workers being hired. Views differ sharply among economists, however, concerning how large a reduction in employment the minimum wage causes. For instance, Anindya Sen, Kathleen Rybczynski, and Corey Van De Wall have studied the impact of minimum wages in Canada between 1981 and 2004. They have found that a 10 percent increase in the minimum wage results in a 3–5 percent decrease in teen employment. Other economists have examined similar data and found that increases in the minimum wage have no impact on employment.

Whatever the extent of employment losses from the minimum wage, because it is a price floor, it will cause a deadweight loss, just as a price floor in the milk market does. Therefore, many economists favour alternative policies for attaining the goal of raising the incomes of low-skilled workers. One policy many economists support is an earned income tax credit. The earned income tax credit reduces the amount of tax that low-income wage earners would otherwise pay. Workers with very low incomes who do not owe any tax receive a payment from the government. Compared with the minimum wage, the earned income tax credit can increase the incomes of low-skilled workers without reducing employment. The earned income tax credit also places a lesser burden on the small businesses that employ many low-skilled workers, and it may cause a smaller loss of economic efficiency.

Based on Sen, A., Rybczynski, K., & Waal, V. D. (2011). Teen employment, poverty, and the minimum wage: Evidence from Canada. *Labour Economics, 18*(1), 36-47. doi:10.1016/j.labeco.2010.06.003

MyEconLab   **Your Turn:** Test your understanding by doing related problem 3.2 on page 120 at the end of this chapter.

Price Ceilings: Government Rent Control Policy in Housing Markets

Support for governments setting price floors typically comes from sellers, and support for governments setting price ceilings typically comes from consumers. For example, when there is a sharp increase in gasoline prices, there are often proposals for the government to impose a price ceiling on the market for gasoline. As we saw in the chapter opener, British Columbia, Manitoba, Ontario, and Quebec impose rent control, which puts a ceiling on the maximum rent that landlords can charge for an apartment. Figure 4.9 shows the market for apartments in a city that has rent control.

Without rent control, the equilibrium rent would be $1,500 per month, and 2,000 apartments would be rented. With a maximum legal rent of $1,000 per month, landlords reduce the quantity of apartments supplied to 1,900. The fall in the quantity of apartments supplied can be the result of landlords converting some apartments into offices, selling some off as condominiums, or converting some small apartment buildings into single-family homes. Over time, landlords may even abandon some apartment buildings. At one time in New York City, which famously imposes rent controls, rent control resulted in landlords abandoning whole city blocks because they were unable to cover their costs with the rents the government allowed them to charge. In London, when rent

Figure 4.9

The Economic Effect of a Rent Ceiling

Without rent control, the equilibrium rent is $1,500 per month. At that price, 2,000 apartments would be rented. If the government imposes a rent ceiling of $1,000, the quantity of apartments supplied falls to 1,900, and the quantity of apartments demanded increases to 2,100, resulting in a shortage of 200 apartments. Producer surplus equal to the area of the blue rectangle *A* is transferred from landlords to renters, and there is a deadweight loss equal to the areas of yellow triangles *B* and *C*.

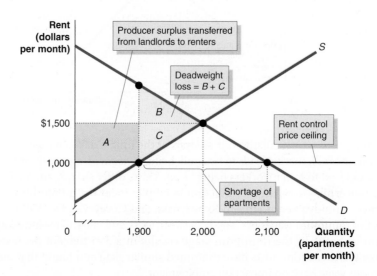

Don't Let This Happen to You

Don't Confuse "Scarcity" With "Shortage"

At first glance, the following statement seems correct: "There is a shortage of every good that is scarce." In everyday conversation, we describe a good as "scarce" if we have trouble finding it. For instance, if you are looking for a gift for a child, you might call the latest hot toy "scarce" if you are willing to buy it at its listed price but can't find it online or in any store. But economists have a broad definition of *scarce*. In the economic sense, almost everything—except undesirable things like garbage—is scarce. A shortage of a good occurs only if the quantity demanded is greater than the quantity supplied at the current price. Therefore, the preceding statement— "There is a shortage of every good that is scarce"—is incorrect. In fact, there is no shortage of most scarce goods.

MyEconLab

---

controls were applied to rooms and apartments located in a landlord's own home, the quantity of these apartments supplied dropped by 75 percent.

In Figure 4.9, with the rent ceiling of $1,000, the quantity of apartments demanded rises to 2,100. There is a shortage of 200 apartments. Consumer surplus increases by rectangle *A* and falls by triangle *B*. Rectangle *A* would have been part of producer surplus if rent control were not in place. With rent control, it is part of consumer surplus. Rent control causes the producer surplus received by landlords to fall by rectangle *A* plus triangle *C*. Triangles *B* and *C* represent the deadweight loss. There is a deadweight loss because rent control has reduced the amount of economic surplus in the market for apartments. Rent control has caused the marginal benefit of the last apartment rented to be greater than the marginal cost of supplying it. We can conclude that a price ceiling, such as rent control, reduces economic efficiency.

Renters as a group benefit from rent controls—total consumer surplus is larger—but landlords lose. Because of the deadweight loss, the total loss to landlords is greater than the gain to renters. Notice also that although renters as a group benefit, the number of renters is reduced, so some renters are made worse off by rent controls because they are unable to find an apartment at the legal rent.

Black Markets

To this point, our analysis of rent controls is incomplete. In practice, renters may be worse off and landlords may be better off than Figure 4.9 makes it seem. We have assumed that renters and landlords actually abide by the price ceiling, but sometimes they don't. Because rent control leads to a shortage of apartments, renters who would otherwise not be able to find apartments have an incentive to offer landlords rents above the legal maximum. When governments try to control prices by setting price ceilings or price floors, buyers and sellers often find a way around the controls. The result is a **black market** where buying and selling take place at prices that violate government price regulations.

In a housing market with rent controls, the total amount of consumer surplus received by renters may be reduced and the total amount of producer surplus received by landlords may be increased if apartments are being rented at prices above the legal price ceiling.

Rent controls can also lead to an increase in racial and other types of discrimination. With rent controls, more renters are looking for apartments than there are apartments to rent. Landlords can afford to indulge their prejudices by refusing to rent to people they don't like. In cities without rent controls, landlords face more competition, which makes it more difficult to turn down tenants on the basis of irrelevant characteristics, such as race.

Black market A market in which buying and selling take place at prices that violate government price regulations.

Solved Problem **4.3**

What's the Economic Effect of a Black Market for Apartments?

In many cities that have rent controls, the actual rents paid can be much higher than the legal maximum. Because rent controls cause a shortage of apartments, desperate tenants are often willing to pay landlords rents that are higher than the law allows, perhaps by writing a cheque for the legally allowed rent and paying an additional amount in cash. Look again at Figure 4.9 on page 106. Suppose that competition among tenants results in the black market rent rising to $2,000 per month. At this rent, tenants demand 1,900 apartments. Use a graph showing the market for apartments to compare this situation with the one shown in Figure 4.9. Be sure to note any differences in consumer surplus, producer surplus, and deadweight loss.

Solving the Problem

Step 1: **Review the chapter material.** This problem is about price controls in the market for apartments, so you may want to review the section "Price Ceilings: Government Rent Control Policy in Housing Markets," which begins on page 106.

Step 2: **Draw a graph similar to Figure 4.9, with the addition of the black market price.**

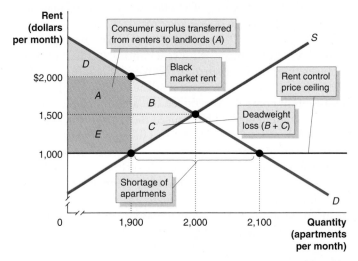

Step 3: **Analyze the changes from Figure 4.9.** The black market rent is now $2,000—even higher than the original competitive equilibrium rent shown in Figure 4.9. So, consumer surplus declines by an amount equal to the red rectangle *A* plus the red rectangle *E*. The remaining consumer surplus is the blue triangle *D*. Note that the rectangle *A*, which would have been part of consumer surplus without rent control, represents a transfer from renters to landlords. Compared with the situation shown in Figure 4.9, producer surplus has increased by an amount equal to rectangles *A* and *E*, and consumer surplus has declined by the same amount. Deadweight loss is equal to triangles *B* and *C*, the same as in Figure 4.9.

Extra Credit: This analysis leads to a surprising result: With an active black market in apartments, rent control may leave renters as a group worse off—with less consumer surplus—than if there were no rent control. There is one more possibility to consider, however. If enough landlords become convinced that they can get away with charging rents above the legal ceiling, the quantity of apartments supplied will increase. Eventually, the market could even end up at the competitive equilibrium, with an equilibrium rent of $1,500 and equilibrium quantity of 2,000 apartments. In that case, the rent control price ceiling becomes nonbinding, not because it was set below the equilibrium price but because it was not legally enforced.

MyEconLab   **Your Turn:** For more practice, do related problem 3.6 on page 120 at the end of this chapter.

The Results of Government Price Controls: Winners, Losers, and Inefficiency

When the government imposes price floors or price ceilings, three important results occur:

- Some people win.

- Some people lose.

- There is a loss of economic efficiency.

The winners with rent control are the people who are paying less for rent because they live in rent-controlled apartments. Landlords may also gain if they break the law by charging rents above the legal maximum for their rent-controlled apartments, provided that those illegal rents are higher than the competitive equilibrium rents would be. The losers from rent control are the landlords of rent-controlled apartments who abide by the law and renters who are unable to find apartments to rent at the controlled price. Rent control reduces economic efficiency because fewer apartments are rented than would be rented in a competitive market (refer again to Figure 4.9, on page 106). The resulting deadweight loss measures the decrease in economic efficiency.

Positive and Normative Analysis of Price Ceilings and Price Floors

Are rent controls, milk price controls, and other price ceilings and price floors bad? As we saw in Chapter 1, questions of this type have no right or wrong answers. Economists are generally skeptical of government attempts to interfere with competitive market equilibrium. Economists know the role competitive markets have played in raising the average person's standard of living. They also know that too much government intervention has the potential to reduce the ability of the market system to produce similar increases in living standards in the future.

But recall from Chapter 1 the difference between positive and normative analysis. Positive analysis is concerned with *what is*, and normative analysis is concerned with *what should be*. Our analysis of rent control and of the farm programs in this chapter is positive analysis. We discussed the economic results of these programs. Whether these programs are desirable or undesirable is a normative question. Whether the gains to the winners more than make up for the losses to the losers and for the decline in economic efficiency is a matter of judgment and not strictly an economic question. Price ceilings and price floors continue to exist partly because people who understand their downside still believe they are good policies and therefore support them. The policies also persist because many people who support them do not understand the economic analysis in this chapter and so do not understand the drawbacks to these policies.

The Economic Impact of Taxes

4.4 LEARNING OBJECTIVE

Analyze the economic impact of taxes.

When the government taxes a good or service, it affects the market equilibrium for that good or service. Just as with a price ceiling or price floor, one result of a tax is a decline in economic efficiency. Analyzing taxes is an important part of the field of economics known as *public finance*. In this section, we will use the model of demand and supply and the concepts of consumer surplus, producer surplus, and deadweight loss to analyze the economic impact of taxes.

The Effect of Taxes on Economic Efficiency

Whenever a government taxes a good or service, less of that good or service will be produced and consumed. For example, a tax on cigarettes will raise the cost of smoking and reduce the amount of smoking that takes place. We can use a demand and supply graph to illustrate this point. Figure 4.10 shows the market for cigarettes.

Figure 4.10

The Effect of a Tax on the Market for Cigarettes

Without the tax, market equilibrium occurs at point *A*. The equilibrium price of cigarettes is $10.00 per pack, and 4 million packs of cigarettes are sold per year. A $1.00-per-pack tax on cigarettes will cause the supply curve for cigarettes to shift up by $1.00, from S_1 to S_2. The new equilibrium occurs at point *B*. The price of cigarettes will increase by $0.90, to $10.90 per pack, and the quantity sold will fall to 3.7 million packs. The tax on cigarettes has increased the price paid by consumers from $10.00 to $10.90 per pack. Producers receive a price of $10.90 per pack (point *B*), but after paying the $1.00 tax, they are left with $9.90 (point *C*). The government will receive tax revenue equal to the green-shaded box. Some consumer surplus and some producer surplus will become tax revenue for the government, and some will become deadweight loss, shown by the yellow-shaded area.

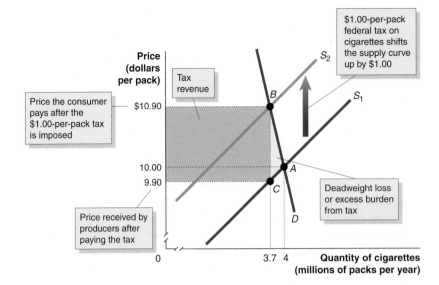

Without the tax, the equilibrium price of cigarettes would be $10.00 per pack, and 4 million packs of cigarettes would be sold per year (point *A*). If the government requires sellers of cigarettes to pay a $1.00-per-pack tax, then their cost of selling cigarettes will increase by $1.00 per pack. This increase in costs causes the supply curve for cigarettes to shift up by $1.00 because sellers will now require a price that is $1.00 greater to supply the same quantity of cigarettes. In Figure 4.10, the supply curve shifts up by $1.00 to show the effect of the tax, and there is a new equilibrium price of $10.90 and a new equilibrium quantity of 3.7 million packs (point *B*).

The government will collect tax revenue equal to the tax per pack multiplied by the number of packs sold, or $3.7 million. The area shaded in green in Figure 4.10 represents the government's tax revenue. Consumers will pay a higher price of $10.90 per pack. Although sellers appear to be receiving a higher price per pack, once they have paid the tax, the price they receive falls from $10.00 per pack to $9.90 per pack. There is a loss of consumer surplus because consumers are paying a higher price. The price producers receive falls, so there is also a loss of producer surplus. Therefore, the tax on cigarettes has reduced *both* consumer surplus and producer surplus. Some of the reduction in consumer and producer surplus becomes tax revenue for the government. The rest of the reduction in consumer and producer surplus is equal to the deadweight loss from the tax, shown by the yellow-shaded triangle in the figure.

We can conclude that the true burden of a tax is not just the amount consumers and producers pay the government but also includes the deadweight loss. The deadweight loss from a tax is referred to as the *excess burden* of the tax. *A tax is efficient if it imposes a small excess burden relative to the tax revenue it raises.* One contribution economists make to government tax policy is to advise policymakers on which taxes are most efficient.

Tax Incidence: Who Actually Pays a Tax?

The answer to the question "Who pays a tax?" seems obvious: Whoever is legally required to send a tax payment to the government pays the tax. But there can be an important difference between who is legally required to pay the tax and who actually *bears the burden* of the tax. The actual division of the burden of a tax between buyers and sellers is referred to as **tax incidence**. The federal government currently levies an excise tax of 10 cents per litre of gasoline sold. Gas station owners collect this tax and forward it to the federal government, but who actually bears the burden of the tax?

Tax incidence The actual division of the burden of a tax between buyers and sellers in a market.

Determining Tax Incidence on a Demand and Supply Graph Suppose that currently the federal government does not impose a tax on gasoline. In Figure 4.11,

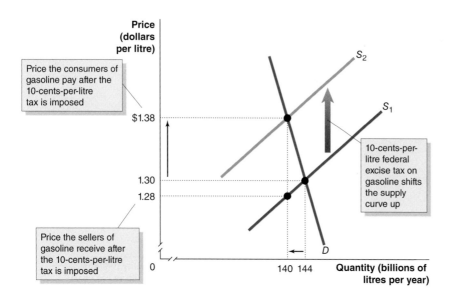

Price the consumers of gasoline pay after the 10-cents-per-litre tax is imposed

Price the sellers of gasoline receive after the 10-cents-per-litre tax is imposed

Figure 4.11

The Incidence of a Tax on Gasoline

With no tax on gasoline, the price would be $1.30 per litre, and 144 billion litres of gasoline would be sold each year. A 10-cents-per-litre excise tax shifts up the supply curve from S_1 to S_2, raises the price consumers pay from $1.30 to $1.38, and lowers the price sellers receive from $1.30 to $1.28. Therefore, consumers pay 8 cents of the 10-cents-per-litre tax on gasoline, and sellers pay 2 cents.

equilibrium in the retail market for gasoline occurs at the intersection of the demand curve and supply curve, S_1. The equilibrium price is $1.30 per litre, and the equilibrium quantity is 144 billion litres. Now suppose that the federal government imposes a 10-cents-per-litre tax. As a result of the tax, the supply curve for gasoline will shift up by 10 cents per litre. At the new equilibrium, where the demand curve intersects the supply curve, S_2, the price has risen by 8 cents per litre, from $1.30 to $1.38. Notice that only in the extremely unlikely case that demand is a vertical line will the market price rise by the full amount of the tax. Consumers are paying 8 cents more per litre. Sellers of gasoline receive a new higher price of $1.38 per litre, but after paying the 10-cents-per-litre tax, they are left with $1.28 per litre, or 2 cents less than they were receiving in the old equilibrium.

Although the sellers of gasoline are responsible for collecting the tax and sending the tax receipts to the government, they do not bear most of the burden of the tax. In this case, consumers pay 8 cents of the tax because the market price has risen by 8 cents, and sellers pay 2 cents of the tax because after sending the tax to the government, they are receiving 2 cents less per litre of gasoline sold. Expressed in percentage terms, consumers pay 80 percent of the tax, and sellers pay 20 percent of the tax.

Solved Problem **4.4**

When Do Consumers Pay All of a Sales Tax Increase?

A student makes the following statement: "If the federal government raises the sales tax on gasoline by $0.25, then the price of gasoline will rise by $0.25. Consumers can't get by without gasoline, so they have to pay the whole amount of any increase in the sales tax." Under what circumstances will the student's statement be true? Illustrate your answer with a graph of the market for gasoline.

Solving the Problem

Step 1: **Review the chapter material.** This problem is about tax incidence, so you may want to review the section "Tax Incidence: Who Actually Pays a Tax?"

Step 2: **Draw a graph like Figure 4.11 to illustrate the circumstances when consumers will pay all of an increase in a sales tax.**

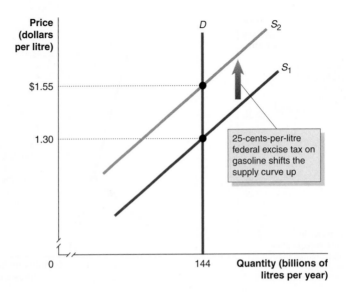

Step 3: Use the graph to evaluate the statement. The graph shows that consumers will pay all of an increase in a sales tax only if the demand curve is a vertical line. It is very unlikely that the demand for gasoline would look like this because we expect that for every good, an increase in price will cause a decrease in the quantity demanded. Because the demand curve for gasoline is not a vertical line, the statement is incorrect.

MyEconLab   **Your Turn:** For more practice, do related problems 4.2 and 4.3 on pages 122 and 123 at the end of the chapter.

Does It Make a Difference Whether the Government Collects a Tax From Buyers or Sellers? We have already seen the important distinction between the true burden of a tax and whether buyers or sellers are legally required to pay a tax. We can reinforce this point by noting explicitly that the incidence of a tax does *not* depend on whether the government collects a tax from the buyers of a good or from the sellers. Figure 4.12 illustrates this point by showing the effect on equilibrium in the market for gasoline if a 10-cents-per-litre tax is imposed on buyers rather than on sellers. That is, we are now assuming that instead of sellers having to collect the 10-cents-per-litre tax at the pump, buyers are responsible for keeping track of how many litres of gasoline they purchase and sending the tax to the government. (Of course, it would be very difficult for buyers to keep track of their purchases or for the government to check whether they were paying all of the taxes they owe. That is why the government collects the tax on gasoline from sellers.)

Figure 4.12 is similar to Figure 4.11 except that it shows the gasoline tax being imposed on buyers rather than sellers. In Figure 4.12, the supply curve does not shift because nothing has happened to change the quantity of gasoline sellers are willing to supply at any given price. The demand curve has shifted, however, because consumers now have to pay a 10-cent tax on every litre of gasoline they buy. Therefore, at every quantity, they are willing to pay a price 10 cents less than they would have without the tax. In the figure, we indicate the effect of the tax by shifting the demand curve down by 10 cents, from D_1 to D_2. Once the tax has been imposed and the demand curve has shifted down, the new equilibrium quantity of gasoline is 140 billion litres, which is exactly the same as in Figure 4.11.

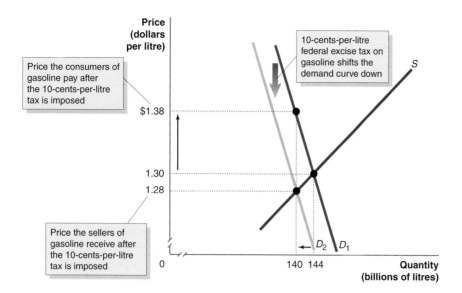

Price the consumers of gasoline pay after the 10-cents-per-litre tax is imposed

10-cents-per-litre federal excise tax on gasoline shifts the demand curve down

Price the sellers of gasoline receive after the 10-cents-per-litre tax is imposed

Figure 4.12

The Incidence of a Tax on Gasoline Paid by Buyers

With no tax on gasoline, the demand curve is D_1. If a 10-cents-per-litre tax is imposed that consumers are responsible for paying, the demand curve shifts down by the amount of the tax, from D_1 to D_2. In the new equilibrium, consumers pay a price of $1.38 per litre, including the tax. Producers receive $1.28 per litre. This is the same result we saw when producers were responsible for paying the tax.

The new equilibrium price after the tax is imposed appears to be different in Figure 4.12 than in Figure 4.11, but if we include the tax, buyers will pay the same price and sellers will receive the same price in both figures. To see this, notice that in Figure 4.11, buyers pay sellers a price of $1.38 per litre. In Figure 4.12, they pay sellers only $1.28, but they must also pay the government a tax of 10 cents per litre. So, the total price buyers pay remains $1.38 per litre. In Figure 4.11, sellers receive $1.38 per litre from buyers, but after they pay the tax of 10 cents per litre, they are left with $1.28, which is the same amount they receive in Figure 4.12.

Making the Connection | How Is the Burden of Employment Insurance Premiums Shared Between Workers and Firms?

Most people who receive paycheques have several different taxes (provincial and federal income tax) and fees (Canada Pension Plan contributions, Employment Insurance premiums, etc.) withheld from them by their employers, who forward these taxes and fees directly to the government. In fact, many people are shocked after getting their first job when they discover the gap between their gross pay and their net pay (pay after taxes and fees have been deducted). Employment Insurance (EI) premiums are one of the fees that employers pay to the government on behalf of their employees. While not exactly a tax, EI premiums are seen by many workers in the same light as a tax.

In addition to the 1.83 percent of earnings a worker pays in EI premiums (up to a maximum of $839.97 in 2013), the employer pays 2.56 percent of the employee's gross pay to the federal government (up to a maximum of $1,175.96 in 2013). This arrangement means that employees directly pay about 40 percent of the cost of the Employment Insurance program.

But do employees really carry only 40 percent of the burden of EI? Our discussion of taxes shows that the answer is no. In the labour market, employers are buyers, and workers are sellers. As we saw in the example of the federal tax on gasoline, whether the tax is collected from buyers or from sellers does not affect the incidence of the tax. Most economists believe that the burden of payroll taxes and deductions like EI premiums falls almost entirely on workers. The following figure, which shows the market for labour, illustrates why.

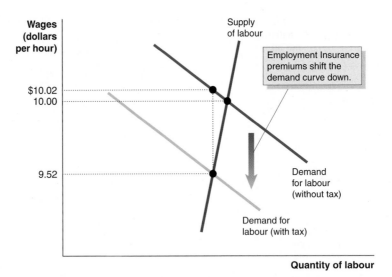

(a) Employment Insurance premium paid by employers

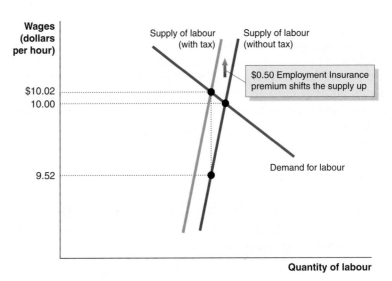

(b) Employment Insurance premium paid by workers

In the market for labour, the demand curve represents the quantity of labour demanded by employers at various wages, and the supply curve represents the quantity of labour supplied by workers at various wages. The intersection of the demand curve and the supply curve determines the equilibrium wage. In both panels we assume the equilibrium wage without EI deductions to be $10.00 per hour. For simplicity, let's assume that the EI premium is $0.50 per hour of work. In panel (a), we assume that employers must pay the tax. The tax causes the demand for labour curve to shift down by $0.50 at every quantity of labour because firms now must pay an extra $0.50 in EI premiums for every hour of labour they hire. We have drawn the supply curve as being very steep because most economists believe that the quantity of labour supplied by workers does not change much as the wage rate changes. Workers pay $0.48 of the tax because their wages fall from $10.00 before EI premiums to $9.52 after EI premiums. Firms pay only $0.02 of the tax because the amount they pay for an hour of labour increases from $10.00 before EI premiums to $10.02 after premiums. In panel (a), after EI premiums are imposed, the equilibrium wage declines from $10.00 per hour to $9.52 per hour. Firms are now paying a total of $10.02 for every hour of work they hire: $9.52 in wages and $0.50 in EI premiums. In other words, workers have paid $0.48 of the $0.50 premium and firms have paid only $0.02.

Panel (b) shows that this result is exactly the same if the premium is imposed on workers rather than on firms. In this case, paying EI premiums causes the supply curve for labour to shift up by $0.50 at every quantity of labour because workers must now pay a premium of $0.50 for every hour they work. After the premiums are collected, the equilibrium wage increases to $10.02 per hour. But workers only get to keep $9.52 after they have paid the $0.50 premium. Once again, workers have paid $0.48 of the $0.50 premium, and firms have paid only $0.02.

Although the figure presents a simplified analysis, it reflects the conclusions of most economists who have studied taxes and fees imposed on wages: *Even when the fees are officially split between workers and firms, the burden falls almost entirely on workers.* This conclusion would not be changed even if the government passed a law to require either employers or workers to pay all of the tax. The forces of demand and supply in the labour market, and not the government, determine the incidence of the tax.

Your Turn: Test your understanding by doing related problem 4.4 on page 123 at the end of this chapter.

MyEconLab

Economics in Your Life

Does Rent Control Make It Easier for You to Find an Affordable Apartment?

At the beginning of the chapter, we posed the following question: If you have two job offers in different cities, one with rent control and one without, will you be more likely to find an affordable apartment in the city with rent control? In answering the question, this chapter has shown that although rent control can keep rents lower than they might otherwise be, it can also lead to a permanent shortage of apartments. You may have to search for a long time to find a suitable apartment, and landlords may even ask you to give them payments "under the table," which would make your actual rent higher than the controlled rent. Finding an apartment in a city without rent control should be much easier, although the rent may be higher.

Conclusion

The model of demand and supply introduced in Chapter 3 showed that markets free from government intervention eliminate surpluses and shortages and do a good job of responding to the wants of consumers. We have seen in this chapter that both consumers and firms sometimes try to use the government to change market outcomes in their favour. The concepts of consumer and producer surplus and deadweight loss allow us to measure the benefits consumers and producers receive from competitive market equilibrium. These concepts also allow us to measure the effects of government price floors and price ceilings and the economic impact of taxes.

Read *An Inside Look* on the next page for an example of the debate around implementing rent controls in the Canadian setting.

LEADER–POST

Rent Control Could Be Dangerous: Saskatchewan Premier Brad Wall

REGINA — Premier Brad Wall on Monday dismissed rent control as a "dangerous" approach while the NDP used the first question period of the spring sitting to hammer home the party's call for a legislated cap on increases.

Wall said a system of rent control would discourage the addition of rental units, an argument that has also been put forward by a Regina landlords group as well as other opponents of the idea.

"We have to focus on supply. We fundamentally believe rent controls actually hurt long-term supply," Wall told reporters at the legislature.

"You're going to see us moving ahead with the Headstart initiative that addresses supply. Working with municipalities we're going to open up new units," said the premier, making reference to the Headstart for a Home program that is supposed to see 1,000 affordable homes constructed over the next five years.

The details of the initiative promised in last fall's throne speech haven't yet been announced.

But the NDP said rent control deserves a second look in the current climate of low vacancy and rental rates that have markedly increased in the past few years.

"As many provinces across Canada, we're looking at next generation, second generation rent control," said Opposition MLA David Forbes. "Often people who talk about problems with rent controls are talking about the first generation but we see provinces that have been able to mature and respond to issues around tenancies and apartment blocks."

The Opposition cited a report indicating a record number of new rental units were under construction last year in Winnipeg, located in a province that caps rent increases.

"They've achieved a neat balance I think of having a cap on existing stock of rental units, but also have an exclusion (from rent control rules) for 20 years for those people who want to build new units. I like that style," said NDP Leader Dwain Lingenfelter, who acknowledged his party has yet to propose the details of how a rent control plan could work in Saskatchewan.

But Social Services Minister June Draude also turned to Manitoba as an example of why rent control doesn't work, noting Winnipeg's rental vacancy rate has fallen to less than one per cent.

The crunch has eased a bit in Saskatchewan, said Draude, with Canada Mortgage and Housing Corp. reporting last fall that the average vacancy rates in centres with 10,000 people or more rose to 2.5 per cent from 1.9 per cent a year earlier.

"I don't understand where the Opposition is coming from. They had the opportunity to put rent controls in place in 2007 after they cut them in 1992. They looked at it and decided it wasn't the right thing to do so all of a sudden they're talking about it again and it surprises me," Draude said.

Draude said a summit to be held next month should produce a new housing strategy for the province by the end of June.

Source: Rent control could be dangerous: Saskatchewan Premier Brad Wall by Angela Hall from LeaderPost.com, March 7, 2011. Material reprinted with the express permission of: Leader-Post, a division of Postmedia Network Inc.

Key Points in the Article

When regions experience rapid economic growth, prices for commodities such as rent increase very quickly. Saskatchewan's economy had grown very quickly in the years prior to 2011. As a result, rents in both Saskatoon and Regina rose rapidly, as people moving into the cities began to compete for places to live. One proposed solution to this rapid increase was to limit the rate at which landlords could increase rent. An alternative was to enact programs to encourage the development of new rental units.

Analyzing the News

(a) Brad Wall, the premier of Saskatchewan at the time of the election, argued against rent control on the grounds that it would reduce the supply of apartments and houses available for rent. As we saw in Chapter 3 and in this chapter, when the price of a product falls, the supply falls as well. When governments restrict prices for a good or service below the equilibrium price, producers are less likely to produce it.

(b) Government policies don't have to be as simple as the price ceilings and price floors presented in this chapter. "Second generation" rent controls often involve restricting the rate at which rents can increase for the same tenant, but allow the landlord to charge the market price to new tenants. This is effectively a price ceiling only on some parts of the market, which can limit the impact on supply.

(c) Rapidly changing prices are a signal to suppliers to increase production. When prices are prevented from increasing by government action, suppliers have to turn to other sources of information about the market to make their decisions about how much to produce and the price they could receive if they did produce. This uncertainty can make new firms less likely to enter the market and existing firms less likely to offer more products for sale.

Thinking Critically

1. One consequence of rent controls is a shortage of apartments, which is shown in the figure below. This reduction in quantity means that some people will have a hard time finding a place to live. Suppose rent control also leads to a reduction in the supply of affordable apartments. Use the figure to illustrate the effects of a reduction in supply, and explain what will happen to the shortage of apartments.

2. One reason some economists are critical of rent control laws is that they create a deadweight loss. Using the figure on this page, identify the area representing the deadweight loss. What causes the deadweight loss? What would the supply curve have to look like for the deadweight loss to equal zero?

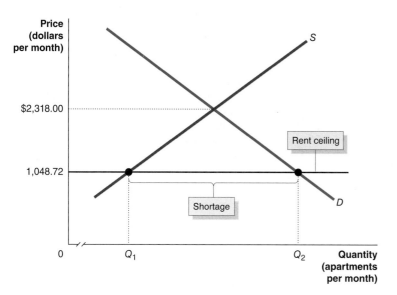

The effect of rent control laws on the supply of affordable apartments.

Chapter Summary and Problems

Key Terms

Black market, p. 107

Consumer surplus, p. 96

Deadweight loss, p. 102

Economic efficiency, p. 103

Economic surplus, p. 102

Marginal benefit, p. 96

Marginal cost, p. 99

Price ceiling, p. 96

Price floor, p. 96

Producer surplus, p. 99

Tax incidence, p. 110

Summary

*LO 4.1 Although most prices are determined by demand and supply in markets, the government sometimes imposes *price ceilings* and *price floors*. A **price ceiling** is a legally determined maximum price that sellers may charge. A **price floor** is a legally determined minimum price that sellers may receive. Economists analyze the effects of price ceilings and price floors using *consumer surplus* and *producer surplus*. **Marginal benefit** is the additional benefit to a consumer from consuming one more unit of a good or service. The demand curve is also a marginal benefit curve. **Consumer surplus** is the difference between the highest price a consumer is willing to pay for a good or service and the price the consumer actually pays. The total amount of consumer surplus in a market is equal to the area below the demand curve and above the market price. **Marginal cost** is the additional cost to a firm of producing one more unit of a good or service. The supply curve is also a marginal cost curve. **Producer surplus** is the difference between the lowest price a firm is willing to accept for a good or service and the price it actually receives.

LO 4.2 Equilibrium in a competitive market is economically efficient. **Economic surplus** is the sum of consumer surplus and producer surplus. **Economic efficiency** is a market outcome in which the marginal benefit to consumers from the last unit produced is equal to the marginal cost of production and where the sum of consumer surplus and producer surplus is at a maximum. When the market price is above or below the equilibrium price, there is a reduction in economic surplus. The reduction in economic surplus

resulting from a market not being in competitive equilibrium is called the **deadweight loss**.

LO 4.3 Producers or consumers who are dissatisfied with the market outcome can attempt to convince the government to impose price floors or price ceilings. A price floor usually increases producer surplus, decreases consumer surplus, and causes a deadweight loss. A price ceiling usually increases consumer surplus, reduces producer surplus, and causes a deadweight loss. The results of the government imposing price ceilings and price floors are that some people win, some people lose, and a loss of economic efficiency occurs. Price ceilings and price floors can lead to a **black market**, where buying and selling take place at prices that violate government price regulations. Positive analysis is concerned with what is, and normative analysis is concerned with what should be. Positive analysis shows that price ceilings and price floors cause deadweight losses. Whether these policies are desirable or undesirable, though, is a normative question.

LO 4.4 Most taxes result in a loss of consumer surplus, a loss of producer surplus, and a deadweight loss. The true burden of a tax is not just the amount paid to the government by consumers and producers, but also includes the deadweight loss. The deadweight loss from a tax is the excess burden of the tax. **Tax incidence** is the actual division of the burden of a tax. In most cases, consumers and firms share the burden of a tax levied on a good or service.

MyEconLab   Log in to MyEconLab to complete these exercises and get instant feedback.

Review Questions

LO 4.1

1.1 What is marginal benefit? Why is the demand curve referred to as a marginal benefit curve?

1.2 What is marginal cost? Why is the supply curve referred to as a marginal cost curve?

1.3 What is consumer surplus? How does consumer surplus change as the equilibrium price of a good rises or falls?

1.4 What is producer surplus? How does producer surplus change as the equilibrium price of a good rises or falls?

LO 4.2

2.1 Define *economic surplus* and *deadweight loss*.

2.2 What is economic efficiency? Why do economists define *efficiency* in this way?

LO 4.3

3.1 Why do some consumers tend to favour price controls while others tend to oppose them?

3.2 Do producers tend to favour price floors or price ceilings? Why?

3.3 Can economic analysis provide a final answer to the question of whether the government should intervene in markets by imposing price ceilings and price floors? Briefly explain.

LO 4.4

4.1 What is meant by *tax incidence*?

4.2 What do economists mean by *an efficient tax*?

4.3 Does who is legally responsible for paying a tax—buyers or sellers—make a difference in the amount of tax each pays? Briefly explain.

*'Learning Objective' is abbreviated to 'LO' in the end of chapter material.

Problems and Applications

LO 4.1

1.1 Suppose that a frost in Florida reduces the size of the orange crop, which causes the supply curve for oranges to shift to the left. Briefly explain whether consumer surplus will increase or decrease and whether producer surplus will increase or decrease. Use a demand and supply graph to illustrate your answers.

1.2 A student makes the following argument: "When a market is in equilibrium, there is no consumer surplus. We know this because in equilibrium, the market price is equal to the price consumers are willing to pay for the good." Briefly explain whether you agree with the student's argument.

1.3 How does consumer surplus differ from the total benefit consumers receive from purchasing products? Similarly, how does producer surplus differ from the total revenue that firms receive from selling products? Under what special case will consumer surplus equal the total benefit consumers receive from consuming a product? Under what special case will producer surplus equal the total revenue firms receive from selling a product?

1.4 The following graph illustrates the market for a breast cancer–fighting drug, without which breast cancer patients cannot survive. What is the consumer surplus in this market? How does it differ from the consumer surplus in the markets you have studied up to this point?

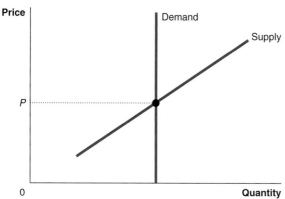

1.5 The graph shows the market for tickets to a concert that will be held in a local arena that seats 15,000 people. What is the producer surplus in this market? How does it differ from the producer surplus in the markets you have studied up to this point?

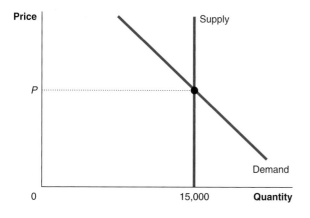

1.6 A study estimates that the total consumer surplus gained by people participating in auctions on eBay in a recent year was $7 billion. Is it likely that the total consumer surplus for the items bought in these auctions was higher or lower than it would have been if consumers had purchased these items for fixed prices in retail stores?

Based on Ravi Bapna, Wolfgang Jank, and Galit Shmueli, "Consumer Surplus in Online Auctions," *Information Systems Research*, Vol. 19, No. 4, December 2008, pp. 400–416.

LO 4.2

2.1 Briefly explain whether you agree with the following statement: "A lower price in a market always increases economic efficiency in that market."

2.2 Briefly explain whether you agree with the following statement: "If at the current quantity marginal benefit is greater than marginal cost, there will be a deadweight loss in the market. However, there is no deadweight loss when marginal cost is greater than marginal benefit."

2.3 Using a demand and supply graph, illustrate and briefly explain the effect on consumer surplus and producer surplus of a price below the equilibrium price. Show any deadweight loss on your graph.

2.4 Briefly explain whether you agree with the following statement: "If consumer surplus in a market increases, producer surplus must decrease."

2.5 Does an increase in economic surplus in a market always mean that economic efficiency in the market has increased? Briefly explain.

2.6 Using the graph below, explain why economic surplus would be smaller if Q_1 or Q_3 was the quantity produced than if Q_2 was the quantity produced.

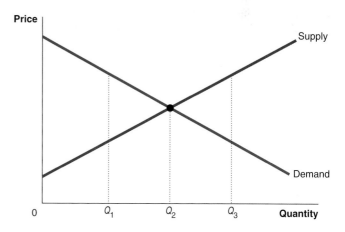

LO 4.3

3.1 The graph below shows the market for apples. Assume that the government has imposed a price floor of $10 per crate.
   a. How many crates of apples will be sold after the price floor has been imposed?
   b. Will there be a shortage or a surplus? If there is a shortage or a surplus, how large will it be?
   c. Will apple producers benefit from the price floor? If so, explain how they will benefit.

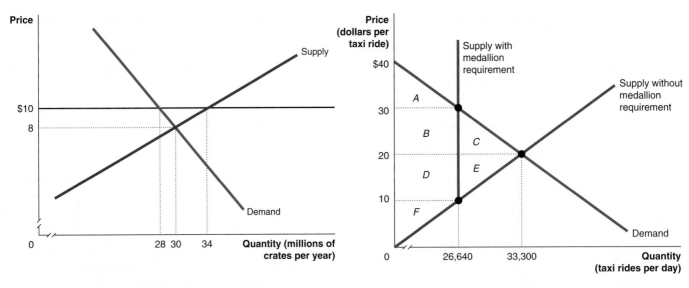

3.2 Suppose that the government sets a price floor for milk that is above the competitive equilibrium price.

    a. Draw a graph showing this situation. Be sure your graph shows the competitive equilibrium price, the price floor, the quantity that would be sold in competitive equilibrium, and the quantity that would be sold with the price floor.

    b. Compare the economic surplus in this market when there is a price floor and when there is no price floor.

3.3 Provincial regulators control the price and supply of milk to ensure that dairy farmers receive a fair and consistent income. Is providing dependable income to dairy farmers a good policy goal for provincial governments? How are provincial governments likely to meet this policy objective? Do you think provincial governments should pursue this objective for all businesses? Explain.

3.4 During 2007, the Venezuelan government allowed consumers to buy only a limited quantity of sugar. The government also imposed a ceiling on the price of sugar. As a result, both the quantity of sugar consumed and the market price of sugar were below the competitive equilibrium price and quantity. Draw a graph to illustrate this situation. On your graph, be sure to indicate the areas representing consumer surplus, producer surplus, and deadweight loss.

3.5 Taxis operating in Montreal must have a licence issued by the Bureau du taxi et du remorquage, which regulates both taxis and towing. This branch of the government has limited the number of vehicles licensed as taxis to 4,440. Let's assume that this puts an absolute limit on the number of taxi rides that can be supplied in Montreal on any day because no one breaks the law and operates an unlicensed taxi. Let's also assume that each taxi can provide 6 trips per

day. In that case, the supply of taxi rides is fixed at 26,640 (or 6 rides per taxi × 4,440 taxis). We show this in the above graph, with a vertical line at this quantity. *Assume there are no government controls on the prices that drivers can charge for rides.* Use the graph above to answer the following questions.

    a. What would the equilibrium price and quantity be in this market if there were no licence requirement?

    b. What are the price and quantity in this market with the licence requirement?

    c. Indicate on the graph the areas representing consumer surplus and producer surplus if there were no licence requirement.

    d. Indicate on the graph the areas representing consumer surplus, producer surplus, and deadweight loss with the licence requirement. Calculate the values of consumer surplus, producer surplus, and deadweight loss.

3.6 [**Related to** Solved Problem 4.3 **on page 108**] Use the information on the market for apartments in Bay City in the table to answer the following questions.

Rent	Quantity Demanded	Quantity Supplied
$ 500	375,000	225,000
600	350,000	250,000
700	325,000	275,000
800	300,000	300,000
900	275,000	325,000
1,000	250,000	350,000

a. In the absence of rent control, what is the equilibrium rent, and what is the equilibrium quantity of apartments rented? Draw a demand and supply graph of the market for apartments to illustrate your answer. In equilibrium, will there be any renters who are unable to find an apartment to rent, or any landlords who are unable to find a renter for an apartment?

b. Suppose the government sets a ceiling on rents of $600 per month. What is the quantity of apartments demanded, and what is the quantity of apartments supplied?

c. Assume that all landlords abide by the law. Use a demand and supply graph to illustrate the effect of this price ceiling on the market for apartments. Be sure to indicate on your graph each of the following: (i) the area representing consumer surplus after the price ceiling has been imposed, (ii) the area representing producer surplus after the price ceiling has been imposed, and (iii) the area representing the deadweight loss after the ceiling has been imposed.

d. Assume that the quantity of apartments supplied is the same as you determined in part (b). But now assume that landlords ignore the law and rent this quantity of apartments for the highest rent they can get. Briefly explain what this rent will be.

3.7 A student makes the following argument:

A price floor reduces the amount of a product that consumers buy because it keeps the price above the competitive market equilibrium. A price ceiling, on the other hand, increases the amount of a product that consumers buy because it keeps the price below the competitive market equilibrium.

Do you agree with the student's reasoning? Use a demand and supply graph to illustrate your answer.

3.8 The Calgary Stampede draws millions of people to Calgary each year. Demand for hotel rooms during Stampede week rises dramatically. Hotel management responds to the increase in demand by increasing the price for a room. Periodically, there is an outcry against the higher prices and accusations of "price gouging."

a. Draw a demand and supply graph of the market for hotel rooms in Calgary during the Stampede and another graph for weeks without the Stampede. If Calgary city council were to pass a law stating that prices for rooms are not allowed to rise during the Stampede, what would happen to the market for hotel rooms during the Stampede? Show your answer on your graph.

b. If the prices of hotel rooms are not allowed to increase, what will be the effect on out-of-town Stampede goers?

c. How might the city council's law affect the supply of hotel rooms over time? Briefly explain.

d. Calgary during the Stampede is not the only place that faces peak and non-peak "seasons." Can you think of other locations that face a large increase in demand for hotel rooms during particular times of the year? Why do we typically not see laws limiting the prices hotels can charge during peak seasons?

3.9 **[Related to the** Chapter Opener **on page 95]** The cities of Peabody and Woburn are 10 kilometres apart. Woburn enacts a rent control law that puts a ceiling on rents well below their competitive market value. Predict the effect of this law on the competitive equilibrium rent in Peabody, which does not have a rent control law. Illustrate your answer with a demand and supply graph.

3.10 **[Related to the** Chapter Opener **on page 95]** The competitive equilibrium rent in the city of Lowell is currently $1,000 per month. The government decides to enact rent control and to establish a price ceiling for apartments of $750 per month. Briefly explain whether rent control is likely to make each of the following people better or worse off.

a. Someone currently renting an apartment in Lowell

b. Someone who will be moving to Lowell next year and who intends to rent an apartment

c. A landlord who intends to abide by the rent control law

d. A landlord who intends to ignore the law and illegally charge the highest rent possible for his apartments

3.11 Suppose that initially the gasoline market is in equilibrium, at a price of $1.50 per litre and a quantity of 45 million litres per month. Then a war in the Middle East disrupts exports from the region, shifting the supply curve for gasoline from S_1 to S_2. The price of gasoline begins to rise, and consumers protest. The federal government responds by setting a price ceiling of $1.50 per litre. Use the graph to answer the following questions.

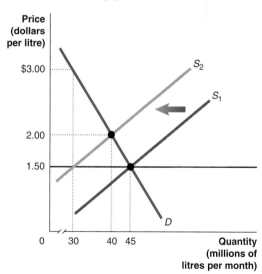

a. If there were no price ceiling, what would be the equilibrium price of gasoline, the quantity of gasoline demanded, and the quantity of gasoline supplied? Now assume that the price ceiling is imposed and that there is no black market in gasoline. What are the price of gasoline, the quantity of gasoline demanded, and the quantity of gasoline supplied? How large is the shortage of gasoline?

b. Assume that the price ceiling is imposed, and there is no black market in gasoline. Show on the graph the areas representing consumer surplus, producer surplus, and deadweight loss.

c. Now assume that there is a black market, and the price of gasoline rises to the maximum that consumers are willing to pay for the amount supplied by producers at $1.50 per litre. Show on the graph the areas representing producer surplus, consumer surplus, and deadweight loss.

d. Are consumers made better off with the price ceiling than without it? Briefly explain.

3.12 An editorial in *The Economist* magazine discusses the fact that in most countries—including Canada—it is illegal for individuals to buy or sell body parts, such as kidneys.

a. Draw a demand and supply graph for the market for kidneys. Show on your graph the legal maximum price of zero and indicate the quantity of kidneys supplied at this price. (*Hint:* Because some kidneys are donated, the quantity supplied will not be zero.)

b. The editorial argues that buying and selling kidneys should be legalized:

With proper regulation, a kidney market would be a big improvement over the current sorry state of affairs. Sellers could be checked for disease and drug use, and cared for after operations. … Buyers would get better kidneys, faster. Both sellers and buyers would do better than in the illegal market, where much of the money goes to middlemen.

Do you agree with this argument? Should the government treat kidneys like other goods and allow the market to determine the price?

From "Psst, Wanna Buy a Kidney?" *The Economist*, November 18, 2006, p. 15.

LO 4.4

4.1 Suppose the current equilibrium price of a quarter-pound hamburger is $5, and 10 million quarter-pound hamburgers are sold per month. After the federal government imposes a tax of $0.50 per hamburger, the equilibrium price of a hamburger rises to $5.20, and the equilibrium quantity falls to 9 million. Illustrate this situation with a demand and supply graph. Be sure your graph shows the equilibrium price before and after the tax, the equilibrium quantity before and after the tax, and the areas representing consumer surplus after the tax, producer surplus after the tax, tax revenue collected by the government, and deadweight loss.

4.2 Use the graph of the market for cigarettes below to answer the following questions.

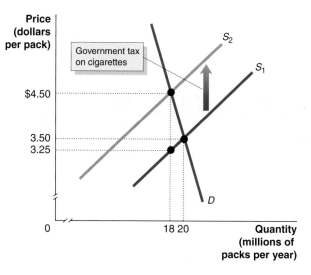

a. According to the graph, how much is the government tax on cigarettes?
b. What price do producers receive after paying the tax?
c. How much tax revenue does the government collect?

4.3 Consider the graph of the market for cigarettes in problem 4.2, where it is assumed that the government collects the tax from the producers of cigarettes.
  a. How would the graph be different if the tax were collected from the buyers of cigarettes?
  b. What would be the new equilibrium price that buyers pay producers of cigarettes?
  c. Including the tax, what would be the total amount that cigarette buyers pay per pack?

4.4 [**Related to the** Making the Connection **on page 113**] If the price consumers pay and the price sellers receive are not affected by whether consumers or sellers collect a tax on a good or service, why does the government usually require sellers and not consumers to collect a tax?

MyEconLab   MyEconLab is an online tool designed to help you master the concepts covered in your course. It will create an adaptive, highly personalized study plan to stimulate and measure your learning. Log in to take advantage of this powerful study aid, and to access quizzes and other valuable course-related material.

Externalities, Environmental Policy, and Public Goods

Chapter Outline and Learning Objectives

Henry Stockton/Shutterstock

Can Government Policies Help Protect the Environment?

Pollution is a part of life. Consumers create air pollution by burning gasoline to power their cars and natural gas to heat their homes. Firms create air pollution when they produce plastics, use pesticides, or refine raw materials. Governments create pollution when they burn fossil fuels to generate electricity.

Government policies to reduce pollution have proven to be controversial. In December 2011, the federal government of Canada announced that it was withdrawing from the Kyoto Protocol, an agreement between countries that required rich countries to reduce their emissions of carbon dioxide (a greenhouse gas). Canada was to reduce its emissions to 6 percent below 1990 levels. While some countries have stuck with the Kyoto Protocol and a few have met their targets, the U.S. has not ratified the agreement and China was exempted from reducing its emissions as a developing country. The move to withdraw from the agreement had both supporters and critics.

Despite the fact that the federal government decided not to pursue policies to reduce emissions of greenhouse gases through the Kyoto Protocol, provinces can still pursue their own environmental policies. British Columbia has done exactly that. On July 1, 2008, the province introduced a tax on fossil fuels in order to reduce the emissions of carbon dioxide. On July 1, 2012, the final planned increase in the tax took effect, so that drivers in B.C. pay an extra 7 cents per litre for gasoline.

By requiring consumers in B.C. to pay more for gas, the provincial government hopes to make the costs of burning fossil fuels closer to the actual costs—including climate changing pollution. As we will see in this chapter, economic analysis can play a significant role in evaluating the effects of environmental policies.

AN INSIDE LOOK on **page 150** discusses arguments for and against such carbon tax in British Columbia.

Economics in Your Life

What's the "Best" Level of Pollution?

Policymakers debate alternative approaches for achieving the goal of reducing carbon dioxide emissions. But how do we know the "best" level of carbon emissions? If carbon dioxide emissions hurt the environment, should the government take action to eliminate them completely? As you read the chapter, see if you can answer these questions. You can check your answers against those we provide on page 148 at the end of this chapter.

Externality A benefit or cost that affects someone who is not directly involved in the production or consumption of a good or service.

Pollution is just one example of an *externality*. An **externality** is a benefit or cost that affects someone who is not directly involved in the production or consumption of a good or service. In the case of air pollution, there is a *negative externality* because, for example, people with asthma may bear a cost even though they were not involved in the buying or selling of the electricity that caused the pollution. *Positive externalities* are also possible. For instance, medical research can provide a positive externality because people who are not directly involved in producing it or paying for it can benefit. A competitive market usually does a good job of producing the economically efficient amount of a good or service. This may not be true, though, if there is an externality in the market. When there is a negative externality, the market may produce a quantity of the good that is greater than the efficient amount. When there is a positive externality, the market may produce a quantity that is less than the efficient amount. In Chapter 4, we saw that government interventions in the economy—such as price floors on agricultural products or price ceilings on rents—can reduce economic efficiency. But when there are externalities, government intervention may actually increase economic efficiency and enhance the well-being of society. The way in which government intervenes is important, however. Economists can help policymakers ensure that government programs are as efficient as possible.

In this chapter, we explore how best to deal with the problem of pollution and other externalities. We also look at *public goods*, which are goods that may not be produced at all unless the government produces them.

Identify examples of positive and negative externalities and use graphs to show how externalities affect economic efficiency.

Externalities and Economic Efficiency

When you consume a Tim Hortons coffee, only you benefit, but when you consume a postsecondary education, other people also benefit. Postsecondary-educated people are less likely to commit crimes and, by being better-informed voters, they are more likely to contribute to better government policies. So, although you capture most of the benefits of your postsecondary education, you do not capture all of them.

When you buy a Tim Hortons coffee, the price you pay covers all of Tim Hortons' costs of producing the coffee. When you buy electricity from a utility that burns coal and generates sulphur dioxide–causing acid rain, or contributes to global warming through significant carbon dioxide emissions, the price you pay for the electricity does not cover the cost of the damage caused by the acid rain or global warming.

So, there is a *positive externality* in the production of postsecondary educations because people who do not pay for postsecondary educations will nonetheless benefit from them. There is a *negative externality* in the generation of electricity because, for example, people in different countries might have to deal with more extreme weather due to climate change from carbon dioxide emissions, even though they might not have bought their electricity from the polluting utility.

The Effect of Externalities

Private cost The cost borne by the producer of a good or service.

Social cost The total cost of producing a good or service, including both the private cost and any external cost.

Private benefit The benefit received by the consumer of a good or service.

Social benefit The total benefit from consuming a good or service, including both the private benefit and any external benefit.

Externalities interfere with the *economic efficiency* of a market equilibrium. We saw in Chapter 4 that a competitive market achieves economic efficiency by maximizing the sum of consumer surplus and producer surplus. *But that result holds only if there are no externalities in production or consumption.* An externality causes a difference between the *private cost* of production and the *social cost*, or the *private benefit* from consumption and the *social benefit*. The **private cost** is the cost borne by the producer of a good or service. The **social cost** is the total cost of producing a good or service, and it is equal to the private cost plus any external cost, such as the cost of pollution. Unless there is an externality, the private cost and the social cost are equal. The **private benefit** is the benefit received by the consumer of a good or service. The **social benefit** is the total benefit from consuming a good or service, and it is equal to the private benefit plus any external benefit, such as the benefit

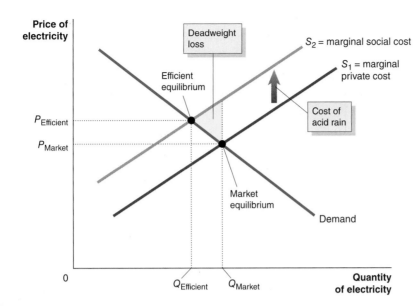

Figure 5.1

The Effect of Pollution on Economic Efficiency

Because utilities do not bear the cost of acid rain, they produce electricity beyond the economically efficient level. Supply curve S_1 represents just the marginal private cost that the utility has to pay. Supply curve S_2 represents the marginal social cost, which includes the costs to those affected by acid rain. The figure shows that if the supply curve were S_2, rather than S_1, market equilibrium would occur at price $P_{Efficient}$ and quantity $Q_{Efficient}$, the economically efficient level of output. But when the supply curve is S_1, the market equilibrium occurs at price P_{Market} and quantity Q_{Market}, where there is a deadweight loss equal to the area of the yellow triangle. Because of the deadweight loss, this equilibrium is not efficient.

to others resulting from your postsecondary education. Unless there is an externality, the private benefit and the social benefit are equal.

How a Negative Externality in Production Reduces Economic Efficiency

Consider how a negative externality in production affects economic efficiency. In Chapters 3 and 4, we assumed that the producer of a good or service must bear all the costs of production. We now know that this is not always true. In producing electricity, private costs are borne by the utility, but some external costs of pollution are borne by people who are not customers of the utility. The social cost of producing electricity is the sum of the private cost plus the external cost. Figure 5.1 shows the effect on the market for electricity of a negative externality in production.

S_1 is the market supply curve and represents only the private costs that utilities have to bear in generating electricity. As we saw in Chapter 4, firms will supply an additional unit of a good or service only if they receive a price equal to (or greater than) the additional cost of producing that unit, so a supply curve represents the *marginal cost* of producing a good or service. If utilities also had to bear the cost of pollution, the supply curve would be S_2, which represents the true marginal social cost of generating electricity. The equilibrium with price $P_{Efficient}$ and quantity $Q_{Efficient}$ is efficient. The equilibrium with price P_{Market} and quantity Q_{Market} is not efficient. To see why, remember from Chapter 4 that an equilibrium is economically efficient if economic surplus—which is the sum of consumer surplus plus producer surplus—is at a maximum. When economic surplus is at a maximum, the net benefit to society from the production of the good or service is at a maximum. With an equilibrium quantity of $Q_{Efficient}$, economic surplus is at a maximum, so this equilibrium is efficient. But with an equilibrium quantity of Q_{Market}, economic surplus is reduced by the deadweight loss, shown in Figure 5.1 by the yellow triangle, and the equilibrium is not efficient. The deadweight loss occurs because the supply curve is above the demand curve for the production of the units of electricity between $Q_{Efficient}$ and Q_{Market}. That is, the additional cost—including the external cost—of producing these units is greater than the marginal benefit to consumers, as represented by the demand curve. In other words, because of the cost of the pollution, economic efficiency would be improved if less electricity were produced.

We can conclude the following: *When there is a negative externality in producing a good or service, too much of the good or service will be produced at market equilibrium.*

How a Positive Externality in Consumption Reduces Economic Efficiency

We have seen that a negative externality interferes with achieving economic efficiency. The same holds true for a positive externality. In Chapters 3 and 4, we assumed that the

Figure 5.2

The Effect of a Positive Externality on Economic Efficiency

People who do not get a postsecondary education can still benefit from them. As a result, the marginal social benefit from a postsecondary education is greater than the marginal private benefit to postsecondary students. Because only the marginal private benefit is represented in the market demand curve D_1, the number of people with postsecondary education (quantity produced), Q_{Market}, is too low. If the market demand curve were D_2 instead of D_1, the number of people with postsecondary education would be $Q_{Efficient}$, which is the efficient level. At the market equilibrium of Q_{Market}, there is a deadweight loss equal to the area of the yellow triangle.

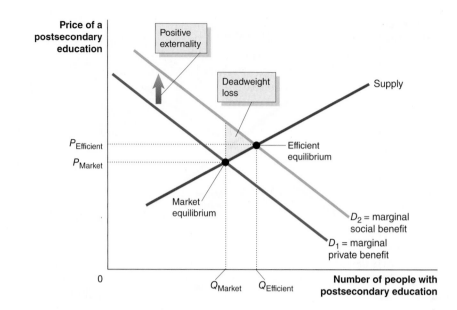

demand curve represents all the benefits that come from consuming a good. But we have seen that a postsecondary education generates benefits that are not captured by the student receiving the education and so are not included in the market demand curve for postsecondary education. Figure 5.2 shows the effect of a positive externality in consumption on the market for postsecondary education.

If students receiving a postsecondary education could capture all its benefits, the demand curve would be D_2, which represents the marginal social benefits. The actual demand curve is D_1, however, which represents only the marginal private benefits received by students. The efficient equilibrium would come at price $P_{Efficient}$ and quantity $Q_{Efficient}$. At this equilibrium, economic surplus is maximized. The market equilibrium, at price P_{Market} and quantity Q_{Market}, will not be efficient because the demand curve is above the supply curve for production of the units between Q_{Market} and $Q_{Efficient}$. That is, the marginal benefit—including the external benefit—for producing these units is greater than the marginal cost. As a result, there is a deadweight loss equal to the area of the yellow triangle. Because of the positive externality, economic efficiency would be improved if more postsecondary educations were produced. We can conclude the following: *When there is a positive externality in consuming a good or service, too little of the good or service will be produced at market equilibrium.*

Externalities and Market Failure

We have seen that because of externalities, the efficient level of output may not occur in either the market for electricity or the market for postsecondary educations. These are examples of **market failure**: situations in which the market fails to produce the efficient level of output. Later, we will discuss possible solutions to problems of externalities. But first we need to consider why externalities occur.

What Causes Externalities?

We saw in Chapter 2 that governments need to guarantee *property rights* in order for a market system to function well. **Property rights** refers to the rights individuals or businesses have to the exclusive use of their property, including the right to buy or sell it. Property can be tangible, physical property, such as a store or factory. Property can also be intangible, such as the right to an idea. Most of the time, the Canadian government and the governments of other high-income countries do a good job of enforcing property rights, but in certain situations, property rights do not exist or cannot be legally enforced.

Market failure A situation in which the market fails to produce the efficient level of output.

Property rights The rights individuals or businesses have to the exclusive use of their property, including the right to buy or sell it.

Consider the following situation: Lee owns land that includes a lake. A paper company wants to lease some of Lee's land to build a paper mill. The paper mill will discharge pollutants into Lee's lake. Because Lee owns the lake, he can charge the paper company the cost of cleaning up the pollutants. The result is that the cost of the pollution is a private cost to the paper company and is included in the price of the paper it sells. There is no externality, the efficient level of paper is produced, and there is no market failure.

Now suppose that the paper company builds its paper mill on privately owned land on the banks of a lake with poorly defined or enforced property rights. In the absence of any government regulations, the company will be free to discharge pollutants into the lake. The cost of the pollution will be external to the company because it doesn't have to pay the cost of cleaning it up. More than the economically efficient level of paper will be produced, and a market failure will occur. Or, suppose that Lee owns the lake, but the pollution is caused by acid rain generated by an electric utility hundreds of miles away. The law does not allow Lee to charge the electric utility for the damage caused by the acid rain. Even though someone is damaging Lee's property, the law does not allow him to enforce his property rights in this situation. Once again, there is an externality, and the market failure will result in an insufficient level of post-secondary education being acquired.

Similarly, if you buy a house, the government will protect your right to exclusive use of that house. No one else can use the house without your permission. Because of your property rights in the house, your private benefit from the house and the social benefit are the same. When you pay for a postsecondary education, however, other people are, in effect, able to benefit from your postsecondary education. You have no property right that will enable you to prevent them from benefiting or to charge them for the benefits they receive. As a result, there is a positive externality, and the market failure will result in too few postsecondary educations being supplied.

We can conclude the following: *Externalities and market failures result from incomplete property rights or from the difficulty of enforcing property rights in certain situations.*

Private Solutions to Externalities: The Coase Theorem

5.2 LEARNING OBJECTIVE

Discuss the Coase theorem and explain how private bargaining can lead to economic efficiency in a market with an externality.

As noted at the beginning of this chapter, government intervention may actually increase economic efficiency and enhance the well-being of society when externalities are present. It is also possible, however, for people to find private solutions to the problem of externalities.

Can the market cure market failure? In an influential article written in 1960, Ronald Coase, winner of the 1991 Nobel Prize in Economics, argued that under some circumstances, private solutions to the problem of externalities will occur. To understand Coase's argument, it is important to recognize that completely eliminating an externality usually is not economically efficient. Consider pollution, for example. There is, in fact, an *economically efficient level of pollution reduction*. At first, this seems paradoxical. Pollution is bad, and you might think the efficient amount of a bad thing is zero. But it isn't zero.

The Economically Efficient Level of Pollution Reduction

Chapter 1 introduced the important idea that the optimal decision is to continue any activity up to the point where the marginal benefit equals the marginal cost. This applies to reducing pollution just as much as it does to other activities. Sulphur dioxide emissions, produced particularly by coal-fired electricity generating stations, contribute to smog and acid rain. As sulphur dioxide emissions—or any other type of pollution—decline, society benefits: Fewer trees die, fewer buildings are damaged, and fewer people suffer breathing problems. But a key point is that the additional benefit—that is, the *marginal benefit*—received from eliminating another tonne of sulphur dioxide declines as sulphur dioxide emissions are reduced. To see why this is true, consider what happens with no reduction in sulphur dioxide emissions. In this situation, many smoggy days will occur. Even healthy people may experience breathing problems. As sulphur dioxide emissions are reduced, the number of smoggy days will fall, and healthy people will no longer experience breathing problems. Eventually, if emissions of sulphur dioxide fall to low levels, even people with asthma will no longer be affected. Further reductions in sulphur dioxide will have little additional benefit. The same will be true of the other benefits from reducing sulphur dioxide emissions: As the reductions increase, the additional benefits from fewer buildings and trees being damaged and lakes polluted will decline.

Making
the
Connection

The Montreal Protocol: Reducing Your Chances of Getting Skin Cancer

Earth is surrounded by a layer of ozone (a specific molecule of oxygen, O_3), which prevents most of the sun's ultraviolet light (UV-B) from reaching the surface of the planet. Too much exposure to UV-B has been linked to skin cancer in people and is known to damage plants. In 1979, it was discovered that a number of chemicals—including chlorofluorocarbon (CFC), commonly used in air conditioners, refrigerators, and foam insulation and packaging—were destroying the ozone layer around the Earth. The chlorine released when CFCs reach the upper atmosphere acts as a catalyst that causes ozone molecules to form a more common oxygen molecule (O_2) that does not offer the same UV protection.

While only those involved in the production of CFCs got to decide how much damage was done to the ozone layer, everyone on Earth suffered the consequences. This is clearly a negative externality. After an international meeting held in Montreal in 1987, an agreement was made to eliminate the production of CFCs and other ozone-depleting chemicals. As the graphs show, the Montreal Protocol (in addition to later agreements) and the subsequent individual government policies have led to a drastic reduction in the production of ozone-depleting chemicals, and a reduction in the amount of ozone-depleting chlorine in the atmosphere. The second graph shows the reduction in new skin cancer cases as a result of decreasing the damage to the ozone layer, projected to be about 60 million fewer cases in 2020.

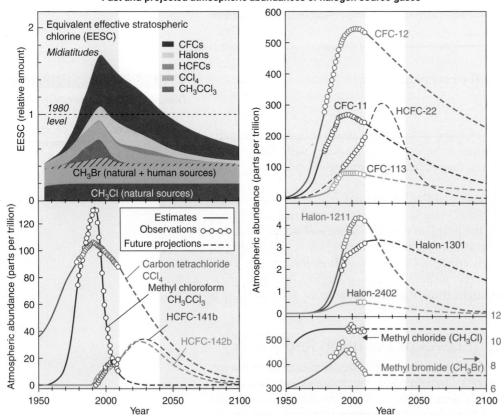

Past and projected atmospheric abundances of halogen source gases

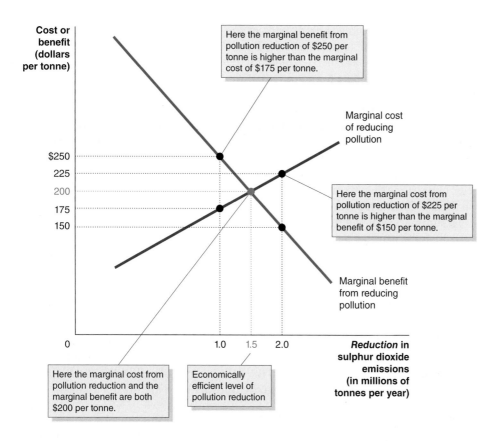

Cost or benefit (dollars per tonne)

Here the marginal benefit from pollution reduction of $250 per tonne is higher than the marginal cost of $175 per tonne.

Marginal cost of reducing pollution

$250
225
200
175
150

Here the marginal cost from pollution reduction of $225 per tonne is higher than the marginal benefit of $150 per tonne.

Marginal benefit from reducing pollution

0   1.0   1.5   2.0   *Reduction* in sulphur dioxide emissions (in millions of tonnes per year)

Here the marginal cost from pollution reduction and the marginal benefit are both $200 per tonne.

Economically efficient level of pollution reduction

Figure 5.3

The Marginal Benefit from Pollution Reduction Should Equal the Marginal Cost

If the reduction of sulphur dioxide emissions is at 1.0 million tonnes per year, the marginal benefit of $250 per tonne is greater than the marginal cost of $175 per tonne. Further reductions in emissions will increase the net benefit to society. If the reduction of sulphur dioxide emissions is at 2.0 million tonnes, the marginal cost of $225 per tonne is greater than the marginal benefit of $150 per tonne. An increase in sulphur dioxide emissions will increase the net benefit to society. Only when the reduction is at 1.5 million tonnes is the marginal benefit equal to the marginal cost. This level is the economically efficient level of pollution reduction.

What about the marginal cost to electric utilities of reducing pollution? To reduce sulphur dioxide emissions, utilities have to switch from burning high-sulphur coal to burning more costly fuel, or they have to install pollution control devices, such as scrubbers. As the level of pollution falls, further reductions become increasingly costly. Reducing emissions to very low levels can require complex and expensive new technologies. For example, Arthur Fraas and Vincent Munley have shown that the marginal cost of removing 97 percent of pollutants from municipal wastewater is more than twice as high as the marginal cost of removing 95 percent.

The *net benefit* to society from reducing pollution is equal to the difference between the benefit of reducing pollution and the cost. To maximize the net benefit to society, sulphur dioxide emissions—or any other type of pollution—should be reduced up to the point where the marginal benefit from another tonne of reduction is equal to the marginal cost. Figure 5.3 illustrates this point.

In Figure 5.3, we measure *reductions* in sulphur dioxide emissions on the horizontal axis. We measure the marginal benefit and marginal cost in dollars from eliminating another tonne of sulphur dioxide emissions on the vertical axis. As reductions in pollution increase, the marginal benefit declines and the marginal cost increases. The economically efficient amount of pollution reduction occurs where the marginal benefit equals the marginal cost. The figure shows that in this case, the economically efficient reduction of sulphur dioxide emissions is 1.5 million tonnes per year. At that level of emission reduction, the marginal benefit and the marginal cost of the last tonne of sulphur dioxide emissions eliminated are both $200 per tonne. Suppose instead that the emissions target was only 1.0 million tonnes. The figure shows that, at that level of reduction, the last tonne of reduction has added $250 to the benefits received by society, but it has added only $175 to the costs of utilities. There has been a net benefit to society from this tonne of pollution reduction of $75. In fact, the figure shows a net benefit to society from pollution reduction for every tonne from 1.0 million to 1.5 million. Only when sulphur dioxide emissions are reduced by 1.5 million tonnes per year will marginal benefit fall enough and marginal cost rise enough that the two are equal.

Now suppose the government had set the target for sulphur dioxide emissions reduction at 2.0 million tonnes per year. Figure 5.3 shows that the marginal benefit at that level of reduction has fallen to only $150 per tonne and the marginal cost has risen to $225 per tonne. The last tonne of reduction has actually *reduced* the net benefit to society by $75 per tonne. In fact, every tonne of reduction beyond 1.5 million reduces the net benefit to society.

Canada and the U.S. agreed in 1991 to reduce their emissions of sulphur dioxide and nitrogen oxides, in an effort to eliminate the negative externalities of acid rain. The Canadian government now imposes a cap on sulphur dioxide emissions of 3.2 million tonnes per year. The cap represents a reduction of 1.5 million tonnes. For the sake of simplicity, let's assume that 3.2 million tonnes is the economically efficient level of emissions, even though Canadian producers now emit much less sulphur dioxide than the cap.

To summarize: If the marginal benefit of reducing sulphur dioxide emissions is greater than the marginal cost, further reductions will make society better off. But if the marginal cost of reducing sulphur dioxide emissions is greater than the marginal benefit, reducing sulphur dioxide emissions will actually make society worse off.

Data from Canada–United States Air Quality Agreement Progress Report 2010, http://www.ec.gc.ca/Publications/4B98B185-7523-4CFF-90F2-5688EBA89E4A%5CCanadaUnitedStatesAirQualityAgreementProgressReport2010.pdf

The Basis for Private Solutions to Externalities

In arguing that private solutions to the problem of externalities were possible, Ronald Coase emphasized that when more than the optimal level of pollution is occurring, the benefits from reducing the pollution to the optimal level are greater than the costs. Figure 5.4 illustrates this point.

The marginal benefit curve shows the additional benefit from each reduction in a tonne of sulphur dioxide emissions. The area under the marginal benefit curve between

Figure 5.4

The Benefits of Reducing Pollution to the Optimal Level Are Greater Than the Costs

Increasing the reduction in sulphur dioxide emissions from 1.0 million tonnes to 1.5 million tonnes results in total benefits equal to the sum of the areas *A* and *B* under the marginal benefits curve. The total cost of this decrease in pollution is equal to the area *B* under the marginal cost curve. The total benefits are greater than the total costs by an amount equal to the area of triangle *A*. Because the total benefits from reducing pollution are greater than the total costs, it's possible for those receiving the benefits to arrive at a private agreement with polluters to pay them to reduce pollution.

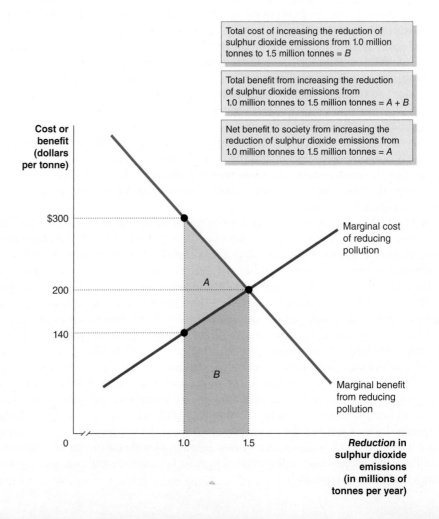

Don't Let This Happen to You

Remember That It's the *Net* Benefit That Counts

Why would we not want to *completely* eliminate anything unpleasant? As long as any person suffers any unpleasant consequences from air pollution, the marginal benefit of reducing air pollution will be positive. So, removing every particle of air pollution results in the largest *total* benefit to society. But removing every particle of air pollution is not optimal for the same reason that it is not optimal to remove every particle of dirt or dust from a home when cleaning it. The cost of cleaning your house is not just the price of the cleaning products but also the opportunity cost of your time. The more time you devote to cleaning your house, the less time you have for other activities.

As you devote more and more additional hours to cleaning your house, the alternative activities you have to give up are likely to increase in value, raising the opportunity cost of cleaning: Cleaning instead of watching TV may not be too costly, but cleaning instead of eating any meals or getting any sleep is very costly. Optimally, you should eliminate dirt in your home up to the point where the marginal benefit of the last dirt removed equals the marginal cost of removing it. Society should take the same approach to air pollution. The result is the largest *net* benefit to society.

MyEconLab
Your Turn: Test your understanding by doing related problem 2.2 on page 153 at the end of this chapter.

---

the two emission levels is the *total* benefit received from reducing emissions from one level to another. For instance, in Figure 5.4, the total benefit from increasing the reduction in sulphur dioxide emissions from 1.0 million tonnes to 1.5 million tonnes is the sum of the areas of A and B. The marginal cost curve shows the additional cost from each reduction in a tonne of emissions. The *total* cost of reducing emissions from one level to another is the area under the marginal cost curve between the two emissions levels. The total cost from increasing the reduction in emissions from 1.0 million tonnes to 1.5 million tonnes is the area B. The net benefit from reducing emissions is the difference between the total cost and the total benefit, which is equal to the area of triangle A.

In Figure 5.4, the benefits from further reductions in sulphur dioxide emissions are much greater than the costs. In the appendix to Chapter 1, we reviewed the formula for calculating the area of a triangle, which is ½ × Base × Height, and the formula for the area of a rectangle, which is Base × Height. Using these formulas, we can calculate the value of the total benefits from the reduction in emissions and the value of the total costs. The value of the benefits (A + B) is $125 million. The value of the costs (B) is $85 million. If the people who would benefit from a reduction in pollution could get together, they could offer to pay the electric utilities $85 million to reduce the pollution to the optimal level. After making the payment, they would still be left with a net benefit of $40 million. In other words, a private agreement to reduce pollution to the optimal level is possible, without any government intervention.

| Making the Connection | **The Fable of the Bees** |

Apple trees must be pollinated by bees in order to bear fruit. Bees need the nectar from apple trees (or other plants) to produce honey. In an important article published in the early 1950s, the British economist James Meade, winner of the 1977 Nobel Prize in Economics, argued that there were positive externalities in both apple growing and beekeeping. The more apple trees growers planted, the more honey would be produced in the hives of local beekeepers. And the more hives beekeepers kept, the larger the apple crops in neighbouring apple orchards. Meade assumed that beekeepers were not being compensated by apple growers for the pollination services they were providing to apple growers and that apple growers were not being compensated by beekeepers for the use of their nectar in honey making. Therefore, he concluded that unless the government intervened, the market would not supply enough apple trees and beehives.

Steven Cheung showed, however, that government intervention was not necessary because beekeepers and apple growers had long since arrived at private agreements.

Some farmers and greenhouses make private agreements with beekeepers to arrive at an economically efficient outcome.

In fact, there is a thriving industry raising bees either for sale or for rent. CanAgro Produce Ltd., which runs greenhouses in B.C., uses several hundred colonies of 60 bumblebees at a time. The colonies are replaced every two or three months at a cost of $275. These bumblebees are estimated to add roughly $6 million in value to the hothouse tomato crop every year.

Farmers across the country also make heavy use of bees for pollination, utilizing approximately 600,000 honeybee hives a year. Hives rent for an average $120 each. With a cost of $90 to pollinate blueberries and up to $150 to pollinate canola, in helping pollinate more than 45 different crops honeybees add around $2 billion to the value of Canadian agricultural produce every year.

Based on J. E. Meade, "External Economies and Diseconomies in a Competitive Situation," *Economic Journal*, Vol. 62, March 1952, pp. 54–67; Steven N. S. Cheung, "The Fable of the Bees: An Economic Investigation," *Journal of Law and Economics*, Vol. 16, 1973, pp. 11–33; "Vitamin Bee: A New Attempt to Save the Most Vital Workers in the Orchards," *Economist*, March 4, 2010; Garry Hamilton, "Bees for Hire," *Canadian Geographic*, July/August 2000, accessed at http://www.canadiangeographic.ca/wildlife-nature/articles/pdfs/honeybee-bees-for-hire.pdf; and Canadian Honey Council http://www.honeycouncil.ca/honey_industry_overview.php.

MyEconLab   **Your Turn:** Test your understanding by doing related problem 2.5 on page 153 at the end of this chapter.

Do Property Rights Matter?

In discussing the bargaining between the electric utilities and the people suffering the effects of the utilities' pollution, we assumed that the electric utilities were not legally liable for the damage they were causing. In other words, the victims of pollution could not legally enforce the right of their property not to be damaged, so they would have to pay the utilities to reduce the pollution. But would it make any difference if the utilities were legally liable for the damages? Surprisingly, as Coase was the first to point out, it does not matter for the amount of pollution reduction. The only difference would be that now the electric utilities would have to pay the victims of pollution for the right to pollute, rather than the victims having to pay the utilities to reduce pollution. Because the marginal benefits and marginal costs of pollution reduction would not change, the bargaining should still result in the efficient level of pollution reduction—in this case, 1.5 million tonnes.

In the absence of the utilities being legally liable, the victims of pollution have an incentive to pay the utilities to reduce pollution up to the point where the marginal benefit of the last tonne of reduction is equal to the marginal cost. If the utilities are legally liable, they have an incentive to pay the victims of pollution to allow them to pollute up to the same point.

The Problem of Transactions Costs

Transactions costs The costs in time and other resources that parties incur in the process of agreeing to and carrying out an exchange of goods or services.

Unfortunately, there are frequently practical difficulties that interfere with a private solution to the problem of externalities. In cases of pollution, for example, there are often both many polluters and many people suffering from the negative effects of pollution. Bringing together all those suffering from pollution with all those causing the pollution and negotiating an agreement often fails due to *transactions costs*. **Transactions costs** are the costs in time and other resources that parties incur in the process of agreeing to and carrying out an exchange of goods or services. In this case, the transactions costs would include the time and other costs of negotiating an agreement, drawing up a binding contract, purchasing insurance, and monitoring the agreement. Unfortunately, when many people are involved, the transactions costs are often higher than the net benefits from reducing the externality. In that case, the cost of transacting ends up exceeding the gain from the transaction, and a private solution to an externality problem is not feasible.

The Coase Theorem

Coase's argument that private solutions to the problem of externalities are possible is summed up in the **Coase theorem**: *If transactions costs are low, private bargaining will result in an efficient solution to the problem of externalities.* We have seen the basis for the Coase theorem in the preceding example of pollution by electric utilities: Because the benefits from reducing an externality are often greater than the costs, private bargaining can lead to an efficient outcome. But we have also seen that this outcome will occur only if transactions costs are low, and in the case of pollution, they usually are not. In general, private bargaining is most likely to reach an efficient outcome if the number of parties bargaining is small.

In practice, we must add a couple of other qualifications to the Coase theorem. In addition to low transactions costs, private solutions to the problem of externalities will occur only if all parties to the agreement have full information about the costs and benefits associated with the externality, and all parties must be willing to accept a reasonable agreement. For example, if those suffering from the effects of pollution do not have information on the costs of reducing pollution, it is unlikely that the parties can reach an agreement. Unreasonable demands can also hinder an agreement. For instance, in the example of pollution by electric utilities, we saw that the total benefit of reducing sulphur dioxide emissions was $125 million. Even if transactions costs are very low, if the utilities insist on being paid more than $125 million to reduce emissions, no agreement will be reached because the amount paid exceeds the value of the reduction to those suffering from the emissions.

> **Coase theorem** The argument of economist Ronald Coase that if transactions costs are low, private bargaining will result in an efficient solution to the problem of externalities.

Government Policies to Deal with Externalities

When private solutions to externalities are not feasible, how should the government intervene? The first economist to analyze market failure systematically was A. C. Pigou, a British economist. Pigou argued that to deal with a negative externality in production, the government should impose a tax equal to the cost of the externality. The effect of such a tax is shown in Figure 5.5, which reproduces the negative externality from acid rain shown in Figure 5.1 on page 127.

By imposing a tax on the production of electricity equal to the cost of acid rain, the government will cause electric utilities to *internalize* the externality. As a consequence, the cost of the acid rain will become a private cost borne by the utilities, and the supply curve for electricity will shift from S_1 to S_2. The result will be a decrease in the equilibrium output of electricity from Q_{Market} to the efficient level, $Q_{\text{Efficient}}$. The price

> **5.3 LEARNING OBJECTIVE**
>
> Analyze government policies to achieve economic efficiency in a market with an externality.

Figure 5.5

When There Is a Negative Externality, a Tax Can Lead to the Efficient Level of Output

Because utilities do not bear the cost of acid rain, they produce electricity beyond the economically efficient level. If the government imposes a tax equal to the cost of acid rain, the utilities will internalize the externality. As a consequence, the supply curve will shift up, from S_1 to S_2. The market equilibrium quantity changes from Q_{Market}, where an inefficiently high level of electricity is produced, to $Q_{\text{Efficient}}$, the economically efficient equilibrium quantity. The price of electricity will rise from P_{Market}—which does not include the cost of acid rain—to $P_{\text{Efficient}}$—which does include the cost. Consumers pay the price $P_{\text{Efficient}}$, while producers receive a price P, which is equal to $P_{\text{Efficient}}$ minus the amount of the tax.

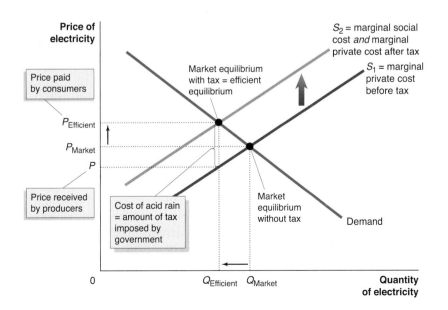

Solved Problem **5.3**

Using a Tax to Deal with a Negative Externality

Companies that produce toilet paper bleach the paper to make it white. Some paper plants discharge the bleach into rivers and lakes, causing substantial environmental damage. Suppose the following graph illustrates the situation in the toilet paper market.

Explain how the federal government can use a tax on toilet paper to bring about the efficient level of production. What should the value of the tax be?

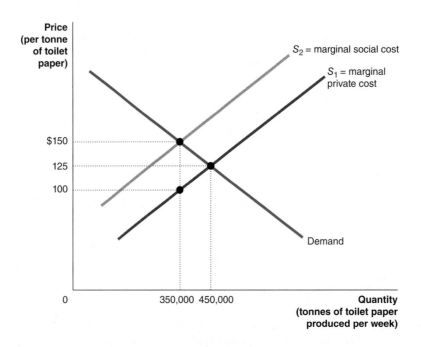

Solving the Problem

Step 1: Review the chapter material. This problem is about the government using a tax to deal with a negative externality in production, so you may want to review the section "Government Policies to Deal with Externalities."

Step 2: Use the information from the graph to determine the necessary tax. The efficient level of toilet paper production will occur where the marginal social benefit from consuming toilet paper, as represented by the demand curve, is equal to the marginal social cost of production. The graph shows that this will occur at a price of $150 per tonne and production of 350,000 tonnes. In the absence of government intervention, the price will be $125 per tonne, and production will be 450,000 tonnes. It is tempting—but incorrect!—to think that the government could bring about the efficient level of production by imposing a per-tonne tax equal to the difference between the price when production is at its optimal level and the current market price. But this would be a tax of only $25. The graph shows that at the optimal level of production, the difference between the marginal private cost and the marginal social cost is $50. Therefore, a tax of $50 per tonne is required to shift the supply curve up from S_1 to S_2.

MyEconLab **Your Turn:** For more practice, do related problem 3.3 on page 154 at the end of this chapter.

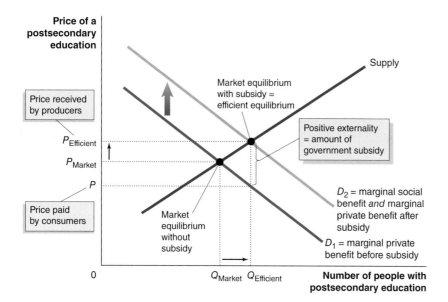

Figure 5.6

When There Is a Positive Externality, a Subsidy Can Bring About the Efficient Level of Output

People who do not consume postsecondary educations can benefit from them. As a result, the social benefit from a postsecondary education is greater than the private benefit to postsecondary students. If the government pays a subsidy equal to the external benefit, students will internalize the externality. The subsidy will cause the demand curve to shift up, from D_1 to D_2. As a result, the market equilibrium quantity will shift from Q_{Market}, where an inefficiently low level of postsecondary educations is supplied, to $Q_{Efficient}$, the economically efficient equilibrium quantity.

Producers receive the price $P_{Efficient}$, while consumers pay a price P, which is equal to $P_{Efficient}$ minus the amount of the subsidy.

consumers pay for electricity will rise from P_{Market}—which does not include the cost of acid rain—to $P_{Efficient}$—which does include the cost. Producers will receive a price P, which is equal to $P_{Efficient}$ minus the amount of the tax.

Pigou also argued that the government can deal with a positive externality in consumption by giving consumers a subsidy, or payment, equal to the value of the externality. The effect of the subsidy is shown in Figure 5.6, which reproduces the positive externality from postsecondary education shown in Figure 5.2 on page 128.

By paying postsecondary students a subsidy equal to the external benefit from a postsecondary education, the government will cause students to *internalize* the externality. That is, the external benefit from a postsecondary education will become a private benefit received by postsecondary students, and the demand curve for postsecondary educations will shift from D_1 to D_2. The equilibrium number of postsecondary educations supplied will increase from Q_{Market} to the efficient level, $Q_{Efficient}$. Producers receive the price $P_{Efficient}$, while consumers pay a price P, which is equal to $P_{Efficient}$ minus the amount of the subsidy. In fact, the government does heavily subsidize postsecondary educations. Most of the universities and colleges in Canada receive approximately half of their funding from provincial governments. The provincial and federal governments also provide students with low-interest loans that subsidize postsecondary education. The economic justification for these subsidies is that postsecondary education provides an external benefit to society.

Because Pigou was the first economist to propose using government taxes and subsidies to deal with externalities, they are sometimes referred to as **Pigovian taxes and subsidies**. Note that a Pigovian tax eliminates deadweight loss and improves economic efficiency. This situation is the opposite of the one we saw in Chapter 4, in which we discussed how most taxes reduce consumer surplus and producer surplus and create a deadweight loss. In fact, one reason that economists support Pigovian taxes as a way to deal with negative externalities is that the government can use the revenues raised by Pigovian taxes to lower other taxes that reduce economic efficiency. For instance, the province of British Columbia has enacted a Pigovian tax on emissions of carbon dioxide and uses the revenue raised to reduce personal income taxes.

Pigovian taxes and subsidies
Government taxes and subsidies intended to bring about an efficient level of output in the presence of externalities.

Making the Connection | Should the Government Tax Soft Drinks?

Typically, governments use Pigovian taxes to deal with negative externalities in *production*. Governments also impose taxes—sometimes called "sin taxes"—on products such as cigarettes and liquor. Some policymakers have argued that these products generate negative externalities in

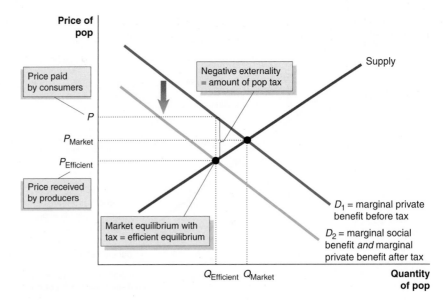

consumption, so a tax on them can increase economic efficiency. Recently, nutrition advocates have argued that governments should tax sweetened soft drinks, on the grounds that these soft drinks cause a negative externality by raising medical costs. Just as governments can deal with a positive externality in consumption by giving consumers a subsidy, they can deal with a negative externality by imposing a tax. The effect of a tax on pop is shown in the figure. By imposing a tax on pop, the government will cause consumers to internalize the externality. That is, the external cost to drinking pop will become a private cost paid by consumers. Because consumers now have to pay a tax on pop, at every quantity they are willing to pay less than they would have without the tax, so the demand curve for pop will shift down by the amount of the tax, from D_1 to D_2. The equilibrium quantity of soft drinks consumed will decrease from Q_{Market} to the efficient level, $Q_{Efficient}$. (Note that as we saw in Chapter 4, pages 110–113, we get the same result whether the government imposes a tax on the buyers of a good or on the sellers.)

But do people actually cause a negative externality by drinking sugary pop? It might seem that they don't because pop drinkers bear the costs of any health problems they experience. However, because provincial governments pay for health care expenses by taxing income, the increased medical costs associated with consuming a lot of pop (such as obesity, for example) are an externality to everyone who pays income tax or needs health care.

There is a complication to this conclusion, however: People who are obese tend to die early. This tragic outcome means that the obese may have been paying taxes to help pay for social benefits that they will never receive. They may also have made payments into company and public employee pension plans and purchased long-term care insurance, but they may not have lived long enough to receive many pension payments or to have spent time in a nursing home. So, there are offsetting effects: While alive, obese people may impose costs on others who bear the expense of their higher medical costs, but because they are likely to die early, they provide a financial gain to recipients of publicly funded health care, company and public employee pension plans, and purchasers of long-term care insurance. Studies of obesity have arrived at somewhat conflicting results: A study of obesity in the Netherlands found that the cost savings from premature death offset the additional lifetime medical costs of obese people. But another study on U.S. data found that obesity did lead to a net increase in lifetime medical costs, even taking into account the shorter average life spans of obese people.

There may also be costs to obesity beyond additional medical costs. Airlines have noted that they spend more on fuel costs because of the increasing weight of passengers.

In the end, economists and policymakers continue to debate whether the government should use taxes to deal with negative externalities in consumption.

Based on David Leonhardt, "The Battle over Taxing Soda," *New York Times*, May 18, 2010; Pieter H. M. van Baal, et al., "Lifetime Medical Costs of Obesity: Prevention No Cure for Increasing Health Expenditure," *PLoS Medicine*, Vol. 5, No. 2, February 2008, pp. 242–249; Pierre-Carl Michaud, "Understanding the Economic Consequences of Shifting Trends in Population Health," National Bureau of Economic Research Working Paper 15231, August 2009; and "Feds Say Obesity Epidemic Hurts Airlines by Increasing Fuel Costs," *Associated Press*, November 5, 2004.

Your Turn: Test your understanding by doing related problem 3.5 on page 154 at the end of this chapter.

MyEconLab

Command-and-Control versus Market-Based Approaches

Although the federal government has sometimes used taxes and subsidies to deal with externalities, in dealing with pollution it has traditionally used a *command-and-control approach* with firms that pollute. A **command-and-control approach** to reducing pollution involves the government imposing quantitative limits on the amount of pollution firms are allowed to generate, or requiring firms to install specific pollution-control devices.

For example, the federal government has imposed on coal-fired power generating stations new pollution standards that are expected to reduce carbon dioxide emissions by 214 megatonnes over 21 years. Many Canadian policies to reduce pollution take the form of command-and-control regulations, and generally identify a specific technology to be used by firms or prescribe a maximum level of emissions for any one facility.

An alternative would be to tax firms based on the amount of carbon dioxide they emit. By charging firms a tax, the government makes emitting carbon dioxide (or any other pollutant) into the atmosphere costly. As firms want to avoid costs, they will pollute less. There are difficulties with the taxation approach as well. It increases costs for all firms, and governments have no way of knowing how much emissions will fall until well after the tax is implemented.

Command and control and taxation aren't the only possible approaches to reducing emissions; the federal government could have used a market-based approach instead. Under a market-based approach, the government identifies an acceptable level of emissions and issues or sells a number of permits equal to this amount (many people believe that selling the permits is preferable to the government giving them away). Firms can choose to reduce their emissions to match the number of permits they have, they can buy permits from other firms (meaning they reduce their emissions by less), or they can reduce their emissions by more and sell unused permits to other firms.

While Canada doesn't currently take a market-based approach to reducing emissions, other states have employed it quite successfully. The European Union uses a market for carbon dioxide emissions to reduce the amount of the greenhouse gas put into the atmosphere. The U.S. uses a market for sulphur dioxide to reduce acid rain.

The main advantage of the market-based approach over command and control is cost. By allowing different firms to use different technologies and thus emit different amounts of sulphur dioxide, the U.S. government reduced acid rain–causing emissions much more cheaply than was predicted. In 1990, just before the program for reducing emissions was put into place, the Edison Electric Institute estimated that the cost of reducing emissions would be US$7.4 billion by 2010. By 1994, the United States' General Accounting Office estimated that the cost would be less than US$2 billion. In practice, the US$870 million actual cost appears to have been about 90 percent less than the initial estimate.

Are Tradable Emissions Allowances Licences to Pollute?

Some environmentalists have criticized tradable emissions allowances, labelling them "licences to pollute." They argue that just as the government does not issue licences to rob banks or to drive drunk, it should not issue licences to pollute. But this criticism ignores one of the central lessons of economics: Resources are scarce, and trade-offs exist. Resources that are spent on reducing one type of pollution are not available to reduce other types of pollution or for any other use. Because reducing acid rain using

Command-and-control approach
An approach that involves the government imposing quantitative limits on the amount of pollution firms are allowed to emit, or requiring firms to install specific pollution control devices.

tradable emissions allowances has cost utilities in the United States US$870 million, rather than US$7.4 billion, as originally estimated, the United States has saved more than US$6.5 billion per year.

Making
the
Connection

Can a Cap-and-Trade System Reduce Global Warming?

In the past 35 years, the global surface temperature has increased about 0.40 degree Centigrade compared with the average for the period between 1951 and 1980. The following graph shows changes in temperature over the years since 1880.

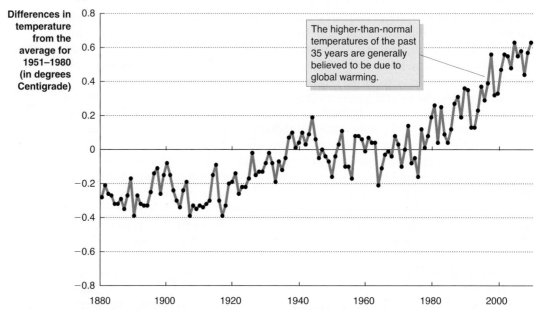

From NASA, Goddard Institute for Space Studies, http://data.giss.nasa.gov/gistemp/graphs/.

Over the centuries, global temperatures have gone through many long periods of warming and cooling. Nevertheless, many scientists are convinced that the recent warming trend is not part of the natural fluctuations in temperature but is instead primarily due to the burning of fossil fuels, such as coal, natural gas, and petroleum. Burning these fuels releases carbon dioxide, which accumulates in the atmosphere as a "greenhouse gas." Greenhouse gases cause some of the heat released from Earth to be reflected back, increasing temperatures. Annual emissions of carbon dioxide have increased from about 50 million tonnes of carbon in 1850 to 1,600 million tonnes in 1950 and to nearly 8,500 million tonnes in 2008.

If greenhouse gases continue to accumulate in the atmosphere, according to some estimates global temperatures could increase by 1.5 degrees Celsius or more during the next 100 years. Such an increase in temperature could lead to significant changes in climate, which might result in more hurricanes and other violent weather conditions, disrupt farming in many parts of the world, and raise sea levels, causing flooding in coastal areas.

Although most economists and policymakers agree that emitting carbon dioxide results in a significant negative externality, there has been a long and heated debate over which policies should be adopted. Part of the debate arises from disagreements over how rapidly global warming is likely to occur and what the economic cost will be. In addition, carbon dioxide emissions are a global problem; sharp reductions in carbon dioxide emissions only in Canada, the United States, and Europe, for instance, would not be enough to eliminate global warming. But coordinating policy across countries has proven difficult. Finally, policymakers and economists debate the relative effectiveness of different policies.

Several approaches to reducing carbon dioxide emissions have been used. As mentioned earlier, British Columbia has introduced a Pigovian tax on carbon dioxide emissions. Cap-and-trade policies, similar to the one used successfully in the United States to reduce sulphur dioxide emissions, have also been tried. In 2005, 24 countries in the European Union set up a cap-and-trade system called the European Union Emissions Trading Scheme. Under this program, each country issues emission allowances that can be freely traded over time. Although carbon dioxide emissions rose slightly during the first few years of the plan, over time, as the number of emission allowances is reduced, emissions should decline.

The debate over which policies to use in reducing carbon dioxide emissions will likely continue for many years.

Based on Gabriel Nelson, "Wrapped Up in Politics, Granddaddy of Cap-and-Trade Plans Has an Uncertain Future," *New York Times*, July 19, 2011; Juliet Eilperin, "New Jersey Gov. Chris Christie Pulls Out of Greenhouse Gas Effort," *Washington Post*, May 26, 2011; "Cap-and-Trade's Last Hurrah," *Economist*, May 18, 2010; and Tom Boden, Gregg Marland, and Bob Andres, "Global Carbon Dioxide Emissions from Fossil-Fuel Burning, Cement Manufacture, and Gas Flaring: 1751-2008," Carbon Dioxide Information Analysis Center, Oak Ridge National Laboratory, June 10, 2011.

Your Turn: Test your understanding by doing related problem 3.5 on page 154 at the end of this chapter.

MyEconLab

Four Categories of Goods

5.4 LEARNING OBJECTIVE

Explain how goods can be categorized on the basis of whether they are rival or excludable and use graphs to illustrate the efficient quantities of public goods and common resources.

We can explore further the question of when the market is likely to succeed in supplying the efficient quantity of a good by understanding that goods differ on the basis of whether their consumption is *rival* and *excludable*. **Rivalry** occurs when one person's consuming a unit of a good means no one else can consume it. If you consume a Big Mac, for example, no one else can consume it. **Excludability** means that anyone who does not pay for a good cannot consume it. If you don't pay for a Big Mac, McDonald's can exclude you from consuming it. The consumption of a Big Mac is therefore rival and excludable. The consumption of some goods, however, can be either *nonrival* or *nonexcludable*, or *both*. Nonrival means that one person's consumption does not interfere with another person's consumption. Nonexcludable means that it is impossible to exclude others from consuming the good, whether they have paid for it or not. Figure 5.7 shows four possible categories into which goods can fall.

We next consider each of the four categories:

1. *Private goods.* A good that is both rival and excludable is a **private good**. Food, clothing, haircuts, and many other goods and services fall into this category. One person's consuming a unit of these goods precludes other people from consuming that unit, and no one can consume these goods without buying them. Although we didn't state it explicitly, when we analyzed the demand for and supply of goods and services in Chapter 3, we assumed that the goods and services were all private goods.

2. *Public goods.* A **public good** is both nonrival and nonexcludable. Public goods are often, although not always, supplied by a government rather than by private firms. The classic example of a public good is national defence. Your consuming national defence does not interfere with your neighbour's consuming it, so consumption is nonrival. You also cannot be excluded from consuming it, whether you pay for it or not. No private firm would be willing to supply national defence because everyone can consume national defence without paying for it. The behaviour of consumers in this situation is referred to as *free riding*. **Free riding** involves individuals benefiting from a good—in this case, the provision of national defence—without paying for it.

Rivalry The situation that occurs when one person's consuming a unit of a good means no one else can consume it.

Excludability The situation in which anyone who does not pay for a good cannot consume it.

Private good A good that is both rival and excludable.

Public good A good that is both nonrival and nonexcludable.

Free riding Benefiting from a good without paying for it.

Figure 5.7

Four Categories of Goods

	Excludable	Nonexcludable
Rival	**Private Goods** *Examples:* *Big Macs* *Running shoes*	**Common Resources** *Examples:* *Tuna in the ocean* *Public pasture land*
Nonrival	**Quasi-Public Goods** *Examples:* *Cable TV* *Toll road*	**Public Goods** *Examples:* *National defence* *Court system*

Goods and services can be divided into four categories on the basis of whether people can be excluded from consuming them and whether they are rival in consumption. A good or service is rival in consumption if one person consuming a unit of a good means that another person cannot consume that unit.

3. *Quasi-public goods.* Some goods are excludable but not rival. An example is cable television. People who do not pay for cable television do not receive it, but one person's watching it doesn't affect other people's watching it. The same is true of a toll road. Anyone who doesn't pay the toll doesn't get on the road, but one person using the road doesn't interfere with someone else using the road (unless so many people are using the road that it becomes congested). Goods that fall into this category are called *quasi-public goods.*

4. *Common resources.* If a good is rival but not excludable, it is a **common resource**. Forest land in many poor countries is a common resource. If one person cuts down a tree, no one else can use the tree. But if no one has a property right to the forest, no one can be excluded from using it. As we will discuss in more detail later, people often overuse common resources.

Common resource A good that is rival but not excludable.

We discussed the demand for and supply of private goods in Chapter 3. For the remainder of this chapter, we focus on the categories of public goods and common resources. To determine the optimal quantity of a public good, we have to modify the demand and supply analysis of Chapter 3 to take into account that a public good is both nonrival and nonexcludable.

The Demand for a Public Good

We can determine the market demand curve for a good or service by adding up the quantity of the good demanded by each consumer at each price. To keep things simple, let's consider the case of a market with only two consumers. Figure 5.8 shows that the market demand curve for hamburgers depends on the individual demand curves of Jill and Joe.

At a price of $4.00, Jill demands 2 hamburgers per week and Joe demands 4. Adding horizontally, the combination of a price of $4.00 per hamburger and a quantity demanded of 6 hamburgers will be a point on the market demand curve for hamburgers. Similarly, adding horizontally at a price of $1.50, we have a price of $1.50 and a quantity demanded of 11 as another point on the market demand curve. A consumer's demand curve for a good represents the marginal benefit the consumer receives from the good, so when we add together the consumers' demand curves, we have not only the market demand curve but also the marginal social benefit curve for this good, assuming that there is no externality in consumption.

How can we find the demand curve or marginal social benefit curve for a public good? Once again, for simplicity, assume that Jill and Joe are the only consumers. Unlike with a private good, where Jill and Joe can end up consuming different quantities, with

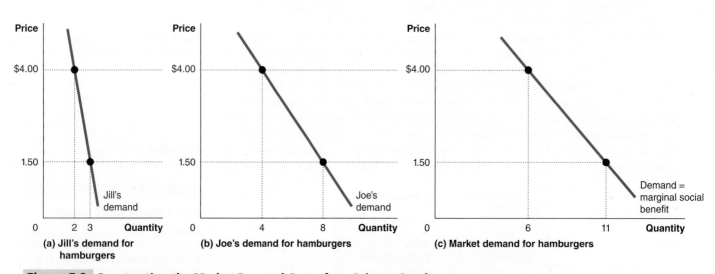

Figure 5.8 Constructing the Market Demand Curve for a Private Good

The market demand curve for private goods is determined by adding horizontally the quantity of the good demanded at each price by each consumer. For instance, in panel (a), Jill demands 2 hamburgers when the price is $4.00, and in panel (b), Joe demands 4 hamburgers when the price is $4.00. So, a quantity of 6 hamburgers and a price of $4.00 is a point on the market demand curve in panel (c).

a public good, they will consume *the same quantity*. Suppose that Jill owns a service station on an isolated rural road, and Joe owns a car dealership next door. These are the only two businesses around for kilometres. Both Jill and Joe are afraid that unless they hire a security guard at night, their businesses may be robbed. Like national defence, the services of a security guard are in this case a public good: Once hired, the guard will be able to protect both businesses, so the good is nonrival. It also will not be possible to exclude either business from being protected, so the good is nonexcludable.

To arrive at a demand curve for a public good, we don't add quantities at each price, as with a private good. Instead, we add the price each consumer is willing to pay for each quantity of the public good. This value represents the total dollar amount consumers as a group would be willing to pay for that quantity of the public good. Put another way, to find the demand curve, or marginal social benefit curve, for a private good, we add the demand curves of individual consumers horizontally; for public goods, we add individual demand curves vertically. Figure 5.9 shows how the marginal social benefit curve for security guard services depends on the individual demand curves of Jill and Joe.

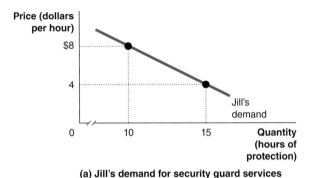

(a) Jill's demand for security guard services

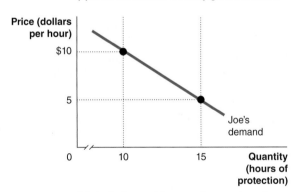

(b) Joe's demand for security guard services

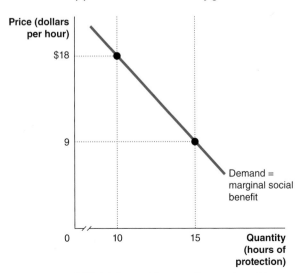

(c) Total demand for security guard services

Figure 5.9

Constructing the Demand Curve for a Public Good

To find the demand curve for a public good, we add up the price at which each consumer is willing to purchase each quantity of the good. In panel (a), Jill is willing to pay $8 per hour for a security guard to provide 10 hours of protection. In panel (b), Joe is willing to pay $10 for that level of protection. Therefore, in panel (c), the price of $18 per hour and the quantity of 10 hours will be a point on the demand curve for security guard services.

The figure shows that Jill is willing to pay $8 per hour for the guard to provide 10 hours of protection per night. Joe would suffer a greater loss from a burglary, so he is willing to pay $10 per hour for the same amount of protection. Adding the dollar amount that each is willing to pay gives us a price of $18 per hour and a quantity of 10 hours as a point on the marginal social benefit curve for security guard services. The figure also shows that because Jill is willing to spend $4 per hour for 15 hours of guard services and Joe is willing to pay $5, a price of $9 per hour and a quantity of 15 hours is another point on the marginal social benefit curve for security guard services.

The Optimal Quantity of a Public Good

We know that to achieve economic efficiency, a good or service should be produced up to the point where the sum of consumer surplus and producer surplus is maximized, or, alternatively, where the marginal social cost equals the marginal social benefit. Therefore, the optimal quantity of security guard services—or any other public good—will occur where the marginal social benefit curve intersects the supply curve. As with private goods, in the absence of an externality in production, the supply curve represents the marginal social cost of supplying the good. Figure 5.10 shows that the optimal quantity of security guard services supplied is 15 hours, at a price of $9 per hour.

Will the market provide the economically efficient quantity of security guard services? One difficulty is that the individual preferences of consumers, as shown by their demand curves, are not revealed in this market. This difficulty does not arise with private goods because consumers must reveal their preferences in order to purchase private goods. If the market price of a hamburger is $4.00, Joe either reveals that he is willing to pay that much by buying it or does without it. In our example, neither Jill nor Joe can be excluded from consuming the services provided by a security guard once either hires one, and, therefore, neither has an incentive to reveal her or his preferences. In this case, though, with only two consumers, it is likely that private bargaining will result in an efficient quantity of the public good. This outcome is not likely for a public good—such as national defence—that is supplied by the government to millions of consumers.

Governments sometimes use *cost–benefit analysis* to determine what quantity of a public good should be supplied. For example, before building a dam on a river, the federal government will attempt to weigh the costs against the benefits. The costs include the opportunity cost of other projects the government cannot carry out if it builds the dam. The benefits include improved flood control or new recreational opportunities on the lake formed by the dam. However, for many public goods, including national defence, the government does not use a formal cost–benefit analysis. Instead, the quantity of national defence supplied is determined by a political process involving

Figure 5.10

The Optimal Quantity of a Public Good

The optimal quantity of a public good is produced where the sum of consumer surplus and producer surplus is maximized, which occurs where the demand curve intersects the supply curve. In this case, the optimal quantity of security guard services is 15 hours, at a price of $9 per hour.

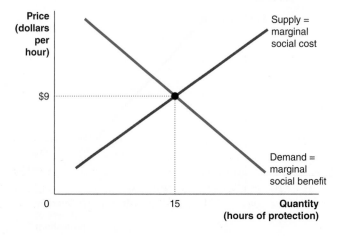

Parliament. Even here, politicians realize that trade-offs are involved: The more resources used for national defence, the fewer resources available for other public goods or for private goods.

Solved Problem **5.4**

Determining the Optimal Level of Public Goods

Suppose, once again, that Jill and Joe run businesses that are next door to each other on an isolated road and both are in need of the services of a security guard. Their demand schedules for security guard services are as follows:

Joe

Price (dollars per hour)	Quantity (hours of protection)
$20	0
18	1
16	2
14	3
12	4
10	5
8	6
6	7
4	8
2	9

Jill

Price (dollars per hour)	Quantity (hours of protection)
$20	1
18	2
16	3
14	4
12	5
10	6
8	7
6	8
4	9
2	10

The supply schedule for security guard services is as follows:

Price (dollars per hour)	Quantity (hours of protection)
$8	1
10	2
12	3
14	4
16	5
18	6
20	7
22	8
24	9

a. Draw a graph that shows the optimal level of security guard services. Be sure to label the curves on the graph.

b. Briefly explain why 8 hours of security guard protection is not an optimal quantity.

Solving the Problem

Step 1: Review the chapter material. This problem is about determining the optimal level of public goods, so you may want to review the section "The Optimal Quantity of a Public Good," which begins on page 144.

Step 2: Begin by deriving the demand curve or marginal social benefit curve for security guard services. To calculate the marginal social benefit of guard services, we need to add the prices that Jill and Joe are willing to pay at each quantity:

Demand or Marginal Social Benefit	
Price (dollars per hour)	Quantity (hours of protection)
$38	1
34	2
30	3
26	4
22	5
18	6
14	7
10	8
6	9

Step 3: **Answer part (a) by plotting the demand (marginal social benefit) and supply (marginal social cost) curves.** The graph shows that the optimal level of security guard services is 6 hours.

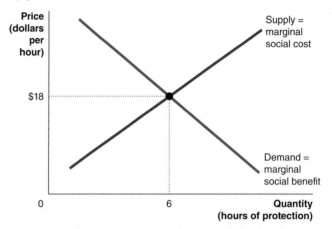

Step 4: **Answer part (b) by explaining why 8 hours of security guard protection is not an optimal quantity.** For each hour beyond 6, the supply curve is above the demand curve. Therefore, the marginal social benefit received will be less than the marginal social cost of supplying these hours. This results in a deadweight loss and a reduction in economic surplus.

MyEconLab   **Your Turn:** For more practice, do related problem 4.1 on page 154 at the end of this chapter.

Common Resources

In England during the Middle Ages, each village had an area of pasture, known as a *commons*, on which any family in the village was allowed to graze its livestock without charge. Of course, the grass one family's animal ate was not available for another family's animal, so consumption was rival. But every family in the village had the right to use the commons, so it was nonexcludable. Without some type of restraint on usage, the commons would be overgrazed. To see why, consider the economic incentives facing a family that was thinking of buying another cow and grazing it on the commons. The family would gain the benefits from increased milk production, but adding another cow to the commons would create a negative externality by reducing the amount of grass available for the livestock of other families. Because this family—and the other families in the village—did not take this negative externality into account when deciding whether to add another animal to the commons, too many animals would be added. The grass on the commons would eventually be depleted, and no family's livestock would get enough to eat.

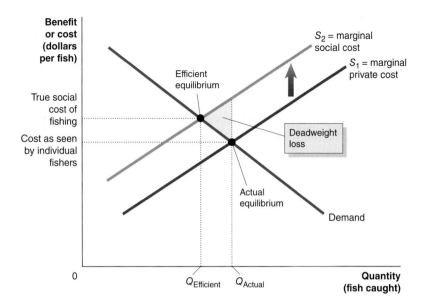

Figure 5.11

Overuse of a Common Resource

For a common resource such as fish from the ocean, the efficient level of use, $Q_{\text{Efficient}}$, is determined by the intersection of the demand curve—which represents the marginal benefit received by consumers—and S_2, which represents the marginal social cost of fishing. Because each individual fisher ignores the external cost, the equilibrium quantity of fish caught is Q_{Actual}, which is greater than the efficient quantity. At the actual equilibrium level of output, there is a deadweight loss, as shown by the yellow triangle.

The Tragedy of the Commons   The tendency for a common resource to be over-used is called the **tragedy of the commons**.

Fisheries around the world are a modern example. Fishers take into account the benefits of having more fish to eat or sell, but do not consider the impact of depleted fish stocks in the ocean. The Grand Banks off Newfoundland were once teeming with cod, which supported commercial fishing for almost 500 years. Each fishing crew caught as many fish as it could without considering what impact the catch would have on other boats. On the basis of individual boats, the improvements in fishing technology and increased catch from the 1960s to the 1990s wouldn't have harmed the fishery. Considering the number of boats and commensurate size of the catch overall, the impact was devastating. Today, there aren't enough fish to support a commercial fishery of any size: In 1992 the federal government declared a moratorium on fishing for Northern Atlantic cod, essentially closing the fishery and most of the communities that depended on it.

Figure 5.11 shows that with a common resource such as fish caught in the ocean, the efficient level of use, $Q_{\text{Efficient}}$, is determined by the intersection of the demand curve—which represents the marginal social benefit received by consumers—and S_2, which represents the marginal social cost of fishing. As in our discussion of negative externalities, the social cost is equal to the private cost of fishing plus the external cost. In this case, the external cost represents the fact that the more fish each person catches, the less fish there are available for others and the greater the depletion of the fish stock, which increases the chance of complete collapse. Because each individual fisher ignores the external cost, the equilibrium quantity of fish caught is Q_{Actual}, which is greater than the efficient quantity. At the actual equilibrium level of output, there is a deadweight loss, as shown in Figure 5.11 by the yellow triangle.

Is There a Way Out of the Tragedy of the Commons?   Notice that our discussion of the tragedy of the commons is very similar to our earlier discussion of negative externalities. The source of the tragedy of the commons is the same as the source of negative externalities: lack of clearly defined and enforced property rights. For instance, suppose that instead of being held as a collective resource, a piece of pasture land is owned by one person. That person will take into account the effect of adding another animal on the food available to livestock already using the pasture. As a result, the optimal number of animals will be placed on the pasture. Over the years, most of the commons lands in England were converted to private property. Similarly, most countries around the world limit fishing in their territorial waters.

In some situations, though, enforcing property rights is not feasible. An example is the oceans. Because no country owns the oceans beyond its own coastal waters, the

Tragedy of the commons   The tendency for a common resource to be overused.

fish and other resources of the ocean will remain a common resource. In situations in which enforcing property rights is not feasible, two types of solutions to the tragedy of the commons are possible. If the geographic area involved is limited and the number of people involved is small, access to the commons can be restricted through community norms and laws. If the geographic area or the number of people involved is large, legal restrictions on access to the commons are required. As an example of the first type of solution, the tragedy of the commons was avoided in the Middle Ages by traditional limits on the number of animals each family was allowed to put on the common pasture. Although these traditions were not formal laws, they were usually enforced adequately by social pressure.

With the second type of solution, the government imposes restrictions on access to the common resources. These restrictions can take several different forms, of which taxes, quotas, and tradable permits are the most common. By setting a tax equal to the external cost, governments can ensure that the efficient quantity of a resource is used. Quotas, or legal limits, on the quantity of the resource that can be taken during a given time period have been used in Canada to limit access to pools of oil that are beneath property owned by many different persons. The governments of Canada, New Zealand, and Iceland have used a system of tradable permits to restrict access to ocean fisheries. Under this system, a total allowable catch (TAC) limits the number of fish that fishers can catch during a season. The fishers are then assigned permits called individual transferable quotas (ITQs) that are equal to the total allowable catch. This system operates like the tradable emissions allowances described earlier in this chapter. The fishers are free to use the ITQs or to sell them, which ensures that the fishers with the lowest costs use the ITQs.

Economics in Your Life

What's the "Best" Level of Pollution?

At the beginning of the chapter, we asked you to think about what the "best" level of carbon dioxide emissions is. Conceptually, this is a straightforward question to answer: The efficient level of carbon dioxide emissions is the level for which the marginal benefit of reducing carbon dioxide emissions exactly equals the marginal cost of reducing carbon dioxide emissions. In practice, however, this is a very difficult question to answer. Scientists disagree about how much carbon dioxide emissions are contributing to climate change and what the damage from climate change will be. In addition, the cost of reducing carbon dioxide emissions depends on the method of reduction used. As a result, neither the marginal cost curve nor the marginal benefit curve for reducing carbon dioxide emissions is known with certainty. This uncertainty makes it difficult for policymakers to determine the economically efficient level of carbon dioxide emissions and is the source of much of the current debate. In any case, economists agree that the total cost of *completely* eliminating carbon dioxide emissions is much greater than the total benefit.

Conclusion

In Chapter 4, we saw that government intervention in the economy can reduce economic efficiency. In this chapter, however, we have seen that the government plays an indispensable role in the economy when the absence of well-defined and enforceable property rights keeps the market from operating efficiently. For instance, because no one has a property right for clean air, in the absence of government intervention, firms will produce too great a quantity of products that generate air pollution. We have also seen that public goods are nonrival and nonexcludable and are, therefore, often supplied directly by the government.

Read *An Inside Look* on the next page for a discussion of B.C.'s carbon tax.

Assessing Pros and Cons of a Government Carbon Tax

THE VANCOUVER SUN

B.C.'s Final Carbon Tax Lift Brings Questions over Tax's Future

VICTORIA — B.C.'s carbon tax will increase Sunday for the fourth time in as many years, meaning consumers will be paying almost seven cents for every litre of gasoline they pump into their cars.

The move is the last scheduled lift for the four-year-old tax and firmly places the province ahead of all other North American jurisdictions when it comes to placing a price on carbon.

"British Columbia is a climate action leader around the world," Environment Minister Terry Lake said this week, pointing out that prominent articles in the *Economist* magazine, the *New York Times* and the *L.A. Times* have all pointed to the success of B.C. policies.

But with other provinces and states struggling to catch up, and with worldwide economies still sputtering, many in British Columbia are asking a key question: what now?

Some, like B.C. Conservative leader John Cummins, are calling for the carbon tax to be scrapped altogether, saying B.C. gas taxes are already too high.

Others are suggesting the carbon tax should be broadened to cover other sources of greenhouse gases, such as the heavy industrial emissions the province once planned to control through a system of cap and trade.

Suggestions have also been made to dedicate some revenue from the carbon tax to programs that help people reduce their carbon footprint, instead of giving all the proceeds back through tax cuts, as the government does now.

Speaking to reporters this week, Lake made clear the carbon tax is here to stay, but opened the door for a wide swath of possible changes.

"We want to continue to be a leader on climate action policy, but when you're a leader, you expect others to follow and when other jurisdictions are not following you do get into a problem of competitiveness," Lake said.

"We have to be careful not to get too far ahead of the curve because that will definitely hurt competitiveness, and that costs families jobs and opportunities."

To that end, the B.C. government last February announced a massive review of the carbon tax, one that began in earnest this week.

"Four years in, the revenue-neutral carbon tax remains the only one of its kind in North America and this is a good time to pause and examine how the carbon tax is affecting our economic competitiveness," Finance Minister Kevin Falcon said in a written statement this week as he asked the public for submissions in the review.

Lest anyone think government has already made up its mind to water down the tax, Lake said he thinks the carbon tax has disproven the doomsday crowd who saw carbon pricing as a weapon against productivity.

"When people talk about pricing carbon, the argument has always been you can't do that and have a growing economy," he said.

"We've shown that actually, in British Columbia, with the kind of policies we have—a carbon tax that is revenue neutral—that in fact we can achieve both an increase in our economic picture as well as a reduction of our greenhouse gases."

With the review officially kicking off this week, groups across the province are now having their say.

The opposition New Democratic Party—which ran in the 2009 election on a platform to "axe" the carbon tax—have for a while promised they would keep the tax, adding they would also strip away some of the corporate tax cuts that were introduced to make it revenue neutral.

The idea, they say, is to invest the extra money into projects that will help reduce emissions.

"I think B.C.'s carbon tax is going to continue to underperform if it's not linked directly to investment in activities and green infrastructure that are proven to reduce emissions," NDP environment critic Rob Fleming said Friday.

He added the money gained from reversing corporate tax cuts—more than $200 million per year—would go toward green investments such as transit, where the province can offer environmentally friendly alternatives instead of just punishing pollution.

"So long as the carbon tax isn't linked to those kind of green investments, B.C.'s emissions are going to continue to be unnecessarily large and it's going to be difficult to meet the legislated targets," he said.

The message is similar at the B.C. Trucking Association, which initially opposed the carbon tax, largely because it punished truckers at the front end of a major economic downturn. On Friday, president and CEO Louise Yako said her association would like to see the government introduce incentive programs that help truck drivers and operators become more fuel efficient.

"If you're trying to incent a certain behaviour and you're penalizing people for doing a certain thing, that makes sense. But for the trucking industry, they really have no choice. It's not like we could use public transportation to carry our boxes," she said.

"For us, it was imposing a cost without really causing a change in behaviour. So that's really why we opposed it. The fact the government is reconsidering it now I think is quite a good sign," she added.

"We're very hopeful they will make a decision that is reasonable."

Amid this discussion, Lake this week agreed that while B.C. has made promising headway so far on reducing its greenhouse gas emissions, the province will need to do more if it is to meet its legislated targets. Provincial law required B.C. to make a 33-percent reduction in emissions by 2020, and an 80-percent reduction by 2050. The baseline for all targets is 2007, and as of 2010, the province had seen a reduction of 4.5 percent.

"It certainly is something we are going to have to put our minds to. We expect our economy to grow, we expect our population to grow," Lake said, adding there will be other challenges as well, such as an emerging liquefied natural gas (LNG) industry.

"I don't doubt or deny that meeting those 2020 targets is going to be a challenge, but I think it's one that British Columbians are ready to face."

Source: Jonathan Fowlie, "B.C.'s Final Carbon Tax Lift Brings Questions Over Tax's Future," *The Vancouver Sun*, June 29, 2012, accessed at http://www.vancouversun.com/technology/final+carbon+lift+brings+questions+over+future/6864802/story.html#ixzz27PiEpqG0. Copyright © 2012 by *The Vancouver Sun*.

Key Points in the Article

British Columbia's provincial government has set targets for reducing emissions of greenhouse gases in the province. The law requires that emissions be reduced by 33 percent of 2007 level by 2020 and by 80 percent by 2050. As part of its efforts to meet these targets, in 2008 B.C.'s provincial government introduced a new tax on gasoline that was intended to increase the cost of emitting carbon dioxide. The economic justification for the tax is the same as any other tax on an activity that creates a negative externality: A tax increases the cost to consumers, causing them to consume less of the product. In order to consume less gasoline, B.C.'s consumers will have to drive less or buy more fuel-efficient cars.

Analyzing the News

ⓐ B.C.'s additional tax on gasoline can be viewed in much the same way as the tax on the production of electricity. People in B.C. pay seven cents more per litre of gasoline as the provincial government tries to reduce emissions. The tax was initially set at a much lower level in order to allow people to get used to the idea and to give them time to make changes in their lives. The results of the tax have been a reduction in the amount of carbon dioxide emitted.

ⓑ One of the concerns raised in debates over environmental policy is the cost of the policies. Clearly a tax raises the cost of gasoline for everyone in B.C. By increasing the cost of an essential input into production and distribution, the provincial government risked making B.C. firms more

expensive than firms in other jurisdictions that don't have to pay a carbon tax. While small differences in taxation are unlikely to make most firms uncompetitive, large differences in taxation can cause firms to relocate or go out of business.

ⓒ In an effort to limit the impact of the carbon tax on people and firms, the provincial government has made the tax "revenue neutral" by reducing another tax (that didn't encourage a reduction in pollution) to allow room for the new tax. This can mean that an average person's total tax bill doesn't change, even when a new tax is introduced. By reducing a tax that didn't penalize pollution and introducing one that does, a tax can reduce the amount of a negative externality produced without making people worse off.

Thinking Critically

1. Instead of imposing a tax on gasoline to reduce consumption (and emissions of carbon dioxide), the provincial government could have taken a command-and-control approach and limited the amount of gasoline one person could legally purchase. Explain why this approach would not be the most economically efficient solution to the pollution problem.

2. B.C.'s government has taken steps to make the tax revenue neutral. Draw a graph that shows how much gasoline would be purchased without the tax, how much gasoline would be purchased with the tax, and how much revenue the government will collect with the tax.

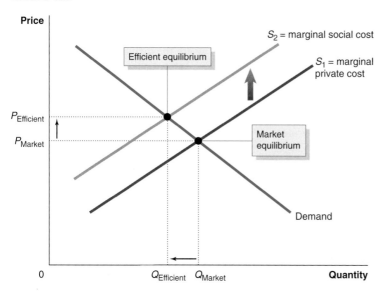

With the implementation of new pollution regulations, producers would bear more of the external cost of pollution.

Chapter Summary and Problems

Key Terms

Summary

*LO 5.1 An **externality** is a benefit or cost to parties who are not involved in a transaction. Pollution and other externalities in production cause a difference between the **private cost** borne by the producer of a good or service and the **social cost**, which includes any external cost, such as the cost of pollution. An externality in consumption causes a difference between the **private benefit** received by the consumer and the **social benefit**, which includes any external benefit. If externalities exist in production or consumption, the market will not produce the optimal level of a good or service. This outcome is referred to as **market failure**. Externalities arise when property rights do not exist or cannot be legally enforced. **Property rights** are the rights individuals or businesses have to the exclusive use of their property, including the right to buy or sell it.

LO 5.2 Externalities and market failures result from incomplete property rights or from the difficulty of enforcing property rights in certain situations. When a negative externality exists, and the efficient quantity of a good is not being produced, the total cost of reducing the externality is usually less than the total benefit. According to the **Coase theorem**, if **transactions costs** are low, private bargaining will result in an efficient solution to the problem of externalities.

LO 5.3 When private solutions to externalities are unworkable, the government sometimes intervenes. One way to deal with a negative externality in production is to impose a tax equal to the cost of the externality. The tax causes the producer of the good to internalize the externality. The government can deal with a positive externality in consumption by giving consumers a subsidy, or payment, equal to the value of the externality. Government taxes and subsidies intended to bring about an efficient level of output in the presence of externalities are called **Pigovian taxes and subsidies**. Although the federal government has sometimes used subsidies and taxes to deal with externalities, in dealing with pollution it has more often used a command-and-control approach. A **command-and-control approach** involves the government imposing quantitative limits on the amount of pollution allowed or requiring firms to install specific pollution control devices. Direct pollution controls of this type are not economically efficient, however. Governments can also use a system of tradable emissions allowances to deal with pollution, such as that used in the U.S. to deal with sulphur dioxide emissions or the European Union to deal with carbon dioxide emissions.

LO 5.4 There are four categories of goods: private goods, public goods, quasi-public goods, and common resources. **Private goods** are both rival and excludable. **Rivalry** means that when one person consumes a unit of a good, no one else can consume that unit. **Excludability** means that anyone who does not pay for a good cannot consume it. **Public goods** are both nonrival and nonexcludable. Private firms are usually not willing to supply public goods because of free riding. **Free riding** involves benefiting from a good without paying for it. Quasi-public goods are excludable but not rival. **Common resources** are rival but not excludable. The **tragedy of the commons** refers to the tendency for a common resource to be overused. The tragedy of the commons results from a lack of clearly defined and enforced property rights. We find the market demand curve for a private good by adding the quantity of the good demanded by each consumer at each price. We find the demand curve for a public good by adding vertically the price each consumer would be willing to pay for each quantity of the good. The optimal quantity of a public good occurs where the demand curve intersects the curve representing the marginal cost of supplying the good.

MyEconLab   Log in to MyEconLab to complete these exercises and get instant feedback.

Review Questions

LO 5.1

1.1 What is an externality? Give an example of a positive externality, and give an example of a negative externality.

1.2 When will the private cost of producing a good differ from the social cost? Give an example. When will the private benefit from consuming a good differ from the social benefit? Give an example.

1.3 What is market failure? When is market failure likely to arise?

LO 5.2

2.1 What do economists mean by "an economically efficient level of pollution"?

*'Learning Objective' is abbreviated to 'LO' in the end of chapter material.

2.2 What is the Coase theorem? Why do the parties involved in an externality have an incentive to reach an efficient solution?

2.3 What are transactions costs? When are we likely to see private solutions to the problem of externalities?

LO 5.3

3.1 What is a Pigovian tax? At what level must a Pigovian tax be set to achieve efficiency?

3.2 What does it mean for a producer or consumer to internalize an externality? What would cause a producer or consumer to internalize an externality?

3.3 Why do most economists prefer tradable emissions allowances to the command-and-control approach to pollution?

LO 5.4

4.1 Define *rivalry* and *excludability* and use these terms to discuss the four categories of goods.

4.2 What is a public good? What is free riding? How is free riding related to the tendency of a public good to create market failure?

4.3 What is the tragedy of the commons? How can it be avoided?

Problems and Applications

LO 5.1

1.1 The chapter states that your consuming a Tim Hortons coffee does not create an externality. But suppose you arrive at your favourite Tim's and get in a long line to be served. By the time you reach the counter, there are 10 people in line behind you. Because you decided to have a decaf coffee—instead of, say, a regular double double—each of those 10 people must wait in line an additional two minutes. Is it still correct to say that your consuming a coffee creates no externalities? Might there be a justification here for the government to intervene in the market for coffee? Briefly explain.

1.2 A neighbour's barking dog can be both a positive externality and a negative externality. Under what circumstances would the barking dog serve as a positive externality? Under what circumstances would the barking dog be a negative externality?

1.3 The Rocky Mountains are bear country. Parks Canada states the following about camping and fishing in bear country: "Dispose of fish offal in fast moving streams or the deep part of a lake, never along stream sides or lake shores." What negative externality does disposing of fish remains near camp sites have for other campers? What negative externality would such an action have for bears?

From Parks Canada, "Bears and People," http://www.pc.gc.ca/eng/pn-np/mtn/ours-bears/sec7/og-bm7.aspx, accessed October 4, 2012.

1.4 The Canadian Radio-television and Telecommunications Commission (CRTC) decided in 2012 that people should be able to subscribe to individual channels rather than being forced to purchase bundles or packages of channels, which is the practice for many cable TV providers. However, the fewer channels a customer opts for, the more they have to pay for each one.

Suppose you're a fan of *The Daily Show* with Jon Stewart, which airs on Comedy, but the only way you could get it before the CRTC ruling was as part of a package of 30 other channels. If you decide to buy the package just so you can watch *The Daily Show*, not all of the money you pay goes to Comedy, but is shared by all networks in the package.

By packaging Comedy with other channels, does your cable provider create a positive externality for you? Does it create a positive externality for the networks? Do you think the CRTC ruling solves the problem of the externality?

Based on Steve Ladurantaye, "CRTC gives TV subscribers more control, with a catch," *Globe and Mail*, July 20, 2012.

LO 5.2

2.1 Is it ever possible for an *increase* in pollution to make society better off? Briefly explain, using a graph like Figure 5.3 on page 131.

2.2 [**Related to the** Don't Let This Happen to You **on page 133**] If the marginal cost of reducing a certain type of pollution is zero, should all of that type of pollution be eliminated? Briefly explain.

2.3 [**Related to the** Making the Connection **on page 130**] Even though governments around the world have eliminated or drastically reduced the amount of CFCs released into the atmosphere, the excess risk of skin cancer due to depleted ozone has not fallen to zero. Should the government take further action to protect the ozone layer? How should government go about deciding this question?

2.4 According to the Coase theorem, why would a steel plant that creates air pollution agree to curtail production (and therefore pollution) if it were not legally liable for the damage the pollution was causing? Must the property right to clean air be assigned to the victims of air pollution to get the steel plant to reduce pollution?

2.5 [**Related to the** Making the Connection **on page 134**] We know that owners of apple orchards and owners of beehives are able to negotiate private agreements. Is it likely that as a result of these private agreements, the market supplies the efficient quantities of apple trees and beehives? Are there any real-world difficulties that might stand in the way of achieving this efficient outcome?

LO 5.3

3.1 Health Canada's nutrition guidelines urge adults to eat at least five servings of fruits and vegetables each day. Does consuming fruits and vegetables have a positive externality? Should the government subsidize the consumption of fruits and vegetables? Briefly explain.

3.2 Many antibiotics that once were effective in eliminating infections no longer are because bacteria have evolved to become resistant to them. Some bacteria are now resistant to all but one or two existing antibiotics. Some policymakers have argued that pharmaceutical companies should receive subsidies for developing new antibiotics. A newspaper article states:

While the notion of directly subsidizing drug companies may be politically unpopular in many quarters, proponents say it is necessary to bridge the gap between the high value that new antibiotics have for society and the low returns they provide to drug companies.

Is there a positive externality in the production of antibiotics? Should firms producing every good where there is a gap between the value of the good to society and the profit to the firms making the good receive subsidies? Briefly explain.

From Andrew Pollack, "Antibiotics Research Subsidies Weighed by U.S.," *The New York Times*, November 5, 2010.

3.3 [**Related to** Solved Problem 5.3 **on page 136**] Draw a graph showing the deadweight loss from a negative externality in production and illustrate how a Pigovian tax eliminates the deadweight loss. Draw another graph showing the deadweight loss from a positive externality in consumption and illustrate how a Pigovian subsidy eliminates the deadweight loss. Briefly explain how the Pigovian tax and subsidy eliminate the deadweight loss.

3.4 Assume the private marginal benefit from a good can be represented by the inverse demand equation, $P = 100 - Q$. Assume the private marginal cost of producing the good can be represented by the supply equation, $P = 3Q$. If consuming the good generates a negative externality of $10 for each unit consumed, calculate:
 a. The privately optimal level of consumption and production
 b. The socially optimal level of consumption and production
 c. The deadweight loss to society if no action is taken

3.5 [**Related to the** Making the Connection **on page 137**] Draw a graph for the market for soft drinks and assume that consumption of sugary pop causes a negative externality by raising medical costs. Draw both the actual demand curve representing the marginal private benefits and the demand curve representing the marginal social benefit. Show the deadweight loss caused by the externality.
 a. Should the government prohibit pop consumption if it causes a negative externality by raising medical costs?
 b. How could the government get pop drinkers to incorporate in their consumption decisions the cost they impose by raising medical costs?

3.6 [**Related to the** Chapter Opener **on page 125**] As discussed in the Chapter Opener, British Columbia has introduced a tax on gasoline. Some people argue that the revenue generated from this tax should be spent on subsidies to firms developing "green" energy. What sort of positive externality would a "green" energy firm produce? Explain how a subsidy could improve economic efficiency.

LO 5.4

4.1 [**Related to** Solved Problem 5.4 **on page 145**] Suppose that Jill and Joe are the only two people in the small town of Andover. Andover has land available to build a park of no more than 9 hectares. Jill and Joe's demand schedules for the park are as follows:

Joe

Price per Hectare	Number of Hectares
$10	0
9	1
8	2
7	3
6	4
5	5
4	6
3	7
2	8
1	9

Jill

Price per Hectare	Number of Hectares
$15	0
14	1
13	2
12	3
11	4
10	5
9	6
8	7
7	8
6	9

The supply curve is as follows:

Price	Number of Acres
$11	1
13	2
15	3
17	4
19	5
21	6
23	7
25	8
27	9

 a. Draw a graph showing the optimal size of the park. Be sure to label the curves on the graph.
 b. Briefly explain why a park of 2 hectares is not optimal.

4.2 The more frequently bacteria are exposed to antibiotics, the more quickly the bacteria will develop resistance to the antibiotics. Health Canada states:

> There is an increasing concern around the world that organisms like bacteria, viruses, fungi, and parasites are becoming resistant to the drugs used to fight them. An example of this is the increasing resistance to antibiotics used to treat bacterial infections. When this occurs, it can mean there are fewer effective antibiotics available to prevent and treat infections and infectious diseases more difficult.

Briefly discuss in what sense antibiotics can be considered a common resource.

Healthy Living Antibiotic Resistance – It's Your Health, http://www.hc-sc.gc.ca/hl-vs/iyh-vsv/med/antibio-eng.php.

4.3 Put each of these goods or services into one of the boxes in Figure 5.7 on page 141. That is, categorize them as private goods, public goods, quasi-public goods, or common resources.
   a. A television broadcast of the Stanley Cup playoff game
   b. Home mail delivery
   c. Hiking in a park not surrounded by a fence
   d. An apple

4.4 In the early 1800s, more than 60 million American bison (commonly known as the buffalo) roamed the Great Plains. By the late 1800s, the buffalo was nearly extinct. Considering the four categories of goods discussed in the chapter, why might it be that hunters nearly killed buffalo to extinction but not cattle?

4.5 William Easterly, in *The White Man's Burden*, shares the following account by New York University Professor Leonard Wantchekon of how Professor Wantchekon's village in Benin, Africa, managed the local fishing pond when he was growing up.

> To open the fishing season, elders performed ritual tests at Amlé, a lake 15 kilometres from the village. If the fish were large enough, fishing was allowed for two or three days. If they were too small, all fishing was forbidden, and anyone who secretly fished the lake at this time was outcast, excluded from the formal and informal groups that formed the village's social structure. Those who committed this breach of trust were often shunned by the whole community; no one would speak to the offender, or even acknowledge his existence for a year or more.

What economic problem were the village elders trying to prevent? Do you think their solution would have worked?

William Easterly, *The White Man's Burden: Why the West's Efforts to Aid the Rest Have Done So Much Ill and So Little Good* (New York: Penguin Books, 2006), p. 94.

MyEconLab   MyEconLab is an online tool designed to help you master the concepts covered in your course. It will create an adaptive, highly personalized study plan to stimulate and measure your learning. Log in to take advantage of this powerful study aid, and to access quizzes and other valuable course-related material.

Elasticity: The Responsiveness of Demand and Supply

Chapter Outline and Learning Objectives

© WavebreakMediaMicro/Fotolia

Do People Respond to Changes in the Price of Gasoline?

Some people have argued that consumers don't vary the quantity of gas they buy as the price changes because the distance they need to drive is roughly constant. Evidence from newspaper articles, however, suggests the opposite.

A 2012 *Globe and Mail* article reported that sales of smaller, more fuel-efficient hybrids such as the Toyota Prius were increasing compared with sales in previous years. This is an indication that, over time, consumers will find other ways to reduce gasoline expenditure, and it is not the first time that automobiles have changed with fuel prices. Ask your parents (or grandparents) about the "muscle cars" that were around from 1968 to 1973 when oil was $6 per barrel and gasoline was about $0.10 per litre.

During the summer of 2005, when the price of gasoline soared to a national average of $1.23 per litre from the effects of Hurricane Katrina, consumers certainly responded. According to Jason Toews, co-founder of Gasbuddy.com, "People were really upset by the high gas prices and they're talking about boycotting the oil companies and gas stations." In 2005, consumers seemed to be sensitive to the price of gasoline. More recently, gasoline price variations have been more common.

A *Calgary Herald* article from 2008 tells the story of the price spike in the summer of that year. Sales of gasoline fell by 4.5 percent between June 2007 and June 2008 as the rising price of oil pushed up gasoline prices. "Canadian sales of gasoline and diesel are plummeting as sky-high prices curb purchases as consumers rethink their automobile preferences, adjust their travel and commuting habits, and reduce energy consumption to protect their wallets..." said the article. Consumers were finding many ways to cut back the volume of gasoline they purchased by moving closer to work, or moving to a job closer to home.

All businesses have a strong interest in knowing how much less they will sell as prices rise. Governments are also interested in knowing how consumers will react if the price of a product such as gasoline increases following a tax increase. In this chapter, we will explore what determines the responsiveness of the quantity demanded and the quantity supplied to changes in the market price. **AN INSIDE LOOK** on **page 182** discusses the causes and effects of higher gas prices in 2012.

Based on Lauren Grugel, "Canada Gas Prices: Consumers Becoming Desensitized to Jumps, Says Gasbuddy. com," Canadian Press, September 14, 2012; G. S. Cotton, "High Prices Cut Fuel Sales," *Calgary Herald*, August 11, 2008; Jeremy Cato, "Toyota Pushes Hybrid Sales to Retake 'Green' Auto Crown," *The Globe and Mail*, July 4, 2012, accessed at http://www.theglobeandmail.com/globe-drive /driving-it-home/toyota-pushes-hybrid-sales-to-retake -green-auto-crown/article4390398/; and data on gasoline prices from Natural Resources Canada.

Economics in Your Life

How Much Do Gas Prices Matter to You?

What factors would make you more or less responsive to price when purchasing gasoline? Have you responded differently to price changes during different periods of your life? Why do consumers seem to respond more to changes in gas prices at a particular service station but seem less sensitive when gas prices rise or fall at all service stations? As you read the chapter, see if you can answer these questions. You can check your answers against those we provide on page 180 at the end of this chapter.

Elasticity A measure of how much one economic variable responds to changes in another economic variable.

W hether you are managing a service station, a bookstore, or a coffee shop, you need to know how an increase or a decrease in the price of your products will affect the quantity consumers are willing to buy. We saw in Chapter 3 that cutting the price of a good increases the quantity demanded and raising the price reduces the quantity demanded. But the critical question is this: *How much* will the quantity demanded change as a result of a price increase or decrease? Economists use the concept of **elasticity** to measure how one economic variable—such as the quantity demanded—responds to changes in another economic variable—such as the price. For example, the responsiveness of the quantity demanded of a good to changes in its price is called the *price elasticity of demand*. Knowing the price elasticity of demand allows you to compute the effect of a price change on the quantity demanded.

We saw in Chapter 3 that the quantity of a good that consumers demand depends not just on the price of the good but also on consumer income and on the prices of related goods. As a manager, you would also be interested in measuring the responsiveness of demand to these other factors. As we will see, we can use the concept of elasticity here as well. We are also interested in the responsiveness of the quantity supplied of a good to changes in its price, which is called the *price elasticity of supply*.

Elasticity is an important concept not just for business managers but for policymakers as well. If the government wants to discourage smoking, it can raise the price of cigarettes by increasing the tax on them. If we know the price elasticity of demand for cigarettes, we can calculate how many fewer packs of cigarettes will be demanded at a higher price. In this chapter, we will also see how policymakers use the concept of elasticity.

6.1 LEARNING OBJECTIVE

Define price elasticity of demand and understand how to measure it.

The Price Elasticity of Demand and Its Measurement

We know from the law of demand that when the price of a product falls, the quantity demanded of the product increases. But the law of demand tells firms only that the demand curves for their products slope downward. More useful is a measure of the responsiveness of the quantity demanded to a change in price. This measure is called the **price elasticity of demand**.

Price elasticity of demand The responsiveness of the quantity demanded to a change in price, measured by dividing the percentage change in the quantity demanded of a product by the percentage change in the product's price.

Measuring the Price Elasticity of Demand

We might measure the price elasticity of demand by using the slope of the demand curve because the slope of the demand curve tells us how much quantity changes as price changes. Using the slope of the demand curve to measure price elasticity has a drawback, however: The measurement of slope is sensitive to the units chosen for quantity and price. For example, suppose a $0.20 per litre decrease in the price of gasoline leads to an increase in the quantity demanded from 10.1 million litres to 10.2 million litres per day. The change in quantity is 0.1 million litres and the change in price is −$0.20, so the slope is $0.1/-0.20 = -0.5$. But if we measure price in cents, rather than dollars, the slope is $0.1/-20 = -0.005$. If we measure price in dollars and litres in thousands, instead of millions, the slope is $100/-0.20 = -500$. Clearly, the value we compute for the slope can change dramatically, depending on the units we use for quantity and price.

To avoid this confusion over units, economists use *percentage changes* when measuring the price elasticity of demand. Percentage changes are not dependent on units of measurement. (For a review of calculating percentage changes, see the appendix to Chapter 1.) No matter what units we use to measure the quantity of gasoline, 10 percent more gasoline is 10 percent more gasoline. Therefore, the price elasticity of demand is measured by dividing the percentage change in the quantity demanded by the percentage change in the price. Or:

$$\text{Price elasticity of demand} = \frac{\text{Percentage change in quantity demanded}}{\text{Percentage change in price}}.$$

It's important to remember that *the price elasticity of demand is not the same as the slope of the demand curve.*

If we calculate the price elasticity of demand for a price cut, the percentage change in price will be negative, and the percentage change in quantity demanded will be positive. Similarly, if we calculate the price elasticity of demand for a price increase, the percentage change in price will be positive, and the percentage change in quantity demanded will be negative. Therefore, the price elasticity of demand is always negative. In comparing elasticities, though, we are usually interested in their relative size. So, we often drop the minus sign and compare their *absolute values*. In other words, although −3 is actually a smaller number than −2, a price elasticity of −3 is larger than a price elasticity of −2.

Elastic Demand and Inelastic Demand

If the quantity demanded is very responsive to changes in price, the percentage change in quantity demanded will be *greater* than the percentage change in price, and the price elasticity of demand will be greater than 1 in absolute value. In this case, demand is **elastic**. For example, if a 10 percent decrease in the price of bagels results in a 20 percent increase in the quantity of bagels demanded, then:

$$\text{Price elasticity of demand} = \frac{20\%}{-10\%} = -2,$$

and we can conclude that the demand for bagels is elastic.

When the quantity demanded is not very responsive to price, however, the percentage change in quantity demanded will be *less* than the percentage change in price, and the price elasticity of demand will be less than 1 in absolute value. In this case, demand is **inelastic**. For example, if a 10 percent decrease in the price of wheat results in a 5 percent increase in the quantity of wheat demanded, then:

$$\text{Price elasticity of demand} = \frac{5\%}{-10\%} = -0.5,$$

and we can conclude that the demand for wheat is inelastic.

In the special case in which the percentage change in the quantity demanded is equal to the percentage change in price, the price elasticity of demand equals −1 (or 1 in absolute value). In this case, demand is **unit elastic**.

An Example of Computing Price Elasticities

Suppose you own a service station, and you are trying to decide whether to cut the price you are charging for a litre of gas. You are currently at point *A* in Figure 6.1: selling 1,000 litres per day at a price of $1.25 per litre. How many more litres you will sell by cutting the price to $1.15 depends on the price elasticity of demand for gasoline at your service station. Let's consider two possibilities: If D_1 is the demand curve for gasoline at your station, your sales will increase to 1,200 litres per day, point *B*. But if D_2 is your demand curve, your sales will increase only to 1,050 litres per day, point *C*. We might expect—correctly, as we will see—that between these points, demand curve D_1 is *elastic*, and demand curve D_2 is *inelastic*.

To confirm that D_1 is elastic between these points and that D_2 is inelastic, we need to calculate the price elasticity of demand for each curve. In calculating price elasticity between two points on a demand curve, though, we run into a problem because we get a different value for price increases than for price decreases. For example, suppose we calculate the price elasticity for D_1 as the price is cut from $1.25 to $1.15. This reduction is an 8 percent price cut that increases the quantity demanded from 1,000 litres to

Elastic demand Demand is elastic when the percentage change in quantity demanded is *greater* than the percentage change in price, so the price elasticity is *greater* than 1 in absolute value.

Inelastic demand Demand is inelastic when the percentage change in quantity demanded is *less* than the percentage change in price, so the price elasticity is *less* than 1 in absolute value.

Unit-elastic demand Demand is unit elastic when the percentage change in quantity demanded is *equal to* the percentage change in price, so the price elasticity is equal to 1 in absolute value.

Figure 6.1

Elastic and Inelastic Demand

Along D_1, cutting the price from $1.25 to $1.15 increases the number of litres sold from 1,000 per day to 1,200 per day, so demand is elastic between point A and point B. Along D_2, cutting the price from $1.25 to $1.15 increases the number of litres sold from 1,000 per day only to 1,050 per day, so demand is inelastic between point A and point C.

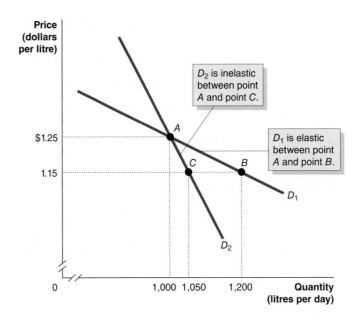

1,200 litres, or by 20 percent. Therefore, the price elasticity of demand between points A and B is 20/−8 = −2.5. Now let's calculate the price elasticity for D_1 as the price is *increased* from $1.15 to $1.25. This is an 8.7 percent price increase that decreases the quantity demanded from 1,200 litres to 1,000 litres, or by 16.7 percent. So, now our measure of the price elasticity of demand between points A and B is −16.7/8.7 = −1.9. It can be confusing to have different values for the price elasticity of demand between the same two points on the same demand curve. As we will see in the next section, to avoid this confusion, economists often use a particular formula when calculating elasticities.

The Midpoint Formula

We can use the *midpoint formula* to ensure that we have only one value of the price elasticity of demand between the same two points on a demand curve. The midpoint formula uses the *average* of the initial and final quantities and the initial and final prices. If Q_1 and P_1 are the initial quantity and price and Q_2 and P_2 are the final quantity and price, the midpoint formula is:

$$\text{Price elasticity of demand} = \frac{(Q_2 - Q_1)}{\left(\dfrac{Q_1 + Q_2}{2}\right)} \div \frac{(P_2 - P_1)}{\left(\dfrac{P_1 + P_2}{2}\right)}.$$

The midpoint formula may seem challenging at first, but the numerator is just the change in quantity divided by the average of the initial and final quantities, and the denominator is just the change in price divided by the average of the initial and final prices.

Let's apply the formula to calculating the price elasticity of D_1 in Figure 6.1. Between point A and point B on D_1, the change in quantity is 200, and the average of the two quantities is 1,100. Therefore, there is an 18.2 percent change in quantity. The change in price is −$0.10, and the average of the two prices is $1.20. Therefore, there is a −8.3 percent change in price. So, the price elasticity of demand is 18.2/−8.3 = −2.2. Notice these three results from calculating the price elasticity of demand using the midpoint formula: First, as we suspected from examining Figure 6.1, demand curve D_1 is elastic between points A and B. Second, our value for the price elasticity calculated using the midpoint formula is between the two values we calculated earlier. Third, the midpoint formula will give us the same value whether we are moving from the higher price to the lower price or from the lower price to the higher price.

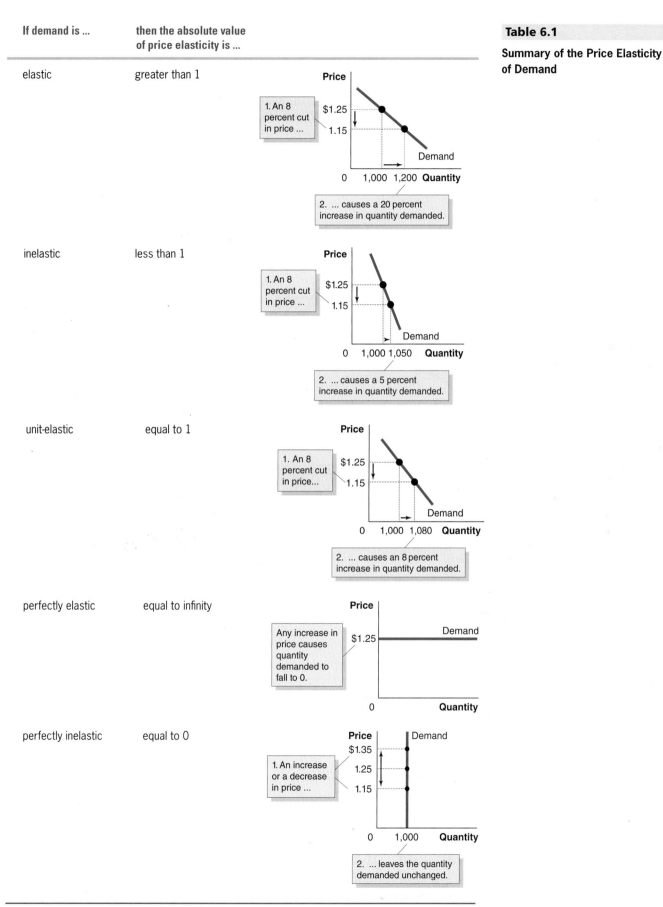

If demand is ...	then the absolute value of price elasticity is ...
elastic	greater than 1
inelastic	less than 1
unit-elastic	equal to 1
perfectly elastic	equal to infinity
perfectly inelastic	equal to 0

Table 6.1

Summary of the Price Elasticity of Demand

Note: The percentage changes shown in the boxes in the graphs were calculated using the midpoint formula and are rounded to the nearest whole number.

Don't Let This Happen to You

Don't Confuse *Inelastic* with *Perfectly Inelastic*

You may be tempted to simplify the concept of elasticity by assuming that any demand curve described as being inelastic is *perfectly* inelastic. You should never assume this because perfectly inelastic demand curves are rare. For example, consider the following problem: "Use a demand and supply graph to show how a decrease in supply affects the equilibrium quantity of gasoline. Assume that the demand for gasoline is inelastic." The following graph would be an *incorrect* answer to this problem.

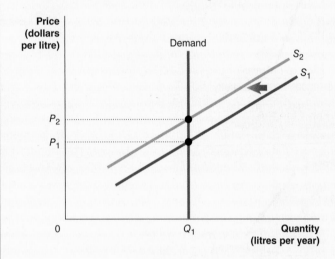

The demand for gasoline is inelastic, but it is not *perfectly* inelastic. When the price of gasoline rises, the quantity demanded falls. So, the graph that would be the correct answer to this problem would show a typical downward-sloping demand curve rather than a vertical demand curve.

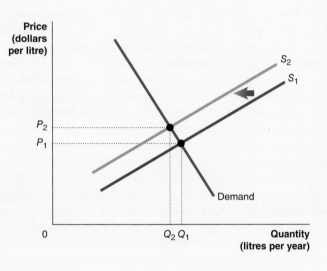

MyEconLab

Your Turn: Test your understanding by doing related problem 1.4 on page 185 at the end of this chapter.

6.2 LEARNING OBJECTIVE
Understand the determinants of the price elasticity of demand.

The Determinants of the Price Elasticity of Demand

We have seen that the demand for some products may be elastic, while the demand for other products may be inelastic. In this section, we examine why price elasticities differ among products. The key determinants of the price elasticity of demand are as follows:

* Availability of close substitutes

* Passage of time

* Luxuries versus necessities

* Definition of the market

* Share of a good in the consumer's budget

Availability of Close Substitutes

The availability of substitutes is the most important determinant of price elasticity of demand because how consumers react to a change in the price of a product depends on what alternatives they have. When the price of gasoline rises, consumers have few alternatives, so the quantity demanded falls only a little. But if the price of pizza rises, consumers have many alternative foods they can eat instead, so the quantity demanded is likely to fall substantially. In fact, a key constraint on a firm's pricing policies is how many close substitutes exist for its product. In general, *if a product has more substitutes available, it will have more elastic demand. If a product has fewer substitutes available, it will have less elastic demand.*

Passage of Time

It usually takes consumers some time to adjust their buying habits when prices change. If the price of chicken falls, for example, it takes a while before consumers decide to change from eating chicken for dinner once per week to eating it twice per week. If the price of gasoline increases, it also takes a while for consumers to decide to begin taking public transportation, to buy more fuel-efficient cars, or to find new jobs closer to where they live. *The more time that passes, the more elastic the demand for a product becomes.*

Luxuries versus Necessities

Goods that are luxuries usually have more elastic demand curves than goods that are necessities. For example, the demand for bread is inelastic because bread is a necessity, and the quantity that people buy is not very dependent on its price. Tickets to a concert are a luxury, so the demand for concert tickets is much more elastic than the demand for bread. *The demand curve for a luxury is more elastic than the demand curve for a necessity.*

Definition of the Market

In a narrowly defined market, consumers have more substitutes available. For example, if you own a service station and raise the price you charge for gasoline, many of your customers will switch to buying from a competitor. So, the demand for gasoline at one particular station is likely to be elastic. The demand for gasoline as a product, on the other hand, is inelastic because consumers have few alternatives (in the short run) to buying it. *The more narrowly we define a market, the more elastic demand will be.*

Share of a Good in a Consumer's Budget

Goods that take only a small fraction of a consumer's budget tend to have less elastic demand than goods that take a large fraction. For example, most people buy table salt infrequently and in relatively small quantities. The share of the average consumer's budget that is spent on salt is very low. As a result, even a doubling of the price of salt is likely to result in only a small decline in the quantity of salt demanded. "Big-ticket items," such as houses, cars, and furniture, take up a larger share in the average consumer's budget. Increases in the prices of these goods are likely to result in significant declines in quantity demanded. In general, *the demand for a good will be more elastic the larger the share of the good in the average consumer's budget.*

Some Estimated Price Elasticities of Demand

Table 6.2 shows some estimated short-run price elasticities of demand. It's important to remember that estimates of the price elasticities of different goods can vary, depending

Table 6.2

Estimated Real-World Price Elasticities of Demand

Product	Estimated Elasticity	Product	Estimated Elasticity
Books (Barnes & Noble)	−4.00	Bread	−0.40
Books (Amazon)	−0.60	Water (residential use)	−0.38
DVDs (Amazon)	−3.10	Chicken	−0.37
Post Raisin Bran	−2.50	Cocaine	−0.28
Automobiles	−1.95	Cigarettes	−0.25
Tide (liquid detergent)	−3.92	Beer	−0.23
Coca-Cola	−1.22	Residential natural gas	−0.09
Grapes	−1.18	Gasoline	−0.06
Restaurant meals	−0.67	Milk	−0.04
Health insurance (low-income households)	−0.65	Sugar	−0.04

Based on Kelly D. Brownell and Thomas R. Frieden, "Ounces of Prevention—The Public Policy Case for Taxes on Sugared Beverages," *New England Journal of Medicine*, April 30, 2009; Sheila M. Olmstead and Robert N. Stavins, "Comparing Price and Non-Price Approaches to Urban Water Conservation," Resources for the Future, Discussion paper 08-22, June 2008; Jonathan E. Hughes, Christopher R. Knittel, and Daniel Sperling, "Evidence of a Shift in the Short-Run Price Elasticity of Gasoline Demand," Research Report UCD-ITS-RR-06-16 (University of California, Davis: Institute of Transportation Studies, 2006); Robert P. Trost, Frederick Joutz, David Shin, and Bruce McDonwell, "Using Shrinkage Estimators to Obtain Regional Short-Run and Long-Run Price Elasticities of Residential Natural Gas Demand in the U.S." George Washington University Working Paper, March 13, 2009; Lesley Chiou, "Empirical Analysis of Competition Between Wal-Mart and Other Retail Channels," *Journal of Economics and Management Strategy*, forthcoming; Judith Chevalier and Austan Goolsbee, "Price Competition Online: Amazon versus Barnes and Noble," *Quantitative Marketing and Economics*, Vol. 1, no. 2, June 2003; Henry Saffer and Frank Chaloupka, "The Demand for Illicit Drugs," *Economic Inquiry*, Vol. 37, No. 3, July 1999; "Response to Increases in Cigarette Prices by Race/Ethnicity, Income, and Age Groups—United States, 1976–1993," *Morbidity and Mortality Weekly Report*, July 31, 1998; James Wetzel and George Hoffer, "Consumer Demand for Automobiles: A Disaggregated Market Approach," *Journal of Consumer Research*, Vol. 9, No. 2, September 1982; Jerry A. Hausman, "The Price Elasticity of Demand for Breakfast Cereal," in Timothy F. Bresnahan and Robert J. Gordon, eds., *The Economics of New Goods*, Chicago: University of Chicago Press, 1997; X. M. Gao, Eric J. Wailes, and Gail L. Cramer, "A Microeconometric Model Analysis of U.S. Consumer Demand for Alcoholic Beverages," *Applied Economics*, January 1995; and U.S. Department of Agriculture, Economic Research Service.

on the data used and the time period over which the estimates were made. The results given in the table are consistent with our discussion of the determinants of price elasticity. Goods for which there are few substitutes, such as cigarettes, gasoline, and health insurance, are price inelastic, as are broadly defined goods, such as bread or beer. Particular brands of products, such as Coca-Cola, Tide, or Post Raisin Bran, are price elastic. (This point is discussed further in the *Making the Connection* on the price elasticity of breakfast cereal.)

The table shows that the demand for books or DVDs bought from a particular retailer is typically price elastic. Note, though, that demand for books from Amazon is inelastic, which indicates that consumers do not consider ordering from other online sites to be good substitutes for ordering from Amazon.

An increase in the price of grapes will lead some consumers to substitute other fruits, so demand for grapes is price elastic. Similarly, an increase in the price of new automobiles will lead some consumers to buy used automobiles or to continue driving their current cars, so demand for automobiles is also price elastic. The demand for necessities, such as natural gas and water, is price inelastic.

Making
the
Connection

The Price Elasticity of Demand for Breakfast Cereal

MIT economist Jerry Hausman has estimated the price elasticity of demand for breakfast cereal. He divided breakfast cereals into three categories: children's cereals, such as Trix and Froot Loops; adult cereals, such as Special K and Grape-Nuts; and family cereals, such as Corn Flakes and Raisin Bran. Some of the results of his estimates are given in the following table.

Cereal	Price Elasticity of Demand
Post Raisin Bran	−2.5
All family breakfast cereals	−1.8
All types of breakfast cereals	−0.9

Data from Jerry A. Hausman, "Valuation of New Goods under Perfect and Imperfect Competition," in Timothy F. Bresnahan and Robert J. Gordon, eds., *The Economics of New Goods* (Chicago: University of Chicago Press, 1997), p. 226.

Just as we would expect, the price elasticity for a particular brand of raisin bran was larger in absolute value than the elasticity for all family cereals, and the elasticity for all family cereals was larger than the elasticity for all types of breakfast cereals. If Post increases the price of its Raisin Bran by 10 percent, sales will decline by 25 percent, as many consumers switch to another brand of raisin bran. If the prices of all family breakfast cereals rise by 10 percent, sales will decline by 18 percent, as consumers switch to child or adult cereals. In both of these cases, demand is elastic. But if the prices of all types of breakfast cereals rise by 10 percent, sales will decline by only 9 percent. Demand for all breakfast cereals is inelastic.

Based on Jerry A. Hausman, "Valuation of New Goods under Perfect and Imperfect Competition," in Timothy F. Bresnahan and Robert J. Gordon, eds., *The Economics of New Goods* (Chicago: University of Chicago Press, 1997).

Your turn: Test your understanding by doing related base align problem 2.2 on page 185 at the end of this chapter.

MyEconLab

The Relationship Between Price Elasticity of Demand and Total Revenue

6.3 LEARNING OBJECTIVE
Understand the relationship between the price elasticity of demand and total revenue.

A firm is interested in price elasticity because it allows the firm to calculate how changes in price will affect its **total revenue**, which is the total amount of funds it receives from selling a good or service. Total revenue is calculated by multiplying price per unit by the number of units sold. When demand is inelastic, price and total revenue move in the same direction: An increase in price raises total revenue, and a decrease in price reduces total revenue. When demand is elastic, price and total revenue move inversely: An increase in price reduces total revenue, and a decrease in price raises total revenue.

Total revenue The total amount of funds received by a seller of a good or service, calculated by multiplying price per unit by the number of units sold.

To understand the relationship between price elasticity and total revenue, consider Figure 6.2. Panel (a) shows a demand curve for gasoline (as in Figure 6.1 on page 160). This demand curve is inelastic between point A and point B. The total revenue received by the service station owner at point A equals the price of $1.25 multiplied by the 1,000 litres sold, or $1,250. This amount equals the areas of the rectangles C and D in the figure because together the rectangles have a height of $1.25 and a base of 1,000 litres. Because this demand curve is inelastic between point A and point B (it was demand curve D_2 in Figure 6.1), cutting the price to $1.15 (point B) reduces total revenue. The new total revenue is shown by the areas of rectangles D and E and is equal to $1.15 multiplied by 1,050 litres, or $1,207.50. Total revenue falls because the increase in the quantity demanded is not large enough to make up for the decrease in price. As a result,

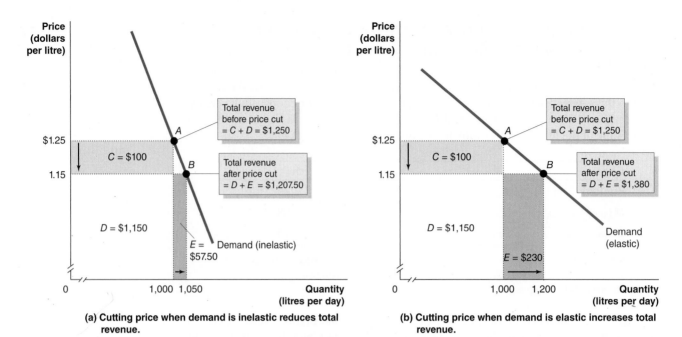

Figure 6.2 **The Relationship Between Price Elasticity and Total Revenue**

When demand is inelastic, a cut in price will decrease total revenue. In panel (a), at point A, the price is $1.25, 1,000 litres are sold, and total revenue received by the service station equals $1.25 × 1,000 litres, or $1,250. At point B, cutting the price to $1.15 increases the quantity demanded to 1,050 litres, but the fall in price more than offsets the increase in quantity. As a result, revenue falls to $1.15 × 1,050 litres, or $1,207.50. When demand is elastic, a cut in the price will increase total revenue. In panel (b), at point A, the area of rectangles C and D is still equal to $1,250. But at point B, the area of rectangles D and E is equal to $1.15 × 1,200 litres, or $1,380. In this case, the increase in the quantity demanded is large enough to offset the fall in price, so total revenue increases.

the $57.50 increase in revenue gained as a result of the price cut—dark-green rectangle *E*—is less than the $100 in revenue lost—light-green rectangle *C*.

Panel (b) of Figure 6.2 shows a demand curve that is elastic between point *A* and point *B*. (It was demand curve *D*₁ in Figure 6.1.) In this case, cutting the price increases total revenue. At point *A*, the areas of rectangles *C* and *D* are still equal to $1,250, but at point *B*, the areas of rectangles *D* and *E* are equal to $1.15 multiplied by 1,200 litres, or $1,380. Here, total revenue rises because the increase in the quantity demanded is large enough to offset the lower price. As a result, the $230 increase in revenue gained as a result of the price cut—dark-green rectangle *E*—is greater than the $100 in revenue lost—light-green rectangle *C*.

The third, less common possibility is that demand is unit elastic. In that case, a small change in price is exactly offset by a proportional change in quantity demanded, leaving revenue unaffected. Therefore, when demand is unit elastic, neither a decrease in price nor an increase in price affects revenue. Table 6.3 summarizes the relationship between price elasticity and revenue.

Elasticity and Revenue with a Linear Demand Curve

Along most demand curves, elasticity is not constant at every point. For example, a straight-line, or linear, demand curve for gasoline is shown in panel (a) of Figure 6.3. (For simplicity, prices used are large and the quantities used are small.) The numbers from the table are plotted in the graphs. The demand curve shows that when the price drops by $1 per gasoline, consumers always respond by buying 2 more gasoline per day. When the price is high and the quantity demanded is low, demand is elastic. Demand is elastic because a $1 drop in price is a smaller percentage change when the price is high, and an increase of 2 gasoline is a larger percentage change when the quantity of gasoline purchased is small. By similar reasoning, we can see why demand is inelastic when the price is low and the quantity demanded is high.

If demand is ...	then ...	because ...
elastic	an increase in price reduces revenue	the decrease in quantity demanded is proportionally *greater* than the increase in price.
elastic	a decrease in price increases revenue	the increase in quantity demanded is proportionally *greater* than the decrease in price.
inelastic	an increase in price increases revenue	the decrease in quantity demanded is proportionally *smaller* than the increase in price.
inelastic	a decrease in price reduces revenue	the increase in quantity demanded is proportionally *smaller* than the decrease in price.
unit elastic	an increase in price does not affect revenue	the decrease in quantity demanded is proportionally *the same as* the increase in price.
unit elastic	a decrease in price does not affect revenue	the increase in quantity demanded is proportionally *the same as* the decrease in price.

Table 6.3

The Relationship Between Price Elasticity and Revenue

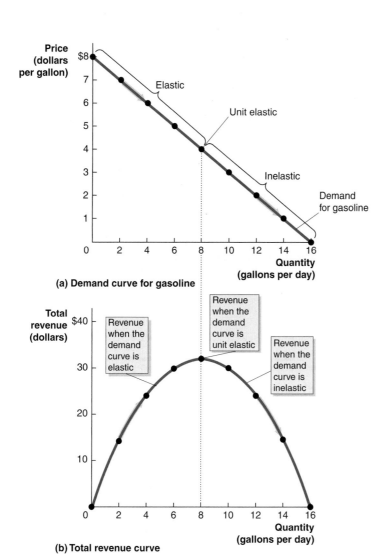

Price	Quantity Demanded	Total Revenue
$8	0	$ 0
7	2	14
6	4	24
5	6	30
4	8	32
3	10	30
2	12	24
1	14	14
0	16	0

(a) Demand curve for gasoline

(b) Total revenue curve

Figure 6.3 **Elasticity Is Not Constant Along a Linear Demand Curve**

The data from the table are plotted in the graphs. Panel (a) shows that as we move down the demand curve for gasoline, the price elasticity of demand declines. In other words, at higher prices, demand is elastic, and at lower prices, demand is inelastic. Panel (b) shows that as the quantity of gasoline purchased increases from 0, revenue will increase until it reaches a maximum of $32 when 8 gallons are purchased. As purchases increase beyond 8 gallons, revenue falls because demand is inelastic on this portion of the demand curve.

Panel (a) in Figure 6.3 shows that when price is between $8 and $4 and quantity demanded is between 0 and 8 gallons, demand is elastic. Panel (b) shows that over this same range, total revenue will increase as price falls. For example, in panel (a), as price falls from $7 to $6, quantity demanded increases from 2 to 4, and in panel (b), total revenue increases from $14 to $24. Similarly, when price is between $4 and $0 and quantity demanded is between 8 and 16, demand is inelastic. Over this same range, total revenue will decrease as price falls. For example, as price falls from $3 to $2 and quantity demanded increases from 10 to 12, total revenue decreases from $30 to $24.

Solved Problem **6.3**

Price and Revenue Don't Always Move in the Same Direction

Briefly explain whether you agree or disagree with the following statement: "The only way to increase the revenue from selling a product is to increase the product's price."

Solving the Problem

Step 1: Review the chapter material. This problem deals with the effect of a price change on a firm's revenue, so you may want to review the section "The Relationship Between Price Elasticity of Demand and Total Revenue," which begins on page 167.

Step 2: Analyze the statement. We have seen that a price increase will increase revenue only if demand is inelastic. In Figure 6.3, for example, increasing the price of gasoline from $1 per gallon to $2 per gallon *increases* revenue from $14 to $24 because demand is inelastic along this portion of the demand curve. But increasing the price from $5 to $6 *decreases* revenue from $30 to $24 because demand is elastic along this portion of the demand curve. If the price is currently $5, increasing revenue would require a price *cut*, not a price increase. As this example shows, the statement is incorrect, and you should disagree with it.

MyEconLab   **Your Turn:** For more practice, do related problems 3.2 and 3.3 on page 186 at the end of this chapter.

Estimating Price Elasticity of Demand

To estimate the price elasticity of demand, a firm needs to know the demand curve for its product. For a well-established product, economists can use historical data to statistically estimate the demand curve. To calculate the price elasticity of demand for a new product, firms often rely on market experiments. With market experiments, firms try different prices and observe the change in quantity demanded that results.

Making the Connection | ## Determining the Price Elasticity of Demand Through Market Experiments

Firms usually have a good idea of the price elasticity of demand for products that have been on the market for at least a few years. For new products, however, firms often experiment with different prices to determine the price elasticity. For example, Apple introduced the first-generation iPhone in June 2007, at a price of US$599. But demand for the iPhone was more elastic than Apple had expected, and when sales failed to reach Apple's projections, the company cut the price to US$399 just two months later. Similarly, when 3D televisions were introduced into the U.S. market in early 2010, Sony and other manufacturers believed that sales would be strong despite prices being several hundred dollars higher than for other high-end ultra-thin televisions. Once again, though, demand turned out to be more elastic than expected, and by December firms were cutting prices 40 percent or more in an effort to increase revenue.

The price elasticity of demand for 3D televisions was higher than Sony had expected.

Since electronic books (e-books) became popular after Amazon introduced the Kindle e-reader, firms have experimented with different prices in trying to determine the relevant price elasticity. Amazon had originally priced most best selling e-books at $9.99, but when Apple introduced the iPad in 2010, Apple negotiated contracts with publishers that raised prices for e-books. Amazon and Barnes & Noble eventually signed similar contracts, and the prices for best selling e-books rose from $9.99 to $12.99 or $14.99. Publishers hoped that a low price elasticity of demand for e-books would result in the price increase leading to higher revenues. Many buyers, however, claimed that rather than pay higher prices, they would go back to reading printed books. Economist Joel Waldfogel raised the possibility that the higher prices might lead some readers to illegally download pirated e-books, in violation of the publishers' copyrights. Although piracy has been a problem with music and movies, it had not yet been a problem with books. Waldfogel argued that, "I would be scared to death about a culture of piracy taking hold. I wouldn't mess around with price increases." Whether the demand for e-books turns out to be elastic or inelastic may depend on how many readers consider printed books or pirated e-books to be close substitutes for legally downloaded e-books.

Based on Daisuke Wakabayashi and Miguel Bustillo, "TV Makers Can't Hold Line on 3-D Prices," *Wall Street Journal*, December 20, 2010; Motoko Rich and Brad Stone, "Cost of an e-Book Will Be Going Up," *New York Times*, February 11, 2010; and Kate Hafner and Brad Stone, "iPhone Owners Crying Foul over Price Cut," *New York Times*, September 7, 2007.

Your turn: Test your understanding by doing related problem 3.5 on page 186 at the end of this chapter.

MyEconLab

Other Demand Elasticities

6.4 LEARNING OBJECTIVE
Define cross-price elasticity of demand and income elasticity of demand and understand their determinants and how they are measured.

Elasticity is an important concept in economics because it allows us to quantify the responsiveness of one economic variable to changes in another economic variable. In addition to price elasticity, two other demand elasticities are important: *cross-price elasticity of demand* and *income elasticity of demand*.

Cross-Price Elasticity of Demand

Suppose you work at Apple, and you need to predict the effect of an increase in the price of Samsung's Galaxy Tab on the quantity of iPads demanded, holding other factors constant. You can do this by calculating the **cross-price elasticity of demand**, which is the percentage change in the quantity of iPads demanded divided by the percentage change in the price of Galaxy Tabs—or, in general:

Cross-price elasticity of demand
The percentage change in quantity demanded of one good divided by the percentage change in the price of another good.

$$\text{Cross-price elasticity of demand} = \frac{\text{Percentage change in quantity demanded of one good}}{\text{Percentage change in price of another good}}.$$

Table 6.4

Summary of Cross-Price Elasticity of Demand

If the products are ...	then the cross-price elasticity of demand will be ...	Example
substitutes	positive.	Two brands of tablet computers
complements	negative.	Tablet computers and applications downloaded from online stores
unrelated	zero.	Tablet computers and peanut butter

The cross-price elasticity of demand is positive or negative, depending on whether the two products are substitutes or complements. Recall that substitutes are products that can be used for the same purpose, such as two brands of tablet computers. Complements are products that are used together, such as tablet computers and applications that can be downloaded from online stores. An increase in the price of a substitute will lead to an increase in quantity demanded, so the cross-price elasticity of demand will be positive. An increase in the price of a complement will lead to a decrease in the quantity demanded, so the cross-price elasticity of demand will be negative. Of course, if the two products are unrelated—such as tablet computers and peanut butter—the cross-price elasticity of demand will be zero. Table 6.4 summarizes the key points concerning the cross-price elasticity of demand.

Cross-price elasticity of demand is important to firm managers because it allows them to measure whether products sold by other firms are close substitutes for their products. For example, Pepsi-Cola and Coca-Cola spend heavily on advertising with the hope of convincing consumers that each cola tastes better than its rival. How can these firms tell whether or not their advertising campaigns have been effective? One way is by seeing whether the cross-price elasticity of demand has changed. If, for instance, Coca-Cola has a successful advertising campaign, then when it increases the price of Coke, the percentage increase in sales of Pepsi should be smaller. In other words, the value of the cross-price elasticity of demand should have declined.

Income Elasticity of Demand

Income elasticity of demand A measure of the responsiveness of quantity demanded to changes in income, measured by the percentage change in quantity demanded divided by the percentage change in income.

The **income elasticity of demand** measures the responsiveness of quantity demanded to changes in income. It is calculated as follows:

$$\text{Income elasticity of demand} = \frac{\text{Percentage change in quantity demanded}}{\text{Percentage change in income}}.$$

As we saw in Chapter 3, if the quantity demanded of a good increases as income increases, then the good is a *normal good*. Normal goods are often further subdivided into *luxuries* and *necessities*. A good is a luxury if the quantity demanded is very responsive to changes in income, so that a 10 percent increase in income results in more than a 10 percent increase in quantity demanded. Expensive jewellery and vacation homes are examples of luxuries. A good is a necessity if the quantity demanded is not very responsive to changes in income, so that a 10 percent increase in income results in less than a 10 percent increase in quantity demanded. Food and clothing are examples of necessities. A good is *inferior* if the quantity demanded falls when income increases. Ground beef with a high fat content is an example of an inferior good. We should note that *normal good*, *inferior good*, *necessity*, and *luxury* are just labels economists use for goods with different income elasticities; the labels are not intended to be value judgments about the worth of these goods.

If the income elasticity of demand is ...	then the good is ...	Example
positive but less than 1	normal and a necessity.	Bread
positive and greater than 1	normal and a luxury.	Caviar
negative	inferior.	High-fat meat

Table 6.5

Summary of Income Elasticity of Demand

Because most goods are normal goods, during periods of economic expansion, when consumer income is rising, most firms can expect—holding other factors constant—that the quantity demanded of their products will increase. Sellers of luxuries can expect particularly large increases. During recessions, falling consumer income can cause firms to experience increases in demand for inferior goods. For example, the demand for bus trips increases as consumers cut back on air travel, and supermarkets find that the demand for hamburger increases relative to the demand for steak. Table 6.5 summarizes the key points about the income elasticity of demand.

Making the Connection | ## Price Elasticity, Cross-Price Elasticity, and Income Elasticity in the Market for Alcoholic Beverages

Many public policy issues are related to the consumption of alcoholic beverages. These issues include underage drinking, drunk driving, and the possible beneficial effects of red wine in lowering the risk of heart disease. Economist X. M. Gao and two colleagues have estimated statistically the following elasticities. (*Spirits* refers to all beverages that contain alcohol, other than beer and wine.)

Price elasticity of demand for beer	−0.23
Cross-price elasticity of demand between beer and wine	0.31
Cross-price elasticity of demand between beer and spirits	0.15
Income elasticity of demand for beer	−0.09
Income elasticity of demand for wine	5.03
Income elasticity of demand for spirits	1.21

The demand for beer is inelastic. A 10 percent increase in the price of beer will result in a 2.3 percent decline in the quantity of beer demanded. Not surprisingly, both wine and spirits are substitutes for beer. A 10 percent increase in the price of wine will result in a 3.1 percent *increase* in the quantity of beer demanded. A 10 percent increase in income will result in a little less than a 1 percent *decline* in the quantity of beer demanded. So, beer is an inferior good. Both wine and spirits are categorized as luxuries because their income elasticities are greater than 1.

Based on X. M. Gao, Eric J. Wailes, and Gail L. Cramer, "A Microeconometric Model Analysis of U.S. Consumer Demand for Alcoholic Beverages," *Applied Economics*, January 1995.

Your turn: Test your understanding by doing related problem 4.4 on page 187 at the end of this chapter.

MyEconLab

Using Elasticity to Analyze the Disappearing Family Farm

The concepts of price elasticity and income elasticity can help us understand many economic issues. For example, some people are concerned that the family farm is becoming an endangered species. Although food production continues to grow rapidly, the number of farms and the number of farmers continue to dwindle.

In 1931, when the farm population count was compiled for the first time, Canada was home to 728,623 farms (with an average of 91 hectares [224 acres] per farm), and close to 3.3 million people (about 31.7 percent of the population) lived on farms. According to the 2011 Census of Agriculture by Statistics Canada, by 2011 only about 205,730 farms remained (with an average of 315 hectares [778 acres] per farm), and about 2 percent of the Canadian population lived on them. However, even though the total land area devoted to growing wheat declined, because of the development of superior strains of wheat and improvements in farming techniques, total wheat production rose from about 320 million bushels in 1931 to about 930 million bushels in 2011. Similar trends occurred in the United States.

Unfortunately for farmers, this increase in wheat production resulted in a substantial decline in wheat prices. Two key factors explain this decline: (1) The demand for wheat is inelastic, and (2) the income elasticity of demand for wheat is low. Even though the Canadian population has increased greatly since 1960 and the income of the average Canadian is much higher than it was in 1960, the demand for wheat has increased only moderately. For all of the additional wheat to be sold, the price has had to decline. Because the demand for wheat is inelastic, the price decline has been substantial. Figure 6.4 illustrates these points for Canada.

A large shift in supply, a small shift in demand, and an inelastic demand curve combined to drive down the price of wheat from $498.80 per bushel in 1960 to $367.23 per bushel in 2013. (The 1960 price is measured in terms of prices in 1960, to adjust for the general increase in prices since 1960.) With low prices, only the most efficiently run farms have been able to remain profitable. Small family-run farms have found it difficult to survive, and many of these farms have disappeared. The markets for most other food products are similar to the market for wheat. They are characterized by rapid output growth and low income and price elasticities. The result is the paradox of North American farming: ever more abundant and cheaper food, supplied by fewer and fewer farms. North American consumers have benefited, but most family farmers have not.

Figure 6.4

Elasticity and the Disappearing Family Farm

In 1960, Canadian farmers produced 14,108,000 tonnes of wheat at a price of $498.80 per tonne. Over the next 50 years, rapid increases in farm productivity caused a large shift to the right in the supply curve for wheat. Production in 2013 is estimated at 27 million tonnes. The income elasticity of demand for wheat is low, so the demand for wheat increased relatively little over this period. Because the demand for wheat is also price inelastic, the large shift in the supply curve and the small shift in the demand curve resulted in a sharp decline in the price of wheat, from $498.80 per bushel in 1960 to $367.23 per bushel in 2013. (All prices are in 2013 Canadian dollars.)

Data from Statistics Canada, Bank of Canada, and World Bank.

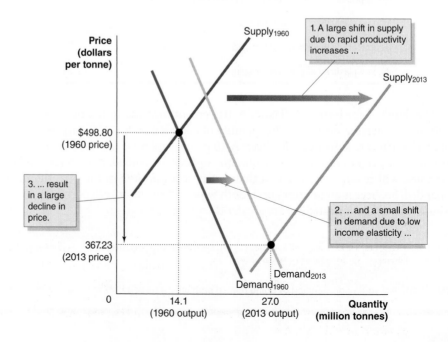

Solved Problem **6.5**

Using Price Elasticity to Analyze a Policy of Taxing Gasoline

In Chapter 5, we saw that if the consumption of a product results in a negative externality, taxing the product may improve economic efficiency. Some economists and policymakers argue that driving cars and trucks involves a negative externality because burning gasoline increases emissions of greenhouse gases and contributes to the congestion that clogs many highways in and around big cities. Some economists have suggested substantially increasing the federal excise tax on gasoline, which in 2011 was 10 cents per litre. How much the tax would cause consumption to fall and how much revenue the tax would raise depend on the price elasticity of demand. Suppose that the price of gasoline is currently $1.25 per litre, the quantity of

gasoline demanded is 140 billion litres per year, the price elasticity of demand for gasoline is −0.06, and the federal government decides to increase the excise tax on gasoline by $0.20 per litre. We saw in Chapter 4 that the price of a product will not rise by the full amount of a tax increase unless the demand for the product is perfectly inelastic. In this case, suppose that the price of gasoline increases by $0.10 per litre after the $0.20 excise tax is imposed.

a. What is the new quantity of gasoline demanded after the tax is imposed? How effective would a gas tax be in reducing consumption of gasoline in the short run?

b. How much revenue does the federal government receive from the tax?

Solving the Problem

Step 1: **Review the chapter material.** This problem deals with applications of the price elasticity of demand formula, so you may want to review the section "Measuring the Price Elasticity of Demand," which begins on page 158.

Step 2: **Answer the first question in part (a) using the formula for the price elasticity of demand to calculate the new quantity demanded.**

$$\text{Price elasticity of demand} = \frac{\text{Percentage change in quantity demanded}}{\text{Percentage change in price}}.$$

We can plug into the midpoint formula the values given for the price elasticity, the original price of $1.25, and the new price of $1.35 (= $1.25 + $0.10):

$$-0.06 = \frac{\text{Percentage change in quantity demanded}}{\dfrac{(\$1.35 - \$1.25)}{\left(\dfrac{\$1.25 + \$1.35}{2}\right)}}.$$

Or, rearranging and writing out the expression for the percentage change in quantity demanded:

$$-0.005 = \frac{(Q_2 - 140 \text{ billion})}{\left(\dfrac{140 \text{ billion} + Q_2}{2}\right)}.$$

Solving for Q_2, the new quantity demanded:

$$Q_2 = 139.5 \text{ billion litres}$$

Step 3: **Answer the second question in part (a).** Because the price elasticity of demand for gasoline is so low (−0.06) even a substantial increase in the gasoline tax of $0.20 per litre would reduce gasoline consumption by only a small amount: from 140 billion litres of gasoline per year to 139.5 billion litres. Note, though, that price elasticities typically increase over time. Economists estimate that the long-run price elasticity of gasoline is in the range of −0.40 to −0.60, so in the long run, the decline in the consumption of gasoline would be larger.

Step 4: Calculate the revenue earned by the federal government to answer part (b). The federal government would collect an amount equal to the tax per litre multiplied by the number of litres sold: $0.20 per litre $\times$ 139.5 billion litres = $27.86 billion.

Extra Credit: We can conclude that raising the federal excise tax on gasoline would be a good way to raise revenue for the federal government, but, at least in the short run, increasing the tax would not greatly reduce the quantity of gasoline consumed. Notice that if the demand for gasoline were elastic, this result would be reversed: The quantity of gasoline consumed would decline much more, but so would the revenue that the federal government would receive from the tax increase.

MyEconLab   **Your Turn:** For more practice, do related problem 5.1 on page 187 at the end of this chapter.

6.6 LEARNING OBJECTIVE
Define price elasticity of supply and understand its main determinants and how it is measured.

The Price Elasticity of Supply and Its Measurement

We can use the concept of elasticity to measure the responsiveness of firms to a change in price, just as we used it to measure the responsiveness of consumers. We know from the law of supply that when the price of a product increases, the quantity supplied increases. To measure how much the quantity supplied increases when price increases, we use the *price elasticity of supply*.

price elasticity of supply The responsiveness of the quantity supplied to a change in price, measured by dividing the percentage change in the quantity supplied of a product by the percentage change in the product's price.

Measuring the Price Elasticity of Supply

Just as with the price elasticity of demand, we calculate the **price elasticity of supply** by using percentage changes:

$$\text{Price elasticity of supply} = \frac{\text{Percentage change in quantity supplied}}{\text{Percentage change in price}}.$$

Notice that because supply curves are upward sloping, the price elasticity of supply will be a positive number. We categorize the price elasticity of supply the same way we categorized the price elasticity of demand: If the price elasticity of supply is less than 1, then supply is *inelastic*. For example, the price elasticity of supply of gasoline is about 0.20, and so it is inelastic; a 10 percent increase in the price of gasoline will result in only a 2 percent increase in the quantity supplied. If the price elasticity of supply is greater than 1, then supply is *elastic*. If the price elasticity of supply is equal to 1, the supply is *unit elastic*. As with other elasticity calculations, when we calculate the price elasticity of supply, we hold constant the values of other factors.

Determinants of the Price Elasticity of Supply

Whether supply is elastic or inelastic depends on the ability and willingness of firms to alter the quantity they produce as price increases. Often, firms have difficulty increasing the quantity of the product they supply during any short period of time. For example, a pizza restaurant cannot produce more pizzas on any one night than is possible using the ingredients on hand. Within a day or two, it can buy more ingredients, and within a few months, it can hire more cooks and install additional ovens. As a result, the supply curve for pizza and most other products will be inelastic if we measure it over a short period of time, but the supply curve will be increasingly elastic the longer the period of time over which we measure it. Products that require resources that are themselves in fixed supply are an exception to this rule. For example, a winery may rely on a particular variety of grape. If all the land on which that grape can be grown is already planted in vineyards, then the supply of that wine will be inelastic even over a long period.

Making the Connection	## Why Are Oil Prices So Unstable?

Bringing oil to market is a long process. Oil companies hire geologists to locate fields for exploratory oil well drilling. If significant amounts of oil are present, the company begins full-scale development of the field. The process from exploration to pumping significant amounts of oil can take years. This long process is why the price elasticity of supply for oil is very low.

During the period from 2003 to mid-2008, the worldwide demand for oil increased rapidly as India, China, and some other developing countries increased both their manufacturing production and their use of automobiles. As the graph below shows, when supply is inelastic, an increase in demand can cause a large increase in price. The shift in the demand curve from D_1 to D_2 causes the equilibrium quantity of oil to increase only by 5 percent, from 80 million barrels per day to 84 million, but the equilibrium price rises by 75 percent, from $80 per barrel to $140 per barrel.

The world oil market is heavily influenced by the Organization of the Petroleum Exporting Countries (OPEC). OPEC has 11 members, including Saudi Arabia, Kuwait, Iran, Venezuela, and Nigeria. Together OPEC members own 75 percent of the world's proven oil reserves. Periodically, OPEC has attempted to force up the price of oil by reducing the quantity of oil its members supply. Since the 1970s, OPEC's attempts to reduce the quantity of oil on world markets have been successful only sporadically. As a result, the supply curve for oil shifts fairly frequently. Combined with the low price elasticities of oil supply and demand, these shifts in supply have caused the price of oil to fluctuate significantly over the past 30 years, from as low as $10 per barrel to more than $140 per barrel.

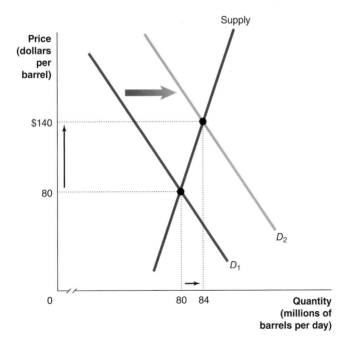

Beginning in mid-2008, the financial crisis that had begun in the United States had spread to other countries, resulting in a severe recession. As production and incomes fell during the recession, the worldwide demand for oil declined sharply. Over the space of a few months, the equilibrium price of oil fell from $140 per barrel to $40 per barrel. As the graph

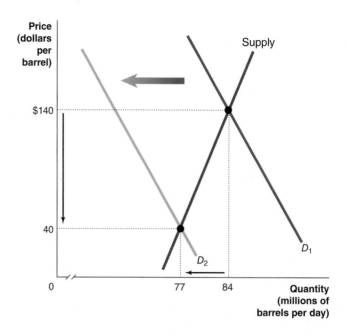

above shows, once again, the extent of the price change reflected not only the size of the decline in demand but also oil's low price elasticity of supply.

MyEconLab   **Your turn:** Test your understanding by doing related problem 6.1 on page 187 at the end of this chapter.

Polar Cases of Perfectly Elastic and Perfectly Inelastic Supply

Although it occurs infrequently, it is possible for supply to fall into one of the polar cases of price elasticity. If a supply curve is a vertical line, it is *perfectly inelastic*. In this case, the quantity supplied is completely unresponsive to price, and the price elasticity of supply equals zero. Regardless of how much price may increase or decrease, the quantity remains the same. Over a brief period of time, the supply of some goods and services may be perfectly inelastic. For example, a parking lot may have only a fixed number of parking spaces. If demand increases, the price to park in the lot may rise, but no more spaces will become available. Of course, if demand increases permanently, over a longer period of time, the owner of the lot may buy more land and add additional spaces.

If a supply curve is a horizontal line, it is *perfectly elastic*. In this case, the quantity supplied is infinitely responsive to price, and the price elasticity of supply equals infinity. If a supply curve is perfectly elastic, a very small increase in price causes a very large increase in quantity supplied. Just as with demand curves, it is important not to confuse a supply curve being elastic with its being perfectly elastic and not to confuse a supply curve being inelastic with its being perfectly inelastic. Table 6.6 summarizes the different price elasticities of supply.

Using Price Elasticity of Supply to Predict Changes in Price

Figure 6.5 illustrates the important point that, when demand increases, the amount by which price increases depends on the price elasticity of supply. The figure shows the demand and supply for parking spaces at a beach resort. In panel (a), on a typical summer weekend, equilibrium occurs at point *A*, where Demand$_{\text{Typical}}$ intersects a supply curve that is inelastic. The increase in demand for parking spaces on July 1 (Canada Day) shifts the demand curve to the right, moving the equilibrium to point *B*. Because the supply curve is inelastic, the increase in demand results in a large increase in price—from $2.00 per hour to $4.00—but only a small increase in the quantity of spaces supplied—from 1,200 to 1,400.

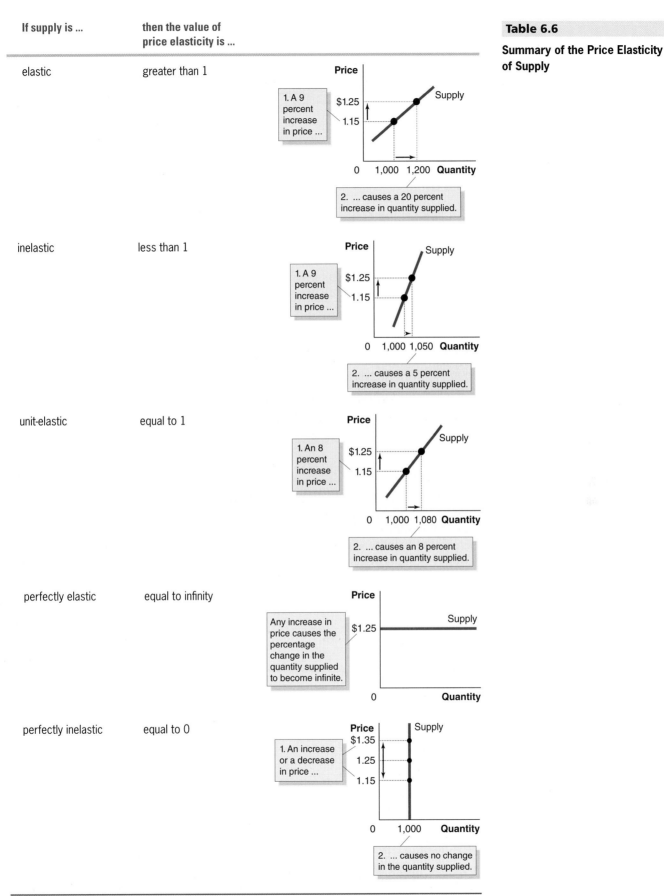

If supply is ...	then the value of price elasticity is ...	
elastic	greater than 1	
inelastic	less than 1	
unit-elastic	equal to 1	
perfectly elastic	equal to infinity	
perfectly inelastic	equal to 0	

Table 6.6

Summary of the Price Elasticity of Supply

Note: The percentage increases shown in the boxes in the graphs were calculated using the midpoint formula, given on page 160.

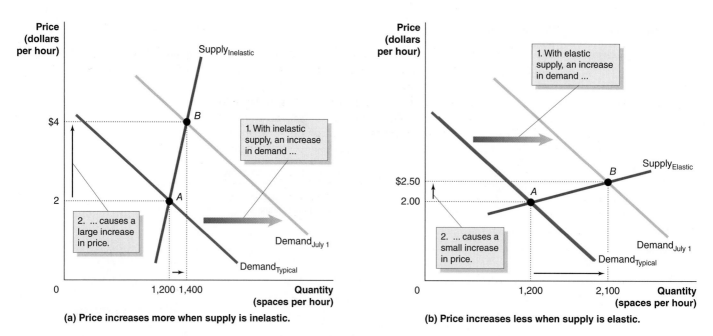

(a) Price increases more when supply is inelastic.

(b) Price increases less when supply is elastic.

Figure 6.5 **Changes in Price Depend on the Price Elasticity of Supply**

In panel (a), Demand_Typical represents the typical demand for parking spaces on a summer weekend at a beach resort. Demand_July 1 represents demand on Canada Day. Because supply is inelastic, the shift in equilibrium from point *A* to point *B* results in a large increase in price—from $2.00 per hour to $4.00—but only a small increase in the quantity of spaces supplied—from

1,200 to 1,400. In panel (b), supply is elastic. As a result, the change in equilibrium from point *A* to point *B* results in a smaller increase in price and a larger increase in the quantity supplied. An increase in price from $2.00 per hour to $2.50 is sufficient to increase the quantity of parking supplied from 1,200 to 2,100.

In panel (b), supply is elastic, perhaps because the resort has vacant land that can be used for parking during periods of high demand. As a result, the change in equilibrium from point *A* to point *B* results in a smaller increase in price and a larger increase in the quantity supplied. An increase in price from $2.00 per hour to $2.50 is sufficient to increase the quantity of parking spaces supplied from 1,200 to 2,100. Knowing the price elasticity of supply makes it possible to predict more accurately how much price will change following an increase or a decrease in demand.

Economics in Your Life

How Much Do Gas Prices Matter to You?

At the beginning of the chapter, we asked you to think about three questions: What factors would make you more or less sensitive to price when purchasing gasoline? Have you responded differently to price changes during different periods of your life? And why do consumers seem to respond more to changes in gas prices at a particular service station but seem less sensitive when gas prices rise or fall at all service stations? A number of factors are likely to affect your sensitivity to changes in gas prices, including how high your income is (and, therefore, how large a share of your budget is taken up by gasoline purchases), whether you live in an area with good public transportation (which can be a substitute for having to use your own car), and whether you live within walking distance of your school or job. Each of these factors may change over the course of your life, making you more or less sensitive to changes in gas prices. Finally, consumers respond to changes in the price of gas at a particular service station because gas at other service stations is a good substitute. But there are currently few good substitutes for gasoline as a product.

Conclusion

In this chapter, we have explored the important concept of elasticity. Table 6.7 summarizes the various elasticities we discussed. Computing elasticities is important in economics because it allows us to measure how one variable changes in response to changes in another variable. For example, by calculating the price elasticity of demand for its product, a firm can make a quantitative estimate of the effect of a price change on the revenue it receives. Similarly, by calculating the price elasticity of demand for cigarettes, the government can better estimate the effect of an increase in cigarette taxes on smoking.

Before going further in analyzing how firms decide on the prices to charge and the quantities to produce, we need to look at how firms are organized. We do this in the next chapter. Read *An Inside Look* on the next page for a discussion of the effect of higher gas prices on consumer and business spending.

Table 6.7

Summary of Elasticities

Price Elasticity of Demand

Formula: $\dfrac{\text{Percentage change in quantity demanded}}{\text{Percentage change in price}}$

Midpoint Formula: $\dfrac{(Q_2 - Q_1)}{\left(\dfrac{Q_2 + Q_1}{2}\right)} \div \dfrac{(P_2 - P_1)}{\left(\dfrac{P_1 + P_2}{2}\right)}$

	Absolute Value of Price Elasticity	Effect on Total Revenue of an Increase in Price
Elastic	Greater than 1	Total revenue falls
Inelastic	Less than 1	Total revenue rises
Unit elastic	Equal to 1	Total revenue unchanged

Cross-Price Elasticity of Demand

Formula: $\dfrac{\text{Percentage change in quantity demanded of one good}}{\text{Percentage change in price of another good}}$

Types of Products	Value of Cross-Price Elasticity
Substitutes	Positive
Complements	Negative
Unrelated	Zero

Income Elasticity of Demand

Formula: $\dfrac{\text{Percentage change in quantity demanded}}{\text{Percentage change in income}}$

Types of Products	Value of Income Elasticity
Normal and a necessity	Positive but less than 1
Normal and a luxury	Positive and greater than 1
Inferior	Negative

Price Elasticity of Supply

Formula: $\dfrac{\text{Percentage change in quantity supplied}}{\text{Percentage change in price}}$

	Value of Price Elasticity
Elastic	Greater than 1
Inelastic	Less than 1
Unit elastic	Equal to 1

Peaking Gas Prices Set New Records

CBC NEWS

Breaking Down the Price of Gasoline

As Canadian drivers prepare for what analysts say will be a month of record-breaking gas prices, we take a look at what exactly goes into determining the price of a litre of gas at the pump.

Prices were up in several parts of the country Wednesday, but not as high as some predicted.

In Toronto, they reached a high of 140.1 cents a litre for regular gas, an eight per cent increase over this time last year even with crude oil prices being lower than a year ago.

In Montreal, prices declined somewhat but were still the highest in the country at 147.9 cents a litre, according to the sites GasBuddy.com and Tomorrow's Gas Price Today, which track local pump prices.

Prices across the country vary widely because of different provincial and territorial tax regimes, but analyst Roger McKnight of Oshawa, Ont.-based En-Pro International Inc. has predicted that prices in southern Ontario could hit record highs between 143 and 147 cents a litre by the end of April.

Prior to this week, Canadian gas prices peaked in July 2008, based on a weekly average. Natural Resources Canada had the average price at 140.1 cents/litre the week of July 15, 2008, and M. J. Ervin and Associates had it at 141.3 cents/litre the week before that.

Geopolitical Factors

(a) It's usual for gas prices to rise in the spring as refineries shut down to convert from producing diesel to gasoline as the summer driving and vacation months approach, but this year, prices have been affected by several other factors, too:

- Shutdowns at four refineries in Pennsylvania and five in Europe have restricted North American supplies.
- Tensions over a possible conflict between the West and Iran have (b) affected supplies and oil futures markets. The U.S. has restricted Tehran's financial transactions with U.S. banks, and the EU has placed an embargo on the import of Iranian crude oil and petroleum products as of July 1. Some insurance companies have stopped insuring tankers transporting oil from Iran, which has reduced the number of supertankers going there.
- Reductions in exports from conflict-ridden Syria, Yemen and South Sudan have disrupted global supply. (c)

The price at the pump for a litre of gasoline is determined by the price of crude oil, the cost of refining that crude, marketing and distribution costs, taxes and, of course, profits all along the way—for everyone from those who extract the oil to those who pump the end product into your automobile.

Components of the Pump Price

M. J. Ervin and Associates of London, Ont., consultants to the petroleum industry, have been tracking the price movements of oil for over 20 years. Using their data for February 2012, here's the breakdown for the average cost of a litre of gasoline in Canada:

The refiner's operating margin, which is the difference between what the refiner pays for the crude and the wholesale price, varies from 6.6 cents/litre in Halifax and St. John's to 20.7 cents in Vancouver.

The marketing operating margin, which includes the costs of distribution and retail, in the major cities in the country's provinces ranges from 3.9 cents/litre in Calgary to 9.8 cents in St. John's but is much higher in the north, with Yellowknife the highest at 36.7 cents/litre.

Despite these fluctuations and the general upward trend of prices in recent years and the predictable griping they bring from consumers, some

Price Component	% of Pump Price (Feb. 2012)	Amount (Feb. 2012)	% of Price (Feb. 2002)	Amount (Feb. 2002)	% of Price (Feb. 1992)	Amount (Feb. 1992)
Crude costs	53	66.7 cents	34	20.4 cents	25	13.2 cents
Refiner's operating margin	12	14.7 cents	11	6.3 cents	16	8.37 cents
Marketing operating margin	5	6.8 cents	6	3.4 cents	10	5.33 cents
Taxes	31	38.9 cents	49	29.3 cents	49	25.7 cents
Pump price	101*	127 cents	100	59.4 cents	100	52.6 cents

Source: M. J. Ervin and Associates. *Percentages are rounded so might not add up to 100.

studies have shown that increases in prices at the pump don't actually affect personal spending habits that much.

The New York Times recently reported on one study, by economists Lutz Kilian at the University of Michigan and Paul Edelstein of the consulting firm IHS Global Insight, that found that periods when energy prices were high did not coincide with a significant decline in spending on recreational activities such as movies, gambling, spectator sports, and sightseeing—the areas that were most likely to be cut back to offset higher fuel costs.

Those findings seem to indicate that prices at the pump will have to get a lot higher before consumers start driving less.

Source: "Breaking down the price of gasoline," April 4, 2012. Used by permission of The Canadian Broadcasting Company (CBC).

Key Points in the Article

Rapidly increasing prices for crude oil during the first quarter of 2012 and other factors translated into higher prices at the gas pump. Crude oil prices, taxes, refiners' margins, and retail margins all contribute to the market price of gasoline. Some of these affect the supply side of the market by increasing transportation costs, and some affect the demand side by reducing the discretionary income of consumers. Analysts are concerned that the higher costs to businesses and cuts in consumer spending could be detrimental to the economic recovery, and the overall effect of the higher gas prices may take months to become evident in the economy.

Analyzing the News

(a) According to the article, oil refineries shut down for a period every year to change from producing diesel fuel to producing gasoline. A reduction in the number of firms producing oil shifts the oil supply curve to the left. In 2012, reduced oil from Iran, Syria, Yemen, and South Sudan also caused the oil supply curve to shift left. As the supply of oil falls, the price of oil rises. The table in the article indicates that the price of crude oil accounts for just over 50 percent of the retail price of gasoline. Together, the closing of the refineries and

the reduction in foreign oil production caused the price of oil to increase. The increase in oil prices reduced gasoline supply and accounted for part of the increase in gasoline prices.

(b) A second component to the price of gasoline is the retail markup—the difference between the wholesale cost and the retail price. The maximum price that a retailer can charge for a litre of gasoline depends on how much consumers require gasoline, and the number of substitutes. In places that have little or no public transit, the primary means of transportation is the private automobile. We expect that the demand for gasoline in such areas should be inelastic. In places where there are several gasoline retailers, the demand should be more elastic and the markup on gasoline should be lower. Information in the article indicates that the markups in Vancouver and Calgary are much lower than the markup in either St. John's or Yellowknife. This is consistent with demand being more elastic in the bigger cities, as expected.

(c) When the demand for a product, such as gasoline, is inelastic, an increase in its price causes expenditure on that product to rise. Consumption on all other products should fall. The study by economists Lutz Kilian and Paul Edelstein quoted in the article seems to suggest that just the opposite is true. Consumption of gasoline is not declining as price rises, which is consistent with an inelastic demand. However, there is no indication that spending on other goods has

been decreasing. Either the demand for gasoline is elastic, or consumers are earning more, or they are taking on more debt. The article is not clear on this point, so we will leave it up to the reader to decide which case is more likely.

Thinking Critically

1. Joe Ferris owns Joe's Gas-and-Go service station. Joe reads a newspaper article in which an economist describes the demand for gasoline as price inelastic. Remembering his principles of economics course from college, Joe comes to the following conclusion: "Because the demand for gasoline is inelastic, if I increase the price I charge, I will lose a few customers, but the price increase will more than compensate for the fact that I will be selling a smaller quantity of gasoline. Therefore, the revenue I earn from gasoline sales will increase." Briefly explain whether you agree with Joe's reasoning.

2. Suppose that initially the only sellers of gasoline in a town are conventional service stations. Then Walmart and Costco decide to begin selling gasoline. They install service islands near their stores and sell gasoline for lower prices than the conventional service stations. What effect do these new gasoline sellers have on the demand curves faced by the conventional service stations?

The demand for gasoline becomes more elastic over time.

Chapter Summary and Problems

Key Terms

Cross-price elasticity of demand, p. 171

Elastic demand, p. 159

Elasticity, p. 158

Income elasticity of demand, p. 172

Inelastic demand, p. 159

Perfectly elastic demand, p. 162

Perfectly inelastic demand, p. 162

Price elasticity of demand, p. 158

Price elasticity of supply, p. 176

Total revenue, p. 167

Unit-elastic demand, p. 159

Summary

*LO **6.1 Elasticity** measures how much one economic variable responds to changes in another economic variable. The **price elasticity of demand** measures how responsive quantity demanded is to changes in price. The price elasticity of demand is equal to the percentage change in quantity demanded divided by the percentage change in price. If the quantity demanded changes more than proportionally when price changes, the price elasticity of demand is greater than 1 in absolute value, and demand is **elastic**. If the quantity demanded changes less than proportionally when price changes, the price elasticity of demand is less than 1 in absolute value, and demand is **inelastic**. If the quantity demanded changes proportionally when price changes, the price elasticity of demand is equal to 1 in absolute value, and demand is **unit elastic**. **Perfectly inelastic demand** curves are vertical lines, and **perfectly elastic demand** curves are horizontal lines. Relatively few products have perfectly elastic or perfectly inelastic demand curves.

LO **6.2** The main determinants of the price elasticity of demand for a product are the availability of close substitutes, the passage of time, whether the good is a necessity or a luxury, how narrowly the market for the good is defined, and the share of the good in the consumer's budget.

LO **6.3** **Total revenue** is the total amount of funds received by a seller of a good or service. When demand is inelastic, a decrease in price reduces total revenue, and an increase in price increases total revenue. When demand is elastic, a decrease in price increases

total revenue, and an increase in price decreases total revenue. When demand is unit elastic, an increase or a decrease in price leaves total revenue unchanged.

LO **6.4** In addition to the elasticities already discussed, other important demand elasticities are the **cross-price elasticity of demand**, which is equal to the percentage change in quantity demanded of one good divided by the percentage change in the price of another good, and the **income elasticity of demand**, which is equal to the percentage change in the quantity demanded divided by the percentage change in income.

LO **6.5** Price elasticity and income elasticity can be used to analyze many economic issues. One example is the disappearance of the family farm. Because the income elasticity of demand for food is low, the demand for food has not increased proportionally as incomes have grown. As farmers have become more productive, they have increased the supply of most foods. Because the price elasticity of demand for food is low, increasing supply has resulted in significantly falling food prices.

LO **6.6** The **price elasticity of supply** is equal to the percentage change in quantity supplied divided by the percentage change in price. The supply curves for most goods are inelastic over a short period of time, but they become increasingly elastic over longer periods of time. Perfectly inelastic supply curves are vertical lines, and perfectly elastic supply curves are horizontal lines. Relatively few products have perfectly elastic or perfectly inelastic supply curves.

MyEconLab   Log in to MyEconLab to complete these exercises and get instant feedback.

Review Questions

LO **6.1**

1.1 Write the formula for the price elasticity of demand. Why isn't elasticity just measured by the slope of the demand curve?

1.2 If a 10 percent increase in the price of Cheerios causes a 25 percent reduction in the number of boxes of Cheerios demanded, what is the price elasticity of demand for Cheerios? Is the demand for Cheerios elastic or inelastic?

1.3 What is the midpoint method for calculating price elasticity of demand? How else can you calculate the price elasticity of demand? What is the advantage of the midpoint method?

1.4 Draw a graph of a perfectly inelastic demand curve. Think of a product that would have a perfectly inelastic demand

curve. Explain why demand for this product would be perfectly inelastic.

LO **6.2**

2.1 Is the demand for most agricultural products elastic or inelastic? Why?

2.2 What are the key determinants of the price elasticity of demand for a product? Which determinant is the most important?

LO **6.3**

3.1 If the demand for orange juice is inelastic, will an increase in the price of orange juice increase or decrease the revenue received by orange juice sellers?

3.2 The price of organic apples falls, and apple growers find that their revenue increases. Is the demand for organic apples elastic or inelastic?

*'Learning Objective' is abbreviated to 'LO' in the end of chapter material.

LO 6.4

4.1 Define the *cross-price elasticity of demand*. What does it mean if the cross-price elasticity of demand is negative? What does it mean if the cross-price elasticity of demand is positive?

4.2 Define the *income elasticity of demand*. Use income elasticity to distinguish a normal good from an inferior good. Is it possible to tell from the income elasticity of demand whether a product is a luxury good or a necessity good?

LO 6.5

5.1 The demand for agricultural products is inelastic, and the income elasticity of demand for agricultural products is low. How do these facts help explain the decline of the family farm?

LO 6.6

6.1 Write the formula for the price elasticity of supply. If an increase of 10 percent in the price of frozen pizzas results in a 9 percent increase in the quantity of frozen pizzas supplied, what is the price elasticity of supply for frozen pizzas? Is the supply of pizzas elastic or inelastic?

6.2 What is the main determinant of the price elasticity of supply?

Problems and Applications

LO 6.1

1.1 The following table gives data on the price of rye and the number of bushels of rye sold in 2010 and 2011.

Year	Price (dollars per bushel)	Quantity (bushels)
2010	$3.00	8 million
2011	2.00	12 million

a. Calculate the change in the quantity of rye demanded divided by the change in the price of rye. Measure the quantity of rye in bushels.

b. Calculate the change in the quantity of rye demanded divided by the change in the price of rye, but this time measure the quantity of rye in millions of bushels. Compare your answer to the one you computed in part (a).

c. Assuming that the demand curve for rye did not shift between 2010 and 2011, use the information in the table to calculate the price elasticity of demand for rye. Use the midpoint formula in your calculation. Compare the value for the price elasticity of demand to the values you calculated in parts (a) and (b).

1.2 [**Related to** Solved Problem 6.1 **on page 161**] You own a hot dog stand that you set up outside the student union every day at lunchtime. Currently, you are selling hot dogs for a price of $3 each, and you sell 30 hot dogs a day. You are considering cutting the price to $2. Following graph shows two possible increases in the quantity sold as a result of your price cut. Use the information in the graph to calculate the price elasticity between these two prices on each of the demand curves. Use the midpoint formula to calculate the price elasticities.

1.3 In 1916, in the United States, the Ford Motor Company sold 500,000 Model T Fords at a price of $440 each. Henry Ford believed that he could increase sales of the Model T by 1,000 cars for every dollar he cut the price. Use this information to calculate the price elasticity of demand for Model T Fords. Use the midpoint formula based on a $10 change in price for your calculation.

1.4 [**Related to the** Don't Let This Happen to You **on page 164**] The publisher of a magazine gives his staff the following information.

Current price	$2.00 per issue
Current sales	150,000 copies per month
Current total costs	$450,000 per month

He tells the staff, "Our costs are currently $150,000 more than our revenues each month. I propose to eliminate this problem by raising the price of the magazine to $3.00 per issue. This will result in our revenue being exactly equal to our cost." Do you agree with the publisher's analysis? Explain. (*Hint:* Remember that a firm's revenue is equal to the price of the product multiplied by the quantity sold.)

LO 6.2

2.1 Briefly explain whether the demand for each of the following products is likely to be elastic or inelastic.

a. Milk

b. Frozen cheese pizza

c. Cola

d. Prescription medicine

2.2 [**Related to the** Making the Connection **on page 167**] One study found that the price elasticity of demand for pop is −0.78, while the price elasticity of demand for Coca-Cola is −1.22. Coca-Cola is a type of pop, so why isn't its price elasticity the same as the price elasticity for pop as a product?

Based on Kelly D. Brownell and Thomas R. Frieden, "Ounces of Prevention—The Public Policy Case for Taxes on Sugared Beverages," *New England Journal of Medicine*, April 30, 2009, pp. 1805–1808.

2.3 The entrance fee into Yellowstone National Park is "$25 for a private, noncommercial vehicle; $20 for each snowmobile or motorcycle; or $12 for each visitor 16 and older entering by foot, bike, ski, etc." The fee provides the visitor with a seven-day entrance permit into Yellowstone and nearby Grand Teton National Park.

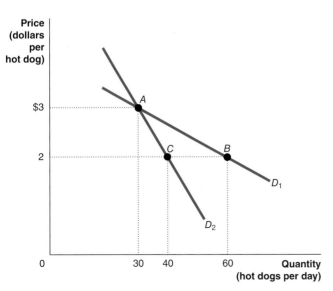

a. Would you expect the demand for entry into Yellowstone National Park for visitors in private, noncommercial vehicles to be elastic or inelastic? Briefly explain.

b. Of the three ways to enter the park—in a private, noncommercial vehicle; on a snowmobile or motorcycle; and by foot, bike, or ski—which way would you expect to have the largest price elasticity of demand, and which way would you expect to have the smallest price elasticity of demand? Briefly explain.

Based on National Park Service, Yellowstone National Park, "Fees, Reservations, and Permits," http://www.nps.gov/yell/planyourvisit/backcountryhiking.htm, August 16, 2011.

LO 6.3

3.1 Use the graph below for Yolanda's Frozen Yogurt Stand to answer the questions.

a. Use the midpoint formula to calculate the price elasticity of demand for D_1 between point A and point C and the price elasticity of demand for D_2 between point A and point B. Which demand curve is more elastic, D_1 or D_2? Briefly explain.

b. Suppose Yolanda is initially selling 200 cones per day at a price of $3.00 per cone. If she cuts her price to $2.50 per cone and her demand curve is D_1, what will be the change in her revenue? What will be the change in her revenue if her demand curve is D_2?

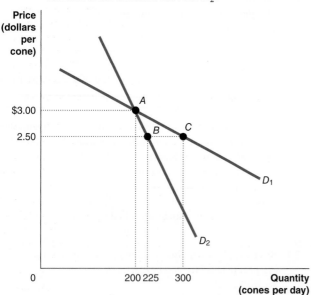

3.2 [**Related to** Solved Problem 6.3 **on page 170**] Briefly explain whether you agree or disagree with Manager 1's reasoning:

Manager 1: "The only way we can increase the revenue we receive from selling our frozen pizzas is by cutting the price."
Manager 2: "Cutting the price of a product never increases the amount of revenue you receive. If we want to increase revenue, we have to increase price."

3.3 [**Related to** Solved Problem 6.3 **on page 170**] If a firm increases the price of its product and its total revenue increases, will further increases in its price necessarily lead to further increases in its total revenue? Briefly explain.

3.4 Consider the following description of a pricing decision by an academic book publisher:

A publisher may have issued a monograph several years ago, when both costs and book prices were

lower, and priced it at $19.95. The book is still selling reasonably well and would continue to do so even at $29.95. Why not, then, raise the price? The only danger is miscalculation: By raising the price you may reduce sales to the point where you make less money overall, even while making more per copy.

Assume that the situation described in the last sentence happens. What does this tell us about the price elasticity of demand for that book? Briefly explain.

From Beth Luey, *Handbook for Academic Authors*, Fifth Edition, (Cambridge, UK: Cambridge University Press, 2010), p. 220.

3.5 [**Related to the** Making the Connection **on page 170**] A publisher was quoted as saying the following about the pricing of e-books: "We may introduce [an e-book] at $14.95 for a year and then move the book to $9.99 when we would have put out the trade paperback edition. I suspect you're going to see a fair amount of experimentation." Why would issuing a paperback version of a book affect the price a publisher would charge for an e-book? Why would publishers be experimenting with the prices of e-books?

From Motoko Rich and Brad Stone, "Cost of an e-Book Will Be Going Up," *New York Times*, February 11, 2010.

LO 6.4

4.1 In the graph below, the demand for hot dog buns has shifted outward because the price of hot dogs has fallen from $2.20 to $1.80 per package. Calculate the cross-price elasticity of demand between hot dogs and hot dog buns.

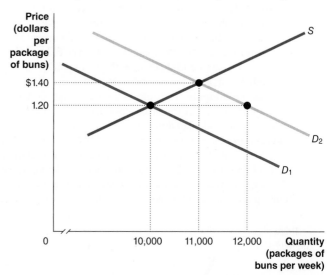

4.2 Are the cross-price elasticities of demand between the following pairs of products likely to be positive or negative? Briefly explain.

a. Iced coffee and iced tea
b. French fries and ketchup
c. Steak and chicken
d. Blu-ray players and Blu-ray discs

4.3 Rank the following four goods from lowest income elasticity of demand to highest income elasticity of demand. Briefly explain your ranking.

a. Bread
b. Pepsi
c. Mercedes-Benz automobiles
d. Laptop computers

4.4 [**Related to the** Making the Connection **on page 173**] Is the cross-price elasticity of demand between wine and spirits likely to be positive or negative? Can you think of reasons why the income elasticity of demand for wine is so much higher than the income elasticity of demand for spirits?

4.5 Consider firms selling three goods—one firm sells a good with an income elasticity of demand less than zero, one firm sells a good with an income elasticity of demand greater than zero but less than one, and one firm sells a good with an income elasticity of demand greater than one. In a recession, which firm is likely to see its sales decline the most? Which firm is likely to see its sales increase the most? Briefly explain.

LO 6.5

5.1 [**Related to** Solved Problem 6.5 **on page 175**] Suppose that the long-run price elasticity of demand for gasoline is −0.55. Assume that the price of gasoline is currently $1.15 per litre, the quantity of gasoline is 140 billion litres per year, and the federal government decides to increase the excise tax on gasoline by $0.30 per litre. Suppose that in the long run the price of gasoline increases by $0.25 per litre after the $0.30 excise tax is imposed.

   a. What is the new quantity of gasoline demanded after the tax is imposed? How effective would a gas tax be in reducing consumption of gasoline in the long run?

   b. How much does the federal government receive from the tax?

   c. Compare your answers to those in Solved Problem 6.5.

5.2 Corruption has been a significant problem in Iraq. Opening and running a business in Iraq usually requires paying multiple bribes to government officials. We can think of there being a demand and supply for bribes, with the curves having the usual shapes: The demand for bribes will be downward sloping because the smaller the bribe, the more business owners will be willing to pay it. The supply of bribes will be upward sloping because the larger the bribe, the more government officials will be willing to run the risk of breaking the law by accepting the bribe. Suppose that the Iraqi government introduces a new policy to reduce corruption that raises the cost to officials of accepting bribes—perhaps by increasing the jail term for accepting a bribe. As a result, the supply curve for bribes will shift to the left. If we measure the burden on the economy from corruption by the total value of the bribes paid, what must be true of the demand for bribes if the government policy is to be effective? Illustrate your answer with a demand and supply graph. Be sure to show on your graph the areas representing the burden of corruption before and after the government policy is enacted.

Based on Frank Gunter, "Corruption in Iraq: Poor Data, Questionable Policies," Working Paper, March 2009.

5.3 The head of the United Kumquat Growers Association makes the following statement:

> The federal government is considering implementing a price floor in the market for kumquats. The government will not be able to buy any surplus kumquats produced at the price floor or to pay us any other subsidy. Because the demand for kumquats is elastic, I believe this program will make us worse off, and I say we should oppose it.

Explain whether you agree or disagree with this reasoning.

5.4 Will there be a greater loss of economic efficiency from a price ceiling when demand is elastic or inelastic? Illustrate your answer with a demand and supply graph.

LO 6.6

6.1 [**Related to the** Making the Connection **on page 177**] Refer again to the first graph in the Making the Connection on page 177. Suppose that demand had stayed at the level indicated in the graph, with the equilibrium price of oil remaining at $140 per barrel. Over long periods of time, high oil prices lead to greater increases in the quantity of oil supplied. In other words, the price elasticity of supply for oil increases. This happens because higher prices provide an economic incentive to recover oil from more costly sources, such as under the oceans, from tar sands, or at greater depths in the earth. If the supply of oil becomes more elastic, explain how the increase in demand shown in the figure will result in a lower equilibrium price than $140 per barrel and a higher equilibrium quantity than 84 million barrels per day. Illustrate your answer with a demand and supply graph.

6.2 Use the midpoint formula for calculating elasticity to calculate the price elasticity of supply between point *A* and point *B* for each panel of Figure 6.5.

6.3 Briefly explain whether you agree with the following statement: "The longer the period of time following an increase in the demand for apples, the greater the increase in the equilibrium quantity of apples and the smaller the increase in the equilibrium price."

6.4 Consider an increase in the demand for petroleum engineers in Canada. How would the supply of these engineers respond in the short run and in the long run? Conversely, consider a decrease in demand for lawyers. How would the supply of lawyers respond in the short run and in the long run?

6.5 On most days, the price of a rose is $1, and 8,000 roses are purchased. On Valentine's Day, the price of a rose jumps to $2, and 30,000 roses are purchased.

   a. Draw a demand and supply graph that shows why the price jumps.

   b. Based on this information, what do we know about the price elasticity of demand for roses? What do we know about the price elasticity of supply for roses? Calculate values for the price elasticity of demand and the price elasticity of supply or explain why you can't calculate these values.

CHAPTER 7

Comparative Advantage and the Gains from International Trade

Chapter Outline and Learning Objectives

nex999/Shutterstock

Is "Buying Canadian" a Good Idea for Your Community?

With unemployment rising and incomes falling through 2009 and 2010, many countries debated laws designed to limit the amount of foreign produced goods and services their citizens purchased. When the U.S. federal government tried to stimulate its economy in 2009, it included a "Buy American" provision intended to prevent companies based in other countries (including Canada) from participating in the government's planned infrastructure projects. The idea was that if other countries were prevented from participating in the U.S. economy, more jobs would be created for Americans. The U.S. wasn't the only country considering restricting international trade; China and Russia, for example, also limited trade.

Canada, in particular, advocated against the U.S. government's "Buy American" policy, arguing that the policy violated the North American Free Trade Agreement (NAFTA). The U.S. is Canada's biggest trading partner and trade (imports and exports) plays a massive role in the Canadian economy. Interestingly, Canada wasn't alone in lobbying against the "Buy American" policy. Caterpillar Inc., which produces heavy equipment for mining and construction and is based in Peoria, Illinois, also lobbied for free trade.

When one country prevents foreign countries from doing business in its domestic market, other countries tend to do the same.

The result is a reduction in all economic activity around the world. When a country's firms are cut off from their markets, people lose their jobs and stop buying things.

In April 2013, Canada was raising the prospect of tariffs on American agricultural products in retaliation for labelling restrictions and other non-tariff barriers the U.S. has put on Canadian and Mexican exports of pork and beef. Some estimate the cost of the retaliatory measures at approximately $1 billion.

Are "Buy Canadian" and other policies designed to protect Canadian firms from foreign competition good ideas? As we will see in this chapter these policies create winners (the firms that are sheltered from international competition) and losers (Canadian consumers and Canadian firms trying to sell to foreign markets). In this chapter we will explore who wins and who loses from international trade and review some of the political debate over restricting international trade. There are trade-offs in government policies toward other countries.

AN INSIDE LOOK on **page 212** looks more closely at the Government of Canada's attempts to prevent restrictions on international trade.

Source: Michael Comte (AFP), "Canada Warns Against Protectionism," June 22, 2010, accessed at http://www.google.com/hostednews/afp/article/ALeqM5iHZZ-T1sFigbijwjkWBfiXCE57PA

Economics in Your Life

Have You Ever Been Urged to "Buy Canadian"?

Politicians often support restrictions on trade to convince people to vote for them. The workers in the industries these restrictions protect are likely to vote for the politicians because the workers think trade restrictions will protect their jobs. But most people are not workers in industries protected from foreign competition by trade restrictions. Many people work for firms that sell goods or services in foreign markets. These workers risk losing their jobs if foreign countries retaliate against Canadian attempts to reduce the number of imported goods we consume. In the case of "Buy Canadian" arguments, millions of consumers would have to accept higher prices for Canadian-made electronics, cars, clothes, and many other goods if foreign-made goods were excluded from the market. How do politicians become convinced to restrict international trade? As you read the chapter, see if you can answer this question. You can check your answer against the one we provide on page 211 at the end of the chapter.

Trade is simply the act of buying or selling. Is there a difference between trade that takes place within a country and international trade? Within Canada, domestic trade makes it possible for people in Saskatchewan to eat salmon farmed in New Brunswick, or for people in the Northwest Territories to drive cars made in Ontario. Similarly, international trade makes it possible for consumers in Canada to drink wine from France or watch movies made in Hollywood on a Blu-ray player manufactured in Japan. One significant difference between domestic trade and international trade is that international trade is more controversial. At one time, most of the things Canadians bought—televisions, toys, shoes, food, cars, etc.—were produced in Canada. Today, these goods are produced mainly by firms in other countries. This change has benefited Canadian consumers because we are able to purchase the things we want either more cheaply or at a higher quality than before. At the same time, many Canadian firms that produced these goods have gone out of business, and their workers have had to search for other jobs. It isn't surprising that people who support reducing international trade do so because they believe less international trade will mean more Canadian jobs. But is this belief correct?

We can use the tools of demand and supply we developed in Chapter 3 to analyze markets for internationally traded goods and services. We saw in Chapter 2 that trade in general—whether between next-door neighbours or between countries—is based on the principle of comparative advantage. In this chapter, we look more closely at the role of comparative advantage in international trade. We also introduce and use the concepts of consumer surplus, producer surplus, and deadweight loss to analyze government policies that restrict trade. With this background we can return to the political debate over whether Canada benefits from international trade. We begin by looking at how large a role international trade plays in the Canadian economy.

Discuss the role of international trade in the Canadian economy.

Tariff A tax imposed by a government on imports.

Imports Goods and services bought domestically but produced in other countries.

Exports Goods and services produced domestically but sold in other countries.

Canada and the International Economy

International trade has grown tremendously over the past 50 years. The increase in trade is the result of decreased costs of shipping products around the world, widespread availability of inexpensive and reliable communications, and changes in government policies. Firms can use large container ships to send their products around the world at low cost. Businesspeople today can travel to Europe or Asia using fast, inexpensive, and reliable air transportation. The Internet, cell phones, email, and text messaging allow managers to communicate instantly and at a very low cost with customers and suppliers all over the globe. These and other improvements in transportation and communication have created a global marketplace that earlier generations would have found hard to imagine.

In addition, over the past 50 years, many governments have changed policies to facilitate international trade. For example tariff rates have fallen. A **tariff** is a tax imposed by a government on *imports* of a good into a country. **Imports** are goods and services bought domestically but produced in other countries. In the 1930s, tariffs of 50 percent of the value of a product, or more, were common. Now tariffs are much lower, if they exist at all. Most tariffs among Canada, the United States, and Mexico were eliminated in the North American Free Trade Agreement (NAFTA) signed in 1994. Twenty-seven countries in Europe have formed the European Union, which has eliminated most tariffs among member countries, greatly increasing both imports and *exports*. **Exports** are goods and services produced domestically but sold in other countries.

The Importance of Trade to the Canadian Economy

International trade has always been an important part of the Canadian economy. When the country was first colonized by Europeans, furs and agricultural products were exported and consumer goods were imported. Canadians today buy a remarkable

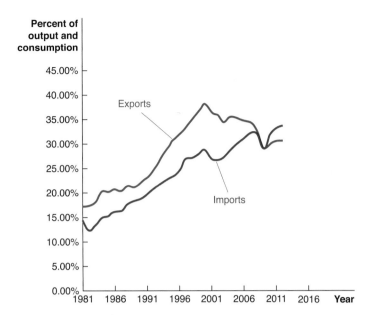

Figure 7.1

Canadian Imports and Exports as a Percent of GDP

Source: Data from Cansim Table 380-0002.

quantity of goods and services produced in other countries. Take a look at the tags on your clothes; the odds are good that what you're wearing was not made in Canada. At the same time, Canadian firms sell large quantities of goods and services to consumers in other countries. Figure 7.1 shows that even after the large drop-off that occurred between 2000 and 2009, we export and import a greater share of the goods and services we produce and consume than we did in the past. Currently, about one third of what we produce is sold to other countries, and one third of what we spend our money on comes from other countries.

Canadian International Trade in a World Context

Relative to other countries—like the U.S., Germany, and China—Canada's exports are small. The single biggest exporter in the world is China, followed by the United States and Germany. Figure 7.2 illustrates Canada's place in relation to other world exporters. Even though exports account about for 30 percent of what we produce, Canada's exports are 2.5 percent of international exports.

China has only recently surpassed Germany and the United States to become the world's largest exporter. Despite remaining a country with relatively poor regions, China is also one of the world's largest economies.

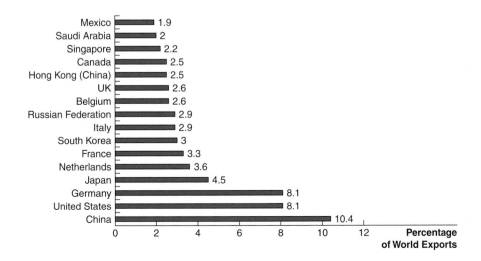

Figure 7.2

World Exports by Country

Source: Data from World Trade Organization, International Trade Statistics 2012.

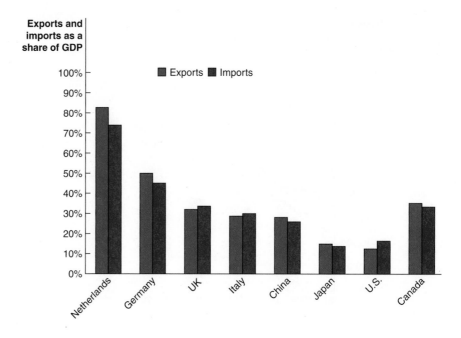

Figure 7.3 shows the importance of exports and imports to the economies of different countries. The Netherlands is remarkably dependent on markets outside its own borders, doing most of its trade with other European countries. Trade plays a much smaller role in the U.S. and Italian economies. Even though the U.S. is the world's second biggest exporter, its exports only account for about 13 percent of what it produces. Exports and imports play a relatively large role in the Canadian economy, with exports accounting for roughly one third of everything we produce and imports accounting for about one third of what we spend our money on.

7.2 LEARNING OBJECTIVE

Understand the difference between absolute and comparative advantage in international trade.

Comparative Advantage in International Trade

Why have businesses around the world increasingly looked for markets in other countries? Why have consumers increasingly purchased goods and services made in other countries? People trade for one reason: Trade makes them better off. Whenever a buyer and seller voluntarily agree to a sale, they must both believe they will be better off; otherwise, they wouldn't agree to trade. This outcome must hold whether the buyer and the seller live in the same city or in different countries. As we will see, governments are more likely to intervene to prevent international trade than trade between citizens. We'll see that the reasons for this are generally political, not economic.

A Brief Review of Comparative Advantage

In Chapter 2, we discussed the key economic concept of *comparative advantage*. **Comparative advantage** is the ability of an individual, firm, or country to produce a good or service at a lower opportunity cost than others. Recall that **opportunity cost** is the highest-valued alternative that must be given up to engage in an activity. People, firms, and countries specialize in economic activities in which they have a comparative advantage. In trading we benefit from the comparative advantage of others and they benefit from our comparative advantage.

A good way to think of comparative advantage is to recall the example in Chapter 2 about you and your neighbour picking fruit. You and your neighbour both have both apple and cherry trees on your property, and you pick your apples and trade them for her cherries. Your neighbour is better at picking both types of fruit than you are. Why, then, wouldn't your neighbour be better off by picking all her own fruit and ignoring

Comparative advantage The ability of an individual, a firm, or a country to produce a good or service at a lower opportunity cost than competitors.

Opportunity cost The highest-valued alternative that must be given up to engage in an activity.

	Output per Hour of Work	
	Cell Phones	Televisions
Canada	4	2
South Korea	6	12

Table 7.1

An Example of South Korean Workers Being More Productive Than Canadian Workers

you? The opportunity cost of picking apples is very high for her: she is very good at picking cherries and every hour spent picking apples means she has to give up all the cherries she could have picked. You can pick apples at a much lower opportunity cost than your neighbour, so you have a comparative advantage in picking apples. Your neighbour can pick cherries at a much lower opportunity cost than you can, so she has the comparative advantage in picking cherries. You both are better off if you specialize in picking apples and she specializes in picking cherries. You can then trade her some apples for some cherries, and in the end you both end up with more of each type of fruit.

Comparative Advantage in International Trade

The principle of comparative advantage can explain why people pursue different occupations. It can also explain why countries produce different goods and services. International trade involves many countries importing and exporting many different goods and services. The people in these countries are better off if they specialize in producing the goods for which they have a comparative advantage and trading for the goods in which other countries have a comparative advantage.

We can illustrate why specializing on the basis of comparative advantage makes people in different countries better off with a simple example involving just two countries and two products. Suppose Canada and South Korea can produce only cell phones and televisions. Assume that each country uses only labour to produce each good and that Canadian and South Korean cell phones and televisions are exactly the same. Table 7.1 shows how much of each good these countries can produce with one hour of labour.

Notice that Korean workers are more productive than Canadian workers in making both goods in this example. In one hour of work, Korean workers can make six times as many televisions and one and one-half times as many cell phones as Canadian workers. South Korea has an *absolute advantage* over Canada in producing both goods. **Absolute advantage** is the ability to produce more of something than others when using the same amount of resources. In this case, South Korea can produce more of both goods using the same amount of labour as Canada.

It might seem at first that Koreans have nothing to gain from trading with Canadians because they have an absolute advantage in producing both goods. However, South Korea should specialize and produce only televisions and get the cell phones it wants by exporting televisions to Canada and importing Canadian cell phones. The reason that Koreans benefit from trade is that although they have an absolute advantage in producing both goods, they have a *comparative advantage* only in the production of televisions. Canada has the comparative advantage in producing cell phones.

If it seems counterintuitive that Koreans should import cell phones from Canada even though they can produce more cell phones per hour of work, think about the opportunity cost to each country of producing each good. If Koreans want to produce more cell phones, some workers have to stop making televisions. Every hour of labour switched from producing televisions to producing cell phones increases cell phone production by 6, but reduces television production by 12. Koreans have to give up 12 televisions for every 6 cell phones they produce. Therefore, the opportunity cost to Koreans of a cell phone is 12/6, or 2 televisions per cell phone.

If a Canadian spends one hour fewer making televisions to spend that hour making cell phones, television production falls by 2, and production of cell phones rises by 4. Therefore, the opportunity cost to Canadians of producing one more cell phone is 2/4, or 0.5 televisions per cell phone. Canadians have a lower opportunity cost of producing cell phones and, thus, have a comparative advantage in producing cell phones.

Absolute advantage The ability to produce more of a good or service than competitors when using the same amount of resources.

Table 7.2

The Opportunity Costs of Producing Cell Phones and Televisions

	Opportunity Costs	
	Cell Phones	Televisions
Canada	0.5 televisions	2 cell phones
South Korea	2 televisions	0.5 cell phones

By similar reasoning we can see that Koreans, in this example, have a comparative advantage in producing televisions. Table 7.2 summarizes the opportunity costs people in each country face in producing televisions and cell phones. For example, the entry in the first row and second column shows that Canada must give up 2 cell phones for every television it produces.

Explain how countries gain from international trade.

Autarky A situation in which a country does not trade with other countries.

Terms of trade The ratio at which a country can trade its exports for imports from other countries.

How Countries Gain from International Trade

Can Koreans really gain from producing only televisions and trading with Canadians for cell phones? To see that they can, assume first that Koreans and Canadians don't trade with each other. A situation in which a country doesn't trade with other countries is called **autarky**. Assume that in autarky the citizens of each country have 1,000 hours of labour available to produce the two goods, and produce the quantities shown in Table 7.3. As there is no trade between countries, these quantities also represent the consumption.

Increasing Consumption Through Trade

Suppose now that Koreans and Canadians begin to trade with each other. The **terms of trade** is the ratio at which one country's exports trade for imports from other countries. For simplicity, let's assume that the terms of trade end up with Koreans and Canadians trading one cell phone for one television.

Once trade has begun, Canadians and Koreans can exchange cell phones for televisions or televisions for cell phones. For example, if Koreans specialize by using all available 1,000 hours to produce televisions they will be able to produce 12,000. Koreans could then export 1,500 televisions to Canada in exchange for 1,500 cell

Table 7.3

Gains from Trade for Canada and South Korea

	Without Trade	
	Production and Consumption	
	Televisions	Cell Phones
Canada	1,500	1,000
South Korea	9,000	1,500

	With Trade					
	Production		Trade		Consumption	
	Televisions	Cell Phones	Televisions	Cell Phones	Televisions	Cell Phones
Canada	0	4,000	**Import** 1,500	**Export** 1,500	1,500	2,500
South Korea	12,000	0	**Export** 1,500	**Import** 1,500	10,500	1,500

Gains from Trade: Increased Consumption	
Canada	1,500 cell phones
South Korea	1,500 televisions

phones. (Remember we assumed that the terms of trade were one cell phone per television.) Koreans end up with 10,500 televisions and 1,500 cell phones. Compared with autarky (the situation before trade), Koreans have the same number of cell phones, but 1,500 televisions. If Canadians specialize in producing cell phones, they will be able to produce 4,000. They could then export 1,500 cell phones in exchange for 1,500 televisions. Canadians end up with 2,500 cell phones and 1,500 televisions. Compared with autarky, Canadians get the same number of televisions, but more cell phones. Trade has allowed the people of both countries to increase the quantities of both goods they get to consume. Table 7.3 summarizes the gains from trade for Canadians and Koreans.

By trading, Koreans and Canadians are able to consume more than they could without trade. This outcome is possible because world production of both goods increases after trade. (Remember, in this example, our world consists of just South Korea and Canada.)

Why does total production of cell phones and televisions increase when Canadians specialize in producing cell phones and Koreans specialize in producing televisions? A domestic analogy helps to answer this question: If a company shifts production from an old factory to a more efficient modern factory, its output will increase. In effect the same thing happens in our example. Producing televisions in Canada and cell phones in Korea is inefficient. Shifting production to the more efficient country—the one whose people have a comparative advantage—increases total production. The key point is this: *People in different countries gain from specializing in producing goods in which they have a comparative advantage, and trading for goods in which people in other countries have a comparative advantage.*

Making the Connection | **Magna International Depends on International Trade**

You may not have heard of Magna International, but you've probably seen its products. This maker of auto parts has its headquarters in Aurora, Ontario, and employs almost 55,000 people in North America alone. You might think that a company like Magna would be interested in having the Canadian or North American auto parts market protected from foreign competition, but such a move would likely be very damaging to Magna and its employees. If the Canadian or North American auto parts market were closed to foreign firms, other countries would likely respond by preventing Magna from selling parts in their markets. You see, Magna doesn't just make parts for the North American automakers, GM, Fiat/Chrysler, and Ford; Magna also makes parts for BMW, Volkswagen, and Daimler.

You can see from the graph that Magna sells just 54 percent of what it makes in North America (only 22 percent in Canada). The remaining 46 percent is sold to other countries. In fact, if just the European markets were closed to Magna, it would lose over 40 percent of its sales. If Magna were to lose access to markets outside Canada or North America, it would have to lay off many of its Canadian workers. Companies like Magna and their employees clearly benefit from international trade.

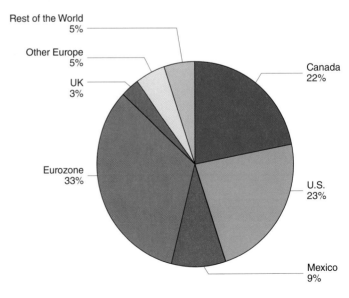

Magna International Sales by Country

Rest of the World 5%
Other Europe 5%
UK 3%
Eurozone 33%
Canada 22%
U.S. 23%
Mexico 9%

Source: Data from Magna International 2010 Annual Report.

Your Turn: Test your understanding by doing related problem 3.1 on page 215 at the end of this chapter.   MyEconLab

Solved Problem **7.3**

Gains from Trade

The first discussion of comparative advantage appears in *On the Principles of Political Economy and Taxation*, a book written by David Ricardo in 1817. Ricardo provided a famous example of the gains from trade, using wine and cloth production in Portugal and England. The following table is adapted from Ricardo's example, with cloth measured in sheets and wine measured in kegs.

	Output per Year of Labour	
	Cloth	Wine
Portugal	100	150
England	90	60

a. Explain which country has an absolute advantage in the production of each good.

b. Explain which country has a comparative advantage in the production of each good.

c. Suppose that Portugal and England currently do not trade with each other. Each country has 1,000 workers, so each has 1,000 years of labour time to use producing cloth and wine, and the countries are currently producing the amounts of each good shown in the following table.

	Total Current Output	
	Cloth	Wine
Portugal	18,000	123,000
England	63,000	18,000

Show that Portugal and England can both gain from trade. Assume that the terms of trade are that one sheet of cloth can be traded for one keg of wine.

d. Which workers in Portugal will have to change jobs? Which workers in England will have to change jobs?

Solving the Problem

Step 1: **Review the chapter material.** This problem is about absolute and comparative advantage and the gains from trade, so you may want to review the section "Comparative Advantage in International Trade" and the section "How Countries Gain from International Trade."

Step 2: **Answer part (a) by determining which country has an absolute advantage.** Remember that a country has an absolute advantage over another country when it can produce more of a good using the same resources. The first table in the problem shows that Portugal can produce more cloth *and* more wine with one year's labour than England can. Thus, Portugal has the absolute advantage in the production of both goods and, therefore, England does not have an absolute advantage in the production of either good.

Step 3: **Answer part (b) by determining which country has a comparative advantage.** A country has a comparative advantage when it can produce a good at a lower opportunity cost. To produce 100 sheets of cloth, Portugal must give up 150 kegs of wine. Therefore, the opportunity cost to Portugal of producing 1 sheet of cloth is 150/100, or 1.5 kegs of wine per sheet of cloth. England has to give up 60 kegs of wine to produce 90 sheets of cloth, so its opportunity cost of producing 1 sheet of cloth is 60/90, or 0.67 kegs of wine per sheet of cloth. The opportunity cost of producing wine can be calculated in the same way. The following table shows the opportunity cost to Portugal and England of producing each good.

	Opportunity Costs	
	Cloth	Wine
Portugal	1.5 kegs of wine	0.67 sheets of cloth
England	0.67 kegs of wine	1.5 sheets of cloth

Portugal has a comparative advantage in wine because its opportunity cost is lower. England has the comparative advantage in cloth as it has the lower opportunity cost.

Step 4: **Answer part (c) by showing that both countries can benefit from trade.** By now it should be clear that both countries will be better off if they specialize where they have a comparative advantage and trade for the other product. The following table is very similar to Table 7.3 and shows one example of trade making both countries better off. (To test your understanding, construct another example.)

Without Trade

	Production and Consumption	
	Cloth	Wine
Portugal	18,000	123,000
England	63,000	18,000

With Trade

	Production		Trade		Consumption	
	Cloth	Wine	Cloth	Wine	Cloth	Wine
Portugal	0	150,000	**Import** 18,000	**Export** 18,000	18,000	132,000
England	90,000	0	**Export** 18,000	**Import** 18,000	72,000	18,000

Gains from Trade: Increased Consumption

Portugal	9,000 cloth
England	9,000 wine

Step 5: **Answer part (d) by considering the changes in production.** As Portugal is specializing in the production of wine, Portuguese weavers will have to learn how to make wine. As England is specializing in making cloth, English wine makers will have to learn how to weave.

Your Turn: Test your understanding by doing related problems 3.2 and 3.3 on pages 215 and 216 at the end of this chapter.

MyEconLab

Why Don't We Observe Complete Specialization?

In our example of two countries producing only two products, each country specializes in producing one of the goods. In the real world, many goods and services are produced in more than one country. For example, Canada and South Korea both produce cars. We do not see complete specialization in the real world for three main reasons:

- **Not all goods and services are traded internationally**. Even if, for example, South Korea had a comparative advantage in the production of medical services, it would be difficult for South Korea to specialize in producing medical services and exporting them. There is no easy way for Canadian patients who need appendectomies to receive them from a surgeon in South Korea.

- **Production of most goods and services involves increasing opportunity costs**. Production of most goods involves increasing opportunity costs. As a result, when Canada devotes more workers to producing cell phones, the opportunity cost of producing more cell phones will increase. At some point, the opportunity cost of producing cell phones in Canada may rise to the level of opportunity cost of producing them in Korea. When that happens, international trade will no longer push Canada further toward complete specialization. The same will be true of South Korea: Increasing opportunity cost will cause South Korea to stop short of complete specialization in televisions.

- **Tastes for products differ**. Most products are *differentiated*. Cell phones, televisions, cars, and wine—to name a few products—come with a wide variety of features. When buying cars, some people look for reliability and fuel efficiency, others look for room to carry seven passengers, and still others want styling and performance. As a result of different tastes, some people will want a Toyota Prius, others SUVs, and still others a BMW, allowing Canada, the U.S., Germany, and Japan each to have a comparative advantage in producing different types of cars.

Does Anyone Lose as a Result of International Trade?

In our cell phone and television example, consumption increases for people in both Canada and South Korea as a result of trade. Everyone gains, and no one loses. Or do they? In our example we talked about people in different countries producing goods, and they could simply switch from producing one good to another. This isn't always how it happens. Keeping with the example, the Korean firms that were making cell phones would likely go out of business and their workers would lose their jobs. Making a transition from working in one industry to another isn't easy and can take a long time. The owners of the Korean cell phone firms also lose when trade occurs. Just like everything else in life, there are costs to trade. The people who face these costs are likely to do their best to convince their government not to allow international trade.

Don't Let This Happen to You

Remember That Trade Creates BOTH Winners and Losers

International trade is often referred to as a "win–win situation" as both countries benefit from trade. People sometimes take statements like this to mean that there are no losers from international trade. But notice that the statement refers to countries and not to individual people. When countries participate in trade, they make consumers there better off by increasing the quantity of goods and services available to them. As we have seen, expanding trade eliminates the jobs of workers employed at companies that are less efficient than foreign companies. Trade also creates

new jobs at companies that export to foreign markets. It is often difficult for workers who lose their jobs because of trade to find a new job in an industry that is growing due to trade. That's why the federal and provincial governments have sponsored programs designed to help people who lose their jobs to develop new skills in fields that are expanding due to trade. Such programs—and those like them in other countries—recognize that international trade has costs as well as benefits.

MyEconLab
Your Turn: Test your understanding by doing related problem 3.7 on page 216 at the end of this chapter.

Where Does Comparative Advantage Come From?

Some of the main sources of comparative advantage are:

- **Climate and natural resources.** This source of comparative advantage is the most obvious. Because of geology, Alberta has a comparative advantage in producing oil. Due to climate and soil conditions, Costa Rica has a comparative advantage in producing bananas.

- **Relative abundance of labour and capital.** Some countries, such as Canada, have highly skilled workers and a great deal of machinery. Other countries, such as Vietnam, have many unskilled workers and relatively little machinery. As a result, Canada has a comparative advantage in producing goods that require highly skilled workers and/or machines—things like aircraft, car parts, cell phone designs, and so on. Vietnam has a comparative advantage in producing goods, such as clothing or children's toys, that require unskilled workers and relatively few machines.

- **Technology.** Broadly defined, *technology* is the process firms use to turn inputs into goods and services. At any given time, firms in different countries do not all have access to the same technologies. In part, this difference is the result of past investments countries have made in supporting higher education or in providing support for research and development. Some countries are strong in *product technologies,* which involve the ability to develop new products. For example, firms in the U.S. have pioneered the tablet computer. Other countries are strong in *process technologies,* which involve the ability to improve the processes used to make existing products, For example, Japanese firms such as Toyota and Honda have succeeded by greatly improving the processes for designing and manufacturing cars.

- **External economies.** It is difficult to explain the location of some industries on the basis of climate, natural resources, the relative abundance of labour and capital, or technology. For example, why does California's "silicon valley" have a comparative advantage in computer software design, or Toronto in providing banking services, or Switzerland in making watches? The answer is that once an industry becomes established in an area, firms that locate in that area gain advantages over firms located in other places. The advantages might include the availability of skilled workers, the opportunity to interact with other firms in the same industry, and proximity to suppliers. These advantages result in lower costs to firms located in the area. Because these lower costs result from increases in the size of the industry in an area, economists refer to them as **external economies**.

External economies Reductions in a firm's costs that result from an increase in the size of an industry.

Comparative Advantage over Time: The Rise and Fall of North American Manufacturing

A country may develop a comparative advantage in the production of a good, and then, as time passes and circumstances change, the country may lose its comparative advantage. For decades North American firms dominated global manufacturing. This was particularly true of early electronics; the best radios, televisions, and stereos were made in Canada and the United States. The comparative advantage for the United States arose because much of the original research that makes these goods possible was done in the U.S., and because North America had some of the best factories and one of the most skilled labour pools in the world. Gradually, other countries (Japan in particular) gained access to the technology, built modern factories, and developed the skilled work force necessary for the manufacture of consumer electronics. As mentioned earlier, Japanese firms have excelled in process technologies, which involve the ability to improve the processes used to make existing products. By the 1970s and 1980s, Japanese firms were able to produce better and cheaper products than their North American competitors. The comparative advantage in consumer electronics shifted to Japan.

Recently, the development of a new generation of consumer electronics has allowed North American firms to regain a comparative advantage. The iPad developed by Apple was the first commercially successful tablet computer. For years, Black-Berry dominated the business cell phone/smart phone market. These new products are based in large part on North America's new comparative advantage in computer and software design.

Once a country has lost its comparative advantage in producing a good, its people will have higher incomes (on average) and its economy will be more efficient if it switches from producing the good to importing it, as Canada has done with most older style electronic devices. As we will see in the next section, however, there is often political pressure on governments to attempt to preserve industries that have lost their comparative advantage.

Government Policies That Restrict International Trade

Free trade, or trade between countries that is without government restrictions, makes consumers better off. To expand on this idea we need to review the concepts of *consumer surplus* and *producer surplus*.

7.4 LEARNING OBJECTIVE
Analyze the economic effects of government policies that restrict international trade.

Free trade Trade between countries that is without government restrictions.

Figure 7.4

The Canadian Market for T-shirts In Autarky

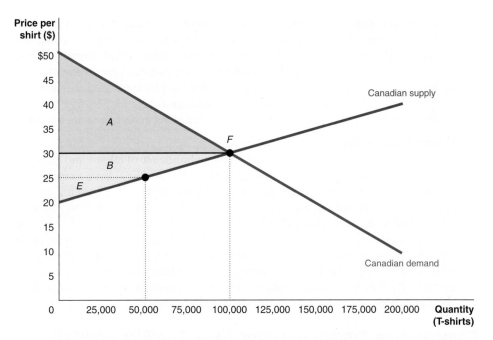

The Benefits of Trade—Imports

Figure 7.4 shows the Canadian market for T-shirts in autarky (no trade with other countries). You can see that the equilibrium price is $30 and the equilibrium quantity exchanged is 100,000. The blue-shaded area represents the consumer surplus, and the yellow-shaded area the producer surplus.

Assume that Canada starts to import T-shirts from Indonesia and other countries that produce T-shirts for $25.00 each. As Canada has a small population, we could buy all the T-shirts we wanted on the world market without having an impact on the world price. This also means that Canadian firms will not be able to sell their shirts for more than $25.00. The Canadian price will now be the same as the world price. At the world price of $25.00, Canadian manufacturers are only willing to sell 50,000 T-shirts but Canadians want to buy 125,000! In autarky this would mean a shortage of 75,000 T-shirts. Instead of a shortage, Canadians import the 75,000 T-shirts Canadian producers are unwilling to supply at the world price of $25.00.

Figure 7.5 shows the impact on the market, including the impact of imports on the consumer surplus and the producer surplus. In autarky the consumer surplus is the area

Figure 7.5

The Canadian Market for T-shirts After Trade

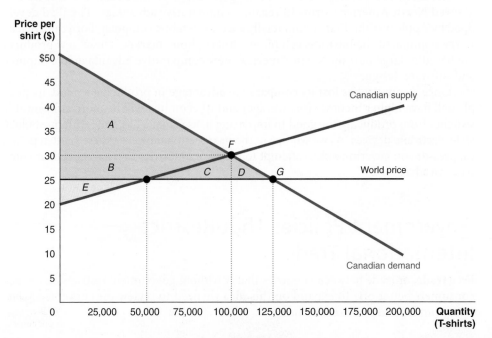

labelled *A* and the producer surplus is the sum of the areas labelled *A* and *E*. This means the total economic surplus from the T-shirt market in autarky is *A* + *B* + *E*.

After trade, the producer surplus is much smaller, simply area *E*. Consumer surplus is now much larger; it is the sum of areas *A*, *B*, *C*, and *D*. It isn't hard to see that the new total economic surplus is larger than it was in autarky. Canadians have gained an amount equal to the area of *C* + *D*.

We should note that not everyone gains from trade in this example. The Canadian producers of T-shirts and their employees have lost. The producer surplus is smaller than it used to be; in autarky, the producer surplus was area *E* + *B*, whereas now it is only area *E*. Canadian manufacturers are not only selling fewer T-shirts, but are selling them for less. This will likely lead to firms closing and some people losing their jobs.

It's important to notice that the areas *C* and *D* in this example were not benefits to anyone before international trade started. This is another illustration of how trade can create wealth.

The Gains from Trade—Exports

Canadians not only rely on imports for many consumer goods, but also export a great deal of what we produce. In this way, Canadians are very much dependent on international trade for employment. We've seen that consumers benefit from imports, but who benefits from exports? Canadian producers benefit from access to larger markets and increased demand for their products as a result of exports. These benefits aren't without a cost, however. As we'll see in this example, exports mean higher prices for Canadian consumers and thus a lower consumer surplus. Figure 7.6 shows the market for paper. Assume, to start, that Canadians are not allowed to buy paper from or sell paper to people in other countries (autarky). Without trading, the equilibrium market price is $4.00 per package of paper and 6 million packages of paper are exchanged every day. Once again, the blue-shaded area is the consumer surplus and the yellow-shaded area is the producer surplus.

Assume that Canada begins to sell its paper to Japan, the European Union, and countries all over the world that pay $6.00 per package for paper. As Canada is a small country, we can sell as much paper as we want on the world market without having an impact on the price. This also means that Canadian firms will be able to charge $6.00 per package in the domestic market and Canadian consumers will have to pay $6.00. At a price of $6.00, Canadian consumers would buy only 4 million packages but Canadian

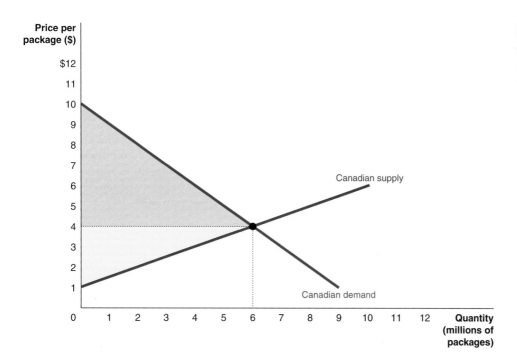

Figure 7.6

The Canadian Paper Market in Autarky

Figure 7.7

The Canadian Paper Market After Trade

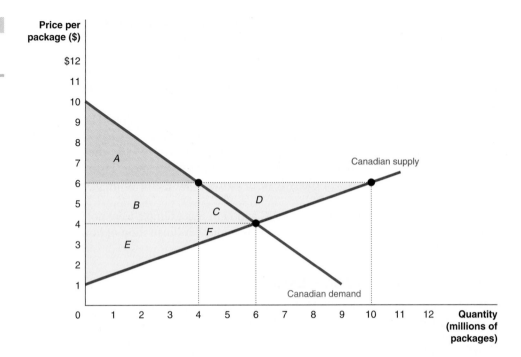

producers would sell 10 million packages. In autarky, such a price would result in a surplus of 6 million packages of paper on the market. In this scenario, we export 6 million packages.

Figure 7.7 shows the impact of participating in international trade on the Canadian paper market. In autarky, the consumer surplus is the sum of the areas A, B, and C, while the producer surplus would be the sum of areas E and F. The total economic surplus of the paper market in Canada is the sum of all these areas, or $A + B + C + E + F$.

After trade, the consumer surplus is much smaller as Canadian consumers buy less paper and pay more for it. In this example, the consumer surplus shrinks by areas $B + C$. This loss in consumer surplus is actually compensated for by the increase in producer surplus. By selling paper internationally at the higher world price, Canadian firms are not only able to sell more paper, but get more for all the paper they sell. The result is an increase in producer surplus equal to $B + C + D$. Overall, Canadians are better off by an area equal to D.

Once again, this gain isn't completely free: Canadian consumers have a smaller consumer surplus than they did in autarky. This loss is more than made up for by the increase in producer surplus. Canadian paper firms can now expand their operations from producing 6 million packages to producing 10 million and that likely means hiring more workers and using more capital.

The fact that some people lose from international trade means that governments can sometimes be persuaded to prevent some international trade from taking place. In many cases, domestic firms that will face difficult foreign competition and their workers lobby the government to restrict international trade. These policies generally take one of two forms: (1) tariffs, or (2) quotas and voluntary export restraints.

Tariffs *Tariffs* are one of the most common forms of government restrictions on international trade. A tariff is simply a tax imposed by a government on goods imported into a country. Like any other tax, a tariff increases the cost of a good. Figure 7.8 shows the impact of a tariff of $2.50 per T-shirt on the Canadian T-shirt market. As a result of the tariff, the price of T-shirts rises to $27.50 and quantity consumed falls to 112,500, making consumer surplus shrink by an amount equal to the shaded areas ($A + B + C + D$).

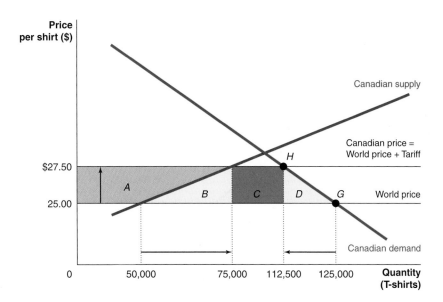

Figure 7.8

The Canadian T-shirt Market with a Tariff

Imposing the tariff allows Canadian T-shirt makers to increase their output from 50,000 to 75,000. Canadian producers also get more ($2.50 more) for each T-shirt they sell. The tariff increases the producer surplus by an amount equal to the red-shaded area (A).

After the tariff is imposed, however, Canadian consumers will be paying more for their T-shirts: $2.50 more. This means the consumer surplus will fall under a tariff. This increase in price for consumers causes them to buy fewer T-shirts in total, purchases fall from 125,000 to 112,500, and the consumer surplus falls by an amount equal to the sum of the yellow- and green-shaded areas (B + C + D).

The government will receive revenue from the tariff. By charging a tariff of $2.50 on each imported T-shirt, the government generates revenue of $93,750—you can find this amount as imports times the tariff or (112,500 – 75,000) × 2.5. We've shown this as the green-shaded area (C).

When we consider all the changes, you should notice that areas A and C are gains to producers and government made at the expense of consumers. Essentially, the tariff transfers some of the benefit of a market from consumers to producers and government. The areas B and D aren't transferred, however; the benefits consumers used to get are lost to society. Area B is the loss to society due to supporting inefficient producers, and area D is loss due to the reduction in consumption.

A tariff will benefit Canadian T-shirt makers, but as you have seen, such benefits are not free. They come at the cost of a reduced consumer surplus and lower total economic surplus for Canadians. And we've only considered the costs and benefits to Canadians: A tariff will reduce the total economic surplus from the T-shirt market for our trading partners as well.

Quotas and Voluntary Export Restraints A **quota** is a numerical limit on the quantity of a good that can be imported, and has an effect similar to a tariff. A quota is generally imposed by the government of the importing country (though some countries do use quotas to restrict exports of agricultural products or natural resources). A **voluntary export restraint (VER)** is an agreement negotiated between two countries that places a numerical limit on the quantity of a good that can be imported by one country from the other country. In the early 1980s, the U.S. and Japan negotiated a VER that limited the number of Japanese cars imported by Americans. The Japanese government went along with the VER largely because it feared that the U.S. would impose a high tariff on all imports of Japanese cars if they did not cooperate. Quotas and VERs have similar economic effects.

The main purpose of most tariffs and quotas is to reduce the foreign competition that domestic firms face. Historically, Canada has imposed tariffs on things like sugar, textiles, and some other finished goods, but not on the raw materials that go into

Quota A numerical limit a government imposes on the quantity of a good that can be imported into the country.

Voluntary export restraint (VER) An agreement negotiated between two countries that places a numerical limit on the quantity of a good that can be imported by one country from the other country.

Figure 7.9

**The Canadian Sugar Market
with a Quota**

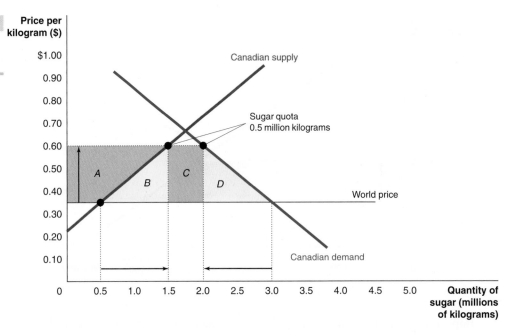

making these goods. These trade restrictions were generally intended to generate Canadian-based industries in processing the raw materials that go into making these goods. It is not uncommon to see old textile mills and sugar refineries throughout eastern Canada and parts of Ontario.

Measuring the Economic Effect of an Import Quota We can use the concepts of consumer surplus, producer surplus, and total economic surplus to measure the economic impact of a quota. We'll use the market for sugar as an example. Figure 7.9 shows the impact a quota would have on the Canadian market for sugar.

Without a sugar quota, Canadians would pay the world price of $0.35 per kilogram and purchase 3 million kilograms of sugar, importing 2.5 million kilograms. To find the price of sugar in the Canadian market after a quota of 0.5 million kilograms has been imposed, we need to look for a price at which the quantity demanded by Canadians is 0.5 million kilograms more than the quantity supplied by Canadian firms. The excess demand will be made up by imports. Thus, after the federal government imposes an import quota of 0.5 million kilograms, Canadians will have to pay $0.6 per kilogram for sugar, and they will buy only 2 million kilograms. The price increase that results from the import quota means consumer surplus will fall by the area $A + B + C + D$.

The area A of lost consumer surplus is captured by the producers that are now able to sell their output at the higher price. Area C is received by the *foreign* producers lucky enough to have gotten an import quota. They are now able to sell their products to Canadians at a price much greater than the world price. Areas B and D are losses to Canadian consumers that are not captured by anyone.

Solved Problem **7.4**

Measuring the Effect of a Quota

Suppose that Canada currently produces and imports apples. The Canadian government decides to restrict international trade in apples by imposing a quota that allows imports of only 4 million boxes of apples into

Canada each year. The figure shows the results of imposing the quota.

Complete the following table, using the prices, quantities, and letters in the figure.

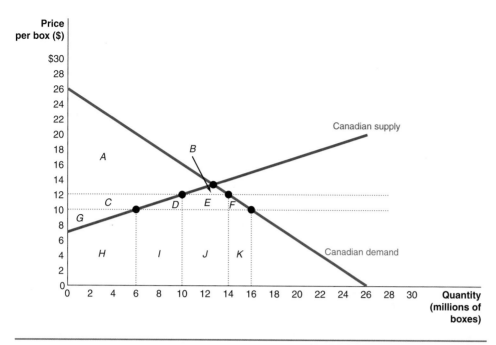

	Without Quota	With Quota
World price of apples		
Canadian price of apples		
Quantity supplied by Canadian growers		
Quantity demanded by Canadian consumers		
Quantity imported		
Area of consumer surplus		
Area of producer surplus		
Area of lost total economic surplus		

Solving the Problem

Step 1: **Review the chapter material.** This problem is about measuring the economic effects of a quota, so you may want to review the sections "Quotas and Voluntary Export Restraints," and "Measuring the Economic Effect of an Import Quota."

Step 2: **Fill in the table.** After studying Figure 7.9, you should be able to complete the table. Remember that consumer surplus is the area below the demand curve and above the market price.

	Without Quota	With Quota
World price of apples	$10 per box	$10 per box
Canadian price of apples	$10 per box	$12 per box
Quantity supplied by Canadian growers	6 million boxes	10 million boxes
Quantity demanded by Canadian consumers	16 million boxes	14 million boxes
Quantity imported	10 million boxes	4 million boxes
Area of consumer surplus	A + B + C + D + E + F	A + B
Area of producer surplus	G	G + C
Area of lost total economic surplus	None	D + F

Your Turn: Test your understanding by doing related problem 4.7 on page 216 at the end of this chapter.   MyEconLab

The High Cost of Preserving Jobs with Tariffs and Quotas

Many countries still use tariffs and quotas to protect jobs, despite the costs associated with doing so. Economists have actually estimated the cost of using tariffs and quotas to protect jobs in the U.S. and Japan, and Table 7.4 shows some of these estimates.

Consider the cost of saving just one job growing rice in Japan for a single year: US$51,233,000. This extraordinary cost is based on the fact that Japanese consumers (who consider rice a key part of their diet) must pay a lot more every time they purchase rice.

Things aren't that much better when we start to consider the impact of American restrictions on international trade. For example, by restricting international trade in products such as softwood lumber, not only do the American consumers lose, as they have to pay US$1,044,271 for each job that is "saved," but Canadian producers lose out as that saved job is a lost Canadian job.

All of these estimated costs are based on the assumption that America's (and Japan's) trading partners do not respond to these trade restrictions by imposing restrictions on the products that the U.S. (Japan) exports. If the trading partners retaliate, the tariffs and quotas won't just hurt domestic consumers, but will also harm domestic producers. For a country like Canada, losing access to major international markets, like the U.S., would be devastating to our exporters.

Gains from Unilateral Elimination of Tariffs and Quotas

Some people argue that Canada can benefit from eliminated tariffs and quotas only if other countries eliminate their own restrictions on international trade in exchange. For politicians, it is easier to gain support for reducing or eliminating tariffs or quotas if it is done as part of an agreement with other countries that involves their eliminating some of their tariffs or quotas. This was part of the reason behind the North American Free Trade Agreement (NAFTA). But as we've seen throughout this chapter, *Canadians would gain from the elimination of tariffs and quotas even if other countries did not reduce their tariffs and quotas.*

Other Barriers to Trade

In addition to tariffs and quotas, governments can restrict international trade using a variety of other tools. For example, all governments require that imports meet certain health

Table 7.4

Costs of Protecting Jobs with Tariffs and Quotas in Japan and the U.S.

Product	Country	Number of Jobs Saved	Cost to Consumers per Saved Job (US$ per year)
Benzenoid chemicals	U.S.	216	1,376,435
Luggage	U.S.	226	1,285,078
Softwood lumber	U.S.	605	1,044,271
Dairy products	U.S.	2,378	685,323
Frozen orange juice	U.S.	609	635,103
Ball bearings	U.S.	146	603,368
Machine tools	U.S.	1,556	479,452
Women's handbags	U.S.	773	263,535
Canned tuna	U.S.	390	257,640
Rice	Japan		51,233,000
Natural gas	Japan		27,987,000
Gasoline	Japan		6,329,000
Paper	Japan		3,813,000
Beef, pork, and poultry	Japan		1,933,000
Cosmetics	Japan		1,778,000
Radio and TV sets	Japan		915,000

Sources: Federal Reserve Bank of Dallas, 2002 Annual Report; and Yoko Sazabami, Shujiro Urata, and Hiroki Kawai, *Measuring the Cost of Protection in Japan*, Washington, D.C.: Institute for International Economics, 1995.

and safety requirements. While health and safety standards are generally a good idea, governments can and sometimes do use these requirements to shield domestic producers from foreign competition. This is clearly what is happening when governments impose stricter health and safety requirements on imported products than on domestically produced ones.

Many governments also restrict imports of certain products for national security reasons. The argument is that in a time of war, a country should not be dependent on imports of critical war materials. Once again, these restrictions make sense but can be subject to abuse as the definition of critical wartime materials can be extended to include computers and software, cars, and even textiles.

The Arguments over Trade Policies and Globalization

7.5 LEARNING OBJECTIVE
Evaluate the arguments over trade policies and globalization.

The arguments over the regulation of trade in Canada and around the world date back to the time when Canada was still controlled by Britain. Even though Canada's trade barriers are much smaller than they have been in the past, there have been calls for the federal government to restrict international trade in the wake of the global recession triggered by the 2007 U.S. financial crisis.

To understand why restricting international trade in response to an economic downturn is a really bad idea, we can explore the attempt to protect domestic industries that took place during the 1930s. During what's come to be known as the Great Depression, the U.S. and many other countries thought they could reduce the impact of the depression on their economies by restricting international trade. To accomplish this, the U.S. government passed legislation known as the Smoot-Hawley Act of 1930, which increased the average U.S. tariff by more than 50 percent. Canada and virtually all of America's trading partners retaliated by increasing tariffs on America's exports by a similar amount. The result was a collapse of international trade. Many have argued that it was the Smoot-Hawley Act of 1930 that turned what would have been a deep recession into one of the worst economic disasters in modern history.

As World War II ended in 1945, Allied governments were looking for ways to reduce tariffs and revive international trade. To help achieve this goal, the General Agreement on Tariffs and Trade (GATT) was set up in 1948. Countries joining GATT agreed not to impose new tariffs or import quotas. In addition, a series of multilateral negotiations, called trade rounds, took place in which countries agreed to reduce tariffs from the very high levels seen in the 1930s.

As international trade has grown and evolved, trade between countries has expanded to include not only the goods covered under GATT but services as well. A new, broader agreement was reached in 1995 in which GATT was replaced by the **World Trade Organization (WTO)**, which currently has more than 150 member countries.

World Trade Organization (WTO) An international organization that oversees international trade agreements.

Why Do Some People Oppose the World Trade Organization?

In the years immediately after World War II, many low-income, or developing, countries erected high tariffs and restricted investment by foreigners. In the 1980s, when these policies failed to deliver the economic growth their proponents promised, many of the countries involved decided to become more open to foreign trade and investment, joining the WTO and following its policies. This process has become known as **globalization.**

Globalization The process of countries becoming more open to foreign trade and investment.

During the 1990s, however, opposition to globalization began to increase. In 1999, this opposition took the form of violent protests at a WTO meeting in Seattle. Though the protests began as a peaceful demonstration they turned into rioting and looting. Since 1999, meetings of the WTO and other organizations devoted to international cooperation have continued to see protests—some peaceful and others quite violent.

Why do some people find the idea of reducing barriers to international trade worthy of such violent opposition? There are a lot of different sources to the opposition to the WTO, but we'll explore three of the major ones. First, some opponents are specifically against the globalization process that began in the 1980s and became widespread in the 1990s. Second, other opponents have the same core motivation as those promoting trade barriers in 1930—to protect domestic producers from foreign competition. Third, some critics of the WTO support globalization in principle but believe the WTO favours the interests of high-income countries at the expense of lower-income countries. We'll explore some of these objections below.

Anti-Globalization   Many of those who protest at WTO meetings distrust globalization. Some believe that free trade and foreign investment destroy the distinctive cultures of many countries. As developing countries began to open their economies to imports from other countries, particularly to cultural goods from the U.S., these imports began to replace the local equivalent products. So a teen in Thailand might be sitting in a McDonald's wearing Levi's jeans, while listening to American music on an iPod. Globalization has increased the variety of products available to consumers in developing countries, but some people argue that the resulting homogenization of global culture is too high a price to pay for increased variety.

Globalization has also allowed multinational corporations to relocate factories from high-income countries to low-income countries. These new factories in Indonesia, Mexico, and China pay lower wages than those paid to workers in countries like Canada. Further, the environmental regulations and working conditions are often much worse than they are in developed countries. Factories in some of these countries have even used child labour—which would be illegal in most developed countries. Some people have argued that firms with factories in developing countries should pay workers wages as high as those paid in high-income countries. They also believe these firms should abide by the health, safety, and environmental regulations that exist in the high-income countries.

The governments of most developing countries have resisted these proposals. They argue that when the currently rich countries were themselves poor, they also lacked environmental or safety standards and their workers were paid low wages. They argue that it is easier for rich countries to afford high wages, good environmental standards, and safety regulations than it is for poor countries. They also point out that many jobs that seem to have very low wages based on high income country standards are often much better than these workers were able to get before globalization.

| Making
the
Connection | **The Unintended Consequences of Banning Goods Made with Child Labour** |

In many developing countries—such as Indonesia, Thailand, and Peru—children as young as 7 or 8 work for 10 or more hours a day. Reports of very young workers labouring long hours producing goods for export are troubling to people with a Canadian standard of living. In Canada, stores selling products made by young workers have been boycotted. Many of those promoting the boycotts assume that if child workers in developing countries weren't working in factories making clothes, toys, or other products, they would be in school just like Canadians the same age.

In fact, children in developing countries don't often have positive alternatives to working. Schooling is frequently available for only a few months each year, and even children who do attend school rarely do so for more than 10 years. Poor families are often unable to afford even the small costs associated with sending a child to school (such as the cost of school supplies over the years). Families sometimes rely

Would eliminating child labour, such as stitching soccer balls, improve the quality of children's lives?

on the earnings of children to survive, as poor families in Canada, Europe, and Japan once did. There is substantial evidence that as incomes begin to rise in poor countries, families rely less on child labour. Today, children under the age of 14 cannot be employed in most businesses (family-owned or family-run businesses and farms can be exceptions). In many countries where child labour is common, producing goods for export often pays better and is safer for children than the alternatives.

As preparations began for the 1998 World Cup in France, there were protests that Baden Sports—the main supplier of soccer balls—was purchasing balls from suppliers in Pakistan that used child workers. France decided to ban all use of soccer balls made by child workers. As a result, Baden Sports moved production from Pakistan, where the balls were hand-stitched by child workers, to China, where the balls were machine-stitched in a factory employing only adults. There was some criticism of the boycott at the time. In a broad study of child labour, three economists argued:

> Of the array of possible employment in which impoverished children might engage, soccer ball stitching is probably one of the most benign... [In Pakistan] children generally work alongside other family members in the home or in small workshops... Nor are the children exposed to toxic chemicals, hazardous tools or brutal working conditions. Rather, the only serious criticism concerns the length of the typical child stitcher's work-day and the impact on formal education.

In fact, the alternatives to soccer ball stitching for child workers in Pakistan turned out to be grim. According to economist Keith Maskus and the World Bank, a "large proportion" of the children who lost their jobs stitching soccer balls ended up begging or in prostitution.

Sources: Drusilla K. Brown, Alan V. Deardorff, and Robert M. Stern, "U.S. Trade and Other Policy Options to Deter Foreign Exploitation of Child Labor," in Magnus Blomstron and Linda S. Goldberg, eds., *Topics in Empirical International Economics: A Fetschrift in Honor of Bob Lipsey,* Chicago: University of Chicago Press, 2001; Tomas Larsson, *The Race to the Top: The Real Story of Globalization,* Washington, DC: Cato Institute, 2001, p. 48; and Eric V. Edmonds and Nina Pavcnik, "Child Labor in the Global Economy," *Journal of Economic Perspectives,* Vol. 19, No. 1, Winter 2005, pp. 199–220.

Your Turn: Test your understanding by doing related problem 5.1 on page 217 at the end of this chapter.   MyEconLab

---

"Old Fashioned" Protectionism   The anti-globalization argument against free trade and the WTO is relatively new. Another argument against free trade, called *protectionism*, has been around for centuries. **Protectionism** is the use of trade barriers to shield domestic producers from foreign competitors. For as long as international trade has been taking place, governments have attempted to restrict it to protect domestic firms. As we saw with the analysis of quotas, protectionism causes losses to consumers. In addition, by reducing the ability of countries to produce according to comparative advantage, protectionism reduces well-being in all countries that could be involved in trade.

Given these costs, why do so many people promote protectionist policies? The use of protectionism is usually justified on the basis of one of the following arguments:

- **Saving jobs.** Supporters of protectionism argue that free trade reduces employment by driving domestic firms out of business. It is true that when more efficient foreign firms drive less efficient firms out of business, jobs are lost, but jobs are also created in expanding export industries. Every day, firms go out of business and new ones start up; in any healthy economy, jobs are continually being created and destroyed. Things can get difficult when the shrinking industries are very different from the ones that are expanding, but this problem is best addressed through education and training programs, not barriers to trade.

- **Protecting high wages.** Some people worry that firms in high-income countries will have to start paying much lower wages to compete with firms in developing countries. This fear is misplaced, however, because free trade actually raises living standards by increasing economic efficiency. When a country practises protectionism and produces goods and services it could get more cheaply from other

Protectionism The use of trade barriers to shield domestic firms from foreign competition.

countries, it reduces its standard of living. For example, Canada could ban the import of bananas and grow them locally in greenhouses. Obviously this would entail very high opportunity costs, and bananas grown in this way would have to be sold at a very high price to cover these costs. Assume that the Government of Canada decided to ban the import of bananas: Eliminating the ban at some point in the future would eliminate the jobs of Canadian banana growers, but the standard of living in Canada would rise as banana prices fell and labour, machinery, and other resources moved out of banana growing and into producing goods and services for which Canada has a comparative advantage.

- **Protecting infant industries.** It is possible that firms in a country may have a comparative advantage in producing a good, but because the country began production of a good later than other countries, its firms initially have higher costs. In producing some goods and services, substantial "learning by doing" occurs. As workers and firms produce more of the good or service, they gain experience and become more productive. As a result of learning by doing, costs and prices fall. As the firms in the "infant industry" gain experience, their costs will fall, and they will be able to compete successfully with foreign producers. Under free trade, such companies would never get the chance to develop into competitive firms, as experienced foreign competitors could undercut the new firms' prices and drive them out of business before they gained enough experience to compete. To economists, this is one of the most persuasive of the protectionist arguments. There is a significant drawback to the infant industry argument—tariffs used to protect an infant industry eliminate the need for the firm to become internationally competitive. Eliminating tariffs protecting firms that do not become as efficient as their foreign competitors can be exceptionally difficult for politicians.

- **Protecting national security.** As we already discussed, a country should not rely on other countries for goods that are critical to its military defence. For example, the U.S. probably should not import fighter planes from China. The Canadian situation is slightly different from that of many other countries as Canada's national defence is highly integrated with and dependent on the U.S. and NATO. For countries that do use the national defence argument for raising barriers to trade, making a cogent case can be difficult. It is rare for an industry to ask for protection without raising the issue of national security in the U.S. even when its products are primarily civilian in nature.

Dumping Selling a product for a price below its cost of production.

Dumping In recent years countries have made use of a provision in the WTO agreement to impose tariffs on products that foreign firms are *dumping*. **Dumping** is selling a product for a price below its cost of production. Although allowable under the WTO, using tariffs to offset the effects of dumping is controversial.

In practice, determining whether foreign companies are dumping their products or are simply much more efficient producers is very difficult, because most firms are not eager to share their true costs of production with foreign governments. As a result, the WTO allows countries to determine that dumping has occurred if a product is exported for a lower price than it sells for on the home market. As usual, this approach has a weakness: Goods are likely to sell for different prices in different markets. For example, one would expect the price of Niagara Falls souvenirs to be higher in Niagara Falls than in China (where many of the souvenirs are made). This isn't dumping, just the reality of different markets. Some firms also offer "loss leaders"—products sold below cost—when introducing a new product or to attract consumers who will also buy other products at full price. These actions are part of normal business strategy for domestic and foreign producers alike, and therefore can't truly be considered dumping.

Positive versus Normative Analysis (Once Again)

Economists emphasize the burden on the economy imposed by tariffs, quotas, and other restrictions on international trade. Does it follow that these restrictions are bad? Recall from Chapter 1 the distinction between *positive analysis* and *normative analysis*.

Positive analysis concerns what is. Normative analysis is about what someone thinks *ought to be*. Measuring the cost to consumers of "saving" one job (as in Table 7.4) is an example of positive analysis. Asserting that all tariffs are bad and should be eliminated is normative analysis. Any tariff or quota makes some people better off and others worse off and we've shown that such restrictions on trade reduce total income and consumption. Whether increasing the profits and employment of firms in a protected industry justifies the costs to everyone in the country is a normative question.

Most economists tend not to support restrictions on international trade. There are, of course, exceptions. The use of trade restrictions to help end apartheid in South Africa is an often cited example. It may also be that eliminating trade restrictions too quickly would be too expensive in terms of adjustment costs, as workers losing jobs would have to search for work in an industry in which they don't have the needed skills.

The success of industries in getting the government to erect barriers to foreign competition depends partly on some members of the public knowing full well the costs of trade barriers but supporting them anyway. However, there are other factors at work:

1. The costs that tariffs and quotas impose on consumers tend to be small per person, despite being large in total. A cost of $35,000,000 on Canadian consumers is only about $1 per person. Most people don't worry too much about such small costs, even when they know the costs exist.
2. The jobs lost to foreign competition are easy to identify, but the jobs created by foreign trade can be harder to spot.

In other words, the industries that benefit from trade restrictions benefit a lot, while those that are harmed by trade restrictions lose only a little (though there are a lot more people who lose as a result of trade restrictions). This concentration of benefits and wide dispersal of burdens makes it easy to understand why governments receive strong pressure from some industries for protection and little pressure from the public to reduce tariffs.

Economics in Your Life

At the beginning of the chapter, we asked you to consider how some companies convince government to support trade restrictions. In the chapter, we saw that trade restriction tend to preserve relatively few jobs in protected industries, while costing consumers billions in higher prices. This might seem to increase the mystery of why governments pursue protectionist policies. We have also seen that, per person, the burden of a specific tariff, quota, or other trade restriction is generally small. Not many people will take the trouble of lobbying a politician for a benefit of only a few dollars a year. In many cases, it is this distribution of costs and benefits (with benefits concentrated to a few producers and the costs shared among millions of consumers) that causes Canadian and foreign politicians to erect trade barriers.

Conclusion

There are few issues economists agree upon more than the economic benefits of trade. However, there are few political issues as controversial as government policy toward international trade. Many people who would be reluctant to see government restrictions on domestic trade are quite willing to promote restrictions on international trade. However, the damage that high tariffs inflicted on the world population during the 1930s shows what can happen when governments around the world aggressively restrict international trade. Whether trade restrictions will become more or less common is subject to some doubt as pressure mounts on many governments to build barriers to international trade.

Read *An Inside Look* on the next page for a close look at the Canadian federal government's attempt to promote free trade in the wake of the global financial crisis of 2007.

AGENCE FRANCE-PRESSE

Canada Warns Against Protectionism

OTTAWA—Pockets of protectionism are hurting the global recovery, Canada's trade minister warned Tuesday, days before Canada hosts a G20 summit.

Most G20 countries have held firm on their commitments made at last year's summit in Pittsburgh not to impose new trade barriers, he said in an interview with AFP.

"Overall, we haven't had a wave of protectionism that was feared," he said. "But there have been some elements of backsliding," Peter Van Loan added, pointing to China, Russia and the United States.

In Toronto on June 26–27, G20 countries "will be called to account for what they've done, and (host Canada) will try to keep countries focused on the right path for the future," said the minister.

Earlier, Van Loan told the American Chamber of Commerce in Canada in Toronto that a lasting economic recovery "depends on free trade."

"This is the message we will be delivering to our existing and future trade partners at the upcoming G20 meeting," he said in a speech.

Canadian Prime Minister Stephen Harper's administration, since coming to power in 2006, has signed free trade agreements with Colombia, Peru, Jordan, Panama and the European Free Trade Association: Iceland, Liechtenstein, Norway and Switzerland.

In February, the United States and Canada ended a year-old dispute as Washington agreed to waive "Buy American" provisions barring Canadian firms from projects under a massive stimulus package.

The controversial US provisions were part of the nearly 800-billion-dollar US stimulus package adopted last year and drew criticism from various countries which branded them as a protectionist measure.

Under the deal reached between the United States and Canada, Washington would provide Canadian suppliers access to state and local public works projects under the American Recovery and Reinvestment Act of 2009 aimed at stimulating the world's largest economy out of recession.

In return, Ottawa would also provide US suppliers with access to construction contracts across its provinces and territories, as well as in a number of municipalities—seen as a breakthrough by Washington.

But new measures in other countries have cost Canadian companies billions of dollars in exports, Van Loan lamented.

Russia imposed merchandise tariffs on agricultural machinery, for example, "in response to the crisis." "We've had issues with canola access in China that cost us 1.2 billion dollars in exports to China."

"Historically, protection has caused economic slowdowns and freer trade has lead [sic] to economic growth, so that's the most important reason in the global economic context for resisting protectionism," Van Loan said.

"For Canada, which is two-thirds trade dependent, our economic recovery depends on being able to trade freely and to seek further trading opportunities."

Source: Michel Comte, "Canada Warns Against Protectionism," Agence France-Presse, June 22, 2010, accessed at http://www.google.com/hostednews/afp/article/ALeqM5iHZZ-T1sFigbijwjkWBfiXCE57PA

Key Points in the Article

This article discusses the Canadian government's efforts at the G20 meetings to prevent countries from erecting barriers to international trade. In general these efforts have been successful as the wave of tariffs, quotas, and other trade restrictions that some people feared has not arisen. While some countries have enacted policies to restrict international trade, there has not been much retaliation from their trading partners. The policy that was of primary concern to Canadian businesses was the so called "Buy American" provisions of the U.S. stimulus package. This policy required that the U.S. infrastructure projects (roads, bridges, etc.) hire only American firms. Such a policy would represent a major barrier to trade between Canada and the U.S.

Analyzing the News

a The economies of the developed world are highly integrated. Many firms with their headquarters in Canada or the U.S. or Germany sell their products not just in their home country but all over the world. This interconnectedness was increasing before the financial crisis. For example, the American firm Caterpillar makes heavy equipment (bulldozers, excavators, etc.) and sells its products in countries all around the globe. For the economies of the U.S. and Canada to recover, they cannot be cut off from their consumers in other countries. If suddenly Caterpillar could not sell machinery outside the U.S., or Bombardier couldn't sell outside Canada, these companies would have to lay off hundreds, if not thousands of workers, making the recession even worse.

b The "Buy American" provision of the U.S. stimulus package was designed to ensure that the government spending on new roads, bridges, and buildings went only to American firms. Such a policy would have meant that Canadian firms normally able to export their services and knowledge to the U.S. could no longer do so. The result would be less employment and profit at those firms. These firms would be likely to lobby the Canadian government for similar rules that denied American firms access to the Canadian stimulus spending taking place at the same time. Instead of preventing firms on both sides of the U.S.–Canada border from applying their expertise to infrastructure projects, the governments agreed to allow firms from the other country to work on domestic projects.

c Even though the U.S. and Canada managed to come to an agreement to avoid raising trade barriers, not all countries have maintained free trade. Russia and China have both taken steps to restrict trade with Canada. The Chinese restriction on the canola trade is estimated to have cost Canadian producers $1.2 billion. The reduction of trade barriers tends to be tied to periods of increasing economic wealth, as more efficient firms replace less efficient ones. International trade is a key reason that Canada is one of the wealthiest nations in the world. If international trade were suddenly to stop, a great many Canadians would become unemployed at the same time as they had to pay a lot more for the things they use every day.

Thinking Critically

1. "Buy Local" provisions, as well as tariffs and quotas on imports, are intended to save jobs. Do they in fact save jobs? Would you support a tariff on imported passenger planes to protect Bombardier? Why or why not?

2. Give examples of goods you think Canadian firms have a comparative advantage in producing. In producing what goods do you think other countries have a comparative advantage (relative to Canada)? (Give examples.)

Chapter Summary and Problems

Key Terms

Absolute advantage, p. 193

Autarky, p. 194

Comparative advantage, p. 192

Dumping, p. 210

Exports, p. 190

External economies, p. 199

Free trade, p. 199

Globalization, p. 207

Imports, p. 190

Opportunity cost, p. 192

Protectionism, p. 209

Quota, p. 203

Tariff, p. 190

Terms of trade, p. 194

Voluntary export restraint (VER), p. 203

World Trade Organization (WTO), p. 207

Summary

*LO **7.1** International trade has been increasing in recent decades, in part because of reductions in tariffs and other barriers to trade. A **tariff** is a tax imposed by a government on imports. The quantity of goods and services that Canada imports and exports has been continually increasing. **Imports** are goods and services bought domestically but produced in other countries. **Exports** are goods and services produced domestically and sold to other countries. Currently, we export about 40 percent of everything we produce, and exports from Canada account for 2.6 percent of global trade around the world.

LO **7.2** **Comparative advantage** is the ability of an individual, a business, or a country to produce a good or service at the lowest opportunity cost. **Opportunity cost** is the highest-valued alternative that must be given up to engage in an activity. **Absolute advantage** is the ability to produce more of a good or service than competitors when using the same amount of resources. Countries trade on the basis of comparative advantage, not on the basis of absolute advantage.

LO **7.3** **Autarky** is a situation in which a country does not trade with other countries. The **terms of trade** is the ratio at which a country can trade its exports for imports from other countries. When a country specializes in producing goods where it has a comparative advantage and trades for the other goods it needs, the country will have a higher level of income and consumption. We do not see complete specialization in production for three reasons: (1) Not all goods and services are traded internationally; (2) production of most goods involves increasing opportunity costs; and (3) tastes for products differ. Although the population of a country as a whole benefits from trade, companies—and their workers—that are unable to compete with lower-cost foreign producers lose. Among the main sources of comparative advantage are climate and natural

resources, relative abundance of labour and capital, technology, and external economies. **External economies** are reductions in a firm's costs that result from an increase in the size of an industry. A country may develop a comparative advantage in the production of a good, and then as time passes and circumstances change, the country may lose its comparative advantage in producing that good and develop a comparative advantage in producing other goods.

LO **7.4** **Free trade** is trade between countries without government restrictions. Government policies that interfere with trade usually take the form of tariffs, quotas, or voluntary export restraints (VERs). A tariff is a tax imposed by a government on imports. A **quota** is a numeric limit imposed by a government on the quantity of a good that can be imported into the country. A **voluntary export restraint (VER)** is an agreement negotiated between two countries that places a numerical limit on the quantity of a good that can be imported by one country from the other country. Saving jobs by using tariffs and quotas is often very expensive.

LO **7.5** The **World Trade Organization (WTO)** is an international organization that enforces international trade agreements. The WTO has promoted **globalization**, the process of countries becoming more open to foreign trade and investment. Some critics of the WTO argue that globalization has damaged local cultures around the world. Other critics oppose the WTO because they believe in **protectionism**, which is the use of trade barriers to shield domestic firms from foreign competition. The WTO allows countries to use tariffs in cases of **dumping**, when an imported product is sold for a price below its cost of production. Economists can point out the burden imposed on the economy by tariffs, quotas, and other government interferences with free trade. But whether these policies should be used is a normative decision.

MyEconLab   Log in to MyEconLab to complete these exercises and get instant feedback.

Review Questions

LO **7.1**

1.1 Briefly explain whether the value of Canadian exports is typically larger or smaller than the value of Canadian imports.

1.2 Briefly explain whether you agree with the following statement: "International trade is more important to the Canadian economy than to most other economies."

*'Learning Objective' is abbreviated to 'LO' in the end of chapter material.

LO **7.2**

2.1 What is the difference between absolute advantage and comparative advantage? Will a country always be an exporter of a good for which it has an absolute advantage in production? Briefly explain.

2.2 A WTO publication calls comparative advantage "arguably the single most powerful insight in economics." What is comparative advantage? What makes it such a powerful insight?

Based on World Trade Organization, "Understanding the WTO," www.wto.org/english/thewto_e/whatis_e/tif_e/fact3_e.htm.

LO 7.3

3.1 What is meant by a country "specializing in the production of a good"? Is it typical for countries to be completely specialized? Briefly explain.

3.2 Does everyone gain from international trade? If not, explain which groups lose.

LO 7.4

4.1 What is a tariff? What is a quota? Give an example, other than a quota, of a non-tariff barrier to trade.

4.2 Who gains and who loses when a country imposes a tariff or a quota on imports of a good?

LO 7.5

5.1 What is globalization? Why are some people opposed to globalization?

5.2 What is protectionism? Who benefits and who loses from protectionist policies? What are the main arguments people use to justify protectionism?

Problems and Applications

LO 7.1

1.1 If Canada were to stop trading goods and services with other countries, which Canadian industries would be likely to see their sales decline the most? Briefly explain.

1.2 Why might a smaller country, such as the Netherlands, be more likely to import and export larger fractions of its GDP than would a larger country, such as China or the United States?

LO 7.2

2.1 Why do the goods that countries import and export change over time? Use the concept of comparative advantage in your answer.

2.2 Briefly explain whether you agree with the following argument: "Unfortunately, Bolivia does not have a comparative advantage with respect to Canada in the production of any good or service." (Hint: You do not need any specific information about the economies of Bolivia and Canada to be able to answer this question.)

2.3 The following table shows for Greece and Italy the hourly output per worker measured as quarts of olive oil and pounds of pasta.

	Output per Hour of Work	
	Olive Oil	Pasta
Greece	4	2
Italy	4	8

Calculate the opportunity cost of producing olive oil and pasta in both Greece and in Italy.

2.4 Some of those arguing against the Canadian government's efforts to increase trade ties with other regions and countries state that removing trade barriers will mean losing jobs in Canada. What do you think people mean by "losing jobs in Canada"? Using the economic concept of comparative advantage, explain under what circumstances it would make sense for Canada to produce all of a specific good—say, T-shirts—in Canada. Do you agree with the lost jobs objection to free trade? Explain.

LO 7.3

3.1 [**Related to the** Making the Connection **on page 195**] Like Magna International, many American firms depend on being able to export their products to the world market. When the U.S. was debating restricting participation in

new government infrastructure development program to U.S. firms in 2008–09, both General Electric and Caterpillar opposed the "Buy American" provision. Douglas Irwin wrote in the *New York Times*:

> General Electric and Caterpillar have opposed the Buy American provision because they fear it will hurt their ability to win contracts abroad…. Once we get through the current economic mess, China, India and other countries are likely to continue their large investments in building projects. If such countries also adopt our preferences for domestic producers, then America will be at a competitive disadvantage in bidding for those contracts.

What are "preferences for domestic producers"? Why would these preferences put U.S. firms at a "competitive disadvantage"? Why might "having difficulty making sales in China and India" be a particular problem for Caterpillar?

"If We Buy American, No One Else Will," by Douglas A. Irwin from *New York Times*, January 31, 2009. Copyright © 2009 by Douglas A. Irwin.

3.2 [**Related to** Solved Problem 7.3 **on page 196**] The following table shows the hourly output per worker in two industries in Chile and Argentina.

	Output per Hour of Work	
	Hats	Beer
Chile	8	6
Argentina	1	2

a. Explain which country has an absolute advantage in the production of hats and which country has an absolute advantage in the production of beer.

b. Explain which country has a comparative advantage in the production of hats and which country has a comparative advantage in the production of beer.

c. Suppose that Chile and Argentina currently do not trade with each other. Each has 1,000 hours of labour to use producing hats and beer, and the countries are currently producing the amounts of each good shown in the following table.

	Output per Hour of Work	
	Hats	Beer
Chile	7,200	600
Argentina	600	800

Using this information, give a numerical example of how Chile and Argentina can both gain from trade. Assume that after trading begins, one hat can be exchanged for one barrel of beer.

3.3 [**Related to** Solved Problem 7.3 **on page 196**] A political commentator makes the following statement:

> The idea that international trade should be based on the comparative advantage of each country is fine for rich countries like Canada and Japan. Rich countries have educated workers and large quantities of machinery and equipment. These advantages allow them to produce every product more efficiently than poor countries can. Poor countries like Kenya and Bolivia have nothing to gain from international trade based on comparative advantage.

Do you agree with this argument? Briefly explain.

3.4 Briefly explain whether you agree with the following statement: "Most countries exhaust their comparative advantage in producing a good or service before they reach complete specialization."

3.5 Is free trade likely to benefit a large, populous country more than a small country with fewer people? Briefly explain.

3.6 Economist Hal Varian has made two observations about international trade:
  a. Trade allows a country "to produce more with less."
  b. There is little doubt who wins [from trade] in the long run: consumers.

Briefly explain whether you agree with either or both of these observations.

Based on Hal R. Varian, "The Mixed Bag of Productivity," *New York Times*, October 23, 2003, accessed September 6, 2013, at http://www.nytimes.com/2003/10/23/business/23SCEN.html.

3.7 [**Related to** Don't Let This Happen to You **on page 198**] In 2012, the Canadian government was pursuing trade deals with the European Union, India, China, and many other countries. Governments generally promote such trade deals as "win–win" with both countries involved. Is everyone in both countries likely to win from the agreement? Briefly explain.

LO 7.4

4.1 In a recent public opinion poll, 61 percent of people responding supported increasing trade with Asia. At the same time, 59 percent of those polled don't support the idea of a free trade agreement with China. What is "free trade"? Do you believe it helps or hurts an economy? (Be sure you define what you mean by "helps" or "hurts".) Why do you think Canadians might support the idea of more trade with Asia but oppose a free trade agreement (like the one Canada already has with the U.S. and Mexico) with China?

Based on Mark Kennedy, "Canadians want Stephen Harper to block foreign investment: poll." PostMedia News, December 18, 2012. http://www.canada.com/Canadians+want+Stephen+Harper+block+foreign+investment+poll/7716805/story.html

4.2 The G20 is a group of central bankers and finance ministers from 19 countries and the European Union who have a common goal of promoting global economic stability. In a letter to the editor of the *New York Times*, Victor K. Fung, the chairman of the International Chamber of Commerce, commented on the 2009 G20 summit in London:

> While global leaders promise to fight protectionism when they gather at summit meetings, they must also resist intense pressure back home to adopt populist policies that will most certainly protract the recession.

What does Fung mean by "fighting protectionism"? What does he mean by "populist policies"? How might populist trade policies extend a period of high unemployment and low production, such as the 2007–09 recession?

Based on Victor K. Fung, "Resist Protectionism," Letter to the Editor, *New York Times*, March 30, 2009.

4.3 Canada produces beef and also imports beef from other countries.
  a. Draw a graph showing the demand and supply of beef in Canada. Assume that Canada can import as much as it wants at the world price of beef without causing the world price of beef to increase. Be sure to indicate on the graph the quantity of beef imported.
  b. Now show on your graph the effect of Canada imposing a tariff on beef. Be sure to indicate on your graph the quantity of beef sold by Canadian producers before and after the tariff is imposed, the quantity of beef imported before and after the tariff, and the price of beef in Canada before and after the tariff.
  c. Discuss who benefits and who loses when Canada imposes a tariff on beef.

4.4 [**Related to the** Chapter Opener **on page 189**] Which U.S. firms are most likely to be unfavourably affected by a provision that only U.S. firms can participate in programs financed by federal spending?

4.5 A student makes the following argument:

> Tariffs on imports of foreign goods into Canada will cause the foreign companies to add the amount of the tariff to the prices they charge in Canada for those goods. Instead of putting a tariff on imported goods, we should ban importing them. Banning imported goods is better than putting tariffs on them because Canadian producers benefit from the reduced competition, and Canadian consumers don't have to pay the higher prices caused by tariffs.

Briefly explain whether you agree with the student's reasoning.

4.6 Suppose China decides to pay large subsidies to any Chinese company that exports goods or services to Canada. As a result, these companies are able to sell products in Canada at far below their cost of production. In addition, China decides to bar all imports from Canada. The dollars that Canada pays to import Chinese goods are left in banks in China. Will this strategy raise or lower the standard of living in China? Will it raise or lower the standard of living in Canada? Briefly explain. Be sure to provide a definition of "standard of living" in your answer.

4.7 [**Related to** Solved Problem 7.4 **on page 204**] Suppose that Canada currently both produces kumquats and imports them. The Canadian government then decides to restrict international trade in kumquats by imposing a quota that allows imports of only 6 million pounds of kumquats into Canada each year. The figure shows the results of imposing the quota.

Fill in the table using the letters in the figure.

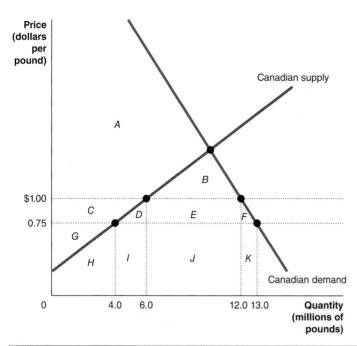

	Without Quota	With Quota
World price of kumquats		
Canadian price of kumquats		
Quantity supplied by Canadian firms		
Quantity demanded		
Quantity imported		
Area of consumer surplus		
Area of domestic producer surplus		
Area of deadweight loss		

LO 7.5

5.1 **[Related to the** Making the Connection **on page 208]** The following excerpt is from a newspaper story on former U.S. President Bill Clinton's proposal to create a group within the World Trade Organization (WTO) responsible for developing labour standards. The story was published just before the 1999 WTO meeting in Seattle that ended in rioting:

> [President Clinton proposed that] core labor standards ... become "part of every trade agreement. And ultimately I would favor a system in which sanctions would come for violating any provision of a trade agreement." ... But the new U.S. stand is sure to meet massive resistance from developing countries, which make up more than 100 of the 135 countries in the WTO. They are not interested in adopting tough U.S. labor standards ....

What did Clinton mean by "core labor standards"? Why would developing countries resist adopting these standards?

From Terence Hunt, "Salute to Trade's Benefits Turns into 'Kind of Circus,'" Associated Press, December 2, 1999, accessed September 6, 2013, at http://www.southcoasttoday.com/apps/pbcs.dll /article?AID=/19991202/NEWS/312029966&cid=sitesearch.

5.2 Suppose you are explaining the benefits of free trade and someone states, "I don't understand all the principles of comparative advantage and gains from trade. I just know that if I buy something produced in Canada, I create a job for a Canadian, and if I buy something produced in Brazil, I create a job for a Brazilian." Do you agree with this statement? When Canada imports products in which it does not have a comparative advantage, does that mean that there are fewer jobs in Canada? In the example in the text with South Korea and Canada producing and trading cell phones and televisions, when Canada imports televisions from South Korea, does the number of jobs in Canada decline?

5.3 Often federal opposition parties resist free trade agreements with other countries. One of the reasons these political parties cite for resisting free trade agreements is that "free trade hurts Canadian workers." Is it likely that trade agreements that reduce tariffs and quotas will harm Canadian workers? Briefly explain.

CHAPTER 8

Consumer Choice and Behavioural Economics

Chapter Outline and Learning Objectives

Christopher Polk/Getty Images

Can Justin Bieber and Ozzy Osbourne Get You to Shop at Best Buy?

Managers at Best Buy had an idea they believed people would love: The company would buy any cell phone or other electronic product back from its customers, within two years of purchase, and allow them to upgrade to a newer model. To announce this Buy Back program, Best Buy ran a new commercial during the 2011 Super Bowl, an opportunity to reach over 110 million viewers. This commercial featured an unlikely pair of celebrities: aging rock star Ozzie Osbourne and teenage singing sensation Justin Bieber. Although many Best Buy customers are old enough to be the teenage Bieber's parents, demand for mobile and technology-related products was growing more than the demand for televisions and stereos that had fuelled Best Buy's past growth. The retailer was anxious to change its image. "Justin Bieber is the biggest star out there…" explained marketing chief Drew Panayiotou. "He… represents something important to the brand message."

In 2012, *Forbes* magazine ranked Justin Bieber as the third most powerful celebrity in the world, behind only Jennifer Lopez and Oprah Winfrey, and ahead of stars like Rihanna, Lady Gaga, Simon Cowell, and Steven Spielberg. It was Bieber's third time on the magazine's "Celebrity 100" list of the world's most powerful celebrities. Do celebrity endorsements affect consumer behaviour? When asked in surveys, many consumers claim that celebrity endorsements don't influence their buying decisions.

Marc Babej, an authority on marketing strategy, argues that survey responses are unreliable because advertisements appeal to the subconscious as well as the conscious mind. To be successful, Babej believes that celebrity endorsements must be relevant to the advertised product:

> In… image-driven consumer categories such as fashion, perfume or liquor, celebrity endorsements can be credible. For sporting goods, endorsement by an athlete can work wonders…. But in [other] categories… a celebrity endorser isn't likely to have much of a positive impact…[because] movie stars or athletes aren't considered authorities in these areas.

Will Justin Bieber's endorsement increase Best Buy's sales of cell phones? In this chapter, we will examine how consumers make decisions about which products to buy. Firms must understand consumer behaviour to determine what strategies are likely to be most effective in selling their products.

AN INSIDE LOOK on **page 242** discusses whether endorsements from celebrities ranging from Jennifer Lopez to Charlie Sheen can help or hurt a brand.

Based on Marc E. Babej, "Poll: Celebrity Endorsements Don't Work… Don't Tell Angelina," *Forbes*, June 14, 2011; Amanda Massa, "Justin Bieber Leads List of Celebrity 100 Newcomers," *forbes.com*, May 18, 2011; Dorothy Pamerantz (ed.), "The World's Most Powerful Celebrities," Forbes.com (www.forbes.com/celebrities), May 16, 2012, accessed November 19, 2012; and Bruce Horovitz, "Justin Bieber…and Ozzy?… to Star in Best Buy Super Bowl Ad," *USA Today*, January 27, 2011.

Economics in Your Life

Do You Make Rational Decisions?

Economists generally assume that people make decisions in a rational, consistent way. But are people actually as rational as economists assume? Consider the following situation: You and your friend are discussing going to a sold-out concert. You have the opportunity to buy a ticket online for $100 but declare that you wouldn't pay $100 to see that band. Later in the day, you win a ticket to the concert by being the thirteenth caller in a contest on the radio. Your friend offers you $100 for the ticket you just won. Would you sell your ticket to your friend? Would an economist think it is rational to sell your ticket? As you read the chapter, see if you can answer these questions. You can check your answers against those we provide on page 241 at the end of this chapter.

W
e begin this chapter by exploring how consumers make decisions. In Chapter 1, we saw that economists usually assume that people act in a rational, self-interested way. In explaining consumer behaviour, this means economists believe consumers make choices that will leave them as satisfied as possible, given their *tastes*, their *incomes*, and the *prices* of the goods and services available to them. We will see how downward-sloping demand curves we encountered in Chapters 3 through 5 result from the economic model of consumer behaviour. We will also explore how in certain situations, knowing which decision is the best one can be difficult. In these cases, economic reasoning provides a powerful tool for consumers to improve their decision making. Finally, we will see that *experimental economics* has shown that factors such as social pressure and notions of fairness can affect consumer behaviour. We will look at how businesses take these factors into account when setting prices. In Appendix D (available online), we extend the analysis by using indifference curves and budget lines to understand consumer behaviour.

Utility and Consumer Decision Making

8.1 LEARNING OBJECTIVE
Define utility and explain how consumers choose goods and services to maximize their utility.

We saw in Chapter 3 that the model of demand and supply is a powerful tool for analyzing how prices and quantities are determined. We also saw that, according to the *law of demand*, whenever the price of a good falls, the quantity demanded increases. In this section, we will show how the economic model of consumer behaviour leads to the law of demand.

The Economic Model of Consumer Behaviour in a Nutshell

Imagine walking through a shopping mall, trying to decide how to spend your clothing budget. If you had an unlimited budget, your decision would be easy: Just buy as much of everything as you want. Given that you have a limited budget, what do you do? Economists assume that consumers act so as to make themselves as well off as possible. Therefore, you should choose the one combination of clothes that makes you as well off as possible from among those combinations that you can afford. Stated more generally, the economic model of consumer behaviour predicts that consumers will choose to buy the combination of goods and services that makes them as well off as possible from among all the combinations that their budgets allow them to buy.

This prediction may seem obvious and not particularly useful. But as we explore the implication of this prediction, we will see that it leads to conclusions that are useful but not obvious.

Utility

How much satisfaction you receive from consuming a particular combination of goods and services depends on your tastes or preferences. There is an old saying—"There's no accounting for tastes"—and economists don't try to. If you buy a can of Red Bull energy drink instead of a can of Monster Energy, even though Monster Energy has a lower price, you must receive more enjoyment or satisfaction from drinking Red Bull. Economists refer to the enjoyment or satisfaction people receive from consuming goods and services as **utility**. So we can say that the goal of a consumer is to spend available income so as to maximize utility. But utility is a difficult concept to measure because there is no way of knowing exactly how much enjoyment or satisfaction someone receives from consuming a product. Similarly, it is not possible to compare utility across consumers. There is no way of knowing for sure whether Jill receives more or less satisfaction than Jack from drinking a can of Red Bull.

Hundreds of years ago, economists hoped to measure utility in units called *utils*. The util would be an objective measure in the same way that temperature is: If it is 24 degrees Celsius in St. John's and 24 degrees Celsius in Vancouver, it is just as warm in both cities. These economists wanted to say that if Jack's utility from drinking a can of Red Bull is

Utility The enjoyment or satisfaction people receive from consuming goods and services.

10 utils and Jill's utility is 5 utils, then Jack receives exactly twice the satisfaction from drinking a can of Red Bull as Jill does. In fact, it is *not* possible to measure utility across people. It turns out that none of the important conclusions of the economic model of consumer behaviour depend on utility being directly measurable (a point we demonstrate in Appendix D). Nevertheless, the economic model of consumer behaviour is easier to understand if we assume that utility is something directly measurable, like temperature.

The Principle of Diminishing Marginal Utility

To make the model of consumer behaviour more concrete, let's see how a consumer makes decisions in a case involving just two products: pepperoni pizza and Coke. To begin, consider how the utility you receive from consuming a good changes with the quantity of the good you consume. For example, suppose that you have just arrived at a Grey Cup party, where the hosts are serving pepperoni pizza, and you are very hungry. In this situation, you are likely to receive quite a lot of enjoyment, or utility, from consuming the first slice of pizza. Suppose this satisfaction is measurable and is equal to 20 units of utility, or *utils*. After eating the first slice, you decide to have a second slice. Because you are no longer as hungry, the satisfaction you receive from eating the second slice of pizza is less than the satisfaction you received from eating the first slice. Consuming the second slice increases your utility by only an *additional* 16 utils, which raises your *total* utility from eating the 2 slices to 36 utils. If you continue eating slices, each additional slice gives you less and less additional satisfaction.

The table in Figure 8.1 shows the relationship between the number of slices of pizza you consume while watching the Grey Cup and the amount of utility you receive. The second column in the table shows the total utility you receive from eating a particular number of slices. The third column shows the additional utility, or **marginal utility** (*MU*), you receive from consuming one additional slice. (Remember that in economics, *marginal* means *additional*.) For example, as you increase your consumption from 2 slices to 3 slices, your total utility increases from 36 to 46, so your marginal utility from consuming the third slice is 10 utils. As the table shows, by the time you eat the fifth slice of pizza that evening, your marginal utility is very low: only 2 utils. If you were to eat a sixth slice, you would become slightly ill, and your marginal utility would actually be a *negative* 3 utils.

Figure 8.1 also plots the numbers from the table as graphs. Panel (a) shows how your total utility rises as you eat the first 5 slices of pizza and then falls as you eat the sixth slice. Panel (b) shows how your marginal utility declines with each additional slice you eat and finally becomes negative when you eat the sixth slice and you wouldn't voluntarily eat it. The height of the marginal utility line at any quantity of pizza in panel (b) represents the change in utility as a result of consuming that additional slice. For example, the change in utility as a result of consuming 4 slices instead of 3 is 6 utils, so the height of the marginal utility line in panel (b) is 6 utils.

The relationship illustrated in Figure 8.1 between consuming additional units of a product during a period of time and the marginal utility received from consuming each additional unit is referred to as the **law of diminishing marginal utility**. For nearly every good or service, the more you consume during a period of time, the less you increase your total satisfaction from each additional unit you consume.

The Rule of Equal Marginal Utility per Dollar Spent

The key challenge for consumers is to decide how to allocate their limited incomes among all the products they wish to buy. Every consumer has to make trade-offs: If you have $100 to spend on entertainment for the month, then the more movies you buy online, the fewer movies you can see in the theatre. Economists refer to the limited amount of income you have available to spend on goods and services as your **budget constraint**. The principle of diminishing marginal utility helps us understand how consumers can best spend their limited incomes on the products available to them.

Suppose you attend a Grey Cup party at a restaurant, and you have $10 to spend on refreshments. Pizza is selling for $2 per slice, and Coke is selling for $1 per cup.

Marginal utility (*MU*) The change in total utility a person receives from consuming one additional unit of a good or service.

Law of diminishing marginal utility The principle that consumers experience diminishing additional satisfaction as they consume more of a good or service during a given period of time.

Budget constraint The limited amount of income available to consumers to spend on goods and services.

Figure 8.1

Total and Marginal Utility from Eating at a Grey Cup Party

The table shows that for the first 5 slices of pizza, the more you eat, the more your total satisfaction, or utility, increases. If you eat a sixth slice, you start to feel ill from eating too much pizza, and your total utility falls. Each additional slice increases your utility by less than the previous slice, so your marginal utility from each slice is less than the one before. Panel (a) shows your total utility rising as you eat the first 5 slices and falling with the sixth slice. Panel (b) shows your marginal utility falling with each additional slice you eat and becoming negative with the sixth slice. The height of the marginal utility line at any quantity of pizza in panel (b) represents the change in utility as a result of consuming that additional slice. For example, the change in utility as a result of consuming 4 slices instead of 3 is 6 utils, so the height of the marginal utility line in panel (b) for the fourth slice is 6 utils.

Number of Slices	Total Utility from Eating Pizza	Marginal Utility from the Last Slice Eaten
0	0	—
1	20	20
2	36	16
3	46	10
4	52	6
5	54	2
6	51	−3

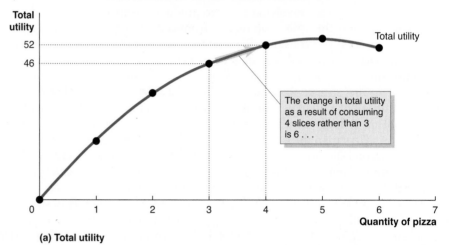

(a) Total utility

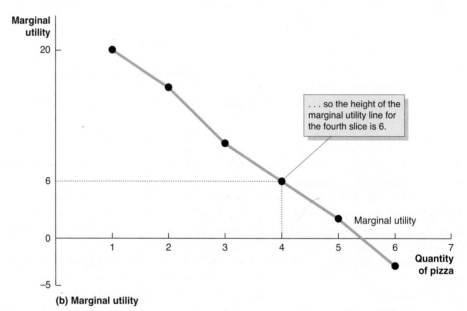

(b) Marginal utility

Table 8.1 shows the relationship between the amount of pizza you eat, the amount of Coke you drink, and the amount of satisfaction, or utility, you receive. The values for pizza are repeated from the table in Figure 8.1. The values for Coke also follow the principle of diminishing marginal utility.

How many slices of pizza and how many cups of Coke do you buy if you want to maximize your utility? If you did not have a budget constraint, you would buy 5 slices of pizza and 5 cups of Coke because that would give you total utility of 107 (= 54 + 53), which is the maximum utility you can achieve. Eating another slice of pizza or drinking another cup of Coke during the evening would lower your utility. Unfortunately, you do have a budget constraint: You have only $10 to spend. To buy 5 slices of pizza (at $2 per slice) and 5 cups of Coke (at $1 per cup), you would need $15.

Table 8.1

Total Utility and Marginal Utility from Eating Pizza and Drinking Coke

Number of Slices of Pizza	Total Utility from Eating Pizza	Marginal Utility from the Last Slice	Number of Cups of Coke	Total Utility from Drinking Coke	Marginal Utility from the Last Cup
0	0	—	0	0	—
1	20	20	1	20	20
2	36	16	2	35	15
3	46	10	3	45	10
4	52	6	4	50	5
5	54	2	5	53	3
6	51	−3	6	52	−1

To select the best way to spend your \$10, remember this key economic principle: *Optimal decisions are made at the margin.* That is, most of the time, economic decision makers—consumers, firms, and the government—are faced with decisions about whether to do a little more of one thing or a little more of an alternative. In this case, you are choosing to consume a little more pizza or a little more Coke. Parliament chooses to spend more for research on heart disease or more for research on breast cancer. Everyone faces a budget constraint, and everyone faces trade-offs.

The key to making the best consumption decision is to maximize utility by following the *rule of equal marginal utility per dollar spent.* As you decide how to spend your income, you should buy pizza and Coke up to the point where the last slice of pizza purchased and the last cup of Coke purchased give you equal increases in utility *per dollar.* By doing this, you will have maximized your total utility.

It is important to remember that to follow this rule, you must equalize your marginal utility per dollar spent, *not* your marginal utility from each good. Buying season tickets for your favorite hockey team or for the symphony or buying a BMW may give you a lot more satisfaction than drinking a cup of Coke, but the hockey tickets may well give you less satisfaction *per dollar spent.* To decide how many slices of pizza and how many cups of Coke to buy, you must convert the values for marginal utility in Table 8.1 into marginal utility per dollar. You can do this by dividing marginal utility by the price of each good, as shown in Table 8.2.

In column (3), we calculate marginal utility per dollar spent on pizza. Because the price of pizza is \$2 per slice, the marginal utility per dollar from eating 1 slice of pizza equals 20 divided by \$2, or 10 utils per dollar. Similarly, we show in column (6) that because the price of Coke is \$1 per cup, the marginal utility per dollar from drinking 1 cup of Coke equals 20 divided by \$1, or 20 utils per dollar. To maximize the total utility you receive, you must make sure that the utility per dollar of pizza for the last slice of pizza is equal to the utility per dollar of Coke for the last cup of Coke. Table 8.2 shows that there are three combinations of slices of pizza and cups of Coke where marginal

Table 8.2

Converting Marginal Utility to Marginal Utility per Dollar

(1) Slices of Pizza	(2) Marginal Utility (MU_{Pizza})	(3) Marginal Utility per Dollar $\left(\dfrac{MU_{Pizza}}{P_{Pizza}}\right)$	(4) Cups of Coke	(5) Marginal Utility (MU_{Coke})	(6) Marginal Utility per Dollar $\left(\dfrac{MU_{Coke}}{P_{Coke}}\right)$
1	20	10	1	20	20
2	16	8	2	15	15
3	10	5	3	10	10
4	6	3	4	5	5
5	2	1	5	3	3
6	−3	−1.5	6	−1	−1

Table 8.3 **Equalizing Marginal Utility per Dollar Spent**	Combinations of Pizza and Coke with Equal Marginal Utilities per Dollar	Marginal Utility per Dollar (*MU/P*)	Total Spending	Total Utility
	1 slice of pizza and 3 cups of Coke	10	$2 + $3 = $5	20 + 45 = 65
	3 slices of pizza and 4 cups of Coke	5	$6 + $4 = $10	46 + 50 = 96
	4 slices of pizza and 5 cups of Coke	3	$8 + $5 = $13	52 + 53 = 105

utility per dollar is equalized. Table 8.3 lists the combinations, the total amount of money needed to buy each combination, and the total utility received from consuming each combination.

If you buy 4 slices of pizza, the last slice gives you 3 utils per dollar. If you buy 5 cups of Coke, the last cup also gives you 3 utils per dollar, so you have equalized your marginal utility per dollar. Unfortunately, as the third column in the table shows, to buy 4 slices and 5 cups, you would need $13, and you have only $10. You could also equalize your marginal utility per dollar by buying 1 slice and 3 cups, but that would cost just $5, leaving you with $5 to spend. Only when you buy 3 slices and 4 cups have you equalized your marginal utility per dollar and spent neither more nor less than the $10 available.

We can summarize the two conditions for maximizing utility:

1. $\dfrac{MU_{Pizza}}{P_{Pizza}} = \dfrac{MU_{Coke}}{P_{Coke}}$

2. Spending on pizza + Spending on Coke = Amount available to be spent

The first condition shows that the marginal utility per dollar spent must be the same for both goods. The second condition is the budget constraint, which states that total spending on both goods must equal the amount available to be spent. Of course, these conditions for maximizing utility apply not just to pizza and Coke but to any two pairs of goods.

Solved Problem **8.1**

Finding the Optimal Level of Consumption

The following table shows Lee's utility from consuming ice cream cones and cans of Lime Fizz pop:

Number of Ice Cream Cones	Total Utility from Ice Cream Cones	Marginal Utility from Last Cone	Number of Cans of Lime Fizz	Total Utility from Cans of Lime Fizz	Marginal Utility from Last Can
0	0	—	0	0	—
1	30	30	1	40	40
2	55	25	2	75	35
3	75	20	3	101	26
4	90	15	4	119	18
5	100	10	5	134	15
6	105	5	6	141	7

a. Ana inspects this table and concludes, "Lee's optimal choice would be to consume 4 ice cream cones and 5 cans of Lime Fizz because with that combination, his marginal utility from ice cream cones is equal to his marginal utility from Lime Fizz." Do you agree with Ana's reasoning? Briefly explain.

b. Suppose that Lee has an unlimited budget to spend on ice cream cones and cans of Lime Fizz. Under these circumstances, how many ice cream cones and how many cans of Lime Fizz will he consume? (Assume that Lee cannot consume more than 6 ice cream cones or 6 cans of Lime Fizz.)

c. Suppose that Lee has $7 per week to spend on ice cream cones and Lime Fizz. The price of an ice cream cone is $2, and the price of a can of Lime Fizz is $1. If Lee wants to maximize his utility, how many ice cream cones and how many cans of Lime Fizz should he buy?

Solving the Problem

Step 1: **Review the chapter material.** This problem involves finding the optimal consumption of two goods, so you may want to review the section "The Rule of Equal Marginal Utility per Dollar Spent," which begins on page 221.

Step 2: **Answer part (a) by analyzing Ana's reasoning.** Ana's reasoning is incorrect. To maximize utility, Lee needs to equalize marginal utility per dollar for the two goods.

Step 3: **Answer part (b) by determining how Lee would maximize utility with an unlimited budget.** With an unlimited budget, consumers maximize utility by continuing to buy each good as long as their utility is increasing. In this case, Lee will maximize utility by buying 6 ice cream cones and 6 cans of Lime Fizz, given that we are assuming he can't buy more than 6 units of either good.

Step 4: **Answer part (c) by determining Lee's optimal combination of ice cream cones and cans of Lime Fizz.** Lee will maximize his utility if he spends his $7 per week so that the marginal utility of ice cream cones divided by the price of ice cream cones is equal to the marginal utility of Lime Fizz divided by the price of Lime Fizz. We can use the following table to solve this part of the problem:

	Ice Cream Cones		Cans of Lime Fizz	
Quantity	MU	$\dfrac{MU}{P}$	MU	$\dfrac{MU}{P}$
1	30	15	40	40
2	25	12.5	35	35
3	20	10	26	26
4	15	7.5	18	18
5	10	5	15	15
6	5	2.5	7	7

Lee will maximize his utility by buying 1 ice cream cone and 5 cans of Lime Fizz. At this combination, the marginal utility of each good divided by its price equals 15. He has also spent all of his $7.

Your Turn: For more practice, do related problem 1.3 on page 245 at the end of this chapter.   MyEconLab

What If the Rule of Equal Marginal Utility per Dollar Does Not Hold?

The idea of getting the maximum utility by equalizing the ratio of marginal utility to price for the goods you are buying can be difficult to grasp, so it is worth thinking about in another way. Suppose that instead of buying 3 slices of pizza and 4 cups of Coke, you buy 4 slices and 2 cups. Four slices and 2 cups cost $10, so you would meet your budget constraint by spending all the money available to you, but would you have gotten the maximum amount of utility? No, you wouldn't have. From the information in Table 8.1 on page 223, we can list the additional utility per dollar you are getting from the last slice and the last cup and the total utility from consuming 4 slices and 2 cups:

Marginal utility per dollar for the fourth slice of pizza = 3 utils per dollar

Marginal utility per dollar for the second cup of Coke = 15 utils per dollar

Total utility from 4 slices of pizza and 2 cups of Coke = 87 utils

Obviously, the marginal utilities per dollar are not equal. The last cup of Coke gave you considerably more satisfaction per dollar than did the last slice of pizza. You could raise your total utility by buying less pizza and more Coke. Buying 1 less slice of pizza frees up $2 that will allow you to buy 2 more cups of Coke. Eating 1 less slice of pizza reduces your utility by 6 utils, but drinking 2 additional cups of Coke raises your utility by 15 utils (make sure you see this), for a net increase of 9. You end up equalizing your marginal utility per dollar (5 utils per dollar for both the last slice and the last cup) and raising your total utility from 87 utils to 96 utils.

The Income Effect and Substitution Effect of a Price Change

We can use the rule of equal marginal utility per dollar to analyze how consumers adjust their buying decisions when a price changes. Suppose you are back at the restaurant for the Grey Cup party, but this time the price of pizza is $1.50 per slice, rather than $2. You still have $10 to spend on pizza and Coke.

Income effect The change in the quantity demanded of a good that results from the effect of a change in price on consumer purchasing power, holding all other factors constant.

When the price of pizza was $2 per slice and the price of Coke was $1 per cup, your optimal choice was to consume 3 slices of pizza and 4 cups of Coke. The fall in the price of pizza to $1.50 per slice has two effects on the quantity of pizza you consume: the *income effect* and the *substitution effect*. First, consider the income effect. When the price of a good falls, you have more purchasing power. In our example, 3 slices of pizza and 4 cups of Coke now cost a total of only $8.50 instead of $10.00. An increase in purchasing power is essentially the same thing as an increase in income. The change in the quantity of pizza you will demand because of this increase in purchasing power—holding all other factors constant—is the **income effect** of the price change. Recall from Chapter 3 that if a product is a *normal good*, a consumer increases the quantity demanded as the consumer's income rises, but if a product is an *inferior good*, a consumer decreases the quantity demanded as the consumer's income rises. So, if we assume that for you pizza is a normal good, the income effect of a fall in price causes you to consume more pizza. If pizza were an inferior good for you, the income effect of a fall in the price would have caused you to consume less pizza.

Substitution effect The change in the quantity demanded of a good that results from a change in price making the good more or less expensive relative to other goods, holding constant the effect of the price change on consumer purchasing power.

The second effect of the price change is the substitution effect. When the price of pizza falls, pizza becomes cheaper *relative* to Coke, and the marginal utility per dollar for each slice of pizza you consume increases. If we hold constant the effect of the price change on your purchasing power and just focus on the effect of the price being lower relative to the price of the other good, we have isolated the **substitution effect** of the price change. The lower price of pizza relative to the price of Coke has lowered the *opportunity cost* to you of consuming pizza because now you have to give up less Coke to consume the same quantity of pizza. Therefore, the substitution effect from the fall in the price of pizza relative to the price of Coke causes you to eat more pizza and drink less Coke. In this case, both the income effect and the substitution effect of the fall in price cause you to eat more pizza. If the price of pizza had risen, both the income effect and the substitution effect would have caused you to eat less pizza. Table 8.4 summarizes the effect of a price change on the quantity demanded.

We can use Table 8.5 to determine the effect of the fall in the price of pizza on your optimal consumption. Table 8.5 has the same information as Table 8.2, with one change: The marginal utility per dollar from eating pizza has been changed to reflect

Table 8.4

Income Effect and Substitution Effect of a Price Change

When price...	consumer purchasing power...	The income effect causes quantity demanded to...	The substitution effect causes the opportunity cost of consuming a good to...
decreases,	increases.	increase, if a normal good, and decrease, if an inferior good.	decrease when the price decreases, which causes the quantity of the good demanded to increase.
increases,	decreases.	decrease, if a normal good, and increase, if an inferior good.	increase when the price increases, which causes the quantity of the good demanded to decrease.

(1) Slices of Pizza	(2) Marginal Utility (MU_{Pizza})	(3) Marginal Utility per Dollar $\left(\dfrac{MU_{Pizza}}{P_{Pizza}}\right)$	(4) Cups of Coke	(5) Marginal Utility (MU_{Coke})	(6) Marginal Utility per Dollar $\left(\dfrac{MU_{Coke}}{P_{Coke}}\right)$
1	20	13.33	1	20	20
2	16	10.67	2	15	15
3	10	6.67	3	10	10
4	6	4	4	5	5
5	2	1.33	5	3	3
6	−3	−1.5	6	−1	−1

Table 8.5

Adjusting Optimal Consumption to a Lower Price of Pizza

the new lower price of $1.50 per slice. Examining the table, we can see that the fall in the price of pizza will result in your eating 1 more slice of pizza, so your optimal consumption now becomes 4 slices of pizza and 4 cups of Coke. You will be spending all of your $10, and the last dollar you spend on pizza will provide you with about the same marginal utility per dollar as the last dollar you spend on Coke. You will not be receiving exactly the same marginal utility per dollar spent on the two products. As Table 8.5 shows, the last slice of pizza gives you 4 utils per dollar, and the last cup of Coke gives you 5 utils per dollar. But this is as close as you can come to equalizing marginal utility per dollar for the two products, unless you can buy a fraction of a slice of pizza or a fraction of a cup of Coke.

Where Demand Curves Come From

According to the *law of demand*, whenever the price of a product falls, the quantity demanded increases. Now that we have covered the concepts of total utility, marginal utility, and the budget constraint, we can look more closely at why the law of demand holds.

In our example of optimal consumption of pizza and Coke at the Grey Cup party, we found the following:

Price of pizza = $2 per slice ⟹ Quantity of pizza demanded = 3 slices
Price of pizza = $1.50 per slice ⟹ Quantity of pizza demanded = 4 slices

In panel (a) of Figure 8.2, we plot the two points showing the optimal number of pizza slices you choose to consume at each price. In panel (b) of Figure 8.2, we draw a line connecting the two points. This downward-sloping line represents your demand curve for pizza. We could find more points on the line by changing the price of pizza and using the information in Table 8.2 to find the new optimal number of slices of pizza you would demand at each price.

To this point in this chapter, we have been looking at an individual demand curve. As we saw in Chapter 3, however, economists are typically interested in market demand curves. We can construct the market demand curve from the individual demand curves for all the consumers in the market. To keep things simple, let's assume that there are only three consumers in the market for pizza: you, David, and Lori. The table in Figure 8.3 shows the individual demand schedules for the three consumers. Because consumers differ in their incomes and their preferences for products, we would not expect every consumer to demand the same quantity of a given product at each price. The final column gives the market demand, which is simply the sum of the quantities demanded by each of the three consumers at each price. For example, at a price of $1.50 per slice, your quantity demanded is 4 slices, David's quantity demanded is 6 slices, and Lori's quantity demanded is 5 slices. So, at a price of $1.50, a quantity of 15 slices is demanded in the market. The graphs in the figure show that we can obtain the market demand curve by adding horizontally the individual demand curves.

8.2 LEARNING OBJECTIVE

Use the concept of utility to explain the law of demand.

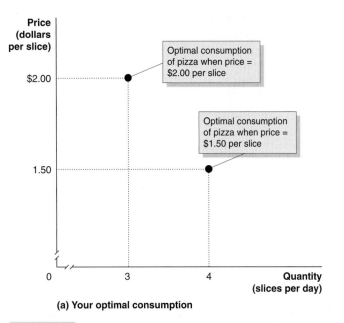

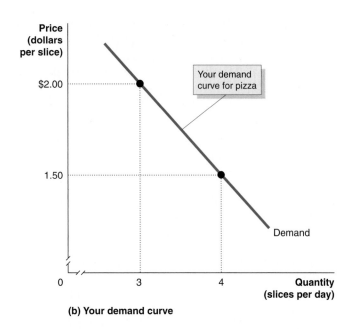

(a) Your optimal consumption   **(b) Your demand curve**

Figure 8.2 Deriving the Demand Curve for Pizza

A consumer responds optimally to a fall in the price of a product by consuming more of that product. In panel (a), the price of pizza falls from $2 per slice to $1.50, and the optimal quantity of slices consumed rises from 3 to 4. When we graph this result in panel (b), we have the consumer's demand curve

Price (dollars per slice)	Quantity (slices per day)			
	You	David	Lori	Market
$2.50	2	4	1	7
2.00	3	5	3	11
1.50	4	6	5	15
1.00	5	7	7	19
0.50	6	8	9	23

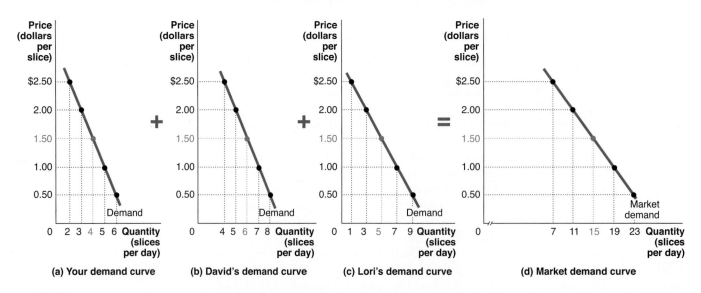

(a) Your demand curve   **(b) David's demand curve**   **(c) Lori's demand curve**   **(d) Market demand curve**

Figure 8.3 Deriving the Market Demand Curve from Individual Demand Curves

The table shows that the total quantity demanded in a market is the sum of the quantities demanded by each buyer. We can find the market demand curve by adding horizontally the individual demand curves in panels (a), (b), and (c). For instance, at a price of $1.50, your quantity demanded is 4 slices, David's quantity demanded is 6 slices, and Lori's quantity demanded is 5 slices. Therefore, panel (d) shows that a price of $1.50 and a quantity demanded of 15 is a point on the market demand curve.

Remember that according to the law of demand, market demand curves always slope downward. We now know that this is true because the income and substitution effects of a fall in price cause consumers to increase the quantity of the good they demand. There is a complicating factor, however. As we discussed earlier, only for normal goods will the income effect result in consumers increasing the quantity of the good they demand when the price falls. If the good is an inferior good, the income effect leads consumers to *decrease* the quantity of the good they demand. The substitution effect, on the other hand, results in consumers increasing the quantity they demand of both normal and inferior goods when the price falls. So, when the price of an inferior good falls, the income effect and substitution effect work in opposite directions: The income effect causes consumers to decrease the quantity of the good they demand, whereas the substitution effect causes consumers to increase the quantity of the good they demand. Is it possible, then, that consumers might actually buy less of a good when the price falls? If this happened, the demand curve would be upward sloping.

Making the Connection | Are There Any Upward-Sloping Demand Curves in the Real World?

For a demand curve to be upward sloping, the good would have to be an inferior good and the income effect would have to be larger than the substitution effect. Economists have understood the conditions for an upward-sloping demand curve since the possibility was first discussed by the British economist Alfred Marshall in the 1890s. Marshall wrote that his friend, Sir Robert Giffen, had told him that when the price of bread rose, very poor people in British cities would actually buy more bread rather than less because the rise in the price of bread meant that these people could no longer afford other types of food. Since that time, goods with upward-sloping demand curves have been referred to as *Giffen goods.*

For more than a century, finding an actual Giffen good proved impossible. A close examination of the data showed that Giffen had been mistaken and that poor people in British cities bought less bread when prices rose, so their demand curves were downward sloping. Other possible candidates for being Giffen goods were also found to actually have downward-sloping demand curves. Finally, in 2006, Robert Jensen and Nolan Miller discovered two Giffen goods. Jensen and Miller reasoned that to be a Giffen good, with an income effect larger than its substitution effect, a good must be inferior and make up a very large portion of consumers' budgets. Jensen and Miller knew that very poor people in the Hunan region of China spent most of their incomes on rice, while in the Gansu province, very poor people spent most of their income on wheat-based foods, such as buns and noodles. In both places, poor people ate meat when their incomes allowed it because they preferred the taste of meat even though it did not supply as many calories as the rice or wheat they could purchase for the same price.

Jensen and Miller carried out the following experiment: In Hunan, for a five-month period they gave a selected number of poor families coupons that would allow them to buy rice at a lower price. Families could not use the coupons for any other purpose. In Gansu, Jensen and Miller gave a selected number of poor families coupons to buy wheat at a lower price. Jensen and Miller then observed the purchases of the families during the time they received the coupons and during the period immediately thereafter. In Hunan, during the months they received the coupons, the families bought less rice and more meat, and in Gansu, they bought less wheat and more meat. Because in Hunan families bought less rice when the price was lower, their demand curves for rice were upward sloping. Similarly, in Gansu, families bought less wheat when the price was lower, so their demand curves for wheat were upward sloping. After more than a century of searching, economists had finally discovered examples of a Giffen good.

Rice is a Giffen good in poor parts of China.

Gianni Baldizzone/Corbis

Based on Robert T. Jensen and Nolan H. Miller, "Giffen Behavior and Subsistence Consumption," *American Economic Review*, Vol. 98, No. 4, September 2008, pp. 1553–1577.

MyEconLab **Your Turn:** Test your understanding by doing related problem 2.4 on page 245 at the end of this chapter.

8.3 LEARNING OBJECTIVE

Explain how social influences can affect consumption choices.

Social Influences on Decision Making

Sociologists and anthropologists have argued that social factors such as culture, customs, and religion are very important in explaining the choices consumers make. Economists have traditionally seen such factors as being relatively unimportant, if they take them into consideration at all. Recently, however, some economists have begun to study how social factors influence consumer choice.

For example, people seem to receive more utility from consuming goods they believe are popular. As the economists Gary Becker and Kevin Murphy put it:

> The utility from drugs, crime, going bowling, owning a Rolex watch, voting Democratic, dressing informally at work, or keeping a neat lawn depends on whether friends and neighbours take drugs, commit crimes, go bowling, own Rolex watches, vote Democratic, dress informally, or keep their lawns neat.

This reasoning can help to explain why one restaurant is packed, while another restaurant that serves essentially the same food and has similar décor has many fewer customers. Consumers decide which restaurant to go to partly on the basis of food and décor but also on the basis of the restaurant's popularity. People receive utility from being seen eating at a popular restaurant because they believe it makes them appear knowledgeable and fashionable. Whenever consumption takes place publicly, many consumers base their purchasing decisions on what other consumers are buying. Examples of public consumption include eating in restaurants, attending sporting events, wearing clothes or jewellery, and driving cars. In all these cases, the decision to buy a product depends partly on the characteristics of the product and partly on how many other people are buying the product.

The Effects of Celebrity Endorsements

In many cases, it is not just the number of people who use a product that makes it desirable but the types of people who use it. If consumers believe that media stars or professional athletes use a product, demand for the product will often increase. This may be partly because consumers believe public figures are particularly knowledgeable about products: "Justin Bieber probably knows more about cell phones and other electronics than I do, so I'll buy these products at Best Buy because he does." But many consumers also feel more fashionable and closer to famous people if they use the same products. These considerations help to explain why companies such as Best Buy are willing to pay millions of dollars to have celebrities endorse their products. Some companies, such as Coca-Cola, have been using celebrities in their advertising for decades.

Making the Connection | **Why Do Firms Pay Sidney Crosby to Endorse Their Products?**

Sidney Crosby is one of the biggest stars in the National Hockey League (NHL). Playing for the Pittsburgh Penguins, he has won the Stanley Cup (the league championship), the Maurice "Rocket" Richard Trophy for most goals scored in a season, the Art Ross Trophy for most points scored in a season, and the Hart Memorial Trophy as the league's most valuable player.

Given this list of awards, it may not be surprising that many companies have paid Crosby to endorse their products. His endorsements include Tim Hortons, Bell, Sport Chek, Gatorade, and Reebok. Reebok in particular was so eager to have him endorse its products that, in 2010, Crosby signed a contract to receive $1.4 million a year for between five and seven years to endorse Reebok sporting goods.

Sidney Crosby is clearly a talented hockey player, but why should consumers care which products he uses? There seems to be little doubt that consumers do in fact care, but why? It might be that they believe Crosby to have better information than they do about the products he endorses. The average amateur player and hockey fan might believe that, if Crosby endorses Reebok equipment, maybe Reebok actually makes better equipment. It also seems likely that people buy products associated with Sidney Crosby or other celebrities because using these products makes them feel closer to the celebrity or because it makes them appear fashionable.

Based on Ken Campbell, "Sidney Crosby to Sign Richest Endorsement Deal in NHL History," *The Hockey News*, May 29, 2010.

nLab   **Your turn:** Test your understanding by doing related problem 3.3 on page 246 at the end of this chapter.

Michael Stuparyk/Getty Images

Are you more likely to purchase a product based on Sidney Crosby's endorsement?

Network Externalities

Technology can play a role in explaining why consumers buy products that many other consumers are already buying. There is a **network externality** in the consumption of a product if the usefulness of the product increases with the number of consumers who use it. For example, if you owned the only phone in the world, it would not be very useful. The usefulness of phones increases as the number of people who own them increases. Similarly, your willingness to buy an Apple iPad depends in part on the number of other people who own iPads. The more people who own iPads, the more applications, or apps, other firms will produce for the iPad, and the more novels, textbooks, newspapers, and magazines publishers will make available for downloading to the iPad, and, therefore, the more useful an iPad is to you.

Some economists have suggested the possibility that network externalities may have a significant downside because they might result in consumers buying products that contain inferior technologies. This outcome could occur because network externalities can create significant *switching costs* related to changing products: When a product becomes established, consumers may find it too costly to switch to a new product that contains a better technology. The selection of products may be *path dependent*. This means that because of switching costs, the technology that was first available may have advantages over better technologies that were developed later. In other words, the path along which the economy has developed in the past is important.

One example of path dependence and the use of an inferior technology is the QWERTY order of the letters along the top row of most computer keyboards. This order became widely used when manual typewriters were developed in the late nineteenth century. The metal keys on manual typewriters would stick together if a user typed too fast, and the QWERTY keyboard was designed to slow down typists and minimize the problem of the keys sticking together. With computers, the problem that QWERTY was developed to solve no longer exists, so keyboards could be changed to have letters in a more efficient layout. But because the overwhelming majority of people have learned to use keyboards with the QWERTY layout, there might be significant costs to them if they had to switch, even if a new layout ultimately made them faster typists.

Other products that supposedly embodied inferior technologies are VHS video recorders—supposedly inferior to Sony Betamax recorders—and the Windows

Network externality A situation in which the usefulness of a product increases with the number of consumers who use it.

computer operating system—supposedly inferior to the Macintosh operating system. Some economists have argued that because of path dependence and switching costs, network externalities can result in *market failures*. As we saw in Chapter 5, a market failure is a situation in which the market fails to produce the efficient level of output. If network externalities result in market failure, government intervention in these markets might improve economic efficiency. Many economists are skeptical, however, that network externalities really do lead to consumers being locked into products with inferior technologies. In particular, economists Stan Leibowitz and Stephen Margolis have argued that, in practice, the gains from using a superior technology are larger than the losses due to switching costs. After carefully studying the cases of the QWERTY keyboard, VHS videocassette recorder, and Windows computer operating system, they have concluded that there is no good evidence that the alternative technologies were actually superior. The implications of network externalities for economic efficiency remain controversial among economists.

Does Fairness Matter?

If people were only interested in making themselves as well off as possible in a material sense, they would not be concerned with fairness. There is a great deal of evidence, however, that people like to be treated fairly and that they usually attempt to treat others fairly, even if doing so makes them worse off financially. Tipping servers in restaurants is an example. In Canada, diners in restaurants typically add 15 to 20 percent to their food bills as tips to their servers. Tips are not *required*, but most people see it as very unfair not to tip, unless the service has been exceptionally bad. You could argue that people leave tips not to be fair but because they are afraid that if they don't leave a tip, the next time they visit the restaurant they will receive poor service. A 2004 study by Boyes, Mounts, and Sowell has shown, however, that most people leave tips at restaurants even while on vacation or in other circumstances where they are unlikely to visit the restaurant again.

There are many other examples where people willingly part with money when they are not required to do so and when they receive nothing material in return. The most obvious example is making donations to charity. Apparently, donating money to charity or leaving tips in restaurants that they will never visit again gives people more utility than they would receive from keeping the money and spending it on themselves.

A Test of Fairness in the Economic Laboratory: The Ultimatum Game Experiment Economists have used experiments to increase their understanding of the role that fairness plays in consumer decision making. *Experimental economics* has been widely used during the past two decades, and a number of experimental economics laboratories exist in North America and Europe. Economists Maurice Allais, Reinhard Selten, and Vernon Smith were awarded the 2002 Nobel Prize in Economics in part because of their contributions to experimental economics. Experiments make it possible to focus on a single aspect of consumer behaviour. The *ultimatum game*, first popularized by Werner Güth of the Max Planck Institute of Economics, is an experiment that tests whether fairness is important in consumer decision making. Various economists have conducted the ultimatum game experiment under slightly different conditions, but with generally the same result. In this game, a group of volunteers—often university or college students—are divided into pairs. One member of each pair is the "allocator," and the other member of the pair is the "recipient."

Each pair is given an amount of money, say, $20. The allocator decides how much of the $20 each member of the pair will get. There are no restrictions on how the allocator divides up the money. He or she could keep it all, give it all to the recipient, or anything in between. The recipient must then decide whether to accept the allocation or reject it. If the recipient decides to accept the allocation, each member of the pair gets to keep his or her share. If the recipient decides to reject the allocation, both members of the pair receive nothing.

If neither the allocator nor the recipient cares about fairness, optimal play in the ultimatum game is straightforward: The allocator should propose a division of the money in which the allocator receives $19.99 and the recipient receives $0.01. The allocator has maximized his or her gain. The recipient should accept the division because the alternative is to reject the division and receive nothing at all: Even a penny is better than nothing.

In fact, when the ultimatum game experiment is carried out, both allocators and recipients act as if fairness is important. Allocators usually offer recipients at least a 40 percent share of the money, and recipients almost always reject offers of less than a 10 percent share. Why do allocators offer recipients more than a negligible amount? It might be that allocators do not care about fairness but fear that recipients do care and will reject offers they consider unfair. This possibility was tested in an experiment known as the *dictator game* carried out by Daniel Kahneman (a psychologist who shared the Nobel Prize in Economics), Jack Knetsch, and Richard Thaler, using students. In this experiment, the allocators were given only two possible divisions of $20: either $18 for themselves and $2 for the recipient or an even division of $10 for themselves and $10 for the recipient. One important difference from the ultimatum game was that *the recipient was not allowed to reject the division.* Of the 161 allocators, 122 chose the even division of the $20. Because there was no possibility of the $18/$2 split being rejected, the allocators must have chosen the even split because they valued acting fairly.

Why would recipients in the ultimatum game ever reject any division of the money in which they receive even a very small amount, given that even a small amount of money is better than nothing? Apparently, most people value fairness enough that they will refuse to participate in transactions they consider unfair, even if they are worse off financially as a result.

Are the Results of Economic Experiments Reliable? Because economists have conducted the ultimatum game and the dictator game many times in different countries using different groups of people, most economists believe that the results of the game provide strong evidence that people value fairness. Recently, however, some economists have begun to question this conclusion. To begin with, the experimental situation is artificial, so results obtained from experiments may not hold up in the real world. Although allocators in the dictatorship game give money to the other player, whose identity is not known to the allocator, in the real world people rarely just hand money to strangers. So, it is possible that the fairness observed in the experiments may be the result of people wanting to avoid appearing selfish rather than people valuing fairness. For instance, in the ultimatum game, anyone who kept $19.99 and gave the other person only $0.01 might be afraid of appearing selfish in the eyes of the economist conducting the experiment. Particularly because the dollar amounts involved in the experiment are small, wanting to please the person conducting the experiment may be the main motive behind the choices made.

John List has carried out variations of the dictator game. When he gave every player $5 and followed the usual procedure of having half the players act as dictators in dividing up the $5, he found the usual result, with 71 percent of dictators allocating some money to the other player. But when he gave the dictator the choice of either giving money to the other player or *taking* up to $5 from the other player, only 10 percent of dictators gave the other player any money, and more than half the dictators took money from the other player. When List asked players to work for 30 minutes at a simple task to earn the $5 before playing the game, two-thirds of the dictators neither gave anything nor took anything from the other player. This last result may indicate that the source of the money being allocated matters.

List's results do not completely reverse the usual interpretation of the results of the ultimatum and dictator games. They do show, however, that the results of those games are not as clear-cut as many economists had thought. They also show that the details of an economic experiment can have a significant effect on its results.

Business Implications of Fairness If consumers value fairness, how does this affect firms? One consequence is that firms will sometimes not raise prices of goods and services, even when there is a large increase in demand, because they are afraid their customers will consider the price increases unfair and may buy elsewhere.

Consider several examples where it seems that businesses could increase their profits by raising prices. In October of 2012, Justin Bieber performed in Calgary. Tickets originally sold for $106 each. Demand for tickets was so large, however, that they sold out in a matter of minutes. Many people who were willing to pay the original price for tickets couldn't get them, and shortly after official ticket sales closed at 10:00 a.m., some tickets were being sold online for as much as $5,000. Why didn't Justin Bieber, his manager, or the concert promoter charge more for the tickets? Other examples are sports tickets and university educations. Each year, particularly when the Leafs are playing well, many more people would like to buy tickets to Toronto Maple Leafs games than there are tickets available. Many universities have more applications than space for students. Why don't the Toronto Maple Leafs or universities raise their prices?

In each of these cases, it appears that a firm could increase its profits by raising prices. The seller would be selling the same quantity—of seats at a concert or in a hockey arena or university educations—at a higher price, so profits should increase. Economists have provided two explanations for why firms sometimes do not raise prices in these situations. Gary Becker, who was awarded the Nobel Prize in Economics, has suggested that the products involved—concerts, hockey games, or university educations—are all products that buyers consume together with other buyers. In those situations, the amount consumers wish to buy may be related to how much of the product other people are consuming. People like to consume, and be seen consuming, a popular product. If entertainers, sports teams, and universities increased their prices enough to equate the quantity of their product demanded with the quantity supplied, they might find that they had also eliminated their popularity.

Daniel Kahneman, Jack Knetsch, and Richard Thaler have offered another explanation for why firms don't always raise prices when doing so would seem to increase their profits. In surveys of consumers, these researchers found that most people considered it fair for firms to raise their prices following an increase in costs but unfair to raise prices following an increase in demand. For example, Kahneman, Knetsch, and Thaler conducted a survey in which people were asked their opinion of the following situation: "A hardware store has been selling snow shovels for $15. The morning after a large snowstorm, the store raises the price to $20." Eighty-two percent of those surveyed responded that they considered the hardware store's actions to be unfair. Kahneman, Knetsch, and Thaler have concluded that firms may sometimes not raise their prices even when the quantity demanded of their product is greater than the quantity supplied out of fear that in the long run, they will lose customers who believe the price increases were unfair.

In analyzing the pricing of Super Bowl tickets, economist Alan Krueger provided some support for Kahneman, Knetsch, and Thaler's explanation of why companies do not always raise prices when the quantity demanded is greater than the quantity supplied. In 2011, the NFL charged $1,200 for the best seats and $600 for most of the rest. Many of these tickets were resold online for as much as $5,000 each. Krueger decided to survey football fans attending the Super Bowl to see if their views could help explain why the NFL didn't charge higher prices for the tickets. When asked whether it would "be fair for the NFL to raise the [price of tickets] to $1,500 if that is still less than the amount most people are willing to pay for tickets," 92 percent of the fans surveyed answered "no." Even 83 percent of the fans who had paid more than $1,500 for their tickets answered "no." Krueger concluded that whatever the NFL might gain in the short run from raising ticket prices, it would more than lose in the long run by alienating football fans.

These explanations for why firms don't always raise prices to a level that would equate the quantity demanded with the quantity supplied share the same basic idea: Sometimes firms will give up some profits in the short run to keep their customers happy and increase their profits in the long run.

Making the Connection

What's Up With "Fuel Surcharges"?

Ordinarily, when firms present their customers with a bill, they don't itemize the costs of producing the good or service: Restaurants don't list on their menus the costs of the lettuce and tomatoes in a salad, and automobile companies don't list on their window price stickers the prices they paid their suppliers for the transmission or the tires. As oil prices began to rise in 2008, however, a number of companies began adding a line for "fuel surcharge" to their bills. For instance, WestJet, the second largest airline in Canada, includes a fuel surcharge in the price of its tickets, adding $23 to the price of a ticket from Vancouver to St. John's. The same is true of Air Canada, which adds a $46 surcharge on flights from Vancouver to St. John's. Canada Post and FedEx both include fuel surcharges on shipping in some cases. If firms don't increase their prices in response to increases in costs their profits decrease, but increasing prices reduces sales.

It isn't uncommon for firms to raise their prices or include surcharges for fuel when the price of oil rises quickly. It is less common for firms to remove these surcharges when the price of oil falls, although many firms do review their surcharges regularly. The mystery of why the prices of airline tickets don't fall as quickly as the price of oil falls in some cases can be solved by considering why airlines started itemizing a fuel surcharge to begin with. As the research of Kahneman, Knetsch, and Thaler has shown, consumers see it as fair for firms to raise prices after an increase in costs. When consumers view a price increase as unfair, they are much more likely to buy from a competing firm. By explicitly including a fuel surcharge in their prices, the airlines—and other firms that added fuel surcharges to their bills—were able to increase prices without consumers seeing the increases as being unfair.

We know, though, that the prices of airline tickets and other goods and services are determined by the interaction of demand and supply. A decline in oil prices, like the one that occurred in the summer of 2011, reduces an airline's costs, thereby shifting the supply curve for airline tickets to the right. As the Canadian economy recovered from the 2008–2009 recession, the demand for airline tickets increased during the same period of time (summer 2011), shifting the demand curve to the right. As a result, the price of most airline tickets did not decline as the price of oil declined. The figure below illustrates this

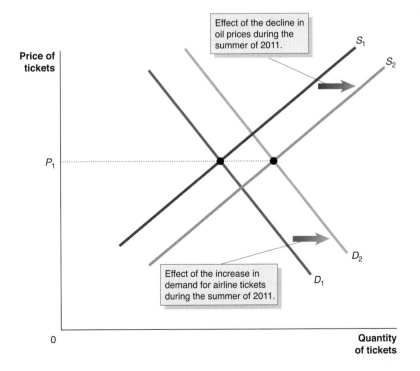

point by showing the price of tickets remaining at P_1 despite the shifts in the demand and supply curves.

Prices are determined by *all* of the factors that affect demand and supply. Airlines and other firms began singling out fuel costs in their prices only because they knew that doing so would make consumers believe that the price increases were fair.

Based on Timothy W. Martin and Jennifer Levitz, "Oil Falls, but Surcharges Stay Aloft," *Wall Street Journal*, August 11, 2011; and Daniel Kahneman, Jack Knetsch, and Richard Thaler, "Fairness as a Constraint on Profit Seeking: Entitlements in the Market," *American Economic Review*, Vol. 76, No. 4, September 1986, pp. 728–741.

MyEconLab   **Your Turn:** Test your understanding by doing related problem 3.5 on page 246 at the end of this chapter.

8.4 LEARNING OBJECTIVE
Describe the behavioural economics approach to understanding decision making.

Behavioural Economics: Do People Make Their Choices Rationally?

Behavioural economics The study of situations in which people make choices that do not appear to be economically rational.

When economists say that consumers and firms are behaving "rationally," they mean that consumers and firms are taking actions that are appropriate to reach their goals, given the information available to them. In recent years, some economists have begun studying situations in which people do not appear to be making choices that are economically rational. This new area of economics is called **behavioural economics**. Why might consumers or businesses not act rationally? The most obvious reason would be that they do not realize that their actions are inconsistent with their goals. As we discussed in Chapter 1, one of the objectives of economics is to suggest ways to make better decisions. In this section, we discuss ways in which consumers can improve their decisions by avoiding some common pitfalls.

Consumers commonly commit the following three mistakes when making decisions:

1. They take into account monetary costs but ignore nonmonetary opportunity costs.
2. They fail to ignore sunk costs.
3. They are unrealistic about their future behaviour.

Ignoring Nonmonetary Opportunity Costs

Opportunity cost The highest-valued alternative that must be given up to engage in an activity.

Remember from Chapter 2 that the **opportunity cost** of any activity is the highest-valued alternative that must be given up to engage in that activity. For example, if you own something you could sell, using it yourself involves an opportunity cost. It is often difficult for people to think of opportunity costs in these terms.

In 2009, the National Football League in the United States ran a lottery for its fans. Winners of the lottery were given the opportunity to buy tickets to the championship game, the Super Bowl, for the face value of the tickets, either $325 or $400 depending on where in the stadium the seats were located. Alan Krueger surveyed the lottery winners, asking them two questions.

Question 1: If you had not won the lottery, would you have been willing to pay $3,000 for your ticket?
Question 2: If after winning your ticket (and before arriving in Florida for the Super Bowl) someone had offered you $3,000 for your ticket, would you have sold it?

In response to question 1, 94 percent said that if they had not won the lottery, they would not have paid $3,000 for a ticket. In answer to question 2, 92 percent said they would not have sold their ticket for $3,000. These answers are contradictory! If someone offers you $3,000 for your ticket, then by using the ticket rather than selling it you incur an opportunity cost of $3,000. There really is a $3,000 cost involved in using that ticket, even though you did not pay $3,000 in cash. The two alternatives—either paying $3,000 or not receiving $3,000—are really the same thing.

If the ticket is really not worth $3,000 to you, you should sell it. If it is worth $3,000 to you, you should be willing to pay $3,000 in cash to buy it. Not being willing to sell a ticket you already own for $3,000 while at the same time not being willing to buy a ticket for $3,000 if you didn't already own one is inconsistent behaviour. The inconsistency comes from a failure to take into account nonmonetary opportunity costs. Behavioural economists believe this inconsistency is caused by the **endowment effect**, which is the tendency of people to be unwilling to sell a good they already own even if they are offered a price that is greater than the price they would be willing to pay to buy the good if they didn't already own it.

Endowment effect The tendency of people to be unwilling to sell a good they already own even if they are offered a price that is greater than the price they would be willing to pay to buy the good if they didn't already own it.

The failure to take into account opportunity costs is a very common error in decision making. Suppose, for example, that a friend is in a hurry to have his room cleaned—it's the Friday before he's expecting company—and he offers you $50 to do it for him. You turn him down and spend the time cleaning your own room, even though you know somebody down the hall who would be willing to clean your room for $20. Leave aside complicating details—the guy who asked you to clean his room is a real slob, or you don't want the person who offered to clean your room for $20 to go through your stuff—and you should see the point we are making. The opportunity cost of cleaning your own room is $50—the amount your friend offered to pay you to clean his room. It is inconsistent to turn down an offer from someone else to clean your room for $20 when you are doing it for yourself at a cost of $50. The key point here is this: *Nonmonetary opportunity costs are just as real as monetary costs and should be taken into account when making decisions.*

There are many examples of businesses taking advantage of the tendency of consumers to ignore nonmonetary costs. For example, some firms sell products with mail-in rebates. Rather than have a mail-in rebate of $10, why not just cut the price by $10? Companies are relying on the fact that not mailing in a rebate form once you have already paid for a product is a nonmonetary opportunity cost rather than a direct monetary cost. In fact, only a small percentage of customers actually mail in rebates.

Failing to Ignore Sunk Costs

A **sunk cost** is a cost that has already been paid and cannot be recovered. Once you have paid money and can't get it back, you should ignore that money in any later decisions you make. Consider the following two situations:

Sunk cost A cost that has already been paid and cannot be recovered.

Situation 1: You bought a ticket to a play for $75. The ticket is nonrefundable and must be used on Tuesday night, which is the only night the play will be performed. On Monday, a friend calls and invites you to a local comedy club to see a comedian you both like who is appearing only on Tuesday night. Your friend offers to pay the cost of going to the club.

Situation 2: It's Monday night, and you are about to buy a ticket for the Tuesday night performance of the same play as in situation 1. As you are leaving to buy the ticket, your friend calls and invites you to the comedy club.

Would your decision to go to the play or to the comedy club be different in situation 1 than in situation 2? Most people would say that in situation 1, they would go to the play, because otherwise they would lose the $75 they had paid for the ticket. In fact, though, the $75 is "lost" no matter what you do because the ticket is not refundable. The only real issue for you to decide is whether you would prefer to see the play or to go with your friend to the comedy club. If you would prefer to go to the club, the fact that you have already paid $75 for the ticket to the play is irrelevant. Your decision should be the same in situation 1 as in situation 2.

Psychologists Daniel Kahneman and Amos Tversky explored the tendency of consumers not to ignore sunk costs by asking two different samples of people the following questions:

Question 1: "Imagine that you have decided to see a play and have paid the admission price of $10 per ticket. As you enter the theatre, you discover that you have lost the ticket. The seat was not marked, and the ticket cannot be recovered. Would you pay $10 for another ticket?" Of those asked, 46 percent answered "yes," and 54 percent answered "no."

Question 2: "Imagine that you have decided to see a play where admission is $10 per ticket. As you enter the theatre, you discover that you have lost a $10 bill. Would you still pay $10 for a ticket to the play?" Of those asked, 88 percent answered "yes," and 12 percent answered "no."

The situations presented in the two questions are actually the same and should have received the same fraction of yes and no responses. Many people, though, have trouble seeing that in question 1, when deciding whether to see the play, they should ignore the $10 already paid for a ticket because it is a sunk cost.

Making the Connection

A Blogger Who Understands the Importance of Ignoring Sunk Costs

In recent years, many people have started blogs—or, "weblogs"—where they record their thoughts on politics, sports, their favourite hobbies, or anything else that interests them. Some bloggers can spend hours a day writing up their latest ideas and providing links to relevant material on the web. A few blogs become so successful that they attract paid advertising and earn their owners a good income. Arnold Kim began blogging about Apple products in 2000, during his fourth year of medical school. He continued blogging on his site, MacRumors.com, over the next eight years, while pursuing a medical career as a nephrologist—a doctor who treats kidney problems.

Would you give up being a surgeon to start your own blog?

By 2008, Kim's site had become very successful, attracting 4.4 million people and more than 40 million page views each month. Kim was earning more than $100,000 per year from paid advertising by companies such as Verizon, Audible.com, and CDW. But the tasks of compiling rumours about new Apple products, keeping an Apple buying guide up to date, and monitoring multiple discussion boards on the site became more than he could handle as a part-time job. Kim enjoyed working on the website and believed that ultimately it could earn him more than he was earning as a doctor. Still, he hesitated to abandon his medical career because he had invested nearly $200,000 in his education.

But the $200,000, as well as the years he had spent in medical school, completing a residency in internal medicine, and completing a fellowship in nephrology, were sunk costs. Kim realized that he needed to ignore these sunk costs in order to make a rational decision about whether to continue in medicine or to become a full-time blogger. After calculating that he would make more from his website than from his medical career—and taking into account that by working from home he could spend more time with his young daughter—he decided to blog full time. He was quoted as saying, "on paper it was an easy decision." By mid-2011, MacRumors.com was being viewed by more than 9 million people per month, and Kim's income had risen above what he would have made as a doctor.

Knowing that it is rational to ignore sunk costs can be important in making key decisions in life.

Based on Brian X. Chen, "Arnold Kim Celebrates 10 Years as Apple Rumor King," wired.com, February 23, 2010; Brian Stelter, "My Son, the Blogger: An M.D. Trades Medicine for Apple Rumors," *New York Times*, July 21, 2008; Dan Frommer, "Nephrologist to Mac Blogger: The Unlikely Career Path of MacRumors' Arnold Kim," businessinsider.com, July 13, 2008; and "Macrumors Traffic," quantcast.com, August 23, 2011.

MyEconLab **Your Turn:** Test your understanding by doing related problem 4.4 on page 246 at the end of this chapter.

Being Unrealistic About Future Behaviour

Studies have shown that a majority of adults in the United States are overweight. Why do many people choose to eat too much? One possibility is that they receive more utility from eating too much than they would from being thin. A more likely explanation, however, is that many people eat a lot today because they expect to eat less tomorrow. But they never do eat less, and so they end up overweight. (Of course, some people also suffer from medical problems that lead to weight gain.) Similarly, some people continue smoking today because they expect to be able to give it up sometime in the future. Unfortunately, for many people that time never comes, and they suffer the health consequences of prolonged smoking. In both these cases, people are overvaluing the utility from current choices—eating chocolate cake or smoking—and undervaluing the utility to be received in the future from being thin or not getting lung cancer.

Economists who have studied this question argue that many people have preferences that are not consistent over time. In the long run, you would like to be thin or give up smoking or achieve some other goal, but each day, you make decisions (such as to eat too much or to smoke) that are not consistent with this long-run goal. If you are unrealistic about your future behaviour, you underestimate the costs of choices—such as overeating or smoking—that you make today. A key way of avoiding this problem is to be realistic about your future behaviour.

<table>
<tr>
<td>

Making
the
Connection

</td>
<td>

Why Don't Students Study More?

Government statistics show that students who do well in postsecondary education

</td>
</tr>
</table>

earn at least $10,000 more per year than students who fail to graduate or who graduate with low grades. So, over the course of a career of 40 years or more, students who do well in university will have earned upward of $400,000 more than students who failed to graduate or who received low grades. Most universities advise that students study at least two hours outside class for every hour they spend in class. Surveys show that students often ignore this advice.

If the opportunity cost of not studying is so high, why do many students choose to study relatively little? Some students have work or family commitments that limit the amount of time they can study. But many other students study less than they would if they were more realistic about their future behaviour. On any given night, a student has to choose between studying and other activities—such as watching television, going to a movie, or going to a party—that may seem to provide higher utility in the short run. Many students choose one of these activities over studying because they expect to study tomorrow or the next day, but tomorrow they face the same choices and make similar decisions. As a result, they do not study enough to meet their long-run goal of graduating with high grades. If they were more realistic about their future behaviour, they would not make the mistake of overvaluing the utility from activities such as watching television or partying because they would realize that those activities can endanger their long-run goal of graduating with honours.

If the payoff to studying is so high, why don't students study more?

Your Turn: Test your understanding by doing related problem 4.5 on page 246 at the end of this chapter.

MyEconLab

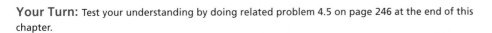

Solved Problem **8.4**

How Do You Get People to Save More of Their Income?

The cost of hiring a worker is usually more than just the worker's pay. In many cases, employers contribute to a pension plan that pays workers after they retire. Under defined benefit pension plans, firms can send some of a worker's pay to a mutual fund or other investment, where its returns will accumulate tax free until the worker retires. In most cases these plans are not voluntary, and all employees are automatically enrolled in the pension plan.

These pension plans are often endorsed by both the union representing workers and the employer. It might be surprising that unions support a program that gives their membership lower pay now and fewer choices. The funds contributed by the employer to the pension plan could be paid to the employee, who could then choose to use a registered retirement savings plan (RRSP) to purchase mutual funds and other investments that will accumulate tax-free returns until the worker retires. The mandatory nature of many pension plans can be explained using research done

by behavioural economists into what determines people's saving behaviour.

a. Why would people opt for a mandatory pension plan, when they could save in very much the same way on their own?

b. One unintended consequence of mandatory pension plans is a reduction in a worker's overall saving rate. When surveyed, many workers participating in an automatic retirement plan with a saving rate of 3 percent of a worker's earnings indicated they would have voluntarily saved more if they hadn't automatically been enrolled in the 3 percent savings plan. Why wouldn't employees enrolled at 3 percent who wanted to save more simply make extra contributions to the savings plan (which is often relatively easy to do)?

Based on Anne Tergesen, "401K Law Suppressed Saving for Retirement," *Wall Street Journal*, July 7, 2011.

Solving the Problem

Step 1: **Review the chapter material.** This problem is about people not always being realistic about their future behaviour, so you may want to review the section "Being Unrealistic About Future Behaviour," which begins on page 239.

Step 2: **Use your understanding of consumer decision making to answer part (a).** Some people appear to have acted irrationally by not taking the minor action of filling out a form to contribute extra to a pension plan. Here is one possible explanation for this puzzle that is consistent with what we have seen about many people being unrealistic about their future behaviour: Some people spend money today that they should be saving for retirement because they expect to increase their saving in the future. If people who act in this way are not automatically enrolled in a plan, they are unlikely to take the steps to enroll because they expect—possibly unrealistically—that in the future they will enroll or save money for retirement in other ways. However, if they are automatically enrolled, then taking the step of opting out of the plan would make it more obvious to themselves that they are behaving in a way that is inconsistent with their long-term goal of saving for retirement. So, once automatically enrolled, most people choose to stay enrolled, even if they would not have taken the necessary action to enroll themselves.

Step 3: **Answer part (b) by explaining why some employees don't raise their saving rate above the default rate of 3 percent.** The answer here is similar to the answer to part (a). Presumably, people who would have chosen a saving rate of 5 percent or 10 percent if they had not been automatically enrolled at 3 percent intend to raise their saving rate in the future. Some may actually do so, but for others the fact that they are at least saving something may disguise the fact that they are spending too much in the present and saving too little to meet their long-run saving goals.

MyEconLab   **Your Turn:** For more practice, do related problems 4.6 and 4.7 on page 247 at the end of this chapter.

Taking into account nonmonetary opportunity costs, ignoring sunk costs, and being more realistic about future behaviour are three ways in which consumers are able to improve the decisions they make.

Economics in Your Life

Do You Make Rational Decisions?

At the beginning of the chapter, we asked you to consider a situation in which you had just won a concert ticket from a local radio station. Before winning the ticket you declared that you would not be willing to pay $100 for a ticket. A friend offers you $100 for your ticket. We posed two questions about this situation: "Would you sell your ticket to your friend?" and "Would an economist think it is rational to sell your ticket?" If you answered that you would sell, then your answer is rational in the sense that economists use the term. Once someone offers you $100 for the ticket, that value becomes the opportunity cost of going to the concert (your best alternative to going is to sell the ticket). Assuming you were being honest when you said you wouldn't pay $100 for a ticket; your friend is offering to pay you more than the ticket is worth to you. However, people often have a harder time giving something up than not getting it in the first place. This can make a concert ticket won in a contest worth more than you would have been willing to pay for the ticket if you hadn't won it. Behavioural economists study situations like this where people make choices that do not appear to be economically rational.

Conclusion

In a market system, consumers are in the driver's seat. Goods are produced only if consumers want them to be. Therefore, how consumers make their decisions is an important area for economists to study. Economists expect that consumers will spend their incomes so that the last dollar spent on each good provides them with equal additional amounts of satisfaction, or utility. In practice, there are significant social influences on consumer decision making, particularly when a good or service is consumed in public. Fairness also seems to be an important consideration for most consumers. Finally, many consumers could improve the decisions they make if they would take into account nonmonetary opportunity costs and ignore sunk costs.

In this chapter, we studied consumers' choices. In the next several chapters, we will study firms' choices. Before moving on to the next chapter, read *An Inside Look* on the next page for a discussion of how celebrity endorsements affect the demand of products—for good and bad.

Adding Value Through Association with Star Power?

CBC NEWS

Celebrity Endorsements: Do They Make Products More Appealing to You?

Companies have relied on celebrities' star power to help sell their products for years.

(a) In 1910, King Edward VII, son of Queen Victoria and Prince Albert, appeared in a print ad endorsing Angelus piano-players, according to the advertising history book *The Age of Persuasion*.

"It's unlikely that the ad was run with the consent of His Highness. To the impudent rascals of Wilcox and White, makers of Angelus player pianos, it was an irresistible opportunity to cash in on the royal persona and an early-twentieth-century example of the power of the celebrity endorsement."

(b) When radio and television arrived in the early 20th century, classic broadcast stars like Jack Benny and Bob Hope were associated with powerful sponsors like Jell-O and Pepsodent and would often plug products during the shows.

These days, it's common to see athletes, musicians, and actors promoting multiple businesses and products. Singer and actress Beyoncé Knowles, for example, has a variety of deals with numerous companies including L'Oreal, Pepsi, Tommy Hilfiger, and even Nintendo.

(c) But a recent trend has seen celebrities moving from merely doing commercials to actually working for companies. Black Eyed Peas front man will.i.am made headlines this week after accepting a job as "director of creative innovation" for computer chip maker Intel Corp.

The artist will collaborate with Intel on creative and technology endeavours across the "compute continuum," according to a company spokesperson. This could include devices such as laptops, smart phones and tablets. He is also already working on music expressly for Intel.

"This partnership is beautiful because we can talk about making products from an artist's perspective," will.i.am said. "We can talk about what fans might want via this partnership. Having that, there is no middle person. It's three people dancing, the fan, the enabler and the creator, and that's amazing."

He's not the only celebrity to get a corporate gig recently. Polaroid made flamboyant pop star Lady Gaga a creative director last year. She appeared at the 2011 Consumer Electronics Show in Las Vegas earlier this month to help introduce the camera company's new Grey Label line.

Source: "Celebrity endorsements: Do they make products more appealing to you?" from POV, January 27, 2011. Used by permission of The Canadian Broadcasting Company (CBC).

Key Points in the Article

Celebrity endorsements aren't new. They go back more than 100 years, ranging from early print advertising through the dawn of both radio and television advertising, up to the current age of infomercials and post-game interviews of sports stars.

One of the recent evolutions of celebrity endorsement is for firms to involve stars directly in the design and distribution of their products.

Analyzing the News

a King Edward VII was featured in an early advertisement for piano-players. The author of *The Age of Persuasion* suspects that the king did not actually agree to the ad. At the time, the British monarchy was very popular and the producers of the piano-player would have believed the association with the king would boost sales.

b Many early radio and television shows were explicitly sponsored by the makers of consumer goods. Advertising on these shows consisted often of simple statements made by the stars or hosts endorsing the products. Even though the nature of many ads has changed, celebrity endorsement is still very common.

c Recently, firms have started to hire celebrities not just to use their products, but to be involved in the entire production process. While the celebrities may well contribute meaningfully to the design and development of products, this approach will also allow firms to tie products more closely to celebrities in the minds of consumers. For example, Intel will be able to say, "Not only is this the computer that will.i.am uses to edit and mix his music, but he helped design it."

Thinking Critically

1. Intel has presumably paid will.i.am a lot of money to become its director of creative innovation, and this has great potential to benefit the company. Hiring celebrities to endorse products can also be risky. Intel is tying people's image of its product to people's image of will.i.am. What do you think would happen to the demand curve for Intel products among aspiring music producers if will.i.am were involved in some embarrassing scandal that destroyed his creative credibility?

2. Firms pay celebrities large amounts of money to endorse their products. Should a firm whose celebrity endorser was just arrested take the money it has already paid the celebrity into account when deciding whether or not to cancel the ad campaign featuring the celebrity? Briefly explain.

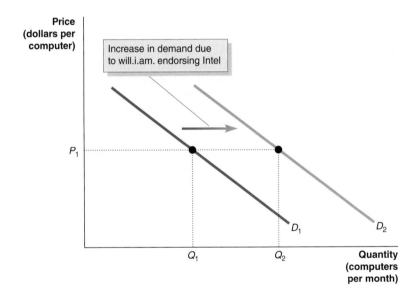

Chapter Summary and Problems

Key Terms

Behavioural economics, p. 236

Budget constraint, p. 221

Endowment effect, p. 237

Income effect, p. 226

Law of diminishing marginal utility, p. 221

Marginal utility (*MU*), p. 221

Network externality, p. 231

Opportunity cost, p. 236

Substitution effect, p. 226

Sunk cost, p. 237

Utility, p. 220

Summary

*LO **8.1 Utility** is the enjoyment or satisfaction that people receive from consuming goods and services. The goal of a consumer is to spend available income so as to maximize utility. **Marginal utility** is the change in total utility a person receives from consuming one additional unit of a good or service. The **law of diminishing marginal utility** states that consumers receive diminishing additional satisfaction as they consume more of a good or service during a given period of time. The **budget constraint** is the amount of income consumers have available to spend on goods and services. To maximize utility, consumers should make sure they spend their income so that the last dollar spent on each product gives them the same marginal utility. The **income effect** is the change in the quantity demanded of a good that results from the effect of a change in the price on consumer purchasing power. The **substitution effect** is the change in the quantity demanded of a good that results from a change in price making the good more or less expensive relative to other goods, holding constant the effect of the price change on consumer purchasing power.

LO **8.2** When the price of a good declines, the ratio of the marginal utility to price rises. This leads consumers to buy more of that good. As a result, whenever the price of a product falls, the quantity demanded increases; this is known as the law of demand. The market demand curve can be constructed from the individual demand curves for all the consumers in the market.

LO **8.3** Social factors can have an effect on consumption. For example, the amount of utility people receive from consuming a good often depends on how many other people they know who also consume the good. There is a **network externality** in the consumption of a product if the usefulness of the product increases with the number of consumers who use it. There is also evidence that people like to be treated fairly and that they usually attempt to treat others fairly, even if doing so makes them worse off financially. This result has been demonstrated in laboratory experiments, such as the ultimatum game. When firms set prices, they take into account consumers' preference for fairness. For example, hardware stores often do not increase the price of snow shovels to take advantage of a temporary increase in demand following a snowstorm.

LO **8.4 Behavioural economics** is the study of situations in which people act in ways that are not economically rational. **Opportunity cost** is the highest-valued alternative that must be given up to engage in an activity. People would improve their decision making if they took into account nonmonetary opportunity costs. People sometimes ignore nonmonetary opportunity costs because of the **endowment effect**—the tendency of people to be unwilling to sell something they already own even if they are offered a price that is greater than the price they would be willing to pay to buy the good if they didn't already own it. People would also improve their decision making if they ignored sunk costs. A **sunk cost** is a cost that has already been paid and cannot be recovered. Finally, people would improve their decision making if they were more realistic about their future behaviour.

MyEconLab   Log in to MyEconLab to complete these exercises and get instant feedback.

Review Questions

LO 8.1

1.1 What is the economic definition of utility? Is utility measurable?

1.2 What is the definition of marginal utility? What is the law of diminishing marginal utility? Why is marginal utility more useful than total utility in consumer decision making?

1.3 What is meant by a consumer's budget constraint? What is the rule of equal marginal utility per dollar spent?

LO 8.2

2.1 Explain how a downward-sloping demand curve results from consumers adjusting their consumption choices to changes in price.

2.2 How is the market demand curve derived from consumers' individual demand curves?

LO 8.3

3.1 Why do consumers pay attention to celebrity endorsements of products?

3.2 What are network externalities? For what types of products are network externalities likely to be important? What is path dependence?

3.3 How does the fact that consumers apparently value fairness affect the pricing decisions that businesses make?

LO 8.4

4.1 What does it mean to be economically rational?

4.2 Define behavioural economics. What are the three common mistakes that consumers often make? Give an example of each mistake.

*'Learning Objective' is abbreviated to 'LO' in the end of chapter material.

Problems and Applications

LO 8.1

1.1 Does the law of diminishing marginal utility hold true in every situation? Is it possible to think of goods for which consuming additional units, at least initially, will result in increasing marginal utility?

1.2 You have six hours to study for two exams tomorrow. The following table shows the relationship between hours of study and test scores:

Economics		Psychology	
Hours	Score	Hours	Score
0	54	0	54
1	62	1	60
2	69	2	65
3	75	3	69
4	80	4	72
5	84	5	74
6	87	6	75

a. Use the rule for determining optimal purchases to decide how many hours you should study each subject. Treat each point on an exam as 1 unit of utility and assume that you consider an extra point on an economics exam to have the same value as an extra point on a psychology exam.

b. Now suppose that you are a psychology major and that you value each point you earn on a psychology exam as being worth three times as much as each point you earn on an economics exam. Now how many hours will you study each subject?

1.3 [**Related to** Solved Problem 8.1 **on page 224**] Joe has $16 to spend on Smarties and chocolate chip cookies. Smarties have a price of $1 per box, and cookies have a price of $2 per pack. Use the information in the following graphs to determine the number of Smarties boxes and the number of cookie packs Joe should buy to maximize his utility. Briefly explain your reasoning.

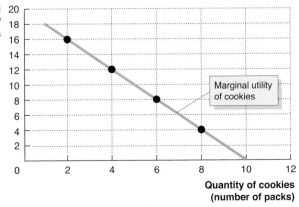

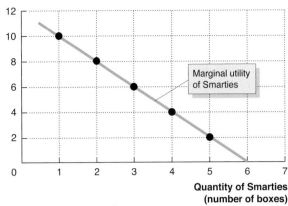

1.4 Suppose the price of a bag of Fritos corn chips declines from $0.69 to $0.59. Which is likely to be larger: the income effect or the substitution effect? Briefly explain.

1.5 When the price of pizza falls in the Grey Cup party example, both the income effect and the substitution effect cause you to want to consume more pizza. If pizza were an inferior good, how would the analysis be changed? In this case, is it possible that a lower price for pizza might lead you to buy less pizza? Briefly explain.

LO 8.2

2.1 The chapter states that "when the price of an inferior good falls, the income effect and substitution effect work in opposite directions." Explain what this statement means.

2.2 Suppose the market for ice cream cones is made up of three consumers: Josh, Jon, and Tim. Use the information in the following table to construct the market demand curve for ice cream cones. Show the information in a table and in a graph.

	Quantity Demanded (cones per week)			
Price	Josh	Jon	Tim	Market Demand
$1.75	2	1	0	
1.50	4	3	2	
1.25	6	4	3	
1.00	7	6	4	
0.75	9	7	5	

2.3 Suppose the wage you are being paid doubles. Is there an income and substitution effect involved in your decision about how many hours you choose to work? If so, what is being substituted for what?

2.4 [**Related to the** Making the Connection **on page 229**] In studying the consumption of very poor families in China, Robert Jensen and Nolan Miller found that in both Hunan and Gansu "Giffen behaviour is most likely to be found among a range of households that are poor (but not too poor or too rich)."

a. What do Jensen and Miller mean by "Giffen behaviour"?

b. Why would the poorest of the poor be less likely than people with slightly higher incomes to exhibit this behaviour?

c. Why must a good make up a very large portion of consumers' budgets in order to be a Giffen good?

Based on Robert T. Jensen and Nolan H. Miller, "Giffen Behavior and Subsistence Consumption," *American Economic Review*, Vol. 98, No. 4, September 2008, p. 1569.

LO 8.3

3.1 Which of the following products are most likely to have significant network externalities? Explain.

a. Tablet computers

b. Dog food

c. Board games

d. LCD televisions

e. 3D televisions

3.2 [**Related to the** Chapter Opener **on page 219**] When asked, most survey respondents claim that celebrity endorsements do not influence their buying decisions. Marketing strategist Marc Babej has argued that these survey responses are unreliable because advertisements appeal to the subconscious as well as the conscious mind. Explain what Babej means by this.

Based on Marc E. Babej, "Poll: Celebrity Endorsements Don't Work … Don't Tell Angelina," *Forbes*, June 14, 2011.

3.3 [**Related to the** Making the Connection **on page 229**] Sidney Crosby is a star NHL centre who knows more than most consumers about hockey and hockey-related products. However, he does not necessarily know more than consumers about cell phones or coffee. Consider the model of utility-maximizing behaviour described in this chapter. For Tim Hortons' use of Sidney Crosby as a celebrity endorser to make economic sense, how must Crosby's endorsement affect the marginal utility that at least some consumers receive from drinking Tim Hortons coffee? What will this do to the demand curve for that coffee?

3.4 Las Vegas is one of the most popular tourist destinations in the United States. In November 2008, the Rio Hotel and Casino in Las Vegas dropped the price of its breakfast buffet to $5.99 for local residents, while keeping the regular price of $14.99 for nonlocals. When setting the price for a meal, why would it matter to the restaurant if the customer is a local resident?

Based on *Las Vegas Advisor*, November 2008.

3.5 [**Related to the** Making the Connection **on page 235**] Suppose that *The Amazing Spider-Man* comes out, and hundreds of people arrive at a theatre only to discover that the movie is already sold out. Meanwhile, the theatre is also showing a boring movie in its third week of release in a mostly empty theatre. Why would this firm charge the same $7.50 for a ticket to either movie, when the quantity of tickets demanded is much greater than the quantity supplied for one movie, and the quantity of tickets demanded is much less than the quantity supplied for the other?

LO 8.4

4.1 Suppose your little brother tells you on Tuesday that one of his friends offered him $80 for his Albert Pujols rookie baseball card, but your brother decides not to sell the card. On Wednesday, your brother loses the card. Your parents feel sorry for him and give him $80 to make up the loss. Instead of buying another Albert Pujols card with the money (which we will assume he could have done), your brother uses the money to buy an iPod shuffle. Explain your brother's actions by using the concepts in this chapter.

4.2 Economist Richard Thaler first used the term *endowment effect* to describe placing a higher value on something already owned than would be placed on the object if not currently owned. According to an article in *The Economist*:

> Dr. Thaler, who recently had some expensive bottles of wine stolen, observes that he is "now confronted with precisely one of my own experiments: these are bottles I wasn't planning to sell and now I'm going to get a cheque from an insurance company and most of these bottles I will not buy. I'm a good enough economist to know there's a bit of an inconsistency there."

Based on Thaler's statement, how do his stolen bottles of wine illustrate the endowment effect, and why does he make the statement: "I'm a good enough economist to know there's a bit of an inconsistency there"?

From "It's Mine, I Tell You," *The Economist*, June 19, 2008.

4.3 Someone who owns a townhouse wrote to a real estate advice columnist to ask whether he should sell his townhouse or wait and sell it in the future when he hoped that prices would be higher. The columnist replied: "Ask yourself: would you buy this townhouse today as an investment? Because every day you don't sell it, you're buying it." Do you agree with the columnist? In what sense are you buying something if you don't sell it? Should the owner's decision about whether or not to sell depend on what price he originally paid for the townhouse?

Edith Lane, "Contract Exclusion OK?" (Allentown, PA) *Morning Call*, May 22, 2011.

4.4 [**Related to the** Making the Connection **on page 238**] After owning a used car for two years, you start having problems with it. You take it into the shop, and a mechanic tells you that repairs will cost $4,000. What factors will you take into account in deciding whether to have the repairs done or to junk the car and buy another one? Will the price you paid for the car be one of those factors? Briefly explain.

4.5 [**Related to the** Making the Connection **on page 239**] Briefly explain whether you agree with the following statement: "If people were more realistic about their future behaviour, the demand curve for potato chips would shift to the left."

4.6 [**Related to** Solved Problem 8.4 **on page 240**] In an article in the *Quarterly Journal of Economics*, Ted O'Donoghue and Matthew Rabin make the following observation: "People have self-control problems caused by a tendency to pursue immediate gratification in a way that their 'long-run selves' do not appreciate." What do they mean by a person's "long-run self"? Give two examples of people pursuing immediate gratification that their long-run selves would not appreciate.

Based on Ted O'Donoghue and Matthew Rabin, "Choice and Procrastination," *Quarterly Journal of Economics*, February 2001, pp. 125–126.

4.7 [**Related to** Solved Problem 8.4 **on page 240**] Data from health clubs show that members who choose a contract with a flat monthly fee over $70 attend, on average, 4.8 times per month. They pay a price per expected visit of more than $14, even though a $10-per-visit fee is also available. Why would these consumers choose a monthly contract when they lose money on it?

MyEconLab   MyEconLab is an online tool designed to help you master the concepts covered in your course. It will create an adaptive, highly personalized study plan to stimulate and measure your learning. Log in to take advantage of this powerful study aid, and to access quizzes and other valuable course-related material.

Technology, Production, and Costs

© Bayne Stanley/Alamy

Chapter Outline and Learning Objectives

Production Costs Determine Oil Sands Investment

As a firm's costs change, how does the firm adjust? This is an important question that companies such as Suncor Energy Inc., Teck Resources Ltd., France's Total SA, and the Canadian arm of Royal Dutch Shell Plc are dealing with when it comes to evaluating investment in Canada's oil sands.

As the cost of wringing oil from Alberta's bitumen deposits continues to edge up, companies are assessing whether to spend billions on new mining projects or pour money into steam-driven extraction.

Competition for materials and labour has significantly increased supply costs for a new oil sands mine (even without an upgrader facility to convert the bitumen to synthetic crude oil). These costs climbed 13.2 percent from 2012 to 2013, according to a study published in July 2013 by the government- and industry-funded Canadian Energy Research Institute (CERI).

"West Texas Intermediate" (WTI) is a grade of crude oil that is used as a benchmark in oil pricing. The break-even WTI price for steam-driven oil sands projects, which use large volumes of steam to melt seams of bitumen buried too deep to mine, falls between $65 and $75 a barrel, according to consultancy IHS-Cera. Mining projects, by comparison, need a WTI price "in the $100 or more range" to make money, said Jackie Forrest, the consultancy's senior director in Calgary. The cost of mining is higher than the cost of steam extraction.

The production cost of a new in-situ oil sands plant rose 6.3 percent to $47.57 a barrel, or $77.85 WTI with transportation and blending costs. The projection includes capital expenditures, operating costs, royalties, and taxes, and assumes a 10 percent return on investment. WTI futures for July delivery (an estimate of the oil company's selling price) were hovering at about $95, according to the CME Group. These numbers are another indication of the high cost of doing business in Alberta's oil sands, the world's No. 3 crude deposit.

"In today's market, I wouldn't say the new projects wouldn't go ahead, but they're at risk," said Dinara Millington, a senior research director with CERI and the report's lead author. She added: "I would be looking into putting my money into in-situ-type projects, which are able to realize higher netbacks for producers."

The tableau presented by CERI is familiar: Competition for scarce resources has long vexed oil sands operators. Moreover, the escalating costs come as the environmental toll of extracting tar-like bitumen from strip mines faces heightened scrutiny from policymakers and the public at large, raising the prospect of delays and increased costs.

The two different technologies have different costs and generate different revenues. Because the firm's objective is to maximize profits, the firm's decision makers must choose the technology that generates the most profits, considering that changing material and labour costs can shift the firms' cost curves and affect their profits. Estimating costs and making investment decisions requires an understanding of what factors determine a firm's cost. This is the subject of this chapter.

Oil production is only one industry that is affected by changing costs. **AN INSIDE LOOK** on **page 270** discusses the potential entry of Verizon to the Canadian wireless market and the effect that that would have on the costs of the three dominant firms in Canada.

From Jeff Lewis, "Oil Sands Mines Face Growing Challenges as Supply Costs Rise," *The Financial Post*, May 29, 2013, accessed at http://www.canada.com/business /sands+mines+face+growing+challenges+supply+costs +rise/8446400/story.html

Economics in Your Life

Using Cost Concepts in Your Own Business

Suppose that you have the opportunity to open a store that sells recliners. You learn that you can purchase the recliners from the manufacturer for $300 each. Bob's Big Chairs is an existing store that is the same size your new store will be. Bob's sells the same recliners you plan to sell and also buys them from the manufacturer for $300 each. Your plan is to sell the recliners for a price of $500. After studying how Bob's is operated, you find that Bob's is selling more recliners per month than you expect to be able to sell and that it is selling them for $450. You wonder how Bob's makes a profit at the lower price. Are there any reasons to expect that because Bob's sells more recliners per month, its costs will be lower than your store's costs? You can check your answer against the one we provide on page 268 at the end of this chapter.

I n Chapter 8, we looked behind the demand curve to better understand consumer decision making. In this chapter, we look behind the supply curve to better understand firm decision making. Supply curves are upward sloping because marginal cost increases as firms increase the quantity of a good that they supply. In this chapter, we look more closely at why this is true. In Appendix C, we extend the analysis by using isoquants and isocost lines to understand the relationship between production and costs. Once we have a good understanding of production and cost, we can proceed to understand how firms decide what level of output to produce and what price to charge.

9.1 LEARNING OBJECTIVE

Define technology and give examples of technological change.

Technology: An Economic Definition

Technology The processes a firm uses to turn inputs into outputs of goods and services.

Technological change A change in the ability of a firm to produce a given level of output with a given quantity of inputs.

The basic activity of a firm is to use *inputs*, such as workers, machines, and natural resources, to produce *outputs* of goods and services. A pizza parlour, for example, uses inputs such as pizza dough, pizza sauce, cooks, and ovens to produce pizza. A firm's **technology** is the processes it uses to turn inputs into outputs of goods and services. Notice that this economic definition of technology is broader than the everyday definition. When we use the word *technology* in everyday language, we usually refer only to the development of new products. In the economic sense, a firm's technology depends on many factors, such as the skills of its managers, the training of its workers, and the speed and efficiency of its machinery and equipment. The technology of pizza production, for example, includes not only the capacity of the pizza ovens and how quickly they bake the pizza but also how quickly the cooks can prepare the pizza for baking, how well the manager motivates the workers, and how well the manager has arranged the facilities to allow the cooks to quickly prepare the pizzas and get them in the ovens.

Whenever a firm experiences positive **technological change,** it is able to produce more output using the same inputs or the same output using fewer inputs. Positive technological change can come from many sources. A firm's managers may rearrange the factory floor or the layout of a retail store in order to increase production and sales. The firm's workers may go through a training program. The firm may install faster or more reliable machinery or equipment. It is also possible for a firm to experience negative technological change. If a firm hires less-skilled workers or if a hurricane damages its facilities, the quantity of output it can produce from a given quantity of inputs may decline.

Making
the
Connection

Just-in-Time Inventory Control at Magna International

Inventories are goods that have been produced but not yet sold. For an automobile parts manufacturer such as Magna International (one of Canada's largest companies and a global automotive supplier), inventories at any point in time include the auto parts in warehouses and distribution centres. Inventories are an input into Magna's output of auto parts sold to its customers. Having money tied up in holding inventories is costly, so firms have an incentive to hold as few inventories as possible and to turn over their inventories as rapidly as possible. Holding too few inventories, however, results in stockouts—that is, sales being lost because the products customers want to buy are not available.

Better inventory controls have helped Magna International and other firms to reduce their costs.

J.P. MOCZULSKI/Corbis

Improvements in inventory control meet the economic definition of positive technological change because they allow firms to produce the same output with fewer inputs. In recent years, many firms have adopted just-in-time inventory systems in which firms accept shipments from suppliers as close as possible to the time they will be needed. The just-in-time system was pioneered by Toyota, which used it to reduce the inventories of parts in its automobile assembly plants. Magna International uses similar inventory control systems.

Magna International actively manages its *supply chain*, which stretches from the manufacturers of the products it sells to its distribution centres. The company has a number of distribution centres spread around the world to supply auto parts to the Big 3 U.S. automakers (General Motors, Ford, and Chrysler) as well as to a large number of other companies, including Volkswagen, BMW, and Toyota. As parts are sold, the *point-of-sale* information is sent electronically to the firm's distribution centres to help managers determine what parts will be shipped. This system allows Magna to minimize its inventory holdings without running the risk of many stockouts occurring.

Technological change has enabled companies like Magna International to boost profits by keeping inventory lean. However, in the aftermath of Iceland's volcanic ash disruption of air transport across Europe in 2010 and Japan's disasters in 2011, the global supply chain has been under great stress. Companies are now also considering "just-in-case" systems to limit the negative effects of supply disruptions of crucial parts and materials.

Your Turn: Test your understanding by doing related problem 1.3 on page 273 at the end of this chapter.

MyEconLab

The Short Run and the Long Run in Economics

When firms analyze the relationship between their level of production and their costs, they separate the time period involved into the short run and the long run. In the **short run**, at least one of the firm's inputs is fixed. In particular, in the short run, the firm's technology and the size of its physical plant—its factory, store, or office—are both fixed, while the number of workers the firm hires is variable. In the **long run**, the firm is able to vary all its inputs and can adopt new technology and increase or decrease the size of its physical plant. Of course, the actual length of calendar time in the short run will be different from firm to firm. A pizza parlour may be able to increase its physical plant by adding another pizza oven and some tables and chairs in just a few weeks. BMW, in contrast, may take more than a year to increase the capacity of one of its automobile assembly plants by installing new equipment.

The Difference Between Fixed Costs and Variable Costs

Total cost is the cost of all the inputs a firm uses in production. We have just seen that in the short run, some inputs are fixed and others are variable. The costs of the fixed inputs are *fixed costs*, and the costs of the variable inputs are *variable costs*. We can also think of

9.2 LEARNING OBJECTIVE

Distinguish between the economic short run and the economic long run.

Short run The period of time during which at least one of a firm's inputs is fixed.

Long run The period of time in which a firm can vary all its inputs, adopt new technology, and increase or decrease the size of its physical plant.

Total cost The cost of all the inputs a firm uses in production.

Variable costs Costs that change as output changes.

Fixed costs Costs that remain constant as output changes.

variable costs as the costs that change as output changes. Similarly, **fixed costs** are costs that remain constant as output changes. A typical firm's variable costs include its labour costs, raw material costs, and costs of electricity and other utilities. Typical fixed costs include lease payments for factory or retail space, payments for fire insurance, and payments for newspaper and television advertising. All of a firm's costs are either fixed or variable, so we can state the following:

Total cost = Fixed cost + Variable cost

or, using symbols:

$$TC = FC + VC$$

The wages of these workers are a variable cost to the publishers who employ them.

Making the Connection | **Fixed Costs in the Publishing Industry**

An editor at Cambridge University Press (the world's oldest publishing house) gives the following estimates of the annual fixed cost for a medium-size academic book publisher:

Cost	Percentage of Total Cost
Salaries and benefits	83.3
Rent	10.0
Utilities	2.7
Supplies	0.8
Postage	0.7
Travel	1.2
Subscriptions, etc.	0.7
Miscellaneous	0.7
Total	100.0

Academic book publishers hire editors, designers, and production and marketing managers who help prepare books for publication. Because these employees work on several books simultaneously, the number of people the company hires does not go up and down with the quantity of books the company publishes during any particular year. Publishing companies therefore consider the salaries and benefits of people in these job categories to be fixed costs.

In contrast, for a company that *prints* books, the quantity of workers varies with the quantity of books printed. The wages and benefits of the workers operating the printing presses, for example, would be a variable cost.

The other costs listed in the table above are typical of fixed costs at many firms.

Handbook for Academic Authors, 5th edition by Beth Lucy. Copyright © 2010 by Cambridge University Press. Reprinted by permission.

MyEconLab

Your Turn: Test your understanding by doing related problems 2.2 and 2.3 on page 273 at the end of this chapter.

Implicit Costs versus Explicit Costs

It is important to remember that economists always measure costs as *opportunity costs*. The **opportunity cost** of any activity is the highest-valued alternative that must be given up to engage in that activity. Costs are either *explicit* or *implicit*. When a firm spends money, it incurs an **explicit cost**. When a firm experiences a nonmonetary opportunity cost, it incurs an **implicit cost**.

For example, suppose that Jill Johnson owns a pizza restaurant. In operating her store, Jill has explicit costs, such as the wages she pays her workers and the payments she makes for rent and electricity. But some of Jill's most important costs are implicit. Before opening her own restaurant, Jill earned a salary of $30,000 per year managing a restaurant for someone else. To start her restaurant, Jill quit her job, withdrew $50,000 from her bank

Opportunity cost The highest-valued alternative that must be given up to engage in an activity.

Explicit cost A cost that involves spending money.

Implicit cost A nonmonetary opportunity cost.

Pizza dough, tomato sauce, and other ingredients	$ 20,000
Wages	48,000
Interest payments on loan to buy pizza ovens	10,000
Electricity	6,000
Lease payment for store	24,000
Forgone salary	30,000
Forgone interest	3,000
Economic depreciation	10,000
Total	$151,000

Table 9.1

Jill Johnson's Costs per Year

account—where it earned her interest of $3,000 per year—and used the funds to equip her restaurant with tables, chairs, a cash register, and other equipment. To open her own business, Jill had to give up the $30,000 salary and the $3,000 in interest. This $33,000 is an implicit cost because it does not represent payments that Jill has to make. Nevertheless, giving up this $33,000 per year is a real cost to Jill. In addition, during the course of the year, the $50,000 worth of tables, chairs, and other physical capital in Jill's store will lose some of its value due partly to wear and tear and partly to better furniture, cash registers, and so forth becoming available. *Economic depreciation* is the difference between what Jill paid for her capital at the beginning of the year and what she could sell the capital for at the end of the year. If Jill could sell the capital for $40,000 at the end of the year, then the $10,000 in economic depreciation represents another implicit cost. (Note that the whole $50,000 she spent on the capital is not a cost because she still has the equipment at the end of the year, although it is now worth only $40,000.)

Table 9.1 lists Jill's costs. The entries in red are explicit costs, and the entries in blue are implicit costs. The rules of accounting generally require that only explicit costs be used for purposes of keeping the company's financial records and for paying taxes. Therefore, explicit costs are sometimes called *accounting costs*. *Economic costs* include both accounting costs and implicit costs.

The Production Function

Let's look at the relationship between the level of production and costs in the short run for Jill Johnson's restaurant. To keep things simpler than in the more realistic situation in Table 9.1, let's assume that Jill uses only labour—workers—and one type of capital— pizza ovens—to produce a single good: pizzas. Many firms use more than two inputs and produce more than one good, but it is easier to understand the relationship between output and cost by focusing on the case of a firm using only two inputs and producing only one good. In the short run, Jill doesn't have time to build a larger restaurant, install additional pizza ovens, or redesign the layout of her restaurant. So, in the short run, she can increase or decrease the quantity of pizzas she produces only by increasing or decreasing the quantity of workers she employs.

The first three columns of Table 9.2 show the relationship between the quantity of workers and ovens Jill uses per week and the quantity of pizzas she can produce.

Quantity of Workers	Quantity of Pizza Ovens	Quantity of Pizzas per Week	Cost of Pizza Ovens (Fixed Cost)	Cost of Workers (Variable Cost)	Total Cost of Pizzas per Week	Cost per Pizza (Average Total Cost)
0	2	0	$800	$0	$800	—
1	2	200	800	650	1,450	$7.25
2	2	450	800	1,300	2,100	4.67
3	2	550	800	1,950	2,750	5.00
4	2	600	800	2,600	3,400	5.67
5	2	625	800	3,250	4,050	6.48
6	2	640	800	3,900	4,700	7.34

Table 9.2

Short-Run Production and Cost at Jill Johnson's Restaurant

Production function The relationship between the inputs employed by a firm and the maximum output it can produce with those inputs.

The relationship between the inputs employed by a firm and the maximum output it can produce with those inputs is called the firm's **production function**. Because a firm's technology is the processes it uses to turn inputs into output, the production function represents the firm's technology. In this case, the first 3 columns of Table 9.2 show Jill's *short-run* production function because we are assuming that the time period is too short for Jill to increase or decrease the quantity of ovens she is using.

A First Look at the Relationship Between Production and Cost

Table 9.2 shows Jill Johnson's costs. We can determine the total cost of producing a given quantity of pizzas if we know how many workers and ovens are required to produce that quantity of pizzas and what Jill has to pay for those workers and pizzas. Suppose Jill has taken out a bank loan to buy two pizza ovens. The cost of the loan is $800 per week. Therefore, her fixed costs are $800 per week. If Jill pays $650 per week to each worker, her variable costs depend on how many workers she hires. In the short run, Jill can increase the quantity of pizzas she produces only by hiring more workers. Table 9.2 shows that if she hires 1 worker, she produces 200 pizzas during the week; if she hires 2 workers, she produces 450 pizzas; and so on. For a particular week, Jill's total cost of producing pizzas is equal to the $800 she pays on the loan for the ovens plus the amount she pays to hire workers. If Jill decides to hire 4 workers and produce 600 pizzas, her total cost is $3,400: $800 to lease the ovens and $2,600 to hire the workers. Her cost per pizza is equal to her total cost of producing pizzas divided by the quantity of pizzas produced. If she produces 600 pizzas at a total cost of $3,400, her cost per pizza, or *average total cost*, is $3,400/600 = $5.67. A firm's **average total cost** is always equal to its total cost divided by the quantity of output produced.

Average total cost Total cost divided by the quantity of output produced.

Panel (a) of Figure 9.1 uses the numbers in the next-to-last column of Table 9.2 to graph Jill's total cost. Panel (b) uses the numbers in the last column to graph her average

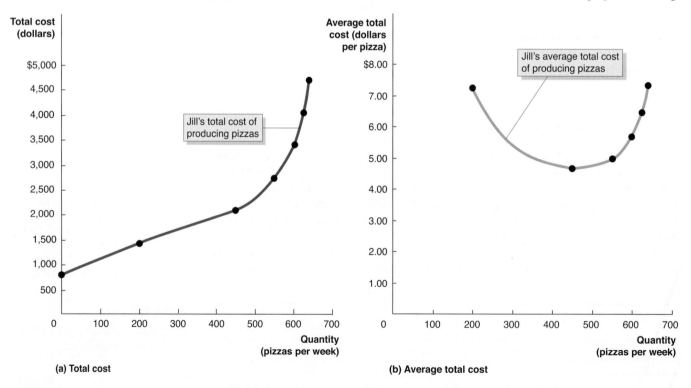

Figure 9.1 Graphing Total Cost and Average Total Cost at Jill Johnson's Restaurant

We can use the information from Table 9.2 to graph the relationship between the quantity of pizzas Jill produces and her total cost and average total cost. Panel (a) shows that total cost increases as the level of production increases. In panel (b), we see that the average total cost is roughly U shaped: As production increases from low levels, average total cost falls before rising at higher levels of production. To understand why average total cost has this shape, we must look more closely at the technology of producing pizzas, as shown by the production function.

total cost. Notice in panel (b) that Jill's average cost has roughly the same U shape as the average cost curve implied by Dinara Millington in the Chapter Opener. As production increases from low levels, average total cost initially falls, and eventually rises. Average total cost then becomes fairly flat, before rising at higher levels of production. To understand why average total cost has this U shape, we first need to look more closely at the technology of producing pizzas, as shown by the production function for Jill's restaurant. Then we need to look at how this technology determines the relationship between production and cost.

The Marginal Product of Labour and the Average Product of Labour

9.3 LEARNING OBJECTIVE
Understand the relationship between the marginal product of labour and the average product of labour.

To better understand the choices Jill faces, given the technology available to her, think first about what happens if she hires only one worker. That one worker will have to perform several different activities, including taking orders from customers, baking the pizzas, bringing the pizzas to the customers' tables, and ringing up sales on the cash register. If Jill hires two workers, some of these activities can be divided up: One worker could take the orders and ring up the sales, and one worker could bake the pizzas. With such a division of tasks, Jill will find that hiring two workers actually allows her to produce more than twice as many pizzas as she could produce with just one worker.

The additional output a firm produces as a result of hiring one more worker is called the **marginal product of labour**. We can calculate the marginal product of labour by determining how much total output increases as each additional worker is hired. We do this for Jill's restaurant in Table 9.3.

Marginal product of labour The additional output a firm produces as a result of hiring one more worker.

When Jill hires only 1 worker, she produces 200 pizzas per week. When she hires 2 workers, she produces 450 pizzas per week. Hiring the second worker increases her production by 250 pizzas per week. So, the marginal product of labour for the first worker is 200 pizzas. For the second worker, the marginal product of labour rises to 250 pizzas. This increase in marginal product results from the *division of labour* and from *specialization*. By dividing the tasks to be performed—the division of labour—Jill reduces the time workers lose moving from one activity to the next. She also allows them to become more specialized at their tasks. For example, a worker who concentrates on baking pizzas will become skilled at doing so quickly and efficiently.

The Law of Diminishing Returns

In the short run, the quantity of pizza ovens Jill leases is fixed, so as she hires more workers, the marginal product of labour eventually begins to decline. This happens because at some point, Jill uses up all the gains from the division of labour and from specialization and starts to experience the effects of the **law of diminishing returns**. This law states that adding more of a variable input, such as labour, to the same amount of a fixed input, such as capital, will eventually cause the marginal product of the variable input to decline. For Jill, the marginal product of labour begins to decline when she hires the third worker. Hiring 3 workers raises the quantity of pizzas she produces from 450 per week

Law of diminishing returns The principle that, at some point, adding more of a variable input, such as labour, to the same amount of a fixed input, such as capital, will cause the marginal product of the variable input to decline.

Quantity of Workers	Quantity of Pizza Ovens	Quantity of Pizzas	Marginal Product of Labour
0	2	0	—
1	2	200	200
2	2	450	250
3	2	550	100
4	2	600	50
5	2	625	25
6	2	640	15

Table 9.3

The Marginal Product of Labour at Jill Johnson's Restaurant

to 550. But the increase in the quantity of pizzas—100—is less than the increase when she hired the second worker—250.

If Jill kept adding more and more workers to the same quantity of pizza ovens, eventually workers would begin to get in each other's way, and the marginal product of labour would actually become negative. When the marginal product is negative, the level of total output declines. No firm would actually hire so many workers as to experience a negative marginal product of labour and falling total output.

Graphing Production

Panel (a) in Figure 9.2 shows the relationship between the quantity of workers Jill hires and her total output of pizzas, using the numbers from Table 9.3. Panel (b) shows the marginal product of labour. In panel (a), output increases as more workers are hired, but the increase in output does not occur at a constant rate. Because of specialization and

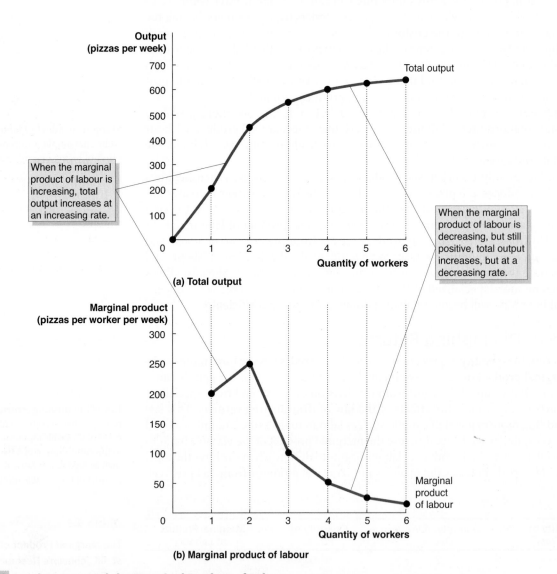

Figure 9.2 Total Output and the Marginal Product of Labour

In panel (a), output increases as more workers are hired, but the increase in output does not occur at a constant rate. Because of specialization and the division of labour, output at first increases at an increasing rate, with each additional worker hired causing production to increase by a *greater* amount than did the hiring of the previous worker. After the third worker has been hired, hiring more workers while keeping the number of pizza ovens constant results in diminishing returns. When the point of diminishing returns is reached, production increases at a decreasing rate. Each additional worker hired after the third worker causes production to increase by a *smaller* amount than did the hiring of the previous worker. In panel (b), the *marginal product of labour* is the additional output produced as a result of hiring one more worker. The marginal product of labour rises initially because of the effects of specialization and division of labour, and then it falls due to the effects of diminishing returns.

the division of labour, output at first increases at an increasing rate, with each additional worker hired causing production to increase by a *greater* amount than did the hiring of the previous worker. But after the second worker has been hired, hiring more workers while keeping the quantity of ovens constant results in diminishing returns. When the point of diminishing returns is reached, production increases at a decreasing rate. Each additional worker hired after the second worker causes production to increase by a *smaller* amount than did the hiring of the previous worker. In panel (b), the marginal product of labour curve rises initially because of the effects of specialization and division of labour, and then it falls due to the effects of diminishing returns.

<table>
<tr><td>Making
the
Connection</td><td>

Adam Smith's Famous Account of the Division of Labour in a Pin Factory

In *The Wealth of Nations*, Adam Smith uses production in a pin factory as an example of the gains in output resulting from the division of labour. The following is an excerpt from his account of
</td></tr>
</table>

how pin making was divided into a series of tasks:

> One man draws out the wire, another straightens it, a third cuts it, a fourth points it, a fifth grinds it at the top for receiving the head; to make the head requires two or three distinct operations; to put it on is a [distinct operation], to whiten the pins is another; it is even a trade by itself to put them into the paper; and the important business of making a pin is, in this manner, divided into eighteen distinct operations.

Because the labour of pin making was divided up in this way, the average worker was able to produce about 4,800 pins per day. Smith speculated that a single worker using the pin-making machinery alone would make only about 20 pins per day. This lesson from the eighteenth century, showing the tremendous gains from division of labour and specialization, remains relevant to most business situations today.

From Adam Smith, *An Inquiry into the Nature and Causes of the Wealth of Nations*, Vol. I (Oxford, UK: Oxford University Press, 1976; original edition, 1776), pp. 14–15.

Your Turn: Test your understanding by doing related problem 3.4 on page 274 at the end of this chapter.

The gains from division of labour and specialization are as important to firms today as they were in the eighteenth century, when Adam Smith first discussed them.

MyEconLab

The Relationship Between Marginal Product and Average Product

The marginal product of labour tells us how much total output changes as the quantity of workers hired changes. We can also calculate how many pizzas workers produce on average. The **average product of labour** is the total output produced by a firm divided by the quantity of workers. For example, using the numbers in Table 9.3 on page 255, if Jill hires 4 workers to produce 600 pizzas, the average product of labour is $600/4 = 150$.

Average product of labour The total output produced by a firm divided by the quantity of workers.

We can state the relationship between the marginal and average products of labour this way: *The average product of labour is the average of the marginal products of labour.* For example, the numbers from Table 9.3 show that the marginal product of the first worker Jill hires is 200, the marginal product of the second worker is 250, and the marginal product of the third worker is 100. Therefore, the average product of labour for three workers is 183.3:

$$183.3 = (200 + 250 + 100)/3$$

| Average product of labour for three workers | Marginal product of labour of first worker | Marginal product of labour of second worker | Marginal product of labour of third worker |

By taking the average of the marginal products of the first three workers, we have the average product of the three workers.

Whenever the marginal product of labour is greater than the average product of labour, the average product of labour must be increasing. This statement is true for the same reason that a person 195 centimetres entering a room where the average height is 160 centimetres raises the average height of people in the room. Whenever the marginal product of labour is less than the average product of labour, the average product of labour must be decreasing. The marginal product of labour equals the average product of labour for the quantity of workers where the average product of labour is at its maximum.

An Example of Marginal and Average Values: University Grades

The relationship between the marginal product of labour and the average product of labour is the same as the relationship between the marginal and average values of any variable. To see this more clearly, think about the familiar relationship between a student's grade point average (GPA) in one semester and his overall, or cumulative, GPA. The table in Figure 9.3 shows Paul's university grades for each semester, beginning with fall 2014. The graph in

Figure 9.3

Marginal and Average GPAs

The relationship between marginal and average values for a variable can be illustrated using GPAs. We can calculate the GPA Paul earns in a particular semester (his "marginal GPA"), and we can calculate his cumulative GPA for all the semesters he has completed so far (his "average GPA"). Paul's GPA is only 1.50 in the fall semester of his first year. In each following semester through the fall of his third year, his GPA for the semester increases—raising his cumulative GPA. In Paul's third year, even though his semester GPA declines from fall to spring, his cumulative GPA rises. Only in the fall of his fourth year, when his semester GPA drops below his cumulative GPA, does his cumulative GPA decline.

	Semester GPA (marginal GPA)	Cumulative GPA (average GPA)
First year		
Fall	1.50	1.50
Spring	2.00	1.75
Second year		
Fall	2.20	1.90
Spring	3.00	2.18
Third year		
Fall	3.20	2.38
Spring	3.00	2.48
Fourth year		
Fall	2.40	2.47
Spring	2.00	2.41

Average GPA continues to rise, although marginal GPA falls.

With the marginal GPA below the average, the average GPA falls.

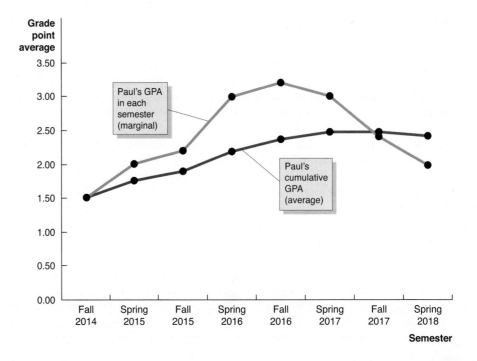

Paul's GPA in each semester (marginal)

Paul's cumulative GPA (average)

Figure 9.3 plots the grades from the table. Just as each additional worker hired adds to a firm's total production, each additional semester adds to Paul's grade point average. We can calculate what each individual worker hired adds to production (marginal product), and we can calculate the average production of the workers hired so far (average product).

Similarly, we can calculate the GPA Paul earns in a particular semester (his "marginal GPA"), and we can calculate his cumulative GPA for all the semesters he has completed so far (his "average GPA"). As the table shows, Paul gets off to a weak start in the fall semester of his first year, earning only a 1.50 GPA. In each subsequent semester through the fall of his third year, his GPA for the semester increases from the previous semester—raising his cumulative GPA. As the graph shows, however, his cumulative GPA does not increase as rapidly as his semester-by-semester GPA because his cumulative GPA is held back by the low GPAs of his first few semesters. Notice that in Paul's third year, even though his semester GPA declines from fall to spring, his cumulative GPA rises. Only in the fall of his fourth year, when his semester GPA drops below his cumulative GPA, does his cumulative GPA decline.

The Relationship Between Short-Run Production and Short-Run Cost

Explain and illustrate the relationship between marginal cost and average total cost.

We have seen that technology determines the values of the marginal product of labour and the average product of labour. In turn, the marginal and average products of labour affect the firm's costs. Keep in mind that the relationships we are discussing are *short-run* relationships: We are assuming that the time period is too short for the firm to change its technology or the size of its physical plant.

At the beginning of this chapter, we saw how Dinara Millington used cost projections to determine optimal investment in oil sands. The average total cost curve Millington implicitly used and the average total cost curve in panel (b) of Figure 9.1 for Jill Johnson's restaurant both have a U shape. As we will soon see, the U shape of the average total cost curve is determined by the shape of the curve that shows the relationship between *marginal cost* and the level of production.

Marginal Cost

One of the key ideas in economics is that optimal decisions are made at the margin. Consumers, firms, and government officials usually make decisions about doing a little more or a little less. As Jill Johnson considers whether to hire additional workers to produce additional pizzas, she needs to consider how much she will add to her total cost by producing the additional pizzas. **Marginal cost** is the change in a firm's total cost from producing one more unit of a good or service. We can calculate marginal cost for a particular increase in output by dividing the change in total cost by the change in output. We can express this idea mathematically (remembering that the Greek letter delta, Δ, means "change in"):

$$MC = \frac{\Delta TC}{\Delta Q}.$$

In the table in Figure 9.4, we use this equation to calculate Jill's marginal cost of producing pizzas. The other values in the table are from Table 9.2 on page 253 and Table 9.3 on page 255.

Marginal cost The change in a firm's total cost from producing one more unit of a good or service.

Why Are the Marginal and Average Cost Curves U Shaped?

Notice in the graph in Figure 9.4 that Jill's marginal cost of producing pizzas declines at first and then increases, giving the marginal cost curve a U shape. The table in Figure 9.4 also shows the marginal product of labour. This table helps us understand the important relationship between the marginal product of labour and the marginal cost of production: The marginal product of labour is *rising* for the first two workers, but the

Figure 9.4

Jill Johnson's Marginal Cost and Average Total Cost of Producing Pizzas

We can use the information in the table to calculate Jill's marginal cost and average total cost of producing pizzas. For the first two workers hired, the marginal product of labour is increasing. This increase causes the marginal cost of production to fall. For the last four workers hired, the marginal product of labour is falling. This causes the marginal cost of production to increase. Therefore, the marginal cost curve falls and then rises—that is, has a U shape—because the marginal product of labour rises and then falls. As long as marginal cost is below average total cost, average total cost will be falling. When marginal cost is above average total cost, average total cost will be rising. The relationship between marginal cost and average total cost explains why the average total cost curve also has a U shape.

Quantity of Workers	Quantity of Pizzas	Marginal Product of Labour	Total Cost of Pizzas	Marginal Cost of Pizzas	Average Total Cost of Pizzas
0	0	—	$ 800	—	—
1	200	200	1,450	$ 3.25	$7.25
2	450	250	2,100	2.60	4.67
3	550	100	2,750	6.50	5.00
4	600	50	3,400	13.00	5.67
5	625	25	4,050	26.00	6.48
6	640	15	4,700	43.33	7.34

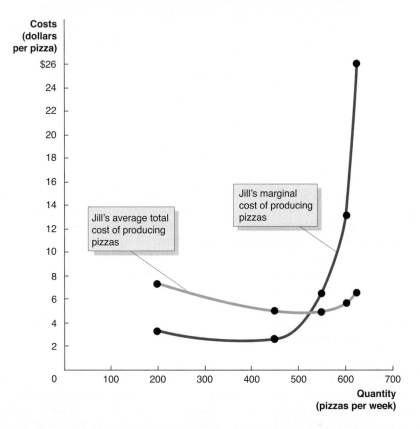

marginal cost of the pizzas produced by these workers is *falling*. The marginal product of labour is *falling* for the last four workers, but the marginal cost of pizzas produced by these workers is *rising*. To summarize this point: *When the marginal product of labour is rising, the marginal cost of output is falling. When the marginal product of labour is falling, the marginal cost of production is rising.*

One way to understand why this point is true is first to notice that the only additional cost to Jill from producing more pizzas is the additional wages she pays to hire more workers. She pays each new worker the same $650 per week. So the marginal cost of the additional pizzas each worker makes depends on that worker's additional output, or marginal product. As long as the additional output from each new worker is rising, the marginal cost of that output is falling. When the additional output from each new worker is falling, the marginal cost of that output is rising. *We can conclude that the marginal cost of production falls and then rises—forming a U shape—because the marginal product of labour rises and then falls.*

The relationship between marginal cost and average total cost follows the usual relationship between marginal and average values. As long as marginal cost is below average total cost, average total cost falls. When marginal cost is above average total cost, average total cost rises. Marginal cost equals average total cost when average total cost is at its lowest point. Therefore, the average total cost curve has a U shape because the marginal cost curve has a U shape.

Solved Problem **9.4**

Calculating Marginal Cost and Average Cost

Santiago Delgado owns a copier store. He leases two copy machines for which he pays $12.50 each per day. He cannot increase the number of machines he leases without giving the office machine company six weeks' notice. He can hire as many workers as he wants, at a cost of $50 per day per worker. These are the only two inputs he uses to produce copies.

1. Fill in the remaining columns in the table below by using the definitions of costs.

2. Draw the average cost curve and marginal cost curve for Santiago's store. Do these curves have the expected shape? Briefly explain.

Quantity of Workers	Quantity of Copies per Day	Fixed Cost	Variable Cost	Total Cost	Average Total Cost	Marginal Cost
0	0					
1	625					
2	1,325					
3	2,200					
4	2,600					
5	2,900					
6	3,100					

Solving the Problem

Step 1: **Review the chapter material.** This problem requires you to understand definitions of costs, so you may want to review the section "The Difference Between Fixed Costs and Variable Costs" and the section "Why Are the Marginal and Average Cost Curves U Shaped?"

Step 2: **Answer part (a) by using the definitions of costs.** Santiago's fixed costs are the costs he pays to lease the copy machines. He uses two copy machines and pays $12.50 each to lease them, so his fixed cost is $25. Santiago's variable costs are the costs he pays to hire workers. He pays $50 per worker per day. His total cost is the sum of his fixed cost and his variable cost. His average total cost is his total cost divided by the quantity of copies he produces that day. His marginal cost is the change in total cost divided by the change in output. So, for example, his marginal cost of producing 1,325 copies per day, rather than 625 copies, is:

$$MC = (\$125 - \$75)/(1,325 - 625) = \$0.07.$$

Quantity of Workers	Quantity of Copies per Day	Fixed Cost	Variable Cost	Total Cost	Average Total Cost	Marginal Cost
0	0	$25	$ 0	$ 25	—	—
1	625	25	50	75	$0.12	$0.08
2	1,325	25	100	125	0.09	0.07
3	2,200	25	150	175	0.08	0.06
4	2,600	25	200	225	0.09	0.13
5	2,900	25	250	275	0.09	0.17
6	3,100	25	300	325	0.10	0.25

Step 3: Answer part (b) by drawing the average total cost and marginal cost curves for Santiago's store and by explaining whether they have the usual shape. You can use the numbers from the table to draw your graph:

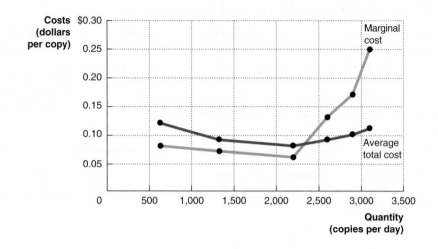

We expect average total cost and marginal cost curves to have a U shape, which Santiago's cost curves do. Both cost curves fall and then rise in the same way as the cost curves in Figure 9.4 on page 260.

MyEconLab **Your Turn:** For more practice, do related problem 4.3 on page 274 at the end of this chapter.

9.5 LEARNING OBJECTIVE

Graph average total cost, average variable cost, average fixed cost, and marginal cost.

Average fixed cost Fixed cost divided by the quantity of output produced.

Average variable cost Variable cost divided by the quantity of output produced.

Graphing Cost Curves

We have seen that we calculate average total cost by dividing total cost by the quantity of output produced. Similarly, we can calculate **average fixed cost** by dividing fixed cost by the quantity of output produced. And we can calculate **average variable cost** by dividing variable cost by the quantity of output produced. Or, mathematically, with Q being the level of output, we have:

$$\text{Average total cost} = ATC = \frac{TC}{Q}$$

$$\text{Average fixed cost} = AFC = \frac{FC}{Q}$$

$$\text{Average variable cost} = AVC = \frac{VC}{Q}.$$

Finally, notice that average total cost is the sum of average fixed cost plus average variable cost:

$$ATC = AFC + AVC.$$

The only fixed cost Jill incurs in operating her restaurant is the $800 per week she pays on the bank loan for her pizza ovens. Her variable costs are the wages she pays her workers. The table and graph in Figure 9.5 show Jill's costs.

We will use graphs like the one in Figure 9.5 to analyze how firms decide the level of output to produce and the price to charge. Before going further, be sure you understand the following three key facts about Figure 9.5:

1. The marginal cost (MC), average total cost (ATC), and average variable cost (AVC) curves are all U shaped, and the marginal cost curve intersects the average

Quantity of Workers	Quantity of Ovens	Quantity of Pizzas	Cost of Ovens (fixed cost)	Cost of Workers (variable cost)	Total Cost of Pizzas	ATC	AFC	AVC	MC
0	2	0	$800	$ 0	$ 800	—	—	—	—
1	2	200	800	650	1,450	$7.25	$4.00	$3.25	$3.25
2	2	450	800	1,300	2,100	4.67	1.78	2.89	2.60
3	2	550	800	1,950	2,750	5.00	1.45	3.54	6.50
4	2	600	800	2,600	3,400	5.67	1.33	4.33	13.00
5	2	625	800	3,250	4,050	6.48	1.28	5.20	26.00
6	2	640	800	3,900	4,700	7.34	1.25	6.09	43.33

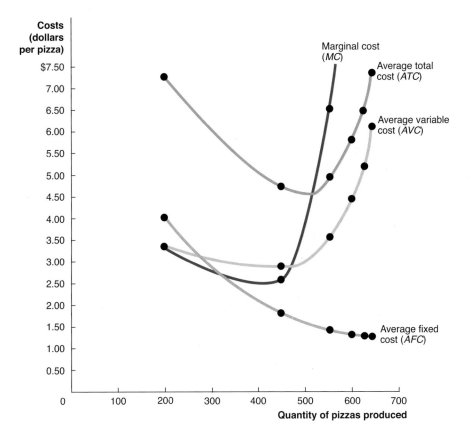

Figure 9.5

Costs at Jill Johnson's Restaurant

Jill's costs of making pizzas are shown in the table and plotted in the graph. Notice three important facts about the graph: (1) The marginal cost (MC), average total cost (ATC), and average variable cost (AVC) curves are all U shaped, and the marginal cost curve intersects both the average variable cost curve and the average total cost curve at their minimum points. (2) As output increases, average fixed cost (AFC) gets smaller and smaller. (3) As output increases, the difference between average total cost and average variable cost decreases. Make sure you can explain why each of these three facts is true. You should spend time becoming familiar with this graph because it is one of the most important graphs in microeconomics.

variable cost curve and average total cost curve at their minimum points. When marginal cost is less than either average variable cost or average total cost, it causes them to decrease. When marginal cost is above average variable cost or average total cost, it causes them to increase. Therefore, when marginal cost equals average variable cost or average total cost, they must be at their minimum points.

2. As output increases, average fixed cost gets smaller and smaller. This happens because in calculating average fixed cost, we are dividing something that gets larger and larger—output—into something that remains constant—fixed cost. Firms often refer to this process of lowering average fixed cost by selling more output as "spreading the overhead" (where "overhead" refers to fixed costs).

3. As output increases, the difference between average total cost and average variable cost decreases. This happens because the difference between average total cost and average variable cost is average fixed cost, which gets smaller as output increases.

9.6 LEARNING OBJECTIVE

Understand how firms use the long-run average cost curve in their planning.

Costs in the Long Run

The distinction between fixed cost and variable cost that we just discussed applies to the short run but *not* to the long run. For example, in the short run, Jill Johnson has fixed costs of $800 per week because she signed a loan agreement with a bank when she bought her pizza ovens. In the long run, the cost of purchasing more pizza ovens becomes variable because Jill can choose whether to expand her business by buying more ovens. The same would be true of any other fixed costs a company like Jill's might have. Once a company has purchased a fire insurance policy, the cost of the policy is fixed. But when the policy expires, the company must decide whether to renew it, and the cost becomes variable. The important point here is this: *In the long run, all costs are variable. There are no fixed costs in the long run.* In other words, in the long run, total cost equals variable cost, and average total cost equals average variable cost.

Managers of successful firms simultaneously consider how they can most profitably run their current store, factory, or office and also whether in the long run they would be more profitable if they became larger or, possibly, smaller. Jill must consider how to run her current restaurant, which has only two pizza ovens, and she must also plan what to do when her current bank loan is paid off and the lease on her store ends. Should she buy more pizza ovens? Should she lease a larger restaurant?

Economies of Scale

Long-run average cost curve A curve that shows the lowest cost at which a firm is able to produce a given quantity of output in the long run, when no inputs are fixed.

Economies of scale The situation when a firm's long-run average costs fall as it increases the quantity of output it produces.

Short-run average cost curves represent the costs a firm faces when some input, such as the quantity of machines it uses, is fixed. The **long-run average cost curve** shows the lowest cost at which a firm is able to produce a given quantity of output in the long run, when no inputs are fixed. A firm may experience **economies of scale**, which means the firm's long-run average costs fall as it increases the quantity of output it produces. We can see the effects of economies of scale in Figure 9.6, which shows the relationship between short-run and long-run average cost curves. Managers can use long-run average cost curves for planning because they show the effect on cost of expanding output by, for example, building a larger factory or store.

Figure 9.6

The Relationship Between Short-Run Average Cost and Long-Run Average Cost

If a small bookstore expects to sell only 1,000 books per month, then it will be able to sell that quantity of books at the lowest average cost of $22 per book if it builds the small store represented by the *ATC* curve on the left of the figure. A larger bookstore will be able to sell 20,000 books per month at a lower cost of $18 per book. A bookstore selling 20,000 books per month and a bookstore selling 40,000 books per month will experience constant returns to scale and have the same average cost. A bookstore selling 20,000 books per month will have reached minimum efficient scale. Very large bookstores will experience diseconomies of scale, and their average costs will rise as sales increase beyond 40,000 books per month.

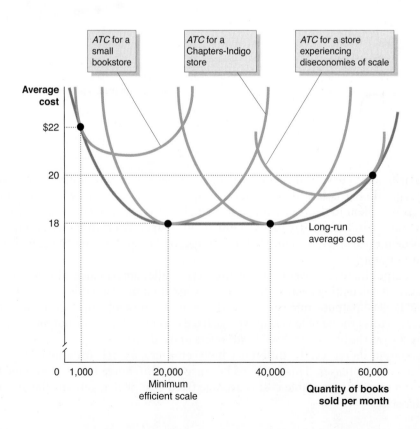

Long-Run Average Cost Curves for Bookstores

Figure 9.6 shows long-run average cost in the retail bookstore industry. If a small bookstore expects to sell only 1,000 books per month, then it will be able to sell that quantity of books at the lowest average cost of $22 per book if it builds the small store represented by the *ATC* curve on the left of the figure. A much larger bookstore, such as one run by a national chain like Chapters-Indigo, will be able to sell 20,000 books per month at a lower average cost of $18 per book. This decline in average cost from $22 to $18 represents the economies of scale that exist in bookselling. Why would the larger bookstore have lower average costs? One important reason is that the Chapters-Indigo store is selling 20 times as many books per month as the small store but might need only six times as many workers. This saving in labour cost would reduce Chapters-Indigo's average cost of selling books.

Firms may experience economies of scale for several reasons. First, as in the case of Chapters-Indigo, the firm's technology may make it possible to increase production with a smaller proportional increase in at least one input. Second, both workers and managers can become more specialized, enabling them to become more productive, as output expands. Third, large firms, like Chapters-Indigo, Hudson's Bay Company, and Bombardier may be able to purchase inputs at lower costs than smaller competitors. In fact, as Hudson's Bay Company expanded, its bargaining power with its suppliers increased, and its average costs fell. Finally, as a firm expands, it may be able to borrow money at a lower interest rate, thereby lowering its costs.

Economies of scale do not continue forever. The long-run average cost curve in most industries has a flat segment that often stretches over a substantial range of output. As Figure 9.6 shows, a bookstore selling 20,000 books per month and a bookstore selling 40,000 books per month have the same average cost. Over this range of output, firms in the industry experience **constant returns to scale**. As these firms increase their output, they have to increase their inputs, such as the size of the store and the quantity of workers, proportionally. The level of output at which all economies of scale are exhausted is known as **minimum efficient scale**. A bookstore selling 20,000 books per month has reached minimum efficient scale.

Very large bookstores experience increasing average costs as managers begin to have difficulty coordinating the operation of the store. Figure 9.6 shows that for sales above 40,000 books per month, firms in the industry experience **diseconomies of scale**. Firms in the auto industry can also experience diseconomies of scale. For instance, Toyota found that as it expanded production at its North American plants and its plants in China, its managers had difficulty keeping average cost from rising. The president of a North American Toyota plant was quoted as saying, "Demand for … high volumes saps your energy. Over a period of time, it eroded our focus … [and] thinned out the expertise and knowledge we painstakingly built up over the years." One analysis of the problems Toyota faced in expanding production concluded: "It is the kind of paradox many highly successful companies face: Getting bigger doesn't always mean getting better."

Constant returns to scale The situation in which a firm's long-run average costs remain unchanged as it increases output.

Minimum efficient scale The level of output at which all economies of scale are exhausted.

Diseconomies of scale The situation in which a firm's long-run average costs rise as the firm increases output.

Solved Problem **9.6**

Using Long-Run Average Cost Curves to Understand Business Strategy

In 2011, the port of Rotterdam in the Netherlands was in the process of expanding its capacity from 9.7 million containers processed per year to 18.2 million containers processed per year. An article in the *Wall Street Journal* described the port as attempting to "provide economies of scale to shippers." Shippers using the port expected that the fees charged to process their containers would decline following the expansion.

a. What does it mean to say that expanding the size of the port will "provide economies of scale to shippers"?

b. Use a long-run average total cost curve to explain why the expansion of the port might result in lower fees to shippers.

Solving the Problem

Step 1: **Review the chapter material.** This problem is about the long-run average cost curve, so you may want to review the material in the section "Costs in the Long Run," which begins on page 264.

Step 2: **Answer part (a) by explaining what it means for the port to "provide economies of scale to shippers."** If by expanding, the port of Rotterdam will lower its average cost of processing a shipping container, then the port was operating at less than minimum efficient scale. In that case, the expansion of the port would provide economies of scale to shippers by lowering the average cost of processing a container.

Step 3: **Draw a long-run average cost graph for the port.** The problem provides us with enough information to draw the following graph:

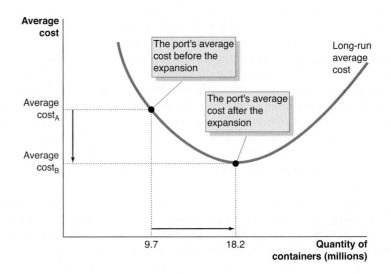

Step 4: **Use your graph to explain why the expansion of the port might result in lower fees to shippers.** Before the expansion, the port was below minimum efficient scale and was processing 9.7 million containers per year, at an average cost of Average cost$_A$. By expanding, the port can move to the minimum efficient scale of 18.2 million containers per year, and average cost falls to Average cost$_B$. (We can't be sure whether the expansion will actually take the port to minimum efficient scale, but it seems likely that the engineers and economists advising the port's managers would suggest an expansion that would raise capacity to that level.) With lower costs, the port may reduce the fees that they charge shippers, which is what shippers were expecting.

Based on John W. Miller, "For Port Expansion, It's Full Speed Ahead," *Wall Street Journal*, October 26, 2010.

MyEconLab **Your Turn:** For more practice, do related problems 6.2 and 6.3 on page 276 at the end of this chapter.

Over time, most firms in an industry will build factories or stores that are at least as large as the minimum efficient scale but not so large that diseconomies of scale occur. In the bookstore industry, stores will sell between 20,000 and 40,000 books per month. However, firms often do not know the exact shape of their long-run average cost curves. As a result, they may mistakenly build factories or stores that are either too large or too small.

Making the Connection	**The Colossal River Rouge:** **Diseconomies of Scale at Ford** **Motor Company**

Was Ford's River Rouge plant too big?

When Henry Ford started the Ford Motor Company in 1903, automobile companies produced cars in small workshops, using highly skilled workers. Ford introduced two new ideas that allowed him to take advantage of economies of scale. First, Ford used identical—or, interchangeable—parts so that unskilled workers could assemble the cars. Second, instead of having groups of workers moving from one stationary automobile to the next, he had the workers remain stationary, while the automobiles moved along an assembly line. Ford built a large factory at Highland Park, outside Detroit, where he used these ideas to produce the famous Model T at an average cost well below what his competitors could match using older production methods in smaller factories.

Ford believed that he could produce automobiles at an even lower average cost by building a still larger plant along the River Rouge in Dearborn, Michigan. Unfortunately, Ford's River Rouge plant was too large and suffered from diseconomies of scale. Ford's managers had great difficulty coordinating the production of automobiles in such a large plant. The following description of the River Rouge comes from a biography of Ford by Allan Nevins and Frank Ernest Hill:

> A total of 93 separate structures stood on the [River Rouge] site.... Railroad trackage covered 93 miles [150 kilometres], conveyors 27 [miles; 44 kilometres]. About 75,000 men worked in the great plant. A force of 5000 did nothing but keep it clean, wearing out 5000 mops and 3000 brooms a month, and using 86 tons [78 tonnes] of soap on the floors, walls, and 330 acres [134 hectares] of windows. The Rouge was an industrial city, immense, concentrated, packed with power.... By its very massiveness and complexity, it denied men at the top contact with and understanding of those beneath, and gave those beneath a sense of being lost in inexorable immensity and power.

Beginning in 1927, Ford produced the Model A—its only car model at that time—at the River Rouge plant. Ford failed to achieve economies of scale and actually *lost money* on each of the four Model A body styles.

Ford could not raise the price of the Model A to make it profitable because at a higher price, the car could not compete with similar models produced by competitors such as General Motors and Chrysler. He eventually reduced the cost of making the Model A by constructing smaller factories spread out across the United States. These smaller factories produced the Model A at a lower average cost than was possible at the River Rouge plant.

From Allan Nevins and Frank Ernest Hill, *Ford: Expansion and Challenge*, 1915–1933, (New York: Scribner, 1957), pp. 293, 295.

Your Turn: Test your understanding by doing related problem 6.4 on page 276 at the end of this chapter.

MyEconLab

Don't Let This Happen to You

Don't Confuse Diminishing Returns with Diseconomies of Scale

The concepts of diminishing returns and diseconomies of scale may seem similar, but, in fact, they are unrelated. Diminishing returns applies only to the short run, when at least one of the firm's inputs, such as the quantity of machinery it uses, is fixed. The law of diminishing returns tells us that in the short run, hiring more workers will, at some point, result in less additional output. Diminishing returns explains why marginal cost curves eventually slope upward. Diseconomies of scale apply only in the long run, when the firm is free to vary all its inputs, can adopt new technology, and can vary the amount of machinery it uses and the size of its facility. Diseconomies of scale explain why long-run average cost curves eventually slope upward.

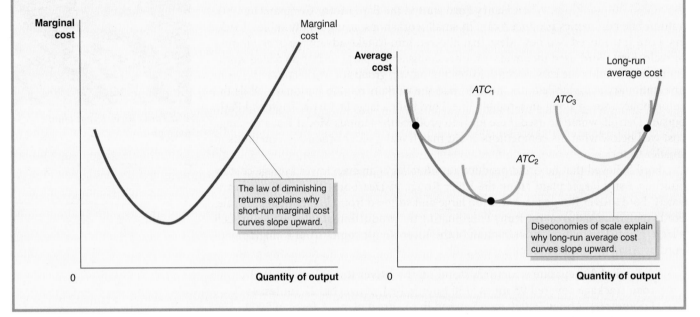

The law of diminishing returns explains why short-run marginal cost curves slope upward.

Diseconomies of scale explain why long-run average cost curves slope upward.

Economics in Your Life

Using Cost Concepts in Your Own Business

At the beginning of the chapter, we asked you to suppose that you are about to open a store to sell recliners. Both you and a competing store, Bob's Big Chairs, can buy recliners from the manufacturer for $300 each. But because Bob's sells more recliners per month than you expect to be able to sell, his costs per recliner are lower than yours. We asked you to think about why this might be true. In this chapter, we have seen that firms often experience declining average costs as the quantity they sell increases. A key reason Bob's average costs might be lower than yours has to do with fixed costs. Because your store is the same size as Bob's store, you may be paying about the same amount to lease the store space. You may also be paying about the same amounts for utilities, insurance, and advertising. All these are fixed costs because they do not change as the quantity of recliners you sell changes. Because Bob's fixed costs are the same as yours, but he is selling more recliners, his average fixed costs are lower than yours, and, therefore, so are his average total costs. With lower average total costs, he can sell his recliners for a lower price than you do and still make a profit.

Conclusion

In this chapter, we discussed the relationship between a firm's technology, production, and costs. In the discussion, we encountered a number of definitions of costs, and it is useful to bring them together in Table 9.4 for you to review.

We have seen the important relationship between a firm's level of production and its costs. Just as this information was vital to Dinara Millington in evaluating the costs of oil extraction, so it remains vital today to all firms as they attempt to decide the optimal level of production and the optimal prices to charge for their products. Read *An Inside Look* on the next page to see how federal subsidies have helped a technology firm lower production costs for solar panels.

Table 9.4

A Summary of Definitions of Cost

Term	Definition	Symbols and Equations
Total cost	The cost of all the inputs used by a firm, or fixed cost plus variable cost	TC
Fixed costs	Costs that remain constant as a firm's level of output changes	FC
Variable costs	Costs that change as the firm's level of output changes	VC
Marginal cost	An increase in total cost resulting from producing another unit of output	$MC = \frac{\Delta TC}{\Delta Q}$
Average total cost	Total cost divided by the quantity of output produced	$ATC = \frac{TC}{Q}$
Average fixed cost	Fixed cost divided by the quantity of output produced	$AFC = \frac{FC}{Q}$
Average variable cost	Variable cost divided by the quantity of output produced	$AVC = \frac{VC}{Q}$
Implicit cost	A nonmonetary opportunity cost	—
Explicit cost	A cost that involves spending money	—

FINANCIAL POST

Telus CEO Entwistle Warns of "Bloodbath" if Verizon Has Advantage in Wireless Spectrum Auction

TORONTO—The head of one of Canada's big three telephone companies warned that the sector faces a "bloodbath" unless rules that could give a U.S. giant preferential treatment in the upcoming spectrum auction are changed in the next two months.

Darren Entwistle, chief executive of Telus Corp., told the *Financial Post* during an editorial board meeting Thursday that the government's campaign to have at least four wireless carriers in every market will lead to overspending by the incumbents, could leave one of them behind technology-wise, and even threaten investment in services for rural communities.

The government plans to auction off wireless spectrum in the prized 700-megahertz frequency band in January but the deadline for deposits is September 17 and Mr. Entwistle is conducting a campaign to convince the public as well as government officials, opposition politicians, and the unions representing telecom employees that the rules need to change before then.

The radio airwaves at stake, which became available after the transition to digital television, are highly prized for their ability to travel long distances and easily penetrate buildings. This type of spectrum is in short supply and wireless carriers are desperate to get their hands on it to build the networks of the future and accommodate the video-streaming and web surfing data demands of the mobile world.

His primary concern is that if a foreign player with massive resources such as Verizon Communications Inc. takes part in the Canadian auction, it would be treated as a "new entrant" and permitted to bid on up to two out of four prime blocks of spectrum.

Verizon chief financial officer Fran Shammo said Thursday during a conference call to discuss the company's quarterly earnings that its interest in Canada is still "exploratory." Still, he acknowledged that the Canadian market could be attractive to the New York-based carrier.

"If you look at the population of Canada, about 70 percent of that population is between Toronto and Quebec. That's adjacent to the Verizon Wireless properties," Mr. Shammo said.

"If Verizon comes to Canada and they focus on Toronto and Montreal as per their comments this morning, then we'll focus on Toronto and Montreal to the detriment of non-urban investment," Mr. Entwistle told the *Financial Post.*

The country's big three providers are up against a federal government that has seized on cellphone bills as an issue that resonates with Canadians.

In early June, Ottawa blocked Telus's $380-million bid to buy Mobilicity's spectrum licences and later that month it released a policy framework stating it would review all transfers on a case-by-case basis to prevent the concentration of too much spectrum in any party's hands.

The Conservative Party of Canada used the Telus decision as an opportunity to highlight its achievements on cellphone bills in an email to supporters, and Prime Minister Stephen Harper addressed the issue on his Facebook page last month.

"Stephen Harper doesn't say a thing without it being well calculated. He's well aware that this is a winner for the government," said Gregory Taylor, principal investigator for Canadian Spectrum Policy Research, a research team at Toronto's Ryerson University.

"If they can score political points while knocking around Rogers and Bell while still allowing Rogers and Bell to reap record profits, it's a great win for the government."

Source: Christine Dobby, "Telus CEO Entwistle Warns of 'Bloodbath' if Verizon Has Advantage in Wireless Spectrum Auction," *Financial Post,* July 18, 2013, accessed at http://business.financialpost.com/2013/07/18/telus-darren-entwistle-wireless-spectrum-verizon/?__lsa=e22b-ab55

Key Points in the Article

The airwaves used by radio and television broadcasters and cellular telephone companies are a public good and, as such, are regulated by the federal government. Recent changes in television broadcast technology have reduced the use of certain frequencies that the government intends to reallocate for use in the cellular industry. To obtain the maximum value for the rights to use these frequencies, the government intends to auction them, selling them to the highest bidder.

The auction is expected to attract the big three Canadian firms—Telus, Rogers, and Bell—as well as the American company, Verizon. It is the expected arrival of Verizon to the Canadian marketplace that has the three Canadian firms upset.

Analyzing the News

a The broadcast industry, including cellular services, is a very capital-intensive industry: It requires large amounts of fixed capital investment, but very little labour. For firms that use a more balanced combination of labour and capital, the average total cost curve has the familiar U shape. For capital-intensive firms, however, the average total cost curve resembles the average fixed cost curve. As output increases, the average production cost continually falls. Firms that have downward-sloping cost curves are often referred to as "natural monopolists" since it is more cost effective to have fewer firms producing large output.

Darren Entwistle, CEO of Telus, believes that allowing new entrants into the market will increase costs. If the number of customers remains unchanged, Entwistle is probably correct. Any new firm would take customers away from the existing firms, and output at these firms would fall. Since the average cost curve is downward sloping, firms would be moving leftward along the curve and average costs would

increase. If, however, the market is expanding and the demand for cellular voice and data services is increasing, Entwistle's concerns may not be valid.

His other two concerns may have more validity. For a new supplier to be able to compete with the incumbents, it must be at least as large. Capital investments are required to get the average cost of any fourth firm to the level of the existing three. Presumably, any new entrant would use state of the art technology and the incumbents would then be required to upgrade their equipment to retain customers. Failure to do so would "leave them behind technology-wise."

The number of customers in rural areas is less than the number in urban areas. With downward-sloping average costs, the average cost of production is higher in rural areas than in urban areas. As demand increases in urban areas, the cellular providers are more likely to invest in those areas and less likely to invest in rural areas.

b Large existing firms typically have an advantage over new entrants when the average cost curve is downward sloping. To reduce this advantage, the auction rules tend to favour new entrants. In the case of the announced auction, there are four blocks of spectrum available, and two of the four are reserved for new entrants with the other two being made available to existing firms.

Entwistle's concern with this arrangement is related to who is likely to be bidding at the auction. At previous auctions, smaller firms were entering the market and were not perceived to be any threat to the big three incumbents. This time, however, it is expected that Verizon will be bidding. Even though Verizon is a large, established wireless provider, it has no operations in Canada. By the government's rules, Verizon is a "new entrant" and can bid on two of the four available blocks. With the vast resources available to Verizon, it will likely

be able to outbid any small domestic entrant. It also means that there are only two blocks available for the big three domestic carriers to fight over, and leaves little chance for existing smaller companies to expand.

c Smaller companies are definitely at a disadvantage in capital-intensive industries. They can rarely get their costs down enough to compete with larger players and quite often don't survive. When a small carrier gets into financial trouble, its best course of action is to sell its assets to a much larger firm. With lower costs, the larger firms can integrate the capital assets and customers of the smaller firms and still earn profits, something the smaller firms could not do. The federal government seems to be concerned with the concentration in the Canadian wireless industry and has implemented rules to try to prevent further amalgamations. In June 2013, Telus tried to purchase the assets of Mobilicity for $380 million, but the sale was rejected by the federal regulators.

Thinking Critically

1. Suppose that Telus can serve 200,000 customers per year at the lowest average total cost if it builds 10 cellular towers. Also suppose that the firm can serve 400,000 customers per year at the lowest average total cost if it builds 15 towers. Draw a graph showing the average total cost curves representing these two alternatives. In drawing the graph, assume that Telus experiences economies of scale over this range of output.

2. Verizon may be the first wireless provider to use the new spectrum. The new spectrum is similar to using a new technology. How might being the first in the market to use this technology be an advantage to Verizon? How might it be a risk?

Chapter Summary and Problems

Key Terms

Average fixed cost, p. 262

Average product of labour, p. 257

Average total cost, p. 254

Average variable cost, p. 262

Constant returns to scale, p. 265

Diseconomies of scale, p. 265

Economies of scale, p. 264

Explicit cost, p. 252

Fixed costs, p. 252

Implicit cost, p. 252

Law of diminishing returns, p. 255

Long run, p. 251

Long-run average cost curve, p. 264

Marginal cost, p. 259

Marginal product of labour, p. 255

Minimum efficient scale, p. 265

Opportunity cost, p. 252

Production function, p. 254

Short run, p. 251

Technological change, p. 250

Technology, p. 250

Total cost, p. 251

Variable costs, p. 252

Summary

*LO 9.1 The basic activity of a firm is to use inputs, such as workers, machines, and natural resources, to produce goods and services. The firm's **technology** is the processes it uses to turn inputs into goods and services. **Technological change** refers to a change in the ability of a firm to produce a given level of output with a given quantity of inputs.

LO 9.2 In the **short run**, a firm's technology and the size of its factory, store, or office are fixed. In the **long run**, a firm is able to adopt new technology and to increase or decrease the size of its physical plant. **Total cost** is the cost of all the inputs a firm uses in production. **Variable costs** are costs that change as output changes. **Fixed costs** are costs that remain constant as output changes. **Opportunity cost** is the highest-valued alternative that must be given up to engage in an activity. An **explicit cost** is a cost that involves spending money. An **implicit cost** is a nonmonetary opportunity cost. The relationship between the inputs employed by a firm and the maximum output it can produce with those inputs is called the firm's **production function**.

LO 9.3 The **marginal product of labour** is the additional output produced by a firm as a result of hiring one more worker. Specialization and division of labour cause the marginal product of labour to rise for the first few workers hired. Eventually, the **law of diminishing returns** causes the marginal product of labour to decline. The **average product of labour** is the total amount of output produced by a firm divided by the quantity of workers hired. When the marginal product of labour is greater than the average product of labour, the average product of labour increases. When the marginal product of labour is less than the average product of labour, the average product of labour decreases.

LO 9.4 The **marginal cost** of production is the increase in total cost resulting from producing another unit of output. The marginal cost curve has a U shape because when the marginal product of labour is rising, the marginal cost of output is falling, and when the marginal product of labour is falling, the marginal cost of output is rising. When marginal cost is less than average total cost, average total cost falls. When marginal cost is greater than average total cost, average total cost rises. Therefore, **average total cost** also has a U shape.

LO 9.5 **Average fixed cost** is equal to fixed cost divided by the level of output. **Average variable cost** is equal to variable cost divided by the level of output. Figure 9.5 shows the relationship among marginal cost, average total cost, average variable cost, and average fixed cost. It is one of the most important graphs in microeconomics.

LO 9.6 The **long-run average cost curve** shows the lowest cost at which a firm is able to produce a given level of output in the long run. For many firms, the long-run average cost curve falls as output expands because of **economies of scale**. **Minimum efficient scale** is the level of output at which all economies of scale have been exhausted. After economies of scale have been exhausted, firms experience **constant returns to scale**, where their long-run average cost curve is flat. At high levels of output, the long-run average cost curve turns up as the firm experiences **diseconomies of scale**.

MyEconLab   Log in to MyEconLab to complete these exercises and get instant feedback.

Review Questions

LO 9.1

1.1 What is the difference between technology and technological change?

1.2 Is it possible for technological change to be negative? If so, give an example.

*'Learning Objective' is abbreviated to 'LO' in the end of chapter material.

LO 9.2

2.1 What is the difference between the short run and the long run? Is the amount of time that separates the short run from the long run the same for every firm?

2.2 Distinguish between a firm's fixed cost and variable cost and give an example of each.

2.3 What are implicit costs? How are they different from explicit costs?

2.4 What is the production function? What does the short-run production function hold constant?

LO 9.3

3.1 Draw a graph that shows the usual relationship between the marginal product of labour and the average product of labour. Why do the marginal product of labour and the average product of labour have the shapes you drew?

3.2 How do specialization and division of labour typically affect the marginal product of labour?

3.3 What is the law of diminishing returns? Does it apply in the long run?

LO 9.4

4.1 What is the difference between the average cost of production and marginal cost of production?

4.2 If the marginal product of labour is rising, is the marginal cost of production rising or falling? Briefly explain.

4.3 Explain why the marginal cost curve intersects the average total cost curve at the level of output where average total cost is at a minimum.

LO 9.5

5.1 As the level of output increases, what happens to the value of average fixed cost?

5.2 As the level of output increases, what happens to the difference between the value of average total cost and average variable cost?

LO 9.6

6.1 What is the difference between total cost and variable cost in the long run?

6.2 What is minimum efficient scale? What is likely to happen in the long run to firms that do not reach minimum efficient scale?

6.3 What are economies of scale? What are four reasons that firms may experience economies of scale?

6.4 What are diseconomies of scale? What is the main reason that a firm eventually encounters diseconomies of scale as it keeps increasing the size of its store or factory?

6.5 Why can short-run average cost never be less than long-run average cost for a given level of output?

Problems and Applications

LO 9.1

1.1 Briefly explain whether you agree with the following observation: "Technological change refers only to the introduction of new products, so it is not relevant to the operations of most firms."

1.2 Which of the following are examples of a firm experiencing positive technological change?
   a. A fall in oil prices leads Air Canada to lower its ticket prices.
   b. A training program makes a firm's workers more productive.
   c. An exercise program makes a firm's workers more healthy and productive.
   d. A firm cuts its workforce and is able to maintain its initial level of output.
   e. A firm rearranges the layout of its factory and finds that by using its initial set of inputs, it can produce exactly as much as before.

1.3 [**Related to the** Making the Connection **on page 251**] The 7-Eleven chain of convenience stores in Japan reorganized its system for supplying its stores with food. This led to a sharp reduction in the number of trucks the company had to use, while increasing the amount of fresh food on store shelves. Someone discussing 7-Eleven's new system argues, "This is not an example of technological change because it did not require the use of new machinery or equipment." Briefly explain whether you agree with this argument.

LO 9.2

2.1 An article in *BusinessWeek* discussed Apple's cost to produce the iPod shuffle: "All told, the cost of the shuffle's components, the headphones, and the packaging it ships in comes to $21.77... That's about 28% of the device's retail price [of $79]." Can we conclude from this information

that Apple is making a profit of about $57 per shuffle? Briefly explain.

Based on Arik Hesseldahl, "Deconstructing Apple's Tiny iPod Shuffle," *BusinessWeek*, April 13, 2009.

2.2 [**Related to the** Making the Connection **on page 252**] Many firms consider their wage costs to be variable costs. Why do publishers usually consider their wage and salary costs to be fixed costs? Are the costs of utilities always fixed, are they always variable, or can they be both? Briefly explain.

2.3 [**Related to the** Making the Connection **on page 252**] For Jill Johnson's pizza restaurant, explain whether each of the following is a fixed cost or a variable cost.
   a. The payment she makes on her fire insurance policy
   b. The payment she makes to buy pizza dough
   c. The wages she pays her workers
   d. The lease payment she makes to the landlord who owns the building where her store is located
   e. The $300-per-month payment she makes to her local newspaper for running her weekly advertisements

2.4 Suppose that Bill owns an automobile collision repair shop. The table below shows how the quantity of cars Bill can repair per month depends on the number of workers that he hires. Assume that he pays each worker $4,000 per month and his fixed cost is $6,000 per month. Using the information provided, complete the table.

Quantity of Workers	Quantity of Cars per Month	Fixed Cost	Variable Cost	Total Cost	Average Total Cost
0	0	$6,000			—
1	20				
2	30				
3	40				
4	50				
5	55				

2.5 Suppose Jill Johnson operates her pizza restaurant in a building she owns in the centre of the city. Similar buildings in the neighbourhood rent for $4,000 per month. Jill is considering selling her building and renting space in the suburbs for $3,000 per month. Jill decides not to make the move. She reasons, "I would like to have a restaurant in the suburbs, but I pay no rent for my restaurant now, and I don't want to see my costs rise by $3,000 per month." Evaluate Jill's reasoning.

LO 9.3

3.1 Fill in the missing values in the following table.

Quantity of Workers	Total Output	Marginal Product of Labour	Average Product of Labour
0	0		
1	400		
2	900		
3	1,500		
4	1,900		
5	2,200		
6	2,400		
7	2,300		

3.2 Use the numbers from problem 3.1 to draw one graph that shows how total output increases with the quantity of workers hired and a second graph that shows the marginal product of labour and the average product of labour.

3.3 A student looks at the data in Table 9.3 and draws this conclusion:

> The marginal product of labour is increasing for the first two workers hired, and then it declines for the next four workers. I guess each of the first two workers must have been hard workers. Then Jill must have had to settle for increasingly poor workers.

Do you agree with the student's analysis? Briefly explain.

3.4 [**Related to the** Making the Connection **on page 257**] Briefly explain whether you agree with the following argument:

> Adam Smith's idea of the gains to firms from the division of labour makes a lot of sense when the good being manufactured is something complex like automobiles or computers, but it doesn't apply in the manufacturing of less complex goods or in other sectors of the economy, such as retail sales.

3.5 Sally looks at her university transcript and says to you, "How is this possible? My grade point average for this semester's courses is higher than my grade point average for last semester's courses, but my cumulative grade point average still went down from last semester to this semester." Explain to Sally how this is possible.

LO 9.4

4.1 Is it possible for average total cost to be decreasing over a range of output where marginal cost is increasing? Briefly explain.

4.2 Suppose a firm has no fixed costs, so all its costs are variable, even in the short run.
  a. If the firm's marginal costs are continually increasing (that is, marginal cost is increasing from the first unit of output produced), will the firm's average total cost curve have a U shape?
  b. If the firm's marginal costs are $5 at every level of output, what shape will the firm's average total cost have?

4.3 [**Related to** Solved Problem 9.4 **on page 261**] Santiago Delgado owns a copier store. He leases two copy machines for which he pays $20 each per day. He cannot increase the number of machines he leases without giving the office machine company six weeks' notice. He can hire as many workers as he wants, at a cost of $40 per day per worker. These are the only two inputs he uses to produce copies.
  a. Fill in the remaining columns in the table below.
  b. Draw the average total cost curve and marginal cost curve for Santiago's store. Do these curves have the expected shape? Briefly explain.

Quantity of Workers	Quantity of Copies per Day	Fixed Cost	Variable Cost	Total Cost	Average Total Cost	Marginal Cost
0	0					
1	600					
2	1,100					
3	1,500					
4	1,800					
5	2,000					
6	2,100					

4.4 Jill Johnson says the following: "I am currently producing 10,000 pizzas per month at a total cost of $50,000.00. If I produce 10,001 pizzas, my total cost will rise to $50,011.00. Therefore, my marginal cost of producing pizzas must be increasing." Is she correct? Draw a graph to illustrate your answer.

4.5 Jill Johnson says the following: "I am currently producing 20,000 pizzas per month at a total cost of $75,000. If I produce 20,001 pizzas, my total cost will rise to $75,002. Therefore, my marginal cost of producing pizzas must be increasing." Is she correct? Illustrate your answer with a graph.

4.6 (This problem is somewhat advanced.) Using symbols, we can write that the marginal product of labour is equal to $\Delta Q/\Delta L$. Marginal cost is equal to $\Delta TC/\Delta Q$. Because fixed costs by definition don't change, marginal cost is also equal to $\Delta VC/\Delta Q$. If Jill Johnson's only variable cost (VC) is labour cost, then her variable cost is just the wage multiplied by the quantity of workers hired, or wL.
  a. If the wage Jill pays is constant, then what is ΔVC in terms of w and L?
  b. Use your answer to part (a) and the expressions given above for the marginal product of labour and the marginal cost of output to find an expression for marginal cost, $\Delta TC/\Delta Q$, in terms of the wage, w, and the marginal product of labour, $\Delta Q/\Delta L$.
  c. Use your answer to part (b) to determine Jill's marginal cost of producing pizzas if the wage is $750 per week and the marginal product of labour is 150 pizzas. If the

wage falls to $600 per week and the marginal product of labour is unchanged, what happens to Jill's marginal cost? If the wage is unchanged at $750 per week and the marginal product of labour rises to 250 pizzas, what happens to Jill's marginal cost?

LO 9.5

5.1 Suppose the total cost of producing 10,000 tennis balls is $30,000, and the fixed cost is $10,000.

   a. What is the variable cost?

   b. When output is 10,000, what are the average variable cost and the average fixed cost?

   c. Assuming that the cost curves have the usual shape, is the dollar difference between the average total cost and the average variable cost greater when the output is 10,000 tennis balls or when the output is 30,000 tennis balls? Explain.

5.2 In the ancient world, a book could be produced either on a scroll or as a codex, which was made of folded sheets glued together, something like a modern book. One scholar has estimated the following variable costs (in Greek drachmas) of the two methods:

	Scroll	Codex
Cost of Writing (wage of a scribe)	11.33 drachmas	11.33 drachmas
Cost of paper	16.50 drachmas	9.25 drachmas

Another scholar points out that a significant fixed cost was involved in producing a codex:

> In order to copy a codex … the amount of text and the layout of each page had to be carefully calculated in advance to determine the exact number of sheets … needed. No doubt, this is more time-consuming and calls for more experimentation than the production of a scroll would. But for the next copy, these calculations would be used again.

   a. Suppose that the fixed cost of preparing a codex was 58 drachmas and that there was no similar fixed cost for a scroll. Would an ancient book publisher who intended to sell 5 copies of a book be likely to publish it as a scroll or as a codex? What if he intended to sell 10 copies? Briefly explain.

   b. Although most books were published as scrolls in the first century A.D., by the third century, most were published as codices. Considering only the factors mentioned in this problem, explain why this change may have taken place.

Based on T. C. Skeat, "The Length of the Standard Papyrus Roll and the Cost-Advantage of the Codex," *Zeitschrift fur Pspyrologie and Epigraphik* (Germany: Rudolph Habelt, 1982), p. 175; and David Trobisch, *The First Edition of the New Testament* (New York: Oxford University Press, 2000), p. 73.

5.3 Use the information in the graph in the next column to find the values for the following at an output level of 1,000.

   a. Marginal cost

   b. Total cost

   c. Variable cost

   d. Fixed cost

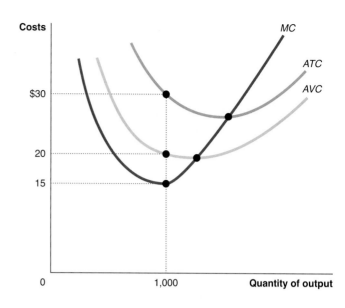

5.4 List the errors in the following graph. Carefully explain why the curves drawn this way are wrong. In other words, why can't these curves be as they are shown in the graph?

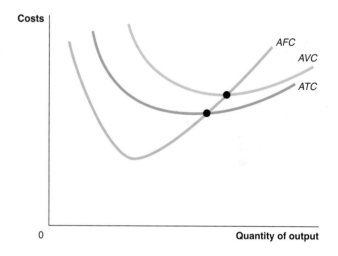

5.5 Explain how the events listed in parts (a) through (d) would affect the following costs at Air Canada:

   1. Marginal cost

   2. Average variable cost

   3. Average fixed cost

   4. Average total cost

     a. Air Canada signs a new contract that requires the airline to increase wages for its flight attendants.

     b. The federal government starts to levy a $20-per-passenger carbon emissions tax on all commercial air travel.

     c. Air Canada decides on an across-the-board 10 percent cut in executive salaries.

     d. Air Canada decides to double its television advertising budget.

LO 9.6

6.1 Factories for producing computer chips are called "fabs." As the semiconductors used in computer chips have become smaller and smaller, the machines necessary to make them have become more and more expensive. According to an article in *The Economist* magazine:

> To reach the economies of scale needed to make such investments pay, chipmakers must build bigger fabs.... In 1966 a new fab cost $14 million. By 1995 the price had risen to $1.5 billion. Today, says Intel, the cost of a leading-edge fab exceeds $6 billion.

Why would the rising costs of chipmaking machines lead chipmaking companies, such as Intel, to build larger factories?

From "The Semiconductor Industry: Under New Management," *The Economist*, April 2, 2009.

6.2 [**Related to** Solved Problem 9.6 **on page 265**] Suppose that Jill Johnson has to choose between building a smaller restaurant and building a larger restaurant. In the following graph, the relationship between costs and output for the smaller restaurant is represented by the curve ATC_1, and the relationship between costs and output for the larger restaurant is represented by the curve ATC_2.

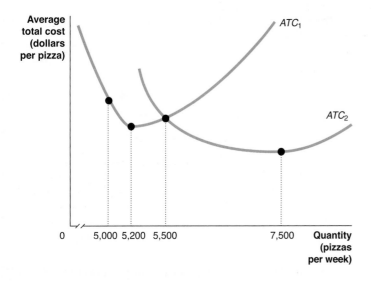

a. If Jill expects to produce 5,100 pizzas per week, should she build a smaller restaurant or a larger restaurant? Briefly explain.

b. If Jill expects to produce 6,000 pizzas per week, should she build a smaller restaurant or a larger restaurant? Briefly explain.

c. A student asks, "If the average cost of producing pizzas is lower in the larger restaurant when Jill produces 7,500 pizzas per week, why isn't it also lower when Jill produces 5,200 pizzas per week?" Give a brief answer to the student's question.

6.3 [**Related to** Solved Problem 9.6 **on page 265**] An account of the difficulties of Japanese mobile phone manufacturers argues that these firms made a mistake by concentrating on selling in high-income countries while making little effort to sell in low-income countries:

> The main growth in the wireless industry overall is in emerging markets, which need cheap phones. The world's top three makers—Nokia, Samsung and Motorola—focus on this segment.... Japanese firms are caught in a vicious circle: because they are not selling to poor countries, their volume stays low, which keeps prices high, which makes selling to poor countries infeasible.

Why would the price of Japanese mobile phones be high because Japanese firms are producing these phones in low volumes? Use a graph like Figure 9.6 to illustrate your answer.

Based on "Dropped Call: Why Japan lost the mobile-phone wars," *The Economist*, March 7, 2008.

6.4 [**Related to the** Making the Connection **on page 267**] Suppose that Henry Ford had continued to experience economies of scale, no matter how large an automobile factory he built. Discuss what the implications of this would have been for the automobile industry.

6.5 [**Related to the** Chapter Opener **on page 249**] Review the discussion at the beginning of the chapter about the oil sands industry in Canada. Suppose that industry executives take Dinara Millington's advice and put more capital into steam extraction. What would be some of the risks that she refers to in her report?

Appendix C

Using Isoquants and Isocost Lines to Understand Production and Cost

LO
Use isoquants and isocost lines to understand production and cost.

Isoquants

In Chapter 9, we studied the important relationship between a firm's level of production and its costs. In this appendix, we will look more closely at how firms choose the combination of inputs to produce a given level of output. Firms usually have a choice about how they will produce their output. For example, Jill Johnson is able to produce 5,000 pizzas per week by using 10 workers and 2 ovens or by using 6 workers and 3 ovens. We will see that firms search for the *cost-minimizing* combination of inputs that will allow them to produce a given level of output. The cost-minimizing combination of inputs depends on two factors: technology—which determines how much output a firm receives from employing a given quantity of inputs—and input prices—which determine the total cost of each combination of inputs.

An Isoquant Graph

We begin by graphing the levels of output that Jill can produce using different combinations of two inputs: labour—the quantity of workers she hires per week—and capital—the quantity of ovens she uses per week. In reality, of course, Jill uses more than just these two inputs to produce pizzas, but nothing important would change if we expanded the discussion to include many inputs instead of just two. Figure 9C.1 measures capital along the vertical axis and labour along the horizontal axis. The curves in the graph are **isoquants**, which show all the combinations of two inputs, in this case capital and labour, that will produce the same level of output.

Isoquant A curve that shows all the combinations of two inputs, such as capital and labour, that will produce the same level of output.

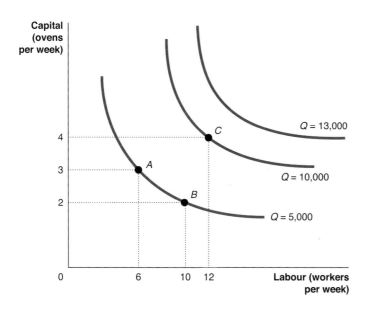

Figure 9C.1

Isoquants

Isoquants show all the combinations of two inputs, in this case capital and labour, that will produce the same level of output. For example, the isoquant labelled $Q = 5,000$ shows all the combinations of ovens and workers that enable Jill to produce that quantity of pizzas per week. At point A, she produces 5,000 pizzas using 3 ovens and 6 workers, and at point B, she produces the same output using 2 ovens and 10 workers. With more ovens and workers, she can move to a higher isoquant. For example, with 4 ovens and 12 workers, she can produce at point C on the isoquant $Q = 10,000$. With even more ovens and workers, she could move to the isoquant $Q = 13,000$.

The isoquant labelled $Q = 5,000$ shows all the combinations of workers and ovens that enable Jill to produce that quantity of pizzas per week. For example, at point A, she produces 5,000 pizzas using 6 workers and 3 ovens, and at point B, she produces the same output using 10 workers and 2 ovens. With more workers and ovens, she can move to a higher isoquant. For example, with 12 workers and 4 ovens, she can produce at point C on the isoquant $Q = 10,000$. With even more workers and ovens, she could move to the isoquant $Q = 13,000$. The higher the isoquant—that is, the further to the upper right on the graph—the more output the firm produces. Although we have shown only three isoquants in this graph, there is, in fact, an isoquant for every level of output.

The Slope of an Isoquant

Remember that the slope of a curve is the ratio of the change in the variable on the vertical axis to the change in the variable on the horizontal axis. Along an isoquant, the slope tells us the rate at which a firm is able to substitute one input for another while keeping the level of output constant. This rate is called the **marginal rate of technical substitution (*MRTS*)**.

We expect that the *MRTS* will change as we move down an isoquant. In Figure 9C.1, at a point like A on isoquant $Q = 5,000$, the isoquant is relatively steep. As we move down the curve, it becomes less steep at a point like B. This shape is the usual one for isoquants: They are bowed in, or convex. The reason isoquants have this shape is that as we move down the curve, we continue to substitute labour for capital. As the firm produces the same quantity of output using less capital, the additional labour it needs increases because of diminishing returns. As a consequence of diminishing returns, for a given decline in capital, increasing amounts of labour are necessary to produce the same level of output. Because the *MRTS* is equal to the change in capital divided by the change in labour, it will become smaller (in absolute value) as we move down an isoquant.

Isocost Lines

A firm wants to produce a given quantity of output at the lowest possible cost. We can show the relationship between the quantity of inputs used and the firm's total cost by using an *isocost* line. An **isocost line** shows all the combinations of two inputs, such as capital and labour, that have the same total cost.

Graphing the Isocost Line

Suppose that Jill has $6,000 per week to spend on capital and labour. Suppose, to simplify the analysis, that Jill can rent pizza ovens by the week. The table in Figure 9C.2 shows the combinations of capital and labour available to her if the rental price of ovens is $1,000 per week and the wage rate is $500 per week. The graph uses the data in the table to construct an isocost line. The isocost line intersects the vertical axis at the maximum number of ovens Jill can rent per week, which is shown by point A. The line intersects the horizontal axis at the maximum number of workers Jill can hire per week, which is point G. As Jill moves down the isocost line from point A, she gives up renting 1 oven for every 2 workers she hires. Any combination of inputs along the line or inside the line can be purchased with $6,000. Any combination that lies outside the line cannot be purchased because it would have a total cost to Jill of more than $6,000.

The Slope and Position of the Isocost Line

The slope of the isocost line is constant and equals the change in the quantity of ovens divided by the change in the quantity of workers. In this case, in moving from any point on the isocost line to any other point, the change in the quantity of ovens equals –1, and the change in the quantity of workers equals 2, so the slope equals –1/2.

Marginal rate of technical substitution (*MRTS*) The rate at which a firm is able to substitute one input for another while keeping the level of output constant.

Isocost line All the combinations of two inputs, such as capital and labour, that have the same total cost.

Combinations of Workers and Ovens with a Total Cost of $6,000			
Point	Ovens	Workers	Total Cost
A	6	0	(6 x $1,000) + (0 x $500) = $6,000
B	5	2	(5 x $1,000) + (2 x $500) = 6,000
C	4	4	(4 x $1,000) + (4 x $500) = 6,000
D	3	6	(3 x $1,000) + (6 x $500) = 6,000
E	2	8	(2 x $1,000) + (8 x $500) = 6,000
F	1	10	(1 x $1,000) + (10 x $500) = 6,000
G	0	12	(0 x $1,000) + (12 x $500) = 6,000

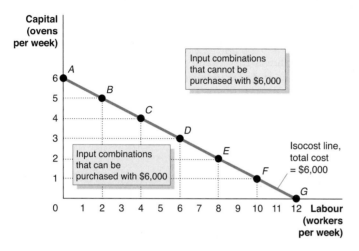

Figure 9C.2

An Isocost Line

The isocost line shows the combinations of inputs with a total cost of $6,000. The rental price of ovens is $1,000 per week, so if Jill spends the whole $6,000 on ovens, she can rent 6 ovens (point *A*). The wage rate is $500 per week, so if Jill spends the whole $6,000 on workers, she can hire 12 workers. As she moves down the isocost line, she gives up renting 1 oven for every 2 workers she hires. Any combinations of inputs along the line or inside the line can be purchased with $6,000. Any combinations that lie outside the line cannot be purchased with $6,000.

Notice that with a rental price of ovens of $1,000 per week and a wage rate for labour of $500 per week, the slope of the isocost line is equal to the ratio of the wage rate divided by the rental price of capital, multiplied by $-1: -\$500/\$1,000 = -1/2$. In fact, this result will always hold, whatever inputs are involved and whatever their prices may be: *The slope of the isocost line is equal to the ratio of the price of the input on the horizontal axis divided by the price of the input on the vertical axis multiplied by -1.*

The position of the isocost line depends on the level of total cost. Higher levels of total cost shift the isocost line outward, and lower levels of total cost shift the isocost line inward. This can be seen in Figure 9C.3, which shows isocost lines for total costs of $3,000, $6,000, and $9,000. We have shown only three isocost lines in the graph, but there is, in fact, a different isocost line for each level of total cost.

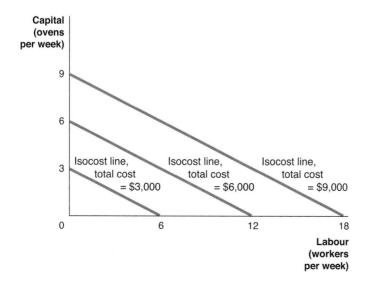

Figure 9C.3

The Position of the Isocost Line

The position of the isocost line depends on the level of total cost. As total cost increases from $3,000 to $6,000 to $9,000 per week, the isocost line shifts outward. For each isocost line shown, the rental price of ovens is $1,000 per week, and the wage rate is $500 per week.

Choosing the Cost-Minimizing Combination of Capital and Labour

Suppose Jill wants to produce 5,000 pizzas per week. Figure 9C.1 shows that there are many combinations of ovens and workers that will allow Jill to produce this level of output. There is only one combination of ovens and workers, however, that will allow her to produce 5,000 pizzas *at the lowest total cost*. Figure 9C.4 shows the isoquant $Q = 5,000$ along with three isocost lines. Point B is the lowest-cost combination of inputs shown in the graph, but this combination of 1 oven and 4 workers will produce fewer than the 5,000 pizzas needed. Points C and D are combinations of ovens and workers that will produce 5,000 pizzas, but their total cost is $9,000. The combination of 3 ovens and 6 workers at point A produces 5,000 pizzas at the lowest total cost of $6,000.

Figure 9C.4 shows that moving to an isocost line with a total cost of less than $6,000 would mean producing fewer than 5,000 pizzas. Being at any point along the isoquant $Q = 5,000$ other than point A would increase total cost above $6,000. In fact, the combination of inputs at point A is the only one on isoquant $Q = 5,000$ that has a total cost of $6,000. All other input combinations on this isoquant have higher total costs. Notice also that at point A, the isoquant and the isocost lines are tangent, so the slope of the isoquant is equal to the slope of the isocost line at that point.

Different Input Price Ratios Lead to Different Input Choices

Jill's cost-minimizing choice of 3 ovens and 6 workers is determined jointly by the technology available to her—as represented by her firm's isoquants—and by input prices—as represented by her firm's isocost lines. If the technology of making pizzas changes, perhaps because new ovens are developed, her isoquants will be affected, and her choice of inputs may change. If her isoquants remain unchanged but input prices change, then her choice of inputs may also change. This fact can explain why firms in different countries that face different input prices may produce the same good using different combinations of capital and labour, even though they have the same technology available.

For example, suppose that in China, pizza ovens are higher priced and labour is lower priced than in Canada. In our example, Jill Johnson pays $1,000 per week to rent pizza ovens and $500 per week to hire workers. Suppose a businessperson in China must pay a price of $1,500 per week to rent the identical pizza ovens but can hire Chinese workers who are as productive as Canadian workers at a wage of $300 per week. Figure 9C.5 shows how the cost-minimizing input combination for the businessperson in China differs from Jill's.

Figure 9C.4

Choosing Capital and Labour to Minimize Total Cost

Jill wants to produce 5,000 pizzas per week at the lowest total cost. Point B is the lowest-cost combination of inputs shown in the graph, but this combination of 1 oven and 4 workers will produce fewer than the 5,000 pizzas needed. Points C and D are combinations of ovens and workers that will produce 5,000 pizzas, but their total cost is $9,000. The combination of 3 ovens and 6 workers at point A produces 5,000 pizzas at the lowest total cost of $6,000.

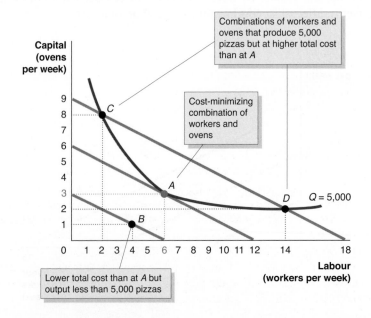

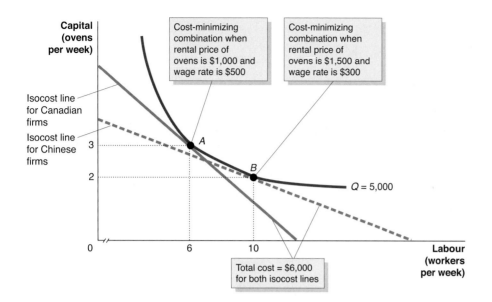

Figure 9C.5

Changing Input Prices Affects the Cost-Minimizing Input Choice

As the graph shows, the input combination at point *A*, which was optimal for Jill, is not optimal for a businessperson in China. Using the input combination at point *A* would cost businesspeople in China more than $6,000. Instead, the Chinese isocost line is tangent to the isoquant at point *B*, where the input combination is 2 ovens and 10 workers. Because ovens cost more in China but workers cost less, a Chinese firm will use fewer ovens and more workers than a Canadian firm, even if it has the same technology as the Canadian firm.

Remember that the slope of the isocost line equals the wage rate divided by the rental price of capital multiplied by 21. The slope of the isocost line that Jill and other Canadian firms face is −$500/$1,000, or −1/2. Firms in China, however, face an isocost line with a slope of −$300/$1,500, or −1/5. As Figure 9C.5 shows, the input combination at point *A*, which was optimal for Jill, is not optimal for a firm in China. Using the input combination at point *A* would cost a firm in China more than $6,000. Instead, the Chinese isocost line is tangent to the isoquant at point *B*, where the input combination is 2 ovens and 10 workers. This result makes sense: Because ovens cost more in China, but workers cost less, a Chinese firm will use fewer ovens and more workers than a Canadian. firm, even if it has the same technology as the Canadian. firm.

Making the Connection | The Changing Input Mix in Walt Disney Film Animation

The inputs used to make feature-length animated films have changed dramatically in the past 15 years. Prior to the early 1990s, the Walt Disney Company dominated the market for animated films. Disney's films were produced using hundreds of animators drawing most of the film by hand. Each film would contain as many as 170,000 individual drawings. Then, two developments dramatically affected how animated films are produced. First, in 1994, Disney had a huge hit with *The Lion King*, which cost only $50 million but earned the company more than $1 billion in profit. As a result of this success, Disney and other film studios began to produce more animated films, increasing the demand for animators and more than doubling their salaries. The second development came in 1995, when Pixar Animation Studios released the film *Toy Story*. This was the first successful feature-length film produced using computers, with no hand-drawn animation. In the following years, technological advance continued to reduce the cost of the computers and software necessary to produce an animated film.

As a result of these two developments, the price of capital—computers and software—fell relative to the price of labour—animators. As the figure shows, the change in the price of computers relative to animators changed the slope of the isocost line and resulted in film studios now producing animated films using many more computers and many fewer animators than in the early 1990s. In 2006, Disney bought Pixar, and within a few years, all the major film studios had converted to computer animation, now referred to as CGI animation, although a few hand-drawn films, such as Disney's film *Winnie the Pooh* released in 2011, continued to be produced.

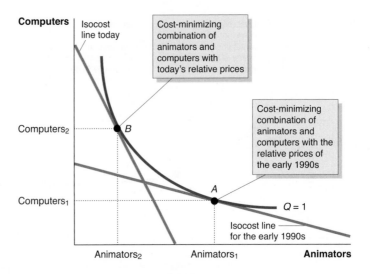

Based on "Magic Restored," *Economist*, April 17, 2008; and Laura M. Holson, "Disney Moves Away from Hand-Drawn Animation," *New York Times*, September 18, 2005.

MyEconLab   **Your Turn:** Test your understanding by doing related problem 9C.8 on page 287 at the end of this appendix.

Another Look at Cost Minimization

Consumers maximize utility when they consume each good up to the point where the marginal utility per dollar spent is the same for every good. We can derive a very similar cost-minimization rule for firms. Remember that at the point of cost minimization, the isoquant and the isocost line are tangent, so they have the same slope. Therefore, *at the point of cost minimization, the marginal rate of technical substitution* (MRTS) *is equal to the wage rate divided by the rental price of capital.*

The slope of the isoquant tells us the rate at which a firm is able to substitute labour for capital, *given existing technology.* The slope of the isocost line tells us the rate at which a firm is able to substitute labour for capital, *given current input prices.* Only at the point of cost minimization are these two rates the same.

When we move from one point on an isoquant to another, we end up using more of one input and less of the other input, but the level of output remains the same. For example, as Jill moves down an isoquant, she uses fewer ovens and more workers but produces the same quantity of pizzas. The *marginal product of labour* (MP_L) is the additional output produced by a firm as a result of hiring one more worker. Similarly, we can define the *marginal product of capital* (MP_K) as the additional output produced by a firm as a result of using one more machine. So, when Jill uses fewer ovens by moving down an isoquant, she loses output equal to:

$$-\text{Change in the quantity of ovens} \times MP_K.$$

But she uses more workers, so she gains output equal to:

$$\text{Change in the quantity of workers} \times MP_L.$$

We know that the gain in output from the additional workers is equal to the loss from the smaller quantity of ovens because total output remains the same along an isoquant. Therefore, we can write:

$$-\text{Change in the quantity of ovens} \times MP_K = \text{Change in the quantity of workers} \times MP_L.$$

If we rearrange terms, we have the following:

$$\frac{-\text{Change in the quantity of ovens}}{\text{Change in the quantity of workers}} = \frac{MP_L}{MP_K}.$$

Because

$$\frac{-\text{Change in the quantity of ovens}}{\text{Change in the quantity of workers}}$$

is the slope of the isoquant, it is equal to the marginal rate of technical substitution (multiplied by -1). So, we can write:

$$\frac{-\text{Change in the quantity of ovens}}{\text{Change in the quantity of workers}} = MRTS = \frac{MP_L}{MP_K}.$$

The slope of the isocost line equals the wage rate (w) divided by the rental price of capital (r). We saw earlier in this appendix that at the point of cost minimization, the *MRTS* equals the ratio of the prices of the two inputs. Therefore:

$$\frac{MP_L}{MP_K} = \frac{w}{r}.$$

We can rewrite this to show that at the point of cost minimization:

$$\frac{MP_L}{w} = \frac{MP_K}{r}.$$

This last expression tells us that to minimize cost for a given level of output, a firm should hire inputs up to the point where the last dollar spent on each input results in the same increase in output. If this equality did not hold, a firm could lower its costs by using more of one input and less of the other. For example, if the left side of the equation were greater than the right side, a firm could rent fewer ovens, hire more workers, and produce the same output at lower cost.

Solved Problem **9C.1**

Determining the Optimal Combination of Inputs

Consider the information in the following table for Jill Johnson's restaurant.

Marginal product of capital	3,000 pizzas per oven
Marginal product of labour	1,200 pizzas per worker
Wage rate	$300 per week
Rental price of ovens	$600 per week

Briefly explain whether Jill is minimizing costs. If she is not minimizing costs, explain whether she should rent more ovens and hire fewer workers or rent fewer ovens and hire more workers.

Solving the Problem

Step 1: Review the appendix material. This problem is about determining the optimal choice of inputs by comparing the ratios of the marginal products of inputs to their prices, so you may want to review the section "Another Look at Cost Minimization."

Step 2: Compute the ratios of marginal product to input price to determine whether Jill is minimizing costs. If Jill is minimizing costs, the following relationship should hold:

$$\frac{MP_L}{w} = \frac{MP_K}{r}.$$

In this case, we have

$$MP_L = 1,200$$

$$MP_K = 3,000$$

$$w = \$300$$

$$r = \$600.$$

So

$$\frac{MP_L}{w} = \frac{1,200}{\$300} = 4 \text{ pizzas per dollar, and } \frac{MP_K}{r} = \frac{3,000}{\$600} = 5 \text{ pizzas per dollar.}$$

Because the two ratios are not equal, Jill is not minimizing cost.

Step 3: Determine how Jill should change the mix of inputs she uses. Jill produces more pizzas per dollar from the last oven than from the last worker. This indicates that she has too many workers and too few ovens. Therefore, to minimize cost, Jill should use more ovens and hire fewer workers.

MyEconLab **Your Turn:** For more practice, do related problems 9C.3 and 9C.4 on page 286 at the end of this appendix.

Did new rules keep the Carolina Panthers from paying Cam Newton too much?

Making the Connection | **Do National Football League Teams Behave Efficiently?**

In the National Football League (NFL), the "salary cap" is the maximum amount each team can spend in a year on salaries for football players. Each year's salary cap results from negotiations between the league and the union representing the players. To achieve efficiency, an NFL team should distribute salaries among players so as to maximize the level of output—in this case, winning football games—given the constant level of cost represented by the salary cap. (Notice that maximizing the level of output for a given level of cost is equivalent to minimizing cost for a given level of output. To see why, think about the situation in which an isocost line is tangent to an isoquant. At the point of tangency, the firm has simultaneously minimized the cost of producing the level of output represented by the isoquant and maximized the output produced at the level of cost represented by the isocost line.)

In distributing salaries, teams should equalize the marginal productivity of players, as represented by their contribution to winning games to the salaries paid. Just as a firm may not use a machine that has a very high marginal product if its rental price is very high, a football team may not want to hire a superstar player if the salary the team would need to pay is too high.

Economists Cade Massey and Richard Thaler have analyzed whether NFL teams distribute their salaries efficiently. NFL teams obtain their players either by signing free agents—who are players whose contracts with other teams have expired—or by signing players chosen in the annual draft of eligible college players. The college draft consists of seven rounds, with the teams with the worst records the previous year choosing first. Massey and Thaler find that, in fact, NFL teams do not allocate salaries efficiently. In particular, the players chosen with the first few picks of the first round of the draft tend to be paid salaries that are much higher relative to their marginal products than are players taken later in the first round. A typical team with a high draft pick would increase its ability to win football games at the constant cost represented by the salary cap if it traded for lower draft picks. Why do NFL teams apparently make the error of not efficiently distributing salaries? Massey and Thaler argue that general managers of NFL teams tend to be overconfident in their ability to forecast how well a college player is likely to perform in the NFL.

General managers of NFL teams are not alone in suffering from overconfidence. Studies have shown that, in general, people tend to overestimate their ability to forecast an uncertain outcome. Because NFL teams tend to overestimate the future marginal productivity of high draft picks, they pay them salaries that are inefficiently high compared to salaries other draft picks receive. NFL teams were aware that they were probably overpaying high draft picks. In 2011, they negotiated a new contract with the NFL Players Union that limited the salaries that drafted players could receive.

This example shows that economic concepts provide powerful tools for analyzing whether firms are operating efficiently.

Based on Cade Massey and Richard Thaler, "The Loser's Curse: Overconfidence vs. Market Efficiency in the National Football League Draft," National Bureau of Economic Research Working Paper 11270, April 8, 2010.

Your Turn: Test your understanding by doing related problem 9C.10 on page 287 at the end of this appendix.

MyEconLab

The Expansion Path

We can use isoquants and isocost lines to examine what happens as a firm expands its level of output. Figure 9C.6 shows three isoquants for a firm that produces bookcases. The isocost lines are drawn under the assumption that the machines used in producing bookcases can be rented for $100 per day and the wage rate is $25 per day. The point where each isoquant is tangent to an isocost line determines the cost-minimizing combination of capital and labour for producing that level of output. For example, 10 machines and 40 workers is the cost-minimizing combination of inputs for producing 50 bookcases per day. The cost-minimizing points A, B, and C lie along the firm's **expansion path**, which is a curve that shows the cost-minimizing combination of inputs for every level of output.

An important point to note is that the expansion path represents the least-cost combination of inputs to produce a given level of output *in the long run*, when the firm is able to vary the levels of all of its inputs. We know, though, that in the short run, at least one input is fixed. We can use Figure 9C.6 to show that as the firm expands in the short run, its costs will be higher than in the long run. For example, suppose that the firm is currently at point B, using 15 machines and 60 workers to produce 75 bookcases per day. The firm wants to expand its output to 100 bookcases per day, but in the short run, it is unable to increase the quantity of machines it uses. Therefore, to expand output, it must hire more workers. The figure shows that in the short run, to produce 100 bookcases per day using 15 machines, the lowest costs it can attain are at point D, where it employs 110 workers. With a rental price of machines of $100 per day and a wage rate of $25 per day, in the short run, the firm will have total costs of $4,250 to produce

Expansion path A curve that shows a firm's cost-minimizing combination of inputs for every level of output.

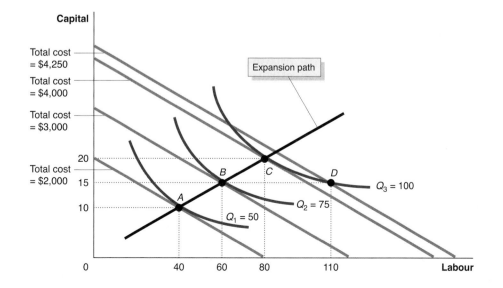

Figure 9C.6

The Expansion Path

The tangency points A, B, and C lie along the firm's expansion path, which is a curve that shows the cost-minimizing combination of inputs for every level of output. In the short run, when the quantity of machines is fixed, the firm can expand output from 75 bookcases per day to 100 bookcases per day at the lowest cost only by moving from point B to point D and increasing the number of workers from 60 to 110. In the long run, when it can increase the quantity of machines it uses, the firm can move from point D to point C, thereby reducing its total costs of producing 100 bookcases per day from $4,250 to $4,000.

100 bookcases per day. In the long run, though, the firm can increase the number of machines it uses from 15 to 20 and reduce the number of workers from 110 to 80. This change allows it to move from point *D* to point *C* on its expansion path and to lower its total costs of producing 100 bookcases per day from $4,250 to $4,000. The firm's minimum total costs of production are lower in the long run than in the short run.

Key Terms

Expansion path, p. 285

Isocost line, p. 278

Isoquant, p. 277

Marginal rate of technical substitution (*MRTS*), p. 278

MyEconLab   Log in to MyEconLab to complete these exercises and get instant feedback.

LO Use isoquants and isocost lines to understand production and cost.

Review Questions

9C.1 What is an isoquant? What is the slope of an isoquant?

9C.2 What is an isocost line? What is the slope of an isocost line?

9C.3 How do firms choose the optimal combination of inputs?

Problems and Applications

9C.1 Draw an isoquant–isocost line graph to illustrate the following situation: Jill Johnson can rent pizza ovens for $400 per week and hire workers for $200 per week. She is currently using 5 ovens and 10 workers to produce 20,000 pizzas per week and has total costs of $4,000. Make sure to label your graph to show the cost-minimizing input combination and the maximum quantity of labour and capital she can use with total costs of $4,000.

9C.2 Use the following graph to answer the questions.

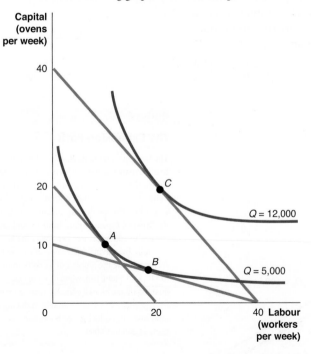

a. If the wage rate and the rental price of ovens are both $100 and total cost is $2,000, is the cost-minimizing point *A*, *B*, or *C*? Briefly explain.

b. If the wage rate is $25, the rental price of ovens is $100, and total cost is $1,000, is the cost-minimizing point *A*, *B*, or *C*? Briefly explain.

c. If the wage rate and the rental price of ovens are both $100 and total cost is $4,000, is the cost-minimizing point *A*, *B*, or *C*? Briefly explain.

9C.3 [**Related to** Solved Problem 9C.1 **on page 283**] Consider the information in the following table for Jill Johnson's restaurant.

Marginal product of capital	4,000
Marginal product of labour	100
Wage rate	$10
Rental price of pizza ovens	$500

Briefly explain whether Jill is minimizing costs. If she is not minimizing costs, explain whether she should rent more ovens and hire fewer workers or rent fewer ovens and hire more workers.

9C.4 [**Related to** Solved Problem 9C.1 **on page 283**] Draw an isoquant–isocost line graph to illustrate the following situation: Jill Johnson can rent pizza ovens for $200 per week and hire workers for $100 per week. Currently, she is using 5 ovens and 10 workers to produce 20,000 pizzas per week and has total costs of $2,000. Jill's marginal rate of technical substitution (*MRTS*) equals 21. Explain why this means that she's not minimizing costs and what she could do to minimize costs.

9C.5 Draw an isoquant–isocost line graph to illustrate the following situation and the change that occurs: Jill Johnson can rent pizza ovens for $2,000 per week and hire workers for $1,000 per week. Currently, she is using 5 ovens and 10 workers to produce 20,000 pizzas per week and has total costs of $20,000. Then Jill reorganizes the way things are done in her business and achieves positive technological change.

9C.6 Use the graph below to answer the following questions about Jill Johnson's isoquant curve.
  a. Which combination of inputs yields more output: combination *A* (3 ovens and 2 workers) or combination *B* (2 ovens and 3 workers)?
  b. What will determine whether Jill selects *A*, *B*, or some other point along this isoquant curve?
  c. Is the marginal rate of technical substitution (*MRTS*) greater at point *A* or point *B*?

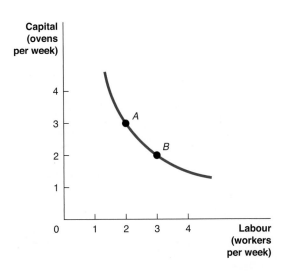

9C.7 Draw an isoquant–isocost line graph to illustrate the following situation: Jill Johnson can rent pizza ovens for $2,000 per week and hire workers for $1,000 per week. She can minimize the cost of producing 20,000 pizzas per week by using 5 ovens and 10 workers, at a total cost of $20,000. She can minimize the cost of producing 45,000 pizzas per week by using 10 ovens and 20 workers, at a total cost of $40,000. She can minimize the cost of producing 60,000 pizzas per week by using 15 ovens and 30 workers, at a total cost of $60,000. Draw Jill's long-run average cost curve and discuss its economies of scale and diseconomies of scale.

9C.8 [**Related to the** Making the Connection **on page 281**] In Brazil, a grove of oranges is picked using 20 workers, ladders, and baskets. In Florida, a grove of oranges is picked using 1 worker and a machine that shakes the oranges off the trees and scoops up the fallen oranges. Using an isoquant–isocost line graph, illustrate why these two different methods are used to pick the same number of oranges per day in these two locations.

9C.9 Jill Johnson is minimizing the costs of producing pizzas. The rental price of one of her ovens is $2,000 per week, and the wage rate is $600 per week. The marginal product of capital in her business is 12,000 pizzas. What must be the marginal product of her workers?

9C.10 [**Related to the** Making the Connection **on page 284**] If Cade Massey and Richard Thaler are correct, should the team that has the first pick in the draft keep the pick or trade it to another team for a lower pick? Briefly explain. Does the 2011 agreement that limits the salaries of drafted players affect your answer?

10

Firms in Perfectly Competitive Markets

© Bill Brooks/Alamy

Chapter Outline and Learning Objectives

Perfect Competition in Farmers' Markets

In recent years, the demand for healthier foods has increased. Sales of organically grown food have increased at a rate of about 20 percent per year. Many people have also begun buying their fruits and vegetables at farmers' markets. At these markets, local farmers come together at a fairground, a city plaza, or some other open space to sell their produce directly to consumers. The advantage to farmers is that they can receive a higher price than they would if they sold their produce to supermarkets. Many consumers prefer to buy from farmers' markets because they believe the produce to be fresher, of higher quality, and healthier or because they want to support local farmers.

According to Farmers' Markets Canada (a national organization dedicated to promoting the growth of the Canadian farmers' market industry), farmers' markets are a great success story. They produce over $1 billion in annual sales, for a total economic impact of about $3 billion. The website www.farmersandfleamarkets.ca lists all of the Canadian cities with active farmers' markets, and includes hundreds of listings from all ten provinces and all three territories.

Not all of the effects have been good, however. The success of farmers' markets has led to problems of parking, increased labour costs, and an increased number of resellers (non-farmers). All of these factors contribute to the profits of the primary producers.

The process of new firms entering a profitable market and driving down prices and profits is not unique to agriculture. Throughout the economy, entrepreneurs are continually introducing new products or new ways of selling products, which—when successful—enable them to earn economic profits in the short run. But in the long run, competition among firms forces prices to the level where they just cover the costs of production. This process of competition is at the heart of the market system and is the focus of this chapter.

AN INSIDE LOOK on **page 314** discusses the steady decline in production and sales of organic food in the United Kingdom after 2008.

Based on http://www.farmersmarketscanada.ca /Upload/files/FMC%20FINAL%20Brochure%202009 -ENG.pdf; http://www.farmersandfleamarkets.ca /provinces.php; and http://www.newswire.ca/en /story/442441/farmers-markets-are-big-business

Economics in Your Life

Are You an Entrepreneur?

Were you an entrepreneur during your high school years? Perhaps you didn't have your own store, but you may have worked as a babysitter, or perhaps you mowed lawns for families in your neighbourhood. While you may not think of these jobs as being small businesses, that is exactly what they are. How did you decide what price to charge for your services? You may have wanted to charge $25 per hour to babysit or mow lawns, but you probably charged much less. As you read the chapter, think about the competitive situation you faced as a teenaged entrepreneur and try to determine why the prices received by most people who babysit and mow lawns are so low. You can check your answers against those we provide on page 313 at the end of this chapter.

F armers' markets are an example of a *perfectly competitive* industry. Firms in perfectly competitive industries are unable to control the prices of the products they sell and are unable to earn an economic profit in the long run for two main reasons: Firms in these industries sell identical products, and it is easy for new firms to enter these industries. Studying how perfectly competitive industries operate is the best way to understand how markets answer the fundamental economic questions:

- What goods and services will be produced?

- How will the goods and services be produced?

- Who will receive the goods and services produced?

In fact, though, most industries are not perfectly competitive. In most industries, firms do *not* produce identical products, and in some industries, it may be difficult for new firms to enter. There are thousands of industries in Canada. Although in some ways each industry is unique, industries share enough similarities that economists group them into four market structures. In particular, any industry has three key characteristics:

1. The number of firms in the industry

2. The similarity of the good or service produced by the firms in the industry

3. The ease with which new firms can enter the industry

Economists use these characteristics to classify industries into the four market structures listed in Table 10.1.

Many industries, including restaurants, clothing stores, and other retailers, have a large number of firms selling products that are differentiated, rather than identical, and fall into the category of *monopolistic competition*. Some industries, such as computers and automobiles, have only a few firms and are *oligopolies*. Finally, a few industries, such as the delivery of mail by Canada Post, have only one firm and are *monopolies*. After discussing perfect competition in this chapter, we will devote a chapter to each of these other market structures.

Table 10.1

The Four Market Structures

	Market Structure			
Characteristic	Perfect Competition	Monopolistic Competition	Oligopoly	Monopoly
Number of firms	Many	Many	Few	One
Type of product	Identical	Differentiated	Identical or differentiated	Unique
Ease of entry	Free entry	Free entry	Low	Entry blocked
Examples of industries	• Wheat farmers • Apple producers	• Clothing stores • Restaurants	• Airlines • Auto industry	• Mail • Tap water

Perfectly Competitive Markets

Why are firms in a **perfectly competitive market** unable to control the prices of the goods they sell, and why are the owners of these firms unable to earn economic profit in the long run? We can begin our analysis by listing the three conditions that make a market perfectly competitive:

1. There must be many sellers and many firms, all of which are small relative to the market.
2. The products sold by all firms in the market must be identical.
3. There must be no barriers to new firms entering the market.

All three of these conditions hold in markets for agricultural products. For example, no single consumer or producer of apples buys or sells more than a tiny fraction of the total apple crop. The apples sold by each apple grower are identical, and there are no barriers to a new firm entering the apple market by purchasing land and planting apple trees. As we will see, it is the existence of many firms, all selling the same good, that keeps any single apple farmer from affecting the price of apples.

Although the market for apples meets the conditions for perfect competition, the markets for most goods and services do not. In particular, the second and third conditions are very restrictive. In most markets that have many buyers and sellers, firms do not sell identical products. For example, not all restaurant meals are the same, nor is all women's clothing the same. In Chapter 11, we will explore the common situation of monopolistic competition where many firms are selling similar but not identical products. In Chapters 12 and 13, we will analyze industries that are oligopolies or monopolies, where it is difficult for new firms to enter. In this chapter, we concentrate on perfectly competitive markets so we can use them as a benchmark to analyze how firms behave when facing strong competitive conditions.

A Perfectly Competitive Firm Cannot Affect the Market Price

Prices in perfectly competitive markets are determined by the interaction of demand and supply for the good or service. The actions of any single consumer or any single firm have no effect on the market price. Consumers and firms have to accept the market price if they want to buy and sell in a perfectly competitive market.

Because a firm in a perfectly competitive market is very small relative to the market and because it is selling exactly the same product as every other firm, it can sell as much as it wants without having to lower its price. But if a perfectly competitive firm tries to raise its price, it won't sell anything at all because consumers will switch to buying the product from the firm's competitors. Therefore, the firm will be a **price taker** and will have to charge the same price as every other firm in the market. Although we don't usually think of firms as being too small to affect the market price, consumers are often in the position of being price takers. For instance, suppose your local supermarket is selling bread for $1.50 per loaf. You can load up your shopping cart with 10 loaves of bread, and the supermarket will gladly sell them all to you for $1.50 per loaf. But if you go to the cashier and offer to buy the bread for $1.49 per loaf, he or she will not sell it to you at that price. As a buyer, you are too small relative to the bread market to have any effect on the equilibrium price. Whether you leave the supermarket and buy no bread or you buy 10 loaves, you are unable to change the market price of bread by even 1 cent.

The situation you face as a bread buyer is the same one a wheat farmer faces as a wheat seller. In 2011, about 52,000 farmers grew wheat in Canada. The market price of wheat is determined not by any individual wheat farmer but by the interaction in the wheat market of all the buyers and all the sellers. If any one wheat farmer has the best crop the farmer has ever had, or if any one wheat farmer stops growing wheat altogether, the market price of wheat will not be affected *because the market supply curve for wheat will not shift by enough to change the equilibrium price by even 1 cent.*

10.1 LEARNING OBJECTIVE

Explain what a perfectly competitive market is and why a perfect competitor faces a horizontal demand curve.

Perfectly competitive market A market that meets the conditions of (1) many sellers, (2) all firms selling identical products, and (3) no barriers to new firms entering the market.

Price taker A buyer or seller that is unable to affect the market price.

A Perfectly Competitive Firm Faces a Horizontal Demand Curve

A firm in a perfectly competitive market is selling exactly the same product as many other firms. Therefore, it can sell as much as it wants at the current market price, but it cannot sell anything at all if it raises the price by even 1 cent. As a result, the demand curve for a perfectly competitive firm's output is a horizontal line. In the figure, whether the wheat farmer sells 6,000 bushels per year or 20,000 bushels has no effect on the market price of $4.

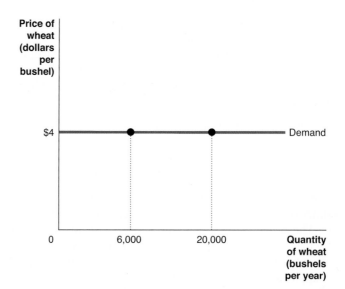

The Demand Curve for the Output of a Perfectly Competitive Firm

Suppose Bill Parker grows wheat on a 100-hectare farm in Saskatchewan. Farmer Parker is selling wheat in a perfectly competitive market, so he is a price taker. Because he can sell as much wheat as he chooses at the market price—but can't sell any wheat at all at a higher price—the demand curve for his wheat has an unusual shape: It is horizontal, as shown in Figure 10.1; that is, the demand curve the firm faces is perfectly elastic at the market price. With a horizontal demand curve, Farmer Parker must accept the market price, which in this case is $4 per bushel. Whether Farmer Parker sells 6,000 bushels per year or 20,000 has no effect on the market price.

The demand curve for Farmer Parker's wheat is very different from the market demand curve for wheat. Panel (a) of Figure 10.2 shows the market for wheat. The demand curve in panel (a) is the *market demand curve for wheat* and has the normal downward slope. Panel (b) of Figure 10.2 shows the demand curve for Farmer Parker's wheat, which is a horizontal line. By viewing these graphs side by side, you can see that the price Farmer Parker receives for his wheat in panel (b) is determined by the interaction of all sellers and all buyers of wheat in the wheat market in panel (a). Keep in mind,

Don't Let This Happen to You

Don't Confuse the Demand Curve for Farmer Parker's Wheat with the Market Demand Curve for Wheat

The demand curve for wheat has the normal downward-sloping shape. If the price of wheat goes up, the quantity of wheat demanded goes down, and if the price of wheat goes down, the quantity of wheat demanded goes up. But the demand curve for the output of a single wheat farmer is *not* downward sloping: It is a horizontal line. If an individual wheat farmer tries to increase the price he charges for his wheat, the quantity demanded falls to zero because buyers will purchase from one of the other 52,000 wheat farmers. But any one farmer can sell as much wheat as the farmer can produce without needing to cut the price. Both of these things are true because

each wheat farmer is very small relative to the overall market for wheat.

When we draw graphs of the wheat market, we usually show the market equilibrium quantity in millions or billions of bushels. When we draw graphs of the demand for wheat produced by one farmer, we usually show the quantity produced in smaller units, such as thousands of bushels. It is important to remember this difference in scale when interpreting these graphs.

Finally, it is not just wheat farmers who have horizontal demand curves for their products; any firm in a perfectly competitive market faces a horizontal demand curve.

MyEconLab

Your Turn: Test your understanding by doing related problem 1.3 on page 317 at the end of this chapter.

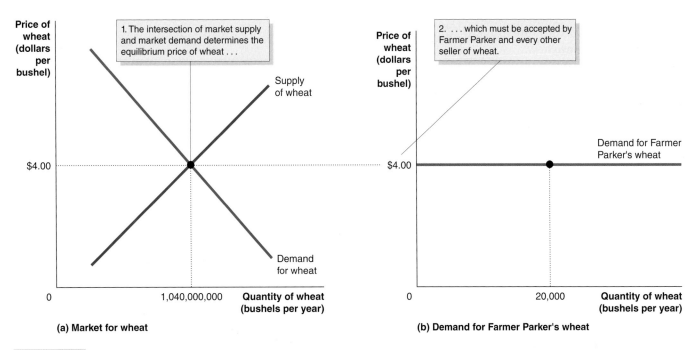

Figure 10.2 The Market Demand for Wheat versus the Demand for One Farmer's Wheat

In a perfectly competitive market, price is determined by the intersection of market demand and market supply. In panel (a), the demand and supply curves for wheat intersect at a price of $4 per bushel. An individual wheat farmer like Farmer Parker cannot affect the market price for wheat. Therefore, as panel (b) shows, the demand curve for Farmer Parker's wheat is a horizontal line. To understand this figure, it is important to notice that the scales on the horizontal axes in the two panels are very different. In panel (a), the equilibrium quantity of wheat is 1.04 *billion* bushels, and in panel (b), Farmer Parker is producing only 20,000 bushels of wheat.

however, that the scales on the horizontal axes in the two panels are very different. In panel (a), the equilibrium quantity of wheat is 1.04 *billion* bushels. In panel (b), Farmer Parker is producing only 20,000 bushels, or less than 0.001 percent of market output. We need to use different scales in the two panels so we can display both of them on one page. Keep in mind this key point: Farmer Parker's output of wheat is very small relative to the total market output.

How a Firm Maximizes Profit in a Perfectly Competitive Market

Explain how a firm maximizes profit in a perfectly competitive market.

We have seen that Farmer Parker cannot control the price of his wheat. In this situation, how does he decide how much wheat to produce? We assume that Farmer Parker's objective is to maximize profit. This is a reasonable assumption for most firms, most of the time. Remember that **profit** is the difference between total revenue (*TR*) and total cost (*TC*):

Profit Total revenue minus total cost.

$$\text{Profit} = TR - TC.$$

To maximize his profit, Farmer Parker should produce the quantity of wheat where the difference between the total revenue he receives and his total cost is as large as possible.

Revenue for a Firm in a Perfectly Competitive Market

To understand how Farmer Parker maximizes profits, let's first consider his revenue. To keep the numbers simple, we will assume that he owns a very small farm and produces at most 10 bushels of wheat per year. Table 10.2 shows the revenue Farmer Parker will earn from selling various quantities of wheat if the market price for wheat is $4.

Table 10.2

Farmer Parker's Revenue from Wheat Farming

Number of Bushels (Q)	Market Price (per bushel) (P)	Total Revenue (TR)	Average Revenue (AR)	Marginal Revenue (MR)
0	$4	$0	—	—
1	4	4	$ 4	$ 4
2	4	8	4	4
3	4	12	4	4
4	4	16	4	4
5	4	20	4	4
6	4	24	4	4
7	4	28	4	4
8	4	32	4	4
9	4	36	4	4
10	4	40	4	4

Average revenue (AR) Total revenue divided by the quantity of the product sold.

The third column in Table 10.2 shows that Farmer Parker's *total revenue* rises by $4 for every additional bushel he sells because he can sell as many bushels as he wants at the market price of $4 per bushel. The fourth and fifth columns in the table show Farmer Parker's *average revenue* and *marginal revenue* from selling wheat. His **average revenue (AR)** is his total revenue divided by the quantity of bushels he sells. For example, if he sells 5 bushels for a total of $20, his average revenue is 20/5 = 4. Notice that his average revenue is also equal to the market price of $4. In fact, for any level of output, a firm's average revenue is always equal to the market price. This equality holds because total revenue equals price times quantity ($TR = P \times Q$), and average revenue equals total revenue divided by quantity ($AR = TR/Q$). So, $AR = TR/Q = (P \times Q)/Q = P$.

Marginal revenue (MR) The change in total revenue from selling one more unit of a product.

Farmer Parker's **marginal revenue (MR)** is the change in his total revenue from selling one more bushel:

$$\text{Marginal revenue} = \frac{\text{Change in total revenue}}{\text{Change in quantity}}, \text{or } MR = \frac{\Delta TR}{\Delta Q}.$$

Because for each additional bushel sold, Farmer Parker always adds $4 to his total revenue, his marginal revenue is $4. Farmer Parker's marginal revenue is $4 per bushel because he is selling wheat in a perfectly competitive market and can sell as much as he wants at the market price. In fact, Farmer Parker's marginal revenue and average revenue are both equal to the market price. This is an important point: *For a firm in a perfectly competitive market, price is equal to both average revenue and marginal revenue.*

Determining the Profit-Maximizing Level of Output

To determine how Farmer Parker can maximize profit, we have to consider his costs as well as his revenue. A wheat farmer has many costs, including the cost of seed and fertilizer, as well as the wages of farm workers. In Table 10.3, we bring together the revenue data from Table 10.2 with cost data for Farmer Parker's farm. Recall that a firm's *marginal cost* is the increase in total cost resulting from producing another unit of output.

We calculate profit in the fourth column by subtracting total cost in the third column from total revenue in the second column. The fourth column shows that as long as Farmer Parker produces between 2 and 8 bushels of wheat, he will earn a profit. His maximum profit is $7.50, which he will earn by producing 6 bushels of wheat. Because Farmer Parker wants to maximize his profits, we would expect him to produce 6 bushels of wheat. Producing more than 6 bushels reduces his profit. For example, if he produces 7 bushels of wheat, his profit will decline from $7.50 to $6.50. The values for marginal cost given in the last column of the table help us understand why Farmer Parker's profits will decline if he produces more than 6 bushels of wheat: After the sixth bushel of wheat, rising marginal cost causes Farmer Parker's profits to fall.

In fact, comparing the marginal cost and marginal revenue at each level of output is an alternative method of calculating Farmer Parker's profits. We illustrate the two methods of

Quantity (bushels) (Q)	Total Revenue (TR)	Total Cost (TC)	Profit (TR − TC)	Marginal Revenue (MR)	Marginal Cost (MC)
0	$ 0.00	$ 2.00	−$ 2.00	—	—
1	4.00	5.00	−1.00	$ 4.00	$ 3.00
2	8.00	7.00	1.00	4.00	2.00
3	12.00	8.50	3.50	4.00	1.50
4	16.00	10.50	5.50	4.00	2.00
5	20.00	13.00	7.00	4.00	2.50
6	24.00	16.50	7.50	4.00	3.50
7	28.00	21.50	6.50	4.00	5.00
8	32.00	28.50	3.50	4.00	7.00
9	36.00	38.00	−2.00	4.00	9.50
10	40.00	50.50	−10.50	4.00	12.50

Table 10.3

Farmer Parker's Profits from Wheat Farming

calculating profits in Figure 10.3. We show the total revenue and total cost approach in panel (a) and the marginal revenue and marginal cost approach in panel (b). Total revenue is a straight line on the graph in panel (a) because total revenue increases at a constant rate of $4 for each additional bushel sold. Farmer Parker's profits are maximized when the vertical distance between the line representing total revenue and the total cost curve is as large as possible. Just as we saw in Table 10.3, his maximum profit occurs at an output of 6 bushels.

The last two columns of Table 10.3 show the marginal revenue (MR) Farmer Parker receives from selling another bushel of wheat and his marginal cost (MC) of producing another bushel of wheat. Panel (b) of Figure 10.3 is a graph of Farmer Parker's marginal revenue and marginal cost. The marginal revenue is the slope of the total revenue line in Figure 10.3, and the marginal cost is the slope of the total cost curve in the same figure. Because marginal revenue is always equal to $4, it is a horizontal line at the market price. We have already seen that the demand curve for a perfectly competitive firm is

(a) Total revenue, total cost, and profit

(b) Marginal revenue and marginal cost

Figure 10.3 The Profit-Maximizing Level of Output

In panel (a), Farmer Parker maximizes his profit where the vertical distance between total revenue and total cost is the largest. This happens at an output of 6 bushels. Panel (b) shows that Farmer Parker's marginal revenue (MR) is equal to a constant $4 per bushel. Farmer Parker maximizes profits by producing wheat up to the point where the marginal revenue of the last bushel produced is equal to its marginal cost, or MR = MC.

In this case, at no level of output does marginal revenue exactly equal marginal cost. The closest Farmer Parker can come is to produce 6 bushels of wheat. He will not want to continue to produce once marginal cost is greater than marginal revenue because that would reduce his profits. Panels (a) and (b) show alternative ways of thinking about how Farmer Parker can determine the profit-maximizing quantity of wheat to produce.

also a horizontal line at the market price. *Therefore, the marginal revenue curve for a perfectly competitive firm is the same as its demand curve.* Farmer Parker's marginal cost of producing wheat first falls and then rises, following the usual pattern.

We know from panel (a) that profit is at a maximum at 6 bushels of wheat. In panel (b), profit is also at a maximum at 6 bushels of wheat. To understand why profit is maximized at the level of output where marginal revenue equals marginal cost, remember a key economic principle that we discussed in Chapter 1: *Optimal decisions are made at the margin.* Firms use this principle to decide what quantity of a good to produce. For example, in deciding how much wheat to produce, Farmer Parker needs to compare the marginal revenue he earns from selling another bushel of wheat to the marginal cost of producing that bushel. The difference between the marginal revenue and the marginal cost is the additional profit (or loss) from producing one more bushel. As long as marginal revenue is greater than marginal cost, Farmer Parker's profits are increasing, and he will want to expand production. For example, he will not stop producing at 5 bushels of wheat because producing and selling the sixth bushel adds $4.00 to his revenue but only $3.50 to his cost, so his profit increases by $0.50. He wants to continue producing until the marginal revenue he receives from selling another bushel is equal to the marginal cost of producing it. At that level of output, he will make no *additional* profit by selling another bushel, so he will have maximized his profits.

By inspecting Table 10.3 on page 295, we can see that there is no level of output at which marginal revenue exactly equals marginal cost. The closest Farmer Parker can come is to produce 6 bushels of wheat. He will not want to produce additional wheat once marginal cost is greater than marginal revenue because that would reduce his profits. For example, the seventh bushel of wheat adds $5.00 to his cost but only $4.00 to his revenue, so producing the seventh bushel *reduces* his profit by $1.00.

From the information in Table 10.3 and Figure 10.3, we can draw the following conclusions:

1. The profit-maximizing level of output is where the difference between total revenue and total cost is the greatest.
2. The profit-maximizing level of output is also where marginal revenue equals marginal cost, or $MR = MC$.

Both of these conclusions are true for any firm, whether or not it is in a perfectly competitive industry. We can draw one other conclusion about profit maximization that is true only of firms in perfectly competitive industries: For a firm in a perfectly competitive industry, price is equal to marginal revenue, or $P = MR$. So, we can restate the $MR = MC$ condition as $P = MC$.

10.3 LEARNING OBJECTIVE

Use graphs to show a firm's profit or loss.

Illustrating Profit or Loss on the Cost Curve Graph

Profit is the difference between total revenue and total cost. We can also express profit in terms of *average total cost* (*ATC*). This allows us to show profit on the cost curve graph.

To begin, we need to work through several steps to determine the relationship between profit and average total cost. Because profit is equal to total revenue minus total cost (*TC*) and total revenue is price times quantity, we can write the following:

$$\text{Profit} = (P \times Q) - TC.$$

If we divide both sides of this equation by Q, we have:

$$\frac{\text{Profit}}{Q} = \frac{(P \times Q)}{Q} - \frac{TC}{Q}$$

or

$$\frac{\text{Profit}}{Q} = P - ATC,$$

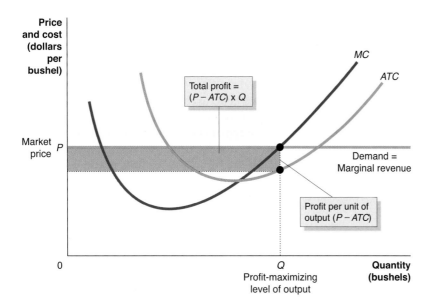

Figure 10.4

The Area of Maximum Profit

A firm maximizes profit at the level of output at which marginal revenue equals marginal cost. The difference between price and average total cost equals profit per unit of output. Total profit equals profit per unit multiplied by the number of units produced. Total profit is represented by the area of the green-shaded rectangle, which has a height equal to $(P - ATC)$ and a width equal to Q.

because TC/Q equals ATC. This equation tells us that profit per unit (or average profit) equals price minus average total cost. Finally, we obtain the equation for the relationship between total profit and average total cost by multiplying again by Q:

$$\text{Profit} = (P - ATC) \times Q.$$

This equation tells us that a firm's total profit is equal to the quantity produced multiplied by the difference between price and average total cost.

Showing a Profit on the Graph

Figure 10.4 shows the relationship between a firm's average total cost and its marginal cost. In this figure, we also show the firm's marginal revenue curve (which is the same as its demand curve) and the area representing total profit. Using the relationship between profit and average total cost that we just determined, we can say that the area representing total profit has a height equal to $(P - ATC)$ and a base equal to Q. This area is shown by the green-shaded rectangle.

Solved Problem **10.3**

Determining Profit-Maximizing Price and Quantity

Suppose that Andy sells wooden hockey sticks in the perfectly competitive hockey stick market. His output per day and his costs are as follows:

Output per Day	Total Cost
0	$10.00
1	20.50
2	24.50
3	28.50
4	34.00
5	43.00
6	55.50
7	72.00
8	93.00
9	119.00

a. Suppose the current equilibrium price in the hockey stick market is $12.50. To maximize profit, how many hockey sticks will Andy produce, what price will he charge, and how much profit (or loss) will he make? Draw a graph to illustrate your answer. Your graph should be labelled clearly and should include Andy's demand, ATC, AVC, MC, and MR curves; the price he is charging; the quantity he is producing; and the area representing his profit (or loss).

b. Suppose the equilibrium price of hockey sticks falls to $6.00. Now how many wooden hockey sticks will Andy produce, what price will he charge, and how much profit (or loss) will he make? Draw a graph to illustrate this situation, using the instructions in part (a).

Solving the Problem

Step 1: **Review the chapter material.** This problem is about using cost curve graphs to analyze perfectly competitive firms, so you may want to review the section "Illustrating Profit or Loss on the Cost Curve Graph" on page 296.

Step 2: **Calculate Andy's marginal cost, average total cost, and average variable cost.** To maximize profit, Andy will produce the level of output where marginal revenue is equal to marginal cost. We can calculate marginal cost from the information given in the table. We can also calculate average total cost and average variable cost in order to draw the required graph. Average total cost (ATC) equals total cost (TC) divided by the level of output (Q). Average variable cost (AVC) equals variable cost (VC) divided by output (Q). To calculate variable cost, recall that total cost equals variable cost plus fixed cost. When output equals zero, total cost equals fixed cost. In this case, fixed cost equals $10.00.

Output per Day (Q)	Total Cost (TC)	Fixed Cost (FC)	Variable Cost (VC)	Average Total Cost (ATC)	Average Variable Cost (AVC)	Marginal Cost (MC)
0	$10.00	$10.00	$0.00	—	—	—
1	20.50	10.00	10.50	$20.50	$10.50	$10.50
2	24.50	10.00	14.50	12.25	7.25	4.00
3	28.00	10.00	18.00	9.33	6.00	3.50
4	34.00	10.00	24.00	8.50	6.00	6.00
5	43.00	10.00	33.00	8.60	6.60	9.00
6	55.50	10.00	45.50	9.25	7.58	12.50
7	72.00	10.00	62.00	10.29	8.86	16.50
8	93.00	10.00	83.00	11.63	10.38	21.00
9	119.00	10.00	109.00	13.22	12.11	26.00

Step 3: **Use the information from the table in Step 2 to calculate how many hockey sticks Andy will produce, what price he will charge, and how much profit he will earn if the market price of hockey sticks is $12.50.** Andy's marginal revenue is equal to the market price of $12.50. Marginal revenue equals marginal cost when Andy produces 6 hockey sticks per day. So, Andy will produce 6 hockey sticks per day and charge a price of $12.50 per hockey stick. Andy's profits are equal to his total revenue minus his total costs. His total revenue equals the 6 hockey sticks he sells multiplied by the $12.50 price, or $75.00. So, his profit equals: $75.00 − $55.50 = $19.50.

Step 4: **Use the information from the table in Step 2 to illustrate your answer to part (a) with a graph.**

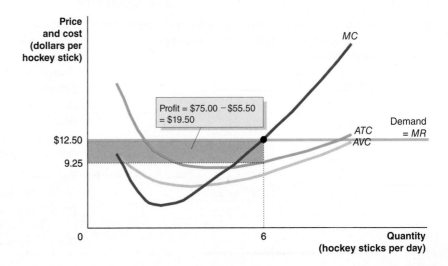

Step 5: **Calculate how many hockey sticks Andy will produce, what price he will charge, and how much profit he will earn when the market price of hockey sticks is $6.00.** Referring to the table in Step 2, we can see that marginal revenue equals marginal cost when Andy produces 4 hockey sticks per day. He charges the market price of $6.00 per hockey stick. His total revenue is only $24.00, while his total costs are $34.00, so he will have a loss of $10.00. (Can we be sure that Andy will continue to produce even though he is operating at a loss? We answer this question in the next section.)

Step 6: **Illustrate your answer to part (b) with a graph.**

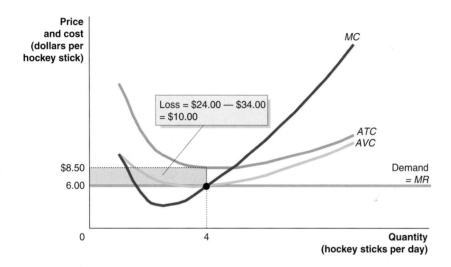

Your Turn: For more practice, do related problems 3.1 and 3.2 on pages 317 and 318 at the end of this chapter.

MyEconLab

Don't Let This Happen to You

Remember That Firms Maximize Their Total Profit, Not Their Profit per Unit

A student examines the following graph and argues, "I believe that a firm will want to produce at Q_1, not Q_2. At Q_1, the distance between price and average total cost is the greatest. Therefore, at Q_1, the firm will be maximizing its profit per unit." Briefly explain whether you agree with the student's argument.

The student's argument is incorrect because firms are interested in maximizing their *total* profit, not their profit per unit. We know that profit is not maximized at Q_1 because at that level of output, marginal revenue is greater than marginal cost. A firm can always increase its profit by producing any unit that adds more to its revenue than it does to its costs. Only when the firm has expanded production to Q_2 will it have produced every unit for which marginal revenue is greater than marginal cost. At that point, it will have maximized profit.

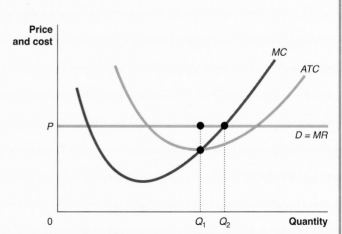

MyEconLab

Your Turn: Test your understanding by doing related problem 3.3 on page 318 at the end of this chapter.

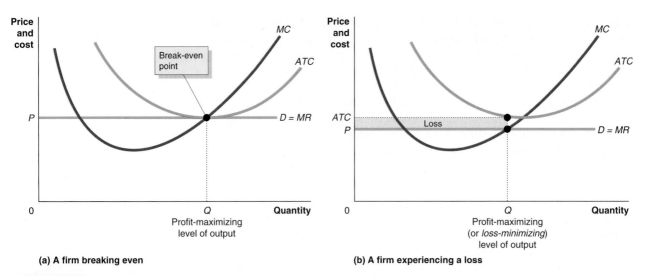

(a) A firm breaking even

(b) A firm experiencing a loss

Figure 10.5 **A Firm Breaking Even and a Firm Experiencing a Loss**

In panel (a), price equals average total cost, and the firm breaks even because its total revenue will be equal to its total cost. In this situation, the firm makes zero economic profit. In panel (b), price is below average total cost, and the firm experiences a loss. The loss is represented by the area of the red-shaded rectangle, which has a height equal to ($ATC - P$) and a width equal to Q.

Illustrating When a Firm Is Breaking Even or Operating at a Loss

We have already seen that to maximize profit, a firm produces the level of output where marginal revenue equals marginal cost. But will the firm actually make a profit at that level of output? It depends on the relationship of price to average total cost. There are three possibilities:

1. $P > ATC$, which means the firm makes a profit
2. $P = ATC$, which means the firm *breaks even* (its total cost equals its total revenue)
3. $P < ATC$, which means the firm experiences a loss

Figure 10.4 on page 297 shows the first possibility, where the firm makes a profit. Panels (a) and (b) of Figure 10.5 show the situations where a firm breaks even or experiences losses. In panel (a) of Figure 10.5, at the level of output at which $MR = MC$, price is equal to average total cost. Therefore, total revenue is equal to total cost, and the firm will break even, making zero economic profit. In panel (b), at the level of output at which $MR = MC$, price is less than average total cost. Therefore, total revenue is less than total cost, and the firm has losses. In this case, maximizing profit amounts to *minimizing* loss.

| Making the Connection | **The Rise and Fall of Canada's Technology Darling** |

In 1984, two university students started a technology company—not in Redmond, Washington, but in Waterloo, Ontario. Mike Lazaridis and Douglas Fregin are the founders of Research In Motion (RIM), the company now known as BlackBerry.

The company was originally involved in the wireless transmission of information using radio waves, concentrating mainly on point-of-sale terminals. By 1992, RIM changed its focus to two-way paging, and Jim Balsillie, who joined the company that year, was determined to find a way to send email using wireless technology. In 1996, RIM introduced the world to the Inter@ctive pager, a handheld wireless device capable of both receiving and sending email.

Two years later, the BlackBerry hit the market. Unique at the time, this device was a handheld wireless computer complete with QWERTY keyboard, that added to RIM's previous offerings the ability to get news, weather, and market data. The demand for the BlackBerry was huge, and by 2004 there were over 1 million subscribers. By 2007, there were over 12 million users and revenue exceeded $1.6 billion. The value of the company soared, and at one point, RIM's market capitalization exceeded that of the Royal Bank of Canada.

RIM's large profits enticed other firms to develop similar products. In June 1997, a California-based company began offering a competing product. You may have heard of Apple's iPhone, which did not offer a keyboard but did have a touchscreen bigger than the BlackBerry and also was capable of operating on the 3G network, could send instant messages, and also had built-in GPS. By the end of 2008, Apple's iPhone was outselling RIM's BlackBerry.

Between 2008 and 2011, Apple continued to outperform RIM. Apple's App Store continued to offer a wider selection of apps, which continued to increase the demand for the iPhone and decrease demand for the BlackBerry. The RIM Playbook, introduced to compete with the iPad, did not have good reviews and sales were poor. Decreased demand resulted in decreased production and lower demand for labour. RIM was forced to lay off 10 percent of its workforce in 2011 and a further 30 percent in 2012. In the fourth quarter of 2012, RIM had slipped to become the seventh-most popular manufacturer of smartphones, behind Samsung, Apple, Huawei, Sony, ZTE, and HTC.

Like many companies before it, RIM's success with the BlackBerry propelled RIM to several years of profitability. Unfortunately for RIM, that success provided the incentive for other firms to develop the technology and introduce smartphones into the marketplace. Increased competition reduces prices and profits. In 2012, RIM introduced its new models, the Z10 and Q10, and it appears that the new models are too little too late. Markets have spoken and competition has prevailed.

Based on "BlackBerry Timeline: A Tech Titan's Roller Coaster Ride: How the Maker of an Iconic Smartphone Rose to Riches, and Why It Faces an Uncertain Future," *CBC News*, May 1, 2013, accessed at http://www.cbc.ca/news/interactives/timeline-rim/

Your Turn: Test your understanding by doing related problem 3.4 on page 318 at the end of this chapter.

MyEconLab

Deciding Whether to Produce or to Shut Down in the Short Run

10.4 LEARNING OBJECTIVE

Explain why firms may shut down temporarily.

In panel (b) of Figure 10.5 on page 300, we assumed that the firm would continue to produce even though it was operating at a loss. In fact, in the short run, a firm experiencing a loss has two choices:

1. Continue to produce
2. Stop production by shutting down temporarily

In many cases, a firm experiencing a loss will consider stopping production temporarily. Even during a temporary shutdown, however, a firm must still pay its fixed costs. For example, if the firm has signed a lease for its building, the landlord will expect to receive a monthly rent payment, even if the firm is not producing anything that month. Therefore, if a firm does not produce, it will suffer a loss equal to its fixed costs. This loss is the maximum the firm will accept. The firm will shut down if producing would cause it to lose an amount greater than its fixed costs.

A firm can reduce its loss below the amount of its total fixed cost by continuing to produce, provided that the total revenue it receives is greater than its variable cost. A firm can use the revenue over and above variable cost to cover part of its fixed cost. In this case, a firm will have a smaller loss by continuing to produce than by shutting down.

In analyzing the firm's decision to shut down, we are assuming that its fixed costs are *sunk costs*. A **sunk cost** is a cost that has already been paid and cannot be recovered. We assume, as is usually the case, that the firm cannot recover its fixed costs by shutting down. For example, if a farmer has taken out a loan to buy land, the farmer is legally

Sunk cost A cost that has already been paid and cannot be recovered.

required to make the monthly loan payment whether he grows any wheat that season or not. The farmer has to spend those funds and cannot get them back, *so the farmer should treat his sunk costs as irrelevant to his decision making.* For any firm, whether total revenue is greater or less than *variable costs* is the key to deciding whether to shut down. As long as a firm's total revenue is greater than its variable costs, it should continue to produce no matter how large or small its fixed costs are.

One option not available to a firm with losses in a perfectly competitive market is to raise its price. If the firm did raise its price, it would lose all its customers, and its sales would drop to zero.

Solved Problem 10.4

When to Pull the Plug on a Movie

When Walt Disney released the film *Mars Needs Moms*, directed by Robert Zemeckis, in March 2011, it did very poorly at the box office. Worldwide, it earned less than $40 million in revenue, even though it cost $175 million to make. A year before the film was released, Disney executives watched the parts of the film that were complete. They were disappointed in what they saw and immediately stopped production on Robert Zemeckis's next film. They did not, however, stop production on *Mars Needs Moms*, on which the company had already spent $100 million. In March 2010, at the time the executives became concerned about the quality of the film, how should Disney have decided whether to finish *Mars Needs Moms* and release it? What role should the $100 million Disney executives had already spent on the film have played in their decision?

Solving the Problem

Step 1: **Review the chapter material.** This problem is about the role of sunk costs in business decision making, so you may want to review the section "Deciding Whether to Produce or to Shut Down in the Short Run," which begins on page 301.

Step 2: **Use your knowledge of the role of sunk costs in decisions about whether to shut down to answer the question.** In this case, Disney was not considering whether to shut down the company but whether to shut down this particular film. By March 2010, Disney had already invested $100 million in *Mars Needs Moms*. It is tempting to argue that unless Disney completed the film, the $100 million would be lost. It is important to see, though, that the $100 million was a sunk cost: Whether Disney shut down the film or finished it and released it to theatres, the company would not be able to get that $100 million back. Therefore, the $100 million was irrelevant to Disney's decision. Instead, Disney should have made the decision based on comparing the additional cost of completing and releasing the film to the revenue the film was expected to earn. In other words, Disney should have completed the film if marginal revenue was expected to be greater than marginal cost, and it should have shut down the film if marginal cost were expected to be greater than marginal revenue.

Although Disney knew the marginal cost of completing and releasing the film, it had to estimate the marginal revenue based on its forecasts of ticket sales and later sales of DVDs and streaming video. Disney decided to finish the film. The film cost an additional $75 million to complete, but it earned only about $39 million at the box office. With hindsight, Disney made the wrong decision, but the company may have overestimated ticket sales or expected sales of DVDs and streaming video to offset poor results at the box office.

Based on Brooks Barnes, "Many Culprits in Fall of a Family Film," *New York Times*, March 14, 2011; revenue and cost data from boxofficemojo.com.

MyEconLab   **Your Turn:** Test your understanding by doing related problem 4.4 on page 319 at the end of this chapter.

The Supply Curve of a Firm in the Short Run

Remember that the supply curve for a firm tells us how many units of a product the firm is willing to sell at any given price. Notice that the marginal cost curve for a firm in a perfectly competitive market tells us the same thing. The firm will produce at the level of output where $MR = MC$. Because price equals marginal revenue for a firm in a perfectly competitive market, the firm will produce where $P = MC$. For any given price, we can determine from the marginal cost curve the quantity of output the firm will supply. *Therefore, a perfectly competitive firm's marginal cost curve is also its supply curve.* There is, however, an important qualification to this fact. We have seen that if a firm is experiencing a loss, it will shut down if its total revenue is less than its variable cost:

$$\text{Total revenue} < \text{Variable cost,}$$

or, in symbols:

$$(P \times Q) < VC$$

If we divide both sides by Q, we have the result that the firm will shut down if

$$P < AVC$$

If the price drops below average variable cost, the firm will have a smaller loss if it shuts down and produces no output. *So, the firm's marginal cost curve is its supply curve only for prices at or above average variable cost.* The red line in Figure 10.6 shows the supply curve for the firm in the short run.

Recall that the marginal cost curve intersects the average variable cost where the average variable cost curve is at its minimum point. Therefore, the firm's supply curve is its marginal cost curve above the minimum point of the average variable cost curve. For prices below minimum average variable cost (P_{MIN}), the firm will shut down, and its output will fall to zero. The minimum point on the average variable cost curve is called the **shutdown point**, and it occurs in Figure 10.6 at output level Q_{SD}.

The Market Supply Curve in a Perfectly Competitive Industry

The market demand curve is determined by adding up the quantity demanded by each consumer in the market at each price. Similarly, the market supply curve is determined by adding up the quantity supplied by each firm in the market at each price. Each firm's marginal cost curve tells us how much that firm will supply at each price. So, the market supply curve can be derived directly from the marginal cost curves of the firms in the market. Panel (a) of Figure 10.7 shows the marginal cost curve for one wheat farmer. At a price of $4, this wheat farmer supplies 20,000 bushels of wheat. If every wheat farmer

Shutdown point The minimum point on a firm's average variable cost curve; if the price falls below this point, the firm shuts down production in the short run.

Figure 10.6

The Firm's Short-Run Supply Curve

The firm will produce at the level of output at which $MR = MC$. Because price equals marginal revenue for a firm in a perfectly competitive market, the firm will produce where $P = MC$. For any given price, we can determine the quantity of output the firm will supply from the marginal cost curve. In other words, the marginal cost curve is the firm's supply curve. But remember that the firm will shut down if the price falls below average variable cost. The marginal cost curve crosses the average variable cost at the firm's shutdown point. This point occurs at output level Q_{SD}. For prices below P_{MIN}, the supply curve is a vertical line along the price axis, which shows that the firm will supply zero output at those prices. The red line in the figure is the firm's short-run supply curve.

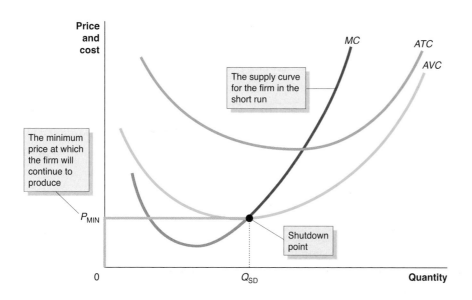

Figure 10.7 **Firm Supply and Market Supply**

We can derive the market supply curve by adding up the quantity that each firm in the market is willing to supply at each price. In panel (a), one wheat farmer is willing to supply 20,000 bushels of wheat at a price of $4 per bushel. If every wheat farmer supplies the same amount of wheat at this price and if there are 52,000 wheat farmers, the total amount of wheat supplied at a price of $4 will equal 20,000 bushels per farmer $\times$ 52,000 farmer$s$ = 1.04 billion bushels of wheat. This is one point on the market supply curve for wheat shown in panel (b). We can find the other points on the market supply curve by determining how much wheat each farmer is willing to supply at each price.

supplies the same amount of wheat at this price and if there are 52,000 wheat farmers, the total amount of wheat supplied at a price of $4 will be

20,000 bushels per farmer $\times$ 52,000 farms = 1.04 billion bushels of wheat.

Panel (b) shows a price of $4 and a quantity of 1.04 billion bushels as a point on the market supply curve for wheat. In reality, of course, not all wheat farms are alike. Some wheat farms supply more at the market price than the typical farm; other wheat farms supply less. The key point is that we can derive the market supply curve by adding up the quantity that each firm in the market is willing and able to supply at each price.

10.5 LEARNING OBJECTIVE

Explain how entry and exit ensure that perfectly competitive firms earn zero economic profit in the long run.

"If Everyone Can Do It, You Can't Make Money at It": The Entry and Exit of Firms in the Long Run

In the long run, unless a firm can cover all its costs, it will shut down and exit the industry. In a market system, firms continually enter and exit industries. In this section, we will see how profits and losses provide signals to firms that lead to entry and exit.

Economic Profit and the Entry or Exit Decision

To begin, let's look more closely at how economists characterize the profits earned by the owners of a firm. Suppose Sacha Gillette decides to start her own business. After considering her interests and preparing a business plan, she decides to start a carrot farm rather than open a restaurant or gift shop. After 10 years of effort, Sacha has saved $100,000 and borrowed another $900,000 from a bank. With these funds, she has bought the land and farm equipment necessary to start her farm. She intends to sell the carrots

Explicit Costs	
Water	$ 10,000
Wages	15,000
Fertilizer	10,000
Electricity	5,000
Payment on bank loan	45,000
Implicit Costs	
Forgone salary	30,000
Opportunity cost of the $100,000 she has invested in her farm	10,000
Total cost	**$125,000**

Table 10.4

Farmer Gillette's Costs per Year

she grows in a local farmers' market. When someone invests her own funds in her firm, the opportunity cost to the firm is the return the funds would have earned in their best alternative use. If Farmer Gillette could have earned a 10 percent return on her $100,000 in savings in their best alternative use—which might have been, for example, to buy a small restaurant—then her carrot business incurs a $10,000 opportunity cost. We can also think of this $10,000 as being the minimum amount that Farmer Gillette needs to earn on her $100,000 investment in her farm to remain in the industry in the long run.

Table 10.4 lists Farmer Gillette's costs. In addition to her explicit costs, we assume that she has two implicit costs: the $10,000 that represents the opportunity cost of the funds she invested in her farm and the $30,000 salary she could have earned managing someone else's farm instead of her own. Her total costs are $125,000. If the market price of carrots is $15 per box and Farmer Gillette sells 10,000 boxes, her total revenue will be $150,000, and her economic profit will be $25,000 (total revenue of $150,000 minus total costs of $125,000). **Economic profit** equals a firm's revenues minus all its costs, implicit and explicit. So, Farmer Gillette is covering the $10,000 opportunity cost of the funds invested in her firm, and she is also earning an additional $25,000 in economic profit.

Economic profit A firm's revenues minus all its costs, implicit and explicit.

Economic Profit Leads to Entry of New Firms
Unfortunately, Farmer Gillette is unlikely to earn an economic profit for very long. Suppose other farmers are just breaking even by selling their carrots to supermarkets. In that case, they will have an incentive to switch to selling at farmers' markets so they can begin earning an economic profit. As we saw in the chapter opener, in recent years, many small farmers have begun to sell in farmers' markets, in the hope of earning higher profits. Remember that the more firms there are in an industry, the farther to the right the market supply curve is. Panel (a) of Figure 10.8 shows that as more farmers begin selling carrots in farmers' markets, the market supply curve shifts to the right. Farmers will continue entering the market until the market supply curve has shifted from S_1 to S_2.

With the supply curve at S_2, the market price will have fallen to $10 per box. Panel (b) shows the effect on Farmer Gillette, who we assume has the same costs as other carrot farmers. As the market price falls from $15 to $10 per box, Farmer Gillette's demand curve shifts down, from D_1 to D_2. In the new equilibrium, Farmer Gillette is selling 8,000 boxes, at a price of $10 per box. She and the other carrot farmers are no longer earning any economic profit. They are just breaking even, and the return on their investment is just covering the opportunity cost of these funds. New farmers will stop entering the market for selling carrots in farmers' markets because the rate of return is no better than they can earn by selling their carrots elsewhere.

Will Farmer Gillette continue to sell carrots at farmers' markets even though she is just breaking even? She will, because selling carrots at farmers' markets earns her as high a return on her investment as she could earn elsewhere. It may seem strange that new firms will continue to enter a market until all economic profits are eliminated and that established firms remain in a market despite not earning any economic profit. But it seems strange only because we are used to thinking in terms of accounting profits rather than *economic* profits. Remember that accounting rules generally

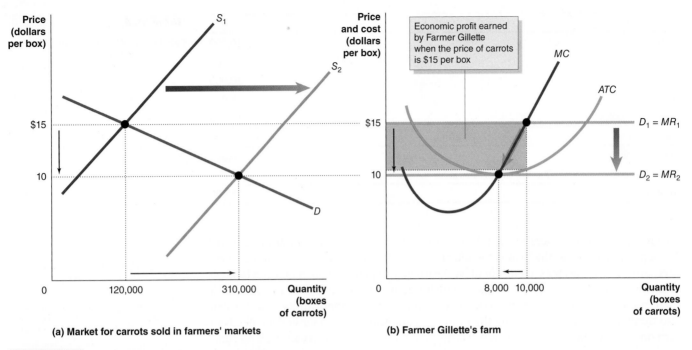

(a) Market for carrots sold in farmers' markets

(b) Farmer Gillette's farm

Figure 10.8 **The Effect of Entry on Economic Profits**

We assume that Farmer Gillette's costs are the same as the costs of other carrot farmers. Initially, she and other farmers selling carrots in farmers' markets are able to charge $15 per box and earn an economic profit. Farmer Gillette's economic profit is represented by the area of the green box. Panel (a) shows that as other farmers begin to sell carrots in farmers' markets, the market supply curve shifts to the right, from S_1 to S_2, and the market price

drops to $10 per box. Panel (b) shows that the falling price causes Farmer Gillette's demand curve to shift down from D_1 to D_2, and she reduces her output from 10,000 boxes to 8,000. At the new market price of $10 per box, carrot growers are just breaking even: Their total revenue is equal to their total cost, and their economic profit is zero. Notice the difference in scale between the graph in panel (a) and the graph in panel (b).

require that only explicit costs be included on a firm's financial statements. The opportunity cost of the funds Farmer Gillette invested in her firm—$10,000—and her forgone salary—$30,000—are economic costs, but neither of them is an accounting cost. So, although an accountant would see Farmer Gillette as earning a profit of $40,000, an economist would see her as just breaking even. Farmer Gillette must pay attention to her accounting profit when preparing her financial statements and when paying her income tax. But because economic profit takes into account all her costs, it gives a more accurate indication of the financial health of her farm.

Economic Losses Lead to Exit of Firms Suppose some consumers decide that there are no important benefits from locally grown produce sold at farmers' markets, and they switch back to buying their produce in supermarkets. Panel (a) of Figure 10.9 shows that the demand curve for carrots sold in farmers' markets will shift to the left, from D_1 to D_2, and the market price will fall from $10 per box to $7. Panel (b) shows that as the price falls, a farmer, like Sacha Gillette, will move down her marginal cost curve to a lower level of output. At the lower level of output and lower price, she will be suffering an **economic loss** because she will not cover all her costs. As long as price is above average variable cost, she will continue to produce in the short run, even when suffering losses. But in the long run, firms will exit an industry if they are unable to cover all their costs. In this case, some farmers will switch back to selling carrots to supermarkets rather than selling them in farmers' markets.

Economic loss The situation in which a firm's total revenue is less than its total cost, including all implicit costs.

Panel (c) of Figure 10.9 shows that as firms exit from selling at farmers' markets, the market supply curve shifts to the left. Firms will continue to exit, and the supply curve will continue to shift to the left until the price has risen back to $10 and the market supply curve is at S_2. Panel (d) shows that when the price is back to $10, the remaining firms in the industry will be breaking even.

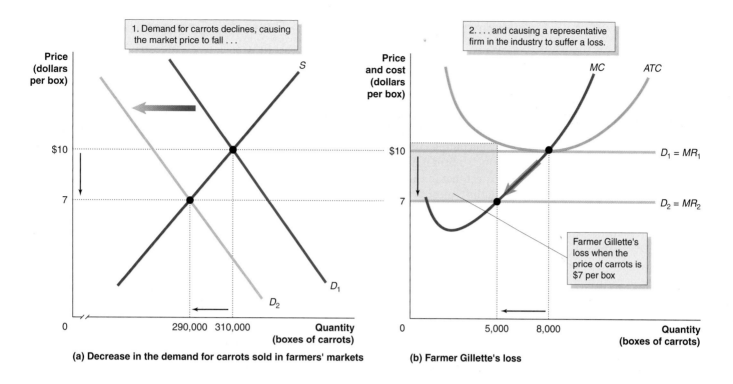

(a) Decrease in the demand for carrots sold in farmers' markets

(b) Farmer Gillette's loss

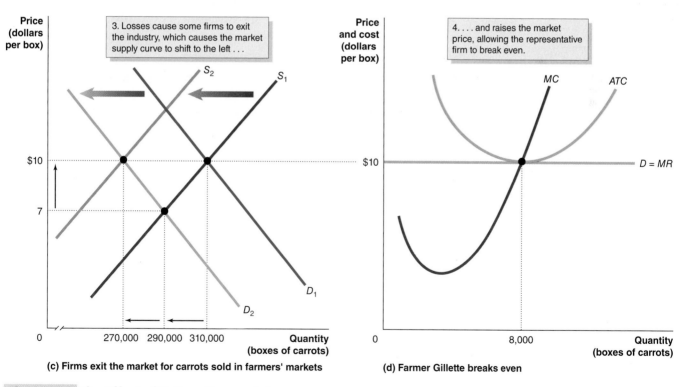

(c) Firms exit the market for carrots sold in farmers' markets

(d) Farmer Gillette breaks even

Figure 10.9 The Effect of Exit on Economic Losses

When the price of carrots is $10 per box, Farmer Gillette and other farmers are breaking even. A total quantity of 310,000 boxes is sold in the market. Farmer Gillette sells 8,000 boxes. Panel (a) shows a decline in the demand for carrots sold in farmers' markets from D_1 to D_2 that reduces the market price to $7 per box. Panel (b) shows that the falling price causes Farmer Gillette's demand curve to shift down from D_1 to D_2 and her output to fall from 8,000 to 5,000 boxes. At a market price of $7 per box,

farmers have economic losses, represented by the area of the red box. As a result, some farmers will exit the market, which shifts the market supply curve to the left. Panel (c) shows that exit continues until the supply curve has shifted from S_1 to S_2 and the market price has risen from $7 back to $10. Panel (d) shows that with the price back at $10, Farmer Gillette will break even. In the new market equilibrium in panel (c), total sales of carrots in farmers' markets have fallen from 310,000 to 270,000 boxes.

Long-Run Equilibrium in a Perfectly Competitive Market

We have seen that economic profits attract firms to enter an industry. The entry of firms forces down the market price until the typical firm is breaking even. Economic losses cause firms to exit an industry. The exit of firms forces up the equilibrium market price until the typical firm is breaking even. This process of entry and exit results in *long-run competitive equilibrium*. In **long-run competitive equilibrium**, entry and exit have resulted in the typical firm breaking even. In the long run, firms can also vary their scale by becoming larger or smaller. The *long-run average cost curve* shows the lowest cost at which a firm is able to produce a given quantity of output in the long run. So, we would expect that in the long run, competition drives the market price to the minimum point on the typical firm's long-run average cost curve.

Long-run competitive equilibrium
The situation in which the entry and exit of firms has resulted in the typical firm breaking even.

Firms in perfectly competitive markets are in a constant struggle to stay one step ahead of their competitors. They are always looking for new ways to provide a product, such as selling carrots in farmers' markets. It is possible for firms to find ways to earn an economic profit for a while, but competition typically competes those profits away in just a few years. This observation is not restricted to agriculture. In any perfectly competitive market, an opportunity to make economic profits never lasts long. As economist Sharon Oster has put it, "If everyone can do it, you can't make money at it."

The Long-Run Supply Curve in a Perfectly Competitive Market

If the typical farmer selling carrots in a farmers' market breaks even at a price of $10 per box, in the long run, the market price will always return to this level. If an increase in demand causes the market price to rise above $10, farmers will be earning economic profits. These profits will attract additional farmers into the market, and the market supply curve will shift to the right until the price is back to $10. Panel (a) in Figure 10.10

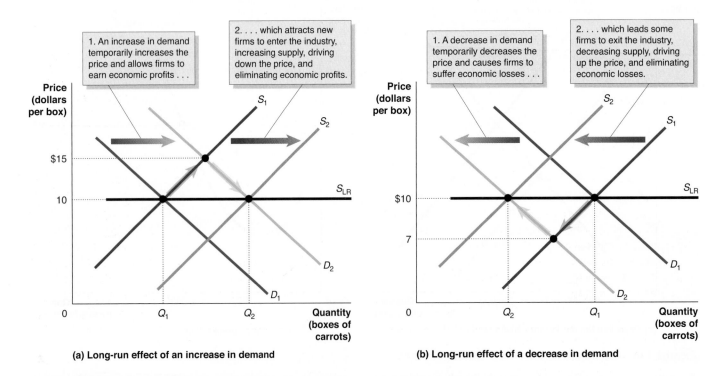

(a) Long-run effect of an increase in demand

(b) Long-run effect of a decrease in demand

Figure 10.10 **The Long-Run Supply Curve in a Perfectly Competitive Industry**

Panel (a) shows that an increase in demand for carrots sold in farmers' markets will lead to a temporary increase in price from $10 to $15 per box, as the market demand curve shifts to the right, from D_1 to D_2. The entry of new firms shifts the market supply curve to the right, from S_1 to S_2, which will cause the price to fall back to its long-run level of $10. Panel (b) shows that a decrease in demand will lead to a temporary

decrease in price from $10 to $7 per box, as the market demand curve shifts to the left, from D_1 to D_2. The exit of firms shifts the market supply curve to the left, from S_1 to S_2, which causes the price to rise back to its long-run level of $10. The long-run supply curve (S_{LR}) shows the relationship between market price and the quantity supplied in the long run. In this case, the long-run supply curve is a horizontal line.

illustrates the long-run effect of an increase in demand. An increase in demand from D_1 to D_2 causes the market price to temporarily rise from \$10 per box to \$15. At this price, farmers are making economic profits selling carrots at farmers' markets, but these profits attract entry of new farmers. The result is an increase in supply from S_1 to S_2, which forces the price back down to \$10 per box and eliminates the economic profits.

Similarly, if a decrease in demand causes the market price to fall below \$10, farmers will experience economic losses. These losses will cause some farmers to exit the market, the supply curve will shift to the left, and the price will return to \$10. Panel (b) in Figure 10.10 illustrates the long-run effect of a decrease in demand. A decrease in demand from D_1 to D_2 causes the market price to fall temporarily from \$10 per box to \$7. At this price, farmers are suffering economic losses, but these losses cause some farmers to exit the market for organic apples. The result is a decrease in supply from S_1 to S_2, which forces the price back up to \$10 per box and eliminates the losses.

The **long-run supply curve** shows the relationship in the long run between market price and the quantity supplied. In the long run, the price will be \$10 per box, no matter how many boxes of carrots are produced. So, as Figure 10.10 shows, the long-run supply curve (S_{LR}) is a horizontal line at a price of \$10. Remember that the reason the price returns to \$10 in the long run is that this is the price at which the typical firm in the industry just breaks even. The typical firm breaks even at this price because it is at the minimum point on the firm's average total cost curve. We can draw the important conclusion that *in the long run, a perfectly competitive market will supply whatever amount of a good consumers demand at a price determined by the minimum point on the typical firm's average total cost curve.*

Because the position of the long-run supply curve is determined by the minimum point on the typical firm's average total cost curve, anything that raises or lowers the costs of the typical firm in the long run will cause the long-run supply curve to shift. For example, if a new disease infects carrots and the costs of treating the disease adds \$2 per box to every farmers' cost of producing carrots, the long-run supply curve will shift up by \$2.

Long-run supply curve A curve that shows the relationship in the long run between market price and the quantity supplied.

| Making the Connection | **In the Apple iPhone App Store, Easy Entry Makes the Long Run Pretty Short** |

The iPhone 5 is the latest version (in fact, the sixth generation) of the iPhone, which was introduced by Apple in June 2007.

Economic profits are rapidly competed away in the iTunes app store.

Although popular, the original iPhone had some drawbacks, including a slow connection to the Internet and an inability to run any applications except those written by Apple. The iPhone 3G, released in July 2008, could connect to the Internet more quickly and easily, had a faster processor, and had a larger capacity. But perhaps most importantly, with the release of the iPhone 3G, Apple announced that a section of its immensely popular iTunes music and video store would be devoted to applications (or "apps") for the iPhone. Independent software programmers would write these iPhone apps. Apple would approve the apps and make them available in the iTunes app store in exchange for receiving 30 percent of the purchase price. Major software companies, as well as individuals writing their first software programs, have posted games, calendars, dictionaries, and many other types of apps to the iTunes store.

Apple sold more than 3 million iPhones within a month of launching the iPhone 3G. Demand for apps from the iTunes store soared along with sales of the iPhone. Ethan Nicholas, who in August 2008 was a programmer at Sun Microsystems but had never written a game before, decided to teach himself the coding language used in iPhone apps. His game, iShoot, with an initial price of \$4.99, was a great success. Within one week of posting to iTunes, enough people had downloaded iShoot to earn Nicholas \$200,000. At the end of five months, he had earned \$800,000.

But could Nicholas's success last? As we have seen, when firms earn economic profits in a market, other firms have a strong economic incentive to enter that market. This is exactly what happened with iPhone apps, and by January 2013, more than 775,000 apps were available in the iTunes store. The cost of entering this market was very small. Anyone with the programming skills and the available time could write an app and have it posted in the store. As a result of this enhanced competition, the ability to get rich quick with a killer app was quickly fading. As an article in the *New York Times* put it: "The chances of hitting the iPhone jackpot keep getting slimmer: the Apple store is already crowded with look-alike games ... and fresh inventory keeps arriving daily. Many of the simple but clever concepts that sell briskly ... are already taken."

To try to maintain sales, Ethan Nicholas was forced to drop the price of iShoot from $4.99 in October 2008 to $2.99 in April 2009 to $1.99 in May 2009, and finally to $0.99 in September 2010 (where it remains today). But his profits from the game continued to decline. In a competitive market, earning an economic profit in the long run is extremely difficult. And the ease of entering the market for iPhone apps has made the long run pretty short.

Based on Jenna Wortham, "The iPhone Gold Rush," *New York Times*, April 5, 2009; and Bruce X. Chen, "Coder's Half-Million-Dollar Baby Proves iPhone Gold Rush Is Still On," wired.com, February 12, 2009.

MyEconLab

Your Turn: Test your understanding by doing related problem 5.4 on page 319 at the end of this chapter.

Increasing-Cost and Decreasing-Cost Industries

Any industry in which the typical firm's average costs do not change as the industry expands production will have a horizontal long-run supply curve, like the one in Figure 10.10. Industries where this holds true (such as the carrot industry) are called *constant-cost industries*. It's possible, however, for the typical firm's average costs to change as an industry expands.

For example, if an input used in producing a good is available in only limited quantities, the cost of the input will rise as the industry expands. If only a limited amount of land is available on which to grow the grapes to make a certain variety of wine, an increase in demand for wine made from these grapes will result in competition for the land and will drive up its price. As a result, more of the wine will be produced in the long run only if the price rises to cover the higher average costs of the typical firm. In this case, the long-run supply curve will slope upward. Industries with upward-sloping long-run supply curves are called *increasing-cost industries*.

Finally, in some cases, the typical firm's costs may fall as the industry expands. Suppose that someone invents a new microwave that uses as an input a specialized memory chip that is currently produced only in small quantities. If demand for the microwave increases, firms that produce microwaves will increase their orders for the memory chip. If there are economies of scale in producing a good, its average cost will decline as output increases. If there are economies of scale in producing this memory chip, the average cost of producing it will fall, and competition will result in its price falling as well. This price decline, in turn, will lower the average cost of producing the new microwave. In the long run, competition will force the price of the microwave to fall to the level of the new lower average cost of the typical firm. In this case, the long-run supply curve will slope downward. Industries with downward-sloping long-run supply curves are called *decreasing-cost industries*.

10.6 LEARNING OBJECTIVE

Explain how perfect competition leads to economic efficiency.

Perfect Competition and Efficiency

Notice how powerful consumers are in a market system. If consumers want more locally grown carrots, the market will supply them. This happens not because a government bureaucrat in Ottawa or an official in a carrot growers' association gives orders. The additional carrots are produced because an increase in demand results in higher prices and a higher rate of return from selling at farmers' markets. Carrot growers, trying to get the highest possible return on their investments, begin to switch from selling to supermarkets to selling at farmers' markets. If consumers lose their taste for locally grown carrots and demand falls, the process works in reverse.

Productive Efficiency

In a market system, consumers get as many carrots as they want, produced at the lowest average cost possible. The forces of competition will drive the market price to the minimum average cost of the typical firm. **Productive efficiency** refers to the situation in which a good or service is produced at the lowest possible cost. As we have seen, perfect competition results in productive efficiency.

> **Productive efficiency** The situation in which a good or service is produced at the lowest possible cost.

The managers of every firm strive to earn an economic profit by reducing costs. But in a perfectly competitive market, other firms quickly copy ways of reducing costs. Therefore, in the long run, only the consumer benefits from cost reductions.

Solved Problem **10.6**

How Productive Efficiency Benefits Consumers

Writing in the *New York Times* on the technology boom of the late 1990s, Michael Lewis argued, "The sad truth, for investors, seems to be that most of the benefits of new technologies are passed right through to consumers free of charge."

a. What do you think Lewis means by the benefits of new technology being "passed right through to consumers free of charge"? Use a graph like Figure 10.8 on page 306 to illustrate your answer.

b. Explain why this result is a "sad truth" for investors.

Solving the Problem

Step 1: **Review the chapter material.** This problem is about perfect competition and efficiency, so you may want to review the section "Perfect Competition and Efficiency."

Step 2: **Use the concepts from this chapter to explain what Lewis means.** By "new technologies," Lewis means new products—such as smartphones or LED television sets—or lower-cost ways of producing existing products. In either case, new technologies will allow firms to earn economic profits for a while, but these profits will lead new firms to enter the market in the long run.

Step 3: **Use a graph like Figure 10.8 on page 306 to illustrate why the benefits of new technologies are "passed right through to consumers free of charge."**

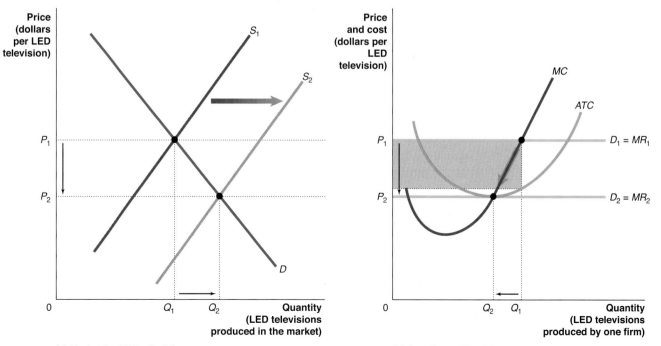

(a) Market for LED televisions

(b) One firm selling LED televisions

Figure 10.8 shows the situation in which a firm is making economic profits in the short run but has these profits eliminated by entry in the long run. We can draw a similar graph to analyze what happens in the long run in the market for LED televisions.

When LED televisions were first introduced, prices were high, and only a few firms were in the market. Panel (a) shows that the initial equilibrium price in the market for LED televisions is P_1. Panel (b) shows that at this price, the typical firm in the industry is earning an economic profit, which is shown by the green-shaded box. The economic profit attracts new firms into the industry. This entry shifts the market supply curve from S_1 to S_2 in panel (a) and lowers the equilibrium price from P_1 to P_2. Panel (b) shows that at the new market price, P_2, the typical firm is breaking even. Therefore, LED televisions are being produced at the lowest possible cost, and productive efficiency is achieved. Consumers receive the new technology "free of charge" in the sense that they only have to pay a price equal to the lowest possible cost of production.

Step 4: Answer part (b) by explaining why the result in part (a) is a "sad truth" for investors. We have seen in answering part (a) that in the long run, firms only break even on their investment in producing high-technology goods. That result implies that investors in these firms are also unlikely to earn an economic profit in the long run.

Extra credit: Lewis is using a key result from this chapter: In the long run, entry of new firms competes away economic profits. We should notice that, strictly speaking, the high-technology industries Lewis is discussing are not perfectly competitive. Smart phones or LED televisions, for instance, are not identical, and each smartphone company produces a quantity large enough to affect the market price. However, these deviations from perfect competition do not change the important conclusion that the entry of new firms benefits consumers by forcing prices down to the level of average cost. In fact, the price of LED televisions dropped by more than 35 percent within three years of their first becoming widely available.

Based on Michael Lewis, "In Defense of the Boom," *New York Times*, October 27, 2002.

MyEconLab **Your Turn:** For more practice, do related problems 6.2 and 6.3 on page 319 at the end of this chapter.

Allocative Efficiency

Not only do perfectly competitive firms produce goods and services at the lowest possible cost, but they also produce the goods and services that consumers value most. Firms will produce a good up to the point where the marginal cost of producing another unit is equal to the marginal benefit consumers receive from consuming that unit. In other words, firms will supply all those goods that provide consumers with a marginal benefit at least as great as the marginal cost of producing them. We know this is true because:

1. The price of a good represents the marginal benefit consumers receive from consuming the last unit of the good sold.
2. Perfectly competitive firms produce up to the point where the price of the good equals the marginal cost of producing the last unit.
3. Therefore, firms produce up to the point where the last unit provides a marginal benefit to consumers equal to the marginal cost of producing it.

These statements are another way of saying that entrepreneurs in a market system efficiently *allocate* labour, machinery, and other inputs to produce the goods and services that best satisfy consumer wants. In this sense, perfect competition achieves **allocative efficiency**. Many goods and services sold in the Canadian economy are not produced in perfectly competitive markets. Nevertheless, productive efficiency and allocative efficiency are useful benchmarks against which to compare the actual performance of the economy.

Allocative efficiency A state of the economy in which production represents consumer preferences; in particular, every good or service is produced up to the point where the last unit provides a marginal benefit to consumers equal to the marginal cost of producing it.

Economics in Your Life

Are You an Entrepreneur?

At the beginning of the chapter, we asked you to think about why you can charge only a relatively low price for performing services such as babysitting or lawn mowing. In the chapter, we saw that firms selling products in competitive markets can't charge prices higher than those being charged by competing firms. The market for babysitting and lawn mowing is very competitive. In most neighbourhoods, there are many teenagers willing to supply these services. The price you can charge for babysitting may not be worth your while at age 20 but is enough to cover the opportunity cost of a 14-year-old eager to enter the market. (Or, as we put it in Table 10.1, the ease of entry into babysitting and lawn mowing is high.) So, in your career as a teenage entrepreneur, you may have become familiar with one of the lessons of this chapter: A firm in a competitive market has no control over price.

Conclusion

The competitive forces of the market impose relentless pressure on firms to produce new and better goods and services at the lowest possible cost. Firms that fail to adequately anticipate changes in consumer tastes or that fail to adopt the latest and most efficient technology do not survive in the long run. In the nineteenth century, the biologist Charles Darwin developed a theory of evolution based on the idea of the "survival of the fittest." Only those plants and animals that are best able to adapt to the demands of their environment are able to survive. Darwin first realized the important role that the struggle for existence plays in the natural world after reading early nineteenth-century economists' descriptions of the role it plays in the economic world. Just as "survival of the fittest" is the rule in nature, so it is in the economic world.

At the start of this chapter, we saw that there are four market structures: perfect competition, monopolistic competition, oligopoly, and monopoly. Now that we have studied perfect competition, in the following chapters we move on to the other three market structures. Before turning to those chapters, read *An Inside Look* on the next page for a discussion of the reasons for the decline in organic farming in the United Kingdom.

Declining Popularity in Organic Farming in the United Kingdom

THE GUARDIAN

Farmers Turn Away From Organic as Sales Drop

Farmers have begun to turn away from organic food production in the face of waning interest from the big supermarkets.

The amount of land being converted to organic cultivation across the UK has dropped by two-thirds since 2007, according to statistics released by the Department for Environment, Food and Rural Affairs, as falling sales of organic products mean fewer farmers are seeing a reason to change.

Sales of organic products fell by 5.9% in the UK last year, according to the Soil Association, from £1.8bn in 2009 to £1.7bn. That continued a decline from record sales of £2.1bn in 2008, and came amid rising food prices. The amount of organic poultry being produced has also fallen steadily.

But many farmers who have gone organic were defiant after publication of the latest figures, arguing that switching to greener methods has drastically cut their costs and that consumer interest is still strong, particularly when farmers can use sales routes other than big supermarket chains.

"There might be lots of farmers who think they can't afford to go organic, because they think the market is restricted, but if they looked into it they would find it can be cost-effective," said Ian Noble, who represents a 12-farm cooperative in south Devon growing organic vegetables. With little or no costs for fertilisers and pesticides, and—at least on smaller farms—most animals fed on grass rather than expensive grain, organic farmers can make savings at a time of high commodity prices. Adrian Dolby, of Barrington Park, said cutting input prices was one of his key reasons for putting 7,000 acres under organic cultivation in 2005.

"If we hadn't gone organic, we would have gone out of business," added Tom Rigby, who farms 160 acres near Warrington, most of it given over to pasture. "We are a small dairy farm and small dairy farmers are going bankrupt every day. I decided that if I was going to go bankrupt, I would rather do it in the way I wanted."

Rigby knows of larger producers that have quit organic methods, such as some bigger dairy farms that found their margins squeezed even on premium organic milk as they needed to import increasingly expensive feed. His smaller grass-fed herd avoids this problem, and his organically cultivated vegetables will be sold to Manchester University.

Oliver Dowding, an organic farmer near Wincanton in Somerset for more than 20 years, blamed waning interest among farmers on the numbers who entered organic cultivation several years ago, attracted by government grants to convert their land and the offers of subsidies, and who have since reverted to conventional farming as the financial support has dried up. This is a widespread view among organic farmers, and seems borne out by figures from Scotland which show a massive decline in the acreage under organic production since the early 2000s.

Last year, across the UK, only 51,000 hectares were in "conversion"—the process farmers need to go through to have their land and practices certified as organic. That is less than half the amount of land in conversion in 2009, itself down markedly from the 2007 peak of 158,000 hectares.... .

For livestock farmers, the picture is mixed. The number of cattle reared organically has risen steadily, to more than 350,000 last year. But despite widespread publicity by food campaigners on the claimed benefits of choosing free range or organic eggs and chickens, more than half a million fewer organic chickens, turkeys and other poultry were produced in the UK last year.

Amid falling sales overall, some specialists are thriving. Abel & Cole, the organic box scheme, expects a 40% increase in sales this year. Keith Abel attributes this to the same reason he believes organic sales have fallen overall—because the big supermarkets have taken organic products off the shelves to make room for cheaper non-organic goods. "It is a self-fulfilling prophecy: they take them off the shelves, and they sell less," he said. "But that's great news for me."

Source: "Farmers Turn Away from Organic as Sales Drop: The Economic Downturn Means Organic Farmers Are Less Likely to Reap Rewards of Premium Prices for Their Produce," by Fiona Harvey from *The Guardian*, August 11, 2011. Copyright © 2011 by Guardian News and Media Ltd. Reprinted by permission.

Key Points in the Article

Since reaching a peak in 2008, organic food production and sales in the United Kingdom have steadily fallen, as has the amount of land farmers have converted to organic cultivation. The recession has been cited as a reason for the drop in sales, with large supermarkets cutting back on their organic selections. With sales numbers declining, many farmers have found it more difficult to justify the added expense of converting to organic production. Some farmers who had switched to organic when the British government was subsidizing conversion and production have since gone back to conventional methods now that subsidies have declined. While organic produce sales have declined in the United Kingdom, organic livestock sales have been mixed, with cattle production on the rise but poultry production falling.

Analyzing the News

ⓐ Organic products usually command a higher price than their non-organic counterparts, and up until 2008, the demand for organic food was increasing in the United Kingdom. The potential for higher profits attracted many farmers to the organic market as demand was increasing. However, the recession coupled with rising food prices had a negative effect on the market for organic food, and sales have declined each year since 2008. The decline in sales is due to a decrease in the overall demand for organic products. Figure 1 shows the market for organically grown corn. The decrease in demand is illustrated as a shift from D_1 to D_2, where both the equilibrium quantity and equilibrium market price decline.

ⓑ With sales falling, fewer farmers are converting to organic production, and some of those who had switched to organic are now reverting to conventional farming methods. The chapter notes that some firms exit a market when they experience economic losses. The decrease in demand in Figure 1 causes the price to decrease from P_1 to P_2. This decrease in price causes the individual farmer's demand curve to shift from D_1 to D_2 in Figure 2. The price per bushel decreases, and the farmer reduces production from q_1 to q_2. At the lower market price of P_2, the farmer has an economic loss represented by the area of the shaded box. Some farmers suffering losses will choose to exit the market.

ⓒ While organic produce and poultry farmers have been experiencing declining sales in the United Kingdom, organic cattle production has continued to rise to keep pace with growing sales. As long as demand continues to increase and organic cattle producers make an economic profit, more producers will have the incentive to enter the market. If the demand starts to decrease, though, as it did in other organic markets, we would expect to eventually see producers of organic cattle begin to exit this market as well.

Thinking Critically

1. The article states that due to declining product demand, farmers are converting from organic production back to conventional methods. Show what will happen in Figure 1 as some farmers exit the organic market, and show how this change will affect the farmer represented by Figure 1.

2. The article indicates that in addition to the decline in demand, the end of government grants and subsidies has contributed to the number of farmers leaving the organic market. How would government grants and subsidies affect this market?

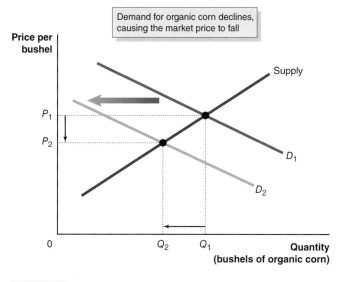

Figure 1

The market for organically grown corn.

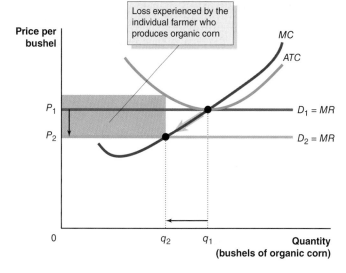

Figure 2

An individual farmer suffering an economic loss in the organic corn market.

Chapter Summary and Problems

Key Terms

Allocative efficiency, p. 313

Average revenue (*AR*), p. 294

Economic loss, p. 306

Economic profit, p. 305

Long-run competitive equilibrium, p. 308

Long-run supply curve, p. 309

Marginal revenue (*MR*), p. 294

Perfectly competitive market, p. 291

Price taker, p. 291

Productive efficiency, p. 311

Profit, p. 293

Shutdown point, p. 303

Sunk cost, p. 301

Summary

*LO 10.1 A **perfectly competitive market** must have many buyers and sellers, firms must be producing identical products, and there must be no barriers to entry of new firms. The demand curve for a good or service produced in a perfectly competitive market is downward sloping, but the demand curve for the output of one firm in a perfectly competitive market is a horizontal line at the market price. Firms in perfectly competitive markets are **price takers** and see their sales drop to zero if they attempt to charge more than the market price.

LO 10.2 **Profit** is the difference between total revenue (*TR*) and total cost (*TC*). **Average revenue (*AR*)** is total revenue divided by the quantity of the product sold. A firm maximizes profit by producing the level of output where the difference between revenue and cost is the greatest. This is the same level of output where marginal revenue is equal to marginal cost. **Marginal revenue (*MR*)** is the change in total revenue from selling one more unit.

LO 10.3 From the definitions of profit and average total cost, we can develop the following expression for the relationship between total profit and average total cost: Profit = $(P - ATC) \times Q$. Using this expression, we can determine the area showing profit or loss on a cost-curve graph: The area of profit or loss is a box with a height equal to price minus average total cost (for profit) or average total cost minus price (for loss) and a base equal to the quantity of output.

LO 10.4 In deciding whether to shut down or produce during a given period, a firm should ignore its *sunk costs*. A **sunk cost** is

a cost that has already been paid and that cannot be recovered. In the short run, a firm continues to produce as long as its price is at least equal to its average variable cost. A perfectly competitive firm's **shutdown point** is the minimum point on the firm's average variable cost curve. If price falls below average variable cost, the firm shuts down in the short run. For prices above the shutdown point, a perfectly competitive firm's marginal cost curve is also its supply curve.

LO 10.5 **Economic profit** is a firm's revenues minus all its costs, implicit and explicit. **Economic loss** is the situation in which a firm's total revenue is less than its total cost, including all implicit costs. If firms make economic profits in the short run, new firms enter the industry until the market price has fallen enough to wipe out the profits. If firms make economic losses, firms exit the industry until the market price has risen enough to wipe out the losses. **Long-run competitive equilibrium** is the situation in which the entry and exit of firms has resulted in the typical firm breaking even. The **long-run supply curve** shows the relationship between market price and the quantity supplied.

LO 10.6 Perfect competition results in **productive efficiency**, which means that goods and services are produced at the lowest possible cost. Perfect competition also results in **allocative efficiency**, which means the goods and services are produced up to the point where the last unit provides a marginal benefit to consumers equal to the marginal cost of producing it.

MyEconLab   Log in to MyEconLab to complete these exercises and get instant feedback.

Review Questions

LO 10.1

1.1 What are the three conditions for a market to be perfectly competitive?

1.2 What is a price taker? When are firms likely to be price takers?

1.3 Draw a graph showing the market demand and supply for corn and the demand for the corn produced by one corn farmer. Be sure to indicate the market price and the price received by the corn farmer.

*'Learning Objective' is abbreviated to 'LO' in the end of chapter material.

LO 10.2

2.1 Explain why it is true that for a firm in a perfectly competitive market, $P = MR = AR$.

2.2 Explain why if the difference between *TR* and *TC* is at its maximum positive value, then *MR* must equal *MC*.

2.3 Explain why it is true that for a firm in a perfectly competitive market, the profit-maximizing condition $MR = MC$ is equivalent to the condition $P = MC$.

LO 10.3

3.1 Draw a graph showing a firm in a perfectly competitive market that is making a profit. Be sure your graph includes the firm's demand curve, marginal revenue curve, marginal cost curve, average total cost curve, and average variable cost curve and make sure to indicate the area representing the firm's profits.

3.2 Draw a graph showing a firm in a perfectly competitive market that is operating at a loss. Be sure your graph includes the firm's demand curve, marginal revenue curve, marginal cost curve, average total cost curve, and average variable cost curve and make sure to indicate the area representing the firm's losses.

LO 10.4

4.1 What is the difference between a firm's shutdown point in the short run and in the long run? Why are firms willing to accept losses in the short run but not in the long run?

4.2 What is the relationship between a perfectly competitive firm's marginal cost curve and its supply curve?

4.3 How is the market supply curve derived from the supply curves of individual firms?

LO 10.5

5.1 When are firms likely to enter an industry? When are they likely to exit an industry?

5.2 Would a firm earning zero economic profit continue to produce, even in the long run?

5.3 Discuss the shape of the long-run supply curve in a perfectly competitive market. Suppose that a perfectly competitive market is initially at long-run equilibrium and then there is a permanent decrease in the demand for the product. Draw a graph showing how the market adjusts in the long run.

LO 10.6

6.1 Why are consumers so powerful in a market system?

6.2 What is meant by allocative efficiency? What is meant by productive efficiency? Briefly discuss the difference between these two concepts.

6.3 How does perfect competition lead to allocative and productive efficiency?

Problems and Applications

LO 10.1

1.1 Explain whether each of the following is a perfectly competitive market. For each market that is not perfectly competitive, explain why it is not.
  a. Corn farming
  b. Retail bookselling
  c. Automobile manufacturing
  d. New home construction

1.2 Why are consumers usually price takers when they buy most goods and services, while relatively few firms are price takers?

1.3 [**Related to the** Don't Let This Happen to You **on page 292**] Explain whether you agree or disagree with the following remark:

> According to the model of perfectly competitive markets, the demand for wheat should be a horizontal line. But this can't be true: When the price of wheat rises, the quantity of wheat demanded falls, and when the price of wheat falls, the quantity of wheat demanded rises. Therefore, the demand for wheat is not a horizontal line.

LO 10.2

2.1 A student argues: "To maximize profit, a firm should produce the quantity where the difference between marginal revenue and marginal cost is the greatest. If a firm produces more than this quantity, then the profit made on each additional unit will be falling." Briefly explain whether you agree with this reasoning.

2.2 Why don't firms maximize revenue rather than profit? If a firm decided to maximize revenue, would it be likely to produce a smaller or larger quantity than if it were maximizing profit? Briefly explain.

2.3 Refer to Table 10.2 and Table 10.3. Suppose the price of wheat rises to $7.00 per bushel. How many bushels of wheat will Farmer Parker produce, and how much profit will he make? Briefly explain.

2.4 Refer to Table 10.2 and Table 10.3. Suppose that the marginal cost of wheat is $0.50 higher for every bushel of wheat produced. For example, the marginal cost of producing the eighth bushel of wheat is now $7.50. Assume that the price of wheat remains $4 per bushel. Will this increase in marginal cost change the profit-maximizing level of production for Farmer Parker? Briefly explain. How much profit will Farmer Parker make now?

LO 10.3

3.1 [**Related to** Solved Problem 10.3 **on page 297**] Frances sells earrings in the perfectly competitive earrings market. Her output per day and her costs are as follows:

Output per Day	Total Cost
0	$1.00
1	2.50
2	3.50
3	4.20
4	4.50
5	5.20
6	6.80
7	8.70
8	10.70
9	13.00

  a. If the current equilibrium price in the market for earrings is $1.80, how many earrings will Frances produce, what price will she charge, and how much profit (or loss) will she make? Draw a graph to illustrate your answer. Your graph should be clearly labelled and should include Frances's demand, *ATC*, *AVC*, *MC*, and *MR* curves; the price she is charging; the quantity she is producing; and the area representing her profit (or loss).

b. Suppose the equilibrium price of earrings falls to $1.00. Now how many earrings will Frances produce, what price will she charge, and how much profit (or loss) will she make? Show your work. Draw a graph to illustrate this situation, using the instructions in part (a).

c. Suppose the equilibrium price of earrings falls to $0.25. Now how many earrings will Frances produce, what price will she charge, and how much profit (or loss) will she make?

3.2 [**Related to** Solved Problem 10.3 **on page 297**] Review Solved Problem 10.3 and then answer the following: Suppose the equilibrium price of hockey sticks falls to $2.50. Now how many hockey sticks will Andy produce? What price will he charge? How much profit (or loss) will he make?

3.3 [**Related to the** Don't Let This Happen to You **on page 299**] A student examines the following graph and argues, "I believe that a firm will want to produce at Q_1, not Q_2. At Q_1, the distance between price and marginal cost is the greatest. Therefore, at Q_1, the firm will be maximizing its profit." Briefly explain whether you agree with the student's argument.

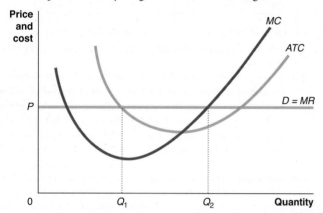

3.4 [**Related to the** Making the Connection **on page 300**] In 2007, Research In Motion's BlackBerry was the dominant handheld communication device. It had 12 million users and $1.6 billion in revenue. By 2012, BlackBerry had fallen to seventh place in rankings of smartphone manufacturers. Explain how this may have been predictable in a competitive market.

Based on "BlackBerry Timeline: A Tech Titan's Roller Coaster Ride: How the Maker of an Iconic Smartphone Rose to Riches, and Why It Faces an Uncertain Future," *CBC News*, May 1, 2013, accessed at http://www.cbc.ca/news/interactives/timeline-rim/

LO 10.4

4.1 Edward Scahill produces table lamps in the perfectly competitive desk lamp market.
   a. Fill in the missing values in the following table.
   b. Suppose the equilibrium price in the desk lamp market is $50. How many table lamps should Scahill produce, and how much profit will he make?
   c. If next week the equilibrium price of desk lamps drops to $30, should Scahill shut down? Explain.

Output per Week	Total Cost	AFC	AVC	ATC	MC
0	$100				
1	150				
2	175				
3	190				
4	210				
5	240				
6	280				
7	330				
8	390				
9	460				
10	540				

4.2 Matthew Rafferty produces hiking boots in the perfectly competitive hiking boot market.
   a. Fill in the missing values in the following table.

Output per Week	Total Cost	AFC	AVC	ATC	MC
0	$100.00				
1	155.70				
2	205.60				
3	253.90				
4	304.80				
5	362.50				
6	431.20				
7	515.10				
8	618.40				
9	745.30				
10	900.00				

   b. Suppose the equilibrium price in the hiking boot market is $100. How many boots should Rafferty produce, what price should he charge, and how much profit will he make?
   c. If next week the equilibrium price of boots drops to $65, how many boots should Rafferty produce, what price should he charge, and how much profit (or loss) will he make?
   d. If the equilibrium price of boots falls to $50, how many boots should Rafferty produce, what price should he charge, and how much profit (or loss) will he make?

4.3 The following graph represents the situation of a perfectly competitive firm.

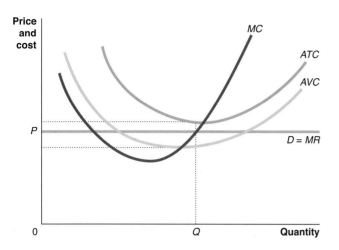

Indicate on the graph the areas that represent the following:
a. Total cost
b. Total revenue
c. Variable cost
d. Profit or loss

Briefly explain whether the firm will continue to produce in the short run.

4.4 [**Related to** Solved Problem 10.4 **on page 302**] An article in the *Wall Street Journal* discussed problems some shopping malls in the United States were having retaining stores. According to the article, some stores that were currently losing money were considering not "sticking around once their leases expire." If the owner of a store that leases space in a mall is suffering a loss at that location, why wouldn't the owner close the store right away rather than wait until the lease expires?

Based on Kris Hudson and Vanessa O'Connell, "Recession Turns Malls into Ghost Towns," *Wall Street Journal*, May 22, 2009.

LO 10.5

5.1 Suppose an assistant professor of economics is earning a salary of $75,000 per year. One day she quits her job, sells $100,000 worth of bonds that had been earning 5 percent per year, and uses the funds to open a bookstore. At the end of the year, she shows an accounting profit of $90,000 on her income tax return. What is her economic profit?

5.2 Why does the entry of firms into an industry decrease the economic profits of the existing firms? Why does the exit of firms from an industry increase the economic profits of the existing firms?

5.3 Consider the following statement: "The products for which demand is the greatest will also be the products that are most profitable to produce." Briefly explain whether you agree with this statement.

5.4 [**Related to the** Making the Connection **on page 309**] Ethan Nicholas developed his first game while still working as a programmer for Sun Microsystems. After his first game was a success, he quit Sun to form his own company—with himself as the only employee. How did Nicholas's quitting Sun to work full time for himself affect the cost to him of developing games?

Based on Jenna Wortham, "The iPhone Gold Rush," *New York Times*, April 5, 2009.

5.5 [**Related to the** Chapter Opener **on page 289**] If in the long run vegetable growers who sell in farmers' markets make no greater rate of return on their investment than vegetable growers who sell to supermarkets, why did a significant number of vegetable growers switch from selling to supermarkets to selling in farmers' markets in the first place?

LO 10.6

6.1 The chapter states, "Firms will supply all those goods that provide consumers with a marginal benefit at least as great as the marginal cost of producing them." A student objects to this statement, arguing, "I doubt that firms will really do this. After all, firms are in business to make a profit; they don't care about what is best for consumers." Evaluate the student's argument.

6.2 [**Related to** Solved Problem 10.6 **on page 311**] Discuss the following statement: "In a perfectly competitive market, in the long run consumers benefit from reductions in costs, but firms don't." Don't firms also benefit from cost reductions because they are able to earn greater profits?

6.3 [**Related to** Solved Problem 10.6 **on page 311**] In 2011, Sony announced that it had lost money selling televisions for the seventh straight year. Given the strong consumer demand for plasma, LCD, and LED television sets, shouldn't Sony have been able to raise prices to earn a profit? Briefly explain.

Based on Daisuke Wakabayashi, "Sony Predicts $1 Billion Loss," *Wall Street Journal*, November 3, 2011.

Monopolistic Competition: The Competitive Model in a More Realistic Setting

Chapter Outline and Learning Objectives

Michele Falzone/Alamy

Starbucks: The Limits to Growth Through Product Differentiation

Like many other large firms, Starbucks started small. In 1971, entrepreneurs Gordon Bowker, Gerald Baldwin, and Zev Siegl opened the first Starbucks in the United States in Seattle, Washington. Current CEO Howard Schultz joined the company 10 years later. Schultz realized that many consumers wanted a coffeehouse where they could sit, relax, read, chat, and drink higher-quality coffee than was typically served in diners or doughnut shops. Designing Starbucks coffeehouses to provide this experience was the key to his success. But it was not difficult for other coffeehouses to copy the Starbucks approach.

By 2009, fierce competition and a weak economy led Starbucks to close hundreds of stores, including seven in Canada, and cut prices as it tried to overcome the impression that it was the "home of the $4 coffee." Starbucks became profitable once more in 2010, opening 51 new stores in Canada alone. Schultz realizes that his company faces a constant challenge to stay ahead of its competitors and satisfy its customers: "I feel it's so important to remind us all of how fleeting success…can be."

Perfectly competitive markets share three key characteristics:
1. There are many firms.
2. All firms sell identical products.
3. There are no barriers to new firms entering the industry.

The market Starbucks competes in shares two of these characteristics: There are many coffeehouses, and the barriers to entering the market are very low. But the coffee at Starbucks is not identical to what competing coffeehouses offer. Selling coffee in coffeehouses is not like selling wheat: The products that Starbucks and its competitors sell are *differentiated* rather than identical. So, the coffeehouse market is *monopolistically competitive* rather than perfectly competitive. As we will see, most monopolistically competitive firms are unable to earn economic profits in the long run.

AN INSIDE LOOK on **page 340** describes how Starbucks acquired a juice maker to expand into areas outside the coffee business.

Based on Claire Cain Miller, "A Changed Starbucks. A Changed C.E.O.," *New York Times*, March 12, 2011; Jason Buckland, "Franchises Closing Stores in Canada: Starbucks," http://money.ca.msn.com/investing/gallery.aspx?cp-documentid=25601800&page=6, September 18, 2010.

Economics in Your Life

Opening Your Own Restaurant

After you graduate, you plan to realize your dream of opening your own Italian restaurant. You are confident that many people will enjoy the pasta prepared with your grandmother's secret sauce. Although your hometown already has three Italian restaurants, you are convinced that you can enter this market and make a profit.

You have many choices to make in operating your restaurant. Will it be "family style," with sturdy but inexpensive furniture, where families with small—and noisy!—children will feel welcome, or will it be more elegant, with nice furniture, tablecloths, and candles? Will you offer a full menu or concentrate on pasta dishes that use your grandmother's secret sauce? These and other choices you make will distinguish your restaurant from competitors. What's likely to happen in the restaurant market in your hometown after you open? How successful are you likely to be? See if you can answer these questions as you read this chapter. You can check your answers against those we provide on page 339 at the end of this chapter.

Monopolistic competition A market structure in which barriers to entry are low and many firms compete by selling similar, but not identical, products.

Many markets in the Canadian economy are similar to the coffeehouse market: They have many buyers and sellers, and the barriers to entry are low, but the goods and services offered for sale are differentiated rather than identical. Examples of these markets include consumer electronics stores, restaurants, movie theatres, supermarkets, and manufacturing men's and women's clothing. In fact, the majority of the firms you patronize are in **monopolistic competition**.

Perfect competition benefits consumers and results in economic efficiency. Will these same desirable outcomes also hold for monopolistically competitive markets? This question is important because monopolistically competitive markets are common.

11.1 LEARNING OBJECTIVE

Explain why a monopolistically competitive firm has downward-sloping demand and marginal revenue curves.

Demand and Marginal Revenue for a Firm in a Monopolistically Competitive Market

If the Starbucks coffeehouse located a kilometre from where you live raises the price of a caffè latte from $3.00 to $3.25, it will lose some, but not all, of its customers. Some customers will switch to buying their coffee at another coffee retailer (Tim Hortons, Second Cup, or McDonald's, perhaps), but other customers will be willing to pay the higher price for a variety of reasons: This store may be closer to them, or they may prefer Starbucks caffè lattes to similar coffees at competing stores. Because changing the price affects the quantity of caffè lattes sold, a Starbucks store will face a downward-sloping demand curve rather than the horizontal demand curve that a wheat farmer faces.

The Demand Curve for a Monopolistically Competitive Firm

Figure 11.1 shows how a change in price affects the quantity of caffè lattes Starbucks sells. The increase in the price from $3.00 to $3.25 decreases the quantity of caffè lattes sold from 3,000 per week to 2,400 per week.

Marginal Revenue for a Firm with a Downward-Sloping Demand Curve

For a firm in a perfectly competitive market, the demand curve and the marginal revenue curve are the same. A perfectly competitive firm faces a horizontal demand curve and does not have to cut the price to sell a larger quantity. A monopolistically competitive firm, on the other hand, must cut the price to sell more, so its marginal revenue curve will slope downward and will be below its demand curve.

Figure 11.1

The Downward-Sloping Demand for Caffè Lattes at a Starbucks

If a Starbucks increases the price of caffè lattes, it will lose some, but not all, of its customers. In this case, raising the price from $3.00 to $3.25 reduces the quantity of caffè lattes sold from 3,000 to 2,400. Therefore, unlike a perfect competitor, a Starbucks coffeehouse faces a downward-sloping demand curve.

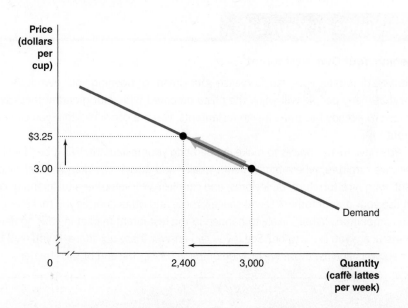

Table 11.1

Demand and Marginal Revenue at a Starbucks

Caffè Lattes Sold per Week (Q)	Price (P)	Total Revenue (TR = P × Q)	Average Revenue $AR = \dfrac{TR}{Q}$	Marginal Revenue $AR = \dfrac{\Delta TR}{\Delta Q}$
0	$6.00	$ 0.00	—	—
1	5.50	5.50	$5.50	$5.50
2	5.00	10.00	5.00	4.50
3	4.50	13.50	4.50	3.50
4	4.00	16.00	4.00	2.50
5	3.50	17.50	3.50	1.50
6	3.00	18.00	3.00	0.50
7	2.50	17.50	2.50	–0.50
8	2.00	16.00	2.00	–1.50
9	1.50	13.50	1.50	–2.50
10	1.00	10.00	1.00	–3.50

The data in Table 11.1 illustrate this point. To keep the numbers simple, let's assume that your local Starbucks coffeehouse is very small and sells at most 10 caffè lattes per week. If Starbucks charges a price of $6.00 or more, all of its potential customers will buy their coffee somewhere else. If it charges $5.50, it will sell 1 caffè latte per week. For each additional $0.50 by which Starbucks reduces the price, it increases the number of caffè lattes it sells by 1. The third column in the table shows how the firm's *total revenue* changes as it sells more caffè lattes. The fourth column shows the firm's revenue per unit, or its *average revenue*. Average revenue is equal to total revenue divided by quantity. Because total revenue equals price multiplied by quantity, dividing by quantity leaves just price. Therefore, *average revenue is always equal to price*. This result will be true for firms selling in any of the four market structures of perfect competition, monopolistic competition, oligopoly, or monopoly.

The last column shows the firm's marginal revenue, or the amount that total revenue changes as the firm sells 1 more caffè latte. For a perfectly competitive firm, the additional revenue received from selling 1 more unit is just equal to the price. That will not be true for Starbucks because to sell another caffè latte, it has to reduce the price. When the firm cuts the price by $0.50, one good thing and one bad thing happen:

- **The good thing.** It sells 1 more caffè latte; we can call this the *output effect*.

- **The bad thing.** It receives $0.50 less for each caffè latte that it could have sold at the higher price; we can call this the *price effect*.

Figure 11.2 illustrates what happens when the firm cuts the price from $3.50 to $3.00. Selling the sixth caffè latte adds the $3.00 price to the firm's revenue; this is the

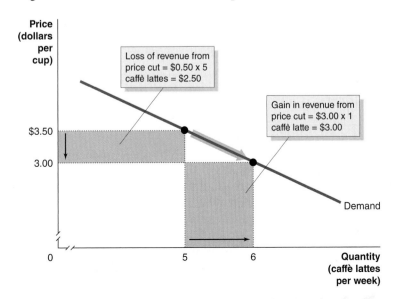

Figure 11.2

How a Price Cut Affects a Firm's Revenue

If a local Starbucks reduces the price of a caffè latte from $3.50 to $3.00, the number of caffè lattes it sells per week will increase from 5 to 6. Its marginal revenue from selling the sixth caffè latte will be $0.50, which is equal to the $3.00 additional revenue from selling 1 more caffè latte (the area of the green box) minus the $2.50 loss in revenue from selling the first 5 caffè lattes for $0.50 less each (the area of the red box).

The Demand and Marginal Revenue Curves for a Monopolistically Competitive Firm

Any firm that has the ability to affect the price of the product it sells will have a marginal revenue curve that is below its demand curve. We plot the data from Table 11.1 to create the demand and marginal revenue curves. After the sixth caffè latte, marginal revenue becomes negative because the additional revenue received from selling 1 more caffè latte is smaller than the revenue lost from receiving a lower price on the caffè lattes that could have been sold at the original price.

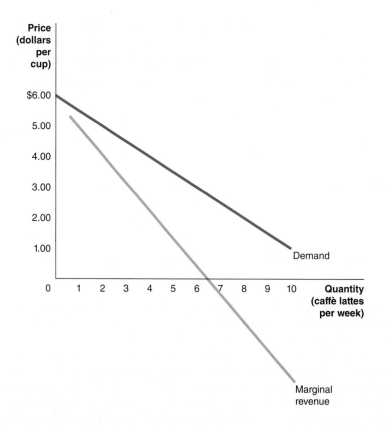

output effect. But Starbucks now receives a price of $3.00, rather than $3.50, on the first 5 caffè lattes sold; this is the price effect. As a result of the price effect, the firm's revenue on these 5 caffè lattes is $2.50 less than it would have been if the price had remained at $3.50. So, the firm has gained $3.00 in revenue on the sixth caffè latte and lost $2.50 in revenue on the first 5 caffè lattes, for a net change in revenue of $0.50. Marginal revenue is the change in total revenue from selling 1 more unit. Therefore, the marginal revenue of the sixth caffè latte is $0.50. Notice that the marginal revenue of the sixth unit is far below its price of $3.00. In fact, for each additional caffè latte Starbucks sells, marginal revenue will be less than price. There is an important general point: *Every firm that has the ability to affect the price of the good or service it sells will have a marginal revenue curve that is below its demand curve*. Only firms in perfectly competitive markets, which can sell as many units as they want at the market price, have marginal revenue curves that are the same as their demand curves.

Figure 11.3 shows the relationship between the demand curve and the marginal revenue curve for the local Starbucks. Notice that after the sixth caffè latte, marginal revenue becomes negative. Marginal revenue is negative because the additional revenue received from selling 1 more caffè latte is smaller than the revenue lost from receiving a lower price on the caffè lattes that could have been sold at the original price.

11.2 LEARNING OBJECTIVE

Explain how a monopolistically competitive firm maximizes profit in the short run.

How a Monopolistically Competitive Firm Maximizes Profit in the Short Run

All firms use the same approach to maximize profits: They produce where marginal revenue is equal to marginal cost. For the local Starbucks, this means selling the quantity of caffè lattes for which the last caffè latte sold adds the same amount to the firm's revenue as to its costs. To begin our discussion of how monopolistically competitive firms maximize profits, let's consider the situation the local Starbucks faces in the short run. In the short run, at least one factor of production is fixed, and there is not enough time for new firms to enter the market. A Starbucks has many costs, including the cost of purchasing the ingredients for its caffè lattes and other coffees, the electricity it uses, and the wages of its employees. Recall that a firm's *marginal cost* is the increase in total cost resulting from producing another unit of output. We have seen that for many firms, marginal cost has a U shape. We will assume that the marginal cost curve for this Starbucks has the usual shape.

In the table in Figure 11.4, we bring together for this Starbucks the revenue data from Table 11.1 with the firm's cost data. The graphs in Figure 11.4 plot the data from the table. In panel (a), we see how Starbucks can determine its profit-maximizing quantity and price. As long as the marginal cost of selling 1 more caffè latte is less than the marginal revenue, the firm should sell additional caffè lattes. For example, increasing the quantity of caffè lattes sold from 3 per week to 4 per week increases total cost by $1.00 but increases total revenue by $2.50; that is, marginal cost is $1 and marginal revenue is $2.50. So, the firm's profits are increased by $1.50 as a result of selling the fourth caffè latte.

Caffè Lattes Sold per Week (Q)	Price (P)	Total Revenue (TR)	Marginal Revenue (MR)	Total Cost (TC)	Marginal Cost (MC)	Average Total Cost (ATC)	Profit
0	$6.00	$0.00	—	$5.00	—	—	−$5.00
1	5.50	5.50	$5.50	8.00	$3.00	$8.00	−2.50
2	5.00	10.00	4.50	9.50	1.50	4.75	0.50
3	4.50	13.50	3.50	10.00	0.50	3.33	3.50
4	4.00	16.00	2.50	11.00	1.00	2.75	5.00
5	3.50	17.50	1.50	12.50	1.50	2.50	5.00
6	3.00	18.00	0.50	14.50	2.00	2.42	3.50
7	2.50	17.50	−0.50	17.00	2.50	2.43	0.50
8	2.00	16.00	−1.50	20.00	3.00	2.50	−4.00
9	1.50	13.50	−2.50	23.50	3.50	2.61	−10.00
10	1.00	10.00	−3.50	27.50	4.00	2.75	−17.50

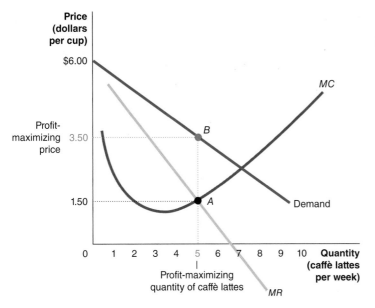

(a) Profit-maximizing quantity and price for a monopolistic competitor

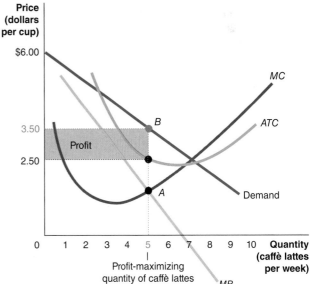

(b) Short-run profits for a monopolistic competitor

Figure 11.4 Maximizing Profit in a Monopolistically Competitive Market

To maximize profit, a Starbucks coffeehouse wants to sell caffè lattes up to the point where the marginal revenue from selling the last caffè latte is just equal to the marginal cost. As the table shows, this happens with the fifth caffè latte—point *A* in panel (a)—which adds $1.50 to the firm's costs and $1.50 to its revenues. The firm then uses the demand curve to find the price that will lead consumers to buy this quantity of caffè lattes (point *B*). In panel (b), the green box represents the firm's profits. The box has a height equal to $1.00, which is the $3.50 price minus the average total cost of $2.50, and it has a base equal to the quantity of 5 caffè lattes. So, this Starbucks's profit equals $1 × 5 = $5.00.

As Starbucks sells more caffè lattes, rising marginal cost eventually equals marginal revenue, and the firm sells the profit-maximizing quantity of caffè lattes. Marginal cost equals marginal revenue with the fifth caffè latte, which adds $1.50 to the firm's costs and $1.50 to its revenues—point *A* in panel (a) of Figure 11.4. The demand curve tells us the price at which the firm is able to sell 5 caffè lattes per week. In Figure 11.4, if we draw a vertical line from 5 caffè lattes up to the demand curve, we can see that the price at which the firm can sell 5 caffè lattes per week is $3.50 (point *B*). We can conclude that for Starbucks, the profit-maximizing quantity is 5 caffè lattes, and the profit-maximizing price is $3.50. If the firm sells more than 5 caffè lattes per week, its profits fall. For example, selling a sixth caffè latte adds $2.00 to its costs and only $0.50 to its revenues. So, its profit would fall from $5.00 to $3.50.

Panel (b) adds the average total cost curve for Starbucks. The panel shows that the average total cost of selling 5 caffè lattes is $2.50.

$$\text{Profit} = (P - ATC) \times Q.$$

In this case, profit = ($3.50 − $2.50) × 5 = $5.00. The green box in panel (b) shows the amount of profit. The box has a base equal to *Q* and a height equal to (*P* − *ATC*), so its area equals profit.

Notice that, unlike a perfectly competitive firm, which produces where *P* = *MC*, a monopolistically competitive firm produces where *P* > *MC*. In this case, Starbucks is charging a price of $3.50, although marginal cost is $1.50. For a perfectly competitive firm, price equals marginal revenue, *P* = *MR*. Therefore, to fulfill the *MR* = *MC* condition for profit maximization, a perfectly competitive firm will produce where *P* = *MC*. Because *P* > *MR* for a monopolistically competitive firm—which results from the marginal revenue curve being below the demand curve—a monopolistically competitive firm will maximize profits where *P* > *MC*.

Solved Problem **11.2**

Does Minimizing Cost Maximize Profits?

Suppose Apple finds that the relationship between the average total cost of producing iPhones and the quantity of iPhones produced is as shown in the following graph.

Will Apple maximize profits if it produces 800,000 iPhones per month? Briefly explain.

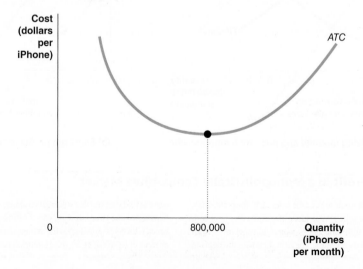

Solving the Problem

Step 1: Review the chapter material. This problem is about how monopolistically competitive firms maximize profits, so you may want to review the section "How a Monopolistically Competitive Firm Maximizes Profit in the Short Run," which begins on page 324.

Step 2: Discuss the relationship between minimizing costs and maximizing profits. Firms often talk about the steps they take to reduce costs. The figure shows that by producing 800,000 iPhones per month, Apple will minimize its average cost of production. But remember that minimizing cost is not the firm's ultimate goal; the firm's ultimate goal is to maximize profits. Depending on demand, a firm may maximize profits by producing a quantity that is either larger or smaller than the quantity that would minimize average total cost.

Step 3: Draw a graph that shows Apple maximizing profit at a quantity where average cost is not minimized. Note that in the graph, average cost reaches a minimum at a quantity of 800,000, but profits are maximized at a quantity of 600,000.

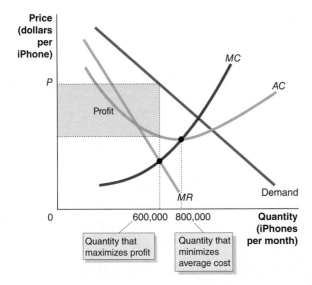

Your Turn: For more practice, do related problem 2.2 on page 343 at the end of this chapter.

MyEconLab

What Happens to Profits in the Long Run?

11. 3 LEARNING OBJECTIVE

Analyze the situation of a monopolistically competitive firm in the long run.

Remember that a firm makes an economic profit when its total revenue is greater than all of its costs, including the opportunity cost of the funds invested in the firm by its owners. Because cost curves include the owners' opportunity costs, the Starbucks coffeehouse represented in Figure 11.4 on page 325 is making an economic profit. This economic profit gives entrepreneurs an incentive to enter this market and establish new firms. If a Starbucks is earning an economic profit selling caffè lattes, new coffeehouses are likely to open in the same area.

How Does the Entry of New Firms Affect the Profits of Existing Firms?

As new coffeehouses open near a local Starbucks, the firm's demand curve will shift to the left. The demand curve will shift because the Starbucks will sell fewer caffè lattes at each price when there are additional coffeehouses in the area selling similar drinks. The demand curve will also become more elastic because consumers have additional coffeehouses from which to buy coffee, so the Starbucks will lose more sales if it raises its prices. Figure 11.5 shows how the demand curve for the local Starbucks shifts as new firms enter its market.

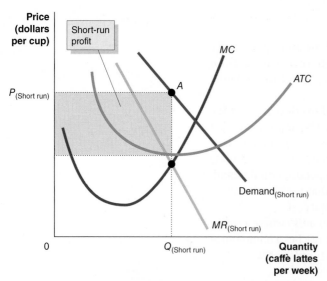

(a) A monopolistic competitor may earn a short-run profit

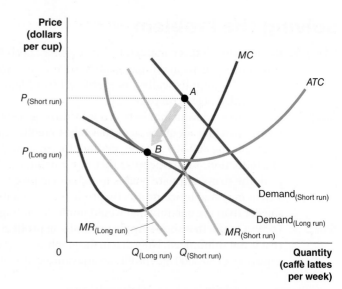

(b) A monopolistic competitor's profits are eliminated in the long run

Figure 11.5 **How Entry of New Firms Eliminates Profits**

Panel (a) shows that in the short run, the local Starbucks faces the demand and marginal revenue curves labelled "Short run." With this demand curve, Starbucks can charge a price above average total cost (point *A*) and make a profit, shown by the green rectangle. But this profit attracts new firms to enter the market, which shifts the demand and marginal revenue curves to the curves labelled "Long run" in panel (b). Because price is now equal to average total cost (point *B*), Starbucks breaks even and no longer earns an economic profit.

In panel (a) of Figure 11.5, the short-run demand curve shows the relationship between the price of caffè lattes and the quantity of caffè lattes Starbucks sells per week before the entry of new firms. With this demand curve, Starbucks can charge a price above average total cost—shown as point *A* in panel (a)—and make a profit. But this profit attracts additional coffeehouses to the area and shifts the demand curve for the Starbucks caffè lattes to the left. As long as Starbucks is making an economic profit, there is an incentive for additional coffeehouses to open in the area, and the demand curve will continue shifting to the left. As panel (b) shows, eventually the demand curve will have shifted to the point where it is just touching—or tangent to—the average total cost curve.

In the long run, at the point at which the demand curve is tangent to the average cost curve, price is equal to average total cost (point *B*), the firm is breaking even, and it no longer earns an economic profit. In the long run, the demand curve is also more

Don't Let This Happen to You

Don't Confuse Zero Economic Profit with Zero Accounting Profit

Remember that economists count the opportunity cost of the owner's investment in a firm as a cost. For example, suppose you invest $200,000 opening a pizza parlour, and the return you could earn on those funds each year in a similar investment—such as opening a sandwich shop—is 10 percent. Therefore, the annual opportunity cost of investing the funds in your own business is 10 percent of $200,000, or $20,000. This $20,000 is part of your profit in the accounting sense, and you would have to pay taxes on it. But in an economic sense, the $20,000 is a cost. In long-run equilibrium, we would expect that entry of new firms would keep you from earning more than 10 percent on your investment. So, you would end up breaking even and earning zero economic profit, even though you were earning an accounting profit of $20,000.

elastic because the more coffeehouses there are in the area, the more sales Starbucks will lose to other coffeehouses if it raises its price.

Of course, it is possible that a monopolistically competitive firm will suffer an economic loss in the short run. As a consequence, the owners of the firm will not be covering the opportunity cost of their investment. We expect that, in the long run, firms will exit an industry if they are suffering economic losses. If firms exit, the demand curve for the output of a remaining firm will shift to the right. This process will continue until the representative firm in the industry is able to charge a price equal to its average cost and break even. Therefore, in the long run, monopolistically competitive firms will experience neither economic profits nor economic losses. Table 11.2 summarizes the short run and the long run for a monopolistically competitive firm.

Table 11.2 The Short Run and the Long Run for a Monopolistically Competitive Firm

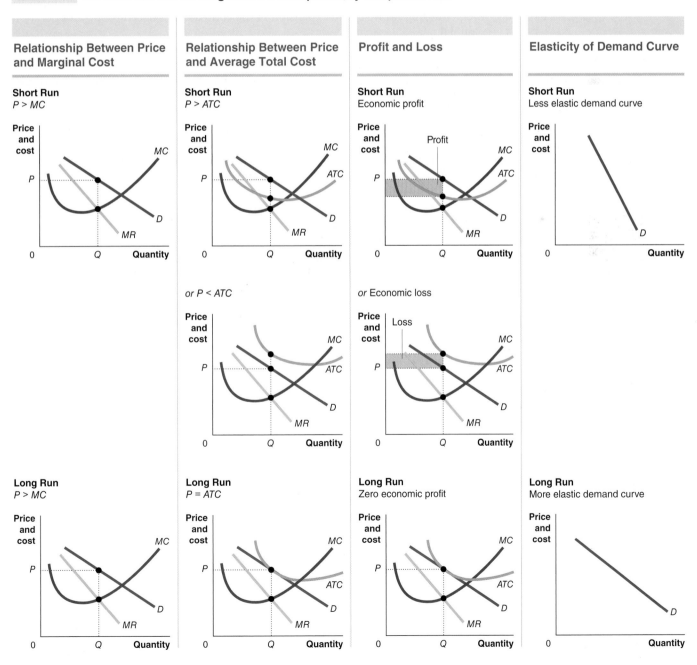

© david pearson/Alam

Making
the
Connection

The Tim Hortons Coffee War in Canadian Cities

On May 8, 2013, an article in the *Financial Post* summed up the situation that Tim Hortons was in: "Tim Hortons Inc., under pressure from a U.S. hedge fund seeking better returns, named a new chief executive on Wednesday as it reported a 3% fall in first-quarter profit. The Canadian coffee and doughnut chain said Marc Caira, a long-time Nestlé SA executive, would take over from interim CEO Paul House on July 2." The success and now struggles of Tim Hortons are a familiar pattern for firms in monopolistically competitive markets.

Tim Hortons was founded in 1964 in Hamilton, Ontario, by the Canadian hockey player Tim Horton and Jim Charade. With 4,071 restaurants (3,355 in Canada, 745 in the United States, 20 in the United Arab Emirates, and 3 in Oman) as of July 1, 2012, Tim Hortons is Canada's largest fast-food service operator and holds over 60 percent of the Canadian coffee market. It managed to generate positive same-store sales growth in both Canada and the United States for 21 years as of 2012. Sales and profits at Tim Hortons were increasing due in part to a broadening of its menu offerings as well as to expansion in the United States and the Gulf Cooperation Council.

The profitability of Tim Hortons has attracted competitors, and today Tim's is facing challenging operating conditions and intense competition from a range of chains, including Starbucks, Second Cup, McDonald's, Wendy's, and Subway. In fact, Starbucks is in direct competition with Tim Hortons. Starbucks is rapidly expanding, with over 18,000 locations around the world (including almost 1,400 locations in Canada). Tim Hortons has many of its stores in Eastern Canada and along the highways between major cities. Starbucks is trying to expand in the cities, opening stores near universities, financial districts, and well-to-do neighbourhoods. Moreover, Starbucks has a strategy that differentiates it from Tim Hortons (and other competitors), offering a European espresso bar atmosphere.

In a monopolistically competitive industry, maintaining profits in the long run is very difficult. Only by constantly innovating and responding to challenging market conditions has Tim Hortons been able to be profitable for nearly 50 years. Now it appears that Tim Hortons is struggling with intense competition from other firms and in particular is fighting a coffee war with Starbucks in the Canadian urban core.

Based on "Meet the New Tim Hortons CEO," *Financial Post*, May 8, 2013; Tim Hortons 2012 *Annual Report*.

MyEconLab

Your Turn: Test your understanding by doing related problem 3.2 on page 344 at the end of this chapter.

Is Zero Economic Profit Inevitable in the Long Run?

The economic analysis of the long run shows the effects of market forces over time. Owners of monopolistically competitive firms, of course, do not have to passively accept this long-run result. The key to earning economic profits is either to sell a differentiated product or to find a way of producing an existing product at a lower cost. If a monopolistically competitive firm selling a differentiated product is earning profits, these profits will attract the entry of additional firms, and the entry of those firms will eventually eliminate the firm's profits. If a firm introduces new technology that allows it to sell a good or service at a lower cost, competing firms will eventually be able to duplicate that technology and eliminate the firm's profits. *But this result holds only if the firm stands still and fails to find new ways of differentiating its product or fails to find new ways of lowering the cost of producing its product.* Starbucks had great initial success, had difficulty maintaining its profitability against the entry of new firms, and then found its way back to profitability by introducing new products and improving its customers' experience through a loyalty program and other innovations. Firms continually struggle to find new ways of differentiating their products as they try to stay one step ahead of other firms that are attempting to copy their success.

The owner of a competitive firm is in a position like that of Ebenezer Scrooge in Charles Dickens's *A Christmas Carol*. When the Ghost of Christmas Yet to Come shows Scrooge visions of his own death, he asks the ghost, "Are these the shadows of the things that Will be, or are they shadows of things that May be, only?" The shadow of the end of their profits haunts owners of every firm. Firms try to avoid losing profits by reducing costs, by improving their products, or by convincing consumers that their products are indeed different from what competitors offer. To stay one step ahead of its competitors, a firm has to offer consumers goods or services that they perceive to have greater *value* than those competing firms offer. Value can take the form of product differentiation that makes the good or service more suited to consumers' preferences, or it can take the form of a lower price.

Solved Problem **11.3**

Can It Be Profitable to Be the High-Price Seller?

During the year ended in March 2011, hhgregg, a U.S. appliance and electronics retailer, reported that its profits had risen 23 percent. During the same period, Best Buy's profits declined by 3 percent. Best Buy is much larger than hhgregg, so it is able to buy its appliances, televisions, and other goods from manufacturers at a low price. Because hhgregg must pay higher prices to manufacturers, it must charge higher prices to consumers. How is hhgregg able to succeed in competition with Best Buy, Walmart, Amazon, and other big retailers, despite charging high prices?

According to an article in the *Wall Street Journal*: "hhgregg's commissioned sales staff is an advantage over national chains with young, lower-paid hourly workers that tend to stay for shorter periods." hhgregg's CEO was quoted as saying: "We have sales people that have been with us 10 to 20 years, and customers who come in and ask for them by name."

Use this information to explain how an hhgregg store might be more profitable than a similar Best Buy store, despite the fact that the hhgregg store charges higher prices. Use a graph for hhgregg and a graph for Best Buy to illustrate your answer.

Solving the Problem

Step 1: Review the chapter material. This problem is about how a monopolistically competitive firm maximizes profits and about how firms attempt to earn economic profits in the long run, so you may want to review the section "How a Monopolistically Competitive Firm Maximizes Profit in the Short Run," which begins on page 324, and the section "Is Zero Economic Profit Inevitable in the Long Run?" on page 330.

Step 2: Explain how hhgregg can remain profitable despite its high costs. If an hhgregg store has higher costs than a comparable Best Buy store, it can have greater profits only if the demand for its goods is higher. According to the *Wall Street Journal* article, hhgregg has differentiated itself from the competition, particularly from large chain stores such as Best Buy, by offering better customer service. By having salespeople who are more knowledgeable and more experienced than the salespeople hired by competitors, hhgregg has attracted consumers who need help in buying televisions and appliances. The higher demand from these consumers must be enough to offset hhgregg's higher costs.

Step 3: Draw graphs to illustrate your argument. For simplicity, the graphs here assume that televisions are the product being sold. Panel (a) shows the situation for hhgregg, and panel (b) shows the situation for Best Buy. The graphs show that the hhgregg store has both greater demand and higher costs than

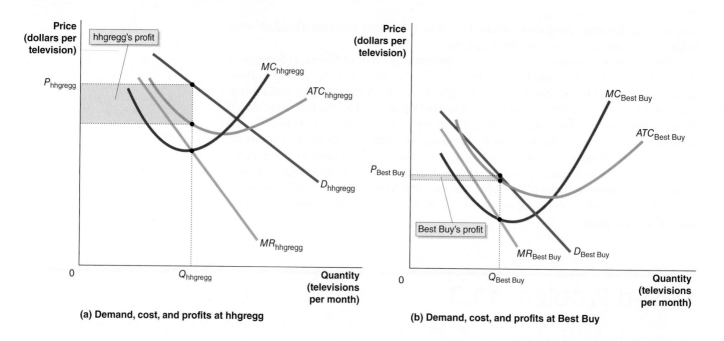

(a) Demand, cost, and profits at hhgregg

(b) Demand, cost, and profits at Best Buy

the Best Buy store. Because the greater demand more than offsets the higher costs, the hhgregg store makes a larger profit.

Extra Credit: As we have seen, firms constantly search for means of differentiating themselves from their competitors. Often, differentiation works for a while but then breaks down as competitors copy the strategy. Providing excellent customer service is more difficult to copy because it can take years to assemble an experienced sales staff and to acquire a reputation for excellent service. In fact, Best Buy, Walmart, and other large chains may not want to compete for customers who are willing to pay a higher price in exchange for more help from the sales staff. In the *Wall Street Journal* article, a spokesperson for Walmart was quoted as saying: "With electronics data so readily available online today, many customers come to us looking for a particular brand or item, knowledge in hand, and may not want or feel comfortable shopping with a salesperson." If the larger firms do not compete on service, smaller firms, such as hhgregg, will have an easier time defending their market niche. For consumers in that niche, hhgregg may charge higher prices, but it still provides these consumers with greater value.

Profit data from *Wall Street Journal;* Scott Tilghman, "hhgregg Could Get a Leg Up," *Barron's,* June 2, 2011; and Miguel Bustillo, "Small Electronics Chains Thrive in Downturn," *Wall Street Journal,* May 27, 2009.

11.4 LEARNING OBJECTIVE

Compare the efficiency of monopolistic competition and perfect competition.

Comparing Monopolistic Competition and Perfect Competition

We have seen that monopolistic competition and perfect competition share the characteristic that in long-run equilibrium, firms earn zero economic profits. As Figure 11.6 shows, however, there are two important differences between the two markets in long-run equilibrium:

- Monopolistically competitive firms charge a price greater than marginal cost.

- Monopolistically competitive firms do not produce at minimum average total cost.

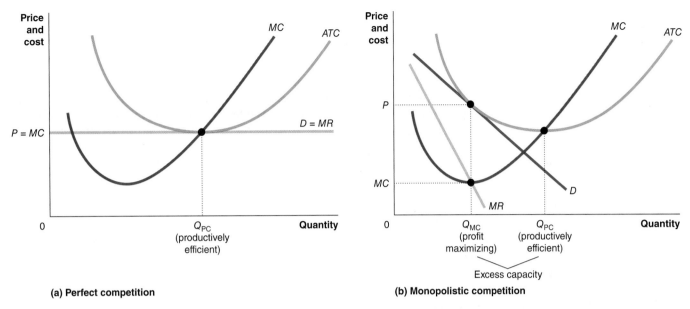

Figure 11.6 **Comparing Long-Run Equilibrium Under Perfect Competition and Monopolistic Competition**

In panel (a), a perfectly competitive firm in long-run equilibrium produces at Q_{PC}, where price equals marginal cost, and average total cost is at a minimum. The perfectly competitive firm is both allocatively efficient and productively efficient. In panel (b), a monopolistically competitive firm produces at Q_{MC}, where price is greater than marginal cost, and average total cost is not at a minimum. As a result, the monopolistically competitive firm is neither allocatively efficient nor productively efficient. The monopolistically competitive firm has excess capacity equal to the difference between its profit-maximizing level of output and the productively efficient level of output.

Excess Capacity Under Monopolistic Competition

Recall that a firm in a perfectly competitive market faces a perfectly elastic demand curve that is also its marginal revenue curve. Therefore, the firm maximizes profit by producing where price equals marginal cost. As panel (a) of Figure 11.6 shows, in long-run equilibrium, a perfectly competitive firm produces at the minimum point of its average total cost curve.

Panel (b) of Figure 11.6 shows that the profit-maximizing level of output for a monopolistically competitive firm comes at a level of output where price is greater than marginal cost, and the firm is not at the minimum point of its average total cost curve. A monopolistically competitive firm has *excess capacity*: If it increased its output, it could produce at a lower average cost.

Is Monopolistic Competition Inefficient?

In Chapter 10, we discussed productive efficiency and allocative efficiency. *Productive efficiency* refers to the situation where a good is produced at the lowest possible cost. *Allocative efficiency* refers to the situation where every good or service is produced up to the point where the last unit provides a marginal benefit to consumers equal to the marginal cost of producing it. For productive efficiency to hold, firms must produce at the minimum point of average total cost. For allocative efficiency to hold, firms must charge a price equal to marginal cost. In a perfectly competitive market, both productive efficiency and allocative efficiency are achieved, but in a monopolistically competitive market, neither is achieved. Does it matter? Economists have debated whether monopolistically competitive markets being neither productively nor allocatively efficient results in a significant loss of well-being to society in these markets compared with perfectly competitive markets.

How Consumers Benefit from Monopolistic Competition

Looking again at Figure 11.6, you can see that the only difference between the monopolistically competitive firm and the perfectly competitive firm is that the demand curve for the monopolistically competitive firm slopes downward, whereas the demand curve for the perfectly competitive firm is a horizontal line. The demand curve for the monopolistically competitive firm slopes downward because the good or service the firm is selling is differentiated from the goods or services being sold by competing firms. The perfectly competitive firm is selling a good or service identical to those being sold by its competitors. A key point to remember is that *firms differentiate their products to appeal to consumers.* When Starbucks coffeehouses begin offering slower-brewed, higher-quality coffees, when Walmart begins carrying more Blu-ray discs and fewer regular DVDs, when General Mills introduces Apple-Cinnamon Cheerios, or when PepsiCo introduces Diet Wild Cherry Pepsi, they are all attempting to attract and retain consumers through product differentiation. The success of these product differentiation strategies indicates that some consumers find these products preferable to the alternatives. Consumers, therefore, are better off than they would have been had these companies not differentiated their products.

We can conclude that consumers face a trade-off when buying the product of a monopolistically competitive firm: They are paying a price that is greater than marginal cost, and the product is not being produced at minimum average cost, but they benefit from being able to purchase a product that is differentiated and more closely suited to their tastes.

Making the Connection	**Netflix: Differentiated Enough to Survive?**

In the late 1990s, the business of renting DVDs was dominated by specialized chain stores such as Rogers and Blockbuster. Some customers were dissatisfied with these stores, however, for two main reasons: (1) After driving to the store, the customer might find that the hoped-for movie was unavailable, and (2) unless the movie was returned on time, the customer would have to pay a late fee that might end up being higher than the price of the movie.

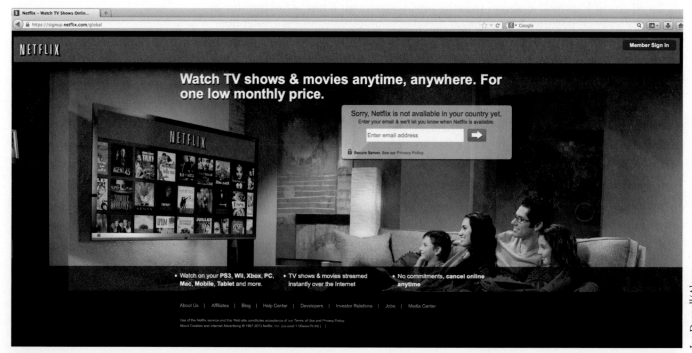

By April 2013, Netflix had more than 36 million streaming subscribers worldwide and revenues in excess of $1 billion in the first quarter of 2013.

In 1997, Reed Hastings had just sold his start-up software firm for $750 million … and he was stuck with a late fee of $40 for having failed to return a copy of *Apollo 13* on time. He decided to start Netflix as a mail-order DVD rental company. For a flat monthly fee, subscribers in the United States could rent a given number of DVDs, with no late fees. Netflix was an immediate success; by 2003, it had 1 million subscribers. But Netflix faced a challenge: Many consumers were switching from renting or buying DVDs to downloading movies or streaming them from the Internet. In 2007, Netflix began offering unlimited streaming of videos in its subscription packages. Because the firm had made agreements with several movie studios and cable channels, its broad selection of films made its streaming service a hit. Netflix launched in Canada in 2010, offering Internet streaming video service (no renting DVDs by mail). By April 2013, Netflix had more than 36 million streaming subscribers worldwide and revenues in excess of $1 billion in the first quarter of 2013.

But would Netflix be able to fight off its many competitors in the business of streaming movies? In the DVD rental business, Netflix had advantages that were hard to duplicate, including a national system of warehouses that allowed it to deliver a DVD the day after a customer ordered it, and an efficient system of processing a returned DVD and mailing out the next DVD in the customer's queue. As a result of these advantages, Walmart, Blockbuster, and other firms were unsuccessful in entering the business of renting DVDs by mail. But some analysts did not believe that Netflix had similar advantages in streaming movies. Many other firms were entering, or had already entered, the business of streaming movies, including Apple, Google, Amazon, Hulu (owned by Disney and News Corp.), and cable companies such as Comcast. These firms were familiar to consumers, were experts in the technology of streaming video, and had access to large selections of movies and television programs. Netflix also upset some consumers in 2011 when it increased price by 60 percent for a subscription to receive DVDs by mail and to stream videos. In late 2011, Netflix announced that it expected to suffer losses for a period during 2012 before returning to profitability.

Indeed, Netflix regained its profitability. In January 2013, it reported a profit of $8 million and its share price increased by 35 percent in one day; on May 10, 2013, the stock closed at $217.69 in the NASDAQ exchange (see the figure). Netflix has also

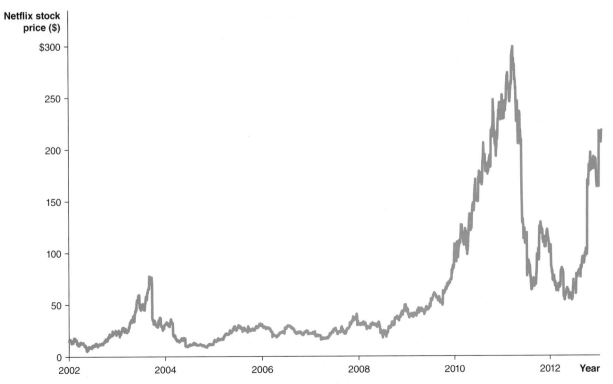

By 2013, Netflix returned to profitability; the stock closed at $217.69 on May 10, 2013.

partnered with a number of hardware providers—including Nintendo, Sony, Apple, and Microsoft—to achieve broad distribution of its product. Its customers can now access the streaming service from gaming and Internet hardware.

Based on Chris Griffiths, "What Netflix Can Teach You About Your Small Business," *The Globe and Mail*, May 28, 2013; Nick Wingfield, "Netflix Warns Price Rise Will Clip Growth," *Wall Street Journal*, July 26, 2011; Matt Phillips, "Netflix: Why One Investor Bets It Gets Crushed," *Wall Street Journal*, December 16, 2010; Reed Hastings and Amy Zipkin, "Out of Africa, Onto the Web," *New York Times*, December 17, 2006; and Reed Hastings and Patrick J. Sauer, "How I Did It: Reed Hastings, Netflix," *Inc.*, December 1, 2005.

MyEconLab

Your Turn: Test your understanding by doing related problem 4.4 on page 345 at the end of this chapter.

11.5 LEARNING OBJECTIVE

Define marketing and explain how firms use marketing to differentiate their products.

Marketing All the activities necessary for a firm to sell a product to a consumer.

How Marketing Differentiates Products

Firms can differentiate their products through marketing. **Marketing** refers to all the activities necessary for a firm to sell a product to a consumer. Marketing includes activities such as determining which product to produce, designing the product, advertising the product, deciding how to distribute the product—for example, in retail stores or through a website—and monitoring how changes in consumer tastes are affecting the market for the product. Peter F. Drucker, a leading business strategist in the United States, described marketing as follows: "It is the whole business seen from the point of view of its final result, that is, from the consumer's point of view…. True marketing… does not ask, 'What do we want to sell?' It asks, 'What does the consumer want to buy?'"

As we have seen, for monopolistically competitive firms to earn economic profits and defend those profits from competitors, they must differentiate their products. Firms use two marketing tools to differentiate their products: brand management and advertising.

Brand Management

Brand management The actions of a firm intended to maintain the differentiation of a product over time.

Once a firm has succeeded in differentiating its product, it must try to maintain that differentiation over time through **brand management**. As we have seen, whenever a firm successfully introduces a new product or a significantly different version of an old product, it earns economic profits in the short run. But the success of the firm inspires competitors to copy the new or improved product and, in the long run, the firm's economic profits will be competed away. Firms use brand management to postpone the time when they will no longer be able to earn economic profits.

Advertising

An innovative advertising campaign can make even long-established and familiar products, such as Coke or McDonald's Big Mac hamburgers, seem more desirable than competing products. When a firm advertises a product, it is trying to shift the demand curve for the product to the right and to make it more inelastic. If the firm is successful, it will sell more of the product at every price, and it will be able to increase the price it charges without losing as many customers. Of course, advertising also increases a firm's costs. If the increase in revenue that results from the advertising is greater than the increase in costs, the firm's profits will rise.

Defending a Brand Name

Once a firm has established a successful brand name, it has a strong incentive to defend it. A firm can apply for a *trademark*, which grants legal protection against other firms using its product's name.

One threat to a trademarked name is the possibility that it will become so widely used for a type of product that it will no longer be associated with the product of a specific company. Courts in Canada and the United States have ruled that when this happens, a firm is no longer entitled to legal protection of the brand name. For example, "aspirin," "escalator," and "thermos" were originally all brand names of the products of particular firms, but each became so widely used to refer to a type of product that none remains a legally protected brand name. Firms spend substantial amounts of money trying to make sure that this does not happen to them. Coca-Cola, for example, employs people to travel to restaurants around the country and order a "Coke" with their meal. If the restaurant serves Pepsi or some other cola, rather than Coke, Coca-Cola's legal department sends the restaurant a letter reminding them that "Coke" is a trademarked name and not a generic name for any cola. Similarly, Xerox Corporation spends money on advertising to remind the public that "Xerox" is not a generic term for making photocopies.

Legally enforcing trademarks can be difficult. Estimates are that each year, Canadian and U.S. firms lose hundreds of billions of dollars in sales worldwide as a result of unauthorized use of their trademarked brand names. Firms often find it difficult to enforce their trademarks in the courts of some foreign countries, although recent international agreements have increased the legal protections for trademarks.

Firms that sell their products through franchises rather than through company-owned stores encounter the problem that if a franchisee does not run his or her business well, the firm's brand may be damaged. Automobile firms send "roadmen" to visit their dealers to make sure the dealerships are clean and well maintained and that the service departments employ competent mechanics and are well equipped with spare parts. Similarly, McDonald's sends employees from corporate headquarters to visit McDonald's franchises to make sure the bathrooms are clean and the french fries are hot.

What Makes a Firm Successful?

11.6 LEARNING OBJECTIVE

Identify the key factors that determine a firm's success.

A firm's owners and managers control some of the factors that make a firm successful and allow it to earn economic profits. The most important of these are the firm's ability to differentiate its product and to produce it at a lower average cost than competing firms. A firm that successfully does these things creates *value* for its customers. Consumers will buy a product if they believe it meets a need not met by competing products or if its price is below that of competitors.

Some factors that affect a firm's profitability are not directly under the firm's control. Certain factors will affect all the firms in a market. For example, rising prices for jet fuel will reduce the profitability of all airlines. If consumers decide that rather than buy DVDs, they would prefer to download or stream movies from Netflix, iTunes, or Amazon, the profitability of all stores selling DVDs will be reduced.

Sheer chance also plays a role in business, as it does in all other aspects of life. A struggling McDonald's franchise may see profits increase dramatically after the government unexpectedly decides to build a new road nearby. Many businesses in New York City, including restaurants, hotels, and theatres, experienced a marked drop in customers and profits following the September 11, 2001, terrorist attacks. Figure 11.7 illustrates the important point that factors within the firm's control and factors outside the firm's control interact to determine the firm's profitability.

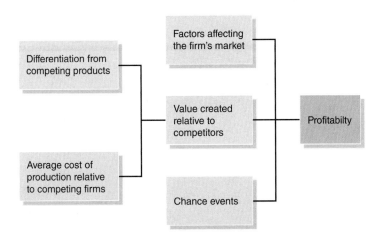

Figure 11.7

What Makes a Firm Successful?

The factors under a firm's control—the ability to differentiate its product and the ability to produce it at lower cost—combine with the factors beyond its control to determine the firm's profitability.

Adapted from Figure 13.3 in David Besanko, David Dranove, Mark Shanley, and Scott Schaefer, *The Economics of Strategy*, 5th ed., New York: John Wiley & Sons, Inc., 2009.

Alamy

Although not first to market, Bic ultimately was more successful than the firm that pioneered ballpoint pens.

Making the Connection | Is Being the First Firm in the Market a Key to Success?

Some business analysts argue that the first firm to enter a market can have important *first-mover advantages*. By being the first to sell a particular good, a firm may find its name closely associated with the good in the public's mind, as, for instance, Amazon is closely associated with ordering books online or eBay is associated with online auctions. This close association may make it more difficult for new firms to enter the market and compete against the first mover.

Surprisingly, though, recent research has shown that the first firm to enter a market often does *not* have a long-lived advantage over later entrants. Consider, for instance, the market for pens. Until the 1940s, the only pens available were fountain pens that had to be refilled frequently from an ink bottle and used ink that dried slowly and smeared easily. In October 1945, entrepreneur Milton Reynolds introduced the first ballpoint pen, which never needed to be refilled. When it went on sale at Gimbel's department store in New York City, it was an instant success. Although the pen had a price of $12.00—the equivalent of about $135.00 at today's prices—hundreds of thousands were sold, and Milton Reynolds became a millionaire. Unfortunately, it didn't last. Although Reynolds had guaranteed that his pen would write for two years—later raised to five years—in fact, the pen often leaked and frequently stopped writing after only limited use. Sales began to collapse, the flood of pens returned under the company's guarantee wiped out its profits, and within a few years, Reynolds International Pen Company stopped selling pens in the United States. By the late 1960s, firms such as Bic, selling inexpensive—but reliable—ballpoint pens, dominated the market.

What happened to the Reynolds International Pen Company turns out to be more the rule than the exception. For example, Apple's iPod was not the first digital music player to appear on the market. Both Seahan's MPMan and Diamond's PMP300 were released in the United States in 1998, three years before the iPod. Similarly, although Hewlett-Packard currently dominates the market for laser printers, with a market share of more than 50 percent, it did not invent the laser printer. Xerox invented the laser printer, and IBM sold the first commercial laser printers. Nor was Procter & Gamble the first firm to sell disposable diapers when it introduced Pampers in 1961. Microsoft's Internet Explorer was not the first Web browser: Before Internet Explorer, there was Netscape; before Netscape, there was Mosaic; and before Mosaic, there were several other Web browsers that for a time looked as if they might dominate the market. In all these cases, the firms that were first to introduce a product ultimately lost out to latecomers who did a better job of providing consumers with products that were more reliable, less expensive, more convenient, or otherwise provided greater value.

Based on Steven P. Schnaars, *Managing Imitation Strategies: How Late Entrants Seize Markets from Pioneers* (New York: The Free Press), 1994; and Gerard J. Tellis and Peter N. Golder, *Will and Vision: How Latecomers Grow to Dominate Markets* (Los Angeles: Figueroa Press), 2002.

MyEconLab

Your Turn: Test your understanding by doing related problem 6.3 on page 345 at the end of this chapter.

Economics in Your Life

Opening Your Own Restaurant

At the beginning of the chapter, we asked you to think about how successful you are likely to be in opening an Italian restaurant in your hometown. As you learned in this chapter, if your restaurant is successful, other people are likely to open competing restaurants, and all your economic profits will eventually disappear. This occurs because economic profits attract entry of new firms into a market. The new restaurants will sell Italian food, but it won't be exactly like your Italian food—after all, they don't have your grandmother's secret sauce recipe! Each restaurant will have its own ideas on how best to appeal to people who like Italian food. Unless your food is very different from your competitors' food—or your service is much better—in the long run you will be unable to charge prices high enough to allow you to earn an economic profit.

In a monopolistically competitive market, free entry will reduce prices and lead to zero economic profits in the long run. In addition to lowering prices, competition benefits consumers by leading firms to offer somewhat different versions of the same product; for example, two Italian restaurants will rarely be exactly alike.

Conclusion

In this chapter, we have applied many ideas about competition to the more common market structure of monopolistic competition. We have seen that these ideas apply to monopolistically competitive markets, just as they do to perfectly competitive markets. The competitive forces of the market impose relentless pressure on firms to produce new and better goods and services at the lowest possible cost. Firms that fail to adequately anticipate changes in consumer tastes or that fail to adopt the latest and most efficient production technology do not survive in the long run. These conclusions are as true for coffeehouses and firms in other monopolistically competitive markets as they are for wheat farmers and carrot growers.

In Chapters 12 and 13, we discuss the remaining market structures: oligopoly and monopoly. Before moving on to those chapters, read *An Inside Look* on the next page for a discussion of how Starbucks began expanding into the juice business in 2011.

Expanding into the Juice Business: Starbucks

ASSOCIATED PRESS

Starbucks Corp. hopes to do for juice what it's done for coffee.

The Seattle-based company that changed the way Americans drink their cup of Joe said Thursday that it acquired juice maker Evolution Fresh Inc. for $30 million as part of a larger effort to move beyond just offering coffee.

Starbucks said it plans to "reinvent" the $1.6 billion super-premium juice segment with its purchase of Evolution, which is based in San Bernardino, Calif. The company plans to open a new chain of health and wellness stores in the coming year that will carry Evolution products such as juices and simple foods. Details are still thin on the new chain, but Starbucks described it as a retail model that has never been seen before.

"We are not just acquiring a juice company," said Starbucks CEO Howard Schultz. "We are using this acquisition to position ourselves, in a broad way, to build a multibillion health and wellness business over time."

The move is the latest by Starbucks to broaden its business as consumers demand healthier products and it faces growing competition from the likes of McDonald's Corp. and Dunkin' Brands Group Inc.'s Dunkin' Donuts chain. Starbucks has rolled out lower-calorie and lower-fat food options and sugar-free syrups and switched from whole milk to 2 percent milk as the default in its drinks. It's also selling more products, like Seattle's Best coffee and Via instant coffee, through grocery stores and other retailers.

Starbucks, which estimates that at some point in the future its consumer products business will rival the size of its café business, said more than a year ago that it would be looking for acquisition candidates. Its last acquisition in 2008 was of The Coffee Equipment Co., which makes the high-end Clover coffee brewing system.

Evolution, started by the founder of Naked Juice, is a logical choice for the chain as it seeks to offer healthier options. Evolution, which makes fresh fruit and vegetable juices, has products that are sold at Whole Foods, Safeway, Costco and other retailers on the West Coast.

Evolution is one of the few larger juice companies that still cracks, peels, presses and squeezes its own fruits and vegetables rather than using pureed or powdered ingredients. It also uses a process called high-pressure pasteurization to make the juice without heating it. Starbucks sees these methods as a competitive edge over juice makers such as Odwalla or Naked Juice, which it currently carries in its stores, as it allows the juice maker to keep a higher nutritional quality in the juice while maintaining the taste.

Starbucks did not disclose how many stores the new chain carrying Evolution products will have or where the locations would be. But the company said the chain will launch on the West Coast and be roughly the size of a traditional Starbucks café. Starbucks also plans to upgrade some of its existing stores to make room for the Evolution products and distribute Evolution's products to other retailers.

Schultz said the company will launch a "full court press" to build the Evolution brand in the coming year, including more details on its new stores. Schultz also dismissed analyst concerns that it might follow in the footsteps of the Jamba Juice chain, which has struggled with soft sales as consumers have cut back on extras like blended fruit drinks. He said Starbucks will be creating an entirely different type of store.

"We understand the beverage business better than anyone else," Schultz told investors Thursday. "We are replicating the understanding we have about beverage capability and adding the theater and romance (of our coffee stores)."

Starbucks did not change its earnings forecast based on the acquisition. It expects Evolution will operate at a moderate loss in the 2012 fiscal year and breakeven in 2013....

Key Points in the Article

With its purchase of Evolution Fresh, Inc., Starbucks is planning to open a chain of health and wellness stores in response to increasing consumer demand for healthier products. While not revealing the number or exact locations of the new stores, the company did say that the first stores will be on the West Coast and will be roughly the size of traditional Starbucks coffeehouses. The juice products are now available in some existing Starbucks locations as well as other retail outlets. Starbucks projected that its Evolution brand would experience moderate losses in 2012 before breaking even in 2013.

Analyzing the News

(a) Facing increased competition in the coffeehouse market, Starbucks has shifted its focus to international expansion, consumer products, and, most recently, the premium juice business. With the acquisition of Evolution, Starbucks plans to open a new chain of health and wellness stores, a market segment it sees as having strong growth potential. If Starbucks is able to capture a significant share of the premium juice market with its new chain, the company has the potential of earning economic profits in this market segment in the short run. Figure 1 represents a Starbucks health

and wellness store earning a short-run economic profit. As long as Starbucks encounters limited competition in the premium juice market, its stores have the potential to earn short-run economic profits. Economic profits will attract competition to the market, and we would expect to eventually see the same result in the premium juice market as in the premium coffee market, with economic profits dropping to zero in the long run.

(b) Due in part to increased competition from companies like Tim Hortons, McDonald's, and Dunkin' Donuts, Starbucks began closing stores in 2008. The increased competition in the coffee business is one reason why Starbucks has decided to expand into other areas. Figure 2 assumes that prior to 2008, an existing Starbucks coffeehouse is earning an economic profit from selling Q_1 cups of coffee and charging a price of P_1 dollars. The profit-maximizing quantity is found where the marginal revenue curve, MR_1, intersects the marginal cost curve, MC. The price is determined by point A on the demand curve, D_1. The firm earns an economic profit equal to the shaded area. Other firms entering the market for premium coffees reduce the demand for Starbucks coffee. The demand and marginal revenue curves for Starbucks shift to the left, from D_1 to D_2 and MR_1 to MR_2. The profit-maximizing level of output is now Q_2,

where MR_2 intersects MC, and the new profit-maximizing price is P_2. At point E, the firm is earning zero economic profit.

(c) While offering few details on its expansion plans for the new chain, Starbucks CEO Howard Schultz did announce that it will begin with locations on the West Coast and that Evolution products will not be limited to just the new stores. Schultz also emphasized that the new business will be an entirely new type of store, and will not follow the model of competitor Jamba Juice, which had been struggling to earn an economic profit.

Thinking Critically

1. Suppose that the federal government required all new coffeehouses to obtain a licence to open (existing coffeehouses would not require a licence) and that the number of licences was limited. How would this requirement affect the equilibrium price and quantity in the coffeehouse market? Who would gain from this requirement and who would lose?

2. Suppose that Starbucks is successful with its chain of health and wellness stores and attracts a significant number of customers from other coffee and juice retailers. How might these other retailers respond to this change in tastes?

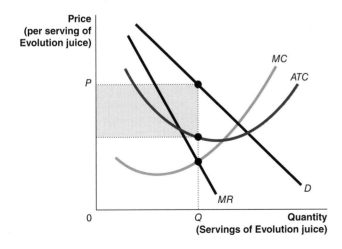

Figure 1

A new chain with short-run economic profit.

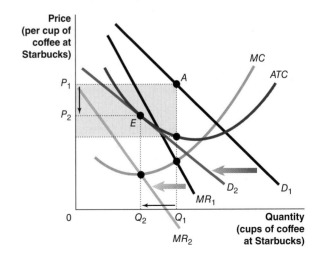

Figure 2

The effect of entry on price, quantity, and profit.

Chapter Summary and Problems

Key Terms

Brand management, p. 336   Marketing, p. 336   Monopolistic competition, p. 322

Summary

*LO 11.1 A firm competing in a **monopolistically competitive** market sells a differentiated product. Therefore, unlike a firm in a perfectly competitive market, it faces a downward-sloping demand curve. When a monopolistically competitive firm cuts the price of its product, it sells more units but must accept a lower price on the units it could have sold at the higher price. As a result, its marginal revenue curve is downward sloping. Every firm that has the ability to affect the price of the good or service it sells will have a marginal revenue curve that is below its demand curve.

LO 11.2 A monopolistically competitive firm maximizes profits at the level of output where marginal revenue equals marginal cost. Price equals marginal revenue for a perfectly competitive firm, but price is greater than marginal revenue for a monopolistically competitive firm. Therefore, unlike a perfectly competitive firm, which produces where $P = MC$, a monopolistically competitive firm produces where $P > MC$.

LO 11.3 If a monopolistically competitive firm is earning economic profits in the short run, entry of new firms will eliminate those profits in the long run. If a monopolistically competitive firm is suffering economic losses in the short run, exit of existing firms will eliminate those losses in the long run. Monopolistically competitive firms continually struggle to find new ways of differentiating their products as they try to stay one step ahead of other firms that are attempting to copy their success.

LO 11.4 Perfectly competitive firms produce where price equals marginal cost and at minimum average total cost. Perfectly competitive firms achieve both allocative and productive efficiency. Monopolistically competitive firms produce where price is greater than marginal cost and above minimum average total cost. Monopolistically competitive firms do not achieve either allocative or productive efficiency. Consumers face a trade-off when buying the product of a monopolistically competitive firm: They are paying a price that is greater than marginal cost, and the product is not being produced at minimum average cost, but they benefit from being able to purchase a product that is differentiated and more closely suited to their tastes.

LO 11.5 Marketing refers to all the activities necessary for a firm to sell a product to a consumer. Firms use two marketing tools to differentiate their products: brand management and advertising. **Brand management** refers to the actions of a firm intended to maintain the differentiation of a product over time. When a firm has established a successful brand name, it has a strong incentive to defend it. A firm can apply for a *trademark*, which grants legal protection against other firms using its product's name.

LO 11.6 A firm's owners and managers control some of the factors that determine the profitability of the firm. Other factors affect all the firms in the market or are the result of chance, so they are not under the control of the firm's owners. The interactions between factors the firm controls and factors it does not control determine its profitability.

MyEconLab   Log in to MyEconLab to complete these exercises and get instant feedback.

Review Questions

LO 11.1

1.1 What are the most important differences between perfectly competitive markets and monopolistically competitive markets? Give two examples of products sold in perfectly competitive markets and two examples of products sold in monopolistically competitive markets.

1.2 Why does a local McDonald's face a downward-sloping demand curve for its Quarter Pounder? If McDonald's raises the price of Quarter Pounders above the prices charged by other fast-food restaurants, won't it lose all its customers?

1.3 With a downward-sloping demand curve, why is average revenue equal to price? Why is marginal revenue less than price?

LO 11.2

2.1 Why doesn't a monopolistically competitive firm produce where $P = MC$, as a perfectly competitive firm does?

*'Learning Objective' is abbreviated to 'LO' in the end of chapter material.

2.2 Stephen runs a pet salon. He is currently grooming 125 dogs per week. If instead of grooming 125 dogs, he grooms 126 dogs, he will add $68.50 to his costs and $60.00 to his revenues. What will be the effect on his profit of grooming 126 dogs instead of 125 dogs?

2.3 If Daniel sells 350 Big Macs at a price of $3.25 each, and his average cost of producing 350 Big Macs is $3.00 each, what is his profit?

2.4 Should a monopolistically competitive firm take into account its fixed costs when deciding how much to produce? Briefly explain.

LO 11.3

3.1 What effect does the entry of new firms have on the economic profits of existing firms?

3.2 Why does the entry of new firms cause the demand curve of an existing firm in a monopolistically competitive market to shift to the left and to become more elastic?

3.3 What is the difference between zero accounting profit and zero economic profit?

3.4 Is it possible for a monopolistically competitive firm to continue to earn economic profits as new firms enter the market?

LO 11.4

4.1 What are the differences between the long-run equilibrium of a perfectly competitive firm and the long-run equilibrium of a monopolistically competitive firm?

4.2 Why is a monopolistically competitive firm not productively efficient? In what sense does a monopolistically competitive firm have excess capacity?

4.3 Why is a monopolistically competitive firm not allocatively efficient?

4.4 Does the fact that monopolistically competitive markets are not allocatively or productively efficient mean that

there is a significant loss in economic well-being to society in these markets? In your answer, be sure to define what you mean by "economic well-being."

LO 11.5

5.1 Define *marketing*. Is marketing just another name for advertising?

5.2 Why are many companies so concerned about brand management?

LO 11.6

6.1 What are the key factors that determine the profitability of a firm in a monopolistically competitive market?

6.2 How might a monopolistically competitive firm continually earn economic profit greater than zero?

Problems and Applications

LO 11.1

1.1 Suppose that Pizza Hut (a Canadian success story) launched a new advertising campaign admitting that its pizzas had not tasted very good, but claiming that a new recipe greatly improved the taste. If Pizza Hut succeeded in convincing consumers that its pizza was significantly better than competing pizzas, would its demand curve become flatter or steeper? Briefly explain.

1.2 Complete the following table, which shows the demand for skiing lessons per day.

Skiing Lessons per Day (Q)	Price (P)	Total Revenue (TR = P×Q)	Average Revenue (AR = TR/Q)	Marginal Revenue (MR = ΔTR/ΔQ)
0	$80.00			
1	75.00			
2	70.00			
3	65.00			
4	60.00			
5	55.00			
6	50.00			
7	45.00			
8	40.00			

1.3 A student makes the following argument:

When a firm sells another unit of a good, the additional revenue the firm receives is equal to the price: If the price is $10, the additional revenue is also $10. Therefore, this chapter is incorrect when it says that marginal revenue is less than price for a monopolistically competitive firm.

Briefly explain whether you agree with this argument.

1.4 There are many wheat farms in the world, and there are also many Starbucks coffeehouses. Why, then, does a Starbucks coffeehouse face a downward-sloping demand curve, while a wheat farmer faces a horizontal demand curve?

1.5 Is it possible for marginal revenue to be negative for a firm selling in a perfectly competitive market? Is it possible for marginal revenue to be negative for a firm selling in a monopolistically competitive market? Briefly explain.

LO 11.2

2.1 Maria manages a bakery that specializes in ciabatta bread, and has the following information on demand and costs:

Ciabatta Bread Sold per Hour (Q)	Price (P)	Total Cost (TC)
0	$6.00	$3.00
1	5.50	7.00
2	5.00	10.00
3	4.50	12.50
4	4.00	14.50
5	3.50	16.00
6	3.00	17.00
7	2.50	18.50
8	2.00	21.00

a. To maximize profit, how many loaves of ciabatta bread should Maria sell per hour, what price should she charge, and how much profit will she make?

b. What is the marginal revenue received by selling the profit-maximizing quantity of ciabatta bread? What is the marginal cost of producing the profit-maximizing quantity of ciabatta bread?

2.2 [**Related to** Solved Problem 11.2 **on page 326**] Suppose a firm producing table lamps has the following costs:

Quantity	Average Total Cost
1,000	$15.00
2,000	9.75
3,000	8.25
4,000	7.50
5,000	7.75
6,000	8.50
7,000	9.75
8,000	10.50
9,000	12.00

Ben and Jerry are managers at the company, and they have this discussion:

Ben: We should produce 4,000 lamps per month because that will minimize our average costs.

Jerry: But shouldn't we maximize profits rather than minimize costs? To maximize profits, don't we need to take demand into account?

Ben: Don't worry. By minimizing average costs, we will be maximizing profits. Demand will determine how high the price we can charge will be, but it won't affect our profit-maximizing quantity.

Evaluate the discussion between the two managers.

2.3 In 1916, Ford Motor Company produced 500,000 Model T Fords, at a price of $440 each. The company made a profit of $60 million that year. Henry Ford told a newspaper reporter that he intended to reduce the price of the Model T to $360, and he expected to sell 800,000 cars at that price. Ford said, "Less profit on each car, but more cars, more employment of labour, and in the end we get all the total profit we ought to make."

a. Did Ford expect the total revenue he received from selling Model Ts to rise or fall following the price cut?

b. Use the information given above to calculate the price elasticity of demand for Model Ts. Use the midpoint formula to make your calculation.

c. What would the average total cost of producing 800,000 Model Ts have to be for Ford to make as much profit selling 800,000 Model Ts as it made selling 500,000 Model Ts? Is this smaller or larger than the average total cost of producing 500,000 Model Ts?

d. Assume that Ford would make the same total profit when selling 800,000 cars as when selling 500,000 cars. Was Henry Ford correct in saying he would make less profit per car when selling 800,000 cars than when selling 500,000 cars?

LO 11.3

3.1 Suppose Angelica opens a small store near campus, selling beef brisket sandwiches. Use the graph, which shows the demand and cost for Angelica's beef brisket sandwiches, to answer the questions that follow.

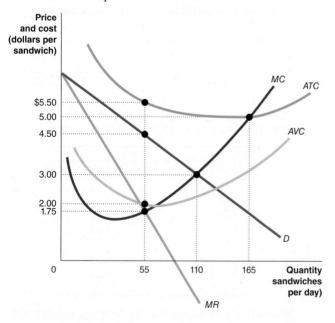

a. If Angelica wants to maximize profits, how many beef brisket sandwiches should she sell per day, and what price should she charge? Briefly explain your answer.

b. How much economic profit (or loss) is Angelica making? Briefly explain.

c. Is Angelica likely to continue selling this number of beef brisket sandwiches in the long run? Briefly explain.

3.2 [**Related to the** Making the Connection **on page 330**] As McDonald's began to increase its competition with Starbucks, Starbucks attempted to fight back with a new advertising campaign. According to an article in the *Wall Street Journal*, one ad proclaimed: "If your coffee isn't perfect, we'll make it over. If it's still not perfect make sure you're in a Starbucks." Starbucks CEO Howard Schultz explained the purpose of the campaign: "We don't want the public to be misled that all coffee is equal, because it's not." Why would it be a problem for Starbucks if consumers came to believe that "all coffee is equal"? How might Starbucks convince consumers that all coffee is not equal?

Based on Julie Jargon, "New Ads Will Stir Up Coffee Wars," *Wall Street Journal*, May 4, 2009.

3.3 [**Related to the** Chapter Opener **on page 321**] John Quelch, a marketing professor at the Harvard Business School, commented on the situation facing Starbucks: "Starbucks is fundamentally selling an experience, but by no means is coffee the only part of the experience." Why might Starbucks have problems if selling coffee were the only part of the Starbucks "experience"?

Based on Sarah Skidmore, "Starbucks Gives Logo a New Look," Associated Press, January 5, 2011.

3.4 The *Wall Street Journal* reported that Western European brewers such as Heineken, Carlsberg, and Anheuser-Busch InBev are increasing their production and marketing of nonalcoholic beer. The article quotes a Carlsberg executive for new-product development as saying:

> Nonalcoholic beer is a largely unexploited opportunity for big brewers. It is quite a natural move when you see that the overall beer market [in Western Europe] is going down. So, of course, we're battling for market share.

The article further states that "brewers are hoping to capitalize on health consciousness" and that "recent brewing advances are helping improve the taste of nonalcoholic beers."

a. In what sense is nonalcoholic beer an "unexploited opportunity" for big brewers?

b. Are the brewers responding to consumer desires, or are brewers exploiting consumers? Briefly explain.

c. How will the "recent brewing advances" that improve taste affect the market for nonalcoholic beer?

Based on Ilan Brat, "Taking the Buzz Out of Beer," *Wall Street Journal*, August 30, 2011.

LO 11.4

4.1 A student makes the following comment:

> I can understand why a perfectly competitive firm will not earn profits in the long run because a perfectly competitive firm charges a price equal to marginal cost. But a monopolistically competitive firm can charge a price greater than marginal cost, so why can't it continue to earn profits in the long run?

How would you answer this question?

4.2 Consider the following graph.

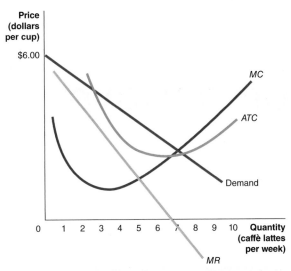

a. Is it possible to say whether this firm is a perfectly competitive firm or a monopolistically competitive firm? If so, explain how you are able to make this determination.

b. Does the graph show a short-run equilibrium or a long-run equilibrium? Briefly explain.

c. What quantity on the graph represents long-run equilibrium if the firm is perfectly competitive?

4.3 Before the fall of Communism, most basic consumer products in Eastern Europe and the Soviet Union were standardized. For example, government-run stores would offer for sale only one type of bar soap or one type of toothpaste. Soviet economists often argued that this system of standardizing basic consumer products avoided the waste associated with the differentiated goods and services produced in Western Europe, Canada, and the United States. Do you agree with this argument?

4.4 [**Related to the** Making the Connection **on page 334**] How will the entry of firms such as Apple, Google, Amazon, Hulu, and Comcast into the business of streaming movies affect Netflix? Why do some analysts question whether Netflix can survive against these competitors? To survive, what must Netflix do?

LO 11.5

5.1 Draw a graph that shows the impact on a firm's profits when it increases spending on advertising and the increased advertising has *no* effect on the demand for the firm's product.

5.2 A skeptic says, "Marketing research and brand management are redundant. If a company wants to find out what customers want, it should simply look at what they're already buying." Do you agree with this comment? Explain.

5.3 The National Football League (NFL) has a trademark on the name "Super Bowl" for its championship game. Advertisers can use "Super Bowl" in their advertising only if they pay the NFL a fee. Many companies attempt to get around this trademark by using the phrase "the big game" in their advertising. For example, a few days before the Super Bowl, a consumer electronics store might have an advertisement with the phrase "Watch the big game on a new LED TV." In 2007, the National Football League considered legal action to have the phrase "the big game" included in its Super Bowl trademark.

a. Why does the government allow firms to trademark their products?

b. Would consumers gain or lose if the NFL were allowed to trademark the phrase "the big game"? Briefly explain.

Based on Craig S. Mende, "On Watching 'The Big Game,'" *Forbes*, February 1, 2008.

5.4 Some companies have done a poor job protecting the images of their products. For example, Hormel's Spam brand name is widely ridiculed and is associated with annoying commercial messages received via email. Think of other cases of companies failing to protect their brand names. What can companies do about the situation now? Should the companies rebrand their products?

LO 11.6

6.1 7-Eleven, Inc., operates more than 20,000 convenience stores worldwide. Edward Moneypenny, 7-Eleven's chief financial officer, was asked to name the biggest risk the company faced. He replied, "I would say that the biggest risk that 7-Eleven faces, like all retailers, is competition… because that is something that you've got to be aware of in this business." In what sense is competition a "risk" to a business? Why would a company in the retail business need to be particularly aware of competition?

Based on Company Report, "CEO Interview: Edward Moneypenny— 7-Eleven, Inc.," The Wall Street Transcript Corporation.

6.2 In 2006, Walmart closed its stores in South Korea and Germany. According to an article in the *New York Times*:

> Wal-Mart's most successful markets, like Mexico, are those in which it started big. There, the company bought the country's largest and best-run retail chain, Cifra, and has never looked back. This year, Wal-Mart is spending more than $1 billion in Mexico to open 120 new stores.

What advantages does Walmart gain from buying large retail chains, as it did in Mexico, rather than small chains, as it did in its unsuccessful attempts to enter the South Korean and German markets?

Based on Mark Landler and Michael Barbaro, "Wal-Mart Finds That Its Formula Doesn't Fit Every Culture," *New York Times*, August 2, 2006.

6.3 [**Related to the** Making the Connection **on page 338**] A firm that is first to market with a new product frequently discovers that there are design flaws or problems with the product that were not anticipated. For example, the ball-point pens made by the Reynolds International Pen Company often leaked. What effect do these problems have on the innovating firm, and how do these unexpected problems open up possibilities for other firms to enter the market?

6.4 An article in the *New York Times* notes that in buying mutual fund shares, "Investors have…[a] problem…: determining whether good returns come from skill or luck." Is it ever easy to determine whether a firm making economic profits is doing so because of the skills of the firm's managers or because of luck? Briefly explain.

From Jeff Brown, "Hedge Funds? Only If You Like Lots of Risk," *New York Times*, August 6, 2009.

Oligopoly: Firms in Less Competitive Markets

Chapter Outline and Learning Objectives

Alamy

Competition in the Computer Market

Many of the largest corporations in the world began as small businesses. In 1975, Bill Gates and Paul Allen founded Microsoft Corporation in Albuquerque, New Mexico, with themselves as the only employees. Steve Jobs and Steve Wozniak formed Apple in 1976, working at first out of Jobs's garage. Jobs and Wozniak were following in the tradition of William Hewlett and David Packard, who founded what became the Hewlett-Packard (HP) company in a garage in Palo Alto, California, in the 1930s. Michael Dell started the Dell computer company in 1984, from his dorm room at the University of Texas. Sam Walton, founder of Walmart, bought his first store in 1945, with $20,000 borrowed from his father-in-law. In Canada, Mike Lazaridis founded Research In Motion (now BlackBerry), the developer of the BlackBerry smartphone and tablet, when he was a University of Waterloo engineering student in 1984.

When each of these firms was founded, their industries included many more firms than they do now. Today, in the software and computer industries, a small number of firms account for the great majority of sales. An industry with only a few firms is an *oligopoly*. In an oligopoly, a firm's profitability depends on its interactions with other firms. In these industries, firms must develop *business strategies*, which involve not just deciding what price to charge and how many units to produce but also how much to advertise, which new technologies to adopt, how to manage relations with suppliers, and which new markets to enter.

Apple has introduced a number of electronic products, including the iPod, iPhone, and iPad. In 2008, Apple introduced the MacBook Air, a very thin and very light laptop computer intended to fill a market niche for students, business travellers, and others needing very lightweight laptops. The MacBook Air posed a challenge to other computer firms: Should they develop models to compete with the MacBook Air or be content to continue producing conventional laptops and desktops? In 2011, Samsung introduced the Series 9 notebook and Dell introduced the XPS 15z laptop, both intended to compete with Apple's MacBook Air. Because there are relatively few firms competing in an oligopolistic industry such as the computer industry, firms must continually react to each other's actions or risk losing significant sales. In this chapter, we focus on strategic interactions among firms.

AN INSIDE LOOK on **page 368** discusses how Intel produced the Ultrabook to respond to consumer demand.

Based on Justin Sheck and Ben Worthen, "Dell Inc. Lowers Its Sights for Gadgets, Consumers," *Wall Street Journal*, May 23, 2011; Doug Aamoth, "Samsung Takes on the MacBook Air," www.techland.time.com, April 28, 2011; and Jared Newman, "Dell's MacBook Air Rival Coming Soon," www.techland.time.com, May 23, 2011.

Economics in Your Life

Why Can't You Find a Cheap PlayStation 4?

You and your roommates have just moved into a great apartment and decide to treat yourselves to a PlayStation 4 game system—provided that you can find one at a relatively low price. First you check Future Shop and find a price of $349.99. Then you check Best Buy, and the price there is also $349.99. Then you check Target; $349.99 again! Finally, you check Walmart, and you find a lower price: $349.96, a whopping discount of $0.03. Why isn't one of these big retailers willing to charge a lower price? What happened to price competition? As you read the chapter, see if you can answer these questions. You can check your answers against those we provide on page 367 at the end of this chapter.

I n Chapters 10 and 11, we studied perfectly competitive and monopolistically competitive industries. Our analysis focused on the determination of a firm's profit-maximizing price and quantity. We concluded that firms maximize profit by producing where marginal revenue equals marginal cost. To determine marginal revenue and marginal cost, we used graphs that included the firm's demand, marginal revenue, and marginal cost curves. In this chapter, we will study oligopoly, a market structure in which a small number of interdependent firms compete. In analyzing oligopoly, we cannot rely on the same types of graphs we used in analyzing perfect competition and monopolistic competition for two reasons.

First, we need to use economic models that allow us to analyze the more complex business strategies of large oligopoly firms. These strategies involve more than choosing the profit-maximizing price and output. Second, even in determining the profit-maximizing price and output for an oligopoly firm, demand curves and cost curves are not as useful as in the cases of perfect competition and monopolistic competition. We are able to draw the demand curves for competitive firms by assuming that the prices these firms charge have no effect on the prices other firms in their industries charge. This assumption is realistic when each firm is small relative to the market. It is not a realistic assumption, however, for firms that are as large relative to their markets as Microsoft, Apple, or Walmart.

When large firms cut their prices, their rivals in the industry often—but not always—respond by also cutting their prices. Because we don't know for sure how other firms will respond to a price change, we don't know the quantity an oligopolist will sell at a particular price. In other words, it is difficult to know what an oligopolist's demand curve will look like. As we have seen, a firm's marginal revenue curve depends on its demand curve. If we don't know what an oligopolist's demand curve looks like, we also don't know what its marginal revenue curve looks like. Because we don't know marginal revenue, we can't calculate the profit-maximizing level of output and the profit-maximizing price the way we do for competitive firms.

The approach we use to analyze competition among oligopolists is called *game theory*. Game theory can be used to analyze any situation in which groups or individuals interact. In the context of economic analysis, game theory is the study of the decisions of firms in industries where the profits of each firm depend on its interactions with other firms. It has been applied to strategies for nuclear war, for international trade negotiations, and for political campaigns, among many other examples. In this chapter, we use game theory to analyze the business strategies of large firms.

12.1 LEARNING OBJECTIVE

Show how barriers to entry explain the existence of oligopolies.

Oligopoly A market structure in which a small number of interdependent firms compete.

Oligopoly and Barriers to Entry

An **oligopoly** is an industry with only a few firms. This market structure lies between the competitive industries, which have many firms, and the monopolies, which have only a single firm. One measure of the extent of competition in an industry is the *concentration ratio*. Every five years, Statistics Canada publishes four-firm concentration ratios that state the fraction of each industry's sales accounted for by its four largest firms. Most economists believe that a four-firm concentration ratio greater than 40 percent indicates that an industry is an oligopoly.

The concentration ratio has some flaws as a measure of the extent of competition in an industry. For example, concentration ratios do not include the goods and services that foreign firms export to Canada. In addition, concentration ratios are calculated for the national market, even though the competition in some industries, such as restaurants or university bookstores, is mainly local. Finally, competition sometimes exists between firms in different industries. For example, Walmart is included in the discount department stores industry but also competes with firms in the supermarket industry and the retail toy store industry. Some economists prefer another measure of competition, known as the *Herfindahl-Hirschman Index*. Despite their shortcomings, concentration ratios can be useful in providing a general idea of the extent of competition in an industry.

Table 12.1

Concentration Ratios for Canadian Industries
Source: Michael Parkin and Robin Bade, *Microeconomics: Canada in the Global Environment*, 8th Canadian Edition. Pearson Canada, 2013, p. 239.

Canadian Industries	
Industry	Four-Firm Concentration Ratio
Sugar	60%
Tobacco products	60%
Beer	60%
Tires	60%
Soft drinks and ice	60%
Ice cream and frozen desserts	60%
Petroleum products	60%
Audio and video equipment	60%
Cookies and crackers	60%
Socks	60%
Paper products	50%
Wooden windows and doors	40%
Pharmaceutical products	39%
Women's and girl's shirts	30%
Printing	28%
Boats	25%
Fabrics	20%
Textiles	18%
Bakery items	15%
Clothing	13%

Table 12.1 list examples of oligopolies in Canadian industries. Industries that produce sugar, tobacco, beer, tires, soft drinks, and ice have a high degree of concentration and are oligopolies. Industries that produce clothing, bakery items, textiles, and fabrics have low concentration measures and are highly competitive. Those industries that produce pharmaceutical products and wooden windows and doors are moderately concentrated and are examples of monopolistic competition.

Barriers to Entry

Why do oligopolies exist? Why aren't there many more firms in the computer industry, the discount department store industry, or the beer industry? Recall that new firms will enter industries where existing firms are earning economic profits. But new firms often have difficulty entering an oligopoly. Anything that keeps new firms from entering an industry in which firms are earning economic profits is called a **barrier to entry**. Three barriers to entry are economies of scale, ownership of a key input, and policy-imposed barriers.

Barrier to entry Anything that keeps new firms from entering an industry in which firms are earning economic profits.

Economies of Scale   The most important barrier to entry is economies of scale. **Economies of scale** exist when a firm's long-run average costs fall as it increases output. The greater the economies of scale, the smaller the number of firms that will be in the industry. Figure 12.1 illustrates this point.

Economies of scale The situation when a firm's long-run average costs fall as the firm increases output.

If economies of scale are relatively unimportant in the industry, the typical firm's long-run average cost curve ($LRAC$) will reach a minimum at a level of output (Q_1 in Figure 12.1) that is a small fraction of total industry sales. The industry will have room for a large number of firms and will be competitive. If economies of scale are significant, the typical firm will not reach the minimum point on its long-run average cost curve (Q_2 in Figure 12.1) until it has produced a large fraction of industry sales. Then the industry will have room for only a few firms and will be an oligopoly.

Economies of scale can explain why there is much more competition in the restaurant industry than in the computer industry. Because very large restaurants do not have lower average costs than smaller restaurants, the restaurant industry has room for many firms. In contrast, large computer firms such as Apple have much lower average costs than small computer firms, partly because large firms can spread the high fixed costs of producing computers—including very large research and development costs—over a much larger quantity of computers.

Figure 12.1

Economies of Scale Help Determine the Extent of Competition in an Industry

An industry will be competitive if the minimum point on the typical firm's long-run average cost curve ($LRAC_1$) occurs at a level of output that is a small fraction of total industry sales, such as Q_1. The industry will be an oligopoly if the minimum point comes at a level of output that is a large fraction of industry sales, such as Q_2.

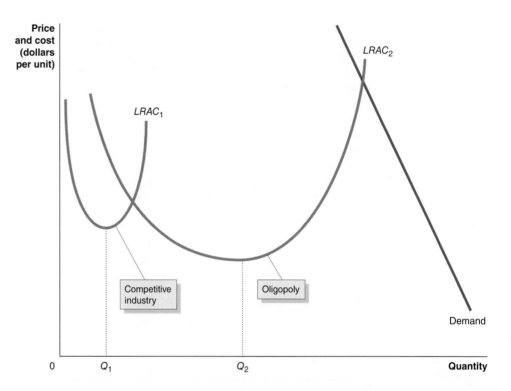

Ownership of a Key Input

If production of a good requires a particular input, then control of that input can be a barrier to entry. The Potash Corporation of Saskatchewan (PotashCorp) has very little competition, because it controls most of the world's supply of potash. Ownership of that input has given the company a strategic advantage over its competitors. In addition, the multibillion-dollar costs and multiyear period required to build a mine have produced significant barriers to entry into the global potash industry. Today, PotashCorp is the world's largest fertilizer company, producing the three primary crop nutrients—potash, phosphate, and nitrogen. The Chalk River Labs, owned and operated by Atomic Energy of Canada Ltd., make radioactive medical products for all of North America and Europe. They have been able to block competition by having unique research facilities and expertise in a number of fields, including physics, chemistry, biology, metallurgy, and engineering. For many years the Aluminum Company of America (Alcoa) controlled most of the world's supply of high-quality bauxite, the mineral needed to produce aluminum. The only way other companies could enter the industry to compete with Alcoa was to recycle aluminum. The De Beers Company of South Africa was able to block competition in the diamond market by controlling the output of most of the world's diamond mines. Until the 1990s, Ocean Spray had very little competition in the market for fresh and frozen cranberries because it controlled almost the entire supply of cranberries. Even today, the company controls about 80 percent of the cranberry crop.

Policy-Imposed Barriers

Firms sometimes try to convince the government to impose barriers to entry. Many large firms employ *lobbyists* to convince provincial legislators and members of Parliament to pass laws favourable to the economic interests of the firms. There are thousands of lobbyists in Ottawa, alone. Top lobbyists command annual salaries of $300,000 or more, which indicates the value firms place on their activities. Examples of government-imposed barriers to entry are patents, licensing requirements, and barriers to international trade.

Patent The exclusive right to a product for a period of 20 years from the date the patent is filed with the government.

A **patent** gives a firm the exclusive right to a new product for a period of 20 years from the date the patent is filed with the government. Governments use patents to encourage firms to carry out research and development of new and better products and better ways of producing existing products. Output and living standards increase faster when firms devote resources to research and development, but a firm that spends money to develop a new product may not earn much profit if other firms can copy the product. For example, the Canadian pharmaceutical company Apotex spends more than $200 million per year on developing new prescription drugs (Merck, an American company and one of the largest in the world, spends more than $3 billion). If rival companies could freely produce these new drugs as soon as Apotex developed them, most of the firm's investment would be wasted. Because Apotex can patent a new drug, the firm can charge higher prices during the years the patent is in force and make an economic profit on its successful innovation.

Governments also restrict competition through *occupational licensing.* Canada currently has a large number of occupational licensing laws. For example, doctors and dentists in every province need licences to practise. The justification for the laws is to protect the public from incompetent practitioners, but by restricting the number of people who can enter the licensed professions, the laws also raise prices.

Governments also provide barriers to entering some industries by imposing tariffs and quotas on foreign competition. A *tariff* is a tax on imports, and a *quota* limits the quantity of a good that can be imported into a country. A quota on foreign sugar imports severely limits competition in the Canadian sugar market. As a result, Canadian sugar companies can charge prices that are more than twice as high as prices companies outside Canada charge.

In summary, to earn economic profits, all firms would like to charge a price well above average cost, but earning economic profits attracts new firms to enter the industry. Eventually, the increased competition forces price down to average cost, and firms just break even. In an oligopoly, barriers to entry prevent—or at least slow down—entry, which allows firms to earn economic profits over a longer period.

Making the Connection | Scale Economies in Canadian Banking?

As of November 2012, there were 78 banks in Canada—24 domestic banks, 25 foreign bank subsidiaries, 24 full-service foreign bank branches, and 5 foreign bank lending branches—managing about $3.9 trillion in assets. However, as shown in the table below, the Big Six—the Royal Bank of Canada (RBC), Canadian Imperial Bank of Commerce (CIBC), Bank of Montreal (BMO), Scotiabank, Toronto Dominion Canada Trust, and the National Bank of Canada—together hold close to 93 percent of the assets in the industry.

There are significant barriers to entry in the Canadian banking industry.

Canadian Banks (as of March 31, 2013)		
Bank	Assets (in millions)	Percent (%) of bank assets
The Big Six		
RBC Financial Group	$ 871,547	22.38
Canadian Imperial Bank of Commerce	408,193	10.48
BMO Financial Group	551,631	14.16
Scotiabank	754,152	19.36
TD Bank Financial Group	833,706	21.41
National Bank of Canada	196,670	5.05
Big Six Subtotal	$3,615,899	92.84
Laurentian Bank of Canada	34,371	0.88
Canadian Western Bank	18,014	0.46
8 Domestic Banks Subtotal	$3,668,284	94.18
Other Banks		
Domestic Banks	36,452	0.94
Foreign Banks	190,117	4.88
Total	$3,894,853	100.00

Source: OSFI web site at www.osfi-bsif.gc.ca. Reprinted with permission.

Although Canadian banks are competitive on some levels (such as, for example, in mortgage lending), they appear to collude on others (such as service fees), suggesting that the Canadian banking industry is an oligopoly.

In fact, in early 1998 four of the largest Canadian commercial banks announced their intention to merge. In particular, the Royal Bank of Canada and the Bank of Montreal made the announcement on January 23, 1998, while the Canadian Imperial Bank of Commerce and the Toronto Dominion Bank followed suit and made a similar announcement on April 17, 1998.

The Competition Bureau reviewed and assessed the proposed mergers at the same time and advised the minister of finance, Paul Martin, against the planned mergers. In fact, in a letter to the presidents of the Royal Bank and the Bank of Montreal on December 11, 1998, it was argued that the merger "… is likely to lead to a substantial lessening or prevention of competition that would cause higher prices and lower levels of service and choice for several key banking services in Canada."

The minister of finance, based on this advice from the Competition Bureau, rejected the mergers in January 1999 in order to prevent reduced competition in the financial services industry and concentration of economic power in the hands of too few banks. The government also issued a statement establishing a process for reviewing mergers involving large financial institutions.

From www.fin.gc.ca/LINKS/mergers_e.html

MyEconLab **Your Turn:** Test your understanding by doing related problem 1.3 on page 371 at the end of this chapter.

12.2 LEARNING OBJECTIVE

Use game theory to analyze the strategies of oligopolistic firms.

Game theory The study of how people make decisions in situations in which attaining their goals depends on their interactions with others; in economics, the study of the decisions of firms in industries where the profits of a firm depend on its interactions with other firms.

Business strategy Actions that a firm takes to achieve a goal, such as maximizing profits.

Using Game Theory to Analyze Oligopoly

As we noted at the beginning of the chapter, economists analyze oligopolies by using *game theory*, which was developed during the 1940s by the mathematician John von Neumann and the economist Oskar Morgenstern. **Game theory** is the study of how people make decisions in situations in which attaining their goals depends on their interactions with others. In oligopolies, the interactions among firms are crucial in determining profitability because the firms are large relative to the market.

In all games—whether poker, chess, or Monopoly—the interactions among the players are crucial in determining the outcome. In addition, games share three key characteristics:

1. *Rules* that determine what actions are allowable
2. *Strategies* that players employ to attain their objectives in the game
3. *Payoffs* that are the results of the interactions among the players' strategies

In business situations, the rules of the "game" include not just laws that a firm must obey but also other matters beyond a firm's control—at least in the short run—such as its production function. A **business strategy** is a set of actions that a firm takes to achieve a goal, such as maximizing profits. The *payoffs* are the profits or market share or income a firm earns as a result of how its strategies interact with the strategies of other firms. The best way to understand the game theory approach is to look at an example.

A Duopoly Game: Price Competition Between Two Firms

In this simple example, we use game theory to analyze price competition in a *duopoly*— an oligopoly with two firms. Suppose we ignore the other firms in the industry and assume that Apple and Dell are the only two firms producing desktop computers. Let's focus on their sales of basic desktop computers. The managers of the two firms have to decide whether to charge $1,200 or $1,000 for their computers. Which price will be more profitable depends on the price the other firm charges. The decision regarding

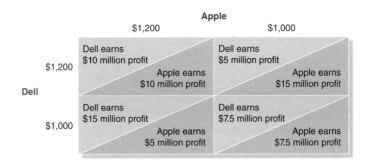

Figure 12.2

A Duopoly Game

Dell's profits are in blue, and Apple's profits are in red. Dell and Apple would each make profits of $10 million per month on sales of desktop computers if they both charged $1,200. However, each firm has an incentive to undercut the other by charging a lower price. If both firms charged $1,000, they would each make a profit of only $7.5 million per month.

what price to charge is an example of a business strategy. In Figure 12.2, we organize the possible outcomes that result from the actions of the two firms into a **payoff matrix**, which is a table that shows the payoffs that each firm earns from every combination of strategies by the firms.

Apple's profits are shown in red, and Dell's profits are shown in blue. If Apple and Dell both charge $1,200 for their computers, each firm will make a profit of $10 million per month. If Apple charges the lower price of $1,000, while Dell charges $1,200, Apple will gain many of Dell's customers. Apple's profits will be $15 million, and Dell's will be only $5 million. Similarly, if Dell charges $1,000 while Apple is charging $1,200, Apple's profits will be only $5 million while Dell's profits will be $15 million. If both firms charge $1,000, each will earn profits of $7.5 million per month.

Clearly, the firms will be better off if they both charge $1,200 for their computers. But will they both charge this price? One possibility is that Apple's managers and Dell's managers will get together and *collude* by agreeing to charge the higher price. **Collusion** is an agreement among firms to charge the same price or otherwise not to compete. Unfortunately for Apple and Dell—but fortunately for their customers—collusion is against the law in most countries. The government can fine companies that collude and send the managers involved to prison.

Apple's managers can't legally discuss their pricing decision with Dell's managers, so they have to predict what the other managers will do. Suppose Apple's managers are convinced that Dell's managers will charge $1,200 for their computers. In this case, Apple's managers will definitely charge $1,000 because that will increase Apple's profit from $10 million to $15 million. But suppose that, instead, Apple's managers are convinced that Dell's managers will charge $1,000. Then Apple's managers also definitely will charge $1,000 because that will increase their profit from $5 million to $7.5 million. In fact, regardless of which price Dell's managers decide to charge, Apple's managers are better off charging $1,000. So, we know that Apple's managers will choose a price of $1,000 for Apple computers.

Now consider the situation of Dell's managers. They are in the same position as Apple's managers, so we can expect them to make the same decision to charge $1,000 for their computers. In this situation, both firms have a *dominant strategy*. A **dominant strategy** is the best strategy for a firm, no matter what strategies other firms use. The result is an equilibrium where both firms charge $1,000 for their computers. This situation is an equilibrium because each firm is maximizing profits, *given the price chosen by the other firm*. In other words, neither firm can increase its profits by changing its price, given the price chosen by the other firm. An equilibrium where each firm chooses the best strategy, given the strategies chosen by other firms, is called a **Nash equilibrium**, named after Nobel Laureate John Nash of Princeton University, a pioneer in the development of game theory.

Payoff matrix A table that shows the payoffs that each firm earns from every combination of strategies by the firms.

Collusion An agreement among firms to charge the same price or otherwise not to compete.

Dominant strategy A strategy that is the best for a firm, no matter what strategies other firms use.

Nash equilibrium A situation in which each firm chooses the best strategy, given the strategies chosen by other firms.

Firm Behaviour and the Prisoner's Dilemma

Notice that the equilibrium in Figure 12.2 is not very satisfactory for either firm. The firms earn $7.5 million in profit each month by charging $1,000, but they could have earned $10 million in profit if they had both charged $1,200. By "cooperating"

Cooperative equilibrium An equilibrium in a game in which players cooperate to increase their mutual payoff.

Noncooperative equilibrium An equilibrium in a game in which players do not cooperate but pursue their own self-interest.

Prisoner's dilemma A game in which pursuing dominant strategies results in noncooperation that leaves both worse off.

and charging the higher price, they would have achieved a *cooperative equilibrium*. In a **cooperative equilibrium**, players cooperate to increase their mutual payoff. We have seen, though, that the outcome of this game is likely to be a **noncooperative equilibrium**, in which each firm pursues its own self-interest.

A situation like this, in which pursuing dominant strategies results in noncooperation that leaves both worse off, is called a **prisoner's dilemma**. The game gets its name from the problem faced by two suspects the police arrest for a crime. If the police lack other evidence, they may separate the suspects and offer each a reduced prison sentence in exchange for confessing to the crime and testifying against the other suspect. Because each suspect has a dominant strategy to confess to the crime, they will both confess and serve a jail term, even though they would have gone free if they had both remained silent.

Don't Let This Happen to You

Don't Misunderstand Why Each Firm Ends Up Charging a Price of $1,000

It is tempting to think that Apple and Dell would each charge $1,000 rather than $1,200 for their computers because each is afraid that the other firm will charge $1,000. In fact, fear of being undercut by the other firm's lower price is not the key to understanding each firm's pricing strategy. Notice that charging $1,000 is the most profitable strategy for each firm, no matter which price the other firm decides to charge. For example, even if Apple's

managers somehow knew for sure that Dell's managers intended to charge $1,200, Apple would still charge $1,000 because its profits would be $15 million instead of $10 million. Dell's managers are in the same situation. That is why charging $1,000 is a dominant strategy for both firms.

MyEconLab

Your Turn: Test your understanding by doing related problem 2.7 on page 373 at the end of the chapter.

Solved Problem **12.2**

Is Advertising a Prisoner's Dilemma for Coca-Cola and Pepsi?

Coca-Cola and Pepsi both advertise aggressively, but would they be better off if they didn't? Their commercials are usually not designed to convey new information about their products. Instead, they are designed to capture each other's customers. Construct a payoff matrix using the following hypothetical information:

- If neither firm advertises, Coca-Cola and Pepsi both earn profits of $750 million per year.
- If both firms advertise, Coca-Cola and Pepsi both earn profits of $500 million per year.
- If Coca-Cola advertises and Pepsi doesn't, Coca-Cola earns profits of $900 million and Pepsi earns profits of $400 million.

- If Pepsi advertises and Coca-Cola doesn't, Pepsi earns profits of $900 million and Coca-Cola earns profits of $400 million.
  a. If Coca-Cola wants to maximize profit, will it advertise? Briefly explain.
  b. If Pepsi wants to maximize profit, will it advertise? Briefly explain.
  c. Is there a Nash equilibrium to this advertising game? If so, what is it?

Solving the Problem

Step 1: **Review the chapter material.** This problem uses payoff matrixes to analyze a business situation, so you may want to review the section "A Duopoly Game: Price Competition Between Two Firms," which begins on page 352.

Step 2: **Construct the payoff matrix.**

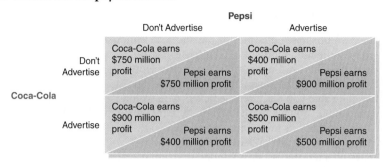

Step 3: **Answer part (a) by showing that Coca-Cola has a dominant strategy of advertising.** If Pepsi doesn't advertise, then Coca-Cola will make $900 million if it advertises but only $750 million if it doesn't. If Pepsi advertises, then Coca-Cola will make $500 million if it advertises but only $400 million if it doesn't. Therefore, advertising is a dominant strategy for Coca-Cola.

Step 4: **Answer part (b) by showing that Pepsi has a dominant strategy of advertising.** Pepsi is in the same position as Coca-Cola, so it also has a dominant strategy of advertising.

Step 5: **Answer part (c) by showing that there is a Nash equilibrium for this game.** Both firms advertising is a Nash equilibrium. Given that Pepsi is advertising, Coca-Cola's best strategy is to advertise. Given that Coca-Cola is advertising, Pepsi's best strategy is to advertise. Therefore, advertising is the optimal decision for both firms, *given the decision by the other firm.*

Extra Credit: This is another example of the prisoner's dilemma game. Coca-Cola and Pepsi would be more profitable if they both refrained from advertising, thereby saving the enormous expense of television and radio commercials and newspaper and magazine ads. Each firm's dominant strategy is to advertise, however, so they end up in an equilibrium where both advertise, and their profits are reduced.

Your Turn: For more practice, do related problems 2.5 and 2.6 on pages 372 at the end of this chapter.

MyEconLab

Making the Connection

Is There a Dominant Strategy for Bidding on eBay?

An auction is a game in which bidders compete to buy a product. The payoff in winning an auction is equal to the difference between the subjective value you place on the product being auctioned and the amount of the winning bid. On the online auction site eBay, more than 200 million items valued at more than $10 billion are auctioned each year.

eBay is run as a *second-price auction*, where the winning bidder pays an amount equal to the bid of the second-highest bidder. If the high bidder on a DVD of *The Dark Knight Rises* bids $12, and the second bidder bids $8, the high bidder wins the auction and pays $8. It may seem that your best strategy when bidding on eBay is to place a bid well below the subjective value you place on the item in the hope of winning it at a low price. In fact, bidders on eBay have a dominant strategy of entering a bid equal to the maximum value they place on the item. For instance, suppose you are looking for a present for your parents'

On eBay, bidding the maximum value you place on an item is a dominant strategy.

Vicki Beaver/Alamy

anniversary. They are U2 fans, and someone is auctioning a pair of U2 concert tickets. If the maximum value you place on the tickets is $200, that should be your bid. To see why, consider the results of strategies of bidding more or less than $200.

There are two possible outcomes of the auction: Either someone else bids more than you do, or you are the high bidder. First, suppose you bid $200 but someone else bids more than you do. If you had bid more than $200, you would still have lost. If you had bid more than $200, you might have been the high bidder, but because your bid would be for more than the value you place on the tickets, you would have a negative payoff. Second, suppose you bid $200 and you are the high bidder. If you had bid less than $200, you would have risked losing the tickets to someone whose bid you would have beaten by bidding $200. You would be worse off than if you had bid $200 and won. If you had bid more than $200, you would not have affected the price you ended up paying—which, remember, is equal to the second-highest bid. Therefore, a strategy of bidding $200—the maximum value you place on the tickets—dominates bidding more or less than $200.

Even though making your first bid your highest bid is a dominant strategy on eBay, many bidders don't use it. After an auction is over, a link leads to a Webpage showing all the bids. In many auctions, the same bidder bids several times, showing that the bidder had not understood his or her dominant strategy.

MyEconLab **Your Turn:** Test your understanding by doing related problem 2.8 on page 373 at the end of this chapter.

Can Firms Escape the Prisoner's Dilemma?

Although the prisoner's dilemma game seems to show that cooperative behaviour always breaks down, we know it doesn't. People often cooperate to achieve their goals, and firms find ways to cooperate by not competing on price. The reason the basic prisoner's dilemma story is not always applicable is that it assumes the game will be played only once. Most business situations, however, are repeated over and over. For example, consider the following situation: Suppose that the only place to buy a Play-Station 4 game console is from either the local Target store or the local Walmart store. (For simplicity, we will ignore the possibility of consumers buying the PlayStation 4 online.) We will assume that the managers will charge either $400 or $300 for the Play-Station. Panel (a) of Figure 12.3 shows the payoff matrix. Examining the matrix shows that, just as with Apple and Dell pricing computers, each manager has an incentive to charge the lower price. Once again, the firms appear caught in a prisoner's dilemma. But the managers will not play this game only once because each month they will decide again what price they will charge for the PlayStation 4. In the language of game theory, the managers are playing a *repeated game*. In a repeated game, the losses from not cooperating are greater than in a game played once, and players can also employ *retaliation strategies* against those who don't cooperate. As a result, we are more likely to see cooperative behaviour.

Panel (a) of Figure 12.3 shows that Walmart and Target are earning $2,500 less per month by both charging $300 instead of $400 for the PlayStation 4. Every month that passes with both stores charging $300 increases the total amount lost: Two years of charging $300 will cause each store to lose $60,000 in profit. This lost profit increases the incentive for the store managers to cooperate by *implicitly* colluding. Remember that *explicit* collusion—such as the managers meeting and agreeing to charge $400—is illegal. But if the managers can find a way to signal each other that they will charge $400, they may be within the law.

Suppose, for example, that Walmart and Target both advertise that they will match the lowest price offered by any competitor—in our simple example, they are each other's only competitor. These advertisements are signals to each other that they intend to charge $400 for the PlayStation. The signal is clear because each store knows that if it charges $300, the other store will automatically retaliate by also lowering its price to $300. The offer to match prices is a good *enforcement mechanism* because it guarantees that if either store fails to cooperate and charges the lower price, the competing store

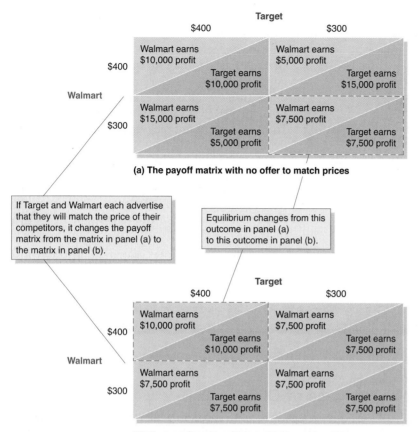

(a) The payoff matrix with no offer to match prices

If Target and Walmart each advertise that they will match the price of their competitors, it changes the payoff matrix from the matrix in panel (a) to the matrix in panel (b).

Equilibrium changes from this outcome in panel (a) to this outcome in panel (b).

(b) The payoff matrix with an offer to match prices

Figure 12.3

Changing the Payoff Matrix in a Repeated Game

Walmart and Target can change the payoff matrix for selling PlayStation 4 game consoles by advertising that each will match its competitor's price. This retaliation strategy provides a signal that one store charging a lower price will be met automatically by the other store charging a lower price. In the payoff matrix in panel (a), there is no matching offer, and each store benefits if it charges $300 when the other charges $400. In the payoff matrix in panel (b), with the matching offer, the companies have only two choices: They can charge $400 and receive a profit of $10,000 per month, or they can charge $300 and receive a profit of $7,500 per month. The equilibrium shifts from the prisoner's dilemma result of both stores charging the low price and receiving low profits to both stores charging the high price and receiving high profits.

will automatically punish that store by also charging the lower price. As Figure 12.3 shows, the stores have changed the payoff matrix they face.

With the original payoff matrix in panel (a), there is no matching offer, and each store makes more profit if it charges $300 when the other charges $400. The matching offer changes the payoff matrix to that shown in panel (b). Now the stores can charge $400 and receive a profit of $10,000 per month, or they can charge $300 and receive a profit of $7,500 per month. The equilibrium shifts from the prisoner's dilemma result of both stores charging the low price and receiving low profits to a result where both stores charge the high price and receive high profits. An offer to match competitors' prices might seem to benefit consumers, but game theory shows that it actually may hurt consumers by helping to keep prices high.

One form of implicit collusion occurs as a result of *price leadership*. With **price leadership**, one firm takes the lead in announcing a price change, which other firms in the industry then match. For example, through the 1970s, General Motors would announce a price change at the beginning of a model year, and Ford and Chrysler would match GM's price change. In some cases, such as in the airline industry, firms have attempted to act as price leaders but failed when other firms in the industry declined to cooperate.

Price leadership A form of implicit collusion in which one firm in an oligopoly announces a price change and the other firms in the industry match the change.

Making the Connection | Canada's Not-So Friendly Skies

In recent years, Canadian consumers have wondered why in-country flights in Canada are significantly more expensive on a per-kilometre basis than in-country flights in the United States and to a larger extent in Europe. Taxes and fees cannot explain the differences. In fact, taxes and fees are higher in Europe than in either Canada or the United States.

The answer is given in a recent report by the Frontier Centre for Public Policy (a Canadian think-tank) and is lack of competition. In particular, since 1997 the

In the Canadian airline industry it doesn't take much competition to greatly reduce opportunities for price collusion.

European Union has had an "open skies" policy that allows any European Union airline to pick up and drop off passengers within any other European Union country. Canada has also had an open skies policy since 2006, but foreign carriers can only fly in and out of Canada, not within Canada. For example, Lufthansa, Air France, or British Airways can fly a passenger from Europe to Toronto, but cannot pick up a passenger in Toronto and fly her to Vancouver.

Because of this restrictive and anticompetitive policy, Canadians end up paying sky-high airfares. Barriers to competition have increased the possibility of implicit collusion by reducing the number of airlines flying between two Canadian cities. Often only one or two airlines will fly on a particular route.

Based on Mark Milke, "Canada's Not-So Friendly Skies: Why Canadian Consumers Pay Sky-High Airfares," *Frontier Centre for Public Policy* Series No. 91, June 2010; *The Economist*, "Airline Competition: No Competition, High Fares," June 28, 2010.

MyEconLab **Your Turn:** Test your understanding by doing related problem 2.9 on page 373 at the end of this chapter.

Cartels: The Case of OPEC

Cartel A group of firms that collude by agreeing to restrict output to increase prices and profits.

In Canada, firms cannot legally meet to agree on what prices to charge and how much to produce. But suppose they could. Would this be enough to guarantee that their collusion would be successful? The example of the Organization of the Petroleum Exporting Countries (OPEC) indicates that the answer to this question is "no." OPEC has 12 members, including Saudi Arabia, Kuwait, and other Arab countries, as well as Iran, Venezuela, Nigeria, and Ecuador. Together, these countries own 75 percent of the world's proven oil reserves, although they pump a smaller share of the total oil sold each year. OPEC operates as a **cartel**, which is a group of firms that collude by agreeing to restrict output to increase prices and profits. The members of OPEC meet periodically and agree on quotas, which are quantities of oil that each country agrees to produce. The quotas are intended to reduce oil production well below the competitive level in order to force up the price of oil and increase the profits of member countries.

Figure 12.4 shows oil prices from 1972 to mid-2013. The line shows the price (in U.S. dollars) of a barrel of oil in each year. Shaded areas represent NBER recessions. Prices in general have risen since 1972, which has reduced the amount of goods and services that consumers can purchase with a dollar. The figure shows that OPEC had considerable success in raising the price of oil during the mid-1970s and early 1980s, although political unrest in the Middle East and other factors also affected the price of oil during these years. Oil prices, which had been below $3 per barrel in 1972, rose to more than $39 per barrel in 1980. The figure also shows that OPEC has had difficulty sustaining the high prices of 1980 in later years, although oil prices rose sharply between 2004 and mid-2008, in part due to increasing demand from China and India.

Game theory helps us understand why oil prices have fluctuated. If every member of OPEC cooperates and produces the low output level dictated by its quota, prices will be high, and the cartel will earn large profits. Once the price has been driven up, however, each member has an incentive to stop cooperating and to earn even higher profits by increasing output beyond its quota. But if no country sticks to its quota, total oil output will increase, and profits will decline. In other words, OPEC is caught in a prisoner's dilemma.

If the members of OPEC always exceeded their production quotas, the cartel would have no effect on world oil prices. In fact, the members of OPEC periodically meet and assign new quotas that, at least for a while, enable them to restrict output

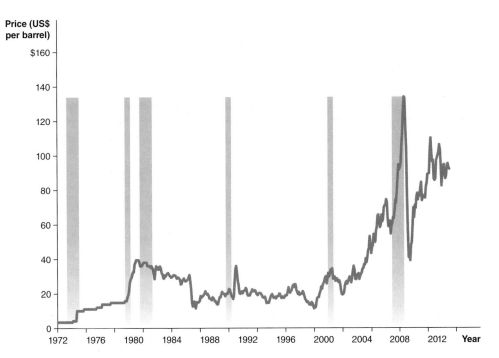

Figure 12.4

Oil Prices, 1972 to mid-2013

The line shows the price of a barrel of oil in each year. Shaded areas represent NBER recessions. By reducing oil production, OPEC was able to raise the world price of oil in the mid-1970s and early 1980s. Sustaining high prices has been difficult over the long run, however, because OPEC members often exceed their output quotas.
Data from Federal Reserve Bank of St. Louis.

enough to raise prices. Two factors explain OPEC's occasional success at behaving as a cartel. First, the members of OPEC are participating in a repeated game. As we have seen, this increases the likelihood of a cooperative outcome. Second, Saudi Arabia has far larger oil reserves than any other member of OPEC. Therefore, it has the most to gain from high oil prices and a greater incentive to cooperate. To see this, consider the payoff matrix shown in Figure 12.5. To keep things simple, let's assume that OPEC has only two members: Saudi Arabia and Nigeria. In Figure 12.5, "Low Output" corresponds to cooperating with the OPEC-assigned output quota, and "High Output" corresponds to producing at maximum capacity. The payoff matrix shows the profits received per day by each country.

We can see that Saudi Arabia has a strong incentive to cooperate and maintain its low output quota. By keeping output low, Saudi Arabia can by itself significantly raise the world price of oil, increasing its own profits as well as those of other members of OPEC. Therefore, Saudi Arabia has a dominant strategy of cooperating with the quota and producing a low output. Nigeria, however, cannot by itself have much effect on the price of oil. Therefore, Nigeria has a dominant strategy of not cooperating and instead producing a high output. The equilibrium of this game will occur with Saudi Arabia producing a low output and Nigeria producing a high output. In fact, OPEC often operates in just this way. Saudi Arabia will cooperate with the quota, while the other 11 members produce at capacity. Because this is a repeated game, however, Saudi Arabia will occasionally produce more oil than its quota to intentionally drive down the price and retaliate against the other members for not cooperating.

Figure 12.5

The OPEC Cartel with Unequal Members

Because Saudi Arabia can produce much more oil than Nigeria, its output decisions have a much larger effect on the price of oil. In the figure, Low Output corresponds to cooperating with the OPEC-assigned output quota, and High Output corresponds to producing at maximum capacity. Saudi Arabia has a dominant strategy to cooperate and produce a low output. Nigeria, however, has a dominant strategy not to cooperate and instead produce a high output. Therefore, the equilibrium of this game will occur with Saudi Arabia producing a low output and Nigeria producing a high output.

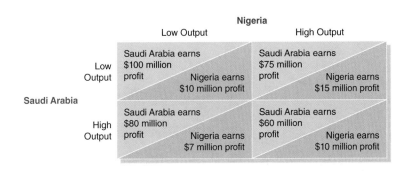

Sequential Games and Business Strategy

We have been analyzing games in which both players move simultaneously. In many business situations, however, one firm will act first, and then other firms will respond. These situations can be analyzed using *sequential games*. We will use sequential games to analyze two business strategies: deterring entry and bargaining between firms. To keep things simple, we consider situations that involve only two firms.

Deterring Entry

We saw earlier that barriers to entry are a key to firms continuing to earn economic profits. Can firms create barriers to deter new firms from entering an industry? Some recent research in game theory has focused on this question. To take a simple example, suppose once again that Apple and Dell are the only makers of very thin and very light laptop computers. Apple has been successfully selling its MacBook Air laptops since 2008. As we saw in the chapter opener, in 2011, Dell finally decided to enter the market for very thin, very light laptops with the XPS 15z laptop. One factor firms consider in pricing a new product is the effect different prices have on the likelihood that competitors will enter the market. A high price might lead to high profits if other firms do not enter the market, but if a high price attracts entry from other firms, it might actually result in lower profits. A low price, by deterring entry, might lead to higher profits. Assume that managers at Apple have developed a very thin, very light laptop before Dell has and are considering what price to charge. To break even by covering the opportunity cost of the funds involved, laptops must provide a minimum rate of return of 15 percent on Apple's investment. If Apple has the market for this type of laptop to itself and charges a price of $800, it will earn economic profits by receiving a return of 20 percent. If Apple charges a price of $1,000 and has the market to itself, it will receive a higher return of 30 percent.

It seems clear that Apple should charge $1,000 for its laptops, but the managers are worried that Dell might also begin selling this type of laptop. If Apple charges $800 and Dell enters the market, Apple and Dell will divide up the market, and both will earn only 5 percent on their investments, which is below the 15 percent return necessary to break even. If Apple charges $1,000 and Dell enters, although the market will still be divided, the higher price means that each firm will earn 16 percent on its investment.

Apple and Dell are playing a sequential game, because Apple makes the first move—deciding what price to charge—and Dell responds. We can analyze a sequential game by using a *decision tree*, like the one shown in Figure 12.6. The boxes in the figure represent *decision nodes*, which are points where the firms must make the decisions contained in the boxes. At the left, Apple makes the initial decision of what price to charge, and

Figure 12.6

The Decision Tree for an Entry Game

Apple earns its highest return if it charges $1,000 for its very thin, very light laptop and Dell does not enter the market. But at that price, Dell will enter the market, and Apple will earn only 16 percent. If Apple charges $800, Dell will not enter because Dell will suffer an economic loss by receiving only a 5 percent return on its investment. Therefore, Apple's best decision is to deter Dell's entry by charging $800. Apple will earn an economic profit by receiving a 20 percent return on its investment. Note that the dashes (—) indicate the situation where Dell does not enter the market and so makes no investment and receives no return.

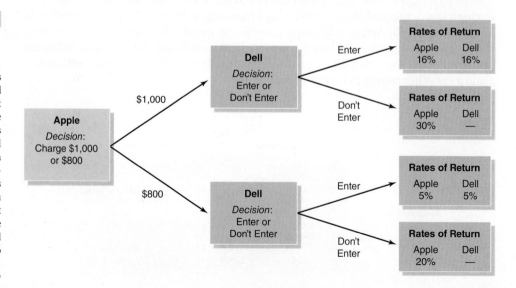

then Dell responds by either entering the market or not. The decisions made are shown beside the arrows. The *terminal nodes*, in green at the right side of the figure, show the resulting rates of return.

Let's start with Apple's initial decision. If Apple charges $1,000, then the arrow directs us to the upper red decision node for Dell. If Dell decides to enter, it will earn a 16 percent rate of return on its investment, which represents an economic profit because it is above the opportunity cost of the funds involved. If Dell doesn't enter, Apple will earn 30 percent, and Dell will not earn anything in this market (indicated by the dash). Apple's managers can conclude that if they charge $1,000 for their laptops, Dell will enter the very thin, very light laptop market, and both firms will earn 16 percent on their investments.

If Apple decides to charge $800, then the arrow directs us to the lower red decision node for Dell. If Dell decides to enter, it will earn only a 5 percent rate of return. If it doesn't enter, Apple will earn 20 percent, and Dell will not earn anything in this market. Apple's managers can conclude that if they charge $800, Dell will not enter, and Apple will earn 20 percent on its investment.

This analysis should lead Apple's managers to conclude that they can charge $1,000 and earn 16 percent—because Dell will enter—or they can charge $800 and earn 20 percent by deterring Dell's entry. Using a decision tree helps Apple's managers to make the correct choice and charge $800 to deter Dell's entry into this market. Note that our discussion is simplified because we are ignoring other characteristics, apart from price, on which the firms also compete. In practice, Apple charged a relatively high price for MacBook Air, which caused Dell to enter the market with the lower-priced XPS 15z. Apple's managers believed that the MacBook Air's features would remain attractive to consumers, despite the XPS 15z having a lower price. Time will tell whether Apple made the correct decision by not charging a low enough price to deter Dell's entry.

Solved Problem **12.3**

Is Deterring Entry Always a Good Idea?

Like any other business strategy, deterring entry is a good idea only if it has a higher payoff than alternative strategies. Use the following decision tree to decide whether Apple should deter Dell from entering the market for very thin, very light laptops. Assume that each firm must earn a 15 percent return on its investment to break even.

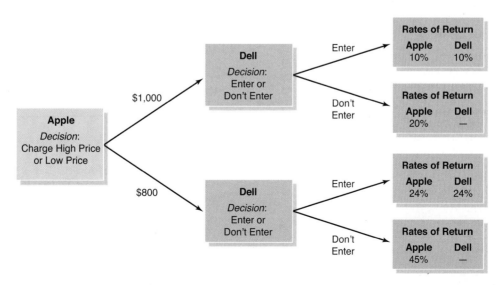

Solving the Problem

Step 1: **Review the chapter material.** This problem is about sequential games, so you may want to review the section "Deterring Entry," which begins on page 360.

Step 2: **Determine how Dell will respond to Apple's decision.** If Apple charges $1,000 for its very thin, very light laptops, Dell will not enter the market because the return on its investment represents an economic loss. If Apple charges $800, Dell will enter because it will earn a return that represents an economic profit.

Step 3: **Given how Dell will react, determine which strategy maximizes profits for Apple.** If Apple charges $1,000, it will have deterred Dell's entry, and the rate of return on its investment will be 20 percent. If Apple charges $800, Dell will enter, but because these low prices will substantially increase the market for these laptops, Apple will actually earn a higher return of 24 percent, splitting the market with Dell at a lower price than it would have earned having the whole market to itself at a high price.

Step 4: **State your conclusion.** Like any other business strategy, deterrence is worth pursuing only if the payoff is higher than for other strategies. In this case, expanding the market for very thin, very light laptops by charging a lower price has a higher payoff for Apple, even given that Dell will enter the market.

MyEconLab   **Your Turn:** For more practice, do related problem 3.1 on page 374 at the end of this chapter.

Bargaining

The success of many firms depends on how well they bargain with other firms. For example, firms often must bargain with their suppliers over the prices they pay for inputs. Suppose that TruImage is a small firm that has developed software that improves how pictures from a digital camera are displayed on computer screens. TruImage currently sells its software only on its website and earns profits of $2 million per year. Dell informs TruImage that it is considering installing the software on every new computer Dell sells. Dell expects to sell more computers at a higher price if it can install TruImage's software on its computers. The two firms begin bargaining over what price Dell will pay TruImage for its software.

The decision tree in Figure 12.7 illustrates this bargaining game. At the left, Dell makes the initial decision about what price to offer TruImage for its software, and

Figure 12.7

The Decision Tree for a Bargaining Game

Dell earns the highest profit if it offers a contract price of $20 per copy and TruImage accepts the contract. TruImage earns the highest profit if Dell offers it a contract of $30 per copy and it accepts the contract. TruImage may attempt to bargain by threatening to reject a $20-per-copy contract. But Dell knows this threat is not credible because once Dell has offered a $20-per-copy contract, TruImage's profits are higher if it accepts the contract than if it rejects it.

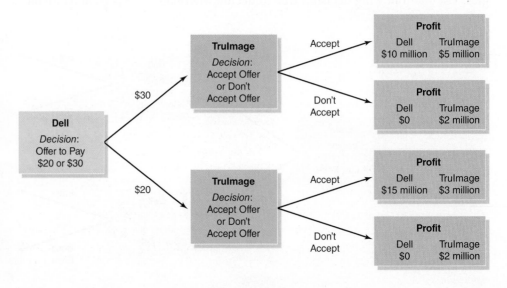

then TruImage responds by either accepting or rejecting the contract offer. First, suppose that Dell offers TruImage a contract price of $30 per copy for its software. If TruImage accepts this contract, its profits will be $5 million per year, and Dell will earn $10 million in additional profits. If TruImage rejects the contract, its profits will be the $2 million per year it earns selling its software on its website, and Dell will earn zero additional profits.

Now, suppose Dell offers TruImage a contract price of $20 per copy. If TruImage accepts this contract, its profits will be $3 million per year, and Dell will earn $15 million in additional profits. If TruImage rejects this contract, its profits will be the $2 million it earns selling its software on its website, and Dell will earn zero additional profits. Clearly, for Dell, a contract price of $20 per copy is more profitable, while for TruImage, a contract price of $30 per copy is more profitable.

Suppose TruImage attempts to obtain a favourable outcome from the bargaining by telling Dell that it will reject a $20-per-copy contract price. If Dell believes this threat, then it will offer TruImage a $30-per-copy contract price because Dell is better off with the $10 million profit that will result from TruImage's accepting the contract than with the zero profits Dell will earn if TruImage rejects the $20-per-copy contract price. This result is a Nash equilibrium because neither firm can increase its profits by changing its choice—*provided that Dell believes TruImage's threat*. But is TruImage's threat credible? Once Dell has offered TruImage the $20 contract price, TruImage's choices are to accept the contract and earn $3 million or reject the contract and earn only $2 million. Because rejecting the contract reduces TruImage's profits, TruImage's threat to reject the contract is not credible, and Dell should ignore it.

As a result, we would expect Dell to use the strategy of offering TruImage a $20-per-copy contract price and TruImage to use the strategy of accepting the contract. Dell will earn additional profits of $15 million per year, and TruImage will earn profits of $3 million per year. This outcome is called a *subgame-perfect equilibrium*. A subgame-perfect equilibrium is a Nash equilibrium in which no player can make himself or herself better off by changing his decision at any decision node. In our simple bargaining game, each player has only one decision to make. As we have seen, Dell's profits are highest if it offers the $20-per-copy contract price, and TruImage's profits are highest if it accepts the contract. Typically, in sequential games of this type, there is only one subgame-perfect equilibrium.

Managers use decision trees like those in Figures 12.6 and 12.7 in business planning because they provide a systematic way of thinking through the implications of a strategy and of predicting the reactions of rivals. We can see the benefits of decision trees in the simple examples considered here. In the first example, Apple's managers can conclude that charging a low price is more profitable than charging a high price. In the second example, Dell's managers can conclude that TruImage's threat to reject a $20-per-copy contract is not credible.

The Five Competitive Forces Model

12.4 LEARNING OBJECTIVE

Use the five competitive forces model to analyze competition in an industry.

We have seen that the number of competitors in an industry affects a firm's ability to charge a price above average cost and earn an economic profit. The number of firms is not the only determinant of the level of competition in an industry, however. Michael Porter of the Harvard Business School has drawn on the research of a number of economists to develop a model that shows how five competitive forces determine the overall level of competition in an industry. Figure 12.8 illustrates Porter's model.

We now look at each of the five competitive forces: (1) competition from existing firms, (2) the threat from potential entrants, (3) competition from substitute goods or services, (4) the bargaining power of buyers, and (5) the bargaining power of suppliers.

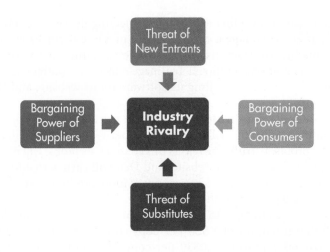

1. Competition from Existing Firms

We have already seen that competition among firms in an industry can lower prices and profits. As another example, Educational Testing Service (ETS) produces the Scholastic Aptitude Test (SAT) and the Graduate Record Exam (GRE). High school students applying to college or university in the United States take the SAT, and students applying to graduate school in the United States and other English-speaking countries (including Canada) take the GRE. In 2011, ETS charged a price of $49 to take the SAT, and it charged $160 to take the GRE. Part of the explanation for this large price difference is that ETS faces competition in the market for tests given to high school students applying to college or university, where the SAT competes with the ACT Assessment, produced by ACT, Inc. But there is no competition for the GRE test. As we saw earlier in this chapter, when there are only a few firms in a market, it is easier for them to implicitly collude and to charge a price close to the monopoly price. In this case, however, competition from a single firm was enough to cause ETS to keep the price of the SAT near the competitive level.

Competition in the form of advertising, better customer service, or longer warranties can also reduce profits by raising costs. For example, online booksellers Amazon.ca and Chapters.Indigo.ca have competed by offering low-cost—or free—shipping, by increasing their customer service staffs, and by building more warehouses to provide faster deliveries. These activities have raised the booksellers' costs and reduced their profits.

2. The Threat from Potential Entrants

Firms face competition from companies that currently are not in the market but might enter. We have already seen how actions taken to deter entry can reduce profits. In our hypothetical example in the previous section, Apple charged a lower price and earned less profit to deter Dell's entry. Business managers often take actions aimed at deterring entry. Some of these actions include advertising to create product loyalty, introducing new products—such as slightly different cereals or toothpastes—to fill market niches, and setting lower prices to keep profits at a level that makes entry less attractive.

3. Competition from Substitute Goods or Services

Firms are always vulnerable to competitors introducing a new product that fills a consumer need better than their current product does. Consider the encyclopedia business. For decades, many parents bought expensive and bulky encyclopedias for their children. By the 1990s, computer software companies were offering electronic encyclopedias that sold for a small fraction of the price of printed encyclopedias.

Encyclopedia Britannica and the other encyclopedia publishers responded by cutting prices and launching advertising campaigns aimed at showing the superiority of printed encyclopedias. Still, profits continued to decline, and by the end of the 1990s, most printed encyclopedias had disappeared.

4. The Bargaining Power of Buyers

If buyers have enough bargaining power, they can insist on lower prices, higher-quality products, or additional services. Automobile companies, for example, have significant bargaining power in the tire market, which tends to lower tire prices and limit the profitability of tire manufacturers. Some retailers have significant buying power over their suppliers. For instance, Walmart has required many of its suppliers to alter their distribution systems to accommodate Walmart's need to control the stocks of goods in its stores.

5. The Bargaining Power of Suppliers

If many firms can supply an input and the input is not specialized, the suppliers are unlikely to have the bargaining power to limit a firm's profits. For instance, suppliers of paper napkins to McDonald's restaurants have very little bargaining power. With only a single or a few suppliers of an input, however, the purchasing firm may face a high price. During the 1930s and 1940s, for example, the Technicolor Company was the only producer of the cameras and film that studios needed to produce colour movies. Technicolor charged the studios high prices to use its cameras, and it had the power to insist that only its technicians could operate the cameras. The only alternative for the movie studios was to make black-and-white movies.

As with other competitive forces, the bargaining power of suppliers can change over time. For instance, when IBM chose Microsoft to supply the operating system for its personal computers, Microsoft was a small company with very limited bargaining power. As Microsoft's Windows operating system became standard in more than 90 percent of personal computers, this large market share increased Microsoft's bargaining power.

Making the Connection	**Can We Predict Which Firms Will Continue to Be Successful?**

For years, economists and business strategists believed that market structure was the most important factor in explaining the ability of some firms to continue earning economic profits. For example, most economists argued that during the first few decades after World War II, steel companies in Canada and the United States earned economic profits because barriers to entry were high, there were few firms in the industry, and competition among firms was low. In contrast, restaurants were seen as less profitable because barriers to entry were low and the industry was intensely competitive. One problem with this approach to analyzing the profitability of firms is that it does not explain how firms in the same industry can have very different levels of profit.

Today, economists and business strategists put greater emphasis on the characteristics of individual firms and the strategies their managers use to continue to earn economic profits. This approach helps explain why Dell, which began as a small company Michael Dell ran from his dorm room at the University of Texas, went on to become extremely profitable and an industry leader, while other computer companies have disappeared. It also explains why Nortel Networks Corporation, a multinational telecommunications equipment manufacturer headquartered in Canada and once the most valuable Canadian company, filed for protection from its creditors on January 14, 2009, and ceased operations in June 2009.

Although its business strategy had once been widely admired, Nortel ceased operations in June 2009.

© Stephen Barnes/Alamy

Is it possible to draw general conclusions about which business strategies are likely to be successful in the future? A number of business analysts have tried to identify strategies that have made firms successful and have recommended those strategies to other firms. Although books with these recommendations are often bestsellers, they have a mixed record in identifying winning strategies. For instance, in 1982, Thomas J. Peters and Robert H. Waterman, Jr., published *In Search of Excellence: Lessons from America's Best-Run Companies*. The book was favourably reviewed by business magazines and sold more than 3 million copies. Peters and Waterman identified 43 companies that were the best at using eight key strategies to "stay on top of the heap." But just two years after the book was published, an article in *BusinessWeek* pointed out that 14 of the 43 companies were experiencing significant financial difficulties. The article noted: "It comes as a shock that so many companies have fallen from grace so quickly—and it also raises some questions. Were these companies so excellent in the first place?"

In 2002, Jim Collins published *Good to Great: Why Some Companies Make the Leap … and Others Don't*, with the goal of determining how companies can "achieve enduring greatness." Although this book also sold 3 million copies, not all of the 11 "great companies" it identified were able to remain successful. For instance, Circuit City was forced to file for bankruptcy in 2009, and Fannie Mae avoided bankruptcy only after the federal government in the United States largely took it over in 2008.

These two books, and many others like them, provide useful analyses of the business strategies of successful firms. That many of the firms highlighted in these books are unable to sustain their success, though, should not be surprising. Many successful strategies can be copied—and, often, improved on—by competitors. Even in oligopolies, competition can quickly erode profits and even turn a successful firm into an unsuccessful one. It remains difficult to predict which currently successful firms will maintain their success.

Based on Thomas J. Peters and Robert H. Waterman, Jr., *In Search of Excellence: Lessons from America's Best-Run Companies* (New York: HarperCollins Publishers, 1982); Jim Collins, *Good to Great: Why Some Companies Make the Leap … and Others Don't* (New York: HarperCollins Publishers, 2001); "Who's Excellent Now?" *BusinessWeek*, November 5, 1984; and Steven D. Leavitt, "From Good to Great … to Below Average," *New York Times*, July 28, 2008.

MyEconLab   **Your Turn:** Test your understanding by doing related problem 4.3 on page 375 at the end of this chapter.

Economics in Your Life

Why Can't You Find a Cheap PlayStation 4?

At the beginning of this chapter, we asked you to consider why the price of the PlayStation 4 game system is almost the same at every large retailer, from Amazon to Walmart. Why don't these retailers seem to compete on price for this type of product? In this chapter, we have seen that if big retailers were engaged in a one-time game of pricing PlayStations, they would be in a prisoner's dilemma and would probably all charge a low price. However, we have also seen that pricing PlayStations is actually a repeated game because the retailers will be selling the game system in competition over a long period of time. In this situation, it is more likely that the retailers will arrive at a cooperative equilibrium, in which they will all charge a high price; this is good news for the profits of the retailers but bad news for consumers! This is one of many insights that game theory provides into the business strategies of oligopolists.

Conclusion

Firms are locked in a never-ending struggle to earn economic profits. As noted in the two preceding chapters, competition erodes economic profits. Even in the oligopolies discussed in this chapter, firms have difficulty earning economic profits in the long run. We have seen that firms attempt to avoid the effects of competition in various ways. For example, they can stake out a secure niche in the market, they can engage in implicit collusion with competing firms, or they can attempt to have the government impose barriers to entry. *An Inside Look* on the next page discusses how Intel produced a new processing chip to remain profitable in the market for laptop computers.

Competing: Intel's "Ultrabook" Against Apple's MacBook Air

ASSOCIATED PRESS

Intel Taps into New Computing at Taiwan Show

Intel Corp. is touting a hybrid laptop 0.8 inches (20 mm) thick with sleek tablet computing features and ultra-sharp visual images that it hopes will create a market bridging traditional PCs and new devices.

The laptop also represents what the U.S. technology giant promises its latest generation of processors will be able to deliver by 2012, when they power new computers produced by companies like Taiwan's AsusTek Computer Inc.

"Computing is taking many forms," Intel executive vice president Sean Maloney said Tuesday at the opening of Taipei's Computex, the world's second-largest computing show.

He said that by the end of 2012, Intel aims to shift 40 percent of consumer laptops to its "Ultrabook" model, a new category of thin and light mobile computers.

Like many other tech companies, Intel is under immense pressure from Apple Inc., whose iPhones and iPads have swept through global markets with the force of a hurricane and show no signs of slowing.

Maloney described the Ultrabook as a laptop-tablet hybrid, featuring touch screens and instant log on, all with a price of less than $1,000.

The projected thickness of the new Intel-powered device would make it the sleekest laptop in the marketplace after Apple's MacBook Air 15 model, which ranges from .11 to .68 inches.

The devices will be based on Intel's "Ivy Bridge," a new generation of chips made with 22 nanometer manufacturing technology and the 3-D transistor the company unveiled early in May. It is slated to be on the market by 2012, Intel said.

The new transistor, with increased density, will make more powerful computing devices, it said.

Also by 2012, a new Intel chip designed for tablets and smartphones, named "Medfield," will be launched. It will give the mobile devices longer use-time, advanced imaging and more power efficiency, the company said.

Intel general manager for the Asia-Pacific region Navin Shenoy acknowledged the market is experiencing significant changes with "the explosion of smartphones and tablets."

"The industry is in constant change," he said. "We're more and more like the fashion industry. Nothing sticks forever."

"We win when we go after and create new markets," he said.

AsusTek is among the Taiwanese computer makers which have pledged to collaborate with Intel.

With the advent of tablets, "the whole industry is reshuffling, including the microprocessors and including

operating systems," said AsusTek Chairman Jonney Shih.

"The boundaries between notebooks, tablets and smartphones are blurring," he told a news conference Monday. Laptops "have to evolve quickly to respond" and become "ultra-thin, ultra-light and ultra-responsive."

Also at Computex, Google Inc. pushed its Chromebook notebook, which is based on its web-browsing-oriented Chrome operating system—an up-and-coming rival in a field long dominated by Microsoft Corp.

Google is partnering with Intel and has engaged South Korea's Samsung Electronics Co. and Taiwan's Acer Inc. to produce the Chromebooks, set to go on sale in June.

Google's Senior Vice President Sundar Pichai said the company has set up a center in Taipei to try to bring more manufacturing partners onboard, but declined to give specifics on his expectations for Chromebook's market share.

"Today my only goal is to make sure we deliver Chromebooks and make customers happy," he said. "That's the only criteria. Focus on quality of experience for consumers rather than quantity."

Key Points in the Article

U.S.-based Intel Corp. introduced new products at Taiwan's Computex computer show: (1) the "Ultrabook," a laptop–tablet hybrid that is 0.8 inches thick and features a touchscreen, excellent image quality, and an updated processor, and (2) a new processing chip for use in tablets and smartphones. Intel noted that to remain successful, it must quickly adapt to the growth and constant changes in the industry. One of Intel's main competitors is Apple, whose MacBook Air, iPhone, and iPad have been highly successful and profitable products. With its new offerings, Intel is positioning itself to compete with Apple with what it believes are better and more advanced products.

Analyzing the News

a When a market is an oligopoly, each firm must take into account the actions of its competitors. With the Ultrabook, Intel expects to compete with firms such as Apple. This means Intel has to account for the likelihood that its rivals will choose to develop models with features similar to those of the Ultrabook. Intel plans to convert 40 percent of consumer laptops to this new model.

b Intel announced that its Ultrabook will be priced under $1,000. In an oligopoly market, a firm's profits depend not only on the price it chooses but also on the price its rivals choose. The figures below illustrate the competition between Intel and Apple, using two possible scenarios. In both figures, we assume that Intel has decided to sell its Ultrabook for $999, and Apple must then decide whether it should also develop a new, comparable computer for the same price. We assume that each company needs a 15 percent return on its investment in these computers to break even. In Figure 1, if Apple decides to develop a new model, both companies will earn a 20 percent return. If Apple decides not to compete with the new Intel model, Intel will earn 30 percent and Apple will earn nothing in this market. Because 20 percent is higher than the minimum 15 percent required return, we can conclude that Apple will enter the market and both firms will earn a 20 percent return.

But suppose that Intel determines that its position relative to Apple is that shown in Figure 2. If Apple enters this market, both Apple and Intel will earn 10 percent returns. If Apple does not enter the market, Intel will earn a 30 percent return. Because 10 percent is below the required return of 15 percent, Apple will not enter the market. In this case, it turns out that whether Figure 1 or Figure 2 more accurately describes the situation in this market is not important for Intel's initial decision to sell the Ultrabook. Whether Apple enters the market or not, Intel will still earn a return greater than 15 percent. Therefore, Intel should sell the Ultrabook.

c Oligopoly firms often try to introduce new products to fill consumer needs better than existing products can, which is what Intel is attempting to do with the Ultrabook. Intel realizes that the computer market changes quickly, and the company must adapt to these rapid changes by introducing new and better products to remain competitive, relevant, and profitable.

Thinking Critically

1. Intel is hoping that its strategy to develop the Ultrabook will increase its share of the laptop computer market. What risks does the company face that could defeat its strategy?
2. Apply the five competitive forces model to Intel. Cite one example of each of the competitive forces that Intel faces.

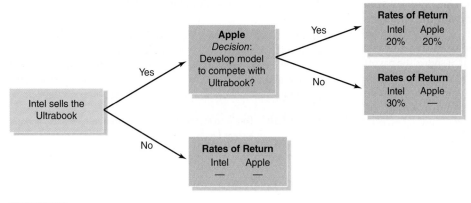

Figure 1

Apple should develop a model to compete with the Ultrabook

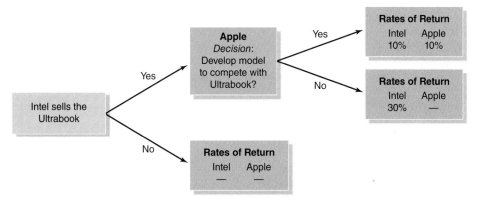

Figure 2

Apple should not develop a model to compete with the Ultrabook

Chapter Summary and Problems

Key Terms

Barrier to entry, p. 349

Business strategy, p. 352

Cartel, p. 358

Collusion, p. 353

Cooperative equilibrium, p. 354

Dominant strategy, p. 353

Economies of scale, p. 349

Game theory, p. 352

Nash equilibrium, p. 353

Noncooperative equilibrium, p. 354

Oligopoly, p. 348

Patent, p. 350

Payoff matrix, p. 353

Price leadership, p. 357

Prisoner's dilemma, p. 354

Summary

*LO 12.1 An **oligopoly** is a market structure in which a small number of interdependent firms compete. **Barriers to entry** keep new firms from entering an industry. The three most important barriers to entry are economies of scale, ownership of a key input, and government barriers. **Economies of scale** exist when a firm's long-run average costs fall as it increases output. Government barriers include patents, licensing, and barriers to international trade. A **patent** is the exclusive right to a product for a period of 20 years from the date the patent is filed with the government.

LO 12.2 Because an oligopoly has only a few firms, interactions among those firms are particularly important. **Game theory** is the study of how people make decisions in situations in which attaining their goals depends on their interactions with others; in economics, it is the study of the decisions of firms in industries where the profits of each firm depend on its interactions with other firms. A **business strategy** refers to actions taken by a firm to achieve a goal, such as maximizing profits. Oligopoly games can be illustrated with a **payoff matrix**, which is a table that shows the payoffs that each firm earns from every combination of strategies by the firms. One possible outcome in oligopoly is **collusion**, which is an agreement among firms to charge the same price or otherwise not to compete. A **cartel** is a group of firms that collude by agreeing to restrict output to increase prices and profits. In a **cooperative**

equilibrium, firms cooperate to increase their mutual payoff. In a **noncooperative equilibrium**, firms do not cooperate but pursue their own self-interest. A **dominant strategy** is a strategy that is the best for a firm, no matter what strategies other firms use. A **Nash equilibrium** is a situation in which each firm chooses the best strategy, given the strategies chosen by other firms. A situation in which pursuing dominant strategies results in noncooperation that leaves everyone worse off is called a **prisoner's dilemma**. Because many business situations are repeated games, firms may end up implicitly colluding to keep prices high. With **price leadership**, one firm takes the lead in announcing a price change, which is then matched by the other firms in the industry.

LO 12.3 Recent work in game theory has focused on actions firms can take to deter the entry of new firms into an industry. Deterring entry can be analyzed using a sequential game, where first one firm makes a decision and then another firm reacts to that decision. Sequential games can be illustrated using decision trees.

LO 12.4 Michael Porter of Harvard Business School argues that the state of competition in an industry is determined by five competitive forces: the degree of competition among existing firms, the threat from new entrants, competition from substitute goods or services, the bargaining power of buyers, and the bargaining power of suppliers.

MyEconLab   Log in to MyEconLab to complete these exercises and get instant feedback

Review Questions

LO 12.1

1.1 What is an oligopoly? Give three examples of oligopolistic industries in Canada.

1.2 What do barriers to entry have to do with the extent of competition in an industry? What are the most important barriers to entry?

1.3 Give an example of a government-imposed barrier to entry. Why would a government be willing to erect barriers to entering an industry?

1.4 What is a patent? If a patent serves as a barrier to entry, why do governments issue patents?

LO 12.2

2.1 Give brief definitions of the following concepts:
  a. Game theory
  b. Cooperative equilibrium
  c. Noncooperative equilibrium
  d. Dominant strategy
  e. Nash equilibrium

2.2 Why do economists refer to the methodology for analyzing oligopolies as game theory?

2.3 Why do economists refer to the pricing strategies of oligopoly firms as a prisoner's dilemma game?

2.4 What is the difference between explicit collusion and implicit collusion? Give an example of each.

2.5 How is the result of the prisoner's dilemma changed in a repeated game?

LO 12.3

3.1 What is a sequential game?

3.2 How are decision trees used to analyze sequential games?

LO 12.4

4.1 List the competitive forces in the five competitive forces model.

4.2 Does the strength of each of the five competitive forces remain constant over time? Briefly explain.

*'Learning Objective' is abbreviated to 'LO' in the end of chapter material.

Problems and Applications

LO 12.1

1.1 In 2009, some analysts of the smartphone industry argued that Apple would be likely to offer a variety of iPhones, each with different features. One observer objected to this argument, though, arguing, " Selling models differentiated by hardware seems unlikely. Different iPhones with very different physical specs could have far-reaching implications for Apple's production methods, volumes and costs." How would Apple's costs be affected by offering different iPhones with "very different specs"? How would this change in costs be likely to affect the prices Apple charged for the iPhone? How would this change in costs be likely to affect the ability of other firms to compete against the iPhone?

Based on James Sherwood, "Apple to Look to Software to Differentiate Multiple iPhone Models," www.reghardware.co.uk, May 18, 2009.

1.2 The graph below illustrates the average total cost curves for two automobile manufacturing firms: Little Auto and Big Auto. Under which of the following conditions would you expect to see the market composed of firms like Little Auto, and under which conditions would you expect to see the market dominated by firms like Big Auto?

   a. When the market demand curve intersects the quantity axis at fewer than 1,000 units

   b. When the market demand curve intersects the quantity axis at more than 1,000 units but fewer than 10,000 units

   c. When the market demand curve intersects the quantity axis at more than 10,000 units

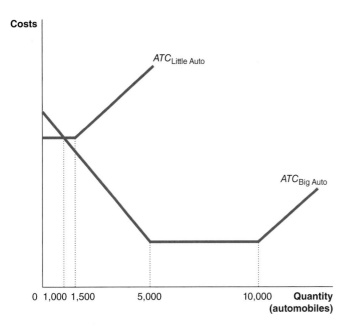

1.3 [**Related to** Making the Connection **on page 351**] The following graph contains two long-run average cost curves. Briefly explain which cost curve would most likely be associated with an oligopoly and which would most likely be associated with a perfectly competitive industry.

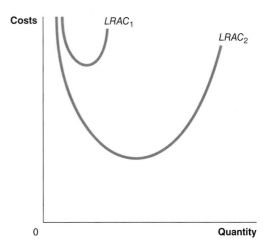

1.4 Alfred Chandler, who was a professor at Harvard Business School, observed, "Imagine the diseconomies of scale—the great increase in unit costs—that would result from placing close to one-fourth of the world's production of shoes, or textiles, or lumber into three factories or mills!" The shoe, textile, and lumber industries are very competitive, with many firms producing each of these products. Briefly explain how Chandler's observation helps explain why these industries are competitive.

From Alfred D. Chandler, Jr., "The Emergence of Managerial Capitalism," in Alfred D. Chandler, Jr., and Richard S. Tedlow, *The Coming of Managerial Capitalism* (New York: Irwin, 1985), p. 406.

1.5 A historical account of the development of the cotton textile industry in England argued:

> The cotton textile industry was shaped by ruthless competition. Rapid growth in demand, low barriers to entry, frequent technological innovations, and a high rate of firm bankruptcy all combined to form an environment in which … oligopolistic competition became almost impossible.

Explain how each of the factors described here would contribute to making oligopolistic competition in the cotton textile industry very difficult.

Based on Thomas K. McCraw, ed., *Creating Modern Capitalism* (Cambridge, MA: Harvard University Press, 1997), pp. 61–62.

LO 12.2

2.1 Bob and Tom are two criminals who have been arrested for burglary. The police put Tom and Bob in separate cells. They offer to let Bob go free if he confesses to the crime and testifies against Tom. Bob also is told that he will serve a 15-year sentence if he remains silent while Tom confesses. If Bob confesses and Tom also confesses, they will each serve a 10-year sentence. Separately, the police make the same offer to Tom. Assume that Bob and Tom know that if they both remain silent, the police have only enough evidence to convict them of a lesser crime, and they will both serve 3-year sentences.

   a. Use the information provided to write a payoff matrix for Bob and Tom.

   b. Does Bob have a dominant strategy? If so, what is it?

   c. Does Tom have a dominant strategy? If so, what is it?

d. What sentences do Bob and Tom serve? How might they have avoided this outcome?

2.2 Explain how collusion makes firms better off. Given the incentives to collude, briefly explain why every industry doesn't become a cartel.

2.3 Baseball players who hit the most home runs *relative to other players* usually receive the highest pay. Beginning in the mid-1990s, the typical baseball player became significantly stronger and more muscular. As one baseball announcer put it, "The players of 20 years ago look like stick figures compared with the players of today." As a result, the average number of home runs hit each year increased dramatically. Some of the increased strength that baseball players gained came from more weight training and better conditioning and diet. As some players admitted, though, some of the increased strength came from taking steroids and other illegal drugs. Taking steroids can significantly increase the risk of developing cancer and other medical problems.

    a. In these circumstances, are baseball players in a prisoner's dilemma? Carefully explain.

    b. Major League Baseball has begun testing players for steroids and fining and suspending players who are caught using steroids (or other illegal muscle-building drugs). Has this testing made baseball players as a group better off or worse off? Briefly explain.

2.4 Soldiers in battle may face a prisoner's dilemma. If all soldiers stand and fight, the chance that the soldiers, as a unit, will survive is maximized. If there is a significant chance that the soldiers will lose the battle, an individual soldier may maximize his chance of survival by running away while the other soldiers hold off the enemy by fighting. If all soldiers run away, however, many of them are likely to be killed or captured by the enemy because no one is left to hold off the enemy. In ancient times, the Roman army practised "decimation." If a unit of soldiers was guilty of running away during a battle or committing other cowardly acts, all would be lined up, and every tenth soldier would be killed by being run through with a sword. No attempt was made to distinguish between soldiers in the unit who had fought well and those who had been cowardly. Briefly explain under what condition the Roman system of decimation was likely to have solved the prisoner's dilemma of soldiers running away in battle.

2.5 [**Related to** Solved Problem 12.2 **on page 354**] Would a ban on advertising beer on television be likely to increase or decrease the profits of beer companies? Briefly explain.

2.6 [**Related to** Solved Problem 12.2 **on page 354**] Radio frequency identification (RFID) tracking tags may ultimately replace bar codes. With this system, a radio signal automatically records the arrival of a product in a warehouse, its shipment to a store, and its purchase by the consumer. Suppose that Walmart and Target are independently deciding whether to stick with bar codes or switch to RFID tags to monitor the flow of products. Because many suppliers sell to both Walmart and Target, it is much less costly for suppliers to use one system or the other rather than to use both. The following payoff matrix shows the profits per year for each company resulting from the interaction of their strategies.

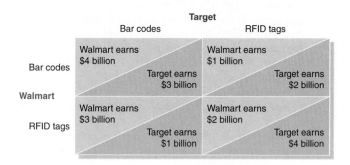

    a. Briefly explain whether Walmart has a dominant strategy.

    b. Briefly explain whether Target has a dominant strategy.

    c. Briefly explain whether there is a Nash equilibrium in this game.

2.7 [**Related to the** Don't Let This Happen to You **on page 354**] A student argues, "The prisoner's dilemma game is unrealistic. Each player's strategy is based on the assumption that the other player won't cooperate. But if each player assumes that the other player *will* cooperate, the 'dilemma' disappears." Briefly explain whether you agree with this argument.

2.8 [**Related to the** Making the Connection **on page 355**] We made the argument that a bidder on an eBay auction has a dominant strategy of bidding only once, with that bid being the maximum the bidder would be willing to pay.

  a. Is it possible that a bidder might receive useful information during the auction, particularly from the dollar amounts other bidders are bidding? If so, how does that change a bidder's optimal strategy?

  b. Many people recommend the practice of "sniping," or placing your bid at the last second before the auction ends. Is there a connection between sniping and your answer to part (a)?

2.9 [**Related to the** Making the Connection **on page 357**] Airlines often find themselves in price wars. Consider the following game: Air Canada and WestJet are the only two airlines flying the route from Calgary to Toronto. Each firm has two strategies: Charge a high price or charge a low price.

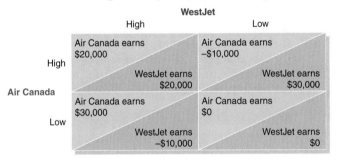

  a. What (if any) is the dominant strategy for each firm?
  b. Is this game a prisoner's dilemma?
  c. How could repeated playing of the game change the strategy each firm uses?

2.10. Finding dominant strategies is often a very effective way of analyzing a game. Consider the following game: Microsoft and Apple are the two firms in the market for operating systems. Each firm has two strategies: Charge a high price or charge a low price.

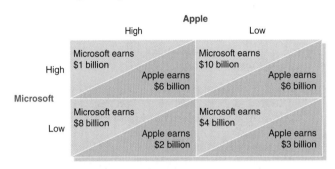

  a. What (if any) is the dominant strategy for each firm?
  b. Is there a Nash equilibrium? Briefly explain.

2.11 A newspaper article referred to Saudi Arabia as "the cartel's enforcer and enabler." What cartel was the article referring to? In what way is Saudi Arabia an enabler and an enforcer?

From Andrew E. Kramer, "Russia Cashes In on Anxiety over Supply of Middle East Oil," *New York Times*, March 7, 2011.

2.12 Refer to Figure 12.5. Consider the entries in the row of the payoff matrix that correspond to Saudi Arabia choosing "low output." Suppose the numbers change so that Nigeria's profit is $15 million when Nigeria chooses "low output" and $10 million when it chooses "high output."

a. Create the payoff matrix for this new situation, assuming that Saudi Arabia and Nigeria choose their output levels simultaneously. Is there a Nash equilibrium to this game? If so, what is it?

b. Draw the decision tree for this situation (using the values from the payoff matrix you created in part a), assuming that Saudi Arabia and Nigeria make their decisions sequentially: First, Saudi Arabia chooses its output level, and then Nigeria responds by choosing its output level. Is there a Nash equilibrium in this game? If so, what is it?

c. Compare your answers to parts (a) and (b). Briefly explain the reason for any differences in the outcomes of these two games.

LO 12.3

3.1. **[Related to** Solved Problem 12.3 **on page 361]** Rockwood is a small town that currently has no fast-food restaurants. McDonald's and Burger King are both considering entering this market. Burger King will wait until McDonald's has made its decision before deciding whether to enter. McDonald's will choose between building a large store and building a small store. Once McDonald's has made its decision about the size of the store it will build, Burger King will decide whether to enter this market. Use the following decision tree to decide the optimal strategy for each company. Does your answer depend on the rate of return that owners of fast-food restaurants must earn on their investments in order to break even? Briefly explain.

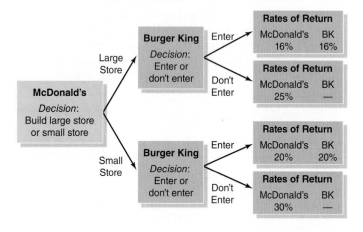

3.2. **[Related to the** Chapter Opener **on page 347]** This chapter describes how firms can create barriers to deter firms from entering an industry:

> One factor firms consider in pricing a new product is the effect different prices have on the likelihood that competitors will enter the market. A high price might lead to high profits if other firms do not enter the market, but if a high price attracts entry from other firms, it might actually result in lower profits. A low price, by deterring entry, might lead to higher profits.

In response to the profits Apple earned from the iPad, other companies, including Dell, Motorola, Research In Motion (now called BlackBerry), and Samsung developed their own tablets. Did Apple make a mistake in not selling its iPads at lower prices in order to prevent other firms from entering the market for tablets?

From "Tablet War Is an Apple Rout," *Wall Street Journal*, August 12, 2011.

3.3. Suppose that in the situation shown in Figure 12.7, TruImage's profits are $1.5 million if the firm accepts Dell's contract offer of $20 per copy. Now will Dell offer TruImage a contract of $20 per copy or a contract of $30 per copy? Briefly explain.

LO 12.4

4.1. Michael Porter argued that in many industries, "strategies converge and competition becomes a series of races down identical paths that no one can win." Briefly explain whether firms in these industries will likely earn economic profits.

Based on Michael E. Porter, "What Is Strategy?" *Harvard Business Review*, November–December 1996, p. 64.

4.2. According to an article in the New York Times, on September 2, 2008, Google released its free Web browser, called Chrome, to directly challenge Microsoft's Internet Explorer and Mozilla Corporation's Firefox browsers. Although Microsoft and Mozilla welcomed the new entry, they also expressed concerns that Google's move will put "more competitive pressure" in an already highly competitive browser landscape.

a. What does the article mean by "competitive pressure"? Which of the five competitive forces is the article referring to?

b. In the long run, will the company that first incorporates new innovations in its browser technology earn economic profits? Which group is likely to benefit the most from these innovations: the browser companies or consumers?

Based on Steve Lohr, "Microsoft Faces New Browser Foe in Google," *New York Times*, September 1, 2008.

4.3. [**Related to the** Making the Connection **on page 365**] In the preface to the 2004 reprint of *In Search of Excellence*, Thomas Peters and Robert Waterman wrote: "Our main detractors point to the decline of some of the companies we featured. They miss the point. . . . We weren't writing *Forever Excellent*, just as it would be absurd to expect any great athlete not to age." Is the analogy the authors make between great firms and great athletes a good one? Should we expect firms to become less successful as they age, just as athletes do?

Based on Thomas Peters and Robert H. Waterman, Jr., "Authors' Note: Excellence 2003," from *In Search of Excellence: Lessons from America's Best-Run Companies* [New York: HarperCollins, 2004 (original edition 1982)].

4.4. The market for electronic readers consists of relatively few firms, including Amazon, Sony, and Plastic Logic. In an interview, Walter Mossberg of the *Wall Street Journal* asked Rich Archuleta, CEO of Plastic Logic, what price the company would be charging for a new electronic reader that it was developing, aimed at business users. Archuleta declined to give a specific price, saying instead, "The market sets pricing. We don't set pricing." But Plastic Logic is competing in an oligopolistic industry, so shouldn't the firm, not the market, be setting the price? Explain why Archuleta made this statement.

Based on "Plastic Logic Shows New E-Book Reader," *Wall Street Journal*, May 27, 2009.

MyEconLab   MyEconLab is an online tool designed to help you master the concepts covered in your course. It will create an adaptive, highly personalized study plan to stimulate and measure your learning. Log in to take advantage of this powerful study aid, and to access quizzes and other valuable course-related material.

Chapter Outline and Learning Objectives

© ONOKY-Photononstop/Alamy

Do Firms Always Compete?

Very few markets today are served by a single private firm, but not that long ago several industries were served by a single firm rather than under competition. Cable television, household mail delivery, and electric power distribution provide excellent examples of markets served by just one firm.

Cable television in Canada offers a great example of a market moving from monopoly to a more competitive structure as technology changes. Television programming was originally broadcast locally at no charge to the user, like radio stations do today. For smaller cities and towns that couldn't support television broadcasters, cable companies were created to rebroadcast programming from larger cities. The Canadian Radio-television and Telecommunications Commission (CRTC), an agency of the federal government, made it illegal for more than one firm to provide cable television services in a given region (typically a city, but not always).

Since the early days of cable television, firms have found ways to compete with cable television providers. Phone companies can now use their lines to provide television packages. Mini satellite dishes offer another alternative. Streaming or downloading programming through the Internet offers yet more options for consumers. As a result of the increase in competition, the price of cable television packages has fallen over time. When prices fall due to increased competition, firms make less profit.

When competition results in low economic profits, firms can sometimes attempt to cooperate to raise prices, a practice known as price fixing. Price fixing is a criminal offence in Canada, but unfortunately, some firms (and the people who work for them) attempt it anyway.

AN INSIDE LOOK on **page 398** discusses the recent case of price fixing in the retail gasoline markets of Kingston and Brockville, Ontario.

Economics in Your Life

Why Does Toronto Have Only One NHL Team?

Toronto Maple Leafs games regularly sell out, and when the Leafs are playing well, it is virtually impossible to get tickets to a game. In a competitive market, such high demand (and presumably profits) should cause someone to form another team in the city. With a population of more than 6 million people, the Greater Toronto Area is home to more than six times as many people as Edmonton (home of the Oilers), so Toronto definitely has the population to support another NHL team. The NHL Board of Governors, made up of representatives of each team, decides on the addition of new teams and any relocation of existing teams. Why would the NHL choose not to have a second franchise in Toronto? Does this decision make economic sense? As you read this chapter, see if you can answer these questions. You can check your answers against those we provide on page 397 at the end of this chapter.

Although few firms are monopolies, the economic model of monopoly can be quite useful. Even though perfectly competitive markets are rare, this market model provides a benchmark for how a firm acts in the most competitive situation possible: when it is in an industry with many firms that all supply the same product. Monopoly provides a benchmark for the other extreme, where a firm is the only one in its market and, therefore, faces no competition from other firms supplying its product. The monopoly model is also useful in analyzing situations in which firms agree to *collude*, or not compete, and act together as if they were a monopoly. As we will discuss in this chapter, collusion is illegal in Canada but it occasionally happens.

Monopolies pose a dilemma for the government. Should the government allow monopolies to exist? Are there circumstances in which the government should actually promote the existence of monopolies? Should the government regulate the prices monopolies charge? If so, will such price regulation increase economic efficiency? In this chapter, we will explore these public policy issues.

13.1 LEARNING OBJECTIVE

Define *monopoly*.

Monopoly A firm that is the only seller of a good or service that does not have a close substitute.

Is Any Firm Ever Really a Monopoly?

A **monopoly** is a firm that is the only seller of a good or service that does not have a close substitute. Because substitutes of some kind exist for just about every product, can any firm really be a monopoly? The answer is "yes," provided that the substitutes are not "close" substitutes. But how do we decide whether a substitute is a close substitute? A narrow definition of monopoly used by some economists is that a firm has a monopoly if it can ignore the actions of all other firms. In other words, other firms must not be producing close substitutes if the monopolist can ignore the other firms' prices. For example, candles are a substitute for electric lights, but your local electric company can ignore candle prices because however low the price of candles becomes, almost no customers will give up using electric lights and switch to candles. Therefore, your local electric company is clearly a monopoly.

Many economists, however, use a broader definition of *monopoly*. For example, suppose Donn Johnson owns the only pizza parlour in a small town. (We will consider later the question of *why* a market may have only a single firm.) Does Donn have a monopoly? Substitutes for pizza certainly exist. If the price of pizza is too high, people will switch to hamburgers or fried chicken or some other food instead. People do not have to eat at Donn's or starve. Donn is in competition with the local McDonald's and KFC, among other firms. So, Donn does not meet the narrow definition of a monopoly. But many economists would still argue that it is useful to think of Donn as having a monopoly.

Although hamburgers and fried chicken are substitutes for pizza, competition from firms selling them is not enough to keep Donn from earning economic profits. When firms earn economic profits, we can expect new firms to enter the industry, and in the long run, the economic profits are competed away. Donn's profits will not be competed away as long as he is the *only* seller of pizza. Using the broader definition, Donn has a monopoly because there are no other firms selling a substitute close enough that his economic profits are competed away in the long run.

Making the Connection | **Is Google a Monopoly?**

As we will discuss later in this chapter, the federal government can take legal action against a firm under the *Competition Act* if the government believes that the firm has created a monopoly. Similar laws exist in every developed country. In mid-2011, the U.S. Federal Trade Commission (FTC) indicated that it was investigating whether Google had violated the antitrust laws. The European Union, which is an organization of 28 European countries, has similar rules against firms forming monopolies. The European Commission enforces these rules. In early 2011, Microsoft filed a complaint with the European Commission that Google was using its dominant position as an Internet search engine to exclude competitors.

But is Google a monopoly? Clearly, Google is not the only Internet search option available. For example, Yahoo! has for a number of years operated a search engine, Microsoft operates the Bing search engine, and there are a number of smaller search engines. Critics point out, though, that Google has a dominant market share of 70 percent in the United States and 90 percent in Europe. Can the other search engines effectively compete with Google? Microsoft argues that Google has taken steps to create an effective monopoly:

Google has a dominant market share in most countries. Can other search engines effectively compete?

> [Google] understands as well as anyone that search engines depend upon the openness of the web in order to function properly…. Unfortunately, Google has engaged in a broadening pattern of walling off access to content and data that competitors need to provide search results to consumers and to attract advertisers.

Microsoft was particularly concerned that Google was limiting the access of other search engines to YouTube, which Google owns: "Without proper access to YouTube, Bing and other search engines cannot stand with Google on an equal footing in returning search results with links to YouTube videos and that, of course, drives more users away from competitors and to Google." Microsoft also complained that Google was limiting the access of other search engines to many of the books that Google had scanned and made available on the web.

Google, naturally, takes a different view of its position. The company argues that its dominant market share is due to the higher quality of its search engine, not any attempts the company has made to reduce the access of other search engines to online content. In a response to the FTC investigation, Google noted, "We want [users of search engines] to stay with us because we're innovating and making our products better—not because [they are] locked in."

As we have seen, many economists consider a firm to have a monopoly if other firms are unable to compete away its profits in the long run. The debate over whether other search engines can compete with Google or whether it is effectively a monopoly is likely to continue.

Based on Thomas Catan, "FTC to Serve Google with Subpoenas in Broad Antitrust Probe," *Wall Street Journal*, June 23, 2011; Miguel Helft, "Google Confirms F.T.C. Antitrust Inquiry," *New York Times*, June 24, 2011; Amit Singhal, "Supporting Choice, Ensuring Economic Opportunity," googleblog.blogspot.com, June 24, 2011; David Goldman, "Microsoft Accuses Google of Antitrust Violations," money.cnn.com, March 31, 2011; and Brad Smith, "Adding Our Voice to Concerns about Search in Europe," blogs.technet.com, March 31, 2011.

Your Turn: Test your understanding by doing related problems 1.3 and 1.4 on page 401 at the end of this chapter.

MyEconLab

Where Do Monopolies Come From?

13.2 LEARNING OBJECTIVE

Explain the four main reasons monopolies arise.

Because monopolies do not face competition, every firm would like to have a monopoly. But to have a monopoly, barriers to entering the market must be so high that no other firms can enter. *Barriers to entry* may be high enough to keep out competing firms for four main reasons:

1. A government blocks the entry of more than one firm into a market.
2. One firm has control of a key resource necessary to produce a good.
3. There are important *network externalities* in supplying the good or service.
4. Economies of scale are so large that one firm has a *natural monopoly*.

Government Action Blocks Entry

As we will discuss later in this chapter, governments ordinarily try to promote competition in markets, but sometimes governments take action to block entry into a market. In Canada, governments block entry in two main ways:

1. By granting a *patent* or *copyright* to an individual or a firm, giving it the exclusive right to produce a product
2. By granting a firm a *public franchise*, making it the exclusive legal provider of a good or service

Patent The exclusive right to a product for a period of 20 years from the date the patent is filed with the government.

Patents and Copyrights The Canadian government grants patents to firms that develop new products or new ways of making existing products. A **patent** gives a firm the exclusive right to a new product for a period of 20 years from the date the patent is filed with the government. Because Microsoft has a patent on the Windows operating system, other firms cannot sell their own versions of Windows. The government grants patents to encourage firms to spend money on the research and development necessary to create new products. If other firms could have freely copied Windows, Microsoft would have been unlikely to spend the money necessary to develop it. Sometimes a firm is able to maintain a monopoly in the production of a good without patent protection, provided that it can keep secret how the product is made.

Patent protection is of vital importance to pharmaceutical firms as they develop new prescription drugs. Pharmaceutical firms start research and development work on a new prescription drug an average of 12 years before the drug is available for sale. A firm applies for a patent about 10 years before it begins to sell the product. The average 10-year delay between the government granting a patent and the firm actually selling the drug is due to the requirement that the firm demonstrate that the drug is both safe and effective. Therefore, during the period before the drug can be sold, the firm will have substantial costs to develop and test the drug. If the drug does not successfully make it to market, the firm will have a substantial loss.

Once a drug is available for sale, the profits the firm earns from the drug will increase throughout the period of patent protection—which is usually about 10 years— as the drug becomes more widely known to doctors and patients. After the patent has expired, other firms are free to legally produce chemically identical drugs called *generic drugs*. Gradually, competition from generic drugs will eliminate the profits the original firm had been earning. For example, when patent protection expired for Glucophage, a diabetes drug manufactured by Bristol-Myers Squibb, sales of the drug declined by more than $1.5 billion in the first year due to competition from 12 generic versions of the drug produced by other firms. When the patent expired on Prozac, an antidepressant drug manufactured by Eli Lilly, sales dropped by more than 80 percent. Most economic profits from selling a prescription drug are eliminated 20 years after the drug is first offered for sale.

Copyright A government-granted exclusive right to produce and sell a creation.

Just as the government grants a new product patent protection, it grants books, films, and pieces of music **copyright** protection. Canadian law grants the creator of a book, film, or piece of music the exclusive right to use the creation during the creator's lifetime. The creator's heirs retain this exclusive right for 50 years after the creator's death. In effect, copyrights create monopolies for the copyrighted items. Without copyrights, individuals and firms would be less likely to invest in creating new books, films, and software.

Making
the
Connection | **The End of the Christmas Plant Monopoly**

In December, the poinsettia plant seems to be almost everywhere, decorating stores, restaurants, and houses. Although it may seem strange that anyone can have a monopoly on the production of a plant, for many years the Paul Ecke Ranch in Encinitas, California, had a monopoly on poinsettias.

The poinsettia is a wildflower native to Mexico. Unlike almost every other flowering plant, the poinsettia blossoms in the winter. This timing, along with the plant's striking red and green colours, makes the poinsettia ideal for Christmas decorating.

Paul Ecke discovered that by grafting together two varieties of poinsettias, it was possible to have multiple branches grow from one stem. The result was a plant that had more leaves and was much more colourful than conventional poinsettias. Paul Ecke did not attempt to patent his new technique for growing poinsettias. But because the Ecke family kept the technique secret for decades, it was able to maintain a monopoly on the commercial production of the plants. Unfortunately for the Ecke family—but fortunately for consumers—a university researcher discovered the technique and published it in an academic journal.

New firms quickly entered the industry, and the price of poinsettias plummeted. Soon consumers could purchase them for as little as $10 for three. At those prices, the Ecke family's firm was unable to earn economic profits. Eventually, Paul Ecke III, the owner of the firm, decided to give up commercial production of poinsettias on his family's ranch. He sold off more than half the firm's land to fund new state-of-the-art greenhouses and research into new varieties of plants that he hoped would earn the firm economic profits once again.

At one time, the Ecke family had a monopoly on growing poinsettias, but many new firms entered the industry.

Based on Adam Kaye, "Ecke Farming Out His Poinsettia Crop," *North County Times*, November 18, 2007; Cynthia Crossen, "Holiday's Ubiquitous Houseplant," *Wall Street Journal*, December 19, 2000; and Mike Freeman and David E. Graham, "Ecke Ranch Plans to Sell Most of Its Remaining Land," *San Diego Union-Tribune*, December 11, 2003.

Your Turn: Test your understanding by doing related problem 2.4 on page 401 at the end of this chapter.

MyEconLab

Public Franchises In some cases, the government grants a firm a **public franchise** that allows it to be the only legal provider of a good or service. For example, provincial governments often designate one company as the sole provider of land telephone lines, natural gas, or electricity.

In many cases, governments decide to provide services to consumers through a *crown corporation*. Most provincial governments provide electricity in this way. As well, some provincial governments provide basic automobile coverage through a crown corporation (Saskatchewan and British Columbia, for example). Some services are simply provided by government without setting up a crown corporation or a public franchise. Most municipal governments provide water, sewer, and waste management services in this way.

Public franchise A government designation that a firm is the only legal provider of a good or service.

Control of a Key Resource

Another way for a firm to become a monopoly is by controlling a key resource. This happens infrequently because most resources, including raw materials such as oil or iron ore, are widely available from a variety of suppliers. There are, however, a few prominent examples of monopolies based on control of a key resource, such as the Aluminum Company of America (Alcoa) and the International Nickel Company of Canada.

For many years until the 1940s, Alcoa either owned or had long-term contracts to buy nearly all of the available bauxite, the mineral needed to produce aluminum. Without access to bauxite, competing firms had to use recycled aluminum, which limited the amount of aluminum they could produce. Similarly, the International Nickel Company of Canada controlled more than 90 percent of available nickel supplies. Competition in the nickel market increased when the Petsamo nickel fields in northern Russia were developed after World War II.

In Canada a key resource for a professional sports team is a large stadium. The teams that make up the major professional sports leagues—Major League Baseball, the National Hockey League, and the National Basketball Association—usually either own or have long-term leases with the stadiums in major cities. Control of these stadiums is a major barrier to new professional baseball, hockey, or basketball leagues forming.

De Beers promoted the sentimental value of diamonds as a way to maintain its position in the diamond market.

Corbis/Fred Prouser

Making the Connection

Are Diamond Profits Forever? The De Beers Diamond Monopoly

The most famous monopoly based on control of a raw material is the De Beers diamond mining and marketing company of South Africa. Before the 1860s, diamonds were extremely rare. Only a few pounds of diamonds were produced each year, primarily from Brazil and India. Then in 1870, enormous deposits of diamonds were discovered along the Orange River in South Africa. It became possible to produce thousands of pounds of diamonds per year, and the owners of the new mines feared that the price of diamonds would plummet. To avoid financial disaster, the mine owners decided in 1888 to merge and form De Beers Consolidated Mines, Ltd.

De Beers became one of the most profitable and longest-lived monopolies in history. The company has carefully controlled the supply of diamonds to keep prices high. As new diamond deposits were discovered in Russia and Zaire, De Beers was able to maintain prices by buying most of the new supplies.

Because diamonds are rarely destroyed, De Beers has always worried about competition from the resale of stones. Heavily promoting diamond engagement and wedding rings with the slogan "A Diamond Is Forever" was a way around this problem. Because engagement and wedding rings have great sentimental value, they are seldom resold, even by the heirs of the original recipients. De Beers advertising has been successful even in some countries, such as Japan, that have had no custom of giving diamond engagement rings. As the populations in De Beers's key markets age, its advertising in recent years has focused on middle-aged men presenting diamond rings to their wives as symbols of financial success and continuing love and on professional women buying "right-hand rings" for themselves.

Over the years, competition has gradually increased in the diamond business. By 2000, De Beers directly controlled only about 40 percent of world diamond production. The company became concerned about the amount it was spending to buy diamonds from other sources to keep them off the market. It decided to abandon its strategy of attempting to control the worldwide supply of diamonds and to concentrate instead on differentiating its diamonds by relying on its name recognition. Each De Beers diamond is now marked with a microscopic brand—a "Forevermark"—to reassure consumers of its high quality. Other firms, such as BHP Billiton, which owns mines in northern Canada, have followed suit by branding their diamonds. Whether consumers will pay attention to brands on diamonds remains to be seen, although through 2011, the branding strategy had helped De Beers to maintain a 35 to 40 percent share of the diamond market.

Based on William J. Holstein, "De Beers Reworks Its Image as Rivals Multiply," *New York Times*, December 12, 2008; Edward Jay Epstein, "Have You Ever Tried to Sell a Diamond?" *Atlantic Monthly*, February 1982; and Donna J. Bergenstock, Mary E. Deily, and Larry W. Taylor, "A Cartel's Response to Cheating: An Empirical Investigation of the De Beers Diamond Empire," *Southern Economic Journal*, Vol. 73, No. 1, July 2006, pp. 173–189.

MyEconLab

Your Turn: Test your understanding by doing related problem 2.5 on page 401 at the end of this chapter.

Network Externalities

Network externalities A situation in which the usefulness of a product increases with the number of consumers who use it.

There are **network externalities** in the consumption of a product if its usefulness increases with the number of people who use it. If you owned the only HD televison in the world, for example, it would not be very valuable because firms would not have an incentive to develop HD programming. The more HD televisions there are in use, the more valuable they become to consumers.

Some economists argue that network externalities can serve as barriers to entry. For example, in the early 1980s, Microsoft gained an advantage over other software companies by developing MS-DOS, the operating system for the first IBM personal computers. Because IBM sold more computers than any other company, software developers wrote many application programs for MS-DOS. The more people who used MS-DOS–based programs, the greater the value to a consumer of using an MS-DOS–based program. By the 1990s, Microsoft had replaced MS-DOS with Windows. Today, Windows has an 85 percent share in the market for personal computer operating systems, with Apple's operating system having a 10 percent share, and other operating systems, including the open-source Linux system, having shares of about 1 percent or less. If another firm introduced a new operating system, some economists argue that relatively few people would use it initially, and few applications would run on it, which would limit the operating system's value to other consumers.

eBay was the first Internet site to attract a significant number of people to its online auctions. Once a large number of people began to use eBay to buy and sell collectibles, antiques, and many other products, it became a more valuable place to buy and sell. Yahoo.com, Amazon.com, and other Internet sites eventually started online auctions, but they had difficulty attracting buyers and sellers. On eBay, a buyer expects to find more sellers, and a seller expects to find more potential buyers than on Amazon or other auction sites.

As these examples show, from a firm's point of view, network externalities can set off a *virtuous cycle*: If a firm can attract enough customers initially, it can attract additional customers because the value of its product has been increased by more people using it, which attracts even more customers, and so on. With products such as computer operating systems and online auctions, it might be difficult for new firms to enter the market and compete away the profits being earned by the first firm in the market.

Economists engage in considerable debate, however, about the extent to which network externalities are important barriers to entry in the business world. Some economists argue that Microsoft and eBay have dominant positions primarily because they are efficient in offering products that satisfy consumer preferences rather than because of the effects of network externalities. In this view, the advantages existing firms gain from network externalities would not be enough to protect them from competing firms offering better products. In other words, a firm entering the operating system market with a program better than Windows or a firm offering an Internet auction site better than eBay would be successful despite the effects of network externalities. In fact, the market shares of both Windows and eBay have been slowly declining in recent years.

Natural Monopoly

Economies of scale exist when a firm's long-run average costs fall as it increases the quantity of output it produces. A **natural monopoly** occurs when economies of scale are so large that one firm can supply the entire market at a lower average total cost than two or more firms. In that case, there is really "room" in the market for only one firm.

Figure 13.1 shows the average total cost curve for a firm producing electricity and the total demand for electricity in the firm's market. Notice that the average total cost curve is still falling when it crosses the demand curve at point *A*. If the firm is a monopoly and produces 30 billion kilowatt-hours of electricity per year, its average total cost of production will be $0.04 per kilowatt-hour. Suppose instead that two firms are in the market, each producing half of the market output, or 15 billion kilowatt-hours per year. Assume that each firm has the same average total cost curve. The figure shows that producing 15 billion kilowatt-hours would move each firm back up its average cost curve so that the average cost of producing electricity would rise to $0.06 per kilowatt-hour (point *B*). In this case, if one of the firms expands production, it will move down the average total cost curve. With lower average costs, it will be able to offer electricity at a lower price than the other firm can offer. Eventually, the other firm will be driven out of business, and the remaining firm will have a monopoly. Because a monopoly would develop automatically—or *naturally*—in this market, it is a natural monopoly.

Natural monopoly A situation in which economies of scale are so large that one firm can supply the entire market at a lower average total cost than can two or more firms.

Figure 13.1

Average Total Cost Curve for a Natural Monopoly

With a natural monopoly, the average total cost curve is still falling when it crosses the demand curve (point *A*). If only one firm is producing electric power in the market, and it produces where the average cost curve intersects the demand curve, average total cost will equal $0.04 per kilowatt-hour of electricity produced. If the market is divided between two firms, each producing 15 billion kilowatt-hours, the average cost of producing electricity rises to $0.06 per kilowatt-hour (point *B*). In this case, if one firm expands production, it can move down the average total cost curve, lower its price, and drive the other firm out of business.

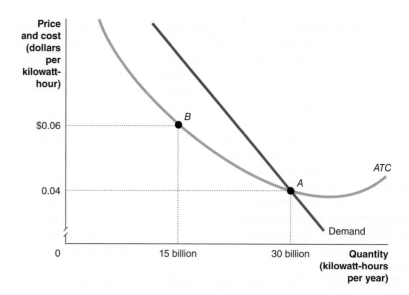

Natural monopolies are most likely to occur in markets where fixed costs are very large relative to variable costs. For example, a firm that produces electricity must make a substantial investment in machinery and equipment necessary to generate the electricity and in the wires and cables necessary to distribute it. Once the initial investment has been made, however, the marginal cost of producing another kilowatt-hour of electricity is relatively small.

Solved Problem 13.2

Is the OpenTable Website a Natural Monopoly?

OpenTable is a website and smartphone application that allows people to make restaurant reservations online. OpenTable charges participating restaurants a fee for each reservation. As business writer James Stewart wrote, "You simply go to the site, choose your neighbourhood, enter your requested date, time, and number of diners, and OpenTable shows all available restaurants with specific times available." Stewart argued that the site is a natural monopoly because "users are attracted to the site with the largest number of listings, and restaurants are attracted to the site with the largest number of users."

a. Assuming that Stewart is correct, draw a graph showing the market for online restaurant reservations. Be sure that the graph contains the demand for online restaurant reservations and OpenTable's average total cost curve. Explain why OpenTable would have lower average costs than would a new site that enters the market to compete against it.

b. Does the number of years OpenTable has been operating affect how you evaluate Stewart's claim that the business is a natural monopoly? Briefly explain.

Solving the Problem

Step 1: Review the chapter material. This problem is about natural monopoly, so you may want to review the section "Natural Monopoly," which begins on page 383.

Step 2: Answer part (a) by drawing a natural monopoly graph and explaining why OpenTable would have lower average costs than new entrants to the market. If Stewart is correct that OpenTable is actually a natural monopoly, the relationship between market demand and its average total costs should look like Figure 13.1.

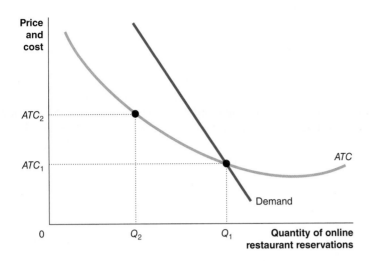

Make sure your average total cost curve is still declining when it crosses the demand curve. As shown in the figure, the market for online reservations is a natural monopoly because if one firm can supply Q_1 online reservations at an average total cost of ATC_1, then dividing the business equally between two firms each supplying Q_2 online reservations would raise average total cost to ATC_2.

OpenTable's fixed costs for servers, software programming, and marketing are very large relative to its variable costs. OpenTable's marginal cost of accommodating one more visitor to its site will be extremely small. Therefore, economies of scale in this market are likely to be so large that a firm that enters and attracts a small number of visitors to its site will have much higher average costs than OpenTable.

Step 3: **Answer part (b) by discussing whether how long OpenTable has been in business is relevant to assessing whether it is a natural monopoly.** If a firm is a natural monopoly, it is unlikely that firms will be able to successfully enter its market. But a firm that is the first to enter a new market may not initially attract competitors. It can take time for potential competitors to decide whether it would be profitable to enter an industry, particularly an industry that might require a substantial initial investment. The longer OpenTable continues to operate without significant competition, the more likely it is that the firm actually is a natural monopoly.

OpenTable began operating in San Francisco in 1999, and it had expanded nationwide by 2003. One restaurant owner was quoted as saying, "All restaurants have to [participate with OpenTable], whether you like it or not. There's no way around it. At this point, there's no other technology or easy solution for making web reservations." This statement indicates that restaurant owners see OpenTable as effectively having a monopoly.

Extra Credit: Keep in mind that competition is not good for its own sake. It is good because it can lead to lower costs, lower prices, and better products. In certain markets, however, cost conditions are such that competition is likely to lead to higher costs and higher prices. These markets are natural monopolies that are best served by one firm. Time will tell whether advances in technology or innovative marketing will make it possible for other firms to successfully compete with OpenTable.

Based on James B. Stewart, "What's New on the Menu: Hot IPO with Rare Quality," *Wall Street Journal*, May 27, 2009; and Katie Hafner, "Restaurant Reservations Go Online," *New York Times*, June 18, 2007.

Your Turn: For more practice, do related problem 2.6 on page 401 at the end of this chapter.　　　MyEconLab

How Does a Monopoly Choose Price and Output?

Like every other firm, a monopoly maximizes profit by producing where marginal revenue equals marginal cost. A monopoly differs from other firms in that *a monopoly's demand curve is the same as the demand curve for the product.* The market demand curve for wheat would be very different from the demand curve for the wheat produced by any one farmer. If, however, one farmer had a monopoly on wheat production, the two demand curves would be exactly the same.

Marginal Revenue Once Again

Firms in perfectly competitive markets—such as a farmer in the wheat market—face horizontal demand curves. They are *price takers*. All other firms, including monopolies, are *price makers*. If price makers raise their prices, they will lose some, but not all, of their customers. Therefore, they face a downward-sloping demand curve and a downward-sloping marginal revenue curve as well. Let's review why a firm's marginal revenue curve slopes downward if its demand curve slopes downward.

Remember that when a firm cuts the price of a product, one good thing happens, and one bad thing happens:

- *The good thing.* It sells more units of the product.

- *The bad thing.* It receives less revenue from each unit than it would have received at the higher price.

For example, consider the table in Figure 13.2, which shows the demand curve for Rogers Communications' basic cable package. For simplicity, we assume that the market has only 10 potential subscribers instead of 2.25 million it actually has. If Rogers Communications charges a price of $60 per month, it won't have any subscribers. If it charges a price of $57, it sells 1 subscription. At $54, it sells 2 subscriptions, and so on. Rogers Communications' total revenue is equal to the number of subscriptions sold per month multiplied by the price. The firm's average revenue—or revenue per subscription sold—is equal to its total revenue divided by the quantity of subscriptions sold. Rogers is particularly interested in marginal revenue because marginal revenue tells the firm how much its revenue will increase if it cuts the price to sell one more subscription.

Notice that Rogers Communications' marginal revenue is less than the price for every subscription sold after the first subscription. To see why, think about what happens if Rogers cuts the price of its basic cable package from $42 to $39, which increases its subscriptions sold from 6 to 7. Rogers increases its revenue by the $39 it receives for the seventh subscription. But it also loses revenue of $3 per subscription on the first 6 subscriptions because it could have sold them at the old price of $42. So, its marginal revenue on the seventh subscription is $39 − $18 = $21 which is the value shown in the table. The graph in Figure 13.2 plots Rogers Communications' demand and marginal revenue curves, based on the information in the table.

Profit Maximization for a Monopolist

Figure 13.3 shows how Rogers Communications combines the information on demand and marginal revenue with information on average and marginal costs to decide how many subscriptions to sell and what price to charge. We assume that the firm's marginal cost and average total cost curves have the usual U shapes. In panel (a), we see how Rogers can calculate its profit-maximizing quantity and price. As long as the marginal cost of selling one more subscription is less than the marginal revenue, the firm should sell additional subscriptions because it is adding to its profits. As Rogers sells more cable subscriptions, rising marginal cost will eventually equal marginal

Subscribers per Month (Q)	Price (P)	Total Revenue (TR = P x Q)	Average Revenue (AR = TR/Q)	Marginal Revenue (MR = ΔTR/ΔQ)
0	$60	$ 0	–	–
1	57	57	$57	$57
2	54	108	54	51
3	51	153	51	45
4	48	192	48	39
5	45	225	45	33
6	42	252	42	27
7	39	273	39	21
8	36	288	36	15
9	33	297	33	9
10	30	300	30	3

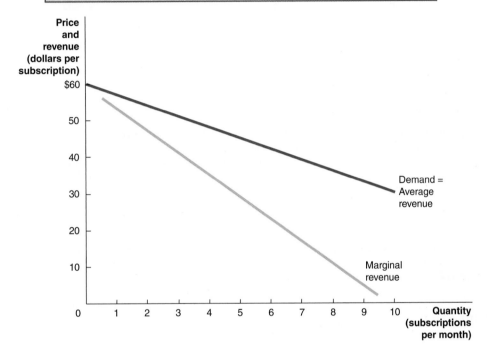

Figure 13.2

Calculating a Monopoly's Revenue

Rogers Communications faces a downward-sloping demand curve for subscriptions to basic cable. To sell more subscriptions, it must cut the price. When this happens, it gains revenue from selling more subscriptions but loses revenue from selling at a lower price the subscriptions that it could have sold at a higher price. The firm's marginal revenue is the change in revenue from selling another subscription. We can calculate marginal revenue by subtracting the revenue lost as a result of a price cut from the revenue gained. The table shows that Rogers' marginal revenue is less than the price for every subscription sold after the first subscription. Therefore, Rogers' marginal revenue curve will be below its demand curve.

revenue, and the firm will be selling the profit-maximizing quantity of subscriptions. This happens with the sixth subscription, which adds $27 to the firm's costs and $27 to its revenues—point *A* in panel (a) of Figure 13.3. The demand curve tells us that Rogers can sell 6 subscriptions for a price of $42 per month. We can conclude that Rogers' profit-maximizing quantity of subscriptions is 6, and its profit-maximizing price is $42.

Panel (b) shows that the average total cost of 6 subscriptions is $30 and that Rogers can sell 6 subscriptions at a price of $42 per month (point *B* on the demand curve). Rogers is making a profit of $12 per subscription—the price of $42 minus the average cost of $30. Its total profit is $72 (= 6 subscriptions × $12 profit per subscription), which is shown by the area of the green-shaded rectangle in the figure. We could also have calculated Rogers' total profit as the difference between its total revenue and its total cost. Its total revenue from selling 6 subscriptions is $252. Its total cost equals its average cost multiplied by the number of subscriptions sold, or $30 × 6 = $180. So, its profit is $252 − $180 = $72.

It's important to note that even though Rogers is earning economic profits, new firms will *not* enter the market. Because Rogers has a monopoly, it will not face competition from other cable operators. Therefore, if other factors remain unchanged, Rogers will be able to continue to earn economic profits, even in the long run.

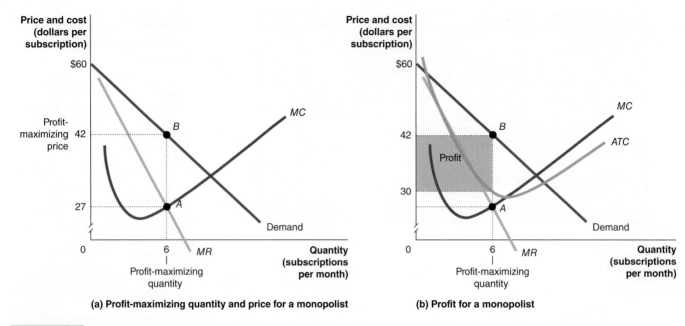

(a) Profit-maximizing quantity and price for a monopolist

(b) Profit for a monopolist

Figure 13.3 **Profit-Maximizing Price and Output for a Monopoly**

Panel (a) shows that to maximize profit, Rogers should sell subscriptions up to the point where the marginal revenue from selling the last subscription equals its marginal cost (point A). In this case, the marginal revenue from selling the sixth subscription and the marginal cost are both $27. Rogers maximizes profit by selling 6 subscriptions per month and charging a price of $42 (point B). In panel (b), the green box represents Rogers' profit. The box has a height equal to $12, which is the price of $42 minus the average total cost of $30, and a base equal to the quantity of 6 cable subscriptions. Rogers' profit therefore equals $12 × 6 = $72.

Solved Problem **13.3**

Finding the Profit-Maximizing Price and Output for a Monopolist

Suppose that Shaw Communications has a cable monopoly in Vancouver. The following table gives Shaw's demand and costs per month for subscriptions to basic cable (for simplicity, we once again keep the number of subscribers artificially small):

Price	Quantity	Total Revenue	Marginal Revenue $\left(MR = \dfrac{\Delta TR}{\Delta Q} \right)$	Total Cost	Marginal Cost $\left(MC = \dfrac{\Delta TC}{\Delta Q} \right)$
$27	3			$ 56	
26	4			73	
25	5			91	
24	6			110	
23	7			130	
22	8			151	

a. Fill in the missing values in the table.

b. If Shaw wants to maximize profits, what price should it charge, and how many cable subscriptions per month should it sell? How much profit will Shaw make? Briefly explain.

c. Suppose the local government imposes a $25-per-month tax on cable companies. Now what price should Shaw charge, how many subscriptions should it sell, and what will its profits be?

Solving the Problem

Step 1: **Review the chapter material.** This problem is about finding the profit-maximizing quantity and price for a monopolist, so you may want to review the section "Profit Maximization for a Monopolist," which begins on page 386.

Step 2: **Answer part (a) by filling in the missing values in the table.** Remember that to calculate marginal revenue and marginal cost, you must divide the change in total revenue or total cost by the change in quantity.

We don't have enough information from the table to fill in the values for marginal revenue and marginal cost in the first row.

Price	Quantity	Total Revenue	Marginal Revenue $\left(MR = \dfrac{\Delta TR}{\Delta Q} \right)$	Total Cost	Marginal Cost $\left(MC = \dfrac{\Delta TC}{\Delta Q} \right)$
$27	3	$ 81	—	$ 56	—
26	4	104	$23	73	$17
25	5	125	21	91	18
24	6	144	19	110	19
23	7	161	17	130	20
22	8	176	15	151	21

Step 3: **Answer part (b) by determining the profit-maximizing quantity and price.** We know that Shaw will maximize profits by selling subscriptions up to the point where marginal cost equals marginal revenue. In this case, that means selling 6 subscriptions per month. From the information in the first two columns, we know Shaw can sell 6 subscriptions at a price of $24 each. Shaw's profits are equal to the difference between its total revenue and its total cost: Profit = $144 – $110 = $34 per month.

Step 4: **Answer part (c) by analyzing the impact of the tax.** This tax is a fixed cost to Shaw because it is a flat $25, no matter how many subscriptions it sells. Because the tax doesn't affect Shaw's marginal revenue or marginal cost, the profit-maximizing level of output has not changed. So, Shaw will still sell 6 subscriptions per month at a price of $24, but its profits will fall by the amount of the tax, from $34 per month to $9.

Your Turn: For more practice, do related problem 3.1 on page 401 and problem 3.2 on page 402 at the end of this chapter.   MyEconLab

---

Don't Let This Happen to You

Don't Assume That Charging a Higher Price Is Always More Profitable for a Monopolist

In answering part (c) of Solved Problem 13.3, it's tempting to argue that Shaw should increase its price to make up for the tax. After all, Shaw is a monopolist, so why can't it just pass along the tax to its customers? The reason it can't is that Shaw, like any other monopolist, must pay attention to demand. Shaw is not interested in charging high prices for the sake of charging high prices; it is interested in maximizing profits. Charging a price of $1,000 for a basic cable subscription sounds nice, but if

no one will buy at that price, Shaw would hardly be maximizing profits.

To look at it another way, before the tax is imposed, Shaw has already determined that $24 is the price that will maximize its profits. After the tax is imposed, it must determine whether $24 is still the profit-maximizing price. Because the tax has not affected Shaw's marginal revenue or marginal cost (or had any effect on consumer demand), $24 is still the profit-maximizing price, and Shaw should continue to charge it. The tax reduces Shaw's profits but doesn't cause it to increase the price of cable subscriptions.

(continued)

The light green shaded area represents the monopolist's pre-tax profit. The darker shaded area represents the monopolist's profit after the tax has been imposed.

MyEconLab

Your Turn: Test your understanding by doing related problem 3.4 on page 402 at the end of this chapter.

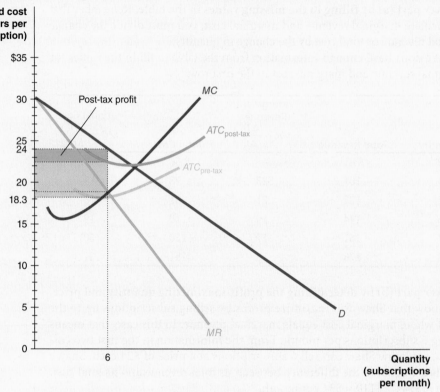

13.4 LEARNING OBJECTIVE

Use a graph to illustrate how a monopoly affects economic efficiency.

Does Monopoly Reduce Economic Efficiency?

A perfectly competitive market is economically efficient. How would economic efficiency be affected if instead of being perfectly competitive, a market were a monopoly? Economic surplus provides a way of characterizing the economic efficiency of a perfectly competitive market: *Equilibrium in a perfectly competitive market results in the greatest amount of economic surplus, or total benefit to society, from the production of a good or service.* What happens to economic surplus under a monopoly? We can begin the analysis by considering the hypothetical case of what would happen if the market for tablet computers begins as perfectly competitive and then becomes a monopoly.

Comparing Monopoly and Perfect Competition

Panel (a) in Figure 13.4 illustrates the situation if the market for tablet computers is perfectly competitive. Price and quantity are determined by the intersection of the demand and supply curves. Remember that none of the individual firms in a perfectly competitive industry has any control over price. Each firm must accept the price determined by the market. Panel (b) shows what happens if the tablet computer industry becomes a monopoly. We know that the monopoly will maximize profits by producing where marginal revenue equals marginal cost. To do this, the monopoly will raise the price and reduce the quantity of tablets, compared to what would have been produced in a perfectly competitive industry. Panel (b) illustrates an important conclusion: *A monopoly will produce less and charge a higher price than would a perfectly competitive industry producing the same good.*

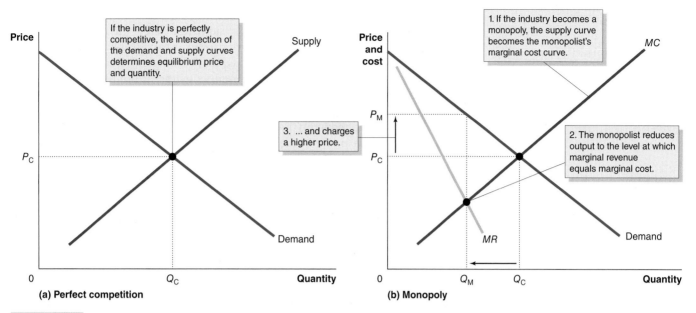

Figure 13.4 What Happens If a Perfectly Competitive Industry Becomes a Monopoly?

In panel (a), the market for tablet computers is perfectly competitive, and price and quantity are determined by the intersection of the demand and supply curves. In panel (b), the perfectly competitive tablet computer industry becomes a monopoly. As a result:

1. The industry supply curve becomes the monopolist's marginal cost curve.
2. The monopolist reduces output to where marginal revenue equals marginal cost, Q_M.
3. The monopolist raises the price from P_C to P_M.

Measuring the Efficiency Losses from Monopoly

Figure 13.5 uses panel (b) from Figure 13.4 to illustrate how monopoly affects consumers, producers, and the efficiency of the economy. *Consumer surplus* measures the net benefit received by consumers from purchasing a good or service. We measure consumer surplus as the area below the demand curve and above the market price. The higher the price, the smaller the consumer surplus. Because a monopoly raises the market price, it reduces consumer surplus. In Figure 13.5, the loss of consumer surplus is equal to rectangle A plus triangle B. Remember that *producer surplus*

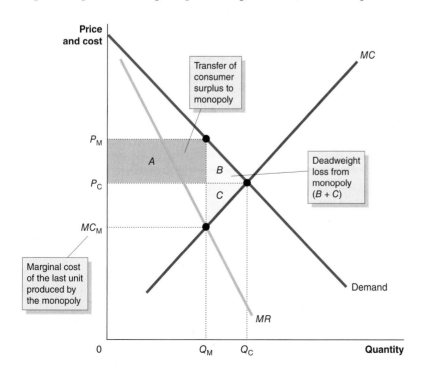

Figure 13.5

The Inefficiency of Monopoly

A monopoly charges a higher price, P_M, and produces a smaller quantity, Q_M, than a perfectly competitive industry, which charges price P_C and produces Q_C. The higher price reduces consumer surplus by the area equal to the rectangle A and the triangle B. Some of the reduction in consumer surplus is captured by the monopoly as producer surplus, and some becomes deadweight loss, which is the area equal to triangles B and C.

measures the net benefit to producers from selling a good or service. We measure producer surplus as the area above the supply curve and below the market price. The increase in price due to monopoly increases producer surplus by an amount equal to rectangle *A* and reduces it by an amount equal to triangle *C*. Because rectangle *A* is larger than triangle *C*, we know that a monopoly increases producer surplus compared with perfect competition.

Economic surplus is equal to the sum of consumer surplus plus producer surplus. By increasing price and reducing the quantity produced, the monopolist has reduced economic surplus by an amount equal to the areas of triangles *B* and *C*. This reduction in economic surplus is called *deadweight loss* and represents the loss of economic efficiency due to monopoly.

The best way to understand how a monopoly causes a loss of economic efficiency is to recall that price is equal to marginal cost in a perfectly competitive market. As a result, a consumer in a perfectly competitive market is always able to buy a good if she is willing to pay a price equal to the marginal cost of producing it. As Figure 13.5 shows, the monopolist stops producing at a point where the price is well above marginal cost. Consumers are unable to buy some units of the good for which they would be willing to pay a price greater than the marginal cost of producing them. Why doesn't the monopolist produce this additional output? Because the monopolist's profits are greater if it restricts output and forces up the price. A monopoly produces the profit-maximizing level of output but fails to produce the efficient level of output from the point of view of society.

We can summarize the effects of monopoly as follows:

1. Monopoly causes a reduction in consumer surplus.
2. Monopoly causes an increase in producer surplus.
3. Monopoly causes a deadweight loss, which represents a reduction in economic efficiency.

How Large Are the Efficiency Losses Due to Monopoly?

Market power The ability of a firm to charge a price greater than marginal cost.

We know that there are relatively few monopolies, so the loss of economic efficiency due to monopoly must be small. Many firms, though, have **market power**, which is the ability of a firm to charge a price greater than marginal cost. The analysis we just completed shows that some loss of economic efficiency will occur whenever a firm has market power and can charge a price greater than marginal cost, even if the firm is not a monopoly. The only firms that do *not* have market power are firms in perfectly competitive markets, which must charge a price equal to marginal cost. Because few markets are perfectly competitive, *some loss of economic efficiency occurs in the market for nearly every good or service.*

Is the total loss of economic efficiency due to market power large or small? It is possible to put a dollar value on the loss of economic efficiency by estimating for every industry the size of the deadweight loss triangle, as in Figure 13.5. The first economist to do this was Arnold Harberger. His original estimates of the cost of market power in the U.S. were small—less than 1 percent of output. Researchers in Canada place the loss to noncompetitive industries at around the same low level.

The loss of economic efficiency is this small primarily because true monopolies are very rare. In most industries, competition keeps price much closer to marginal cost than would be the case in a monopoly. The closer price is to marginal cost, the smaller the size of the deadweight loss.

Market Power and Technological Change

Some economists have raised the possibility that the economy may actually benefit from firms having market power. This argument is most closely identified with Joseph Schumpeter, who argued that economic progress depends on technological change in the form of new products. For example, the replacement of horse-drawn carriages by automobiles, the replacement of ice boxes by refrigerators, and the replacement of mechanical calculators by electronic computers all represent technological changes that significantly raised living standards. In Schumpeter's view, new products unleash a "gale of creative destruction" that drives older products—and, often, the firms that produced them—out of the market. Schumpeter was not concerned that firms with market power would charge higher prices than perfectly competitive firms:

> It is not that kind of [price] competition which counts but the competition from the new commodity, the new technology, the new source of supply, the new type of organization...competition which commands a decisive cost or quality advantage and which strikes not at the margins of the profits and outputs of the existing firms but at their foundations and their very lives.

Economists who support Schumpeter's view argue that the introduction of new products requires firms to spend funds on research and development. It is possible for firms to raise this money by borrowing from investors or from banks. But investors and banks are usually skeptical of ideas for new products that have not yet passed the test of consumer acceptance in the market. As a result, firms are often forced to rely on their profits to finance the research and development needed for new products. Because firms with market power are more likely to earn economic profits than are perfectly competitive firms, they are also more likely to carry out research and development and introduce new products. In this view, the higher prices firms with market power charge are unimportant compared with the benefits from the new products these firms introduce to the market.

Some economists disagree with Schumpeter's views. These economists point to the number of new products developed by smaller firms, including, for example, Steve Jobs and Steve Wozniak inventing the first Apple computer in Jobs's garage, and Larry Page and Sergey Brin inventing the Google search engine as graduate students. As we will see in the next section, government policymakers continue to struggle with the issue of whether, on balance, large firms with market power are good or bad for the economy.

Government Policy Toward Monopoly

Because monopolies reduce consumer surplus and economic efficiency, most governments have policies that regulate their behaviour. **Collusion** refers to an agreement among firms to charge the same price or otherwise not to compete. In Canada, the *Competition Act* is designed to improve monopoly behaviour when it occurs and to prevent collusion. Governments also regulate firms that are natural monopolies, often by controlling the prices they charge.

Collusion An agreement among firms to charge the same price or otherwise not to compete.

Antitrust Laws and Antitrust Enforcement

Antitrust laws aim to eliminate collusion and promote competition among firms. The first important antitrust law regulating monopolies in Canada was enacted in 1889 and is the oldest law of its type in the western world. The *Competition Act* covers a wide variety of competition issues, from price fixing and cartels to requiring the government to review mergers of large or important corporations. The legislation states that the purpose of the Act is to promote efficiency and to provide Canadian consumers with competitive prices and product choices. There are a number of different offences under the Act—for example, price fixing, bid rigging, and predatory pricing are all offences. A person convicted of such offences can be imprisoned for up to 14 years, pay a fine of as much as $25 million, or even both. The *Competition Act*

Antitrust laws Laws aimed at eliminating collusion and promoting competition among firms.

also lays out guidelines for mergers of companies. All large mergers must be approved by the Competition Bureau, and mergers that result in a firm large enough to engage in monopolistic behaviour are unlikely to receive the Bureau's approval.

Mergers: The Trade-off Between Market Power and Efficiency

Horizontal merger A merger between firms in the same industry.

Vertical merger A merger between firms at different stages of production of a good.

The government regulates business mergers because it knows that if firms gain market power by merging, they may use that market power to raise prices and reduce output. As a result, the government is most concerned with **horizontal mergers**, or mergers between firms in the same industry. Horizontal mergers are more likely to increase market power than **vertical mergers**, which are mergers between firms at different stages of the production of a good. An example of a vertical merger would be a merger between a company making personal computers and a company making computer hard drives.

Two factors can complicate regulating horizontal mergers. First, the "market" that firms are in is not always clear. For example, if Hershey Foods wants to merge with Mars, Inc., maker of M&Ms, Snickers, and other candies, what is the relevant market? If the government looks just at the candy market, the newly merged company would have more than 70 percent of the market, a level at which the government would likely oppose the merger. What if the government looks at the broader market for snacks? In this market, Hershey and Mars compete with makers of potato chips, pretzels, and peanuts—and perhaps even producers of fresh fruit. Of course, if the government looked at the very broad market for food, then both Hershey and Mars have very small market shares, and there would be no reason to oppose their merger. In practice, the government defines the relevant market on the basis of whether there are close substitutes for the products being made by the merging firms. In this case, potato chips and the other snack foods mentioned are not close substitutes for candy. So, the government would consider the candy market to be the relevant market and would oppose the merger, on the grounds that the new firm would have too much market power.

The second factor that complicates merger policy is the possibility that the newly merged firm might be more efficient than the merging firms were individually. For example, one firm might have an excellent product but a poor distribution system for getting the product into the hands of consumers. A competing firm might have built a great distribution system but have an inferior product. Allowing these firms to merge might be good for both the firms and consumers. Or, two competing firms might each have an extensive system of warehouses that are only half full, but if the firms merged, they could consolidate their warehouses and significantly reduce their average costs.

Most of the mergers that come under scrutiny by the Competition Bureau are between large firms. For simplicity, though, let's consider a case in which all the firms in a perfectly competitive industry want to merge to form a monopoly. As we saw in Figure 13.5, as a result of this merger, prices will rise and output will fall, leading to a decline in consumer surplus and economic efficiency. But what if the larger, newly merged firm actually is more efficient than the smaller firms were? Figure 13.6 shows a possible result.

If costs aren't affected by the merger, we get the same result as in Figure 13.5: Price rises from P_C to P_M, quantity falls from Q_C to Q_M, consumer surplus is lower, and a loss of economic efficiency results. If the monopoly has lower costs than the competitive firms, it is possible for price to decline and quantity to increase. In Figure 13.6, note where MR crosses MC after the merger—this is the new profit-maximizing quantity, Q_{Merge}. The demand curve shows that the monopolist can sell this quantity at a price of P_{Merge}. Therefore, the price declines after the merger from P_C to P_{Merge}, and quantity increases from Q_C to Q_{Merge}. We have the following seemingly paradoxical result: *Although the newly merged firm has a great deal of market power, because it is more efficient, consumers are better off and economic efficiency is improved.* Of course,

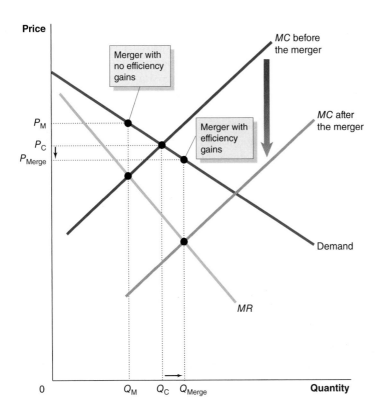

Figure 13.6

A Merger That Makes Consumers Better Off

This figure shows the result of all the firms in a perfectly competitive industry merging to form a monopoly. If costs are unaffected by the merger, the result is the same as in Figure 13.5: Price rises from P_C to P_M, quantity falls from Q_C to Q_M, consumer surplus declines, and a loss of economic efficiency results. If, however, the monopoly has lower costs than the perfectly competitive firms, as shown by the marginal cost curve shifting to MC after the merger, it is possible that the price will actually decline from P_C to P_{Merge} and that output will increase from Q_C to Q_{Merge} following the merger.

sometimes a merged firm will be more efficient and have lower costs, and other times it won't. Even if a merged firm is more efficient and has lower costs, that may not offset the increased market power of the firm enough to increase consumer surplus and economic efficiency.

As you might expect, whenever large firms propose a merger, they claim that the newly merged firm will be more efficient and have lower costs. They realize that without these claims, the Competition Bureau, along with the court system, is unlikely to approve the merger.

The Competition Bureau and Merger Guidelines

Enforcement of the *Competition Act* is the job of the commissioner of competition, who is the head of the Competition Bureau (the Bureau), which has about 400 employees. The Bureau is divided into several departments, each specializing in different types of offences under the Act.

Assessing the impact of mergers on competition is an important activity of the Bureau. When the Bureau finds that a merger will prevent or reduce competition substantially, it can stop the merger from taking place. In order for a merger to prevent or reduce competition, the newly created firm must have significant market power. In considering whether or not the new firm will have market power, the Bureau has to consider two things:

1. Market definition
2. Measure of concentration

Market Definition   The Coca-Cola Company is the only firm in the world that can use its unique recipe to make and sell Coke. Despite this fact, the Coca-Cola Company is not considered by the Bureau to be a monopolist, since Coke isn't in a market all by itself.

Defining a market is actually quite technical and not all economists agree on how to do it. The Competition Bureau has to define markets as part of its work; here, we briefly cover some of the Bureau's method. The Bureau defines a market as all firms making products that consumers see as close substitutes. When substituting between products, there are two dimensions to be considered: (1) the product dimension, which considers only the characteristics of the product (goods that are not similar aren't substitutes); and (2) the geographic dimension, which considers the location of consumers and suppliers (if consumers can't buy from a supplier they are considered to be in a different market).

The product dimension is mostly concerned with the substitutability of one firm's products for those produced by another firm. Identifying a market in this manner begins with the narrowest possible definition of a market by product (say, Coke and Pepsi in the cola market) and tests to see if a monopolist could maintain a small but permanent increase in the price (generally 5 percent, but not always). If the price increase raises profits, the market is considered to be appropriately defined. So if Coca-Cola and Pepsi and all other makers of cola increased their profits by increasing the prices they charged by 5 percent, "cola" would be an appropriate definition of a market. If increasing price reduced the profits of these firms, "cola" would be too narrow a definition for the industry and the Bureau would consider a broader definition of the market—"soft drinks," for example.

Markets also have a geographic element. The Bureau's process for defining a geographic market is similar to how it defines a market in terms of products. A narrow geographic region is defined (say, the Greater Toronto Area), and the impact of an area-wide increase in prices is considered. So, if all the makers of soft drinks in the Greater Toronto Area see profits rise when they increase their prices, the Bureau considers the Greater Toronto Area to be a correctly defined market. If a price increase reduces the profits of these firms, the area is too small and more regions (Hamilton, Barrie, etc.) are added to the market definition. Consumers must have ready access to a supplier for consumers and suppliers to be part of the same market.

Measure of Concentration A market is *concentrated* if a relatively small number of firms have a large share of total sales in the market. A merger between firms in a highly concentrated market is very likely to increase market power. A merger between firms in an industry that has relatively low concentration is unlikely to increase market power, and generally isn't challenged by the commissioner of competition.

A merger that creates a firm with less than 35 percent of the sales does not usually concern the Bureau. Markets in which the share of sales generated by the four largest firms is less than 65 percent are also considered to have low concentration. Even if a merger creates a firm with sales larger than 35 percent of market, or a market in which the largest four firms in the market sell more than 65 percent of the goods in the market, the merger isn't necessarily going to reduce competition, but such mergers will generally be examined more closely.

Regulating Natural Monopolies

If a firm is a natural monopoly, competition from other firms will not play its usual role of forcing price down to the level where the company earns zero economic profit. As a result, public utility boards usually set the prices for natural monopolies, such as firms selling natural gas or electricity. What price should these commissions set? Economic efficiency requires the last unit of a good or service produced to provide an additional benefit to consumers equal to the additional cost of producing it. We can measure the additional benefit consumers receive from the last unit by the price, and we can measure the additional cost to the monopoly of producing the last unit by marginal cost. Therefore, to achieve economic efficiency, regulators should require that the monopoly charge a price equal to its marginal cost. There is, however, an important drawback to doing so, as illustrated in Figure 13.7, which shows the situation of a typical regulated natural monopoly.

Remember that with a natural monopoly, the average total cost curve is still falling when it crosses the demand curve. If unregulated, the monopoly will charge a price equal to P_M and produce Q_M. To achieve economic efficiency, regulators should require

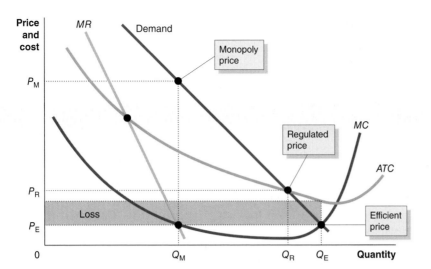

Regulating a Natural Monopoly

A natural monopoly that is not subject to government regulation will charge a price equal to P_M and produce Q_M. If government regulators want to achieve economic efficiency, they will set the regulated price equal to P_E and the monopoly will produce Q_E. Unfortunately, P_E is below average cost, and the monopoly will suffer a loss, shown by the shaded rectangle. Because the monopoly will not continue to produce in the long run if it suffers a loss, government regulators set a price equal to average cost, which is P_R in the figure. The resulting production, Q_R, will be below the efficient level.

the monopoly to charge a price equal to P_E. The monopoly will then produce Q_E. But here is the drawback: P_E is less than average total cost, so the monopoly will be suffering a loss, shown by the area of the red-shaded rectangle. In the long run, the owners of the monopoly will not continue in business if they are experiencing losses. Realizing this, most regulators will set the regulated price, P_R, equal to the level of average total cost at which the demand curve intersects the *ATC* curve. At that price, the owners of the monopoly are able to break even on their investment by producing the quantity Q_R, although this quantity is below the efficient quantity, Q_E.

Economics in Your Life

Why Does Toronto Have Only One NHL Team?

At the beginning of the chapter, we asked why Toronto has only one NHL team. You might think that the NHL would want to have as many teams in the league as possible. But the NHL and its Board of Governors understand that having more teams would lead to there being less revenue per team. Adding another team in Toronto would likely mean that hockey fans would be able to go to more games at a lower price. Lower prices due to competition mean lower profits. So adding another team in Toronto would mean fewer sales and lower prices for the Leafs and possibly even for the nearby Buffalo Sabres, as fans purchased merchandise from the new team instead of their old favourites, and lower earnings as television revenues were shared among more teams. The NHL understands that when you're the only game in town, you can charge a price that is greater than marginal cost (and thus earn economic profits).

Conclusion

The more intense the level of competition among firms is, the better a market works. In this chapter, we have seen that, compared with perfect competition, in a monopoly, the price of a good or a service is higher, output is lower, and consumer surplus and economic efficiency are reduced. Fortunately, true monopolies are rare. Even though most firms resemble monopolies in being able to charge a price above marginal cost, most markets have enough competition to keep the efficiency losses from market power low.

We've seen that barriers to entry are an important source of market power. Read *An Inside Look* on the next page for a discussion of price fixing by gas stations in Ontario.

NATIONAL POST

Three Gas Retailers Fined $2M for Price-Fixing Scheme

Three gas companies admitted guilt in a price-fixing scheme in Kingston and Brockville, Ont. and have been fined a total of $2-million, the Competition Bureau said Tuesday.

(a) The Bureau said it found evidence that local retailers from national chain Canadian Tire Corp. and Ontario-based chains Pioneer Energy LP and Mr. Gas Ltd. phoned each other and settled on the prices to charge customers at the pump in the two Ontario cities from May to November 2007.

"Consumers in Kingston and Brockville were denied a competitive price for gasoline as a result of this criminal price-fixing cartel," said Melanie Aitken, Commissioner of Competition.

Such schemes are difficult to detect, the Bureau said, as high or identical prices are not necessarily evidence of criminal activity.

Gas prices can vary because of a range of factors, including differences in local supply and demand conditions and aggressive price competition in a particular market.

The Bureau continues to investigate potential price-fixing in southeastern Ontario, it said.

Ontario Superior Court in Brockville imposed fines after the three companies pleaded guilty to price-fixing under the Competition Act on Tuesday.

Pioneer and Canadian Tire both admitted price-fixing in Kingston and Brockville and were fined $985,000 and $900,000, respectively.

(b) In June 2008 and July 2010, it laid charges against 38 people and 14 companies accused of conspiring to fix gas prices in the Quebec cities of Victoriaville, Thetford Mines, Sherbrooke and Magog.

As of March 8, 22 of those charged and six companies have pleaded guilty and fines of more than $2.8-million have been imposed. Six individuals have been sentenced to jail terms totalling 54 months.

Some of the stations in that case operated under the names of major oil companies like Ultramar, Shell and Irving, but the Bureau said the local operators were the ones who set the prices at the pumps.

(c) The criminal activity in the Kingston/Brockville case came to light through information obtained under the Bureau's immunity program.

This lets those involved come forward and cooperate in exchange for leniency or immunity from prosecution, something the Bureau said is invaluable in uncovering anticompetitive agreements, which can be hard to discover otherwise.

In recent years the federal government amended the Competition Act to increase the penalties related to anti-competitive behaviours, changes that came into effect in March 2010. The Act now provides for jail terms of up to 14 years, fines of up to $25 million or a combination of both.

However, the scheme in the case occurred before the amendments, so the companies were penalized under the previous version of the Act, which allowed for jail terms of up to five years, fines of up to $10-million or both.

Source: Christine Dobby, "Three gas retailers fined $2M for price-fixing scheme," *Financial Post*, December 3, 2012. Material reprinted with the express permission of: National Post, a division of Postmedia Network Inc.

Key Points in the Article

Price fixing is agreeing with competitors to charge higher prices than would be seen if firms were competing with each other, and is illegal under the *Competition Act*. The Competition Bureau is responsible for identifying and prosecuting firms that engage in price fixing. Gas stations are often accused of price fixing and the Competition Bureau has charged several over the years; the fact that there are few substitutes for gasoline provides an excellent opportunity for gas stations to cooperate and act as if they were a monopoly.

Analyzing the News

ⓐ A group of firms all charging the same price is not evidence of price fixing in itself. There are a lot different reasons why firms might set the same price. More direct evidence is needed before the Competition Bureau can bring charges. The Competition Bureau can use a wide range of evidence to support charges of price fixing. In this case, they found evidence that the three firms involved telephoned each other to agree on what price to charge. This is exactly what the *Competition Act* is intended to prevent or punish when it does occur.

ⓑ Price fixing by gas retailers doesn't just happen in Ontario. Fourteen companies in Quebec were found guilty of fixing the price of gas in four different communities. The punishments were severe, with fines of almost $3 million and some people actually going to prison.

ⓒ Because the Bureau requires direct evidence of price fixing, prosecuting offences can be very difficult. One of the ways the Bureau can get evidence is by offering immunity to someone involved in the price fixing to come forward and provide evidence of wrongdoing. The penalties for price fixing are substantial: A person convicted can be fined up to $25 million, be sent to prison for up to 14 years, or be assigned some combination of both jail time and fines. The large penalties are intended, in part, to make price fixing a less appealing option for firms and their employees.

Thinking Critically

1. Some people argue that the penalties for price fixing and other offences under the *Competition Act* should be even larger. Why would a firm ignore a small fine and engage in an illegal activity?

2. Would entry of new firms in the Brockville gasoline market make it easier or harder for price fixing to occur (as we assume in the figure), with the price always being at the competitive level?

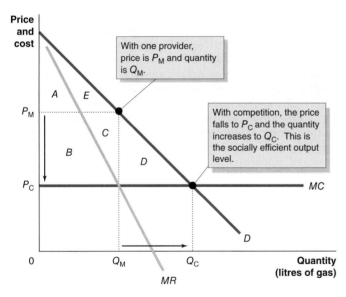

Competition lowers the price of gas and increases economic efficiency.

Chapter Summary and Problems

Key Terms

Summary

*LO 13.1 A **monopoly** exists only in the rare situation in which a firm is producing a good or service for which there are no close substitutes. A narrow definition of monopoly that some economists use is that a firm has a monopoly if it can ignore the actions of all other firms. Many economists favour a broader definition of monopoly. Under the broader definition, a firm has a monopoly if no other firms are selling a substitute close enough that the firm's economic profits are competed away in the long run.

LO 13.2 To have a monopoly, barriers to entering the market must be so high that no other firms can enter. Barriers to entry may be high enough to keep out competing firms for four main reasons: (1) A government blocks the entry of more than one firm into a market by issuing a **patent**, which is the exclusive right to make a product for 20 years, or a **copyright**, which is the exclusive right to produce and sell a creation, or by giving a firm a **public franchise**, which is the right to be the only legal provider of a good or service; (2) one firm has control of a key raw material necessary to produce a good; (3) there are important network externalities in supplying the good or service; or (4) economies of scale are so large that one firm has a natural monopoly. **Network externalities** refer to the situation where the usefulness of a product increases with the number of consumers who use it. A **natural monopoly** is a situation in which economies of scale are so large that one firm can supply the entire market at a lower average cost than can two or more firms.

LO 13.3 Monopolists face downward-sloping demand and marginal revenue curves and, like all other firms, maximize profit by producing where marginal revenue equals marginal cost. Unlike a perfect competitor, a monopolist that earns economic profits does not face the entry of new firms into the market. Therefore, a monopolist can earn economic profits even in the long run.

LO 13.4 Compared with a perfectly competitive industry, a monopoly charges a higher price and produces less, which reduces consumer surplus and economic efficiency. Some loss of economic efficiency will occur whenever firms have **market power** and can charge a price greater than marginal cost. The total loss of economic efficiency in the Canadian economy due to market power is small, however, because true monopolies are very rare. In most industries, competition will keep price much closer to marginal cost than would be the case in a monopoly.

LO 13.5 Because monopolies reduce consumer surplus and economic efficiency, most governments regulate monopolies. Firms that are not monopolies have an incentive to avoid competition by practising **collusion**, or agreeing to charge the same price or otherwise not to compete. **Antitrust laws** such as the *Competition Act* are aimed at deterring monopoly, eliminating collusion, and promoting competition among firms. The Competition Bureau is responsible for enforcing the *Competition Act*, including regulating mergers between firms. A **horizontal merger** occurs between firms in the same industry. A **vertical merger** occurs between firms at different stages of production of a good. Local governments regulate the prices charged by natural monopolies.

MyEconLab   Log in to MyEconLab to complete these exercises and get instant feedback.

Review Questions

LO 13.1
1.1 What is a monopoly? Can a firm be a monopoly if close substitutes for its product exist?
1.2 If you own the only hardware store in a small town, do you have a monopoly?

LO 13.2
2.1 What are the four most important ways a firm becomes a monopoly?
2.2 What is a public franchise? Are all public franchises natural monopolies?
2.3 What is "natural" about a natural monopoly?

LO 13.3
3.1 What is the relationship between a monopolist's demand curve and the market demand curve? What is the relationship between a monopolist's demand curve and its marginal revenue curve?
3.2 Draw a graph that shows a monopolist earning a profit. Be sure your graph includes the monopolist's demand, marginal revenue, average total cost, and marginal cost curves. Be sure to indicate the profit-maximizing level of output and price.

LO 13.4
4.1 Suppose that a perfectly competitive industry becomes a monopoly. Describe the effects of this change on consumer surplus, producer surplus, and deadweight loss.

*'Learning Objective' is abbreviated to 'LO' in the end of chapter material.

4.2 Explain why market power leads to a deadweight loss. Is the total deadweight loss from market power for the economy large or small?

5.1 What is the purpose of the antitrust laws? Who is in charge of enforcing these laws?

5.2 What is the difference between a horizontal merger and a vertical merger? Which type of merger is more likely to increase the market power of a newly merged firm?

5.3 Why would it be economically efficient to require a natural monopoly to charge a price equal to marginal cost? Why do most regulatory agencies require natural monopolies to charge a price equal to average cost instead?

Problems and Applications

1.1 The great baseball player Ty Cobb was known for being very thrifty. Near the end of his life, he was interviewed by a reporter who was surprised to find that Cobb used candles, rather than electricity, to light his home. From Ty Cobb's point of view, was the local electric company a monopoly?

1.2 Some observers say that changes in the past few years have eroded the market power of local cable TV companies, even if no other cable firms have entered their markets. What are these changes? Do these "monopoly" firms still have a lot of market power?

1.3 [**Related to the** Making the Connection **on page 378**] A newspaper article has the headline "Google Says It's Actually Quite Small." According to the article:

> Google rejects the idea that it's in the search advertising business, an industry in which it holds more than a 70 percent share of revenue. Instead, the company says its competition is all advertising, a category broad enough to include newspaper, radio and highway billboards.

Why does Google care whether people think it is large or small? Do highway billboards actually provide competition for Google? Briefly explain.

From Jeff Horwitz, "Google Says It's Actually Quite Small," *Washington Post*, June 7, 2009.

1.4 [**Related to the** Making the Connection **on page 378**] Why is access to YouTube by other search engines such as Yahoo! and Bing relevant to the question of whether Google has a monopoly in the Internet search engine market?

2.1 Canada Post is the only firm offering general mail delivery in Canada. Is Canada Post a natural monopoly? How can we tell?

2.2 Patents are granted for 20 years, but pharmaceutical companies can't use their patent-guaranteed market power for anywhere near this long because it takes several years to acquire Health Canada approval of drugs. Should the life of drug patents be extended to 20 years after Health Canada approval? What would be the costs and benefits of such an extension?

2.3 The German company Koenig & Bauer has 90 percent of the world market for presses that print currency. Discuss the factors that would make it difficult for new companies to enter this market.

2.4 [**Related to the** Making the Connection **on page 380**] Would the Ecke family have been better off if it had patented its process for growing poinsettias? Briefly explain.

2.5 [**Related to the** Making the Connection **on page 382**] Why was De Beers worried that people might resell their old diamonds? How did De Beers attempt to convince consumers that used diamonds were not good substitutes for new diamonds? How did De Beers's strategy affect the demand curve for new diamonds? How did De Beers's strategy affect its profits?

2.6 [**Related to** Solved Problem 13.2 **on page 384**] Suppose that the quantity demanded per day for a product is 90 units when the price is $35. The following table shows costs for a firm with a monopoly in this market:

Quantity (per day)	Total Cost
30	$1,200
40	1,400
50	2,250
60	3,000

Briefly explain whether this firm has a natural monopoly in this market.

3.1 [**Related to** Solved Problem 13.3 **on page 388**] Ed Scahill has acquired a monopoly on the production of baseballs (don't ask how) and faces the demand and cost situation shown in the following table.

Price	Quantity (per week)	Total Revenue	Marginal Revenue	Total Cost	Marginal Cost
$20	15,000			$330,000	
19	20,000			365,000	
18	25,000			405,000	
17	30,000			450,000	
16	35,000			500,000	
15	40,000			555,000	

a. Fill in the remaining values in the table.

b. If Scahill wants to maximize profits, what price should he charge, and how many baseballs should he sell? How much profit (or loss) will he make? Draw a graph to illustrate your answer. Your graph should be clearly labelled and should include: Scahill's demand, *ATC*, *AVC*, *AFC*, *MC*, and *MR* curves, the price he is charging, the quantity he is producing, and the area representing his profit (or loss).

c. Suppose the government imposes a tax of $50,000 per week on baseball production. Now what price should Scahill charge, how many baseballs should he sell, and what will his profit (or loss) be?

d. Suppose that the government raises the tax in part (c) to $70,000. Now what price should Scahill charge, how many baseballs should he sell, and what will his profit (or loss) be? Will his decision on what price to charge and how much to produce be different in the short run than in the long run? Briefly explain.

3.2 [**Related to** Solved Problem 13.3 **on page 388**] Use the information in Solved Problem 13.3 to answer the following questions.

a. What will Shaw do if the tax is $6.00 per month instead of $2.50? (Hint: Will its decision be different in the long run than in the short run?)

b. Suppose that the flat per-month tax is replaced with a tax on the firm of $0.50 per cable subscriber. Now how many subscriptions should Shaw sell if it wants to maximize profit? What price should it charge? What is its profit? (Assume that Shaw will sell only the quantities listed in the table.)

3.3 Before inexpensive pocket calculators were developed, many science and engineering students used slide rules to make numerical calculations. Slide rules are no longer produced, which means nothing prevents you from establishing a monopoly in the slide rule market. Draw a graph showing the situation your slide rule firm would be in. Be sure to include on your graph your demand, marginal revenue, average total cost, and marginal cost curves. Indicate the price you would charge and the quantity you would produce. Are you likely to make a profit or a loss? Show this area on your graph.

3.4 [**Related to the** Don't Let This Happen to You **on page 389**] A student argues, "If a monopolist finds a way of producing a good at lower cost, he will not lower his price. Because he is a monopolist, he will keep the price and the quantity the same and just increase his profit." Do you agree? Use a graph to illustrate your answer.

3.5 Will a monopoly that maximizes profit also be maximizing revenue? Will it be maximizing production? Briefly explain.

LO 13.4

4.1 Review Figure 13.5 on the inefficiency of monopoly. Will the deadweight loss due to monopoly be larger if the demand is elastic or if it is inelastic? Briefly explain.

4.2 Economist Harvey Leibenstein argued that the loss of economic efficiency in industries that are not perfectly competitive has been understated. He argued that when competition is weak, firms are under less pressure to adopt the best techniques or to hold down their costs. He referred to this effect as "x-inefficiency." If x-inefficiency causes a firm's marginal costs to rise, show that the deadweight loss in Figure 13.5 understates the true deadweight loss caused by a monopoly.

4.3 Most cities own the water system that provides water to homes and businesses. Some cities charge a flat monthly fee, while other cities charge by the litre. Which method of pricing is more likely to result in economic efficiency

in the water market? Be sure to refer to the definition of economic efficiency in your answer. Why do you think the same method of pricing isn't used by all cities?

LO 13.5

5.1 Use the graph for a monopoly to answer the questions.

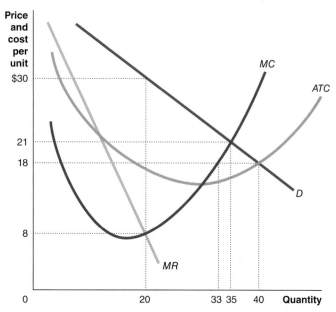

a. What quantity will the monopoly produce, and what price will the monopoly charge?

b. Suppose the government decides to regulate this monopoly and imposes a price ceiling of $18 (in other words, the monopoly can charge less than $18 but can't charge more). Now what quantity will the monopoly produce, and what price will the monopoly charge? Will every consumer who is willing to pay this price be able to buy the product? Briefly explain.

5.2 Consider the natural monopoly shown in Figure 13.7. Assume that the government regulatory agency sets the regulated price, at the level of average total cost at which the demand curve intersects the ATC curve. If the firm knows that it will always be able to charge a price equal to its average total cost, does it have an incentive to reduce its average cost? Briefly explain.

5.3 Draw a graph like Figure 13.6 that shows a merger lowering costs. On your graph, show producer surplus and consumer surplus before a merger and consumer surplus and producer surplus after a merger.

5.4 Look again at the section "The Competition Bureau and Merger Guidelines." Evaluate the following situations.

a. A market initially has 20 firms, each with a 5 percent market share. Of the firms, 4 propose to merge, leaving a total of 17 firms in the industry. Is the Competition Bureau likely to oppose the merger? Briefly explain.

b. A market initially has 5 firms, each with a 20 percent market share. Of the firms, 2 propose to merge, leaving a total of 4 firms in the industry. Is the Competition Bureau likely to oppose the merger? Briefly explain.

Based on www.competitionbureau.gc.ca/eic/site/cb-bc.nsf/eng/03420 .html#s4_3

5.5 The table below shows the market share for companies in the Canadian smartphone market.

Company	Market Share (%)
Apple	32
BlackBerry	23
Samsung	23
Others	22

Use the information in the section "The Competition Bureau and Merger Guidelines" to predict whether the Competition Bureau would be likely to oppose a merger between any of the Canadian distributors of the three firms listed in the table. Assume that "Others" in the table consists of six firms, each of which has approximately a 3.7 percent share of the market.

5.6 The following table gives the approximate market shares of the companies in the Canadian brewing industry for 2012.

Company	Market Share (%)
Anheuser-Busch Inbev (Labatts)	41
Molson Coors	40
Sapporo Breweries (Sleeman)	8
Others	10

Use the information in the section "The Competition Bureau and Merger Guidelines" to predict whether the Competition Bureau would be likely to oppose a merger between any two of the three companies listed. Does your answer depend on how many companies are included in the "Others" category? Briefly explain.

5.7 According to a column in the *New York Times*, the French National Assembly approved a bill:

> …that would require Apple Computer to crack open the software codes of its iTunes music store and let the files work on players other than the iPod….If the French gave away the codes, Apple would lose much of its rationale for improving iTunes.

a. Why would Apple no longer want to improve iTunes if its software codes were no longer secret?

b. Why would the French government believe it was a good idea to require Apple to make the codes public?

Based on Austan Goolsbee, "In iTunes War, France Has Met the Enemy. Perhaps It Is France," *New York Times*, April 27, 2006.

MyEconLab   MyEconLab is an online tool designed to help you master the concepts covered in your course. It will create an adaptive, highly personalized study plan to stimulate and measure your learning. Log in to take advantage of this powerful study aid, and to access quizzes and other valuable course-related material.

The Markets for Labour and Other Factors of Production

Chapter Outline and Learning Objectives

© PCN Photography/Alamy

Hockey and the Canadian Job Market: Can Canadian Workers Make the Playoffs?

"He shoots, he scores! The Calgary Flames are the new Stanley Cup Champions!"

Most Canadian males, and an ever-increasing number of Canadian females, have at some point pretended to be their favourite NHL player, the one who scores the Stanley Cup winning overtime goal. NHL players are celebrities in Canada. Players like Guy Lafleur, Wayne Gretzky, Mario Lemieux, Steve Yzerman, and more recently Jarome Iginla, Sidney Crosby, and Roberto Luongo are national heroes. Not only are these players excellent ambassadors for the game of hockey, but they are viewed by the public as role models of a strong work ethic, grit, determination, and dedication.

And yet if playing in the NHL is a dream of most Canadian kids, few ever achieve it. In the 2011–12 season, only 690 players skated for the 30 NHL teams. Those players that survive the roster cuts make a lot of money relative to the average Canadian, whose salary in 2012 was $46,000. In contrast, for the 2011–12 season, the lowest paid player on the Calgary Flames' roster, Tim Jackman, made $612,500. Jarome Iginla, then Calgary's superstar franchise player, made $7 million, or 152 times the average Canadian salary. The dynamic energy, physical play, and consistent goal scoring of Iginla helped Calgary become a competitive team. Fans identified with him; they purchased Calgary Flames merchandise and tickets or television packages so they could watch him play.

The NHL, and professional sports more broadly, are examples of an industry where there is a tournament structure payoff. There are relatively few winners and they make out extraordinarily well, while the vast majority of those who play hockey never manage to make a significant living from their efforts. Economists describe these industries as lottery, tournament, or "winner-take-all" markets. Historically these lottery markets have been limited to arts and entertainment industries (sports is entertainment) but in recent decades their prevalence has widened to include mainstream businesses.

The shift toward more lottery markets has changed the distribution of income in the economy. What has come to be known in the popular media as the "hollowing out" of the middle class is the trend of disappearing middle class jobs.[*] This trend has led to an economy where increasingly a small portion of the population earns extremely high salaries and the rest of the economy is facing stagnant wages or even unemployment. Income inequality in many countries is now an important political issue. Why do we observe such huge wage differentials?

AN INSIDE LOOK on **page 430** discusses the trend in the economy that more and more labour markets are becoming lottery markets.

[*]See Thomas B. Edsall, "The Hollowing Out," *New York Times*, July 8, 2012.

Economics in Your Life

How Can You Convince Your Boss to Give You a Raise?

Imagine that you have worked for a local sandwich shop for over a year and are preparing to ask for a raise. You might tell the manager that you are a good employee, with a good attitude and work ethic. You might also explain that you have learned more about your job and are now able to make sandwiches more quickly, track inventory more accurately, and work the point-of-sale system more effectively than when you were first hired. Will this be enough to convince your manager to give you a raise? How can you convince your manager that you are worth more money than you are currently being paid? As you read this chapter, see if you can answer these questions. You can check your answers against those we provide on page 429 at the end of this chapter.

Factors of production Labour, capital, natural resources, and other inputs used to produce goods and services.

Firms use **factors of production**—such as labour, capital, and natural resources—to produce goods and services. In this chapter, we will explore how firms choose the profit-maximizing quantity of labour and other factors of production. The interaction between firms' demand for labour and households' supply of labour determines the equilibrium wage rate.

Because there are many different types of labour, there are many different labour markets. The equilibrium wage in the market for baseball players is much higher than the equilibrium wage in the market for college or university professors. We will explore why this is true. We will also explore how factors such as discrimination, unions, and compensation for dangerous or unpleasant jobs help explain differences among wages. We will then look at *personnel economics*, which is concerned with how firms can use economic analysis to design their employee compensation plans. Finally, we will analyze the markets for other factors of production.

Explain how firms choose the profit-maximizing quantity of labour to employ.

Derived demand The demand for a factor of production; it depends on the demand for the good the factor produces.

The Demand for Labour

Up until now, we have concentrated on consumer demand for final goods and services. The demand for labour is different from the demand for final goods and services because it is a *derived demand*. A **derived demand** for a factor of production depends on the demand for the good the factor produces. You demand an Apple iPhone because of the utility you receive from making phone calls, texting, playing games, and listening to music. Apple's demand for the labour to make iPhones is derived from the underlying consumer demand for iPhones. As a result, we can say that Apple's demand for labour depends primarily on two factors:

1. The additional iPhones Apple can produce if it hires one more worker
2. The additional revenue Apple receives from selling the additional iPhones

(In fact, Apple's suppliers, rather than Apple itself, manufacture the iPhone. For simplicity, we are assuming here that Apple does the manufacturing.)

The Marginal Revenue Product of Labour

Let's consider an example. To keep the main point clear, we'll assume that in the short run, Apple can increase production of iPhones only by increasing the quantity of labour it employs. The table in Figure 14.1 shows the relationship between the quantity of workers Apple hires, the quantity of iPhones it produces, the additional revenue from selling the additional iPhones, and the additional profit from hiring each additional worker.

For simplicity, we are keeping the scale of Apple's factory very small. We will also assume that Apple is a perfect competitor both in the market for selling cell phones and in the market for hiring labour. This means that Apple is a *price taker* in both markets. Although this is not realistic, the basic analysis would not change if we assumed that Apple can affect the price of cell phones and the wage paid to workers. Given these assumptions, suppose that Apple can sell as many iPhones as it wants at a price of $200 and can hire as many workers as it wants at a wage of $600 per week. The additional output a firm produces as a result of hiring one more worker is called the **marginal product of labour**. In the table in Figure 14.1, we calculate the marginal product of labour as the change in total output as each additional worker is hired. Because of *the law of diminishing returns*, the marginal product of labour declines as a firm hires more workers.

Marginal product of labour The additional output a firm produces as a result of hiring one more worker.

When deciding how many workers to hire, a firm is not interested in how much *output* will increase as it hires another worker but in how much *revenue* will increase as it hires another worker. In other words, what matters is how much the firm's revenue will rise when it sells the additional output it can produce by hiring one more worker.

Number of Workers	Output of iPhones per Week	Marginal Product of Labour (iPhones per week)	Product Price	Marginal Revenue Product of Labour (dollars per week)	Wage (dollars per week)	Additional Profit from Hiring One More Worker (dollars per week)
L	Q	MP	P	MRP = P x MP	W	MRP – W
0	0	—	$200	—	$600	—
1	6	6	200	$1,200	600	$600
2	11	5	200	1,000	600	400
3	15	4	200	800	600	200
4	18	3	200	600	600	0
5	20	2	200	400	600	–200
6	21	1	200	200	600	–400

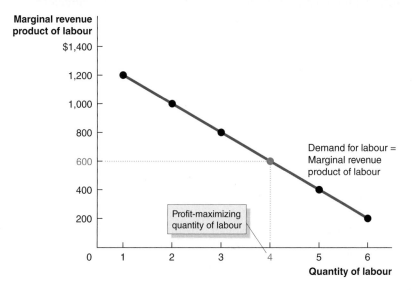

Figure 14.1

The Marginal Revenue Product of Labour and the Demand for Labour

The marginal revenue product of labour equals the marginal product of labour multiplied by the price of the good. The marginal revenue product curve slopes downward because diminishing returns cause the marginal product of labour to decline as more workers are hired. A firm maximizes profits by hiring workers up to the point where the wage equals the marginal revenue product of labour. The marginal revenue product of labour curve is the firm's demand curve for labour because it tells the firm the profit-maximizing quantity of workers to hire at each wage. For example, using the demand curve shown in this figure, if the wage is $600, the firm will hire 4 workers.

We can calculate this amount, which is called the **marginal revenue product of labour** (**MRP**), by multiplying the additional output produced by the product price. For example, consider what happens if Apple increases the number of workers hired from 2 to 3. The table in Figure 14.1 shows that hiring the third worker allows Apple to increase its weekly output of iPhones from 11 to 15, so the marginal product of labour is 4 iPhones. The price of the iPhones is $200, so the marginal revenue product of the third worker is 4 × $200 or $800. In other words, Apple adds $800 to its revenue as a result of hiring the third worker. In the graph, we plot the values of the marginal revenue product of labour at each quantity of labour.

To decide how many workers to hire, Apple must compare the additional revenue it earns from hiring another worker to the increase in its costs from paying that worker. The difference between the additional revenue and the additional cost is the additional profit (or loss) from hiring one more worker. This additional profit is shown in the last column of the table in Figure 14.1 and is calculated by subtracting the wage from the marginal revenue product of labour. As long as the marginal revenue product of labour is greater than the wage, Apple's profits are increasing, and it should continue to hire more workers. When the marginal revenue product of labour is less than the wage, Apple's profits are falling, and it should hire fewer workers. When the marginal revenue product of labour is equal to the wage, Apple has maximized its profits by hiring the optimal number of workers. The values in the table show that Apple should hire 4 workers. If Apple hires a fifth worker, the marginal revenue product of $400 will be less than the wage of $600, and its profits will fall by $200. Table 14.1 summarizes the relationship between the marginal revenue product of labour and the wage.

Marginal revenue product of labour (**MRP**) The change in a firm's revenue as a result of hiring one more worker.

Table 14.1

The Relationship Between the Marginal Revenue Product of Labour and the Wage

When ...	the firm ...
$MRP > W$,	should hire more workers to increase profits.
$MRP < W$,	should hire fewer workers to increase profits.
$MRP = W$,	is hiring the optimal number of workers and is maximizing profits.

We can see from Figure 14.1 that if Apple has to pay a wage of $600 per week, it should hire 4 workers. If the wage were to rise to $1,000, then applying the rule that profits are maximized where the marginal revenue product of labour equals the wage, Apple should hire only 2 workers. Similarly, if the wage is only $400 per week, Apple should hire 5 workers. In fact, the marginal revenue product curve tells a firm how many workers it should hire at any wage rate. In other words, *the marginal revenue product of labour curve is the demand curve for labour.*

Solved Problem **14.1**

Hiring Decisions by a Firm That Is a Price Maker

We have assumed that Apple can sell as many iPhones as it wants to sell, without having to cut the price. This is the case for firms in perfectly competitive markets. These firms are *price takers*. Suppose instead that a firm has market power and is a *price maker*, so that to increase sales, it must reduce the price.

Assume that Apple faces the situation shown in the following table. Fill in the blanks and then determine the profit-maximizing number of workers for Apple to hire. Briefly explain why hiring this number of workers is profit maximizing.

(1) Quantity of Labour	(2) Output of iPhones per Week	(3) Marginal Product of Labour	(4) Product Price	(5) Total Revenue	(6) Marginal Revenue Product of Labour	(7) Wage	(8) Additional Profit from Hiring One Additional Worker
0	0	—	$200		—	$500	—
1	6	6	180			500	
2	11	5	160			500	
3	15	4	140			500	
4	18	3	120			500	
5	20	2	100			500	
6	21	1	80			500	

Solving the Problem

Step 1: **Review the chapter material.** This problem is about determining the profit-maximizing quantity of labour for a firm to hire, so you may want to review the section "The Demand for Labour," which begins on page 406.

Step 2: **Fill in the blanks in the table.** As Apple hires more workers, it sells more iPhones and earns more revenue. You can calculate how revenue increases by multiplying the number of iPhones produced—shown in column (2)—by the price—shown in column (4). Then you can calculate the marginal revenue product of labour as the change in revenue as each additional worker is hired. (Notice that in this case, marginal revenue product is *not* calculated by multiplying the marginal product by the product price. Because Apple is a price maker, its marginal revenue from selling additional iPhones is less than the price of iPhones.) Finally, you can calculate the additional profit from hiring one more worker by subtracting the wage—shown in column (7)—from each worker's marginal revenue product.

(1) Quantity of Labour	(2) Output of iPhones per Week	(3) Marginal Product of Labour	(4) Product Price	(5) Total Revenue	(6) Marginal Revenue Product of Labour	(7) Wage	(8) Additional Profit from Hiring One Additional Worker
0	0	—	$200	$0	—	$500	—
1	6	6	180	1,080	$1,080	500	$580
2	11	5	160	1,760	680	500	180
3	15	4	140	2,100	340	500	−160
4	18	3	120	2,160	60	500	−440
5	20	2	100	2,000	−160	500	−660
6	21	1	80	1,680	−320	500	−820

Step 3: **Use the information in the table to determine the profit-maximizing quantity of workers to hire.** To determine the profit-maximizing quantity of workers to hire, you need to compare the marginal revenue product of labour with the wage. Column (8) makes this comparison by subtracting the wage from the marginal revenue product. As long as the values in column (8) are positive, the firm should continue to hire workers. The marginal revenue product of the second worker is $680, and the wage is $500, so column (8) shows that hiring the second worker will add $180 to Apple's profits. The marginal revenue product of the third worker is $340, and the wage is $500, so hiring the third worker would reduce Apple's profits by $160. Therefore, Apple will maximize profits by hiring 2 workers.

Your Turn: For more practice, do problem 1.2 on page 433 at the end of this chapter.   MyEconLab

The Market Demand Curve for Labour

We can determine the market demand curve for labour in the same way we determine a market demand curve for a good. The market demand curve for a good is determined by adding up the quantity of the good demanded by each consumer at each price. Similarly, the market demand curve for labour is determined by adding up the quantity of labour demanded by each firm at each wage, holding constant all other variables that might affect the willingness of firms to hire workers.

Factors That Shift the Market Demand Curve for Labour

In constructing the demand curve for labour, we held constant all variables—except for the wage—that would affect the willingness of firms to demand labour. An increase or a decrease in the wage causes *an increase or a decrease in the quantity of labour demanded*, which we show by a movement along the demand curve. If any variable other than the wage changes, the result is *an increase or a decrease in the demand for labour*, which we show by a shift of the demand curve. The following are the five most important variables that cause the labour demand curve to shift:

Human capital The accumulated training and skills that workers possess.

1. *Increases in human capital.* **Human capital** represents the accumulated training and skills that workers possess. For example, a worker with a postsecondary education generally has more skills and is more productive than a worker who has only a high school diploma. If workers become more educated and are therefore able to produce more output per day, the demand for their services will increase, shifting the labour demand curve to the right.
2. *Changes in technology.* As new and better machinery and equipment are developed, workers become more productive. This effect causes the labour demand curve to shift to the right over time.
3. *Changes in the price of the product.* The marginal revenue product of labour depends on the price a firm receives for its output. A higher price increases the marginal revenue product and shifts the labour demand curve to the right. A lower price shifts the labour demand curve to the left.
4. *Changes in the quantity of other inputs.* Workers are able to produce more if they have more machinery and other inputs available to them. The marginal product of labour in Canada is higher than the marginal product of labour in most other countries in large part because Canadian firms provide workers with more machinery and equipment. Over time, workers in Canada have had increasing amounts of other inputs available to them, and that has increased their productivity and caused the demand for labour to shift to the right.
5. *Changes in the number of firms in the market.* If new firms enter the market, the demand for labour will shift to the right. If firms exit the market, the demand for labour will shift to the left. This effect is similar to the effect that increasing or decreasing the number of consumers in a market has on the demand for a good.

The Supply of Labour

Having discussed the demand for labour, we can now consider the supply of labour. Of the many trade-offs each of us faces in life, one of the most important is how to divide up the 24 hours in a day between labour and leisure. Every hour spent posting to Facebook, walking on the beach, or in other forms of leisure is one hour fewer spent working. Because in devoting an hour to leisure we give up an hour's earnings from working, the *opportunity cost* of leisure is the wage. The higher the wage we could earn working, the higher the opportunity cost of leisure. Therefore, as the wage increases, we tend to take less leisure and work more. This relationship explains why the labour supply curve for most people is upward sloping, as Figure 14.2 shows.

Figure 14.2

The Labour Supply Curve

As the wage increases, the opportunity cost of leisure increases, causing individuals to supply a greater quantity of labour. Therefore, the labour supply curve is upward sloping.

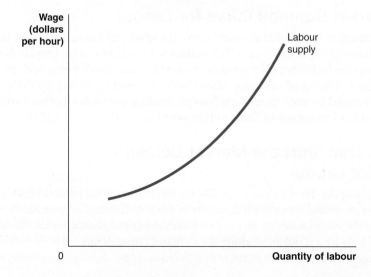

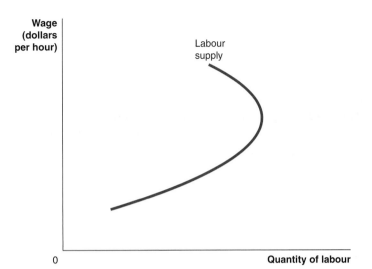

Figure 14.3

A Backward-Bending Labour Supply Curve

As the wage rises, a greater quantity of labour is usually supplied. As the wage climbs above a certain level, the individual is able to afford more leisure even though the opportunity cost of leisure is high. The result may be a smaller quantity of labour supplied.

Although we normally expect the labour supply curve for an individual to be upward sloping, it is possible that at very high wage levels, the labour supply curve of an individual might be *backward bending*, so that higher wages actually result in a *smaller* quantity of labour supplied, as shown in Figure 14.3. To understand why, consider the definitions of the *substitution effect* and the *income effect*. The substitution effect of a price change refers to the fact that an increase in price makes a good more expensive *relative* to other goods. In the case of a wage change, the substitution effect refers to the fact that an increase in the wage raises the opportunity cost of leisure and causes a worker to devote *more* time to working and less time to leisure.

The income effect of a price change refers to the change in the quantity demanded of a good that results from changes in consumer purchasing power as a result of a price change. An increase in the wage will clearly increase a consumer's purchasing power for any given number of hours worked. For a normal good, the income effect leads to a larger quantity demanded. Because leisure is a normal good, the income effect of a wage increase will cause a worker to devote *less* time to working and more time to leisure. So, the substitution effect of a wage increase causes a worker to supply a larger quantity of labour, but the income effect causes a worker to supply a smaller quantity of labour. Whether a worker supplies more or less labour following a wage increase depends on whether the substitution effect is larger than the income effect. Figure 14.3 shows the typical case of the substitution effect being larger than the income effect at low levels of wages—so the worker supplies a larger quantity of labour as the wage rises—and the income effect being larger than the substitution effect at high levels of wages—so the worker supplies a smaller quantity of labour as the wage rises. For example, suppose an attorney has become quite successful and can charge clients very high fees. Or suppose a rock band has become very popular and receives a large payment for every concert it performs. In these cases, there is a high opportunity cost for the lawyer to turn down another client to take a longer vacation or for the band to turn down another concert. But because their incomes are already very high, they may decide to give up additional income for more leisure. For the lawyer or the rock band, the income effect is larger than the substitution effect, and a higher wage causes them to supply *less* labour.

The Market Supply Curve of Labour

We can determine the market supply curve of labour in the same way as we determine a market supply curve of a good. The market supply curve of a good is determined by adding up the quantity of the good supplied by each firm at each price. Similarly, the market supply curve of labour is determined by adding up the quantity of labour supplied by each worker at each wage, holding constant all other variables that might affect the willingness of workers to supply labour.

Factors That Shift the Market Supply Curve of Labour

In constructing the market supply curve of labour, we hold constant all other variables that would affect the willingness of workers to supply labour, except the wage. If any of these other variables change, the market supply curve will shift. The following are the three most important variables that cause the market supply curve of labour to shift:

1. ***Increasing population.*** As the population grows due to the number of births exceeding the number of deaths and due to immigration, the supply curve of labour shifts to the right. The effects of immigration on labour supply are largest in the markets for unskilled workers. In some large cities in Canada, for example, the majority of taxi drivers and workers in hotels and restaurants are immigrants. Some supporters of reducing immigration argue that wages in these jobs have been depressed by the increased supply of labour from immigrants.

2. ***Changing demographics.*** *Demographics* refers to the composition of the population. The more people who are between the ages of 16 and 65, the greater the quantity of labour supplied. During the 1970s and 1980s, the Canadian labour force grew particularly rapidly as members of the *baby boom* generation—born between 1946 and 1964—first began working. In contrast, a low birthrate in Japan has resulted in an aging population. The number of working-age people in Japan actually began to decline during the 1990s, causing the labour supply curve to shift to the left.

3. ***Changing alternatives.*** The labour supply in any particular labour market depends, in part, on the opportunities available in other labour markets. For example, the problems in the financial services industry that began in 2007 reduced the opportunities for investment bankers, stockbrokers, and other financial workers. Many workers left this industry—causing the labour supply curve to shift to the left—and entered other markets, causing the labour supply curves to shift to the right in those markets. Canadians who have lost jobs or who have low incomes are eligible for Employment Insurance benefits and other payments from the government. The more generous these payments are, the less pressure unemployed workers have to quickly find another job. In many European countries, it is much easier than in Canada for unemployed workers to receive a greater replacement of their wage income from government payments. Many economists believe generous unemployment benefits help explain the higher unemployment rates experienced in some European countries.

14.3 LEARNING OBJECTIVE

Explain how equilibrium wages are determined in labour markets.

Equilibrium in the Labour Market

In Figure 14.4, we bring together labour demand and labour supply to determine equilibrium in the labour market. We can use demand and supply to analyze changes in the equilibrium wage and the level of employment for the entire labour market,

Figure 14.4

Equilibrium in the Labour Market

As in other markets, equilibrium in the labour market occurs where the demand curve for labour and the supply curve of labour intersect.

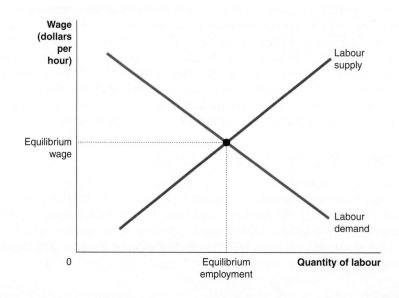

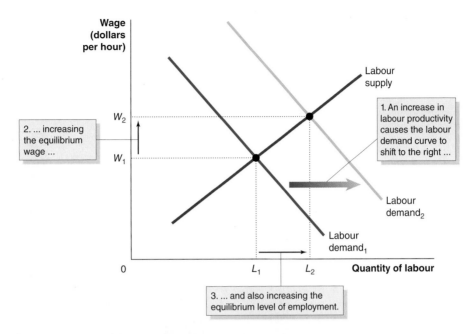

Figure 14.5 The Effect of an Increase in Labour Demand

Increases in labour demand will cause the equilibrium wage and the equilibrium level of employment to rise:

1. If the productivity of workers rises, the marginal revenue product increases, causing the labour demand curve to shift to the right.

2. The equilibrium wage rises from W_1 to W_2.
3. The equilibrium level of employment rises from L_1 to L_2.

and we can also use it to analyze markets for different types of labour, such as baseball players or professors.

The Effect on Equilibrium Wages of a Shift in Labour Demand

In many labour markets, increases over time in labour productivity will cause the demand for labour to increase. As Figure 14.5 shows, if labour supply is unchanged, an increase in labour demand will increase both the equilibrium wage and the number of workers employed.

Making the Connection	**Will Your Future Income Depend on Which Courses You Take in College or University?**

Most people realize the value of a university (or college) education. As the following chart shows, in 2011, full-time Canadian workers aged 17 to 64 with a bachelor's degree earned more per hour than other workers. For example, educated men earned about 1.6 times as much as male high school dropouts, and educated women earned over 1.8 times their uneducated counterparts' wages.

Why do postsecondary graduates earn more than others? The obvious answer would seem to be that a postsecondary education provides skills that increase productivity. Some economists, though, advocate an alternative explanation, known as the *signalling hypothesis*, first proposed by Nobel Laureate A. Michael Spence. This hypothesis is based on the idea that job applicants will always have more information than will potential employers about how productive the applicants are likely to be. Although employers attempt through job interviews and background checks to distinguish "good workers" from "bad workers," they are always looking for more information.

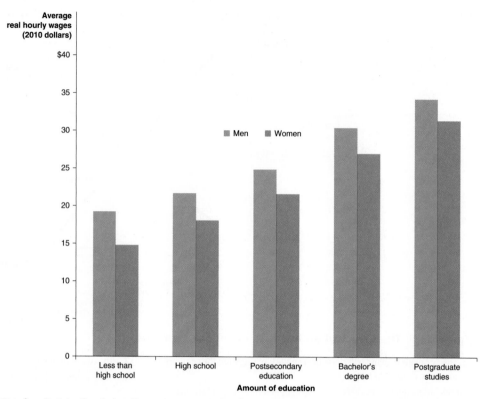

Data from Statistics Canada, http://www.statcan.gc.ca/pub/11f0019m/2013347/t010-eng.htm

Signalling hypothesis The idea that actions taken by people are motivated by the wish to send a positive "signal" to other people.

According to the **signalling hypothesis**, employers see a postsecondary education as a signal that workers possess certain desirable characteristics: self-discipline, the ability to meet deadlines, and the ability to make a sustained effort. Employers value these characteristics because they usually lead to success in any activity. People generally believe that postsecondary graduates possess these characteristics, so employers often require a university degree for their best-paying jobs. In this view, the signal that a postsecondary education sends about a person's inherent characteristics—which the person presumably already possessed *before* entering university—is much more important than any skills the person may have learned in school. Or, as a math professor of one of the authors put it (only half-jokingly): "The purpose of university is to show employers that you can succeed at something that's boring and hard."

Recently, though, several economic studies have provided evidence that the higher incomes of university graduates are due to their greater productivity rather than the signal that a university degree sends to employers. Orley Ashenfelter and Cecilia Rouse studied the relationship between schooling and income among 700 pairs of identical twins. Identical twins have identical genes, so differences in their inherent abilities should be relatively small. Therefore, if they have different numbers of years in school, differences in their earnings should be mainly due to the effect of schooling on their productivity. Ashenfelter and Rouse found that identical twins had returns of about 9 percent per additional year of schooling, enough to account for most of the gap in income between high school graduates and university graduates.

Daniel Hamermesh and Stephen G. Donald studied the determinants of the earnings of university graduates 5 to 25 years after graduation. They collected extensive information on each person in their study, including the person's SAT scores, rank in high school graduating class, grades in every university course taken, and university major. Hamermesh and Donald discovered that, holding constant all other factors, business and engineering majors earned more than graduates with other majors. They also discovered that taking science and math courses has a large effect on future earnings: "A student who takes 15 credits of upper-division science and math courses and obtains a B average in them will earn about 10% more than an otherwise identical student in the same major...who takes no upper-division classes in these areas." This result held even after adjusting for a student's SAT score. The study by Hamermesh and Donald contradicts the signalling hypothesis because if that hypothesis is correct, the choice of courses taken in university should be of minor importance compared with the signal workers send to employers just by having completed university.

Based on Orley Ashenfelter and Cecilia Rouse, "Income, Schooling, and Ability: Evidence from a New Sample of Identical Twins," *Quarterly Journal of Economics*, Vol. 113, No. 1, February 1998, pp. 253–284; and Daniel S. Hamermesh and Stephen G. Donald, "The Effect of College Curriculum on Earnings: An Affinity Identifier for Non-Ignorable Non-Response Bias," *Journal of Econometrics*, Vol. 144, No. 2, June 2008, pp. 479–491.

Your Turn: Test your understanding by doing related problem 3.1 on page 434 at the end of this chapter.

MyEconLab

The Effect on Equilibrium Wages of a Shift in Labour Supply

What is the effect on the equilibrium wage of an increase in labour supply due to population growth? As Figure 14.6 shows, if labour demand is unchanged, an increase in labour supply will decrease the equilibrium wage but increase the number of workers employed.

Whether the wage rises in a market depends on whether demand increases faster than supply. For example, as Facebook, Twitter, Zynga, and other social networking sites became increasingly popular, the demand for software engineers in California's Silicon Valley began to increase faster than the supply of new engineers graduating from university. By 2011, starting salaries for new graduates had increased from about $80,000 in 2009 to as much as $150,000. To keep their engineers from jumping to other employers, Google, Tagged, and other firms had to give their existing employees across-the-board raises. Start-up firms found that the salaries they needed to pay were raising their costs to levels that made it difficult to compete. If these escalating salaries lead more students to graduate with degrees in software engineering, the increased labour supply could eventually bring down salaries.

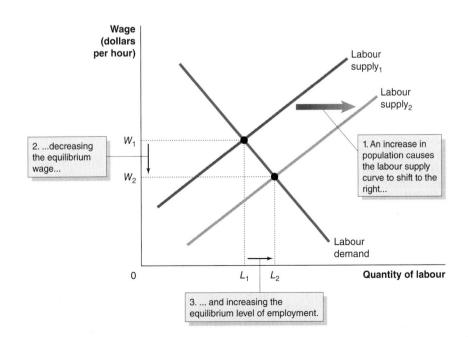

Figure 14.6

The Effect of an Increase in Labour Supply

Increases in labour supply will cause the equilibrium wage to fall but the equilibrium level of employment to rise:

1. As population increases, the labour supply curve shifts to the right.

2. The equilibrium wage falls from W_1 to W_2.

3. The equilibrium level of employment increases from L_1 to L_2.

14.4 LEARNING OBJECTIVE

Use demand and supply analysis to explain how compensating differentials, discrimination, and labour unions cause wages to differ.

Explaining Differences in Wages

A key conclusion of our discussion of the labour market is that the equilibrium wage equals the marginal revenue product of labour. The more productive workers are and the higher the price for which workers' output can be sold, the higher the wages workers will receive. At the beginning of the chapter, we raised the question of why NHL players are paid so much more than most other workers. We are now ready to use demand and supply analysis to answer this question. Figure 14.7 shows the demand and supply curves for NHL players and the demand and supply curves for university professors.

Keeping in mind that each NHL club faces a fixed roster size (so that adding one player requires that a player must leave the roster), consider the marginal revenue product of hockey players, which is the additional revenue a team owner will receive from hiring one more player. Hockey players are hired to produce hockey games that are then sold to fans who pay admission to hockey arenas and to radio and television stations that broadcast the games. Because an NHL team can sell each hockey game for a large amount, the marginal revenue product of hockey players is high. The supply of people with the ability to play in the NHL is also very limited. As a result, the average annual salary of the 690 NHL players was $2.4 million in 2011.

The marginal revenue product of university professors is much lower than for hockey players. University professors are hired to produce degrees and credentials that are sold to students and their parents. Although one year's tuition is quite high at many universities, hiring one more professor allows a university to admit at most a few more students. So, the marginal revenue product of a professor is much lower than the marginal revenue product of a hockey player. There are also many more people who possess the skills to be a university professor than possess the skills to be an NHL player. As a result, the average annual salary of the country's 14,000 full-time university professors was about $115,000 in 2010–11.

This still leaves unanswered some questions raised at the beginning of this chapter: For example, why are the Vancouver Canucks willing to pay Roberto Luongo more than the Florida Panthers, his previous team, were? Luongo's marginal product—which we can think of as the extra games a team will win by employing him—should be about the same in Vancouver as in Miami. But his marginal revenue product will be higher in Vancouver. Because the Vancouver Canucks have fans throughout Canada and the

---

Don't Let This Happen to You

Remember That Prices and Wages Are Determined at the Margin

You have probably heard some variation of the following remark: "We could live without hockey but we can't live without the garbage being hauled away. In a more rational world, garbage collectors would be paid more than hockey players." This remark seems logical: The total value to society of having the garbage hauled away certainly is greater than the total value of hockey. But wages—like prices—do not depend on total value but on *marginal* value. The *additional* hockey games the Pittsburgh Penguins win by having Sidney Crosby (a Canadian hockey player) result in millions of dollars in increased revenue. The supply of people with the ability to play in the NHL is very limited. The supply of people with the ability to be trash haulers is much greater. If a trash-hauling firm hires another worker, the *additional*

trash-hauling services it can now offer will bring in a relatively small amount of revenue. The *total* value of hockey games and the *total* value of trash hauling are not relevant in determining the relative salaries of hockey players and garbage collectors.

This point is related to the diamond and water paradox first noted by Adam Smith. On the one hand, water is very valuable—we literally couldn't live without it—but its price is very low. On the other hand, apart from a few industrial purposes, diamonds are used only for jewellery, yet their prices are quite high. We resolve the paradox by noting that the price of water is low because the supply is very large and the additional benefit consumers receive from the last litre purchased is low. The price of diamonds is high because the supply is very small, and the additional benefit consumers receive from the last diamond purchased is high.

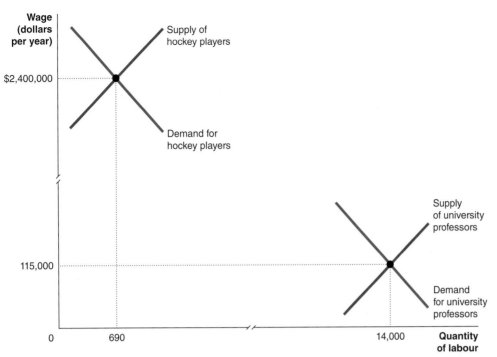

Figure 14.7

Hockey Players Are Paid More Than University Professors

The marginal revenue product of hockey players is very high, and the supply of people with the ability to play in the NHL is low. The result is that the 690 NHL players receive an average wage of $2.4 million. The marginal revenue product of university professors is much lower, and the supply of people with the ability to be professors is much higher. The result is that the approximately 14,000 university professors in Canada receive an average wage of $115,000, far below the average wage of hockey players.

United States, the number of their fans is much greater than the number of Florida Panthers fans, so winning additional games will result in a greater increase in attendance at Vancouver Canucks games than it would at Florida Panthers games. It will also result in a greater increase in viewers for Vancouver Canucks games on television. Therefore, the Vancouver Canucks are able to sell the extra wins that Roberto Luongo produces for much more than the Florida Panthers can. This difference explains why the Vancouver Canucks were willing to pay Roberto Luongo so much more (close to $7 million) than the Florida Panthers were willing to pay him.

Making the Connection | Technology and the Earnings of "Superstars"

The gap between Sidney Crosby's salary and the salary of the lowest-paid hockey players is much greater than the gap between the salaries paid during the 1950s and 1960s to top players such as Jean Beliveau and Maurice Richard and the salaries of the lowest-paid players. Similarly, the gap between the $15 million Angelina Jolie is paid to star in a movie and the salary paid to an actor in a minor role is much greater than the gap between the salaries paid during the 1930s and 1940s to stars such as Clark Gable and Cary Grant and the salaries paid to bit players. In fact, in most areas of sports and entertainment, the highest-paid performers—the "superstars"—now have much higher incomes relative to other members of their professions than was true a few decades ago.

The increase in the relative incomes of superstars is mainly due to technological advances that have increased their bargaining power. The spread of cable television has increased the number of potential viewers of Pittsburgh Penguins games, but many of those viewers will watch only if the Pittsburgh Penguins are winning. This increases the value to the Pittsburgh Penguins of winning games and, therefore, increases Crosby's marginal revenue product and the salary he can earn. That is, superstars possess something unique, which allows them to demand and receive a high price.

With Blu-ray discs, DVDs, Internet streaming video, and pay-per-view cable, the value to movie studios of producing a hit movie has risen greatly. Not surprisingly, movie studios have also increased their willingness to pay large salaries to stars such as

Why does Angelina Jolie earn more today relative to the typical actor than stars did in the 1940s?

Shutterstock

Angelina Jolie and Will Smith because they think these superstars will significantly raise the chances that a film will be successful.

This process has been going on for a long time. For instance, before the invention of the motion picture, anyone who wanted to see a play had to attend the theatre and see a live performance. Limits on the number of people who could see the best actors and actresses perform created an opportunity for many more people to succeed in the acting profession, and the gap between the salaries earned by the best actors and the salaries earned by average actors was relatively small. Today, when a hit movie starring Angelina Jolie is available on DVD or for downloading, millions of people will buy or rent it, and they will not be forced to spend money to see a lesser actress, as their great-great-grandparents might have been.

MyEconLab   **Your Turn:** Test your understanding by doing related problems 4.2 and 4.3 on page 434 at the end of this chapter.

Differences in marginal revenue products are the most important factor in explaining differences in wages, but they are not the whole story. To provide a more complete explanation for differences in wages, we must take into account three important aspects of labour markets: compensating differentials, discrimination, and labour unions. We begin with compensating differentials.

Compensating Differentials

Compensating differentials Higher wages that compensate workers for unpleasant aspects of a job.

Suppose Paul runs a pizza parlour and acquires a reputation for being a bad boss who yells at his workers and is generally unpleasant. Two blocks away, Brendan also runs a pizza parlour, but Brendan is always very polite to his workers. We would expect in these circumstances that Paul will have to pay a higher wage than Brendan to attract and retain workers. Higher wages that compensate workers for unpleasant aspects of a job are called **compensating differentials**.

If working in a dynamite factory requires the same degree of training and education as working in a semiconductor factory but is much more dangerous, a larger number of workers will want to work making semiconductors than will want to work making dynamite. As a consequence, the wages of dynamite workers will be higher than the wages of semiconductor workers. We can think of the difference in wages as being the price of risk. As each worker decides on his or her willingness to assume risk and decides how much higher the wage must be to compensate for assuming more risk, wages will adjust so that dynamite factories will end up paying wages that are just high enough to compensate workers who choose to work there for the extra risk they assume. Only when workers in dynamite factories have been fully compensated with higher wages for the additional risk they assume will dynamite companies be able to attract enough workers.

One surprising implication of compensating differentials is that *laws protecting the health and safety of workers may not make workers better off.* To see this, suppose that dynamite factories pay wages of $25 per hour, and semiconductor factories pay wages of $20 per hour, with the $5 difference in wages being a compensating differential for the greater risk of working in a dynamite factory. Suppose that the government passes a law regulating the manufacture of dynamite in order to improve safety in dynamite factories. As a result of this law, dynamite factories are no longer any more dangerous than semiconductor factories. Once this happens, the wages in dynamite factories will decline to $20 per hour, the same as in semiconductor factories. Are workers in dynamite factories any better or worse off? Before the law was passed, their wages were $25 per hour, but $5 per hour was a compensating differential for the extra risk they were exposed to. Now their wages are only $20 per hour, but the extra risk has been eliminated. The conclusion seems to be that dynamite workers are no better off as a result of the safety legislation.

This conclusion is true, though, only if the compensating differential actually does compensate workers fully for the additional risk. Nobel Laureate George Akerlof and William Dickens have argued that the psychological principle known as *cognitive dissonance* might cause workers to underestimate the true risk of their jobs. According to this principle, people prefer to think of themselves as intelligent and rational and tend to reject evidence that seems to contradict this image. Because working in a very hazardous job may seem irrational, workers in such jobs may refuse to believe that the jobs really are hazardous. Akerlof and Dickens present evidence that workers in chemical plants producing benzene and workers in nuclear power plants underestimate the hazards of their jobs. If this is true, the wages of these workers will not be high enough to compensate them fully for the risk they have assumed. So, in this situation, safety legislation may make workers better off.

Discrimination

Table 14.2 shows that in Canada, white males on average earn more than other groups. One possible explanation for this is **economic discrimination**, which involves paying a person a lower wage or excluding a person from an occupation on the basis of an irrelevant characteristic such as race or gender.

If employers discriminated by hiring only white males for high-paying jobs or by paying white males higher wages than other groups working the same jobs, white males would have higher earnings, as Table 14.2 shows. However, excluding groups from certain jobs or paying one group more than another is illegal in Canada. Nevertheless, it is possible that employers are ignoring the law and practising economic discrimination.

Most economists believe that only part of the gap between the wages of white males and the wages of other groups is due to discrimination. Instead, some of the gap is explained by three main factors:

1. Differences in education
2. Differences in experience
3. Differing preferences for jobs

Differences in Education Some of the difference between the incomes of white workers and the incomes of black workers can be explained by differences in education. Historically, black people have had less schooling than white people, although the gap has closed significantly over the years. Not surprisingly, studies have shown that differing levels of education can account for a significant part of the gap between the earnings of white and black males. Some of the difference in educational levels between black and white people may itself reflect past and current discrimination by governments in failing to provide equal educational opportunities.

Economic discrimination Paying a person a lower wage or excluding a person from an occupation on the basis of an irrelevant characteristic such as race or gender.

Group	Annual Earnings
White males	$33,898
White females	21,164
Black males	22,763
Black females	19,976
South Asian	19,464
Latin American	18,807

Note: The values are median annual earnings for persons who worked full-time, year-round in 2005.
Data from Statistics Canada 2006 Census Dictionary, Catalogue no. 92-566-XWE. http://www12.statcan.gc.ca/census-recensement/2006/dp-pd/tbt/Rp-eng.cfm?LANG=E&APATH=3&DETAIL=0&DIM=0&FL=A&FREE=0&GC=0&GID=0&GK=0&GRP=1&PID=96253&PRID=0&PTYPE=88971,97154&S=0&SHOWALL=0&SUB=812&Temporal=200

Table 14.2

Why Do White Males Earn More Than Other Groups?

Differences in Experience Women are much more likely than men to leave their jobs for a period of time after having a child. Women with several children will sometimes have several interruptions in their careers. Some women leave the workforce for several years until their children are of school age. As a result, on average, women with children have less workforce experience than do men of the same age. Because workers with greater experience are, on average, more productive, the difference in levels of experience helps to explain some of the difference in earnings between men and women.

Differing Preferences for Jobs Significant differences exist between the types of jobs held by women and men. Women represent 90 percent or more of the people employed in some relatively low-paying jobs, such as preschool teachers, dental assistants, and childcare workers, while men represent more than 90 percent of the people employed in some relatively high-paying jobs, such as airline pilots, engineering managers, and electricians. Although the overrepresentation of women in low-paying jobs and men in high-paying jobs may be due in part to discrimination, it is also likely to reflect differences in job preferences between men and women. For example, because many women interrupt their careers—at least briefly—when their children are born, they are more likely to take jobs where work experience is less important. Women may also be more likely to take jobs, such as teaching, that allow them to be home in the afternoons when their children return from school.

Solved Problem **14.4**

Is Passing "Comparable Worth" Legislation a Good Way to Close the Gap Between Men's and Women's Pay?

As we have seen, either because of discrimination or differing preferences, certain jobs are filled primarily by men, and other jobs are filled primarily by women. On average, the "men's jobs" have higher wages than the "women's jobs." Some observers have argued that many "men's jobs" are more highly paid than "women's jobs," despite the jobs being comparable in terms of the education and skills required and the working conditions involved. These observers have argued that the earnings gap between men and women could be closed at least partially if the government required employers to pay the same wages for jobs that have *comparable worth*. Many economists are skeptical

of these proposals because they believe allowing markets to determine wages results in a more efficient outcome.

Suppose that electricians are currently being paid a market equilibrium wage of $800 per week, and dental assistants are being paid a market equilibrium wage of $500 per week. Comparable-worth legislation is passed, and a study finds that an electrician and a dental assistant have comparable jobs, so employers will now be required to pay workers in both jobs $650 per week. Analyze the effects of this requirement on the market for electricians and on the market for dental assistants. Be sure to use demand and supply graphs.

Solving the Problem

Step 1: Review the chapter material. This problem is about economic discrimination, so you may want to review the section "Discrimination," which begins on page 419.

Step 2: Draw the graphs. When the government sets the price in a market, the result is a surplus or a shortage, depending on whether the government-mandated price is above or below the competitive market equilibrium. A wage of $650 per week is below the market wage for electricians and above the market wage for dental assistants. Therefore, we expect the requirement to result in a shortage of electricians and a surplus of dental assistants.

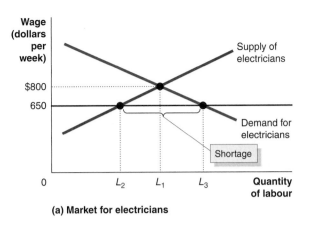

(a) Market for electricians

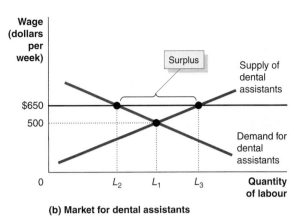

(b) Market for dental assistants

In panel (a), without comparable-worth legislation, the equilibrium wage for electricians is $800, and the equilibrium quantity of electricians hired is L_1. Setting the wage for electricians below equilibrium at $650 reduces the quantity of labour supplied in this occupation from L_1 to L_2 but increases the quantity of labour demanded by employers from L_1 to L_3. The result is a shortage of electricians equal to $L_3 - L_2$, as shown by the bracket in the graph.

In panel (b), without comparable-worth legislation, the equilibrium wage for dental assistants is $500, and the equilibrium quantity of dental assistants hired is L_1. Setting the wage for dental assistants above equilibrium at $650 increases the quantity of labour supplied in this occupation from L_1 to L_3. but reduces the quantity of labour demanded by employers from L_1 to L_2. The result is a surplus of dental assistants equal to $L_3 - L_2$, as shown by the bracket in the graph.

Extra Credit: Most economists are skeptical of government attempts to set wages and prices, as comparable-worth legislation would require. Supporters of comparable-worth legislation, by contrast, see differences between men's and women's wages as being mainly due to discrimination and are looking to government legislation as a solution.

Your Turn: For more practice, do related problem 4.5 on page 434 and problem 4.6 on page 435 at the end of this chapter.

MyEconLab

The Difficulty of Measuring Discrimination When two people are paid different wages, discrimination may be the explanation. But differences in productivity or preferences may also be an explanation. Labour economists have attempted to measure what part of differences in wages between visible minority workers and white workers and between men and women is due to discrimination and what part is due to other factors. Unfortunately, it is difficult to precisely measure differences in productivity or in worker preferences. As a result, we can't know exactly the extent of economic discrimination in Canada today.

Making the Connection	**Does Greg Have an Easier Time Finding a Job Than Jamal?**

One difficulty in accurately measuring economic discrimination is that two workers may differ not only in race and gender but also in characteristics that employers expect will affect the workers' productivity. If Worker A is hired instead of Worker B, is it because A is a white male, while B is a black female, or is it because of A's and B's other characteristics?

Does having an African-American-sounding name make it more difficult to find a job?

Marianne Bertrand and Sendhil Mullainathan found an ingenious way of getting around this difficulty. They responded to help wanted ads in newspapers by sending identical resumes, with the exception that half of the resumes were assigned an African-American–sounding name and half were assigned a white-sounding name. In other words, the characteristics of these fictitious people were the same, except for their names. In the absence of discrimination, resumes with African-American–sounding names, such as Jamal Jones, should have been as likely to get job interviews as the identical resumes with white-sounding names, such as Greg Baker. In fact, though, employers were 50 percent more likely to interview workers with white-sounding names than workers with African-American–sounding names. Bertrand and Mullainathan sent out more than 5,000 resumes to many different employers who were advertising for jobs in sales, administrative support, clerical services, and customer services. Their results were similar across these different types of jobs.

Some economists have questioned whether the study by Bertrand and Mullainathan, as well as other similar studies, actually shows that employers discriminate. They argue that employers may believe that the typical white job applicant and the typical black job applicant have different characteristics, apart from those included in the resumes, that may affect their productivity. If so, the employers may be responding to these differences in productivity rather than solely to the job applicant's race. Because Bertrand and Mullainthan based their artificial resumes on actual resumes, however, the artificial resumes probably include all the characteristics that actual job applicants think are relevant. Bertrand and Mullainathan believe that the results of their experiment show that "differential treatment by race… appears to still be prominent."

Based on Marianne Bertrand and Sendhil Mullainathan, "Are Emily and Greg More Employable Than Lakisha and Jamal? A Field Experiment on Labour Market Discrimination," *American Economic Review*, Vol. 94, No. 4, September 2004, pp. 991–1013; and David Neumark, "Detecting Discrimination in Audit and Correspondence Studies," National Bureau of Economic Research, Working Paper 16448, October 2010.

MyEconLab   **Your Turn:** Test your understanding by doing related problem 4.7 on page 435 at the end of this chapter.

Does It Pay to Discriminate? Many economists believe that in the long run, markets can undermine economic discrimination. One reason is that *employers who discriminate pay an economic penalty*. To see why this is true, let's consider a simplified example. Suppose that men and women are equally qualified to be airline pilots and that, initially, airlines do not discriminate. In Figure 14.8, we divide the airlines into two groups: "A" airlines and "B" airlines. If neither group of airlines discriminates, we would expect them to pay an equal wage of $1,100 per week to both men and women pilots. Now suppose that "A" airlines decide to discriminate and to fire all their women pilots. This action will reduce the supply of pilots to these airlines and, as shown in panel (a), that will force up the wage from $1,100 to $1,300. At the same time, as women fired from the jobs with "A" airlines apply for jobs with "B" airlines, the supply of pilots to "B" airlines will increase, and the equilibrium wage will fall from $1,100 to $900. All the women pilots will end up being employed at the non-discriminating airlines and will be paid a lower wage than the men who are employed by the discriminating airlines.

But this situation cannot persist for two reasons. First, male pilots employed by "B" airlines will also receive the lower wage. This lower wage gives them an incentive to quit their jobs at "B" airlines and apply at "A" airlines, which will shift the labour supply curve for "B" airlines to the left and the labour supply curve for "A" airlines to the right. Second, "A" airlines are paying $1,300 per week to hire pilots who are no more productive than the pilots being paid $900 per week by "B" airlines. As a result, "B" airlines will have lower costs and will be able to charge lower prices. Eventually, "A" airlines will lose their customers to "B" airlines and will be driven out of business. The market will have imposed an economic penalty on the discriminating airlines. So, discrimination will not persist, and the wages of men and women pilots will become equal.

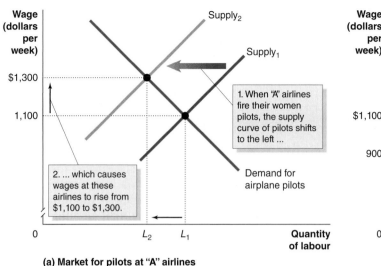

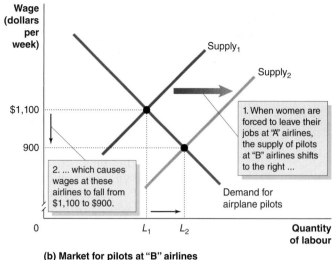

(a) Market for pilots at "A" airlines

(b) Market for pilots at "B" airlines

Figure 14.8 Discrimination and Wages

In this hypothetical example, we assume that initially neither "A" airlines nor "B" airlines discriminate. As a result, men and women pilots receive the same wage of $1,100 per week at both groups of airlines. We then assume that "A" airlines discriminate by firing all their women pilots. Panel (a) shows that this reduces the supply of pilots to "A" airlines and raises the wage paid by these airlines from $1,100 to $1,300. Panel (b) shows that this increases the supply of pilots to "B" airlines and lowers the wage paid by these airlines from $1,100 to $900. All the women pilots will end up being employed at the nondiscriminating airlines and will be paid a lower wage than the men who are employed by the discriminating airlines.

Labour Unions

Workers' wages can differ depending on whether the workers are members of labour unions. **Labour unions** are organizations of employees that have the legal right to bargain with employers about wages and working conditions. If a union is unable to reach an agreement with a company, it has the legal right to call a *strike*, which means its members refuse to work until a satisfactory agreement has been reached. As Figure 14.9 shows, a larger fraction of the Canadian labour force is unionized than in most other high-income countries.

As Table 14.3 shows, in Canada, workers who are in unions receive higher wages than workers who are not in unions. Do union members earn more than nonunion members because they are in unions? The answer might seem to be "yes," but many union workers are in industries, such as automobile manufacturing, in which their marginal revenue products are high, so their wages would be high even if they were

Labour union An organization of employees that has a legal right to bargain with employers about wages and working conditions.

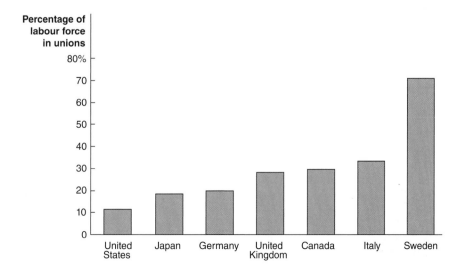

Figure 14.9

Canada Is More Unionized Than Most Other High-Income Countries

The percentage of the labour force belonging to unions is higher in Canada than in most other high-income countries.
Data from Organisation for Economic Co-operation and Development.

	Average Hourly Wage (as of August 2012)
Union workers	$26.97
Nonunion workers	21.98

Table 14.3

Union Workers Earn More Than Nonunion Workers

Note: "Union workers" includes union members as well as workers who are not union members but who are covered by a collective agreement or a union contract.

Data from: http://www.statcan.gc.ca/tables-tableaux/sum-som/l01/cst01/labr69a-eng.htm

not unionized. Economists who have attempted to estimate statistically the effect of unionization on wages have concluded that being in a union increases a worker's wages about 10 percent, holding constant other factors, such as the industry the worker is in. A related question is whether unions raise the total amount of wages received by all workers, whether unionized or not. Because the share of national income received by workers has remained roughly constant over many years, most economists do not believe that unions have raised the total amount of wages received by workers.

Personnel Economics

14.5 LEARNING OBJECTIVE

Discuss the role personnel economics can play in helping firms deal with human resources issues.

Personnel economics The application of economic analysis to human resources issues.

Traditionally, labour economists have focused on issues such as the effects of labour unions on wages or the determinants of changes in average wages over time. They have spent less time analyzing *human resources issues*, which address how firms hire, train, and promote workers and set their wages and benefits. In recent years, some labour economists, including Edward Lazear and William Neilson, have begun exploring the application of economic analysis to human resources issues. This new focus has become known as **personnel economics**.

Personnel economics analyzes the link between differences among jobs and differences in the way workers are paid. Jobs have different skill requirements, require more or less interaction with other workers, have to be performed in more or less unpleasant environments, and so on. Firms need to design compensation policies that take into account these differences. Personnel economics also analyzes policies related to other human resources issues, such as promotions, training, and pensions. In this brief overview, we look only at compensation policies.

Should Workers' Pay Depend on How Much They Work or on How Much They Produce?

One issue personnel economics addresses is when workers should receive *straight-time pay*—a certain wage per hour or salary per week or month—and when they should receive *commission* or *piece-rate pay*—a wage based on how much output they produce.

Suppose, for example, that Anne owns a car dealership and is trying to decide whether to pay her salespeople a salary of $800 per week or a commission of $200 on each car they sell. Figure 14.10 compares the compensation a salesperson would receive under the two systems, according to the number of cars the salesperson sells.

With a straight salary, the salesperson receives $800 per week, no matter how many cars she sells. This outcome is shown by the horizontal line in Figure 14.10. If she receives a commission of $200 per car, her compensation will increase with every car she sells. This outcome is shown by the upward-sloping line. A salesperson who sells fewer than 4 cars per week would earn more by receiving a straight salary of $800 per week. A salesperson who sells more than 4 cars per week would be better off receiving the $200-per-car commission. We can identify two advantages Anne would receive from paying her salespeople commissions rather than salaries: She would attract and retain the most productive employees, and she would provide an incentive to her employees to sell more cars.

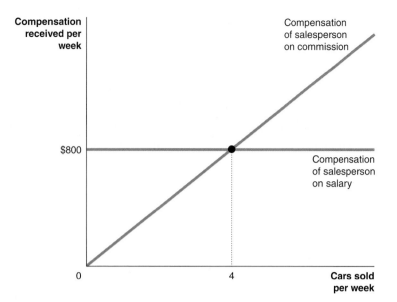

Figure 14.10

Paying Car Salespeople by Salary or by Commission

This figure compares the compensation a car salesperson receives if she is on a straight salary of $800 per week or if she receives a commission of $200 for each car she sells. With a straight salary, she receives $800 per week, no matter how many cars she sells. This outcome is shown by the horizontal line in the figure. If she receives a commission of $200 per car, her compensation will increase with every car she sells. This outcome is shown by the upward-sloping line. If she sells fewer than 4 cars per week, she would be better off with the $800 salary. If she sells more than 4 cars per week, she would be better off with the $200-per-car commission.

Suppose that other car dealerships are all paying salaries of $800 per week. If Anne pays her employees on commission, any of her employees who are unable to sell at least 4 cars per week can improve their pay by going to work for one of her competitors. And any salespeople at Anne's competitors who can sell more than 4 cars per week can raise their pay by quitting and coming to work for Anne. Over time, Anne will find her least productive employees leaving, while she is able to hire new employees who are more productive.

Paying a commission also increases the incentive Anne's salespeople have to sell more cars. If Anne paid a salary, her employees would receive the same amount no matter how few cars they sold. An employee on salary might decide on a particularly hot or cold day that it was less trouble to stay inside the building than to go out on the car lot to greet potential customers. An employee on commission would know that the additional effort expended on selling more cars would be rewarded with additional compensation.

Other Considerations in Setting Compensation Systems

The discussion so far indicates that companies will find it more profitable to use a commission or piece-rate system of compensation rather than a salary system. In fact, many firms continue to pay their workers salaries, which means they are paying their workers on the basis of how long they work rather than on the basis of how much they produce. Firms may choose a salary system for several good reasons:

- *Difficulty measuring output.* Often it is difficult to attribute output to any particular worker. For example, projects carried out by an engineering firm may involve teams of workers whose individual contributions are difficult to distinguish. On assembly lines, such as those used in the automobile industry, the amount produced by each worker is determined by the speed of the line, which is set by managers rather than by workers. Managers at many firms perform such a wide variety of tasks that measuring their output would be costly, if it could be done at all.

- *Concerns about quality.* If workers are paid on the basis of the number of units produced, they may become less concerned about quality. An office assistant who is paid on the basis of the quantity of letters typed may become careless about how many typos the letters contain. In some cases, there are ways around this problem; for example, the assistant may be required to correct the mistakes on his or her own time, without pay.

- *Worker dislike of risk.* Piece-rate or commission systems of compensation increase the risk to workers because sometimes output declines for reasons not connected to the worker's effort. For example, if there is a very snowy winter, few customers may show up at Anne's auto dealership. Through no fault of their own, her salespeople may have great difficulty selling any cars. If they are paid a salary, their income will not be affected, but if they are on commission, their incomes may drop to low levels. The flip side of this is that by paying salaries, Anne assumes a greater risk. During a snowy winter, her payroll expenses will remain high even though her sales are low. With a commission system of compensation, her payroll expenses will decline along with her sales. But owners of firms are typically better able to bear risk than are workers. As a result, some firms may find that workers who would earn more under a commission system will prefer to receive a salary to reduce their risk. In these situations, paying a lower salary may reduce the firm's payroll expenses compared with what they would have been under a commission or piece-rate system.

Personnel economics is a relatively new field, but it holds great potential for helping firms deal more efficiently with human resources issues.

14.6 LEARNING OBJECTIVE

Show how equilibrium prices are determined in the markets for capital and natural resources.

The Markets for Capital and Natural Resources

The approach we have used to analyze the market for labour can also be used to analyze the markets for other factors of production. We have seen that the demand for labour is determined by the marginal revenue product of labour because the value to a firm from hiring another worker equals the increase in the firm's revenue from selling the additional output it can produce by hiring the worker. The demand for capital and natural resources is determined in a similar way.

The Market for Capital

Physical capital includes machines, equipment, and buildings. Firms sometimes buy capital, but we will focus on situations in which firms rent capital. A chocolate manufacturer renting a warehouse and an airline leasing a plane are examples of firms renting capital. Like the demand for labour, the demand for capital is a derived demand. When a firm is considering increasing its capital by, for example, employing another machine, the value it receives equals the increase in the firm's revenue from selling the additional output it can produce by employing the machine. The *marginal revenue product of capital* is the change in the firm's revenue as a result of employing one more unit of capital, such as a machine. We have seen that the marginal revenue product of labour curve is the demand curve for labour. Similarly, the marginal revenue product of capital curve is the demand curve for capital.

Firms producing capital goods face increasing marginal costs, so the supply curve of capital goods is upward sloping, as are the supply curves for other goods and services. Figure 14.11 shows equilibrium in the market for capital. In equilibrium, suppliers of capital receive a rental price equal to the marginal revenue product of capital, just as suppliers of labour receive a wage equal to the marginal revenue product of labour.

The Market for Natural Resources

The market for natural resources can be analyzed in the same way as the markets for labour and capital. When a firm is considering employing more natural resources, the

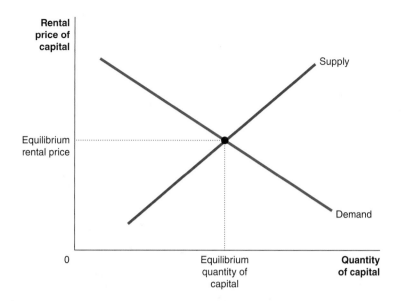

Figure 14.11

Equilibrium in the Market for Capital

The rental price of capital is determined by demand and supply in the market for capital. In equilibrium, the rental price of capital is equal to the marginal revenue product of capital.

value it receives equals the increase in the firm's revenue from selling the additional output it can produce by buying the natural resources. So, the demand for natural resources is also a derived demand. The *marginal revenue product of natural resources* is the change in a firm's revenue as a result of employing one more unit of natural resources, such as a barrel of oil. The marginal revenue product of natural resources curve is also the demand curve for natural resources.

Although the total quantity of most natural resources is ultimately fixed—as Will Rogers once remarked, "Buy land. They ain't making any more of it"—in many cases, the quantity supplied still responds to the price. For example, although the total quantity of oil deposits in the world is fixed, an increase in the price of oil will result in an increase in the quantity of oil supplied during a particular period. The result, as shown in panel (a) of Figure 14.12, is an upward-sloping supply curve. In some cases, however, the quantity of a natural resource that will be supplied is fixed and will not change as the price changes. The land available at a busy intersection is fixed, for example. In panel (b) of Figure 14.12, we illustrate this situation with a supply curve that is a vertical line, or perfectly inelastic. The price received by a factor of production that is in fixed supply is called an **economic rent** (or a **pure rent**) because, in this case, the price of the factor is determined only by demand. For example, if a new highway diverts much of the traffic from a previously busy intersection, the demand for the land will decline, and the price of the land will fall, but the quantity of the land will not change.

Economic rent (or pure rent) The price of a factor of production that is in fixed supply.

Monopsony

In the case of *monopoly*, a firm is the sole *seller* of a good or service. What happens if a firm is the sole *buyer* of a factor of production? This case, which is known as **monopsony**, is comparatively rare. An example is a firm in an isolated town—perhaps a lumber mill in a small town in British Columbia—that is the sole employer of labour in that location. In this case, not only would the firm own the mill, but it would also own the stores and other businesses in the town. Workers would have the choice of working for the sole employer in the town or moving to another town.

Monopsony The sole buyer of a factor of production.

We know that a firm with a monopoly in an output market takes advantage of its market power to reduce the quantity supplied to force up the market price and increase its profits. A firm that has a monopsony in a factor market would employ a similar strategy: It would restrict the quantity of the factor demanded to force down the price of the factor and increase profits. A firm with a monopsony in a labour market will hire

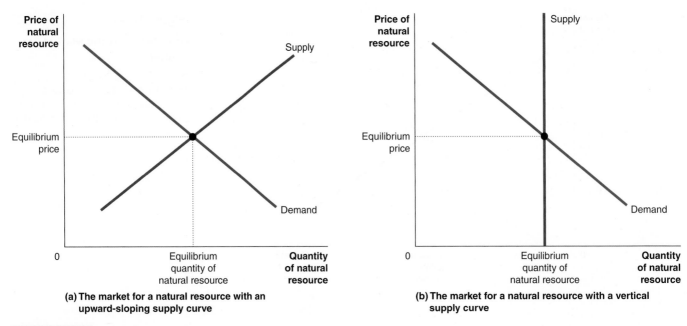

Figure 14.12 Equilibrium in the Market for Natural Resources

In panel (a), the supply curve of a natural resource is upward sloping. The price of the natural resource is determined by the interaction of demand and supply. In panel (b), the supply curve of the natural resource is a vertical line, indicating that the quantity supplied does not respond to changes in price. In this case, the price of the natural resource is determined only by demand. The price of a factor of production with a vertical supply curve is called an *economic rent*, or a *pure rent*.

fewer workers and pay lower wages than would be the case in a competitive market. Because fewer workers are hired than would be hired in a competitive market, monopsony results in a deadweight loss. Monopoly and monopsony have similar effects on the economy: In both cases, a firm's market power results in a lower equilibrium quantity, a deadweight loss, and a reduction in economic efficiency compared with a competitive market.

The Marginal Productivity Theory of Income Distribution

Marginal productivity theory of income distribution The theory that the distribution of income is determined by the marginal productivity of the factors of production that individuals own.

We have seen that in equilibrium, each factor of production receives a price equal to its marginal revenue product. We can use this fact to explain the distribution of income. Marginal revenue product represents the value of a factor's marginal contribution to producing goods and services. Therefore, individuals will receive income equal to the marginal contributions to production from the factors of production they own, including their labour. The more factors of production an individual owns and the more productive those factors are, the higher the individual's income will be. This approach to explaining the distribution of income is called the **marginal productivity theory of income distribution**, and was developed by John Bates Clark.

Economics in Your Life

How Can You Convince Your Boss to Give You a Raise?

At the beginning of the chapter, we asked you to imagine that you work at a local sandwich shop and that you plan to ask your manager for a raise. One way to show the manager your worth is to demonstrate how many dollars your work earns for the sandwich shop: your marginal revenue product. You could certainly suggest that as you have become better at your job and have gained new skills, you have become a more productive employee; but, more importantly, you could say that your productivity results in increased revenue for the sandwich shop or consider a competitive offer elsewhere. By showing how your employment contributes to higher revenue and profit, you may be able to convince your manager to give you a raise.

Conclusion

In this chapter, we used the demand and supply model to explain why wages differ among workers. The demand for workers depends on their productivity and on the price firms receive for the output the workers produce. The supply of workers to an occupation depends on the wages and working conditions offered by employers and on the skills required. The demand and supply for labour can also help us analyze such issues as economic discrimination and the effect of labour unions.

Read *An Inside Look* on the next page to see how labour markets have been changing in recent years.

Buying a Ticket in a Lottery Industry

NEW YORK TIMES

Why Are Harvard Graduates in the Mailroom?

(a) In their book *Freakonomics*, Stephen J. Dubner and Steven D. Levitt explain, among other things, the odd economic behavior that guides many drug dealers. In one gang they described, the typical street-corner guy made less than minimum wage but still worked extremely hard in hopes of someday becoming one of the few wildly rich kingpins. This behavior isn't isolated to illegal activity. There are a number of professions in which workers are paid, in part, with a figurative lottery ticket. The worker accepts a lower-paying job in exchange for a slim but real chance of a large, future payday.

This more or less explains Hollywood. Yes, the Oscars may be an absurd spectacle of remarkably successful people congratulating themselves for work that barely nudges at the borders of meaningful human achievement. But it's also a celebration of a form of meritocratic capitalism. I'm not talking about the fortunes lavished on extremely good looking people; no, I mean the economic system that compels lots of young people to work extremely hard for little pay so that it's possible to lavish fortune on the good-looking people. That's the spirit of meritocratic capitalism!

Hollywood is, in some ways, the model lottery industry. For most companies in the business, it doesn't make economic sense to, as Google does, put promising young applicants through a series of tests and then hire only the small number who pass. Instead, it's cheaper for talent agencies and studios to hire a lot of young workers and run them through a few years of low-paying drudgery. (Actors are another story altogether. Many never get steady jobs in the first place.) This occupational centrifuge allows workers to effectively sort themselves out based on skill and drive. Over time, some will lose their commitment; others will realize that they don't have the right talent set; others will find that they're better at something else.

When it's time to choose who gets the top job or becomes partner, managers subsequently have a lot more information to work with. In the meantime, companies also get the benefit of several years of hard work from determined young people at below-market pay. (Warner Brothers pays its mailroom clerks $25,000 to $30,000, a little more than an apprentice plumber.) While far from perfect, this strategy has done a pretty decent job of pushing those with real promise to the top. Barry Diller and David Geffen each started his career in the William Morris mailroom.

Hollywood is merely the most glamorous industry that puts new entrants—whether they're in the mailroom, picking up dry cleaning for a studio head or waiting on tables between open-call auditions—through a lottery system. Even glamour-free industries offer economic-lottery systems. Young, ambitious accountants who toil away at a Big Four firm may have modest expectations of glory, but they'll be millionaires if they make partner. The same goes at law firms, ad agencies and consulting firms. Startups explicitly use a lottery system, known as stock options, to entice young people to work for nothing. Wall Street, however, is a special case. It offers extremely high entry salaries and enormous potential earnings.

Even professions that can't offer as much in the way of riches operate as a lottery system. Academia, non-profit groups, book publishers and public-radio production companies also put their new recruits through various forms of low-paid hazing, holding out the promise of, well, more low pay but in a job that provides, for some, something more important than money: satisfaction. In the language of economics, these people are consuming their potential wages in happiness. (Honestly, economists talk this way.)

This system is unfair and arbitrary and often takes advantage of many people who don't really have a shot at the big prize. But it is far preferable to the parts of our economy where there are no big prizes waiting. That mailroom clerk at Warner Brothers may make less than a post office clerk (maybe even half as much), but the latter has less chance of a significant promotion. Workers in retail sales, clerical settings, low-skill manufacturing and other fields tend to have loose, uncommitted bonds to their industries, and their employers have even looser commitments to them. These jobs don't offer a bright future precisely because they don't require a huge amount of skill, and therefore there's no need to do much merit-sorting.

But part of the American post–World War II economic miracle was that most people didn't have to choose between a high-stakes-lottery job or a lousy dead-end one.

Steelworkers, midlevel corporate executives, shopkeepers and plumbers were all able to make a decent amount from the start of their careers with steady, but never spectacular, raises throughout. These two tiers actually supported each other. Strivers were able to dream bigger because they had a solid Plan B. New York City and Los Angeles are buoyed by teachers, store owners, arts administrators and others who came to town to make it big in film or music or publishing, eventually gave up on that dream and ended up doing fine in another field.

b Now, many economists fear that the comfortable Plan B jobs are disappearing. Technology and cheaper goods from overseas have replaced many of the not-especially-creative professions. A tax accountant loses clients to TurboTax; many graphic designers have been replaced by Photoshop; and the small shopkeeper by Home Depot, Wal-Mart or Duane Reade. Though a lottery economy is valuable to various industries, the thought of an entire lottery-based economy, in which a few people win big while the rest are forced to toil in an uncertain and not terribly remunerative dead-end labour pool, is unfair and politically scary. If large numbers of people believe they have no shot at a better life in the future, they will work less hard and generate fewer new ideas and businesses. The economy, as a whole, will be poorer.

It's not clear what today's eager 23-year-old will do in 5 or 10 years when she decides that acting (or that accounting partnership) isn't going to work out after all. The best advice may be to accept that economic success in America will come as much from the labour lottery as from hard work and tenacity. The Oscars make clear that there is only so much room at the top. In a lottery-based economy, you need some luck, too; now, perhaps, more than ever. People should be prepared to enter a few different lotteries, because the new Plan B is just going to be another long shot in a different field. The role model of our time should be an actress who was never nominated for an Oscar. Hedy Lamarr did well enough on the screen but, just in case, she spent her free time developing something called frequency-hopping spread-spectrum. It's a wireless-communication technique still in use in Bluetooth and Wi-Fi. Not bad for a fallback.

Key Points in the Article

This article discusses the trend in the economy that more and more labour markets are becoming lottery markets. Lottery markets are characterized by having many workers that earn little to no wages, where talent, effort, and some luck allow few to rise to the top and earn substantial incomes. The article begins by suggesting the drug trade, as characterized in *Freakonomics* by Stephen J. Dubner and Steven D. Levitt, is an example of one such industry. So is Hollywood. As a result of rapid technological progress and globalization, many more traditional industries such as those found in professional services—investment banking, accounting, legal services, and advertising—have become lottery markets. Business start-ups also offer this type of compensation through stock options. Wall Street and Bay Street are special cases that offer both high starting salaries and significant potential (bonus) earnings.

Analyzing the News

a The structure of the labour market is changing significantly in several ways. Rapid changes in technology and globalization are creating a society that is tending towards an increasing number of lottery labour markets. These markets are characterized by job requirements of high levels of relative creativity and productivity, with comparatively few winners who experience enormous economic success while the masses are washed out. The jobs that are being replaced are routine jobs. Workers are being asked increasingly to choose between low paying entry level lottery jobs and low paying (but better than entry level lottery), limited opportunity service jobs.

b The lottery jobs create an oversupply of labour entrants into their market as they attract individuals who have little chance of success. This is what we call a negative externality, and its presence suggests a role for government. Typically, when a negative externality (such as pollution) is present, the efficiency promoting role of government is to tax the activity so less of it is provided. This implies making either income taxes or consumption taxes more progressive (increasing as either income or consumption increases).

But some lottery markets, such as information technology and "junior" resource exploration companies, expand employment through entrepreneurship and new business innovation that creates a positive externality for the economy. In these markets there is a role for government to provide subsidies or support to create incentives to promote efficiency. There is also a role for government to subsidize education in entrepreneurship, the skilled trades, and knowledge intensive careers like engineering and the sciences that are and will be needed by the entrepreneurial class. Government policies that facilitate job market flexibility such as job retraining programs can also help.

Thinking Critically

1. Do an Internet search on "Occupy Wall Street." How does this movement relate to the issue of the financial services industry being a lottery market? What concern of this movement could the government address to make the economy simultaneously more efficient and equitable? Suppose the government had to choose between a significant regulation of either social network sites like Facebook and Twitter or money centre banks like the Big Six. Which should it choose and why? What does your answer imply about government policy toward lottery markets?

2. Canada is a small open economy which, presumably, faces all of the labour market issues that are being faced in the United States. The United States is recognized as the world leader in innovation and international business, with the most world class universities and flexible labour markets. Why then does Canada have lower unemployment than the United States? Does Canada have less of an issue presently than the United States with the trend toward lottery labour markets? Over time, would we expect lottery markets to be a bigger or smaller issue for Canada? What role do federal equalization payments serve?

431

Chapter Summary and Problems

Key Terms

Compensating differentials, p. 418

Derived demand, p. 406

Economic discrimination, p. 419

Economic rent (or pure rent), p. 427

Factors of production, p. 406

Human capital, p. 410

Labour union, p. 423

Marginal product of labour, p. 406

Marginal productivity theory of income distribution, p. 428

Marginal revenue product of labour (*MRP*), p. 407

Monopsony, p. 427

Personnel economics, p. 424

Signalling hypothesis, p. 414

Summary

*LO 14.1 The demand for productive inputs is a **derived demand** because it depends on the demand consumers have for goods and services. The additional output produced by a firm as a result of hiring another worker is called the **marginal product of labour**. The amount by which a firm's revenue will increase as a result of hiring one more worker is called the **marginal revenue product of labour (*MRP*)**. A firm's marginal revenue product of labour curve is its demand curve for labour. Firms maximize profit by hiring workers up to the point where the wage is equal to the marginal revenue product of labour. The market demand curve for labour is determined by adding up the quantity of labour demanded by each firm at each wage, holding constant all other variables that might affect the willingness of firms to hire workers. The most important variables that shift the labour demand curve are changes in human capital, technology, the price of the product, the quantity of other inputs, and the number of firms in the market. **Human capital** is the accumulated training and skills that workers possess.

LO 14.2 As the wage increases, the opportunity cost of leisure increases, causing individuals to supply a greater quantity of labour. Normally, the labour supply curve is upward sloping, but it is possible that at very high wage levels, the supply curve might be backward bending. This outcome occurs when someone with a high income is willing to accept a somewhat lower income in exchange for more leisure. The market labour supply curve is determined by adding up the quantity of labour supplied by each worker at each wage, holding constant all other variables that might affect the willingness of workers to supply labour. The most important variables that shift the labour supply curve are increases in population, changing demographics, and changing alternatives.

LO 14.3 The intersection between labour supply and labour demand determines the equilibrium wage and the equilibrium level of employment. If labour supply is unchanged, an increase in labour demand will increase both the equilibrium wage and the number of workers employed. If labour demand is unchanged, an increase in labour supply will lower the equilibrium wage and increase the number of workers employed.

LO 14.4 The equilibrium wage is determined by the intersection of the labour demand curve and the labour supply curve. Some differences in wages are explained by **compensating differentials**, which are higher wages that compensate workers for unpleasant aspects of a job. Wages can also differ because of **economic discrimination**, which involves paying a person a lower wage or excluding a person from an occupation on the basis of irrelevant characteristics, such as race or gender. **Labour unions** are organizations of employees that have the legal right to bargain with employers about wages and working conditions. Being in a union increases a worker's wages about 10 percent, holding constant other factors, such as the industry in question.

LO 14.5 Personnel economics is the application of economic analysis to human resources issues. One insight of personnel economics is that the productivity of workers can often be increased if firms move from straight-time pay to commission or piece-rate pay.

LO 14.6 The approach used to analyze the market for labour can also be used to analyze the markets for other **factors of production**. In equilibrium, the price of capital is equal to the marginal revenue product of capital, and the price of natural resources is equal to the marginal revenue product of natural resources. The price received by a factor that is in fixed supply is called an **economic rent**, or a **pure rent**. A **monopsony** is the sole buyer of a factor of production. According to the **marginal productivity theory of income distribution**, the distribution of income is determined by the marginal productivity of the factors of production individuals own.

MyEconLab   Log in to MyEconLab to complete these exercises and get instant feedback.

Review Questions

LO 14.1

1.1 In what sense is the demand for labour a derived demand?

1.2 What is the difference between the marginal product of labour and the marginal revenue product of labour?

1.3 Why is the demand curve for labour downward sloping?

1.4 What are the five most important variables that cause the market demand curve for labour to shift?

LO 14.2

2.1 How can we measure the opportunity cost of leisure? What are the substitution effect and the income effect resulting from a wage change? Why is the supply curve of labour usually upward sloping?

2.2 What are the three most important variables that cause the market supply curve of labour to shift?

LO 14.3

3.1 If the labour demand curve shifts to the left and the labour supply curve remains unchanged, what will happen to the equilibrium wage and the equilibrium level of employment? Illustrate your answer with a graph.

3.2 If the labour supply curve shifts to the left and the labour demand curve remains unchanged, what will happen to

*'Learning Objective' is abbreviated to 'LO' in the end of chapter material.

the equilibrium wage and the equilibrium level of employment? Illustrate your answer with a graph.

LO 14.4

4.1 What is a compensating differential? Give an example.

4.2 Define *economic discrimination*. Is the fact that one group in the population has higher earnings than other groups evidence of economic discrimination? Briefly explain.

4.3 In what sense do employers who discriminate pay an economic penalty? Is this penalty enough to eliminate discrimination? Briefly explain.

4.4 Is the fraction of Canadian workers in labour unions larger or smaller than in other countries?

LO 14.5

5.1 What is personnel economics?

5.2 What are the two ways that the productivity of a firm's employees may increase when a firm moves from straight-time pay to commission or piece-rate pay?

5.3 If piece-rate or commission systems of compensating workers have important advantages for firms, why don't more firms use them?

LO 14.6

6.1 In equilibrium, what determines the price of capital? What determines the price of natural resources? What is the marginal productivity theory of income distribution?

6.2 What is an economic rent? What is a monopsony?

Problems and Applications

LO 14.1

1.1 Frank Gunter owns an apple orchard. He employs 87 apple pickers and pays them each $8 per hour to pick apples, which he sells for $1.60 per box. If Frank is maximizing profits, what is the marginal revenue product of the last worker he hired? What is that worker's marginal product?

1.2 [**Related to** Solved Problem 14.1 **on page 408**] Complete the following table for Terrell's Televisions.

Number of Workers (L)	Output of Televisions per Week (Q)	Marginal Product of Labour (television sets per week) (MP)	Product Price (P)	Marginal Revenue Product of Labour (dollars per week)	Wage (dollars per week) (W)	Additional Profit from Hiring One More Worker (dollars per week)
0	0	—	$300	—	$1,800	—
1	8	—	300	—	1,800	—
2	15	—	300	—	1,800	—
3	21	—	300	—	1,800	—
4	26	—	300	—	1,800	—
5	30	—	300	—	1,800	—
6	33	—	300	—	1,800	—

  a. From the information in the table, can you determine whether this firm is a price taker or a price maker? Briefly explain.

  b. Use the information in the table to draw a graph like Figure 14.1 that shows the demand for labour by this firm. Be sure to indicate the profit-maximizing quantity of labour on your graph.

1.3 State whether each of the following events will result in a movement along the market demand curve for labour in electronics factories in China or whether it will cause the market demand curve for labour to shift. If the demand curve shifts, indicate whether it will shift to the left or to the right and draw a graph to illustrate the shift.

  a. The wage rate declines.

  b. The price of televisions declines.

  c. Several firms exit the television market in Japan.

  d. Chinese high schools introduce new vocational courses in assembling electronic products.

LO 14.2

2.1 Daniel was earning $65 per hour and working 45 hours per week. Then Daniel's wage rose to $75 per hour, and as a result, he now works 40 hours per week. What can we conclude from this information about the income effect and the substitution effect of a wage change for Daniel?

2.2 A columnist writing in the *Wall Street Journal* during the recession of 2007–09 made the following observation about the "price of time":

> The recession is doing funny things with the price of time.
>
> Technically it's risen in value. Although hardly anyone seems to have noticed, the government's latest figures show that hourly wages in real terms—which had pretty much stagnated for decades—have just jumped to their highest levels since the 1970s. You can thank cheaper prices in the stores, as well as higher pay.

What is the "price of time"? Is the columnist correct that when real hourly wages rise, the price of time increases? Briefly explain.

"Spend Some Time, Save Some Money," by Brett Arends from *Wall Street Journal*, May 19, 2009. Copyright © 2011 by Dow Jones & Company, Inc.. Reproduced with permission of Dow Jones & Company, Inc.

2.3 Most labour economists believe that many adult males are on the vertical section of their labour supply curves. Use the concepts of income and substitution effects to explain under what circumstances an individual's labour supply curve would be vertical.

Based on Robert Whaples, "Is There Consensus Among American Labour Economists? Survey Results on Forty Propositions," *Journal of Labour Research*, Vol. 17, No. 4, Fall 1996.

2.4 Suppose that a large oil field is discovered in Alberta. By imposing a tax on the oil, the provincial government is able to eliminate the provincial income tax on wages. What is likely to be the effect on the labour supply curve in Alberta?

2.5 The fraction of the Canadian population older than age 65 is increasing. What is the likely effect of the aging of the Canadian population on the supply curve for labour?

2.6 State whether each of the following events will result in a movement along the market supply curve of agricultural labour in Canada or whether it will cause the market supply curve of agricultural labour to shift. If the supply curve

shifts, indicate whether it will shift to the left or to the right and draw a graph to illustrate the shift.
a. The agricultural wage rate declines.
b. Wages outside agriculture increase.
c. The law is changed to allow for unlimited immigration into Canada.

LO 14.3

3.1 [**Related to the** Making the Connection **on page 413**] Over time, the gap between the wages of workers with college or university degrees and the wages of workers without college or university degrees has been increasing. Shouldn't this gap have increased the incentive for workers to earn college or university degrees, thereby increasing the supply of educated workers and reducing the size of the gap?

3.2 Reread the discussion of changes in the salaries of software engineers on page 415. Use a graph to illustrate this situation. Make sure your graph has labour demand and supply curves for 2009 and 2011 and that the equilibrium point for each year is clearly indicated.

3.3 Sean Astin, who played Sam in the *Lord of the Rings* movies, wrote the following about an earlier film he had appeared in: "Now I was in a movie I didn't respect, making obscene amounts of money (five times what a teacher makes, and teachers do infinitely more important work)." Are salaries determined by the importance of the work being done? If not, what are salaries determined by?

From Sean Astin, with Joe Layden, *There and Back Again: An Actor's Tale* (New York: St. Martin's Press, 2004), p. 35.

3.4 A newspaper article summarizes a study showing that "a standout kindergarten teacher is worth about $320,000 a year. That's the present value of the additional money that a full class of students can expect to earn over their careers. This estimate doesn't take into account social gains, like better health and less crime." Why are even standout kindergarten teachers paid salaries much lower than $320,000?

Based on David Leonhardt, "The Case for $320,000 Kindergarten Teachers," *New York Times*, July 27, 2010.

3.5 In 541 A.D., an outbreak of bubonic plague hit the Byzantine Empire. Because the plague was spread by flea-infested rats that often lived on ships, ports were hit particularly hard. In some ports, more than 40 percent of the population died. The emperor, Justinian, was concerned that the wages of sailors were rising very rapidly as a result of the plague. In 544 A.D., he placed a ceiling on the wages of sailors. Use a demand and supply graph of the market for sailors to show the effect of the plague on the wages of sailors. Use the same graph to show the effect of Justinian's wage ceiling. Briefly explain what is happening in your graph.

Based on Michael McCormick, *The Origins of the European Economy: Communications and Commerce, A.D., 300–900* (New York: Cambridge University Press, 2001), p. 109.

LO 14.4

4.1 [**Related to the** Chapter Opener **on page 405**] A student remarks, "I don't think the idea of marginal revenue product really helps explain differences in wages. After all, a ticket to a baseball game costs much less than university tuition, yet baseball players are paid much more than university professors." Do you agree with the student's reasoning?

4.2 [**Related to the** Making the Connection **on page 417**] According to economist Alan Krueger, the share of concert ticket revenue received by the top 1 percent of all acts rose from 26 percent in 1982 to 56 percent in 2003. Does this information indicate that the top acts in 2003 must have been much better performers relative to other acts than was the case in 1982? If not, can you think of another explanation?

Based on Eduardo Porter, "More Than Ever, It Pays to Be the Top Executive," *New York Times*, May 25, 2007.

4.3 [**Related to the** Making the Connection **on page 417**] Why are there superstar basketball players but no superstar plumbers?

4.4 Some policymakers have proposed that all firms be required to make contributions to retirement plans for their employees. If such a proposal is enacted, what is likely to happen to the wages received by workers at firms that currently do not make contributions to their employees' retirement plans? Briefly explain your reasoning.

4.5 [**Related to** Solved Problem 14.4 **on page 420**] Use the following graphs to answer the questions.
a. What is the equilibrium quantity of trash collectors hired, and what is the equilibrium wage?
b. What is the equilibrium quantity of receptionists hired, and what is the equilibrium wage?
c. Briefly discuss why trash collectors might earn a higher weekly wage than receptionists.

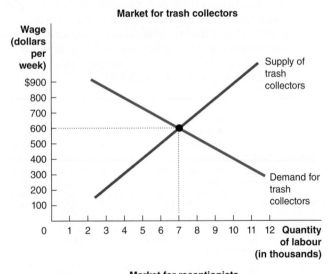

Market for trash collectors

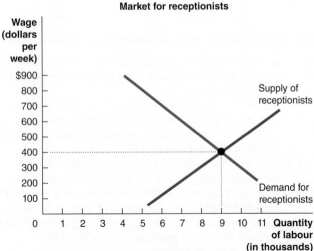

Market for receptionists

d. Suppose that comparable-worth legislation is passed, and the government requires that trash collectors and receptionists be paid the same wage, $500 per week. Now how many trash collectors will be hired and how many receptionists will be hired?

4.6 [**Related to** Solved Problem 14.4 **on page 420**] In most universities, economics professors receive larger salaries than English professors. Suppose that the government requires that from now on, all universities must pay economics professors the same salaries as English professors. Use demand and supply graphs to analyze the effect of this requirement.

4.7 [**Related to the** Making the Connection **on page 421**] Why might employers be more likely to interview a job applicant with a white-sounding name than an applicant with an ethnic minority–sounding name? Leaving aside legal penalties, will employers who follow this practice incur an economic penalty? Briefly explain.

LO 14.5

5.1 According to a study, the number of jobs in which firms used bonuses, commissions, or piece rates to tie workers' pay to their performance increased from an estimated 30 percent of all jobs in the 1970s to 40 percent in the 1990s. Why would systems that tie workers' pay to how much they produce have become increasingly popular with firms? The same study found that these pay systems were more common in higher-paid jobs than in lower-paid jobs. Briefly explain this result.

Based on Thomas Lemieux, W. Bentley MacLeod, and Daniel Parent, "Performance Pay and Wage Inequality," *Quarterly Journal of Economics*, Vol. 124, No. 1, February 2009, pp. 1–49.

5.2 Many companies that pay workers an hourly wage require some minimum level of acceptable output. Suppose a company that has been using this system decides to switch to a piece-rate system under which workers are compensated on the basis of how much output they produce. Is it likely that workers under a piece-rate system will end up choosing to produce less than the minimum output required under the hourly wage system? Briefly explain.

5.3 In most jobs, the harder you work, the more you earn. Some workers would rather work harder and earn more; others would rather work less hard, even though as a result they earn less. Suppose, though, that all workers at a company fall into the "work harder and earn more" group. Suppose also that the workers all have the same abilities. In these circumstances, would output per worker be the same under an hourly wage compensation system as under a piece-rate system? Briefly explain.

5.4 For years, the Goodyear Tire & Rubber Company compensated its sales force by paying a salesperson a salary plus a bonus, based on the number of tires he or she sold. Eventually, Goodyear made two changes to this policy: (1) The basis for the bonus was changed from the *quantity* of tires sold to the *revenue* from the tires sold; and (2) salespeople were required to get approval from corporate headquarters in Akron, Ohio, before offering to sell tires to customers at reduced prices. Explain why these changes were likely to increase Goodyear's profits.

Based on Timothy Aeppel, "Amid Weak Inflation, Firms Turn Creative to Boost Prices," *Wall Street Journal*, September 18, 2002.

5.5 What effect did the incentive pay system have on the marginal cost of planting trees in British Columbia? If all firms that plant trees adopted an incentive pay system, what would happen to the price of planting trees? Who would ultimately benefit?

LO 14.6

6.1 Adam operates a pin factory. Suppose Adam faces the situation shown in the following table and the cost of renting a machine is $550 per week.

Number of Machines	Output of Pins (boxes per week)	Marginal Product of Capital	Product Price (dollars per box)	Total Revenue	Marginal Revenue Product of Capital	Rental Cost per Machine	Additional Profit from Renting One Additional Machine
0	0	—	$100		—	$550	
1	12		100			550	
2	21		100			550	
3	28		100			550	
4	34		100			550	
5	39		100			550	
6	43		100			550	

   a. Fill in the blanks in the table and determine the profit-maximizing number of machines for Adam to rent. Briefly explain why renting this number of machines is profit maximizing.

   b. Draw Adam's demand curve for capital.

6.2 Many people have predicted, using a model like the one in panel (b) of Figure 14.12 that the price of natural resources should rise consistently over time in comparison with the prices of other goods because the demand curve for natural resources is continually shifting to the right, while the supply curve must be shifting to the left as natural resources are used up. However, the relative prices of most natural resources have not been increasing. Draw a graph that shows the demand and supply for natural resources that can explain why prices haven't risen even though demand has.

6.3 In 1879, economist Henry George published *Progress and Poverty*, which became one of the best-selling books of the nineteenth century. In this book, George argued that all existing taxes should be replaced with a single tax on land. Tax incidence is the actual division of the burden of a tax between buyers and sellers in a market. If land is taxed, how will the burden of the tax be divided between the sellers of land and the buyers of land? Illustrate your answer with a graph of the market for land.

6.4 The total amount of oil in the earth is not increasing. Does this mean that in the market for oil, the supply curve is perfectly inelastic? Briefly explain.

6.5 In a competitive labour market, imposing a minimum wage should reduce the equilibrium level of employment. Will this also be true if the labour market is a monopsony? Briefly explain.

MyEconLab   MyEconLab is an online tool designed to help you master the concepts covered in your course. It will create an adaptive, highly personalized study plan to stimulate and measure your learning. Log in to take advantage of this powerful study aid, and to access quizzes and other valuable course-related material.

Public Choice, Taxes, and the Distribution of Income

Chapter Outline and Learning Objectives

Shutterstock

Taxes and Trade-Offs

Taxes can have a large effect on the decisions of people and businesses. The Home Renovation Tax Credit, introduced as a temporary measure in the 2009 budget, caused thousands of Canadians to undertake improvements to their homes. Such tax credits are not without a cost, however; because of them, the federal government won't receive as much revenue to support its spending.

In the lead-up to the 2010 budget, the Conference Board of Canada lobbied the federal government to reduce the corporate income tax rate. Changes in corporate income taxes can induce firms to dramatically change their behaviour. For example, when the United States reduced its corporate income tax rate, Microsoft paid its first ever dividends to shareholders. The Conference Board argues that higher corporate taxes reduce firms' willingness to invest, and lower investment means lower future capital stocks. Lower capital stocks mean lower productivity of labour, lower output, and thus lower living standards for Canadians. However, the revenue collected from corporate income taxes can be used to support social programs, or even simply be given to people with relatively low income. Any decision about taxation is fundamentally a trade-off between costs and benefits.

Given these trade-offs, how should we evaluate tax laws? Tax laws affect economic incentives and economic activity and can also affect fairness. The concerns raised about tax policy (such as the recent proposed reduction in corporate taxes) are not new. Politicians since Sir John A. Macdonald have been debating which types of taxes to use and at what level taxes should be set.

One of the most heated recent debates concerning taxation in Canada was around the creation of the federal goods and services tax (GST). Launched in 1989 by the Progressive Conservative government under Brian Mulroney, this 7 percent consumption tax was to replace a manufacturer's sales tax and a federal communications tax. Widespread opposition to the tax helped the Liberals to defeat the Progressive conservatives in 1993. Despite their vocal opposition to the GST before winning the election, the Liberal government under Jean Chretien did not repeal the tax. The GST remained at 7 percent until the Conservative government reduced it by 1 percent in 2006, and later by another 1 percent in 2008.

How has the GST and its recent changes affected the economy of Canada? Does the current tax structure reduce economic efficiency and growth? Does it actually promote equity?

AN INSIDE LOOK on **page 462** examines the debate about absolute versus relative poverty.

Economics in Your Life

How Much Tax Should You Pay?

Government is ever present in your life. Just today, you likely drove on roads that the government paid to build and maintain. You may attend a public college or university, paid for, at least in part, by government. Where does a government get its money? By taxing citizens. Think of the different taxes you pay. Do you think you pay more than, less than, or just about your fair share in taxes? How do you determine what your fair share is? As you read this chapter, see if you can answer these questions. You can check your answers against those we provide on page 460 at the end of this chapter.

Public choice model A model that applies economic analysis to government decision making.

T
he government plays a significant role in helping the market system work efficiently by providing secure rights to private property and an independent court system to enforce contracts. In addition, the government itself must sometimes supply goods—known as *public goods*—that private firms will not supply. But how do governments decide which policies to adopt? In recent years, economists, led by Nobel Laureate James Buchanan and Gordon Tullock, have developed the **public choice model**, which applies economic analysis to government decision making. In this chapter, we will explore how public choice can help us understand how policymakers make decisions.

We will also discuss some of the principles that governments use to create tax policy. In particular, we will see how economists identify which taxes are most economically efficient. At the end of the chapter, we will discuss the extent to which government policy—including tax policy—affects the distribution of income.

15.1 LEARNING OBJECTIVE

Describe the public choice model and explain how it is used to analyze government decision making.

Public Choice

Households and firms act to make themselves as well off as possible. Households choose the goods they buy to maximize their utility, and firms choose the quantities and prices of the goods they sell to maximize profits. Because government policy plays an important role in the economy, it is important also to consider how government policymakers—such as Members of Parliament, Members of Legislative Assemblies, and municipal councils—arrive at their decisions. One of the key insights from the public choice model is that policymakers are no different from consumers or managers of firms: Policymakers are likely to pursue their own self-interest, even if their self-interest conflicts with the public interest. In particular, we expect that public officials will take actions that are likely to result in their being reelected.

How Do We Know the Public Interest? Models of Voting

It is possible to argue that elected officials simply represent the preferences of the voters who elect them. After all, it would seem logical that voters will not reelect a politician who fails to act in the public interest. A closer look at voting, however, makes it less clear that politicians are simply representing the views of the voters.

The Voting Paradox Many policy decisions involve multiple alternatives. Because the size of the federal budget is limited, policymakers face trade-offs. To take a simple example, suppose that there is $1 billion available in the budget, and Parliament must choose whether to spend it on *only one* of three alternatives: (1) research on breast cancer, (2) subsidies for mass transit, or (3) fighting climate change. Assume that the votes of members of Parliament will represent the preferences of their constituents. We might expect that Parliament will vote for the alternative favoured by a majority of the voters. In fact, though, there are circumstances in which majority voting will fail to result in a consistent decision. For example, suppose for simplicity that there are only three voters, and they have the preferences shown at the top of Table 15.1.

In the table, we show the three policy alternatives in the first column. The remaining columns show the voters' rankings of the alternatives. For example, Lena would prefer to see the money spent on cancer research. Her second choice is mass transit, and her third choice is fighting climate change. What happens if a series of votes are taken in which each pair of alternatives is considered in turn? The bottom of Table 15.1 shows the results of these votes. If the vote is between spending the money on cancer research and spending the money on mass transit, cancer research wins because Lena and David both prefer spending the money on cancer research to spending the money on mass transit. So, if the votes of members of Parliament represent the preferences of voters, we have a clear verdict, and the money is spent on cancer research. Suppose, though, that the vote is between spending the money on mass transit and spending the

Policy	Lena	David	Kathleen
Cancer research	1st	2nd	3rd
Mass transit	2nd	3rd	1st
Fighting climate change	3rd	1st	2nd

Votes	Outcome
Cancer research versus mass transit	Cancer research wins
Mass transit versus fighting climate change	Mass transit wins
Fighting climate change versus cancer research	Fighting climate change wins

Table 15.1

The Voting Paradox

money on fighting climate change. Then, because Lena and Kathleen prefer spending on mass transit to spending on fighting climate change, mass transit wins. Now, finally, suppose the vote is between spending on cancer research and spending on fighting climate change. Surprisingly, fighting climate change wins because that is what David and Kathleen prefer. The outcome of this vote is surprising because if voters prefer cancer research to mass transit and mass transit to fighting climate change, we would expect that consistency in decision making would ensure that they prefer cancer research to fighting climate change. But in this example, the collective preferences of the voters turn out not to be consistent. The failure of majority voting to always result in consistent choices is called the **voting paradox**.

This is an artificial example because we assumed that there were only three alternatives, there were only three voters, and a simple majority vote determined the outcomes. In fact, though, Nobel Laureate Kenneth Arrow has shown mathematically that the failure of majority votes to always represent voters' preferences is a very general result. The **Arrow impossibility theorem** states that no system of voting can be devised that will consistently represent the underlying preferences of voters. This theorem suggests that there is no way through democratic voting to ensure that the preferences of voters are translated into policy choices. In fact, the Arrow impossibility theorem suggests that voting might lead to shifts in policy that may not be efficient. For instance, which of the three alternatives for spending the $1 billion Parliament will actually choose would depend on the order in which the alternatives happen to be voted on, which might change from one year to the next. So, with respect to economic issues, such as providing funding for public goods, we cannot count on the political process to necessarily result in an efficient outcome. In other words, the "voting market"—as represented by elections—may often do a less efficient job of representing consumer preferences than do markets for goods and services.

The Median Voter Theorem In practice, many political issues are decided by a majority vote. In those cases, what can we say about which voters' preferences the outcome is likely to represent? An important result known as the **median voter theorem** states that the outcome of a majority vote is likely to represent the preferences of the voter who is in the political middle. To take another simplified example, suppose there are five voters, and their preferences for spending on breast cancer research are shown in Figure 15.1. Their preferences range from Kathleen, who prefers to spend nothing on breast cancer research—preferring the funds to be spent on other programs or for federal spending to be reduced and taxes lowered—to Lena, who prefers to spend $6 billion.

In this case, David is the median voter because he is in the political middle; two voters would prefer to spend less than he does and two would prefer to spend more. To see why the median voter's preferences are likely to prevail, consider first a vote between David's preferred outcome of spending $2 billion and a proposal to spend $6 billion. Because only Lena favours $6 billion and the other voters all prefer spending less, the proposal to spend $2 billion would win four votes to one. Similarly, consider a vote between spending $2 billion and spending $1 billion. Three voters prefer

Voting paradox The failure of majority voting to always result in consistent choices.

Arrow impossibility theorem A mathematical theorem that holds that no system of voting can be devised that will consistently represent the underlying preferences of voters.

Median voter theorem The proposition that the outcome of a majority vote is likely to represent the preferences of the voter who is in the political middle.

Figure 15.1

The Median Voter Theorem

The median voter theorem states that the outcome of a majority vote is likely to represent the preferences of the voter who is in the political middle. In this case, David is in the political middle because two voters want to spend more on breast cancer research than he does and two voters want to spend less. In any vote between a proposal to spend $2 billion and a proposal to spend a different amount, a proposal to spend $2 billion will win.

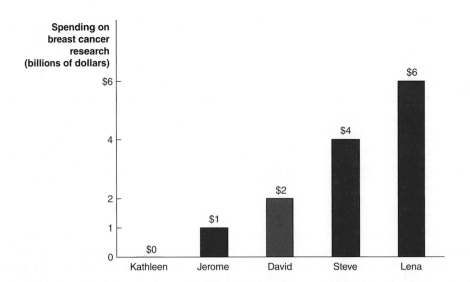

spending more than $1 billion and only two prefer spending $1 billion or less, so the proposal to spend $2 billion will win three votes to two. Only the proposal to spend $2 billion will have the support of a majority when paired with proposals to spend a different amount. Notice also that the amount spent as a result of the voting is less than the amount that would result from taking the simple average of the voters' preferences, which would be $2.6 billion.

One implication of the median voter theorem is that the political process tends to serve individuals whose preferences are in the middle but not those individuals whose preferences are far away from the median. There is an important contrast between the political process, which results in collective actions in which everyone is obliged to participate, and the market process, in which individuals are free to participate or not. For instance, even though Kathleen would prefer not to spend government funds on breast cancer research, once a majority has voted to spend $2 billion, Kathleen is obliged to go along with the spending—and the taxes required to fund the spending. This is in contrast with the market for goods and services, where if, for instance, Kathleen disagrees with the majority of consumers who like iPods, she is under no obligation to buy one. Similarly, even though Lena and Steve might prefer to pay significantly higher taxes to fund additional spending on breast cancer research, they are obliged to go along with the lower level of spending the majority approved. If Lena would like to have her iPod gold plated, she can choose to do so, even if the vast majority of consumers would consider such spending a waste of money.

Government Failure?

The voting models we have just looked at indicate that individuals are less likely to see their preferences represented in the outcomes of government policies than in the outcomes of markets. The public choice model goes beyond this observation to question whether the self-interest of policymakers is likely to cause them to take actions that are inconsistent with the preferences of voters, even where those preferences are clear. There are several aspects of how the political process works that might lead to this outcome.

Rent seeking Attempts by individuals and firms to use government action to make themselves better off at the expense of others.

Rent Seeking Economists usually focus on analyzing the actions of individuals and firms as they attempt to make themselves better off by interacting in markets. The public choice model shifts the focus to attempts by individuals and firms to engage in **rent seeking**, which is the use of government action to make themselves better off at the expense of others. One of the benefits of the market system is that it channels self-interested behaviour in a way that benefits society as a whole. Although Apple developed the iPad to make profits, its actions increased the well-being of millions of consumers. When Samsung introduced the Galaxy Tab to compete with the iPad, it also was motivated by the desire for profit, but it further increased consumer well-being by expanding the choice of tablet computers available. Rent seeking, in contrast, can benefit a few individuals or firms at the expense of all other individuals and firms. For example, the Canadian government restricts the import of cheese with quotas. The quota system has benefited Canadian cheese makers and the people who work for them, but has reduced consumer surplus, hurt Canadian pizza firms and their employees (by increasing the price of essential inputs), and reduced overall economic efficiency.

Because firms can benefit from government intervention in the economy, as the cheese companies have benefited from the cheese quota, they are willing to spend resources to attempt to secure these interventions. Politicians need funds to finance their election campaigns. So, these policymakers may accept campaign contributions from rent-seeking firms and may be willing to introduce *special interest legislation* on their behalf.

Logrolling and Rational Ignorance   Two other factors help explain why rent-seeking behaviour can sometimes succeed. It may seem puzzling that the cheese quota has been enacted when it helped very few workers and firms. Why would members of Parliament vote for the cheese quota if they do not have large numbers of dairy farms in their riding? One possibility is logrolling. *Logrolling* refers to the situation where a member of Parliament votes to approve a bill in exchange for favourable votes from other members on other bills. For example, a member of Parliament from Toronto might vote for the cheese quota, even though none of the member's constituents will benefit from it. In exchange, members of Parliament from districts where dairy farms are located will vote for legislation the member of Parliament from Toronto would like to see passed. This vote trading may result in a majority of Parliament supporting legislation that benefits the economic interests of a few while harming the economic interests of a much larger group.

But if the majority of voters is harmed by rent-seeking legislation, how does it get passed, even given the effects of logrolling? In Chapter 9, we discussed one possible explanation with respect to the Canadian cheese quota. Although, collectively, consumer surplus might decline by $262.5 million per year because of the cheese quota, spread across a population of 35 million, the loss per person is only $7.50. Because the loss is so small, most people do not take it into account when deciding how to vote in elections, and many people are not even aware that the cheese quota exists. Other voters may be convinced to support restrictions on trade because the jobs saved by tariffs and quotas are visible and often highly publicized, while the jobs lost because of these restrictions and the reductions in consumer surplus are harder to detect. Because becoming informed on an issue may require time and effort and the economic payoff is often low, some economists argue that many voters are *rationally ignorant* of the effect of rent-seeking legislation. In this view, because voters frequently lack an economic incentive to become informed about pending legislation, the voters' preferences do not act as a constraint on legislators voting for rent-seeking legislation.

Regulatory Capture   One way in which the government intervenes in the economy is by establishing a regulatory agency or commission that is given authority over a particular industry or type of product. For example, no firm is allowed to sell prescription drugs in Canada without first receiving authorization from Health Canada. Ideally, regulatory agencies will make decisions in the public interest. Health Canada should weigh the benefits to patients from quickly approving a new drug against the costs that the agency may overlook potentially dangerous side effects of the drug if approval is too rapid. However, because the firms being regulated are significantly affected by the regulatory agency's actions, the firms have an incentive to try to influence those actions. In extreme cases, this influence may lead the agency to make decisions that are in the best interests of the firms being regulated, even if these actions are not in the public interest. In that case, the agency has been subject to *regulatory capture* by the industry being regulated. Some economists point to the market for taxis as an example of regulatory capture in Canada. In most major Canadian cities, taxis must be licensed to carry passengers, and the number of licences is controlled by the city. In many of these cities, cabbies actually lobby to keep the number of licences issued small. If few licences (particularly new licences) are issued, those lucky enough to get a licence are protected from extra competition while the public suffers a lower consumer surplus, either as a higher price or a longer wait for a cab. Economists debate the extent to which regulatory capture explains the decisions of some government agencies.

The presence of externalities can lead to market failure, which is the situation where the market does not supply the economically efficient quantity of a good or service. Public choice analysis indicates that *government failure* can also occur. For the reasons we have discussed in this section, it is possible that government intervention in the economy may reduce economic efficiency rather than increase it. Economists disagree about the extent to which government failure results in serious economic inefficiency in the Canadian economy. Most economists, though, accept the basic argument of the public choice model that policymakers may have incentives to intervene in the economy in ways that do not promote efficiency and that proposals for such intervention should be evaluated with care.

Is Government Regulation Necessary?

The public choice model raises important questions about the effect of government regulation on economic efficiency. But can we conclude that Parliament should abolish agencies such as Health Canada, the Canadian Radio-television and Telecommunications Commission, and Transport Canada? In fact, most economists agree that these agencies can serve useful purposes. For instance, government agencies can help correct the effects of production externalities, such as pollution. Regulatory agencies can also improve economic efficiency in markets where consumers have difficulty obtaining the information they need to make informed purchases. For example, consumers have no easy way of detecting bacteria and other contaminants in food or determining whether prescription drugs are safe and effective. Health Canada takes on this role for consumers.

Although government regulation can clearly provide important benefits to consumers, we need to take into account the costs of regulations. Recent estimates indicate that the costs of federal regulations may be several thousand dollars per taxpayer. Economics can help policymakers devise regulations that provide benefits to consumers that exceed their costs.

15.2 LEARNING OBJECTIVE

Understand the tax system in Canada, including the principles that governments use to create tax policy.

The Tax System

However the size of government and the types of activities it engages in are determined, government spending has to be financed. The government primarily relies on taxes to raise the revenue it needs. Some taxes, such as those on cigarettes or alcohol, are intended to discourage consumption of some goods as well as to raise revenues. In 2012, the average Canadian family (of two or more individuals) had an income of $94,259 and paid $41,627 in taxes.

These are the most widely used taxes in Canada:

- *Personal income taxes.* The federal and provincial governments of Canada tax the wages, salaries, and other income of households. Personal income taxes are the largest source of revenue for both the federal and the provincial governments.

- *Corporate income taxes.* The federal and provincial governments also collect taxes on the profits made by corporations.

- *Sales taxes.* The federal government collects the goods and services tax on most purchases of consumer goods. All provinces except Alberta collect taxes on purchases. The importance of sales taxes as a revenue source varies significantly by province.

- *Employment Insurance premiums.* The federal government collects contributions to the Employment Insurance program from every person earning wages in Canada.

- *Property taxes.* Most local governments tax homes, offices, factories, and the land they are built on. In Canada, property taxes are the main source of revenue for municipalities.

- *Excise taxes.* The federal and provincial governments levy excise taxes on specific goods, such as gasoline, cigarettes, and alcohol.

An Overview of the Canadian Tax System

Figure 15.2 shows the revenue sources for the federal, provincial, and municipal governments in 2012. Panel (a) shows that the federal government raises approximately half of its revenue ($498,680 million of $999,080 million) from personal income taxes. Corporate income tax and the GST account for much smaller portions of federal revenues.

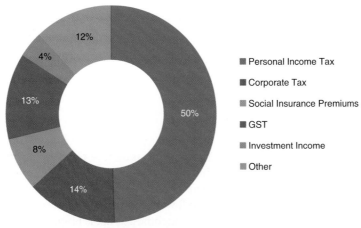

(a) Federal government revenue sources

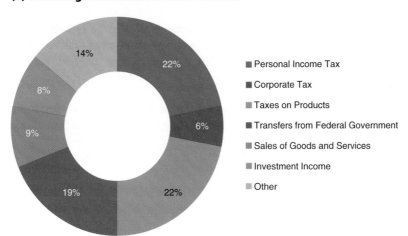

(b) Provincial government revenue sources

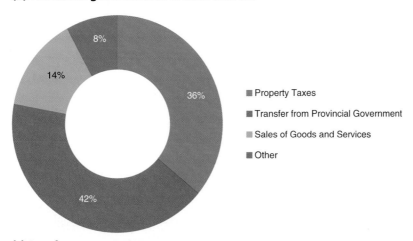

(c) Local government revenue sources

Figure 15.2

Canadian Government Revenue Sources, 2012

Individual income taxes make up the majority of revenue for both federal and provincial governments, with taxes on products (including GST, PST, and HST) important for both. While corporate taxes are important for the federal government, they contribute relatively little to provincial government revenues. Provincial governments also receive significant funding from the federal government through various transfer programs. Municipal governments rely primarily on only two revenue sources: transfers from the provincial government and property taxes.

Panels (b) and (c) show that provincial and local governments receive a lot of their revenue from sources different from the federal government's. One of the major differences is revenue from other levels of government. This is particularly important for municipalities. The major source of funds for local governments is taxes on property and revenue from provincial governments.

Source: Cansim Table 380-0080. This does not constitute an endorsement by Statistics Canada of this product.

Table 15.2

Federal Income Tax Brackets and Tax Rates for Single Taxpayers, 2013

Income	Tax Rate
$0 to $42,707	15%
$42,707 to $85,414	22%
$85,414 to $132,406	26%
$132,407 and up	29%

Data from CRA website: http://www.cra-arc.gc.ca/E/pbg/tf/5000-s1/5000-s1-12e.pdf

Table 15.3

Federal Income Tax Paid on Taxable Income of $100,000

On Matt's ...	Matt Pays ...
First $42,707 of income	$6,406.00
Next $42,707 of income	$9,396.00
Remaining $14,586 of income	$3,792.36

Regressive tax A tax for which people with lower incomes pay a higher percentage of their income in tax than do people with higher incomes.

Progressive tax A tax for which people with lower incomes pay a lower percentage of their income in tax than do people with higher incomes.

Progressive and Regressive Taxes

Economists often categorize taxes on the basis of the amount of tax people with different levels of income pay relative to their incomes. With a **regressive tax**, people with lower incomes pay a higher percentage of their income in tax than do people with higher incomes. With a **progressive tax**, people with lower incomes pay a lower percentage of their income in tax than do people with higher incomes. A tax is *proportional* if people with lower incomes pay the same percentage of their income in tax as do people with higher incomes.

The federal income tax is an example of a progressive tax. To see why, we must first consider the important distinction between a tax rate and a tax bracket. A *tax rate* is the percentage of income paid in taxes. A *tax bracket* refers to the income range within which a tax rate applies. Table 15.2 shows the federal income tax brackets and tax rates for single taxpayers in 2013.

We can use Table 15.2 to calculate what Matt, a single taxpayer with an income of $100,000, pays in federal income tax. This example is somewhat simplified because we are ignoring the *exemptions* and *deductions* that taxpayers can use to reduce the amount of income subject to tax. For example, taxpayers are allowed to exclude from taxation a certain amount of income (called the *personal exemption*) that represents very basic living expenses. Ignoring Matt's exemptions and deductions, he will have to make the tax payment to the federal government showing in Table 15.3. Matt's first $42,707 is in the 15 percent bracket, so he pays $6,406. His next $42,707 of income is in the 22 percent bracket, so he pays $9,396 on this part of his income, bringing his total to $15,802. His remaining $14,586 of income is taxed at a rate of 26 percent, adding another $3,792.36 to his tax bill. Matt's total federal income tax bill will be $19,594.36.

Making the Connection | Which Groups Pay the Most in Federal Taxes?

In this chapter, we have discussed the distribution of tax burden between corporations and people as well as between different people. It is generally agreed that some level of progressiveness is desirable in a tax system, but how progressive is the Canadian tax system? The following table shows the proportion of total income tax revenues paid by group by income. Each group is called a quintile and is one fifth of the population. The lowest quintile is made up of those people in Canada whose income is in the lowest 20 percent. The second quintile is made of people with incomes in the next 20 percent. Those in the highest quintile are those that earn the most in Canada.

	Share of Income Earned, 2010	Share of Income Taxes Paid, 2010
Lowest quintile	4.2%	1.6%
Second quintile	9.6%	4.2%
Third quintile	15.3%	10.8%
Fourth quintile	23.6%	21.6%
Highest quintile	47.3%	61.9%

Source: Statistics Canada, Cansim Tables 202-0501 and 202-0701.

The data in the Share of Income Earned column show that not quite half of all income earned in Canada goes to the 20 percent of the population receiving the highest incomes. The data in the Share of Income Taxes Paid column shows that just over 60 percent of the revenue the government collects in income taxes comes from the same 20 percent of people at the high end of the income distribution. At the same time, those with incomes in the lowest 20 percent pay just 1.6 percent of income tax collected.

The data in the table are a clear indication that the Canadian income tax system is progressive. Remember that a progressive tax system will require those with greater wealth or incomes to pay more than those with lower wealth or incomes. People who have incomes in the top 20 percent of all Canadians pay more than 60 percent of the total income tax bill. Whether or not the Canadian income tax system should be made more or less progressive is a normative debate that is likely to continue well into the future.

Your Turn: Test your understanding by doing related problem 2.5 on page 465 at the end of this chapter.

MyEconLab

Marginal and Average Income Tax Rates

The fraction of each additional dollar of income that must be paid in taxes is called the **marginal tax rate**. The **average tax rate** is the total tax paid divided by total income. When a tax is progressive, as is the federal income tax, the marginal and average tax rates differ. For example, in Table 15.3 Matt had a marginal tax rate of 26 percent because that is the rate he paid on the last dollar of his income. But his average tax rate was:

Marginal tax rate The fraction of each additional dollar of income that must be paid in taxes.

Average tax rate Total tax paid divided by total income.

$$\left(\frac{\$19{,}594.36}{\$100{,}000}\right) \times 100 = 19.6\%.$$

His average tax rate was lower than his marginal tax rate because the first $85,414 of his income was taxed at rates below his marginal rate of 26 percent.

When economists consider a change in tax policy, they generally focus on the marginal tax rate rather than the average tax rate because the marginal tax rate is a better indicator of how a change in a tax will affect people's willingness to work, save, and invest. For example, if Matt is considering working longer hours to raise his income, he will use his marginal tax rate to determine how much extra income he will earn after taxes. He will ignore his average tax rate because it does not represent the taxes he must pay on the *additional* income he earns. The higher the marginal tax rate, the lower the return he receives from working additional hours and the less likely he is to work those additional hours.

The Corporate Income Tax

The federal government taxes the profits earned by corporations under the *corporate income tax*. Unlike the individual income tax, the corporate income tax system is not progressive. The earnings of a corporation have no effect on its income tax rate: All corporations paying the corporate income tax pay the same rate (18 percent rate in 2010, 16.5 percent in 2011, and 15 percent in 2012). Remember that the federal government is not the only government to tax corporations. Provincial governments also collect corporate income taxes, and provinces have different corporate income tax rates and structures.

Economists debate the costs and benefits of a separate tax on corporate profits. The corporate income tax ultimately must be paid by a corporation's owners—which are its shareholders—or by its employees, in the form of lower wages, or by its customers, in the form of higher prices. Some economists argue that if the purpose of the corporate income tax is to tax the owners of corporations, it would be better to do so directly by taxing the owners' incomes rather than by taxing the owners indirectly through the corporate income tax. Individual taxpayers already pay income taxes on the dividends and capital gains they receive from owning stock in corporations. In effect, the corporate income tax "double taxes" earnings on individual shareholders' investments in corporations.

An alternative policy that avoids this double taxation would be for corporations to calculate their total profits each year and send a notice to each shareholder, indicating the shareholder's portion of the profits. The shareholder would then be required to include this amount as taxable income on his or her personal income tax. Under another alternative, the federal government could continue to tax corporate income through the corporate income tax but allow individual taxpayers to receive corporate dividends and capital gains tax-free.

International Comparison of Corporate Income Taxes

In the past 10 years, several countries have cut corporate income taxes to increase investment spending and growth. Table 15.4 compares corporate income tax rates in several high-income countries. The tax rates given in the table include taxes at all levels of government. So, in Canada, for example, they include taxes imposed on corporate profits by provincial governments as well as by the federal government. The table shows that several countries, including Italy, Germany, and Ireland, significantly reduced corporate income tax rates between 2000 and 2013. Ireland, in particular, has been successful in using lower corporate income tax rates to attract foreign corporations to locate facilities there. Lower tax rates have led Microsoft, Intel, and Dell, among other U.S.-based firms, to move some of their operations to Ireland. The table also shows that corporate income tax rates are higher in the United States than in other high-income countries.

Evaluating Taxes

We have seen that governments use a variety of taxes to raise revenue. In selecting which taxes to use, governments take into account the following goals and principles:

- The goal of economic efficiency
- The ability-to-pay principle
- The horizontal-equity principle
- The benefits-received principle
- The goal of attaining social objectives

The Goal of Economic Efficiency Taxes affect economic efficiency: Whenever a government taxes an activity, it raises the cost of engaging in that activity, so less of that activity will occur. Figure 15.3 uses a demand and supply graph to illustrate this point for a sales tax. A sales tax increases the cost of supplying a good, which causes the supply curve to shift up by the amount of the tax. In the figure, the equilibrium price rises from P_1 to P_2, and the equilibrium quantity falls from Q_1 to Q_2. When a good is taxed, less of it is produced.

The government collects tax revenue equal to the tax per unit multiplied by the number of units sold. The green-shaded rectangle in Figure 15.3 represents the government's tax revenue. Although sellers appear to receive a higher price for the good—P_2—the price they receive after paying the tax falls to P_3. Because the price consumers pay has risen, consumer surplus has fallen. Because the price producers receive has also fallen, producer surplus has fallen. Some of the reduction in consumer surplus and

Country	Tax Rate in 2000 (%)	Tax Rate in 2013 (%)
Canada	43	26
France	37	33.33
Germany	52	29.48
Ireland	24	12.5
Italy	41	31.4
Japan	42	38.01
Spain	35	30
Sweden	28	22
United Kingdom	30	24
United States	40	40

Table 15.4

Corporate Income Tax Rates Around the World

Data from KPMG's survey of Corporate Tax Rates, 2009 and 2012. http://www.kpmg.com/Global/en IssuesAndInsights/ArticlesPublications/Documents/KPMG-Corporate-Indirect-Tax-Rate-Survey-2009.pdf and http://www.kpmg.com/global/en/services/tax/tax-tools-and-resources/pages/corporate-tax-rates-table.aspx

producer surplus becomes tax revenue for the government. The rest of the reduction in consumer surplus and producer surplus is equal to the deadweight loss from the tax and is shown in the figure by the yellow-shaded triangle. The deadweight loss from a tax is known as the *excess burden* of the tax. The **excess burden** is a measure of the efficiency loss to the economy that results from the tax having reduced the quantity of the good produced. *A tax is efficient if it imposes a small excess burden relative to the tax revenue it raises.*

To improve the economic efficiency of a tax system, economists argue that the government should reduce its reliance on taxes that have a high deadweight loss relative to the revenue raised. The tax on interest earned from savings is an example of a tax with a high deadweight loss because savings often come from income already taxed once. Therefore, taxing interest earned on savings from income that has already been taxed is essentially double taxation.

There are other examples of significant deadweight losses of taxation. High taxes on work can reduce the number of hours an individual works, as well as how hard the individual works or whether the individual starts a business. In each case, the reduction in the taxed activity—here, work—generates less government revenue, and individuals are worse off because the tax encourages them to change their behaviour.

Excess burden A measure of the efficiency loss to the economy that results from a tax having reduced the quantity of a good produced; also known as the deadweight loss.

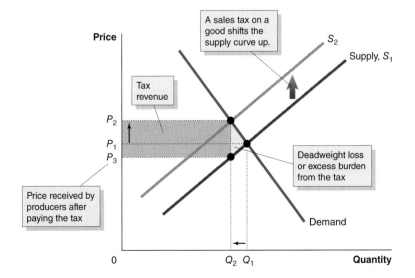

Figure 15.3

The Efficiency Loss from a Sales Tax

A sales tax increases the cost of supplying a good, which causes the supply curve to shift up, from S_1 to S_2. Without the tax, the equilibrium price of the good is P_1, and the equilibrium quantity is Q_1. After the tax is imposed, the equilibrium price rises to P_2, and the equilibrium quantity falls to Q_2. After paying the tax, producers receive P_3. The government receives tax revenue equal to the green-shaded rectangle. Some consumer surplus and some producer surplus become tax revenue for the government, and some become deadweight loss, shown by the yellow-shaded triangle. The deadweight loss is the *excess burden* of the tax.

Taxation can have substantial effects on economic efficiency by altering incentives to work, save, or invest. A good illustration of this effect can be seen in the large differences between annual hours worked in Europe and in the United States. Europeans typically work fewer hours than do Americans. According to an analysis by Nobel Laureate Edward Prescott, this difference was not always present. In the early 1970s, when European and U.S. tax rates on income were comparable, European and U.S. hours worked per employee were also comparable. Prescott finds that virtually all of the difference between labour supply in the United States and labour supply in France and Germany since that time is due to differences in their tax systems.

Anton Gvozdikov/Shutterstock

Would an increase in the GST be more efficient than an increase in income taxes?

Making the Connection | Should the Federal Government Raise Income Taxes or the GST?

In response to the global recession in 2008–09, the federal government increased spending and began to run a deficit. As Canada and other countries recover from the recession, many people are starting to ask how the federal government will return to a balanced budget, and maybe even a surplus (in order to pay back what was borrowed). Should the federal government increase income taxes or consumption taxes (the GST) in an effort to deal with the current budget shortfall? Under the income tax, households pay taxes on income earned. Under the GST, households pay taxes on the part of the income they spend.

We saw that the federal government collects about half of its revenues from income taxes and only about 13 percent from the GST. What would happen if the federal government started to rely more on the GST for its revenues? To answer this question, we need to examine how different taxes change the incentives people face.

We will make this easier by ignoring the existing level of taxation, and will focus only on the potential changes. Consider the following example: Suppose a 20-year-old is deciding whether to save the $1000 bonus she received from her employer. If she saves the $1,000 by purchasing a Canada Savings Bond, both the $1,000 and the interest she earns will be taxed under an income tax, but neither will be taxed if the government relies on the GST. Suppose she earns 6 percent per year on the Canada Savings Bond and keeps it until she retires at age 70. With interest compounding tax-free over 50 years, she will have accumulated $18,420 by age 70. Now suppose that her income is taxed at a total rate of 33 percent. As a result, she will only have $670 of her bonus left after paying the tax. In addition, if she saves the money in a Canada Savings Bond, her after-tax return is only 6 percent × (1 − 0.33) = 4 percent. Now her bonus in a Canada Savings Bond at age 20 yields only $4,761 at age 70. This big difference in accumulation, $13,659, is the tax burden on saving, a burden that makes saving less attractive.

Many economists argue that a taxpayer's well-being is better measured by her consumption (how much she spends) than by her income (how much she earns). Taxing consumption may therefore be more appropriate than taxing income. Also, because the income tax also taxes interest and other returns to saving, it taxes future consumption—the whole point of current saving—more heavily than present consumption. That is, under an income tax, current consumption is taxed more favourably than future consumption, reducing households' willingness to save, as in the example above.

Some economists oppose a shift from reliance on income tax to reliance on consumption tax because they believe a consumption tax will be more regressive than an income tax. These economists argue that people with very low incomes are able to save little or nothing and so would not be able to benefit from the increased incentives for saving that exist under a consumption tax.

Would it be a radical change in the tax system for federal government revenue to shift away from income taxes and toward the GST? For many households, the answer is no. Most taxpayers can already put part or even most of their savings into accounts where the funds deposited and the interest received are not taxed until the funds are withdrawn for retirement spending—for example, RRSP plans and tax-free savings accounts. In effect, individuals whose savings are mainly in these accounts are already paying a consumption tax rather than an income tax.

Your Turn: Test your understanding by doing related problem 2.6 on page 465 at the end of this chapter.

MyEconLab

The administrative burden of a tax represents another example of the deadweight loss of taxation. Individuals spend many hours during the year keeping records for income tax purposes, and they (or a tax preparer) spend many more hours prior to April 30 preparing their tax returns. The opportunity cost of this time is millions of dollars each year and represents an administrative burden of the federal income tax. For corporations, complexity in tax planning arises in many areas. The federal government also has to devote resources to enforcing the tax laws. Although the government collects the revenue from taxation, the resources spent on administrative burdens benefit neither taxpayers nor the government.

Wouldn't tax simplification reduce the administrative burden and the deadweight loss of taxation? Yes. So why is the tax code complicated? In part, complexity arises because the political process has resulted in different types of income being taxed at different rates, requiring rules to limit taxpayers' ability to avoid taxes. In addition, interest groups seek benefits, while the majority of taxpayers, who do not benefit, find it difficult to organize a drive for a simpler tax system.

The Ability-to-Pay Principle

The *ability-to-pay principle* holds that when the government raises revenue through taxes, it is fair to expect a greater share of the tax burden to be borne by people who have a greater ability to pay. Usually this principle means raising more taxes from people with high incomes than from people with low incomes, which is sometimes referred to as **vertical equity principle**. The federal income tax is consistent with the ability-to-pay principle. The GST, in contrast, is not consistent with the ability-to-pay principle because low-income people tend to spend a larger fraction of their income than do high-income people. As a result, low-income people will pay a greater fraction of their income in GST than will high-income people.

Vertical-equity principle The principle that those with more income should carry more of the tax burden.

The Horizontal-Equity Principle

The **horizontal-equity principle** states that people in the same economic situation should be treated equally. Although this principle seems desirable, it is not easy to use in practice because it is sometimes difficult to determine whether two people are in the same economic situation. For example, two people with the same income are not necessarily in the same economic situation. Suppose one person does not work but receives an income of $50,000 per year entirely from interest received on bonds, and another person receives an income of $50,000 per year from working at two jobs 16 hours a day. In this case, we could argue that the two people are in different economic situations and should not pay the same tax. Although policymakers and economists usually consider horizontal equity when evaluating proposals to change the tax system, it is not a principle they can follow easily.

Horizontal-equity principle The principle that people in the same economic situation should be treated identically.

The Benefits-Received Principle

According to the *benefits-received principle*, people who receive the benefits from a government program should pay the taxes that support the program. For example, if a city operates a marina used by private boat owners, the government can raise the revenue to operate the marina by levying a tax on the boat owners. Raising the revenue through a general income tax paid by both boat owners and non-boat owners would be inconsistent with the benefits-received principle. Because the government has many programs, however, it would be impractical to identify and tax the beneficiaries of every program.

The Goal of Attaining Social Objectives Taxes are sometimes used to attain social objectives. For example, the government might want to discourage smoking and drinking alcohol. Taxing cigarettes and alcoholic beverages is one way to help achieve this objective. Taxes intended to discourage certain activities are sometimes referred to as "sin taxes."

15.3 LEARNING OBJECTIVE

Understand the effect of price elasticity on tax incidence.

Tax incidence The actual division of the burden of a tax between buyers and sellers in a market.

Tax Incidence Revisited: The Effect of Price Elasticity

There is a difference between who is legally required to send a tax payment to the government and who actually bears the burden of a tax. The actual division of the burden of a tax between buyers and sellers in a market is known as **tax incidence**. We can go beyond the basic analysis of tax incidence by considering how the price elasticity of demand and price elasticity of supply affect how the burden of a tax is shared between consumers and firms.

In Chapter 4, we discussed whether consumers or firms bear the larger share of a 10-cents-per-litre federal excise tax on gasoline. We saw that consumers paid the majority of the tax. We can expand on this conclusion by stating that consumers of gasoline pay a larger fraction of gasoline taxes than do sellers because the elasticity of demand for gasoline is smaller than the elasticity of supply. In fact, we can draw a general conclusion: *When the demand for a product is less elastic than the supply, consumers pay the majority of the tax on the product. When demand for a product is more elastic than the supply, firms pay the majority of the tax on the product.*

Figure 15.4 shows why this conclusion is correct. In Figure 15.4, D_1 is inelastic between points A and B, and D_2 is elastic between points A and C. With demand curve D_1, the 10-cents-per-litre tax raises the market price of gasoline from \$1.50 (point A) to \$1.58 (point B) per litre, so consumers pay 8 cents of the tax. The amount firms get to keep falls to \$1.48 from \$1.50, so firms pay 2 cents of the tax. With D_2, the market price rises only to \$1.52 (point C) per litre, and consumers pay only 2 cents of the tax. With demand curve D_2, sellers of gasoline receive only \$1.42 per litre after paying the tax. So, the amount they receive per litre after taxes falls from \$1.50 to \$1.42 per litre, and they pay 8 cents of the tax.

Don't Let This Happen to You

Remember Not to Confuse Who Pays a Tax with Who Bears the Burden of the Tax

Consider the following statement: "Of course, I bear the burden of the sales tax on everything I buy. I can show you my sales receipts with the 5 percent GST clearly labelled. The seller doesn't bear that tax. I do."

The statement is incorrect. To understand why it is incorrect, think about what would happen to the price of a product if the sales tax on it were eliminated. Figure 15.4 shows that the price of the product would fall because the supply curve would shift down by the amount of the tax. The equilibrium price, however, would fall by less than the amount of the tax. (If you doubt that this is true, draw

the graph to convince yourself.) So, the gain from eliminating the tax would be received partly by consumers in the form of a lower price but also partly by sellers in the form of a new price that is higher than the amount they received from the old price minus the tax. Therefore, the burden from imposing a sales tax is borne partly by consumers and partly by sellers.

In determining the burden of a tax, what counts is not what is printed on the receipt for a product but what happens to the price of a product as a result of the tax.

MyEconLab

Your Turn: Test your understanding by doing related problem 3.1 on page 465 at the end of this chapter.

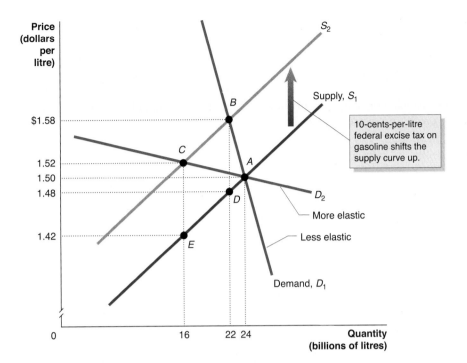

Figure 15.4

The Effect of Elasticity on Tax Incidence

When demand is more elastic than supply, consumers bear less of the burden of a tax. When supply is more elastic than demand, firms bear less of the burden of a tax. D_1 is inelastic between point A and point B, and D_2 is elastic between point A and point C. With demand curve D_1, a 10-cents-per-litre tax raises the equilibrium price from $1.50 (point A) to $1.58 (point B), so consumers pay 8 cents of the tax, and firms pay 2 cents. With D_2, a 10-cents-per-litre tax on gasoline raises the equilibrium price only from $1.50 (point A) to $1.52 (point C), so consumers pay 2 cents of the tax. Because in this case producers receive $1.42 per litre after paying the tax, their share of the tax is 8 cents per litre.

Making the Connection

Do Corporations Really Bear the Burden of the Federal Corporate Income Tax?

During the U.S. 2012 presidential election campaign, hecklers at an Iowa appearance by former Massachusetts Governor Mitt Romney suggested that taxes on corporations be raised. Romney responded by saying, "Corporations are people, my friend." The hecklers responded, "No, they're not!" To which Romney responded, "Of course they are. Everything corporations earn ultimately goes to people. Where do you think it goes?" Romney was correct that corporations are legal persons in the eyes of the law. But what about the larger question: Who actually pays the corporate income tax? The incidence of the corporate income tax is one of the most controversial questions in the economics of tax policy. It is straightforward to determine the incidence of the gasoline tax using demand and supply analysis. Determining the incidence of the corporate income tax is more complicated because economists disagree about how corporations respond to the tax.

Will this consumer be paying part of Apple's corporate income tax when she buys an iPad or an iPhone?

A company might make its cheque payable to the Canada Revenue Agency, but that money has to come from somewhere: from reduced returns to investors, lower wages to workers, or higher prices for consumers.

Most economists agree that some of the burden of the corporate income tax is passed on to consumers in the form of higher prices. There is also some agreement that, because the corporate income tax reduces the rates of return received by investors, it results in less investment in corporations. This reduced investment means workers have less capital available to them. When workers have less capital, their productivity and their wages both fall. In this way, some of the burden of the corporate income tax is shifted from corporations to workers in the form of lower wages. The deadweight loss or excess burden from the corporate income tax is substantial. A survey by PricewaterhouseCoopers Canada found that the average large corporation in Canada spends 1,696 employee-days on tax compliance activities each year; this is the equivalent of eight full-time employees working exclusively on Canadian tax compliance-related issues. Clearly this time investment makes these taxes expensive for firms and, given their complexity, these taxes are also costly for the federal government to collect.

As a consequence, economists have long argued for reform of the system of double taxing income earned on investments that corporations finance by issuing stock. This income is taxed once by the corporate income tax and again by the individual income tax as profits are distributed to shareholders.

Based on Ashley Parker, "'Corporations Are People,' Romney Tells Iowa Hecklers Angry over His Tax Policy," *New York Times*, August 11, 2011; and PricewaterhouseCoopers, "Total Tax Contribution 2008—Canada's Tax Regime: Complexity and Competitiveness in Difficult Times," accessed at http://www.pwc.com/ca/en/corporate-tax/total-contribution-survey.jhtml

MyEconLab   **Your Turn:** Test your understanding by doing related problem 3.4 on page 466 at the end of this chapter.

Solved Problem **15.3**

The Effect of Price Elasticity on the Excess Burden of a Tax

Explain whether you agree or disagree with the following statement: "For a given supply curve, the excess burden of a tax will be greater when demand is less elastic than when it is more elastic." Illustrate your answer with a demand and supply graph.

Solving the Problem

Step 1: **Review the chapter material.** This problem is about both excess burden and tax incidence, so you may want to review the section "Evaluating Taxes," which begins on page 446," and the section "Tax Incidence Revisited: The Effect of Price Elasticity," which begins on page 450.

Step 2: **Draw a graph to illustrate the relationship between tax incidence and excess burden.** Figure 15.4 on page 451 is a good example of the type of graph to draw. Be sure to indicate the areas representing excess burden.

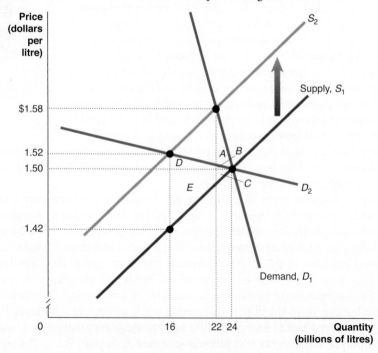

Step 3: Use the graph to evaluate the statement. As we have seen, for a given supply curve, when demand is more elastic, as with demand curve D_2, the fall in equilibrium quantity is greater than when demand is less elastic, as with demand curve D_1. The deadweight loss when demand is less elastic is shown by the area of the triangle made up of A, B, and C. The deadweight loss when demand is more elastic is shown by the area of the triangle made up of B, C, D, and E. The area of the deadweight loss is clearly larger when demand is more elastic than when it is less elastic. Recall that the excess burden of a tax is measured by the deadweight loss. Therefore, when demand is less elastic, the excess burden of a tax is *smaller* than when demand is more elastic. We can conclude that the statement is incorrect.

Your Turn: For more practice, do related problem 3.3 on page 466 at the end of this chapter.

MyEconLab

Income Distribution and Poverty

15.4 LEARNING OBJECTIVE

Discuss the distribution of income in Canada and understand the extent of income mobility.

In practice, in most economies, some individuals will have very high incomes, and some individuals will have very low incomes. But how unequal is the distribution of income in Canada today? How does this compare with the distribution of income in Canada in the past or with the distribution of income in other countries today? What determines the distribution of income? And, to return to an issue raised at the beginning of this chapter, how does the tax system affect the distribution of income? These are questions we will explore in the remainder of this chapter.

Measuring the Income Distribution and Poverty

Table 15.5 clearly shows that income is not evenly distributed within Canada. The majority of Canadians earn less than $40,000 a year, while 5.1 percent of Canadians earn more than $100,000.

Table 15.6 divides the population of Canada into five groups, from the 20 percent with the lowest incomes to the 20 percent with the highest total incomes. The fraction of total income received by each of the five groups is shown for selected years. Table 15.6 reinforces the fact that income is unequally distributed. The first row shows that in 1976 the 20 percent of Canadians with the lowest incomes received only 4.2 percent of all income. Table 15.6 also shows that over time, there have been some changes in the distribution of income. Those with the lowest incomes saw a moderate increase in their share of income received between 1976 and 1985. After 1985, this group of people saw their portion of income received fall back to 4.2 percent. During the same period, those earning the highest 20 percent of incomes saw their share of total

Annual Individual Income	Percentage of All Individuals (%)
Less than $20,000	38.5
$20,000 to $29,000	14.6
$30,000 to $39,999	12.0
$40,000 to $49,999	9.9
$50,000 to $59,999	6.9
$60,000 to $69,999	4.9
$70,000 to $79,999	3.6
$80,000 to $89,999	2.7
$90,000 to $99,999	1.9
Over $100,000	5.1

Table 15.5

Distribution of Individual Income, 2010 (2010 constant dollars)

Source: Cansim Table 202-0402. This does not constitute an endorsement by Statistics Canada of this product.

Table 15.6

How Has the Distribution of Income Changed over Time? (Percentage of total income received)

Year	Lowest 20%	Second 20%	Third 20%	Fourth 20%	Highest 20%
1976	4.2	10.6	17.4	24.7	43.0
1980	4.3	10.9	17.9	25.2	41.8
1985	4.6	10.5	17.1	24.9	42.8
1990	4.6	10.1	16.7	24.8	43.8
1995	4.5	10.0	16.4	24.6	44.4
2000	4.1	9.5	15.6	23.9	47.0
2005	4.1	9.6	15.6	23.9	46.9
2010	4.2	9.6	15.3	23.6	47.3

Source: Cansim Table 202-0701. This does not constitute an endorsement by Statistics Canada of this product.

income received fall between 1976 and 1980 and then rise between 1980 and 2010. We will discuss some of the reasons why income is unevenly distributed among people later in this chapter.

There are a variety of ways to measure poverty, and while there is no officially recognized single measure of poverty in Canada, Statistics Canada publishes information on those who spend 20 percentage points more of their income on food, shelter, and clothing than an average family does—currently the cut-off is families that spend more than 63 percent of their after-tax income on food, shelter, and clothing. This approach is sometimes referred to as the **low income cut-off**. The actual dollar value of the cut-off changes from place to place, due to differences in the cost of living and in the size of the family. Figure 15.5 shows the Canadian **poverty rate**, or the proportion of Canadians with incomes below the low income cut-off. The proportion with after-tax incomes below the cut-off peaked in 1996 at 15.2 percent of people and has since fallen to 9 percent. There are other different factors that influence an individual's likelihood of living in poverty.

Low income cut-off The income level at which a family must spend 20 percentage points more than the average Canadian family of the same size on food, shelter, and clothing.

Poverty rate The proportion of people with incomes below the low income cut-off.

Factors Related to Poverty and Income Inequality

The novelists Ernest Hemingway and F. Scott Fitzgerald supposedly once had a conversation about the rich. Fitzgerald said to Hemingway, "You know, the rich are different from you and me." To which Hemingway replied, "Yes. They have more money." Although witty, Hemingway's joke doesn't help answer the question of why the rich have more money. We provided one part of the answer to this question when we discussed the marginal productivity theory of income distribution. We saw that in equilibrium,

Figure 15.5

Percentage of the Canadian Population with Income Below the Low Income Cut-Off (LICO), 1976–2010

The percentage of people living below the low income cut-off in Canada peaked in 1996 at 15.2 percent. Since then, it has fallen to a low of 9 percent.
Source: Cansim Table 202-0802. This does not constitute an endorsement by Statistics Canada of this product.

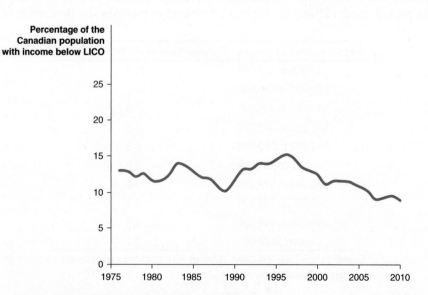

each factor of production receives a payment equal to its marginal revenue product. The more factors of production an individual owns, and the more productive those factors are, the higher the individual's income will be.

For most people, of course, the most important factor of production they own is their labour. Therefore, the income they earn depends on how productive they are and on the prices of the goods and services their labour helps produce. Roberto Luongo, goalie for the Vancouver Canucks, made $6.7 million for the 2012–13 season because he is very productive (or, more accurately, because he prevents opposing players from being productive), and his employer can sell tickets and television rights to hockey games he plays in for a high price. Individuals who help to produce goods and services that can be sold for only a low price earn lower incomes.

Many people own other factors of production as well. For example, many people own capital by owning stock in corporations or by owning shares in mutual funds that buy the stock of corporations. Ownership of capital is not equally distributed, and income earned from capital is more unequally distributed than income earned from labour. Some people supply entrepreneurial skills by starting and managing businesses. Their income is increased by the profits from these businesses.

We saw in Table 15.6 that income inequality has increased during the past 25 years. Two factors that appear to have contributed to this increase are technological change and expanding international trade. Rapid technological change, particularly the development of information technology, has led to the substitution of computers and other machines for unskilled labour. This substitution has caused a decline in the wages of unskilled workers relative to other workers. Expanding international trade has put Canadian workers in competition with foreign workers to a greater extent than in the past. This competition has caused the wages of unskilled workers to be depressed relative to the wages of other workers.

There have been some changes in the federal tax structure and social spending programs in Canada over the period of time covered in Table 15.6. There has been a shift in the share of income received by those with the highest incomes; however, when you consider the proportion of Canadians below the low income cut-off, we see a fall in poverty since the mid-1990s. The tax system changes have been both hailed as favouring the poor and decried as punishing those at the low end of the income distribution.

Finally, like everything else in life, earning an income is subject to good and bad luck. A poor person who becomes a millionaire by winning the lottery is an obvious example, as is a person whose earning power drastically declines as a result of a debilitating illness or accident. So, we can say that as a group, the people with high incomes are likely to have greater-than-average productivity and own greater-than-average amounts of capital. They are also likely to have experienced good luck. As a group, poor people are likely to have lower-than-average productivity and own lower-than-average amounts of capital. They are also likely to have been unlucky.

Showing the Income Distribution with a Lorenz Curve

Figure 15.6 presents the distribution of income using *Lorenz curves*. A **Lorenz curve** shows the distribution of income by arraying incomes from lowest to highest on the horizontal axis and indicating the cumulative fraction of income earned by each fraction of households on the vertical axis. If the distribution of income were perfectly equal, a Lorenz curve would be a straight line because the first 20 percent of households would earn 20 percent of total income, the first 40 percent of households would earn 40 percent of total income, and so on. Panel (a) of Figure 15.6 shows a Lorenz curve for the actual distribution of income in Canada in 1976 and another curve for the distribution of income in 2010, using the data from Table 15.6. We know that income was distributed more unequally in 2010 than in 1976 because the Lorenz curve for 2010 is farther away from the line of equal distribution than is the Lorenz curve for 1976.

Lorenz curve A curve that shows the distribution of income by arraying incomes from lowest to highest on the horizontal axis and indicating the cumulative fraction of income earned by each fraction of households on the vertical axis.

Figure 15.6

The Lorenz Curve and Gini Coefficient

In panel (a), the Lorenz curves show the distribution of income by arraying incomes from the lowest to the highest on the horizontal axis and indicating the cumulative fraction of income by each fraction of households on the vertical axis. The straight line represents perfect income equality. Because the Lorenz curve for 1976 is closer to the line of perfect equality than the Lorenz curve for 2010, we know that income was more equally distributed in 1976 than in 2010. In panel (b), we show the Gini coefficient, which is equal to the area between the line of perfect income equality and the Lorenz curve—area A—divided by the whole area below the line of perfect equality—area A plus area B. The closer the Gini coefficient is to 1, the more unequal the income distribution.

Source: Cansim Table 202-0701. This does not constitute an endorsement by Statistics Canada of this product.

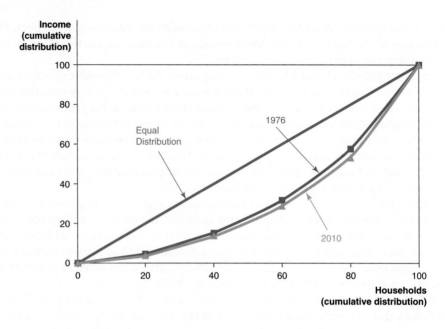

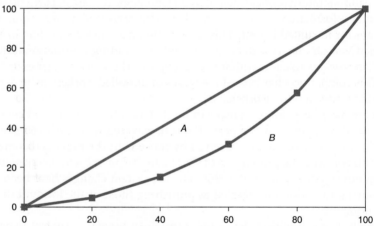

Panel (b) illustrates how to calculate the *Gini coefficient*, which is one way of summarizing the information provided by a Lorenz curve. The Gini coefficient is equal to the area between the line of perfect income equality and the Lorenz curve—area *A* in panel (b)—divided by the whole area below the line of perfect equality—area *A* plus area *B* in panel (b). Or:

$$\text{Gini coefficient} = \left(\frac{A}{A + B}\right).$$

If the income distribution were completely *equal*, the Lorenz curve would be the same as the line of perfect income equality, area *A* would be zero, and the Gini coefficient would be zero. If the income distribution were completely *unequal*, area *B* would be zero, and the Gini coefficient would equal 1. Therefore, the greater the degree of income inequality, the greater the value of the Gini coefficient. In 1976, the Gini coefficient for Canada was 0.304. In 2010, it was 0.324, which tells us again that income inequality increased between 1976 and 2010.

Problems in Measuring Poverty and the Distribution of Income

The measures of poverty and the distribution of income that we have discussed to this point may be misleading for two reasons. First, these measures are snapshots in time that do not take into account income mobility. Second, they ignore the effects of government programs outside the tax system that are designed to reduce the impacts of poverty.

Income Mobility in Canada and Similar Countries   We expect to see income mobility. When students graduate from university, their incomes typically rise as they take up new jobs. A family may be below the low income cut-off one year because its primary wage earner was unemployed, but may be well above the low income cut-off the next. It's also possible that someone with a high income in one year may have a much lower income in future years.

In countries with low income mobility, it is very difficult for someone with poor parents to become a high income earner. In countries with high income mobility, it is much easier for someone to do better (or worse) than their parents. In an attempt to capture this effect, economists calculate the *intergenerational income elasticity*. Intergenerational income elasticity tells you how a difference in incomes will transfer from parents to children. The greater the degree of intergenerational income elasticity, the better parents' income is at predicting the children's income. For example, if a country has an intergenerational income elasticity of 0.5, if parents earn incomes $10,000 less than average, their children will likely earn incomes $5,000 less than average. With an income elasticity of 0.5, it takes many generations for differences in incomes to disappear. The lower the intergenerational income elasticity, the higher the degree of income mobility. You can see the intergenerational income elasticity for 11 different countries in Figure 15.7.

A Fraser Institute study by Charles Lammam, Amela Karabegović, and Niels Veldhuis tracked incomes of the same people from 1990 to 2009 using their tax filings. They found that 87 percent of those with incomes in the lowest 20 percent in 1990 had moved up the income distribution by 2009, and 36 percent of those with incomes in the highest 20 percent of the population in 1990 had moved into a lower income group by 2009.

It's clear that Canada does fairly well in terms of income mobility. A number of different social factors and social programs can have an impact on income mobility. The quality of the public education system and preschool-aged care can be a factor. Better access to higher-quality education makes it more likely that children of poorer parents will have higher incomes later in life, and also reduces the advantages of children of high-income parents, making it more likely that they won't earn as much as their parents. Immigration can also play an important role in income mobility. Those who choose to immigrate to countries like Canada often have lower incomes than the average, although many first-generation Canadians have incomes that are as high as, or higher than, average.

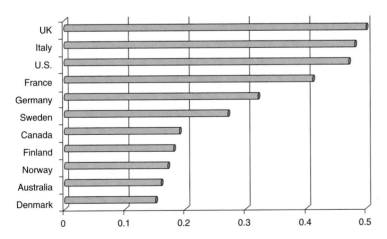

Figure 15.7

Intergenerational Income Elasticity In Wealthy Countries

Canada enjoys relatively high income mobility, with an elasticity of 0.19. Only 19 percent of parental income difference is transferred to children, on average. This means that income differences disappear within three generations. The United Kingdom, on the other hand, suffers from quite low income mobility with an elasticity of 0.5, indicating that it takes about seven generations for a difference in income to disappear. Even Sweden, which is generally known for promoting equality, has a relatively low level of income mobility, with an elasticity of 0.27. In Sweden, it still takes about five generations for a difference in incomes to disappear.

Source: Data from Conference Board of Canada: http://www.conferenceboard.ca/hcp /details/society/intergenerational-income -mobility.aspx#numbers

Solved Problem **15.4**

Are Many Individuals Stuck in Poverty?

Evaluate the following statement:

> Government statistics indicate that 9 percent of the population in Canada is below the low income cut-off. The fraction of the population in poverty has never dropped below 9 percent. Therefore, more than 9 percent of the population must cope with very low incomes year after year.

Solving the Problem

Step 1: Review the chapter material. This problem is about income mobility, so you may want to review the section "Income Mobility in Canada and Similar Countries" on page 457.

Step 2: Use the discussion in this chapter to evaluate the statement. Although it is true that the poverty rate in Canada is never below 9 percent, it is not the same 9 percent of the population that is in poverty each year. A 2012 Fraser Institute study showed that 13 percent of people who were in the lowest 20 percent of the income distribution in 1990 were still in the lowest 20 percent in 2009. Another study showed that it takes only three generations for income differences to disappear. Poverty remains a problem in Canada, but fortunately the number of people who remain in poverty for many years or from one generation to the next is much smaller than the number of people who suffer poverty during any one year.

Based on http://www.fraserinstitute.org/uploadedFiles/fraser-ca/Content/research-news/research/publications/measuring-income-mobility-in-canada.pdf; and http://www.conferenceboard.ca/hcp/details/society/intergenerational-income-mobility.aspx#numbers

MyEconLab   **Your Turn:** For more practice, do related problem 4.1 on page 466 at the end of this chapter.

The Effect of Taxes and Transfers The statistics on poverty presented in this chapter all concern the after-tax distribution of income. The Canadian income tax system is progressive in that it taxes people who earn higher incomes at a higher marginal tax rate. Many people who earn low incomes also receive transfers of money from the government. These social assistance payments and the progressive income tax system mean there is a difference between the incomes people receive from their factors of production and the amount of money they actually have to spend. The income in the tables above does not take a number of these transfers into account when determining the distribution of wealth. While these transfers increase the amount of money those at the low end of the income distribution get to spend, they are unlikely to change the overall distribution of income.

Individuals with low incomes also receive noncash benefits, such as eye care and dental coverage not paid for by general health care, as well as rent subsidies. Because individuals with low incomes are more likely to receive transfer payments and other benefits from the government than are individuals with high incomes, the distribution of income is more equal if we take these benefits into account.

Income Distribution and Poverty Around the World

How does income inequality in Canada compare with income inequality in other countries? Table 15.7 compares the ratio of total income received by the 20 percent of

Country	Ratio of Income Received by Highest 20% to Income Received by Lowest 20%
Bolivia	21.9
Brazil	17.4
Thailand	15.2
Paraguay	15.0
United States	14.8
Chile	13.8
Argentina	12.3
Canada	9.1
Spain	6.0
United Kingdom	5.2
Italy	5.2
Germany	4.5
Ireland	4.2
France	4.4
Sweden	3.7
Japan	3.0

Data from the World Bank, Eurostat, and Statistics Canada.

Table 15.7

Income Inequality Around the World

the population with the lowest incomes and the 20 percent with the highest incomes in several countries. The countries are ranked from most unequal to least unequal. As the table shows, poor countries, such as Bolivia and Paraguay, typically have more unequal distributions of income than does Canada. The distribution of income in Canada is less equal than in some moderate-income countries, such as Spain and the United Kingdom, but it is more equal than in other moderate-income countries, such as Chile and Argentina. The United States has the most unequal distribution of income of any high-income country in the world. Of course, we must be careful with such comparisons because transfer payments are not counted in income. For example, the Social Security and Medicare systems in the United States are much more generous than the corresponding systems in Japan but less generous than those in France and Germany.

Although poverty remains a problem in high-income countries, it is a much larger problem in poor countries. The level of poverty in much of sub-Saharan Africa, in particular, is a human catastrophe. In 2012, the low income cut-off in Canada was approximately $20,000, but economists often use a much lower threshold income of $1 per day when calculating the rate of poverty in poor countries. As Table 15.8 shows, by this measure, according to estimates by Maxim Pinkovskiy and Xavier Sala-i-Martin, poverty declined from about 27 percent of the world population in 1970 to 5 percent in 2006, the most recent year for which statistics are available. The greatest reduction in poverty has taken place in Asia. In East Asia, which includes China, the poverty rate dropped spectacularly from about 60 percent in 1970 to less than 2 percent in 2006. In South Asia, which includes India, poverty rates dropped from 20 percent to less than 3 percent. Even in sub-Saharan Africa, poverty decreased from 40 percent in 1970 to 32 percent in 2006. Why has poverty fallen dramatically more in Asia than in Africa? The key explanation is that the countries of Asia have had higher rates of economic growth than have the countries of sub-Saharan Africa. Recent economic research demonstrates a positive relationship between economic growth and the incomes of lower-income people.

Table 15.8

**Poverty Has Declined
Dramatically Around the World
Since 1970**

	Percentage of the Population in Poverty	
Region	1970	2006
World	26.8%	5.4%
East Asia	58.8	1.7
South Asia	20.1	2.6
Middle East and North Africa	8.4	5.2
Latin America	11.6	3.1
Sub-Saharan Africa	39.9	31.8

Source: Reprinted by permission of Xavier Sala-i-Martin.

Economics in Your Life

How Much Tax Should You Pay?

At the beginning of the chapter, we asked you to think about where government gets the money to provide goods and services and about whether you pay your fair share of taxes. After reading this chapter, you should see that you pay taxes in many different forms. When you work, you pay taxes on your income, both for individual income taxes and social insurance taxes. When you buy gasoline, you pay an excise tax, which, in part, pays for highways. When you buy goods at a local store, you pay federal and provincial (except in Alberta) sales taxes, which the government uses to fund education and other services. Whether you are paying your fair share of taxes is a normative question. The Canadian tax system is progressive, so higher-income individuals pay more in taxes than do lower-income individuals. You may find that you will not pay much in federal income taxes in your first job after university. But as your income grows during your career, so will the percentage of your income you pay in taxes.

Conclusion

The public choice model provides insights into how government decisions are made. The decisions of policymakers will not necessarily reflect the preferences of voters. Attempts by government to intervene in the economy may increase economic efficiency, but they may also lead to government failure and a reduction in economic efficiency.

A saying attributed to Benjamin Franklin states that "nothing in this world is certain but death and taxes." But which taxes? As we saw at the beginning of this chapter, politicians continue to debate whether the government should use the tax system and other programs to reduce the level of income inequality in Canada. The tax system represents a balance among the objectives of economic efficiency, ability to pay, paying for benefits received, and achieving social objectives. Those favouring government intervention to reduce inequality argue that it is unfair for some people to have much higher incomes than others. Others argue that income inequality largely reflects higher incomes resulting from greater skills and from entrepreneurial ability and that higher taxes reduce work, saving, and investment.

Many economists are skeptical of tax policy proposals intended to significantly reduce income inequality. They argue that a market system relies on individuals being willing to work hard and take risks, with the promise of high incomes if they are successful. Taking some of that income from them in the name of reducing income inequality reduces the incentives to work hard and take risks. Policymakers are often faced with a trade-off between economic efficiency and equity. Ultimately, whether policies to reduce income inequality should be pursued is a normative question. Economics alone cannot decide the issue.

An Inside Look on the next page discusses policies for helping the poor.

THE FINANCIAL POST

Focus on Helping the Truly Poor

Most Canadians would never equate the plight of a 20-year-old student who has to scramble to find the money to go out for a beer with friends with the circumstances of a single mother earning the same income. As Anne Golden's column highlights, the Conference Board apparently does.

To most Canadians, poverty is not being able to afford basic necessities such as a nutritious diet, satisfactory housing, clothing, health care, public transportation, household supplies, telephone service, and a host of other goods and services that Canadians need to survive in our society.

(a) The level of income needed to buy these necessities is naturally very different, depending on the makeup of the household (i.e., number of people and dependants) and community in which the household lives (i.e., it is more costly to live in Vancouver, British Columbia, than Brandon, Manitoba). Chris Sarlo, a professor of economics at Nipissing University, estimates "basic needs" income levels for six different family types in over 50 different Canadian cities. By calculating over 300 different poverty lines (incomes needed to buy basic necessities), Sarlo's measurement of poverty is extremely accurate.

Unfortunately, the Conference Board makes none of these distinctions in estimating poverty. It simply defines poverty as those individuals with a disposable income of less than 50% of the median income in a country. The problem with this poverty measure is that it simply shows to what extent some Canadians are less well-off than others and has nothing to do with whether or not individuals can provide themselves with the basic necessities listed above.

Anne Golden and the Conference Board view poverty as a problem of inequality, not insufficiency. As she notes, poverty is an "issue of social exclusion."

Personally, we think that all Canadians should be able to go out for dinner, to the movies, and to buy tickets to watch their favourite NHL team. But if they cannot afford to do so, they should not be considered poor.

(b) Blurring the line between actual poverty and those who can't afford the same level of "social engagement" as others prevents us from identifying those most in need. Not being able to afford basic necessities such as food, shelter, clothing, and health care can lead to malnutrition and many other life-threatening conditions. Real poverty is a serious issue that can have tragic consequences if not addressed.

But according to the Conference Board, relative poverty (being relatively worse off than others) does indeed have long-lasting social consequences. Specifically, they point to the OECD, which found "greater income inequality [i.e., relative poverty] stifles upward mobility between generations."

Interestingly, the Conference Board's own report finds the opposite. It gives Canada a "D" on "poverty" (really inequality) and an "A" on intergenerational income mobility. Put differently, Canada gets a "D" for being unequal but an "A" for upward income mobility between generations.

(c) The discrepancy arises because the Conference Board's poverty measure captures many young Canadians who are starting out with significantly lower incomes than the median Canadian. It also captures many immigrant families who often earn significantly less than the median Canadian during their early days in Canada. Through hard work, saving, and investing, they move up the income ladder, just as students and others do.

Let's not confuse two completely different things: poverty and income inequality. Instead, through accurate measurement of poverty, we can focus on those who need our help the most.

—Niels Veldhuis and Amela Karabegovic are economists with the Fraser Institute.

Source: Niels Veldhuis and Amela Karabegovic, "Focus on Helping the Truly Poor," *Financial Post*, October 6, 2009. Used with permission of the Fraser Institute.

Key Points in the Article

This article presents a side in the ongoing debate about poverty in Canada. The Conference Board of Canada assesses poverty on the basis of the distribution of income—relative poverty—while the economists at the Fraser Institute think poverty should be assessed on the basis of whether or not you can afford the essentials—absolute poverty. Different types of poverty have different implications for those who experience them. Those who experience relative poverty are unlikely to be able to fully participate in their society, missing out on social and cultural experiences that form the common experiences of Canadian society, even if all their basic material needs are met. Those experiencing absolute poverty are not only excluded from social engagement, but also missing out on some of their basic material needs. The authors of the article put forth the argument that worrying about relative poverty when absolute poverty exists reduces our ability to help those missing out on the bare essentials.

Analyzing the News

(a) The level of income needed to assess poverty depends on location and the nature of the family unit being considered. Different people in different phases of life have different needs. Someone with an infant will have needs very different from a single student's. To accurately assess whether or not someone is living in poverty, a lot of different factors have to be taken into consideration. The problem with this approach is that it can make it more difficult to compare the experiences of people living in different places and who have made different choices.

(b) One of the fundamental realizations of economics is the existence of scarcity. If society only has limited resources to devote to dealing with poverty, we need a method of deciding who will be helped and how much. If we consider only relative poverty, some of these resources will go to people who are meeting all of their material needs, leaving less for those who can't afford sufficient food, shelter, or clothing. Targeting spending on those living with absolute poverty is more likely to make dramatic improvements in well-being.

(c) Using a single income level to assess whether or not someone experiences poverty is quite likely to overstate the level of poverty. The authors use the example of a student, who while completing a degree is likely to earn a lot less in income than most of the population. Are most students truly living in poverty? Most students will make significantly more in the future than they are now. Students also have much better access to credit and in many cases are offered lower prices than regular customers. The implications of a low income for a student are very different from the implications of low income for a single parent. We need to consider the specifics of the person's situation before we can assess the type and severity of poverty they experience.

Thinking Critically

1. It is often claimed that the number of Canadians living in poverty has increased over the last 30 years. Based on the information in Figures 15.5 and 15.6, do you think this is true? Why or why not?

2. Social security (welfare) payments in Canada are much higher than the commonly used international poverty line of approximately US$1.50 a day. Do you think this means that people receiving only social security payments in Canada are not truly living in poverty? Why or why not?

Chapter Summary and Problems

Key Terms

Arrow impossibility theorem, p. 439

Average tax rate, p. 445

Excess burden, p. 447

Horizontal-equity principle, p. 449

Lorenz curve, p. 455

Low income cut-off, p. 454

Marginal tax rate, p. 445

Median voter theorem, p. 439

Poverty rate, p. 454

Progressive tax, p. 444

Public choice model, p. 438

Regressive tax, p. 444

Rent seeking, p. 440

Tax incidence, p. 450

Voting paradox, p. 439

Vertical-equity principle, p. 449

Summary

*LO 15.1 The **public choice model** applies economic analysis to government decision making. The observation that majority voting may not always result in consistent choices is called the **voting paradox**. The **Arrow impossibility theorem** states that no system of voting can be devised that will consistently represent the underlying preferences of voters. The **median voter theorem** states that the outcome of a majority vote is likely to represent the preferences of the voter who is in the political middle. Individuals and firms sometimes engage in **rent seeking**, which is the use of government action to make themselves better off at the expense of others. Although government intervention can sometimes improve economic efficiency, public choice analysis indicates that government failure can also occur, reducing economic efficiency.

LO 15.2 Governments raise the funds they need through taxes. The most widely used taxes are income taxes, social insurance taxes, sales taxes, property taxes, and excise taxes. Governments take into account several important objectives when deciding which taxes to use: efficiency, ability to pay, horizontal equity, benefits received, and attaining social objectives. A **regressive tax** is a tax for which people with lower incomes pay a higher percentage of their incomes in tax than do people with higher incomes. A **progressive tax** is a tax for which people with lower incomes pay a lower percentage of their incomes in tax than do people with higher incomes. The **marginal tax rate** is the fraction of each additional dollar of income that must be paid in taxes. The **average tax rate** is the total tax paid divided by total income. When analyzing the impact of taxes on how much people are willing to work or save or invest, economists focus on the marginal tax rate rather than

the average tax rate. The **excess burden** of a tax is the efficiency loss to the economy that results from a tax having reduced the quantity of a good produced.

LO 15.3 **Tax incidence** is the actual division of the burden of a tax. In most cases, buyers and sellers share the burden of a tax levied on a good or service. When the elasticity of demand for a product is smaller than the elasticity of supply, consumers pay the majority of the tax on the product. When the elasticity of demand for a product is larger than the elasticity of supply, sellers pay the majority of the tax on the product.

LO 15.4 No dramatic changes in the distribution of income have occurred over the past 40 years, although there was some increase in inequality between 1976 and today. A **Lorenz curve** shows the distribution of income by arraying incomes from lowest to highest on the horizontal axis and indicating the cumulative fraction of income earned by each fraction of households on the vertical axis. About 9 percent of Canadians are below the **low income cut-off**, which is defined as having to spend 20 percentage points more of income on food, shelter, and clothing than an average family of the same size. Over time, there has been significant income mobility in Canada. The **poverty rate**—the percentage of the population that is poor—has been declining in most countries around the world, with the important exception of Africa. The marginal productivity theory of income distribution states that in equilibrium, each factor of production receives a payment equal to its marginal revenue product. The more factors of production an individual owns and the more productive those factors are, the higher the individual's income will be.

MyEconLab   Log in to MyEconLab to complete these exercises and get instant feedback.

Review Questions

LO 15.1

1.1 What is the public choice model?

1.2 What is the difference between the voting paradox and the Arrow impossibility theorem?

1.3 What is rent seeking, and how is it related to regulatory capture?

LO 15.2

2.1 What is a progressive tax system? What is a regressive tax system?

2.2 What is the difference between a marginal tax rate and an average tax rate? Which is more important in determining the effect of a change in taxes on economic behaviour?

2.3 Briefly discuss each of the five goals and principles governments consider when deciding which taxes to use.

LO 15.3

3.1 What is meant by tax incidence?

3.2 Briefly discuss the effect of price elasticity of supply and demand on tax incidence.

*'Learning Objective' is abbreviated to 'LO' in the end of chapter material.

LO 15.4

4.1 Discuss the extent of income inequality in Canada. Has inequality in the distribution of income in Canada increased or decreased over time?

4.2 Define low income cut-off and poverty rate. How has the poverty rate changed in Canada since 1990?

4.3 What is a Lorenz curve? What is a Gini coefficient? If a country had a Gini coefficient of 0.48 in 1960 and 0.44 in 2012, would income inequality in the country have increased or decreased?

4.4 Describe the trend in the global poverty rate.

Problems and Applications

LO 15.1

1.1 Will the preferences shown in the following table lead to a voting paradox? Briefly explain.

Policy	Lena	David	Kathleen
Cancer research	1st	2nd	3rd
Mass transit	2nd	1st	1st
Climate change	3rd	3rd	2nd

1.2 Many political observers have noted that, when running for their party's leadership, Conservative candidates for prime minister tend to emphasize their right-wing positions and Liberal candidates tend to emphasize their left-wing positions. In the general election, however, Conservative candidates tend to downplay their right-wing positions and Liberal candidates tend to downplay their left-wing positions. Can the median voter theorem help explain this pattern? Briefly explain.

1.3 Briefly explain whether you agree with the following argument.

> The median voter theorem will be an accurate predictor of the outcomes of elections when a majority of voters have preferences very similar to those of the median voter. When the majority of voters have preferences very different from those of the median voter, the median voter theorem will not lead to accurate predictions of the outcomes of elections.

From "The Grabbing Hand," *The Economist*, February 11, 1999.

1.4 An article in *The Economist* magazine made the following observation: "In fact, as public choice theory shows, government has a whole set of special decision-making problems that can make the normal human mistakes of those decision-makers even worse." What "special decision-making problems" does government face according to public choice theory? Why might these problems make the mistakes of government decision makers worse?

From "Problem or Solution?" *The Economist*, February 13, 2007.

1.5 Is the typical person likely to gather more information when buying a new car or when voting for a member of their provincial legislative assembly? Briefly explain.

LO 15.2

2.1 Why does the federal government raise more tax revenue from taxes on individuals than from taxes on businesses?

2.2 According to a World Bank report on the Economics of Tobacco, "[t]here is concern that, as taxes are raised, poor consumers will spend more and more of their income on cigarettes," in countries such as Canada, the U.S., and the UK. Assuming that the above is true, are these taxes progressive or regressive? Be sure to define progressive and regressive taxes in your answer.

From http://www1.worldbank.org/tobacco/book/html/chapter6.htm

2.3 Provincial governments use lotteries to raise revenue. If we think of a lottery as a type of tax, is a lottery likely to be progressive or regressive? What data would you need to determine whether the burden of a lottery is progressive or regressive?

2.4 Use the information in Table 15.2 to calculate the total federal income tax paid, the marginal tax rate, and the average tax rate for people with the following incomes. (For simplicity, assume that these people have no exemptions or deductions from their incomes.)
  a. $25,000
  b. $125,000
  c. $300,000

2.5 [**Related to the** Making the Connection **on page 444**] Given the following data for the Canadian federal tax rates, has the Canadian income tax system been getting more progressive or more regressive?

Quintile	Effective Tax Rate			Proportion of Federal Taxes Paid		
	1997	2001	2007	1997	2001	2007
Lowest	6.2	4.2	6.1	1.4	1.0	1.6
Second	9.2	9.0	8.3	4.5	4.9	4.8
Third	16.0	13.5	12.2	12.5	11.9	11.4
Fourth	15.3	16.7	15.3	24.6	22.5	21.6
Highest	24.5	22.5	21.5	56.9	59.7	60.6

Source: Cansim table 202-0501. This does not constitute an endorsement by Statistics Canada of this product.

2.6 [**Related to the** Making the Connection **on page 448**] Suppose the government eliminates the income tax and replaces it with an increased GST. Think about the effect of this on the market for automobiles. Can you necessarily tell what will happen to the price and quantity of automobiles? Briefly explain.

LO 15.3

3.1 [**Related to** Don't Let This Happen to You **on page 450**] Many economists have been known to argue that there is a difference between who actually pays a tax and who is responsible for writing the cheque to the government. Briefly explain what they mean and discuss whether or not you agree with it.

3.2 Many advocates for lower business taxes argue that only people can pay taxes and that businesses cannot pay taxes. Do you agree that businesses cannot pay taxes? Don't businesses pay federal and provincial corporate income taxes? Briefly explain.

3.3 [**Related to** Solved Problem 15.3 **on page 452**] Explain whether you agree with the following statement: "For a given demand curve, the excess burden of a tax will be greater when supply is less price elastic than when it is more elastic." Illustrate your answer with a demand and supply graph. Hint: This is a lot easier if you go to extremes.

3.4 [**Related to the** Making the Connection **on page 451**] Use a demand and supply model for the labour market to show the effect of the corporate income tax on workers. What factors would make the deadweight loss or excess burden from the tax larger or smaller?

3.5 Governments often have multiple objectives in imposing a tax. In each part of this question, use a demand and supply graph to illustrate your answer.

   a. If the government wants to minimize the excess burden from excise taxes, should these taxes be imposed on goods whose demand is elastic or goods whose demand is inelastic?

   b. Suppose that, rather than minimizing excess burden, the government is most interested in maximizing the revenue it receives from the tax. In this situation, should the government impose excise taxes on goods whose demand is elastic or on goods whose demand is inelastic?

   c. Suppose that the government wants to discourage smoking and drinking alcohol. Will a tax be more effective in achieving this objective if the demand for these goods is elastic or if the demand is inelastic?

LO 15.4

4.1 [**Related to** Solved Problem 15.4 **on page 458**] Evaluate the following statement: "Policies to redistribute income are desperately needed in Canada. Without such policies, the more than 10 percent of the population that is currently poor has no hope of ever climbing out of poverty."

http://www.cbc.ca/news/background/economy/poverty-line.html

4.2 Use the following Lorenz curve graph to answer the questions.

   a. Did the distribution become more equal in 2010 than it was in 2009, or did it become less equal? Briefly explain.

   b. Estimate the value of the Gini coefficient for 2009 and for 2010.

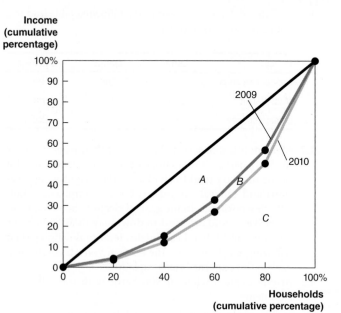

4.3 Draw a Lorenz curve showing the distribution of income for the five people in the following table.

Name	Annual Earnings
Lena	$70,000
David	60,000
Steve	50,000
Jerome	40,000
Lori	30,000

4.4 Why do economists often use a lower poverty threshold for low-income countries than for high-income countries such as Canada? Is there a difference between relative poverty and absolute poverty? Briefly explain.

4.5 Suppose that Parliament decides on a policy of bringing about a perfectly equal distribution of income. What factors might make this policy difficult to achieve? If it were possible to achieve the goal of this policy, would doing so be desirable?

4.6 If everyone had the same income, would everyone have the same level of well-being?

4.7 Suppose that, in Canada, we found a number of households below the low income cut-off that not only owned their own homes, but also had such amenities as air conditioning, cable or satellite television, and high speed Internet, and owned cars. Given that many of these things were rare even for households well above the low income cut-off generations ago, how is it that despite relatively constant poverty rates, there has been such an increase in the ownership of these goods among the poor?

4.8 In the newspaper article cited in *An Inside Look*, Fraser Institute economists argue that the Conference Board of Canada's measure of poverty overstates the true problems of poverty. Suppose that, based on the work by the Conference Board of Canada, the federal government decides to guarantee equality of economic outcomes. What would some of the benefits of this policy be? What would some of the costs be? What impact do you think such a policy would have on intergenerational income mobility?

Based on Niels Veldhuis and Amela Karabegovic, *Financial Post*, October 6, 2009, http://www.financialpost.com/opinion/story .html?id=2069582

MyEconLab   MyEconLab is an online tool designed to help you master the concepts covered in your course. It will create an adaptive, highly personalized study plan to stimulate and measure your learning. Log in to take advantage of this powerful study aid, and to access quizzes and other valuable course-related material.

GLOSSARY

A

Absolute advantage The ability of an individual, a firm, or a country to produce more of a good or service than potential trading partners, using the same amount of resources.

Allocative efficiency A state of the economy in which production is in accordance with consumer preferences; in particular, every good or service is produced up to the point where the last unit provides a marginal benefit to society equal to the marginal cost of producing it.

Antitrust laws Laws aimed at eliminating collusion and promoting competition among firms.

Arrow impossibility theorem A mathematical theorem that holds that no system of voting can be devised that will consistently represent the underlying preferences of voters.

Autarky A situation in which a country does not trade with other countries.

Average fixed cost Fixed cost divided by the quantity of output produced.

Average product of labour The total output produced by a firm divided by the quantity of workers.

Average revenue (AR) Total revenue divided by the quantity of the product sold.

Average tax rate Total tax paid divided by total income.

Average total cost Total cost divided by the quantity of output produced.

Average variable cost Variable cost divided by the quantity of output produced.

B

Barrier to entry Anything that keeps new firms from entering an industry in which firms are earning economic profits.

Behavioural economics The study of situations in which people make choices that do not appear to be economically rational.

Black market A market in which buying and selling take place at prices that violate government price regulations.

Brand management The actions of a firm intended to maintain the differentiation of a product over time.

Budget constraint The limited amount of income available to consumers to spend on goods and services.

Business strategy Actions that a firm takes to achieve a goal, such as maximizing profits.

Cartel A group of firms that collude by agreeing to restrict output to increase prices and profits.

C

Centrally planned economy An economy in which the government decides how economic resources will be allocated.

Ceteris paribus ("all else equal") condition The requirement that when analyzing the relationship between two variables—such as price and quantity demanded—other variables must be held constant.

Circular-flow diagram A model that illustrates how participants in markets are linked.

Coase theorem The argument of economist Ronald Coase that if transactions costs are low, private bargaining will result in an efficient solution to the problem of externalities.

Collusion An agreement among firms to charge the same price or otherwise not to compete.

Command-and-control approach An approach that involves the government imposing quantitative limits on the amount of pollution firms are allowed to emit, or requiring firms to install specific pollution control devices.

Common resource A good that is rival but not excludable.

Comparative advantage The ability of an individual, a firm, or a country to produce a good or service at a lower opportunity cost than potential trading partners or competitors.

Compensating differentials Higher wages that compensate workers for unpleasant aspects of a job.

Competitive market equilibrium A market equilibrium with many buyers and many sellers.

Complements Goods and services that are used together.

Constant returns to scale The situation in which a firm's long-run average costs remain unchanged as it increases output.

Consumer surplus The difference between the highest price a consumer is willing to pay for a good or service and the price the consumer actually pays.

Cooperative equilibrium An equilibrium in a game in which players cooperate to increase their mutual payoff.

Copyright A government-granted exclusive right to produce and sell a creation.

Cross-price elasticity of demand The percentage change in quantity demanded of one good divided by the percentage change in the price of another good.

D

Deadweight loss The reduction in economic surplus resulting from a market not being in competitive equilibrium.

Demand curve A curve that shows the relationship between the price of a product and the quantity of the product demanded.

Demand schedule A table that shows the relationship between the price of a product and the quantity of the product demanded.

Demographics The characteristics of a population with respect to age, race, and gender.

Derived demand The demand for a factor of production; it depends on the demand for the good the factor produces.

Diseconomies of scale The situation in which a firm's long-run average costs rise as the firm increases output.

Dominant strategy A strategy that is the best for a firm, no matter what strategies other firms use.

Dumping Selling a product for a price below its cost of production.

E

Economic discrimination Paying a person a lower wage or excluding a person from an occupation on the basis of an irrelevant characteristic such as race or gender.

Economic efficiency A market outcome in which the marginal benefit to consumers of the last unit produced is equal to its marginal cost of production and in which the sum of consumer surplus and producer surplus is at a maximum.

Economic growth The ability of an economy to produce increasing quantities of goods and services.

Economic loss The situation in which a firm's total revenue is less than its total cost, including all implicit costs.

Economic model A simplified version of reality used to analyze real-world economic situations.

Economic profit A firm's revenues minus all its costs, implicit and explicit.

Economic rent (or pure rent) The price of a factor of production that is in fixed supply.

Economics The study of the choices people make to attain their goals, given their scarce resources.

Economic surplus The sum of consumer surplus and producer surplus.

Economic variable Something measurable that can have different values, such as the price of coffee.

Economies of scale The situation when a firm's long-run average costs fall as it increases the quantity of output it produces.

Elastic demand Demand is elastic when the percentage change in quantity demanded is greater than the percentage change in price, so the price elasticity is greater than 1 in absolute value.

Elasticity A measure of how much one economic variable responds to changes in another economic variable.

Endowment effect The tendency of people to be unwilling to sell a good they already own even if they are offered a price that is greater than the price they would be willing to pay to buy the good if they didn't already own it.

Entrepreneur Someone who operates a business, bringing together factors of production—labour, capital, and natural resources—to produce goods and services.

Equity The fair distribution of economic benefits.

Excess burden A measure of the efficiency loss to the economy that results from a tax having reduced the quantity of a good produced; also known as the deadweight loss.

Excludability The situation in which anyone who does not pay for a good cannot consume it.

Expansion path A curve that shows a firm's cost-minimizing combination of inputs for every level of output.

Explicit cost A cost that involves spending money.

Exports Goods and services produced domestically but sold in other countries.

External economies Reductions in a firm's costs that result from an increase in the size of an industry.

Externality A benefit or cost that affects someone who is not directly involved in the production or consumption of a good or service.

F

Factor market A market for the factors of production, such as labour, capital, natural resources, and entrepreneurial ability.

Factors of production Labour capital, natural resources, and other inputs used to produce goods and services.

Fixed costs Costs that remain constant as output changes.

Free market A market with few government restrictions on how goods or services can be produced or sold, on who can buy or sell goods or services, or on how factors of production can be employed.

Free riding Benefiting from a good without paying for it.

Free trade Trade between countries that is without government restrictions.

G

Game theory The study of how people make decisions in situations in which attaining their goals depends on their interactions with others; in economics, the study of the decisions of firms in industries where the profits of a firm depend on its interactions with other firms.

Globalization The process of countries becoming more open to foreign trade and investment.

H

Horizontal merger A merger between firms in the same industry.

Human capital The accumulated training and skills that workers possess.

I

Implicit cost A nonmonetary opportunity cost.

Imports Goods and services bought domestically but produced in other countries.

Income effect The change in the quantity demanded of a good that results from the effect of a change in price on consumer purchasing power, holding all other factors constant.

Income elasticity of demand A measure of the responsiveness of quantity demanded to changes in income, measured by the percentage change in quantity demanded divided by the percentage change in income.

Inelastic demand Demand is inelastic when the percentage change in quantity demanded is less than the percentage change in price, so the price elasticity is less than 1 in absolute value.

Inferior good A good for which the demand increases as income falls and decreases as income rises.

Isocost line All the combinations of two inputs, such as capital and labour, that have the same total cost.

Isoquant A curve that shows all the combinations of two inputs, such as capital and labour, that will produce the same level of output.

L

Labour union an organization of employees that has a legal right to bargain with employers about wages and working conditions.

Law of demand The rule that, holding everything else constant, when the price of a product falls, the quantity demanded of the product will increase, and when the price of a product rises, the quantity demanded of the product will decrease.

Law of diminishing marginal utility The principle that consumers experience diminishing additional satisfaction as they consume more of a good or service during a given period of time.

Law of diminishing returns The principle that, at some point, adding more of a variable input, such as labour, to the same amount of a fixed input, such as capital, will cause the marginal product of the variable input to decline.

Law of supply The rule that, holding everything else constant, increases in price cause increases in the quantity supplied, and decreases in price cause decreases in the quantity supplied.

Long-run average cost curve A curve that shows the lowest cost at which a firm is able to produce a given quantity of output in the long run, when no inputs are fixed.

Long-run competitive equilibrium The situation in which the entry and exit of firms has resulted in the typical firm breaking even.

Long-run supply curve A curve that shows the relationship in the long run between market price and the quantity supplied.

Long run The period of time in which a firm can vary all its inputs, adopt new technology, and increase or decrease the size of its physical plant.

Lorenz curve A curve that shows the distribution of income by arraying incomes from lowest to highest on the horizontal axis and indicating the cumulative fraction of income earned by each fraction of households on the vertical axis.

Low income cut-off The income level at which a family must spend 20 percentage points more than the average Canadian family of the same size on food, shelter, and clothing.

M

Macroeconomics The study of the economy as a whole, including topics such as inflation, unemployment, and economic growth.

Marginal analysis Analysis that involves comparing marginal benefits and marginal costs.

Marginal benefit The additional benefit to a consumer from consuming one more unit of a good or service.

Marginal cost The additional cost to a firm of producing one more unit of a good or service.

Marginal productivity theory of income distribution The theory that the distribution of income is determined by the marginal productivity of the factors of production that individuals own.

Marginal product of labour The additional output a firm produces as a result of hiring one more worker.

Marginal rate of technical substitution (MRTS) The rate at which a firm is able to substitute one input for another while keeping the level of output constant.

Marginal revenue (MR) The change in total revenue from selling one more unit of a product.

Marginal revenue product of labour (MRP) The change in a firm's revenue as a result of hiring one more worker.

Marginal tax rate The fraction of each additional dollar of income that must be paid in taxes.

Marginal utility (MU) The change in total utility a person receives from consuming one additional unit of a good or service.

Market A group of buyers and sellers of a good or service and the institutions or arrangements by which they come together to trade.

Market demand The demand by all the consumers of a given good or service.

Market economy An economy in which the decisions of households and firms interacting in markets allocate economic resources.

Market equilibrium A situation in which quantity demanded equals quantity supplied.

Market failure A situation in which the market fails to produce the efficient level of output.

Marketing All the activities necessary for a firm to sell a product to a consumer.

Market power The ability of a firm to charge a price greater than marginal cost.

Median voter theorem The proposition that the outcome of a majority vote is likely to represent the preferences of the voter who is in the political middle.

Microeconomics The study of how households and firms make choices, how they interact in markets, and how the government attempts to influence their choices.

Minimum efficient scale The level of output at which all economies of scale are exhausted.

Mixed economy An economy in which most economic decisions result from the interaction of buyers and sellers in markets, but in which the government plays a significant role in the allocation of resources.

Monopolistic competition A market structure in which barriers to entry are low and many firms compete by selling similar, but not identical, products.

Monopoly A firm that is the only seller of a good or service that does not have a close substitute.

Monopsony The sole buyer of a factor of production.

N

Nash equilibrium A situation in which each firm chooses the best strategy, given the strategies chosen by other firms.

Natural monopoly A situation in which economies of scale are so large that one firm can supply the entire market at a lower average total cost than can two or more firms.

Network externality A situation in which the usefulness of a product increases with the number of consumers who use it.

Noncooperative equilibrium An equilibrium in a game in which players do not cooperate but pursue their own self-interest.

Normal good A good for which the demand increases as income rises and decreases as income falls.

Normative analysis Analysis concerned with what ought to be.

O

Oligopoly A market structure in which a small number of interdependent firms compete.

Opportunity cost The highest-valued alternative that must be given up to engage in an activity.

P

Patent The exclusive right to a product for a period of 20 years from the date the patent is filed with the government.

Payoff matrix A table that shows the payoffs that each firm earns from every combination of strategies by the firms.

Perfectly competitive market A market that meets the conditions of (1) many buyers and sellers, (2) all firms selling identical products, and (3) no barriers to new firms entering the market.

Perfectly elastic demand The case where the quantity demanded is infinitely responsive to price, and the price elasticity of demand equals infinity.

Perfectly inelastic demand The case where the quantity demanded is completely unresponsive to price and the price elasticity of demand equals zero.

Personnel economics The application of economic analysis to human resources issues.

Pigovian taxes and subsidies Government taxes and subsidies intended to bring about an efficient level of output in the presence of externalities.

Positive analysis Analysis concerned with.

Poverty rate The proportion of people with incomes below the low income cut-off.

Price ceiling A legally determined maximum price that sellers may charge.

Price elasticity of demand The responsiveness of the quantity demanded to a change in price, measured by dividing the percentage change in the quantity demanded of a product by the percentage change in the product's price.

Price elasticity of supply The responsiveness of the quantity supplied to a change in price, measured by dividing the percentage change in the quantity supplied of a product by the percentage change in the product's price.

Price floor A legally determined minimum price that sellers may receive.

Price leadership A form of implicit collusion in which one firm in an oligopoly announces a price change and the other firms in the industry match the change.

Price taker A buyer or seller that is unable to affect the market price.

Prisoner's dilemma A game in which pursuing dominant strategies results in noncooperation that leaves everyone worse off.

Private benefit The benefit received by the consumer of a good or service.

Private cost The cost borne by the producer of a good or service.

Private good A good that is both rival and excludable.

Producer surplus The difference between the lowest price a firm would be willing to accept for a good or service and the price it actually receives.

Production function The relationship between the inputs employed by a firm and the maximum output it can produce with those inputs.

Production possibilities frontier (PPF) A curve showing the maximum attainable combinations of two products that may be produced with available resources and current technology.

Productive efficiency A situation in which a good or service is produced at the lowest possible cost.

Product market A market for goods—such as computers—or services—such as haircuts.

Profit Total revenue minus total cost.

Progressive tax A tax for which people with lower incomes pay a lower percentage of their income in tax than do people with higher incomes.

Property rights The rights individuals or firms have to the exclusive use of their property, including the right to buy or sell it.

Protectionism The use of trade barriers to shield domestic firms from foreign competition.

Public choice model A model that applies economic analysis to government decision making.

Public franchise A government designation that a firm is the only legal provider of a good or service.

Public good A good that is both nonrival and nonexcludable.

Q

Quantity demanded The amount of a good or service that a consumer is willing and able to purchase at a given price.

Quantity supplied The amount of a good or service that a firm is willing and able to supply at a given price.

Quota A numerical limit a government imposes on the quantity of a good that can be imported into the country.

R

Regressive tax A tax for which people with lower incomes pay a higher percentage of their income in tax than do people with higher incomes.

Rent seeking Attempts by individuals and firms to use government action to make themselves better off at the expense of others.

Rivalry The situation that occurs when one person's consuming a unit of a good means no one else can consume it.

S

Scarcity A situation in which unlimited wants exceed the limited resources available to fulfill those wants.

Shortage A situation in which the quantity demanded is greater than the quantity supplied.

Short run The period of time during which at least one of a firm's inputs is fixed.

Shutdown point The minimum point on a firm's average variable cost curve; if the price falls below this point, the firm shuts down production in the short run.

Social benefit The total benefit from consuming a good or service, including both the private benefit and any external benefit.

Social cost The total cost of producing a good or service, including both the private cost and any external cost.

Substitutes Goods and services that can be used for the same purpose.

Substitution effect The change in the quantity demanded of a good that results from a change in price making the good more or less expensive relative to other goods, holding constant the effect of the price change on consumer purchasing power.

Sunk cost A cost that has already been paid and cannot be recovered.

Supply curve A curve that shows the relationship between the price of a product and the quantity of the product supplied.

Supply schedule A table that shows the relationship between the price of a product and the quantity of the product supplied.

Surplus A situation in which the quantity supplied is greater than the quantity demanded.

T

Tariff A tax imposed by a government on imports.

Tax incidence The actual division of the burden of a tax between buyers and sellers in a market.

Technological change A change in the ability of a firm to produce a given level of output with a given quantity of inputs.

Technological change A change in the quantity of output a firm can produce using a given quantity of inputs.

Technology The processes a firm uses to turn inputs into outputs of goods and services.

Terms of trade The ratio at which a country can trade its exports for imports from other countries.

Total cost The cost of all the inputs a firm uses in production.

Total revenue The total amount of funds received by a seller of a good or service, calculated by multiplying price per unit by the number of units sold.

Trade-off The idea that because of scarcity, producing more of one good or service means producing less of another good or service.

Trade The act of buying and selling.

Tragedy of the commons The tendency for a common resource to be overused.

Transactions costs The costs in time and other resources that parties incur in the process of agreeing to and carrying out an exchange of goods or services.

U

Unit-elastic demand Demand is unit elastic when the percentage change in quantity demanded is equal to the percentage change in price, so the price elasticity is equal to 1 in absolute value.

Utility The enjoyment or satisfaction people receive from consuming goods and services.

V

Variable costs Costs that change as output changes.

Vertical merger A merger between firms at different stages of production of a good.

Voluntary exchange A situation that occurs in markets when both the buyer and seller of a product are made better off by the transaction.

Voluntary export restraint (VER) An agreement negotiated between two countries that places a numerical limit on the quantity of a good that can be imported by one country from the other country.

Voting paradox The failure of majority voting to always result in consistent choices.

W

World Trade Organization (WTO) An international organization that oversees international trade agreements.

Key terms and the page on which they are defined appear in **boldface.**